2011

SHANGHAI

上海统计年鉴

STATISTICAL YEARBOOK

上海市统计局·编

SHANGHAI MUNICIPAL STATISTICS BUREAU

中国统计出版社

China Statistics Press

《上海统计年鉴—2011》编辑委员会 EDITORIAL BOARD

编者说明

一、《上海统计年鉴——2011》是一本信息高度密集的资料工具书。本书收录了2010年上海的经济和社会等各方面的统计数据,以及重要年份和改革开放以来的主要统计数据。

二、全书内容分为23个篇目，即：1. 综合；2. 人口和劳动力；3. 国民经济核算；4. 财政收支；5. 能源生产和消费；6. 固定资产投资；7. 对外经济贸易和旅游；8. 价格水平；9. 人民生活；10. 城市建设；11. 农业；12. 工业；13. 建筑业；14. 交通运输、邮政和信息传输；15. 批发和零售；16. 金融业；17. 房地产业；18. 科学技术；19. 环境保护治理；20. 教育；21. 卫生、社会保障和社会福利业；22. 文化和体育；23. 法律、公证和其他。为便于读者正确地使用资料,各篇目还附有主要统计指标解释。

三、本年鉴数据主要是由我局通过年报调查收集,而不作特别说明以外,凡是由专业部门提供的数据均在表式的注释中说明了数据来源。

四、资料中所使用的度量衡单位均采用国际统一标准计量单位。

五、本年鉴总量指标计算所采用的价格均为现行价格。

六、 本年鉴部分数据合计数或相对数由于单位取舍不同产生的计算误差均未作机械调整。

七、本年鉴表中的符号使用说明：

“…”表示数据不足本表最小计量单位数；

“空格”表示该项统计数据不详或无该项数据；

“#”表示其中的主要项。

八、《上海统计年鉴》公开出版以来,受到了国内外广大读者的关心和支持,对本年鉴的内容和编辑工作提出了许多宝贵的意见,对此我们深表谢意。限于我们的水平,欢迎读者继续对年鉴的不足之处给予批评和指正,帮助我们进一步改进年鉴的编辑工作,以期更好地为广大读者服务。

EDITOR'S NOTE

Ⅰ. Shanghai Statistical Yearbook 2011 contains comprehensive statistics of Shanghai's social and economic development in 2010 and selected data of some important years and of the period since China adopted the policy of reform and opening to the outside world.

Ⅱ. The book is composed of 23 parts viz. 1. General Survey; 2. Population and Labor Force; 3. National Economic Accounting; 4. Fiscal Revenue and Expenditure; 5. Energy Prouduction and Consumption; 6. Investment in Fixed Assets; 7. Foreign Economic Relations, Trade and Tourism; 8. Prices; 9. Living Standards; 10. Urban Construction; 11. Agriculture; 12. Industry; 13. Construction; 14. Transportation, Posts and Information Transmission; 15. Wholesale and Retail; 16. Finance; 17. Real Estate; 18. Science and Technology; 19. Environment Protection and Treatment; 20. Education; 21. Health, Social Security and Social Welfare; 22. Culture, Sports; 23. Laws, Notary and others. In order to make readers using materials correctly, explanations of major statistical indicators are attached after every chapter.

Ⅲ. Main part of the data in this yearbook are investigated and collected by Municipal Statistical Bureau, we havent mentioned especially. As to the data provided by professional bureaus, we especially mentioned the source of data in the notes after the tables.

Ⅳ. The international standard unit of measurement is applied in this book.

Ⅴ. The prices used for gross indicators' calculating in this yearbook are current prices.

Ⅵ. Statistical discrepancies in this book due to rounding are not adjusted.

Ⅶ. Marks in this book: ··· means not large enough to be rounded into the least unit of measurement; Blank space means data are not available; # indicates major item in a category.

Ⅷ. Previous editions of Shanghai Statistical Yearbook have won wide acclaim among the readers. In order to excel, we welcome all candid comments and criticism from our readers.

目录 CONTENTS

第一篇 CHAPTER 1 综合 GENERAL SURVEY

第二篇 CHAPTER 2 人口和劳动力 POPULATION AND LABOUR FORCE

目录

CONTENTS

第三篇 CHAPTER 3 国民经济核算 NATIONAL ECONOMIC ACCOUNTING

目录 CONTENTS

第五篇 CHAPTER 5 能源生产和消费 ENERGY PROUDUCTION AND CONSUMPTION

目录
CONTENTS

第六篇 CHAPTER 6 固定资产投资 INVESTMENT IN FIXED ASSETS

第七篇 CHAPTER 7 对外经济贸易和旅游 FOREIGN ECONOMIC RELATIONS, TRADE AND TOURISM

目录
CONTENTS

第八篇 CHAPTER 8 价格水平 PRICES

第九篇 CHAPTER 9 人民生活 LIVING STANDARDS

第十篇 CHAPTER 10 城市建设 URBAN CONSTRUCTION

第十一篇 CHAPTER 11 农 业 AGRICULTURE

第十二篇 CHAPTER 12 工业 INDUSTRY

第十三篇 CHAPTER 13 建筑业 CONSTRUCTION

目录 CONTENTS

第十五篇 CHAPTER 15 批发和零售 WHOLESALE AND RETAIL

第十六篇 CHAPTER 16 金融业 FINANCE

第十七篇 CHAPTER 17 房地产业 REAL ESTATE

目录
CONTENTS

目录
CONTENTS

第十九篇 CHAPTER 19 环境保护治理 ENVIRONMENT PROTECTION AND TREATMENT

第二十篇 CHAPTER 20 教育 EDUCATION

目录
CONTENTS

第二十一篇 CHAPTER 21 卫生、社会保障和社会福利业 HEALTH,SOCIAL SECURITY AND SOCIAL WELFARE

第二十二篇 CHAPTER 22 文化和体育 CULTURE,SPORTS

目录
CONTENTS

第二十三篇 CHAPTER 23 法律、公证和其他 LAWS,NOTARY AND OTHERS

第一篇

CHAPTER 1

综　　合

GENERAL SURVEY

表 1.1 行政区划（2010）
ADMINISTRATIVE DIVISION

单位:个（unit）

地 区	District	镇 Towns	乡 Township	街道办事处 Urban Sub-district Office	居民委员会 Neighbourhood Committees	村民委员会 Village Committees
全 市	**Total**	**109**	**2**	**99**	**3 671**	**1 739**
浦东新区	Pudong New Area	25		13	708	412
黄 浦 区	Huangpu			6	120	
卢 湾 区	Luwan			4	72	
徐 汇 区	Xuhui	1		12	303	6
长 宁 区	Changning	1		9	175	5
静 安 区	Jing'an			5	73	
普 陀 区	Putuo	3		6	238	7
闸 北 区	Zhabei	1		8	208	1
虹 口 区	Hongkou			8	232	
杨 浦 区	Yangpu	1		11	308	
闵 行 区	Minhang	9		3	361	156
宝 山 区	Baoshan	9		3	302	111
嘉 定 区	Jiading	7		3	120	151
金 山 区	Jinshan	9		1	78	124
松 江 区	Songjiang	11		4	144	114
青 浦 区	Qingpu	8		3	73	184
奉 贤 区	Fengxian	8			86	199
崇 明 县	Chongming	16	2		70	269

注：本表数据由上海市民政局提供。
Note：The figures of land area are provided by Shanghai Civil Affairs Bureau.

表 1.2　主要气象指标 (2010)
MAIN CLIMATE INDICATORS

指　标	Indicators	2010	指　标	Indicators	2010
平均气温(℃)	Annual Average Temperature	17.4	蒸发量(毫米)	Evaporation (mm)	697.4
极端最高气温(℃)	Utmost Highest Air Temperature	40.0	降水量(毫米)	Precipitation(mm)	1 317.3
极端最低气温(℃)	Utmost Lowest Air Temperature	-3.7	降雨日(天)	Annual Rainy Days(day)	137
日照时间 (小时)	Annual Sunshine Time (h)	1 366.8	无霜期(天)	Frost-free Period(day)	290
			晴天天数(天)	Sunshine Days(day)	71

表 1.3　各月主要气象指标(2010)
MAIN CLIMATE INDICATORS OF EVERY MONTH

月　份	Month	平均气温(℃) Annual Average Temperature (℃)	极端最高气温(℃) Utmost Highest Air Temperature(℃)	极端最低气温(℃) Utmost Lowest Air Temperature(℃)	日照时间(小时) Annual Sunshine Time(h)
1 月	Jan.	5.7	19.4	-3.7	28.9
2 月	Feb.	7.7	21.0	-2.2	61.5
3 月	Mar.	9.6	21.7	-2.1	107.9
4 月	Apr.	13.3	25.7	4.4	128.8
5 月	May.	20.9	31.6	14.1	150.5
6 月	Jun.	24.1	36.0	18.1	106.1
7 月	Jul.	28.8	37.4	24.1	150.8
8 月	Aug.	30.9	40.0	23.5	228.6
9 月	Sep.	26.2	35.3	16.4	154.0
10 月	Oct.	19.3	26.7	9.3	102.5
11 月	Nov.	14.2	22.5	8.1	64.7
12 月	Dec.	8.1	19.6	-2.3	82.5

表 1.3 续表 continued

月　份	Month	降水量(毫米) Precipitation (mm)	降雨日(天) Annual Rainy Days (day)	蒸发量(毫米) Evaporation (mm)	晴天(天) Sunny Days (day)
1 月	Jan.	38.8	6	30.2	
2 月	Feb.	82.3	13	25.3	
3 月	Mar.	193.3	16	40.2	10
4 月	Apr.	77.3	16	54.5	8
5 月	May.	86.3	13	82.1	12
6 月	Jun.	93.9	12	65.1	6
7 月	Jul.	208.8	16	91.5	9
8 月	Aug.	145.9	11	123.5	13
9 月	Sep.	248.0	15	67.9	12
10 月	Oct.	67.3	9	51.6	1
11 月	Nov.	11.6	4	33.4	
12 月	Dec.	63.8	6	32.1	

注：本页资料由上海市气象局提供。
Note: Data on this page are provided by Shanghai Meteorological Bureau.

表 1.4 主要年份社会经济主要指标
MAJOR SOCIAL AND ECONOMIC INDICATORS IN MAIN YEARS

指标	Indicators	1990	2000	2009	2010
人口与就业	**Population and Employment**				
人口	**Population**				
年末常住人口(万人)	Year-end Resident Population (10 000 persons)	1 334.00	1 608.60	2 210.28	2 302.66
年末户籍人口 (万人)	Year-end Registered Population(10 000 persons)	1 283.35	1 321.63	1 400.70	1 412.32
#非农业人口	Non-agricultural Population	864.46	986.16	1 236.16	1 254.95
就业	**Employment**				
职工人数(万人)	Staff and Workers(10 000 persons)	508.10	390.14	601.57	648.49
城镇登记失业率(%)	Registered Unemployment Rate in Urban Areas (%)	1.5	3.5	4.3	4.2
宏观经济	**Macro Economy**				
国民经济核算	**Domestic Economic Accounts**				
上海市生产总值(亿元)	Gross Domestic Product (100 million yuan)	781.66	4 771.17	15 046.45	17 165.98
第一产业	Primary Industry	34.24	76.68	113.82	114.15
第二产业	Secondary Industry	505.70	2 207.63	6 001.78	7 218.32
#工业	Industry	469.83	1 998.96	5 408.75	6 536.21
第三产业	Tertiary Industry	241.82	2 486.86	8 930.85	9 833.51
人均生产总值(元)(按常住人口计算)	Per Capita Gross Domestic Product(yuan) (Calculated by Resident Population)	5 911	30 047	69 164	76 074
经济增长贡献率(%)	Contribution Rate of Economic Growth (%)				
第一产业	Primary Industry	2.5	0.6	-0.1	-0.4
第二产业	Secondary Industry	62.6	55.7	19.0	69.2
#工业	Industry	74.6	54.7	14.3	66.6
第三产业	Tertiary Industry	37.2	43.7	81.1	31.2
固定资产投资	**Investment in Fixed Assets**				
全社会固定资产投资总额(亿元)	Total Investment in Fixed Assets(100 million yuan)	227.08	1 869.67	5 273.33	5 317.67
#房地产投资	Investment in Real Estate	8.16	566.17	1 464.18	1 980.68

表 1.4 续表 1　continued

指　标	Indicators	1990	2000	2009	2010
财　政	**Public Finance**				
地方财政收入(亿元)	Local Fiscal Revenue(100 million yuan)	166.99	497.96	2 540.30	2 873.58
地方财政支出(亿元)	Local Fiscal Expenditure(100 million yuan)	75.56	622.84	2 989.65	3 302.89
价　格	**Price**				
居民消费价格指数(上年 = 100)	Consumer Price Index(preceding = 100)	106.3	102.5	99.6	103.1
商品零售价格指数(上年 = 100)	Retail Price Index(preceding = 100)	104.8	96.4	99.4	101.7
外商直接投资	**Foreign Direct Investment**				
签订合同项目(个)	Number of Contracts (unit)	203	1 814	3 090	3 906
签订合同金额(亿美元)	Contractual Foreign Investment (100 million USD)	3.75	63.90	133.01	153.07
实际到位金额(亿美元)	Foreign Investment Actually Absorbed (100 million USD)	1.77	31.60	105.38	111.21
产　业	**Industries**				
农　业	Agriculture				
农业总产值(亿元)	Gross Output Value of Agriculture (100 million yuan)	68.16	216.50	283.15	287.03
工　业	**Industry**				
工业总产值(亿元)	Gross Output Value of Industry (100 million yuan)	1 642.75	7 022.98	24 888.08	31 038.57
轻工业	Light Industry	846.63	2 903.40	5 663.34	6 692.35
重工业	Heavy Industry	796.12	4 119.59	19 224.74	24 346.22
建筑业	**Construction**				
总产值(亿元)	Gross Output Value (100 million yuan)	75.62	631.64	3 830.53	4 300.19
交通运输、邮政业和信息传输	**Transportation, Post and Information Transmission**				
货物运输量(万吨)	Freight Transportation Volume (10000 tons)	22 848	47 954	76 967	81 024
旅客发送量(万人次)	Passenger Departures (10000 person-times)	3 835	6 893	11 136	13 432
港口货物吞吐量(万吨)	Port Cargo throughput (10000 tons)	13 959	20 440	59 205	65 339
国际标准集装箱吞吐量(万 TEU)	International Container Throughput Capacity (10 000TEU)	45.60	561.20	2 500.20	2 906.90
邮电业务总量(亿元)	Revenue from Post and Telecommunications Services (100 million yuan)	10.23	171.65	875.46	1 016.44
年末固定电话用户(万户)	Year-end Installed Telephone Subscribers (10 000 households)	45.69	549.00	935.48	935.91

表 1.4 续表 2 continued

	指 标 Indicators	1990	2000	2009	2010
批发和零售	**Wholesale and Retail**				
社会消费品零售总额（亿元）	Retail Sales of Consumer Goods (100 million yuan)	333.86	1 865.28	5 173.24	6 070.50
批发零售业商品销售总额（亿元）	Total Sales of Wholesale and Retail (100 million yuan)	1 305.41	7 474.81	31 974.39	37 383.25
对外经济贸易	**Foreign Trade**				
上海关区进出口总额(亿美元)	Total Trade Value Through Customs(100 million USD)	172.89	1 093.11	5 154.89	6 846.45
进口额	Imports	86.27	477.39	1 903.61	2 613.05
出口额	Exports	86.62	615.72	3 251.28	4 233.40
上海进出口总额（亿美元）	Total Value of Imports and Exports (100 million USD)	74.31	547.10	2 777.31	3 688.69
进口额	Imports	21.10	293.56	1 358.17	1 880.85
出口额	Exports	53.21	253.54	1 419.14	1 807.84
国际旅游	International Tourism				
上海入境境外旅游者人数（万人次）	Number of Foreign Tourists Through Shanghai Custom (10 000 persons-times)	89.30	181.40	628.92	851.12
国际旅游(外汇)收入（亿美元）	Foreign Exchange Earnings from International Tourism (100 million USD)	2.31	16.13	47.96	64.05
金融保险	**Finance and Insurance**				
金融机构存款余额(亿元)	Total Saving Deposits of Financial Institutions (100 million yuan)	851.51	9 349.83	44 620.27	52 190.04
金融机构贷款余额(亿元)	Total Loan Balance of Financial Institutions (100 million yuan)	1 106.80	7 254.26	29 684.10	34 154.17
有价证券成交总额(亿元)	Total Volume of Priced Security Trade (100 million)		49 901.47	441 874.67	398 395.73
#股 票	Stocks		31 373.86	346 511.90	304 312.01
原保险保费收入（亿元）	Premium of Primary Income(100 million yuan)	8.99	127.23	665.03	883.86
原保险赔付支出（亿元）	Payment of Primary Insurance (100 million yuan)	2.22	36.44	176.74	194.54
教育、科技、文化	**Education, Science&Technology and Culture**				
教 育	**Education**				
在校学生数（万人）	Students Enrollment(10 000 persons)				
高等学校	Institutions of Higher Education	12.13	22.68	51.28	51.57
普通中学	Regular Secondary Schools	48.31	79.54	60.37	59.44
小 学	Primary Schools	110.19	78.86	67.12	70.16
每万人拥有大学生(人)	Number of College and University Students Per 10 000 Persons(person)	90	141	232	224

表 1.4 续表 3　continued

指　标	Indicators	1990	2000	2009	2010
科　技	**Science and Technology**				
科技成果（项）	Achievements in Science and Technology (item)	2 092	1 102	2 166	2 318
研究与试验发展经费支出（亿元）	Research and Development Expenditures (100 million yuan)	10.13	76.73	423.38	480.18
研究与试验发展经费支出相当于上海市生产总值比例(%)	R&D Expenditure as Percentage of Gross Domestic Product(%)	1.30	1.61	2.81	2.80
文　化	**Culture**				
出版数量	Number of Publications				
图　书（亿册、张）	Books (100 million copies)	2.98	2.54	2.74	2.89
期　刊（亿册）	Periodicals (100 million copies)	1.73	1.85	1.79	1.77
报　纸（亿份）	Newspapers (100 million copies)	16.16	16.77	16.33	15.90
故事影片产量（部）	Feature Films Produced(film)	16	10	11	19
家庭、生活、环境	**Family, Living and Environment**				
家　庭	**Household**				
家庭总户数（万户）	Total Households (10 000 households)	415.28	475.73	509.79	519.27
平均每户家庭人口（人）	Average Persons per Household (person)	3.1	2.8	2.7	2.7
婚　姻	**Marriages and Divorces**				
准予登记结婚（万对）	Marriage Registration Permitted (10 000 couples)	10.77	9.31	14.99	13.03
离婚人数（万人）	Divorce (10 000 persons)	3.27	6.36	9.65	9.34
住　宅	**Housing**				
市区人均居住面积(平方米)	Per Capita Net Floor Space of Urban Residents(sq·m)	6.6	11.8	17.2	17.5
农村居民人均居住面积(平方米)	Per Capita Net Floor Space of Rural Residents(sq·m)	37.08	53.58	60.18	59.68
生　活	**Living**				
城市居民人均可支配收入（元）	Per Capita Annual Disposable Income of Urban Households(yuan)	2 183	11 718	28 838	31 838
城市居民人均消费支出（元）	Per Capita Annual Consumption Expenditures of Urban Households(yuan)	1 937	8 868	20 992	23 200
农村居民人均可支配收入（元）	Per Capita Annual Disposable Income of Rural Households(yuan)	1 665	5 565	12 324	13 746
农村居民人均生活消费支出（元）	Per Capita Annual Consumption Expenditure of Rural Households(yuan)	1 262	4 138	9 804	10 225
储蓄存款年末余额（亿元）	Saving Deposits of Urban and Rural Households (100 million yuan)	252.16	2 627.07	14 357.65	16 249.29

表 1.4 续表 4 continued

	指 标 Indicators	1990	2000	2009	2010
工 资	**Wages**				
职工工资总额(亿元)	Total Wages of Staff and Workers(100 million yuan)	146.78	614.53	2 594.21	3 018.55
职工平均工资(元)	Average Wages of Staff and Workers (yuan)	2 917	15 420	42 789	46 757
卫 生	**Health Care**				
医 院(个)	Quantity of Hospitals (unit)	462	459	296	306
医 生(万人)	Doctors (10 000 persons)	5.82	4.99	5.11	5.13
医院床位数(万张)	Quantity of Hospital Beds (10 000 beds)	6.21	7.31	7.95	8.48
每万人拥有医生(人)	Quantity of Doctors Per 10 000 Persons (person)	44	31	23	22
城市建设	**Urban Construction**				
城市基础设施投资额(亿元)	Investment in Urban Infrastructure (100 million yuan)	47.22	449.90	2 113.45	1 497.46
自来水售水量(亿立方米)	Sales Volume of Tap Water (100 million cu. m)	12.25	19.75	24.06	24.44
用电量(亿千瓦时)	Electric Power Consumption (100 million kwh)	264.74	559.51	1 153.38	1 295.87
煤气销售总量(亿立方米)	Total Sales Volume (100 million cu. m)	12.15	18.40	14.19	12.85
年末出租车运营总数(辆)	Year-end Operating Taxi Vehicles (vehicle)	11 298	42 943	49 111	50 007
运营公交车辆数(辆)	Total Number of Public Buses (vehicle)	6 264	17 939	16 272	17 455
道路长度(公里)	Length of Roads (km)	1 631	6 641	16 071	16 687
城市人均公共绿地面积(平方米)	Public Green Areas Per Capita (sq. m)	1.02	4.60	12.80	13.00
城市绿化覆盖率(%)	Coverage Rate of Urban Green Areas (%)	12.4	22.2	38.1	38.2
森林覆盖率(%)	Coverage Rate of Forest(%)	5.5	9.2	11.6	12.6
环境保护投资相当于上海市生产总值比例(%)	Environment Protection Investment as Percentage of Gross Domestic Product (%)		3.10	3.06	2.96
环境空气质量优良率(%)	Rate of Good Ambient Air Quality (%)		80.8	91.5	92.1
火灾、交通事故	**Fires and Traffic Accidents**				
火灾发生数(起)	Quantity of Fires (unit)	2 146	5 164	6 086	5 703
火灾损失额(万元)	Loss of Fires (10 000 yuan)	1 868	1 919	3 990	22 949
交通事故发生数(万起)	Quantity of Traffic Accidents(10 000 unit)	0.76	4.13	0.28	0.22
交通事故损失额(万元)	Loss of Traffic Accidents (10 000 yuan)	1 345	20 391	1 226	967

注：本表总量指标中的价值量指标均按当年价格计算。
Note: The data in value terms in the table are calculated at current prices.

表 1.5　主要年份社会经济主要指标发展速度
GROWTH RATE OF MAJOR SOCIAL AND ECONOMIC INDICATORS IN MAIN YEARS

单位:%

指　标	Indicators	2010 年比下列各年增长 Indicator's Growth Rate Between 2010 and Year Below		
		1990	2000	2009
年末常住人口	Year-end Residnet Population	72.6	43.1	4.2
上海市生产总值	Gross Domestic Product	8.5 倍	2.0 倍	10.3
第一产业	Primary Industry	12.9	-10.9	-6.6
第二产业	Secondary Industry	8.2 倍	2.0 倍	16.8
第三产业	Tertiary Industry	10.4 倍	2.0 倍	5.7
全社会固定资产投资总额	Total Investment in Fixed Assets	22.4 倍	1.8 倍	0.8
地方财政收入	Local Fiscal Revenue	16.2 倍	4.8 倍	13.1
地方财政支出	Local Fiscal Expenditure	42.7 倍	4.3 倍	10.5
农业总产值	Gross Output Value of Agriculture	42.2	-10.2	-5.1
工业总产值	Gross Output Value of Industry	16.7 倍	3.3 倍	22.9
轻工业	Light Industry	7.4 倍	1.6 倍	18.0
重工业	Heavy Industry	25.8 倍	4.4 倍	24.3
货物运输量	Freight Transportation Volume	2.5 倍	69.0	5.3
旅客发送量	Passenger Departures	2.5 倍	94.9	20.6
港口货物吞吐量	Port Cargo Throughput	3.7 倍	2.2 倍	10.4
社会消费品零售总额	Retail Sales of Consumer Goods	17.2 倍	2.3 倍	17.3
上海关区进出口总额	Total Trade Value Through Customs	38.6 倍	5.3 倍	32.8
进口额	Imports	29.3 倍	4.5 倍	37.3
出口额	Exports	47.9 倍	5.9 倍	30.2
上海进出口总额	Total Value of Imports and Exports	48.6 倍	5.7 倍	32.8
进口额	Imports	88.1 倍	5.4 倍	38.5
出口额	Exports	33 倍	6.1 倍	27.4
直接吸收外资	Foreign Direct Investment			
签订合同项目	Number of Contracts	18.2 倍	1.2 倍	26.4
签订合同金额	Contractual Foreign Investment	70.5 倍	1.4 倍	15.1
实际到位金额	Foreign Investment Actually Absorbed	61.8 倍	2.5 倍	5.5
城市居民家庭人均可支配收入	Per Capita Annual Disposable Income of Urban Households	14.8 倍	1.9 倍	10.4
城市居民家庭人均消费支出	Per Capita Annual Consumption Expenditures of Urban Households	10.9 倍	1.6 倍	10.5
农村居民家庭人均可支配收入	Per Capita Annual Disposable Income of Rural Households	7.3 倍	1.5 倍	11.5
农村居民家庭人均生活消费支出	Per Capita Annual Consumption Expenditures of Rural Households	7.1 倍	1.5 倍	4.3
城市基础设施投资额	Investment in Urban Infrastructure	30.7 倍	2.3 倍	-29.1
医　生	Doctors	-11.9	2.8	0.4
高等学校在校学生	Student Enrollment of Institutions of Higher Education	3.3 倍	1.3 倍	0.6

注：本表速度指标中，上海市生产总值及三次产业、工业总产值、农业总产值均按可比价格计算。

Note: The growth rates of the following indicators are calculated by comparable prices: gross domestic product and three industries, gross output value of agriculture and industry.

表 1.5 续表 continued

单位:%

指 标	Indicators	平均每年增长 Indicators'Average Annual Growth Rate 1991 ~ 2010	2001 ~ 2010
年末常住人口	Year-end Resident Population	2.8	3.7
上海市生产总值	Gross Domestic Product	11.9	11.6
第一产业	Primary Industry	0.6	-1.2
第二产业	Secondary Industry	11.7	11.6
第三产业	Tertiary Industry	13.0	11.8
全社会固定资产投资总额	Total Investment in Fixed Assets	20.0	12.2
地方财政收入	Local Fiscal Revenue	15.3	19.2
地方财政支出	Local Fiscal Expenditure	20.8	18.2
农业总产值	Gross Output Value of Agriculture	1.8	-1.1
工业总产值	Gross Output Value of Industry	15.5	15.8
轻工业	Light Industry	11.2	10.0
重工业	Heavy Industry	17.9	18.3
货物运输量	Freight Transportation Volume	6.5	5.4
旅客发送量	Passenger Departures	6.5	6.9
港口货物吞吐量	Port Cargo Throughput	8.0	12.3
社会消费品零售总额	Retail Sales of Consumer Goods	15.6	12.5
上海关区进出口总额	Total Trade Value Through Customs	20.2	20.1
进口额	Imports	18.6	18.5
出口额	Exports	21.5	21.3
上海市进出口总额	Total Value of Imports and Exports	21.6	21.0
进口额	Imports	25.2	20.4
出口额	Exports	19.3	21.7
城市居民家庭人均可支配收入	Per Capita Annual Disposable Income of Urban Households	14.8	10.4
城市居民家庭人均消费支出	Per Capita Annual Consumption Expenditures of Urban Households	13.2	10.0
农村居民家庭人均可支配收入	Per Capita Annual Disposable Income of Rural Households	11.1	9.5
农村居民家庭人均生活消费支出	Per Capita Consumption Expenditure of Rural Households	11.0	9.5
医 生	Doctors	-0.6	0.3
高等学校在校学生	Student Enrollment of Institutions of Higher Education	7.5	8.6
城市基础设施投资额	Investment in Urban Infrastructure	22.3	16.1

表 1.6　主要年份社会经济发展结构指标
STRUCTURAL INDICATORS OF SOCIAL AND ECONOMIC DEVELOPMENT IN MAIN YEARS

单位:%

指　标	Indicators	1990	2000	2009	2010
农业非农业人口结构	Structure of Agriculture and Non-agriculture	100	100	100	100
农　业	Agriculture	32.6	25.4	11.7	11.1
非农业	Non-agriculture	67.4	74.6	88.3	88.9
人口性别结构	Structure of Sex	100	100	100	100
男	Male	50.4	50.4	49.9	51.5
女	Female	49.6	49.6	50.1	48.5
上海市生产总值产业结构	Industrial Structure of GDP	100	100	100	100
第一产业	Primary Industry	4.4	1.6	0.7	0.7
第二产业	Secondary Industry	64.7	46.3	39.9	42.0
第三产业	Tertiary Industry	30.9	52.1	59.4	57.3
上海市生产总值所有制结构	Ownership Structure of GDP	100	100	100	100
公有制经济	Public State-owned	95.4	71.4	51.6	50.5
国有经济	State-owned	71.2	55.0	45.6	45.2
集体经济	Collective-owned	24.2	16.4	6.0	5.3
非公有制经济	Non-state-owned	4.6	28.6	48.4	49.5
全社会固定资产投资所有制结构	Ownership Structure of Total Investment	100	100	100	100
国有经济	State-owned	84.7	44.4	49.7	42.0
非国有经济	Non-State-owned	15.3	55.6	50.3	58.0
地方财政收入结构	Structure of Local Fiscal Revenue	100	100	100	100
#增值税	Value-added Tax		18.8	14.7	13.5
营业税	Business Tax		30.9	33.1	32.5
企业所得税	Enterprise Income Tax		20.7	19.0	21.1
个人所得税	Personal Income Tax		12.1	9.1	9.1
外商直接投资实际吸收外资结构	Foreign Direct Investment Structure of Foreign Investment Actually Absorbed	100	100	100	100
#合资企业	Joint Ventures	61.0	40.9	15.3	16.0
合作企业	Coopراtive Enterprises	37.9	9.5	1.9	1.5
独资企业	Sole-foreign Enterprises	1.1	49.6	82.7	81.6
农业总产值结构	Structure of Gross Output Value of Agriculture	100	100	100	100
#种植业	Planting	42.7	41.5	52.1	54.1
牧　业	Animal Husbandry	44.4	40.3	22.8	21.9
渔　业	Fishery	11.8	17.5	18.9	18.3
工业总产值结构	Structure of Gross Output Value of Industry	100	100	100	100
轻工业	Light Industry	51.5	41.3	22.8	21.6
重工业	Heavy Industry	48.5	58.7	77.2	78.4

表 1.6 续表 continued

单位:%

指 标	Indicators	1990	2000	2009	2010
货物运输总量结构	Structure of Freight Transportation	100	100	100	100
铁 路	Railways	5.5	2.2	1.2	1.2
公 路	Roadways	38.2	59.1	49.1	50.5
水 运	Waterways	56.3	38.5	49.3	47.9
民用航空	Civil Aviation	…	0.2	0.4	0.5
社会消费品零售总额结构	Structure of Retail Sales of Consumer Goods	100	100	100	100
吃	Food	42.6	39.8	31.1	30.1
穿	Clothing	15.7	13.4	11.2	11.3
用	Articles	41.1	46.0	52.5	52.7
烧	Fuels	0.6	0.8	5.2	5.9
上海市出口总额结构	Structure of Exports		100	100	100
#一般贸易	General Trade		40.1	34.4	35
加工贸易	Processing Trade		58.3	57.4	55.5
中资金融机构人民币存款余额结构	Structure of RMB Saving Deposit in Chinese Financial Institution	100	100	100	100
#企业存款	Enterprise Deposits	43.1	56.9	49.1	45.0
储蓄存款	Saving Deposits	41.1	32.5	34.0	33.2
中资金融机构人民币贷款余额结构	Structure of RMB Loans in Chinese Financial Institution	100	100	100	100
#短期贷款	Short Term Loans	75.2	72.9	25.8	24.0
中长期贷款	Medium and Long Term Loans	14.8	18.0	64.4	68.2
在校学生结构	Structure of Students Enrollment	100	100	100	100
大学生	University and College Students	7.1	12.5	28.7	28.5
中学生	Secondary Students	28.3	43.9	33.8	32.8
小学生	Primary Students	64.6	43.6	37.5	38.7
城市居民消费支出结构	Consumption Structure of Urban Households	100	100	100	100
#食 品	Food	56.5	44.5	35.0	33.5
衣 着	Clothing	10.7	6.4	7.6	7.7
家庭设备、用品及服务	Household Facilities, Articles and Services	10.1	7.7	6.5	7.8
交通和通信	Transportation and Communications	3.0	8.6	16.7	17.6
教育文化娱乐服务	Cultural, Education and Recreation Services	11.9	14.5	14.9	14.5
居 住	Residence	4.7	9.0	9.1	9.3
农村居民消费支出结构	Consumption Structure of Rural Households	100	100	100	100
#食 品	Food	46.4	44.0	37.1	37.2
衣 着	Clothing	8.5	4.9	5.1	5.4
家庭设备、用品及服务	Household Facilities, Articles and Services	10.2	5.4	4.9	5.2
交通和通信	Transportation and Communications	0.5	6.7	12.4	14.3
文教娱乐用品及服务	Culture, Education ,Recreation Articles and Services	4.7	13.5	9.6	9.9
居 住	Residence	21.6	17.5	21.5	20.2
卫生机构数结构	Structure of Health Care Institutions	100	100	100	100
#医 院	Hospitals	6.0	10.4	9.8	9.4
卫生技术人员结构	Structure of Medical Professionals	100	100	100	100
#医 生	Doctors	49.2	46.6	39.0	37.9
护师、护士	Senior and Junior Nurses	27.6	34.4	39.9	41.3

表 1.7　各时期社会经济主要指标
MAJOR SOCIAL AND ECONOMIC INDICATORS OF EACH FIVE-YEAR PLAN PERIOD

时　期	Period	上海市生产总值（亿元） Gross Domestic Product (100 million yuan)	其　中 of which 第一产业 Primary Industry	第二产业 Secondary Industry	第三产业 Tertiary Industry	地　方财政收入（亿元） Local Fiscal Revenue (100 million yuan)
"一五"时期	"First Five-year Plan" Period	293.26	12.56	163.89	116.81	14.93
"二五"时期	"Second Five-year Plan" Period	568.99	21.03	412.70	135.26	304.28
1963～1965		304.94	17.28	220.81	66.85	172.51
"三五"时期	"Third Five-year Plan" Period	657.06	37.64	487.88	131.54	374.19
"四五"时期	"Fourth Five-year Plan" Period	918.76	42.75	708.84	167.17	633.79
"五五"时期	"Fifth Five-year Plan" Period	1 309.61	49.26	1 004.23	256.12	797.56
"六五"时期	"Sixth Five-year Plan" Period	1 871.24	74.20	1 349.98	447.06	846.92
"七五"时期	"Seventh Five-year Plan" Period	3 162.79	132.52	2 105.23	925.04	846.96
"八五"时期	"Eighth Five-year Plan" Period	8 017.61	213.47	4 698.27	3 105.87	1 006.06
"九五"时期	"Ninth Five-year Plan" Period	19 157.33	365.76	9 434.90	9 356.67	1 962.85
"十五"时期	"Tenth Five-year Plan" Period	34 965.87	412.41	16 507.97	18 045.49	4 792.94
"十一五"时期	"Eleventh Five-year Program" Period	69 348.55	535.42	29 846.95	38 966.18	11 499.22

表 1.7 续表 continued

时　期	Period	地　方财政支出（亿元） Local Fiscal Expenditure (100 million yuan)	工　业总产值（亿元） Gross Output Value of Industry (100 million yuan)	全社会固定资产投资总额（亿元） Total Investment in Fixed Assets (100 million yuan)	上海市出口总额（亿美元） Total Exports Value (100 million USD)	社会消费品零售总额（亿元） Retail Sales of Consumer Goods (100 million yuan)
"一五"时期	"First Five-year Plan" Period	12.25	512.03	19.29	17.46	121.02
"二五"时期	"Second Five-year Plan" Period	60.79	1 069.50	55.60	31.00	145.82
1963～1965		19.28	596.63	20.29	20.12	79.50
"三五"时期	"Third Five-year Plan" Period	39.41	1 334.94	34.77	43.08	153.86
"四五"时期	"Fourth Five-year Plan" Period	86.78	1 894.01	95.79	92.86	200.62
"五五"时期	"Fifth Five-year Plan" Period	111.30	2 550.91	151.44	150.33	302.07
"六五"时期	"Sixth Five-year Plan" Period	138.52	3 509.15	412.74	180.08	576.32
"七五"时期	"Seventh Five-year Plan" Period	327.68	6 498.13	1 020.34	226.96	1 383.16
"八五"时期	"Eighth Five-year Plan" Period	775.11	17 308.90	3 994.67	403.31	3 408.52
"九五"时期	"Ninth Five-year Plan" Period	2 421.50	29 776.04	9 620.86	880.57	7 874.26
"十五"时期	"Tenth Five-year Plan" Period	5 762.87	59 716.74	13 261.11	2 724.27	12 261.12
"十一五"时期	"Eleventh Five-year Program" Period	12 925.94	124 634.89	23 804.15	7 495.49	23 069.47

表 1.8　各时期社会经济主要指标平均增长率
GROWTH RATE OF MAJOR SOCIAL AND ECONOMIC INDICATORS OF EACH FIVE-YEAR PLAN PERIOD

单位:%

时　期		上海市生产总值 Gross Domestic Product	其　中　of which			地　方财政收入 Local Fiscal Revenue
Period			第一产业 Primary Industry	第二产业 Secondary Industry	第三产业 Tertiary Industry	
"一五"时期	"First Five-year Plan" Period	13.8	3.3	18.4	8.3	12.6
"二五"时期	"Second Five-year Plan" Period	1.6	1.3	4.1	-3.1	57.2
1963 ~ 1965		17.0	11.6	21.8	5.6	12.3
"三五"时期	"Third Five-year Plan" Period	8.7	3.3	9.7	5.7	9.7
"四五"时期	"Fourth Five-year Plan" Period	6.6	-1.6	7.1	6.2	6.4
"五五"时期	"Fifth Five-year Plan" Period	8.4	0.9	8.6	8.6	5.1
"六五"时期	"Sixth Five-year Plan" Period	9.1	4.3	8.3	12.3	1.1
"七五"时期	"Seventh Five-year Plan" Period	5.7	1.2	5.0	8.0	-1.6
"八五"时期	"Eighth Five-year Plan" Period	13.1	1.4	13.9	12.8	6.0
"九五"时期	"Ninth Five-year Plan" Period	11.5	3.4	9.7	15.5	17.0
"十五"时期	"Tenth Five-year Plan" Period	11.9	-1.4	13.1	11.2	23.6
"十一五"时期	"Eleventh Five-year Program " Period	11.2	-0.9	10.2	12.3	14.9

表 1.8 续表 continued

单位:%

时　期 Period		地　方财政支出 Local Fiscal Expenditure	工　业总产值 Gross Output Value of Industry	全社会固定资产投资总额 Total Investment in Fixed Assets	上海市出口总额 Total Exports Value	社会消费品零售总额 Retail Sales of Consumer Goods
"一五"时期	"First Five-year Plan" Period	12.3	14.5	23.1	30.6	5.6
"二五"时期	"Second Five-year Plan" Period	0.6	4.9	26.5	4.2	1.2
1963 ~ 1965		25.2	18.8	31.4	11.4	-0.1
"三五"时期	"Third Five-year Plan" Period	11.2	10.2	-3.6	2.5	3.3
"四五"时期	"Fourth Five-year Plan" Period	15.5	7.5	19.4	20.7	8.4
"五五"时期	"Fifth Five-year Plan" Period	-6.3	7.6	-2.4	14.0	11.0
"六五"时期	"Sixth Five-year Plan" Period	19.2	7.7	20.6	-4.7	16.6
"七五"时期	"Seventh Five-year Plan" Period	10.4	5.9	18.7	9.6	14.0
"八五"时期	"Eighth Five-year Plan" Period	28.8	18.0	45.4	16.8	25.8
"九五"时期	"Ninth Five-year Plan" Period	18.4	12.3	6.2	17.0	12.2
"十五"时期	"Tenth Five-year Plan" Period	21.7	19.2	11.9	29.0	9.8
"十一五"时期	"Eleventh Five-year Program" Period	14.7	12.6	10.0	17.2	15.3

表 1.9　国民经济主要指标比上年增长(1978～2010)
GROWTH RATE OF MAJOR NATIONAL ECONOMIC INDICATORS OVER PRECEDING YEAR

单位:%

年　份 Year	上海市 生产总值 Gross Domestic Product	地　方 财政收入 Local Fiscal Revenue	地　方 财政支出 Local Fiscal Expenditure	工　业 总产值 Gross Output Value of Industry	全社会固定资产 投资总额 Total Investment in Fixed Assets
1978	15.8	14.6	51.4	12.1	55.1
1979	7.4	2.1	4.0	8.6	27.5
1980	8.4	1.2	-29.1	6.5	27.7
1981	5.6	-0.2	-0.6	3.7	20.2
1982	7.2	-3.6	8.5	4.7	30.7
1983	7.8	-6.9	8.3	7.0	6.5
1984	11.6	4.8	35.4	9.9	21.5
1985	13.4	12.4	51.9	13.5	28.5
1986	4.4	-2.6	28.2	5.5	23.9
1987	7.5	-5.8	-8.9	6.7	26.8
1988	10.1	-4.3	22.3	10.5	31.7
1989	3.0	3.3	11.3	3.0	-12.4
1990	3.5	0.1	3.1	4.0	5.7
1991	7.1	5.1	13.9	14.1	13.7
1992	14.8	5.7	10.4	20.2	38.4
1993	15.1	30.6	36.1	20.0	83.0
1994	14.5	-27.7	52.3	18.2	71.8
1995	14.3	29.6	36.0	17.4	42.6
1996	13.1	26.9	27.9	15.5	21.9
1997	12.8	22.1	25.2	14.5	1.3
1998	10.3	11.3	12.1	7.8	-0.6
1999	10.4	10.1	13.7	10.5	-5.5
2000	11.0	15.3	14.0	13.5	0.7
2001	10.5	24.6	16.6	16.4	6.7
2002	11.3	16.1	20.9	14.6	9.6
2003	12.3	24.9	25.6	31.4	12.1
2004	14.2	24.5	26.6	20.3	25.8
2005	11.4	28.7	19.0	13.9	14.8
2006	12.7	11.6	9.2	13.9	10.8
2007	15.2	31.4	21.4	15.7	13.6
2008	9.7	13.3	18.9	8.1	8.3
2009	8.2	7.7	15.3	3.2	9.2
2010	10.3	13.1	10.5	22.9	0.8

表 1.9 续表 continued

单位:%

年份 Year	上海市进出口总额 Total Value of Import and Export	#出口总额 Export	社会消费品零售总额 Retail Sales of Consumer Goods	直接吸收外资合同金额 Contracted Foreign Direct Investment	直接吸收外资实际到位金额 Actually Absorbed Foreign Direct Investment	港口货物吞吐量 Cargo Handled at Ports	城市居民家庭人均可支配收入 Per Capita Annual Disposable Income of Urban Households
1978	30.4	30.3	9.8			30.6	
1979	28.2	27.0	26.2			5.0	
1980	16.2	16.1	17.8			1.6	
1981	-7.9	-10.8	10.3	1.0倍	…	-1.7	
1982	-6.2	-5.3	1.2	1.8倍	…	7.7	3.5
1983	6.3	1.2	12.1	1.8倍	2.7倍	2.4	4.0
1984	6.3	-1.7	22.9	3.1倍	1.5倍	9.5	21.6
1985	17.6	-6.3	40.1	56.4	1.2倍	12.2	28.9
1986	0.6	6.6	13.5	-68.9	58.1	11.6	20.3
1987	15.2	16.1	14.4	35.8	1.2倍	1.8	11.1
1988	20.8	10.7	31.3	28.7	71.7	3.8	19.9
1989	8.3	9.3	12.0	6.6	15.9	9.6	14.6
1990	-5.3	5.7	0.7	20.9	-58.1	-4.4	10.5
1991	8.2	7.9	14.4	30.4	-1.1	5.2	13.9
1992	21.3	14.2	21.7	5.7倍	6.2倍	11.0	21.1
1993	30.5	12.6	45.4	1.0倍	84.1	8.0	42.2
1994	24.6	23.0	23.5	42.3	39.4	-5.8	37.2
1995	19.9	27.5	25.9	0.2	0.6	-0.1	22.2
1996	17.0	14.3	19.7	8.4	45.1	-1.0	13.8
1997	11.2	11.2	14.1	-8.4	2.0	…	3.4
1998	26.6	8.4	11.0	9.9	-24.3	-0.1	4.0
1999	23.2	17.7	8.1	-29.8	-16.2	13.7	24.6
2000	41.7	35.0	8.3	55.7	3.7	9.7	7.2
2001	11.3	9.0	8.1	15.4	39.0	8.1	9.9
2002	19.3	16.0	9.3	43.4	14.5	19.4	11.5
2003	54.7	51.2	9.1	23.5	30.1	19.8	12.2
2004	42.4	51.6	10.5	12.6	11.8	19.8	12.2
2005	16.5	23.4	12.1	18.3	4.7	16.9	11.8
2006	22.1	25.2	13.3	5.4	3.8	21.3	10.8
2007	24.4	26.7	14.8	2.0	11.4	4.5	14.3
2008	13.8	17.7	18.2	15.1	27.3	3.6	12.9
2009	-13.8	-16.2	13.0	-22.3	4.5	1.8	8.1
2010	32.8	27.4	17.3	15.1	5.5	10.4	10.4

表 1.10 上海社会经济主要指标占全国比重(2010) PERCENTAGE OF THE NATIONAL TOTAL OF SHANGHAI'S MAJOR SOCIAL AND ECONOMIC INDICATORS

指 标	Indicators	全 国 Country	上 海 Shanghai	上海占全国比重(%) Percentage of the National Total(%)
土地面积(万平方公里)	Land Area (10 000 sq·km)	960	0.63	0.1
生产总值(亿元)	Gross Domestic Product (100 million yuan)	397 983	17 165.98	4.3
第一产业	Primary Industry	40 497	114.15	0.3
第二产业	Secondary Industry	186 481	7 218.32	3.9
#工 业	Industry	160 030	6 536.21	4.1
第三产业	Tertiary Industry	171 005	9 833.51	5.8
港口货物吞吐量(亿吨)	Port Cargo Handled at Seaports (100 millions tons)	54.54	6.53	11.9
国际标准集装箱吞吐量(万 TEU)	International Container Throughput Capacity (10 000TEU)	14 613	2 906.90	19.9
邮电业务总量(亿元)	Revenue of Post and Telecommunication (100 million yuan)	32 940	1 016.44	3.1
全社会固定资产投资总额(亿元)	Total Investment in Fixed Assets (100 million yuan)	278 140	5 317.67	1.9
社会消费品零售总额(亿元)	Retail Sales of Consumer Goods (100 million yuan)	154 553.70	6 070.50	3.9
上海关区进出口总额(亿美元)	Total Trade Value Through Customs (100 million USD)	29 727.61	6 846.45	23.0
进口额	Imports	13 948.29	2 613.05	18.7
出口额	Exports	15 779.32	4 233.40	26.8
外商直接投资实际到位金额(亿美元)	Foreign Direct Investment Actually Absorbed (100 million USD)	1 057.35	111.21	10.5
国际旅游入境人数(万人次)	Number of International Tourists (10 000 person-times)	13 376.22	851.12	6.4
研究与试验发展经费支出(亿元)	Research and Development Expenditure (100 million yuan)	6 980	480.18	6.9
图书出版量(亿册/张)	Books Published (100 million copies/signatures)	74	2.89	3.9
期 刊(亿册)	Periodicals (100 million copies)	32	1.77	5.5
报纸出版量(亿份)	Newspapers Published (100 million copies)	448	15.90	3.5
医生(万人)	Doctors (10 000 persons)	241.3	5.13	2.1
医院床位数(万张)	Beds in Hospitals (10 000 beds)	440.1	8.48	1.9

表1.11 主要年份人大情况
BASIC STATISTIC OF SHANGHAI MUNICIPAL PEOPLE'S CONGRESS IN MAIN YEARS

类别	Types	2000	2009	2010
全国人大代表人数(人)	Quantity of National Congress(person)	68	66	66
#女　性	Female	17	17	17
全国人大代表提出议案(件)	Proposals Offered by National Congress Representations (case)		21	21
市人大代表人数(人)	Quantity of Municipal CongressRepresentatives(person)	865	867	864
#女　性	Female	203	244	244
市人大常委人数(人)	Quantity of Municipal Standing Committee(person)	65	55	64
#女　性	Female	13	9	9
市人大代表提出议案(件)	Proposals Offered by Municipal CongressRepresentatives (case)		78	78
区县人大代表人数(人)	Quantity of District Level Congress Representatives (person)	4 944	4 651	4 667
#女　性	Female	1 451	1 447	1 454
区县人大常委人数(人)	Quantity of District Level Standing Committee(person)	432	401	414
#女　性	Female	67	90	94

注：本表数据由市人大代表工作委员会提供。
Note: Data in this table are provided by Shanghai Committee of People's Congress.

表1.12 主要年份政协情况
BASIC STATISTICS ON SHANGHAI MUNICIPAL PEOPLE'S POLITICAL CONSULTATIVE CONFERENCE IN MAIN YEARS

类别	Types	2000	2009	2010
全国政协委员人数(人)	Quantity of National Commissary (person)	104	108	109
#女　性	Female	20	18	18
全国政协委员提出议案(件)	Proposals Offered by National Commissary (case)		209	30
市政协委员人数(人)	Quantity of Municipal Commissary(person)	729	816	817
#女　性	Female	120	171	168
市政协常委人数(人)	Quantity of Municipal Standing Committee(person)	121	140	132
#女　性	Female	20	25	24
市政协委员提出提案(件)	Proposals Offered by Municipal Commissary (case)	1 197	1 049	944
区县政协委员人数(人)	Quantity of District Level Commissary(person)	4 802	5 261	5 280
#女　性	Female	1 230	1 444	1 459
区县政协常委人数(人)	Quantity of District Level Standing Committee(person)	707	713	709
#女　性	Female	174	148	154

注：本表数据由市政协提供。
Note: Data in this table are provided by Shanghai Municipal People's Political Consultative Conference.

上 / 海 / 统 / 计 / 年 / 鉴

主要统计指标解释

行政区划

指国家对行政区域的划分。根据宪法规定,我国的行政区域划分如下:(1)全国分为省、自治区、直辖市;(2)省、自治区分为自治州、县、自治县、市;(3)自治州分为县、自治县、市;(4)县、自治县分为乡、民族乡、镇;(5)直辖市和较大的市分为区、县;(6)国家在必要时设立的特别行政区。

气　候

指地球与大气之间长期能量交换与质量交换所形成的一种自然环境状态,它是多种因素综合作用的结果。气候既是人类生活和生产的环境要素之一,又是供给人类生活和生产的重要资源。气温、降水、湿度等气象要素的多年平均值是用来描述一个地区气候状况的主要参数,而各种气象要素某年、某月的平均值(或总量)则可以反映出该时期天气气候状况的重要特征。

气　温

指空气的温度,一般以摄氏度(℃)为单位表示。气象观测的温度表是放在离地面约 1.5 米处通风良好的百叶箱里测量的,因此,通常说的气温指的是离地面 1.5 米处百叶箱中的温度。其统计计算方法为:

月平均气温是将全月各日的平均气温相加,除以该月的天数而得。

年平均气温是将 12 个月的月平均气温累加后除以 12 而得。

降水量

指从天空降落到地面的液态或固态(经融化后)水,未经蒸发、渗透、流失而在地面上积聚的深度。其统计计算方法为:

月降水量是将全月各日的降水量累加而得。

年降水量是将 12 个月的月降水量累加而得。

日照时间

指太阳实际照射地面的时间。其统计方法与降水量相同。

国民经济行业分类

《国民经济行业分类》国家标准于 1984 年首次发布,1994 年对其进行了第一次修订,2002 年为第二次修订。

本年鉴的行业分类使用 2002 年修订的行业分类标准。

2002 年新行业分类标准按照国际通行的经济活动同质性原则划分行业,进一步打破了部门管理界限,对原标准中不符合这一原则的分类进行了调整;根据我国社会经济活动的发展状况,重点加强了第三产业的分类,新增了大量服务业方面的活动类别;对新标准的每一个行业小类,全部与国际标准产业分类的最细一层分类建立了对应关系。新修订的国民经济行业分类主要目的之一是与联合国的《全部经济活动的国际标准产业分类》接轨,准确反映一定时期内国民经济行业的构成状况。

各个计划时期

表内所用各个“时期”代表的年份如下:恢复时期为 1950 到 1952 年;第一个五年计划时期(简称“一五”时期)为 1953 到 1957 年;第二个五年计划时期(简称“二五”时期)为 1958 到 1962 年;第三个五年计划时期(简称“三五”时期)为 1966 到 1970 年;第四个五年计划时期(简称“四五”时期)为 1971 到 1975 年;第五个五年计划时期(简称“五五”时期)为 1976 到 1980 年;第六个五年计划时期(简称“六五”时期)为 1981 到 1985 年;第七个五年计划时期(简称“七五”时期)为 1986 到 1990 年;第八个五年计划时期(简称“八五”时期)为 1991 到 1995 年;第九个五年计划时期(简称“九五”时期)为 1996 到 2000 年;第十个五年计划时期(简称“十五”时期)为 2001 到 2005 年;第十一个五年规划时期(简称“十一五”时期)为 2006 到 2010 年。

指　数

指数是一种表明社会经济现象动态的相对数。运用指数可以测定不能直接相加和直接对比的社会经济现象的总动态;可以分析社会经济现象总变动中各因素变动的影响程度;可以研究总平均指标变动中各组标志水平和总体结构变动的作用。它是在把各个年份的产值换算成可比价格的基础上,根据定基数等于相应各个环比指数的连乘积这个换算关系计算出来的。

本年鉴所列的上海市生产总值、工业总产值、农业总产值等指标增长速度,就是分别使用上海市生产总值指数、工业总产值指数、农业总产值指数直接计算的。

主要统计指标解释

平均每年增长速度

在我国计算平均增长速度有两种方法。一种是习惯上经常使用的“水平法”,又称几何平均法,是以间隔期最后一年的水平同基期水平对比来计算平均每年增长(或下降)速度;另一种是“累计法”,又称代数平均法或方程法,是以间隔期内各年水平的总和同基期水平对比来计算平均每年增长(或下降)速度。

在一般正常情况下，两种方法计算的平均每年增长速度比较接近。但在经济发展不平衡,出现大起大落时,两种方法计算的结果差别较大。

本年鉴内所列的平均每年增长速度,除固定资产投资、直接吸收外资是用“累计法”计算以外,其余均用“水平法”计算。从某年到某年平均增长速度的年份,均不包括基期年在内。如 1991~2009 年平均增长速度是以 1990 年为基期计算的,余类推。

SHANGHAI STATISTICAL YEARBOOK

EXPLANATORY NOTES TO MAJOR STATISTICAL INDICATORS

□ Administrative Division

Administrative Division refers to the division of administrative areas by the state. The Constitution of the People's Republic of China stipulates that the administrative areas in China are divided as: 1) The whole country is divided into provinces, autonomous regions and municipalities directly under the central government; 2)Provinces and autonomous regions are divided into autonomous prefectures, counties, autonomous counties and cities; 3) Autonomous prefectures are divided into counties, autonomous counties and cities; 4) Counties and autonomous counties are divided into townships, nationality townships and towns; 5) Municipalities and large cities are divided into districts and counties, 6) The state shall, when necessary, establish special administrative regions.

□ Climate

Climate refers to the natural environmental status formed by the long-term exchange of energy and mass between the earth and the air, and is the results of interaction of many factors. Climate is both one of the environment factors and the important resources for the living and production activities of the human being. The average values across several years of meteorological factors such as temperature, rainfall and humidity are used as important parameters to describe the climate of a region, while the average values (or total values) of a given year or month of meteorological factors reflect the key characteristics of climate for that period of time.

□ Temperature

Temperature refers to the air temperature. It often uses centigrade as the unit. The thermometry used for weather observation is put in a breezy shutter, which is 1.5 meters high from the ground. Therefore, the commonly used temperature refers to the temperature in the breezy shutter 1.5 meters away from the ground. The calculation method is as follows:

Monthly average temperature is the summation of average daily temperature of one month divided by the actual days of that particular month. Annual average temperature is the summation of monthly average of a year divided by 12 months.

□ Volume of Precipitation

Volume of Precipitation refers to the deepness of liquid state or solid state (thawed) water falling from the sky to the ground that has not been evaporated, infiltrated or run off. The calculation method is as follows:

Monthly precipitation is the summation of daily precipitation of a month.

Annual precipitation is the summation of 12 months precipitation of a year.

□ Sunshine Hours

Sunshine Hours refer to the actual hours of sun irradiating the earth. The calculation method is the same as that of the precipitation.

□ Classification of the Sectors of the National Economy

Classification of the Sectors of the National Economy was first published in 1984 and revisions were made into it in 1994 and 2002 respectively .

This Yearbook follows standards in the 2002 version of the Classification of the Sectors of the National Economy.

In the 2002 version, economic sectors are classified in accordance with the international categories of the economic activities, abolishing in definition between different administrative departments. Given the development of China's social and economic activities, more detailed classification is made of the service sector. The further breakdown of each economic sector in the latest version is geared to the most specific categorization in international practice. The latest version aims at, among others, an objective and precise presentation of the composition of the national economy in a certain period.

□ Various Planning Periods

The conventional division of time period in this statistical yearbook is as follows: Rehabilitation Period, 1950-1952; The First Five-Year Plan period (cited as first-five period), 1953-1957; The Second Five-Year Plan period (cited as second-five period), 1958-1962; The Third Five-Year Plan period (cited as third-five period), 1966-1970; The Fourth Five-Year

EXPLANATORY NOTES TO MAJOR STATISTICAL INDICATORS

Plan period (cited as fourth–five period), 1971–1975; The Fifth Five–Year Plan period (cited as fifth–five period), 1976–1980; The Sixth Five–Year Plan period (cited as sixth–five period), 1981–1985; The Seventh Five–Year Plan period (cited as seventh–five period), 1986–1990; The Eight Five–Year Plan period (cited as eighth–five period), 1991–1995; The Ninth Five–Year Plan period (cited as ninth–five period),1996–2000;The Tenth Five–Year Plan period (cited as tenth–five period),2001–2005; The eleventh Five–Year Plan period (cited as eleventh–five period),2006–2010.

□ Index

Index refers to the relative figures indicating social and economic phenomena and developments. Index is used to evaluate the overall development of social and economic phenomena which can not be determined by simple addition or direct comparison. It is also used to analyze the outcome of various changes in the general phenomenon movement of social and economic development, and to study the level of each sub–index in the changes of general average index and the role of the changes of the overall structure. It is calculated at the comparable prices conversed from the output value of each year, using the formula of index number with fixed base period equal to the continuous product of its relative chain index .

The increases of Shanghai Gross Domestic Product, industrial output value and agricultural output value compared with the previous year, which are listed in this yearbook, are calculated according to Shanghai GDP index, industrial output value index and agricultural output value index.

□ Average Annual Growth Rate

Two methods for calculating Average Annual Growth Rate are applied in China, one is often called "level approach" or geometry average, which is derived by comparing the growth rate for the last year of the interval with that of the beginning year; the other is called "accumulating approach" or algebraic average or equation method, which is calculated by comparing the total growth rate of each year for the interval with that of base year .

Usually the results calculated by the two methods are fairly close, but they differ sharply when imbalance occurred in economic development with striking fluctuations in growth.

The Average Annual Growth Rates listed in this statistical yearbook are calculated by "level approach" except for the growth rate of investment in fixed assets and foreign capital absorbed. The base years are not listed when the years are listed for average annual growth rates for instance, the average annual growth rate of 1991–2009 is calculated with the base year 1990, and the analogy of this is also for the rest.

第二篇

CHAPTER 2

人口和劳动力

POPULATION AND LABOUR FORCE

表2.1 主要年份常住人口
RESIDENT POPULATION IN MAIN YEARS

单位:万人(10 000 persons)

指标	Indicators	2000	2009	2010
年末常住人口	Year-end Resident Population	1 608.60	2 210.28	2 302.66
户籍人口	Year-end Registered Population	1 295.11	1 390.70	1 404.71
外来人口(半年以上人口)	Year-end Floating Population (Above Half Year)	313.49	819.58	897.95

注：本表户籍人口不包括离开上海、外出(市外)半年以上本市户籍人口。
Note: Registered population in this table does not include those outside of Shanghai for over half year.

表2.2 主要年份户籍人口
REGISTERED POPULATION IN MAIN YEARS

单位:万人(10 000 persons)

指标	Indicators	2000	2009	2010
年末户籍人口	Year-end Registered Population	1 321.63	1 400.70	1 412.32
农业人口	Agriculture	335.47	164.54	157.37
非农业人口	Non-agriculture	986.16	1 236.16	1 254.95

注：本表数据由市公安局提供。
Note: Data in this table is provided by Shanghai Municipal Public Security Bureau.

表2.3 主要年份外来人口
FLOATING POPULATION IN MAIN YEARS

单位:万人(10 000 persons)

指标	Indicators	2000	2009	2010
年末外来人口	Floating Population	387.11	1 010.47	1 122.38
半年以下流动人口	Below Half Year	73.62	190.89	224.43
半年及以上常住人口	Above Half Year	313.49	819.58	897.95

表2.4　户数、人口、人口密度和户籍人口期望寿命(1978～2010)
TOTAL HOUSEHOLDS, POPULATION, DENSITY OF REGISTERED POPULATION AND LIFE EXPECTANCY

年　份 Year	总户数 (万户) Total Households (10 000 households)	平均每户人口 (人) Average Persons Per Household (person)	常住人口 (万人) Year-end Resident Population (10 000 persons)	人口密度 (人/平方公里) Density of Population (person/sq. km)	年末户籍人口 (万人) Year-end Registered Population (10 000 persons)	按性别分 Grouped by Sex	
						男　性 Male	女　性 Female
1978	291.69	3.8	1 104.00	1 785	1 098.28	542.70	555.58
1979	296.71	3.8	1 137.00	1 838	1 132.14	560.40	571.74
1980	303.87	3.8	1 152.00	1 862	1 146.52	569.30	577.22
1981	314.56	3.7	1 168.00	1 888	1 162.84	578.76	584.08
1982	321.71	3.7	1 186.00	1 917	1 180.51	588.82	591.69
1983	330.60	3.6	1 201.00	1 942	1 194.01	596.67	597.34
1984	340.78	3.5	1 217.00	1 968	1 204.78	602.59	602.19
1985	351.72	3.5	1 233.00	1 993	1 216.69	609.70	606.99
1986	364.92	3.4	1 249.00	1 970	1 232.33	618.88	613.45
1987	380.19	3.3	1 265.00	1 995	1 249.51	628.78	620.73
1988	394.95	3.2	1 288.00	2 031	1 262.42	635.82	626.60
1989	406.82	3.1	1 311.00	2 067	1 276.45	643.51	632.94
1990	415.28	3.1	1 334.00	2 104	1 283.35	647.13	636.22
1991	425.84	3.0	1 350.00	2 128	1 287.20	649.03	638.17
1992	431.67	3.0	1 365.00	2 154	1 289.37	649.97	639.40
1993	438.69	3.0	1 381.00	2 179	1 294.74	652.92	641.82
1994	444.38	2.9	1 398.00	2 204	1 298.81	655.14	643.67
1995	450.76	2.9	1 414.00	2 230	1 301.37	656.48	644.89
1996	457.49	2.9	1 451.00	2 288	1 304.43	657.86	646.57
1997	461.40	2.8	1 489.00	2 348	1 305.46	657.93	647.53
1998	465.72	2.8	1 527.00	2 409	1 306.58	658.22	648.36
1999	470.11	2.8	1 567.00	2 472	1 313.12	661.19	651.93
2000	475.73	2.8	1 608.60	2 537	1 321.63	665.51	656.12
2001	478.92	2.8	1 668.33	2 631	1 327.14	668.32	658.82
2002	481.77	2.8	1 712.97	2 702	1 334.23	672.05	662.18
2003	486.06	2.8	1 765.84	2 785	1 341.77	675.47	666.30
2004	490.58	2.8	1 834.98	2 894	1 352.39	680.38	672.01
2005	496.69	2.7	1 890.26	2 981	1 360.26	683.51	676.75
2006	499.54	2.7	1 964.11	3 098	1 368.08	686.66	681.42
2007	503.29	2.7	2 063.58	3 255	1 378.86	691.08	687.78
2008	506.64	2.7	2 140.65	3 376	1 391.04	695.57	695.47
2009	509.79	2.7	2 210.28	3 486	1 400.70	699.25	701.45
2010	519.27	2.7	2 302.66	3 632	1 412.32	703.57	708.75

注：户数和年末户籍人口由市公安局提供，户籍人口期望寿命由市卫生局提供。

Note: The figures of household and year-end registered population are provided by Shanghai Municipal Public Security Bureau, and the figures of life expendency are provided by Shanghai Municipal Health Bureau.

表 2.4 续表 continued

年 份 Year	按农业非农业分 Grouped by Agriculture and Non-agriculture		非农业人口占总人口比重（%）Percertage of Non-agriculture Population in Total（%）	户籍人口期望寿命（岁）Life Expectancy of Registered Population（year）	其 中 of which	
	农 业 Agriculture	非农业 Non-agriculture			男 性 Male	女 性 Female
1978	453.05	645.23	58.7	73.35	70.69	74.78
1979	444.76	687.38	60.7	73.14	70.64	75.48
1980	444.09	702.43	61.3	73.33	71.25	75.36
1981	447.76	715.08	61.5	73.38	71.28	75.47
1982	449.20	731.31	61.9	74.04	71.77	76.25
1983	448.15	745.86	62.5	73.23	71.15	75.26
1984	444.03	760.75	63.1	73.90	71.73	76.17
1985	440.32	776.37	63.8	74.27	72.14	76.37
1986	429.77	802.56	65.1	74.71	72.54	76.85
1987	427.20	822.31	65.8	74.46	72.32	76.60
1988	423.49	838.93	66.5	74.63	72.50	76.77
1989	420.61	855.84	67.0	74.98	72.85	77.12
1990	418.89	864.46	67.4	75.46	73.16	77.74
1991	417.32	869.88	67.6	75.79	73.58	77.95
1992	413.82	875.55	67.9	75.97	74.04	77.91
1993	401.28	893.46	69.0	75.97	74.04	77.91
1994	388.32	910.49	70.1	76.26	74.29	78.23
1995	379.67	921.70	70.8	76.03	74.11	77.97
1996	372.29	932.14	71.5	76.11	74.07	78.21
1997	362.43	943.03	72.2	77.20	75.18	79.21
1998	352.93	953.65	73.0	77.03	75.06	79.02
1999	343.49	969.63	73.8	78.44	76.38	80.53
2000	335.47	986.16	74.6	78.77	76.71	80.81
2001	328.07	999.07	75.3	79.66	77.47	81.83
2002	315.42	1 018.81	76.4	79.52	77.36	81.63
2003	300.38	1 041.39	77.6	79.80	77.78	81.81
2004	254.79	1 097.60	81.2	80.29	78.08	82.48
2005	211.32	1 148.94	84.5	80.13	77.89	82.36
2006	194.78	1 173.30	85.8	80.97	78.64	83.29
2007	181.92	1 196.94	86.8	81.08	78.87	83.29
2008	174.48	1 216.56	87.5	81.28	79.06	83.50
2009	164.54	1 236.16	88.3	81.73	79.42	84.06
2010	157.37	1 254.95	88.9	82.13	79.82	84.44

表2.5 各区、县土地面积、常住人口及人口密度（2010）
LAND AREA, RESIDENT POPULATION AND DENSITY OF POPULATION IN DISTRICTS AND COUNTIES

地 区	District	土地面积（平方公里）Land Area (sq. km)	年末常住人口（万人）Year-end Resident Population (10 000 persons)	其中 of which 外来人口 Floating People	人口密度（人/平方公里）Density of Population (person/sq · km)
全 市	**Total**	**6 340.50**	**2 302.66**	**897.95**	**3 632**
浦东新区	Pudong New Area	1 210.41	504.73	202.48	4 170
黄 浦 区	Huangpu	12.41	42.97	13.25	34 625
卢 湾 区	Luwan	8.05	24.87	5.40	30 889
徐 汇 区	Xuhui	54.76	108.52	27.96	19 817
长 宁 区	Changning	38.30	69.06	17.54	18 031
静 安 区	Jing'an	7.62	24.67	5.73	32 373
普 陀 区	Putuo	54.83	128.88	36.31	23 505
闸 北 区	Zhabei	29.26	83.04	20.00	28 379
虹 口 区	Hongkou	23.48	85.23	19.62	36 299
杨 浦 区	Yangpu	60.73	131.30	27.54	21 620
闵 行 区	Minhang	370.75	243.12	120.40	6 558
宝 山 区	Baoshan	270.99	190.56	76.63	7 032
嘉 定 区	Jiading	464.20	147.20	82.84	3 171
金 山 区	Jinshan	586.05	73.25	20.12	1 250
松 江 区	Songjiang	605.64	158.34	93.77	2 614
青 浦 区	Qingpu	670.14	108.19	60.52	1 614
奉 贤 区	Fengxian	687.39	108.41	52.73	1 577
崇 明 县	Chongming	1 185.49	70.34	15.10	593

注：土地面积由市民政局提供。
Note: The figures of land area are provided by Shanghai Civil Affairs Bureau.

表 2.6 主要年份户籍人口出生率、死亡率、自然增长率
BIRTH RATE, DEATH RATE AND NATURAL GROWTH RATE OF POPULATION IN MAIN YEARS

年份 Year	出生 Birth		死亡 Death		自然增长 Natural Growth	
	人数（万人） Population (10 000 persons)	出生率（‰） Birth Rate (‰)	人数（万人） Population (10 000 persons)	死亡率（‰） Death Rate (‰)	人数（万人） Population (10 000 persons)	自然增长率（‰） Natural Growth Rate (‰)
1990	13.12	10.25	8.63	6.74	4.49	3.51
1995	7.11	5.47	9.79	7.53	-2.68	-2.06
1996	6.79	5.21	9.77	7.50	-2.98	-2.29
1997	6.42	4.92	9.57	7.33	-3.15	-2.41
1998	6.17	4.73	10.13	7.75	-3.96	-3.03
1999	6.56	5.01	9.54	7.28	-2.98	-2.27
2000	6.95	5.27	9.45	7.17	-2.50	-1.90
2001	5.76	4.34	9.34	7.05	-3.58	-2.71
2002	6.20	4.66	9.67	7.27	-3.47	-2.61
2003	5.73	4.28	10.07	7.52	-4.34	-3.24
2004	8.09	6.00	9.65	7.16	-1.56	-1.16
2005	8.25	6.08	10.23	7.54	-1.98	-1.46
2006	8.12	5.95	9.80	7.19	-1.68	-1.24
2007	10.08	7.34	10.22	7.44	-0.14	-0.10
2008	9.67	6.98	10.70	7.73	-1.03	-0.75
2009	9.23	6.62	10.67	7.64	-1.44	-1.02
2010	10.02	7.13	10.87	7.73	-0.84	-0.60

表 2.7 主要年份户籍人口迁移
MIGRATION IN MAIN YEARS

年份 Year	迁入 Inflows		迁出 Outflows		机械增长 Mechanical Increase	
	人口（万人） Population (10 000 persons)	迁入率（‰） Rate of Inflows (‰)	人口（万人） Population (10 000 persons)	迁出率（‰） Rate of Outflows (‰)	人口（万人） Population (10 000 persons)	增长率（‰） Growth Rate (‰)
1990	12.18	9.52	10.72	8.38	1.46	1.14
1995	13.12	10.09	6.47	4.98	6.65	5.11
1996	13.01	9.99	6.41	4.92	6.60	5.07
1997	11.47	8.79	5.72	4.38	5.75	4.41
1998	11.73	8.98	5.04	3.86	6.69	5.12
1999	14.06	10.73	5.08	3.88	8.98	6.85
2000	15.16	11.51	5.32	4.04	9.84	7.47
2001	14.63	11.05	5.56	4.20	9.07	6.85
2002	15.41	11.58	4.38	3.29	11.03	8.29
2003	14.92	11.15	3.69	2.76	11.23	8.39
2004	13.93	10.34	2.74	2.03	11.19	8.31
2005	12.96	9.55	3.46	2.55	9.50	7.00
2006	12.86	9.43	3.50	2.57	9.36	6.86
2007	14.69	10.70	3.95	2.88	10.74	7.82
2008	17.28	12.48	4.29	3.10	12.99	9.38
2009	15.72	11.26	4.77	3.42	10.95	7.84
2010	17.22	12.24	4.97	3.53	12.25	8.71

注：本页数据由市公安局提供。
Note: Data on this paper are provided by Shanghai Municipal Public Security Bureau.

表2.8　各区、县户籍人口迁移(2010)
MIGRATION IN DISTRICTS AND COUNTIES

地　区	District	迁　入(人) Inflows(person)		迁　出(人) Outflows(person)	
		市内迁入 From Inside of the City	市外迁入 From Outside of the City	迁往市内 To the Inside of the City	迁往市外 To the Outside of the City
全　市	**Total**	**9 651**	**172 206**	**9 921**	**49 733**
浦东新区	Pudong New Area	595	26 845	685	8 434
黄 浦 区	Huangpu	51	6 110	71	486
卢 湾 区	Luwan	12	3 447	26	603
徐 汇 区	Xuhui	127	16 876	168	5 660
长 宁 区	Changning	71	8 623	117	2 213
静 安 区	Jing'an	20	2 205	28	359
普 陀 区	Putuo	137	10 390	243	1 541
闸 北 区	Zhabei	207	9 680	348	1 180
虹 口 区	Hongkou	200	7 667	293	2 699
杨 浦 区	Yangpu	359	25 617	592	11 410
闵 行 区	Minhang	464	15 595	429	5 014
宝 山 区	Baoshan	1 929	11 624	2 062	2 357
嘉 定 区	Jiading	62	4 022	53	1 051
金 山 区	Jinshan	11	1 238	37	289
松 江 区	Songjiang	61	16 249	67	4 812
青 浦 区	Qingpu	21	1 946	32	446
奉 贤 区	Fengxian	73	2 220	41	874
崇 明 县	Chongming	5 251	1 852	4 629	305

注：本表数据由市公安局提供。
Note: This table is provided by Shanghai Municipal Public Security Bureau.

表2.9 各区、县户籍人口年龄构成(2010)
AGE STRUCTURE OF REGISTERED POPULATION IN DISTRICTS AND COUNTIES

单位:万人(10 000 persons)

地 区	District	合 计 Total	17 岁及以下 17 and below	18 ~ 34 岁 18 ~ 34	35 ~ 59 岁 35 ~ 59	60 岁及以上 60 and above
全 市	**Total**	**1 412.32**	**146.14**	**336.03**	**599.13**	**331.02**
浦东新区	Pudong New Area	275.80	31.49	66.53	116.50	61.28
黄 浦 区	Huangpu	60.19	5.41	14.47	25.76	14.55
卢 湾 区	Luwan	30.44	2.46	7.26	12.67	8.05
徐 汇 区	Xuhui	91.09	9.55	22.77	36.29	22.47
长 宁 区	Changning	61.62	5.35	17.44	24.37	14.46
静 安 区	Jing'an	30.51	2.93	6.93	12.45	8.19
普 陀 区	Putuo	87.89	7.87	20.37	38.18	21.47
闸 北 区	Zhabei	69.21	6.20	16.30	30.20	16.51
虹 口 区	Hongkou	79.06	7.02	18.21	33.88	19.95
杨 浦 区	Yangpu	109.16	8.99	29.26	45.44	25.46
闵 行 区	Minhang	96.75	11.99	23.82	39.46	21.48
宝 山 区	Baoshan	88.29	9.42	20.00	38.64	20.22
嘉 定 区	Jiading	55.75	6.25	12.15	23.73	13.62
金 山 区	Jinshan	51.66	5.95	10.68	23.59	11.43
松 江 区	Songjiang	57.60	7.02	14.93	23.65	12.00
青 浦 区	Qingpu	46.19	5.39	9.87	20.65	10.27
奉 贤 区	Fengxian	52.18	6.15	11.35	23.08	11.61
崇 明 县	Chongming	68.95	6.69	13.68	30.60	17.99

注:本表数据由市公安局提供。
Note: This table is provided by Shanghai Municipal Public Security Bureau.

表 2.10　各区、县户籍老年人口年龄构成(2010)
AGE STRUCTURE OF REGISTERED AGING POPULATION IN DISTRICTS AND COUNTIES

单位:万人(10 000 persons)

地区	District	合计 Total	60～64岁 60～64	65～79岁 65～79	80岁及以上 80 and above
全　市	**Total**	**331.02**	**104.53**	**166.66**	**59.83**
浦东新区	Pudong New Area	61.28	20.11	30.72	10.46
黄 浦 区	Huangpu	14.55	4.64	6.59	3.32
卢 湾 区	Luwan	8.05	2.43	3.81	1.81
徐 汇 区	Xuhui	22.47	6.57	11.55	4.35
长 宁 区	Changning	14.46	4.16	7.45	2.85
静 安 区	Jing'an	8.19	2.48	3.89	1.82
普 陀 区	Putuo	21.47	6.89	10.37	4.22
闸 北 区	Zhabei	16.51	5.26	7.98	3.27
虹 口 区	Hongkou	19.95	6.30	9.57	4.08
杨 浦 区	Yangpu	25.46	7.97	12.58	4.92
闵 行 区	Minhang	21.48	6.92	11.11	3.45
宝 山 区	Baoshan	20.22	6.93	9.87	3.41
嘉 定 区	Jiading	13.62	4.32	7.00	2.30
金 山 区	Jinshan	11.43	3.64	6.21	1.58
松 江 区	Songjiang	12.00	3.74	6.46	1.81
青 浦 区	Qingpu	10.27	3.08	5.62	1.56
奉 贤 区	Fengxian	11.61	3.73	6.23	1.64
崇 明 县	Chongming	17.99	5.35	9.65	2.98

表2.11 各区、县计划生育基本情况(2010)
FAMILY PLANNING IN DISTRICTS AND COUNTIES

地 区 District		出生人数(万人) Birth (10 000 persons)	已婚育龄妇女人数(万人) Married Women at Childbearing Age (10 000 persons)	采取避孕措施人数(万人) Married People Adopting Contraception (10 000 persons)	计划生育率(%) Family Planning Rate (%)	避孕率(%) Comprehensive Contraception Rate (%)
全 市	**Total**	**10.02**	**217.13**	**173.88**	**99.2**	**80.1**
浦东新区	Pudong New Area	2.23	45.08	36.47	99.7	80.9
黄 浦 区	Huangpu	0.42	7.95	5.78	99.4	72.7
卢 湾 区	Luwan	0.21	3.81	2.91	99.5	76.4
徐 汇 区	Xuhui	0.61	11.85	9.24	98.7	78.0
长 宁 区	Changning	0.43	8.50	6.16	98.6	72.5
静 安 区	Jing'an	0.20	3.86	2.91	99.9	75.4
普 陀 区	Putuo	0.59	10.97	8.35	99.8	76.1
闸 北 区	Zhabei	0.48	9.12	6.35	99.1	69.6
虹 口 区	Hongkou	0.52	9.90	7.11	98.5	71.9
杨 浦 区	Yangpu	0.66	13.79	11.42	99.6	82.8
闵 行 区	Minhang	0.95	15.72	12.01	99.7	76.4
宝 山 区	Baoshan	0.64	13.30	11.02	98.8	82.9
嘉 定 区	Jiading	0.37	9.59	8.32	98.7	86.7
金 山 区	Jinshan	0.29	10.16	8.61	97.0	84.8
松 江 区	Songjiang	0.44	10.50	9.17	97.9	87.3
青 浦 区	Qingpu	0.29	9.39	7.66	99.0	81.5
奉 贤 区	Fengxian	0.31	10.04	8.75	99.4	87.2
崇 明 县	Chongming	0.36	13.58	11.62	99.6	85.6

注：本表由市人口和计划生育委员会提供。
Note: This table is provided by Shanghai Municipal Committee of Population and Family Planning.

表 2.12 主要年份婚姻情况
MARRIAGE STATISTICS IN MAIN YEARS

年份 Year	准予登记结婚（万对）Marriage Registration Permitted (10 000 couples)	初婚（万人）First Marriage (10 000 persons)	再婚（万人）Remarriage (10 000 persons)	其中 of which 女性 Female	离婚人数（万人）Divorce (10 000 persons)	其中 of which 民政部门批准 Approved by the Civil Administration	法院调判 Mediated by the Court
1990	10.77	19.49	2.04	1.06	3.27	1.45	1.82
1995	8.40	14.61	2.19	1.09	4.54	1.97	2.57
1996	8.96	14.98	2.31	1.24	4.93	2.14	2.79
1997	8.84	15.12	2.57	1.27	5.46	2.38	3.08
1998	8.57	14.48	2.67	1.28	5.92	2.85	3.07
1999	9.05	15.07	2.46	1.24	6.24	3.39	2.85
2000	9.31	15.08	2.89	1.45	6.36	3.52	2.84
2001	9.30	15.23	2.68	1.40	6.29	3.36	2.93
2002	9.10	14.60	3.05	1.40	5.92	3.08	2.84
2003	10.82	17.20	3.97	2.31	6.60	3.97	2.63
2004	12.49	20.27	4.18	2.05	7.26	5.35	1.91
2005	10.27	16.44	4.09	2.05	7.86	6.21	1.65
2006	16.56	27.29	5.83	2.93	9.43	7.55	1.88
2007	12.01	18.10	5.93	2.95	9.38	7.49	1.88
2008	14.16	22.04	6.28	3.17	9.35	7.44	1.91
2009	14.99	23.33	6.65	3.31	9.65	7.83	1.82
2010	13.03	20.10	5.96	2.98	9.34	7.62	1.72

表 2.13 主要年份涉外婚姻情况
CHINESE-FOREIGN MARRIAGE IN MAIN YEARS

年份 Year	涉外婚姻(对) Chinese-Foreign Marriage (couple)	在涉外婚姻中的国内公民（人）In Chinese-Foreign Marriage Chinese Citizens (person)	在国内公民中 Among the Chinese Citizens 男性 Male	女性 Female
1990	1 345	1 345	136	1 209
1995	3 033	3 030	274	2 756
1996	3 107	3 105	307	2 798
1997	2 839	2 838	298	2 540
1998	2 926	2 923	293	2 630
1999	2 872	2 869	343	2 526
2000	3 187	3 182	374	2 808
2001	3 447	3 438	399	3 039
2002	2 705	2 690	67	2 623
2003	2 418	2 418	367	2 051
2004	2 636	2 623	417	2 206
2005	2 407	2 385	372	2 013
2006	2 943	2 943	540	2 403
2007	2 495	2 483	109	2 374
2008	2 626	2 553	428	2 125
2009	2 492	2 416	305	2 111
2010	2 231	2 144	414	1 730

注：本页数据由市民政局提供。
Note: This table is provided by Shanghai Civil Affairs Bureau.

表2.14 主要年份在沪外国常住人口
RESIDENT FOREIGNERS IN SHANGHAI IN MAIN YEARS

单位：人(person)

类 别	Types	2005	2009	2010
总 计	**Total**	**100 011**	**152 050**	**162 481**
居留许可外国人	**Residence Permitted Foreigners**	**95 384**	**147 213**	**159 303**
按国别(地区)分	Grouped by Country and Region			
#日 本	Japan	27 812	31 490	35 075
韩 国	Republic of Korea	14 047	20 700	21 073
新加坡	Singapore	5 547	7 209	7 545
德 国	Germany	4 591	7 253	8 023
英 国	United Kingdom	2 904	5 137	5 591
加拿大	Canada	4 279	6 121	7 306
美 国	United States	14 329	21 284	24 358
澳大利亚	Australia	3 729	5 257	6 165
法 国	France	4 181	7 437	8 238
按类别分	By Types			
#留学人员及家属	Overseas Students and Relatives	10 224	14 654	16 064
驻华机构代表及家属	Delegate and Relatives of Institutions Stationed in China	9 769	10 754	8 933
外资企业工作人员及家属	Employees and Relatives at Foreign Ventures	60 137	96 750	95 623
外国专家及家属	Foreign Experts and Relatives	4 586	6 582	6 638
永久居留外国人	Permanent Resident Foreigners		715	948
半年以上长期签证外国人	Long-term Vise Foreigners Above Half Year		4 122	2 230

注：本表由市公安局出入境管理局提供。
Note: Figures of this table are provided by Bureau of Exit-Entry Administration Shanghai Municipal Public Security Bureau.

表 2.15 全社会各行业从业人员(2008～2010)
QUANTITY OF WHOLE SOCIAL EMPLOYEES IN DIFFERENT SECTORS

单位:万人(10 000 persons)

行　业	Sector	2008	2009	2010
总　计	**Total**	**1 053.24**	**1 064.42**	**1 090.76**
按产业分	**Grouped by Industry**			
第一产业	Primary Industry	49.38	48.53	37.09
第二产业	Secondary Industry	424.16	423.03	443.74
第三产业	Tertiary Industry	579.7	592.86	609.93
按行业分	**Grouped by Sector**			
农、林、牧、渔业	Farming, Forestry, Animal Husbandry and Fishery	49.38	48.53	37.09
采矿业	Mining	0.08	0.09	0.09
制造业	Manufacturing	348.78	327.86	341.42
电力、燃气及水的生产和供应业	Power, Gas and Water Production and Supply	5.61	5.74	6.14
建筑业	Construction	69.69	89.34	96.09
交通运输、仓储和邮政业	Transportation, Warehousing and Post Industries	55.56	54.28	54.97
信息传输、计算机服务和软件业	Information Transmission, Computer Servcie and Software Industries	13.65	19.03	20.03
#信息传输	Information Transmission	2.81	2.89	2.97
批发和零售业	Retail and Wholesale	172.72	175.32	180.69
住宿和餐饮业	Hoteling and Catering	41.73	42.79	47.52
金融业	Finance	23.19	22.11	24.11
房地产业	Real Estate	37.38	36.55	35.94
租赁和商务服务业	Leasing and Business Service Industries	59.77	55.46	58.86
科学研究、技术服务和地质勘查业	Scientific Research, Technical Service and Geological Prospecting	20.49	33.60	33.11
水利、环境和公共设施管理业	Water Conservancy, Environment and Public Facility Management	12.74	11.36	11.94
#公共设施管理业	Public Facility Management	1.64	2.66	2.60
居民服务和其他服务业	Resident Service and Other Services	63	63.31	62.75
教　育	Education	29.58	29.20	29.02
卫生、社会保障和社会福利业	Health, Social Security and Welfare	19.61	19.58	20.41
文化、体育和娱乐业	Culture, Sports and Entertainment	11.32	11.99	11.91
公共管理和社会组织	Public Administration and Social Organizations	18.96	18.25	18.67

表2.16 各行业职工人数(2010)
STAFF AND WORKERS IN DIFFERENT SECTORS

单位:万人(10 000 persons)

行业	Sector	职工人数 Staff and Workers	按登记注册类型分 Classified According to the Categories of Registration			
			国有单位 State-owned Units	集体单位 Collective-owned Units	港澳台及外商投资单位 Units with Investment from Hong Kong, Macao, Taiwan and Foreign Countries	其他单位 Other Ownership Units
总　计	**Total**	**648.49**	**136.99**	**11.13**	**120.19**	**380.18**
按产业分	**Grouped by Industry**					
第一产业	Primary Industry	1.52	0.52	0.05	0.02	0.93
第二产业	Secondary Industry	293.18	23.25	2.77	92.94	174.22
第三产业	Tertiary Industry	353.79	113.22	8.31	27.23	205.03
按行业分	**Grouped by Sector**					
农、林、牧、渔业	Farming, Forestry, Animal Husbandry and Fishery	1.52	0.52	0.05	0.02	0.93
采矿业	Mining	0.08	0.04			0.04
制造业	Manufacturing	236.51	15.83	2.39	92.06	126.23
电力、燃气及水的生产和供应业	Power, Gas and Water Production and Supply	5.48	3.90	0.09	0.23	1.26
建筑业	Construction	51.11	3.48	0.29	0.65	46.69
交通运输、仓储和邮政业	Transportation, Warehousing and Post Industries	39.87	12.15	0.87	1.93	24.91
信息传输、计算机服务和软件业	Information Transmission, Computer Servcie and Software Industries	13.43	1.75	0.03	3.41	8.23
#信息传输	Information Transmission	2.41	1.48	0.03	0.55	0.36
批发和零售业	Retail and Wholesale	87.02	4.59	1.50	8.89	72.03
住宿和餐饮业	Hoteling and Catering	19.96	1.24	0.12	3.28	15.32
金融业	Finance Inductry	21.64	4.72		1.78	15.14
房地产业	Real Estate	18.17	1.90	0.24	2.76	13.26
租赁和商务服务业	Leasing and Business Service Industries	44.06	9.91	2.10	2.94	29.10
科学研究、技术服务和地质勘查业	Scientific Research, Technical Service and Geological Prospecting	29.65	19.22	0.18	1.24	9.02
水利、环境和公共设施管理业	Water Conservancy, Environment and Public Facility Management	5.24	3.32	0.40	0.02	1.50
#公共设施管理业	Public Facility Management	2.19	0.78	0.06		1.35
居民服务和其他服务业	Resident Service and Other Services	13.72	0.83	0.69	0.56	11.65
教　育	Education	24.13	21.83	0.21	0.04	2.06
卫生、社会保障和社会福利业	Health, Social Security and Welfare	14.19	11.47	1.59	0.05	1.07
文化、体育和娱乐业	Culture, Sports and Entertainment	5.40	3.22	0.15	0.32	1.71
公共管理和社会组织	Public Administration and Social Organizations	17.31	17.08	0.21		0.01

注：本表包括全部城镇私营企业职工。
Note: Data in this table has included those of employees work for private enterprises.

表 2.17 各行业在岗职工人数(2010)
QUANTITY OF WORKING STAFF AND WORKERS IN DIFFERENT SECTORS

单位:万人(10 000 persons)

行业	Sector	职工人数 Staff and Workers	按登记注册类型分 Classified According to the Categories of Registration			
			国有单位 State-owned Units	集体单位 Collective-owned Units	港澳台及外商投资单位 Units with Investment from Hong Kong, Macao, Taiwan and Foreign Countries	其他单位 Other Ownership Units
总计	**Total**	**617.70**	**122.44**	**6.83**	**118.05**	**370.38**
按产业分	**Grouped by Industry**					
第一产业	Primary Industry	1.35	0.44	0.05	0.02	0.84
第二产业	Secondary Industry	280.36	17.86	1.26	91.02	170.22
第三产业	Tertiary Industry	335.99	104.14	5.52	27.01	199.32
按行业分	**Grouped by Sector**					
农、林、牧、渔业	Farming, Forestry, Animal Husbandry and Fishery	1.35	0.44	0.05	0.02	0.84
采矿业	Mining	0.07	0.03			0.04
制造业	Manufacturing	224.75	10.98	0.92	90.17	122.68
电力、燃气及水的生产和供应业	Power, Gas and Water Production and Supply	5.40	3.86	0.08	0.23	1.24
建筑业	Construction	50.14	2.99	0.26	0.62	46.26
交通运输、仓储和邮政业	Transportation, Warehousing and Post Industries	37.07	11.14	0.38	1.91	23.63
信息传输、计算机服务和软件业	Information Transmission, Computer Servcie and Software Industries	13.36	1.74	0.03	3.38	8.22
#信息传输	Information Transmission	2.38	1.47	0.02	0.54	0.35
批发和零售业	Retail and Wholesale	83.44	2.59	0.80	8.79	71.25
住宿和餐饮业	Hoteling and Catering	19.41	1.08	0.07	3.28	14.99
金融业	Finance Inductry	21.34	4.55		1.78	15.00
房地产业	Real Estate	17.33	1.51	0.20	2.75	12.87
租赁和商务服务业	Leasing and Business Service Industries	37.13	6.19	1.25	2.92	26.77
科学研究、技术服务和地质勘查业	Scientific Research, Technical Service and Geological Prospecting	29.38	19.00	0.17	1.21	9.00
水利、环境和公共设施管理业	Water Conservancy, Environment and Public Facility Management	5.04	3.16	0.40	0.02	1.46
#公共设施管理业	Public Facility Management	2.17	0.76	0.06		1.35
居民服务和其他服务业	Resident Service and Other Services	12.60	0.54	0.15	0.56	11.34
教育	Education	23.62	21.41	0.19	0.04	1.98
卫生、社会保障和社会福利业	Health, Social Security and Welfare	13.91	11.24	1.55	0.05	1.07
文化、体育和娱乐业	Culture, Sports and Entertainment	5.13	2.97	0.13	0.32	1.71
公共管理和社会组织	Public Administration and Social Organizations	17.23	17.01	0.21		0.01

注:本表包括全部城镇私营企业职工。
Note: Data in this table has included those of employees work for private enterprises.

表2.18 各行业在岗女职工人数(2010)
QUANTITY OF WORKING FEMALE STAFF AND WORKERS IN DIFFERENT SECTORS

单位:万人(10 000 persons)

行业	Sector	在岗女职工人数 Working Female Staff and Workers	按登记注册类型分 Classified According to the Categories of Registration			
			国有单位 State-owned Units	集体单位 Collective-owned Units	港澳台及外商投资单位 Units with Investment from Hong Kong, Macao, Taiwan and Foreign Countries	其他单位 Other Ownership Units
总　计	**Total**	**191.58**	**49.47**	**2.85**	**54.08**	**85.18**
按产业分	**Grouped by Industry**					
第一产业	Primary Industry	0.21	0.13	0.01	0.01	0.06
第二产业	Secondary Industry	86.23	3.83	0.35	40.80	41.25
第三产业	Tertiary Industry	105.14	45.51	2.49	13.27	43.87
按行业分	**Grouped by Sector**					
农、林、牧、渔业	Farming, Forestry, Animal Husbandry and Fishery	0.21	0.13	0.01	0.01	0.06
采矿业	Mining	0.03	0.01			0.02
制造业	Manufacturing	80.44	2.41	0.29	40.60	37.15
电力、燃气及水的生产和供应业	Power, Gas and Water Production and Supply	1.18	0.88	0.04	0.06	0.20
建筑业	Construction	4.57	0.53	0.02	0.14	3.88
交通运输、仓储和邮政业	Transportation, Warehousing and Post Industries	6.45	1.83	0.11	0.67	3.85
信息传输、计算机服务和软件业	Information Transmission, Computer Servcie and Software Industries	3.20	0.58	0.01	1.32	1.30
#信息传输	Information Transmission	0.89	0.49	0.01	0.24	0.15
批发和零售业	Retail and Wholesale	18.38	0.94	0.29	4.84	12.31
住宿和餐饮业	Hoteling and Catering	7.90	0.42	0.03	1.75	5.70
金融业	Finance Intermendiatry	11.32	2.37	0.00	1.09	7.86
房地产业	Real Estate	4.50	0.46	0.05	0.95	3.04
租赁和商务服务业	Leasing and Business Service Industries	7.64	1.41	0.52	1.57	4.13
科学研究、技术服务和地质勘查业	Scientific Research, Technical Service and Geological Prospecting	11.52	9.57	0.05	0.51	1.39
水利、环境和公共设施管理业	Water Conservancy, Environment and Public Facility Management	1.42	0.88	0.15		0.38
#公共设施管理业	Public Facility Management	0.59	0.21	0.03		0.34
居民服务和其他服务业	Resident Service and Other Services	2.57	0.18	0.08	0.34	1.98
教　育	Education	14.32	13.25	0.13	0.01	0.94
卫生、社会保障和社会福利业	Health, Social Security and Welfare	9.02	7.44	0.95	0.04	0.59
文化、体育和娱乐业	Culture, Sports and Entertainment	1.86	1.22	0.04	0.19	0.41
公共管理和社会组织	Public Administration and Social Organizations	5.02	4.95	0.07		

注：本表包括全部城镇私营企业职工。
Note: Data in this table has included those of employees work for private enterprises.

表 2.19 主要年份城镇新就业人数
NUMBER OF NEW URBAN EMPLOYEES IN MAIN YEARS

单位:万人(10 000 persons)

指 标	Indicators	2000	2009	2010
总 计	**Total**	**49.74**	**62.86**	**70.21**
按主要来源分	**Grouped by Source of Employment**			
城镇劳动力	Urban Labour Force	39.14	22.58	26.80
农村劳动力	Rural Labour Force	1.76	24.55	28.57
大学、中专、技校毕业生	Graduates from Universities, Secondary Technical Schools and Worker Training Schools	4.09	10.17	10.03
其 他	Others	4.75	5.56	4.81
按安置去向分	**Grouped by Employment Assignment**			
国有经济单位	State-owned Units	7.40	12.20	13.15
城镇集体经济单位	Urban Collective-owned Units	1.42	0.84	0.61
其他经济单位	Other Ownership Units	8.60	48.32	54.42
其他劳动者	Others	32.32	1.50	2.03

表 2.20 主要年份城镇登记失业人数和城镇登记失业率
QUANTITY OF URBAN REGISTERED UNEMPLOYED AND URBAN REGISTERED UNEMPLOYMENT RATE IN MAIN YEARS

指 标	Indicators	2000	2009	2010
城镇登记失业人数(万人)	Registered Urban Unemployment (10 000 persons)	20.08	27.87	27.73
区	District	18.86	27.11	26.97
县	County	1.22	0.76	0.76
城镇登记失业率(%)	**Registered Urban Unemployment Rate (%)**	**3.5**	**4.3**	**4.2**

注:本表由市人力资源和社会保障局提供。
Note: This table is provided by Shanghai Municipal Human Resource and Social Security Bureau.

表 2.21 主要年份新增就业岗位
NEWLY ADDED WORKING POST IN MAIN YEARS

指 标	Indicators	2003	2009	2010
新增就业岗位(万个)	Newly Added Working Post (10 000 units)	46.2	59.6	63.15
#农村富余劳动力实现非农就业	Non-agricultural Working Post Gained by Surplus Rural Labor Force	12.5	11.6	12.18

注:本表由市人力资源和社会保障局提供。
Note: This table is provided by Shanghai Municipal Human Resource and Social Security Bureau.

表 2.22　主要年份离休、退休及退职职工人数
QUANTITY OF RETIRED AND RESIGNED PERSONS IN MAIN YEARS

单位:万人(10 000 persons)

指　标	Indicators	2000	2009	2010
总　计	**Total**	**234.23**	**338.85**	**352.02**
国有单位	State-owned Units	165.55	166.04	166.38
离　休	Retired Veteran Cadres	3.39	1.92	1.82
退　休	Retired	161.03	159.95	160.53
退　职	Resigned	1.13	4.17	4.03
集体单位	Collective-owned Units	50.22	46.82	46.97
离　休	Retired Veteran Cadres	0.10	0.04	0.04
退　休	Retired	48.40	44.95	45.15
退　职	Resigned	1.72	1.83	1.78
其他单位	Other Ownership Units	18.46	125.99	138.67
离　休	Retired Veteran Cadres	0.21	0.71	0.68
退　休	Retired	18.05	120.07	132.29
退　职	Resigned	0.20	5.21	5.7

注：本表数据由市人力资源和社会保障局提供。
Note: This table is provided by Shanghai Municipal Labour and Social Security Bureau.

表 2.23　在岗职工人数变动(2010)
CHANGES IN THE NUMBER OF WORKING STAFF AND WORKERS

单位:万人(10 000 persons)

指　标	Indicators	合　计 Total	按登记注册类型划分 Classified According to the Categories of Registration		
			国有单位 State-owned Units	集体单位 Collective-owned Units	其他单位 Other Ownership Units
增加人数	**Increase of Staff and Workers**	**95.59**	**18.41**	**1.01**	**76.17**
从农村招收	Recruited from Rural Areas	35.50	0.62	0.24	34.64
从城镇招收	Recruited from Urban Areas	31.11	9.38	0.20	21.53
录用的复员转业军人	Demobilized Soldiers	0.29	0.18		0.11
录用的大、中专、技工学校毕业生	Graduates from Colleges, Secondary Technical Schools and Worker Training Schools	10.03	2.62	0.12	7.29
调入人数	Number Transferred in	8.83	3.95	0.19	4.69
#市外调入	From Outside Areas	0.60	0.08		0.52
其　他	Others	9.83	1.66	0.26	7.91
减少人数	**Decrease of Staff and Workers**	**86.17**	**15.72**	**1.24**	**69.21**
离休、退休、退职	Retired and Resigned	17.65	3.21	0.39	14.05
开除、除名、辞退	Expelled and Discharged	4.63	0.19	0.02	4.42
终止、解除合同	Contract Terminated	42.30	7.66	0.44	34.20
死　亡	Death	0.20	0.10	0.01	0.09
调出人数	Number Transferred Out	7.14	3.14	0.16	3.84
#调往市外	To Outside Areas	0.29	0.05		0.24
其　他	Others	14.25	1.42	0.22	12.61

表2.24 主要年份离岗职工人数
QUANTITY OF LAID-OFF EMPLOYEES IN MAIN YEARS

单位：万人(10 000 persons)

指 标	Indicators	2000	2009	2010
总 计	**Total**	**83.11**	**35.19**	**30.78**
国有单位	State-owned Units	48.25	17.54	14.55
集体单位	Collective-owned Units	20.87	5.07	4.3
其他单位	Other Ownership Units	13.99	12.58	11.93

表2.25 主要年份职业介绍所
EMPLOYMENT AGENCIES IN MAIN YEARS

单位：万人次(10 000 persons times)

指 标	Indicators	2000	2009	2010
登记招聘人数	**Number of Vacancies Registered**	**54.09**	**123.43**	**158.67**
登记求职人数	**Number of Registered People Seeking a Job**	**54.69**	**161.25**	**177.64**
#女 性	Females	25.45	77.74	77.89
#失业人员	Unemployed	29.86	92.16	95.78
#获得职业资格人员	Personnel with Job Qualifications		24.33	28.71
职业指导人数	**Number of People Receiving Career Training**	**55.58**	**110.27**	**106.95**
介绍成功人数	**Number of People that Got a Job through Employment Agencies**	**28.59**	**49.48**	**53.28**
#女 性	Females	13.87	28.56	22.28
#失业人员	Unemployed	14.33	35.64	39.88
#获得职业资格人员	Personnel with Job Qualifications		16.39	19.18

注：本表由市人力资源和社会保障局提供。
Note: This table is provided by Shanghai Municipal Human Resource and Social Security Bureau.

表 2.26 历次人口普查资料
Basic Statistics on National Population Census

指 标	Indicators	第一次普查(1953 年) First Census
总户数(万户)	Total Households(10 000 households)	131.63
家庭户	Family Households	–
集体户	Collective households	–
平均每户人口(人)	Average Family Household Size(person)	4.7
总人口	Total Population	620.44
#外省市来沪常住人口	Resident Population from Other Provinces	–
按性别分	Population by Gender	
男	Male	331.96
女	Female	288.48
按年龄构成分	Population by Age Group	
0~14 岁	Aged 0~14	204.89
15~59 岁	Aged 15~59	392.74
60 岁及以上	Aged 60 and above	22.81
#百岁老人(人)	Aged 100 and above(person)	1
按民族构成分	Population by Ethnicity	
汉 族	Han	617.29
少数民族	Ethnic Minorities	3.15
每十万人受教育程度(人)	Population with Various Education Attainments Per 100 000 Persons(person)	
小 学	Primary School	–
初 中	Junior Secondary School	–
高 中	Senior Secondary School and Technical Secondary School	–
大专及以上	Junior College and Above	–

单位：万人(10 000 persons)

第二次普查 (1964 年) Second Census	第三次普查 (1982 年) Third Census	第四次普查 (1990 年) Fourth Census	第五次普查 (2000 年) Fifth Census	第六次普查 (2010 年) Sixth Census
240.63	315.17	409.96	564.26	889.35
-	312.71	406.53	529.91	825.33
-	2.46	3.43	34.35	64.02
4.5	3.8	3.3	2.9	2.5
1 081.65	1 185.97	1 334.19	1 640.77	2 301.92
-	-	-	346.49	897.70
536.9	591	680.61	843.03	1 185.49
544.74	594.97	653.58	797.75	1 116.43
457.61	215.42	243.18	201.09	198.29
558.31	834.02	901.89	1 193.92	1 756.66
65.73	136.53	189.12	245.76	346.97
2	20	80	269	928
1 077.28	1 180.99	1 328.03	1 630.38	2 274.30
4.37	4.98	6.16	10.39	27.62
39 154	25 201	22 691	18 934	13 561
12 948	28 036	31 596	36 803	36 519
5 220	20 351	19 539	23 018	20 953
2 205	3 471	6 537	10 940	21 892

上/海/统/计/年/鉴

主要统计指标解释

人　口

人口数为每年12月31日的年末总人口。根据统计口径的不同,分为户籍人口和常住人口。户籍人口是指在公安部门办理了户籍登记的人口。常住人口是指实际上经常居住在一个地方(住所)的人口,一般都以在其住所居住半年以上者为常住人口。

出生率

出生率(又称粗出生率)指在一定时期内(通常为一年)一定地区的出生人数与同期平均人数(或期中人数)之比,一般用千分率表示。计算公式:

$$出生率=\frac{年出生人数}{年平均人数}\times 1000‰$$

出生人数是指活产婴儿,即胎儿脱离母体时(不管怀孕月数),有过呼吸或其他生命现象。年平均人数是年初、年底人口数的平均数,也可用年中人口数代替。

死亡率

死亡率(又称粗死亡率)指在一定时期内(通常为一年)一定地区的死亡人数与同期平均人数(或期中人数)之比,一般用千分率表示。计算公式:

$$死亡率=\frac{年死亡人数}{年平均人数}\times 1000‰$$

人口自然增长率

指在一定时期内(通常为一年)人口自然增加数(出生人数减死亡人数)与该时期内平均人数(或期中人数)之比,一般用千分率表示。计算公式:

$$人口自然增长率=\frac{本年出生人数-年死亡人数}{年平均人数}\times 1000‰$$

人口自然增长率=人口出生率—人口死亡率

户籍人口期望寿命

指在一定年龄组的死亡率水平下,该年龄组人群日后平均可能继续生存的年(岁)数。通常所说的平均期望寿命是指刚出生的一批人平均一生可能存活的年数。

从业人员

指从事一定社会劳动并取得劳动报酬或经营收入的人员,包括在岗职工、再就业的离退休人员、私营业主、个体户主、私营和个体从业人员、乡镇企业从业人员、农村从业人员、其他从业人员(包括民办教师、宗教职业者、现役军人等)。这一指标反映了一定时期内全部劳动力资源的实际利用情况,是研究我国基本国情国力的重要指标。

各单位的从业人员指在各级国家机关、政党机关、社会团体及企业、事业单位中工作,取得工资或其他形式的劳动报酬的全部人员。包括在岗职工、再就业的离退休人员、民办教师以及在各单位中工作的外方人员和港澳台方人员、兼职人员、借用的外单位人员和第二职业者。不包括离开本单位仍保留劳动关系的职工。各单位的就业人员反映了各单位实际参加生产或工作的全部劳动力。

职　工

指在国有、城镇集体、联营、股份制、外商和港、澳、台投资、其他单位及其附属机构工作,并由其支付工资的各类人员。不包括下列人员:(1)乡镇企业就业人员;(2)城镇个体劳动者;(3)离休、退休、退职人员;(4)再就业的离、退休人员;(5)民办教师;(6)在城镇单位中工作的外方及港、澳、台人员;(7)其他按有关规定不列入职工统计范围的人员。(1998年及以后的数据均为在岗职工数据,其他相关指标如职工工资总额,职工平均工资等指标也从1998年按此口径进行了相应调整)。

城镇登记失业人员

指有非农业户口,在一定的劳动年龄内(16岁以上及男50岁以下、女45岁以下),有劳动能力,无业而要求就业,并在当地就业服务机构进行求职登记的人员。

城镇登记失业率

指城镇登记失业人员同城镇单位就业人员、城镇私营企业及个体就业人员(扣除使用的农村劳动力、聘用的离退休人员、港澳台及外方人员)和城镇登记失业人员、城镇单位中的不在岗职工之和的比。计算公式为:

主要统计指标解释

城镇登记失业率＝城镇登记失业人员 /(城镇单位就业人员－使用的农村劳动力－聘用的离退休人员－聘用的港澳台及外方人员)+ 不在岗职工＋城镇私营企业及个体就业人员＋城镇登记失业人员×100%

在岗职工

指在本单位工作并由单位支付工资的人员，以及有工作岗位，但由于学习、病伤产假等原因暂未工作，仍由单位支付工资的人员。

SHANGHAI STATISTICAL YEARBOOK

EXPLANATORY NOTES TO MAJOR STATISTICAL INDICATORS

□ Population

Population refers to the total population by December 31 every year. According to different statistical approaches, there are two definitions of population named as population with registered residence and population with permanent residence. The former refers to the population with registration in the police while the latter refers to the population that actually reside in a place (residence) permanently, usually longer than half a year.

□ Birth Rate

Birth Rate (or gross birth rate) means the ratio of the number of births in a certain period (usually a year) to the average population in the same period (or mid-year figure). It is usually calculated in terms of permillage and its calculating formula is:

$$\text{Birth Rate} = \frac{\text{Number of Births}}{\text{Average Number of Population}} \times 1000‰$$

Number of Births refers to live births, when babies have showed any vital phenomena regardless of the length of pregnancy.

Average Number of Population is the average of the number of population at the beginning of the year and, at the end of the year and sometimes is substituted for with mid-year population.

□ Death Rate

Death Rate (or Gross Death Rate) refers to the ratio of number of deaths to the average population (or mid-year population) during a certain period of time (usually a year), which is often presented as permillage. Its calculating formula is :

$$\text{Death Rate} = \frac{\text{Number of Deaths}}{\text{Average Number of Population}} \times 1000‰$$

□ Natural Growth Rate of Population

Natural Growth Rate of Population refers to the ratio of natural increase in population (number of births minus number of deaths) in a certain period of time (usually a year) to the average population (or mid-year population) of the same period, which is often presented as permillage. The following formula are applied:

Number of Births-Number of Deaths

$$\text{Natural Growth Rate of Population} = \frac{\text{Number of Births} - \text{Number of Deaths}}{\text{Average Number of Population}} \times 1000‰$$

Natural Growth Rate of Population = Birth Rate-Death Rate

□ Life Expectancy of Registered Population

Life Expectancy of Registered Population refers to the average age that an age group may possibly live at a certain mortality rate of the group, in the common knowledge, the average age that a group of new-borns may possibly live.

□ Employees

Employees refer to the persons who are engaged in social working and receive remuneration payment or earn business income, including total staff and workers, re-employed retirees, employers of private enterprises, self-employ ed workers, employees in private enterprises and individual economy, employees in township enterprises, employed persons in the rural areas , and other employed persons (including teachers in the schools run by the local people, people engaged in religious profession and the servicemen, etc.). This indicator reflects the actual utilization of total labour force during a certain period of time and is often used for the research on China's economic situation and national power.

Employees in Various Units refer to all the persons working in government agencies of various levels, political and party organizations, social organizations, enterprises and institutions, and receiving wages or other forms of payment. They include fully-employed staff and workers, re-employed retirees, teachers in schools run by the local people, foreigners and Chinese compatriots from Hong Kong, Macao, and Taiwan working in various units, part -time employees, employees of other units working temporarily at current posts, and employees holding the second job, but exclude staff and workers who have left their working units while keeping their labor contract (employment relation) unchanged. This indicator reflects the total number of laborers actually engaged in production or other operations in various units.

□ Staff and Workers

Staff and Workers refer to persons working in, and receive payment from units of state ownership, collective ownership, joint ownership, share holding ownership, foreign ownership, and ownership by entrepreneurship from Hong Kong, Macao, and Taiwan, and other types of ownership and their affiliated units. They do not

EXPLANATORY NOTES TO MAJOR STATISTICAL INDICATORS

include 1) persons employed in township enterprises, 2) urban self-employed persons, 3) retirees, 4) re-employed retirees, 5) teachers in the schools run by the local people, 6) foreigners and persons from Hong Kong, Macao and Taiwan who work in urban units, and 7) other persons not to be included by relevant regulations.(Data of 1998 and afterward refer to fully employed staff and workers. Other related statistics such as total wages and average wage are adjusted since 1998 accordingly).

□ Registered Urban Unemployment

Registered Urban Unemployment refers to those non-agricultural population within working age (16-50 years for male and 16-45 years for females),who are able and willing to work but unemployed and have registered for job in local employment service agencies.

□ Registered Urban Unemployment Rate

Registered Urban Unemployment Rate refers to the ratio of the number of the registered unemployed to the sum of the number of persons employed in various units (minus the rural labour force, retirees, and Hong Kong, Macao, Taiwan and foreign employees they employ) laid-off workers in urban units, urban self-employed individuals and the registered urban unemployed persons . The formula is as follows:

Registered Urban Unemployment Rate = Number of Registered Urban Unemployed Persons ÷ (Number of Persons Employed in Urban Units – rural labour force employed– retirees employed – Hong Kong, Macao, Taiwan and foreign employees + laid-off workers + Self-employed Individuals in Urban Areas + Number of Registered Urban Unemployed Persons) × 100%.

□ Fully Employed Staff and Workers

Working Staff and Workers refer to persons who work in, and receive wages from their working units, as well as persons who have their work posts, but are temporarily absent from work for reasons of study or on sick, injury or maternal leave and still receive wages from their working units.

第三篇

CHAPTER 3

国民经济核算

NATIONAL ECONOMIC ACCOUNTING

表 3.1 上海市生产总值(1978～2010)
GROSS DOMESTIC PRODUCT

年 份 Year	上海市生产总值(亿元) Gross Domestic Product (100 million yuan)	其 中 of which				
		第一产业 Primary Industry	第二产业 Secondary Industry	其中 of which: 工 业 Industry	其中 of which: 建筑业 Construction	第三产业 Tertiary Industry
1978	272.81	11.00	211.05	207.47	3.58	50.76
1979	286.43	11.39	221.21	216.62	4.59	53.83
1980	311.89	10.10	236.10	230.87	5.23	65.69
1981	324.76	10.58	244.34	237.12	7.22	69.84
1982	337.07	13.31	249.32	240.75	8.57	74.44
1983	351.81	13.52	255.32	246.26	9.06	82.97
1984	390.85	17.26	275.37	263.19	12.18	98.22
1985	466.75	19.53	325.63	311.12	14.51	121.59
1986	490.83	19.69	336.02	318.89	17.13	135.12
1987	545.46	21.60	364.38	336.54	27.84	159.48
1988	648.30	27.36	433.05	399.53	33.52	187.89
1989	696.54	29.63	466.18	432.92	33.26	200.73
1990	781.66	34.24	505.60	469.83	35.77	241.82
1991	893.77	34.06	550.64	514.79	35.85	309.07
1992	1 114.32	34.16	677.39	636.68	40.71	402.77
1993	1 519.23	37.82	902.38	846.71	55.67	579.03
1994	1 990.86	47.61	1 148.45	1 074.37	74.08	794.80
1995	2 499.43	59.82	1 419.41	1 308.20	111.21	1 020.20
1996	2 957.55	68.72	1 596.72	1 452.79	143.93	1 292.11
1997	3 438.79	72.03	1 774.02	1 598.91	175.11	1 592.74
1998	3 801.09	73.84	1 871.89	1 670.19	201.70	1 855.36
1999	4 188.73	74.49	1 984.64	1 787.98	196.66	2 129.60
2000	4 771.17	76.68	2 207.63	1 998.96	208.67	2 486.86
2001	5 210.12	78.00	2 403.18	2 166.74	236.44	2 728.94
2002	5 741.03	79.68	2 622.45	2 368.02	254.43	3 038.90
2003	6 694.23	81.02	3 209.02	2 941.24	267.78	3 404.19
2004	8 072.83	83.45	3 892.12	3 593.25	298.87	4 097.26
2005	9 247.66	90.26	4 381.20	4 036.85	344.35	4 776.20
2006	10 572.24	93.81	4 969.95	4 575.30	394.65	5 508.48
2007	12 494.01	101.84	5 571.06	5 154.42	416.64	6 821.11
2008	14 069.87	111.80	6 085.84	5 576.79	509.05	7 872.23
2009	15 046.45	113.82	6 001.78	5 408.75	593.03	8 930.85
2010	17 165.98	114.15	7 218.32	6 536.21	682.11	9 833.51

表 3.2 上海市生产总值指数(以 1978 年为 100，1978 ~ 2010)
INDEX OF GROSS DOMESTIC PRODUCT (1978 = 100)

年 份 Year	上海市生产总 值 Gross Domestic Product	其 中 of which				
		第一产业 Primary Industry	第二产业 Secondary Industry	其 中 of which		第三产业 Tertiary Industry
				工 业 Industry	建筑业 Construction	
1978	100	100	100	100	100	100
1979	107.4	99.3	108.6	108.8	97.8	103.1
1980	116.4	98.7	115.1	115.4	99.4	126.0
1981	122.9	99.0	120.7	120.1	138.4	137.2
1982	131.7	124.9	126.3	125.1	164.3	155.6
1983	142.0	124.9	135.8	134.5	178.9	170.8
1984	158.5	156.4	149.4	147.5	213.4	195.9
1985	179.7	121.7	171.7	169.6	237.1	224.7
1986	187.6	121.5	178.6	175.9	264.8	238.2
1987	201.7	118.2	191.8	187.9	323.9	259.4
1988	222.1	123.6	209.8	205.4	363.1	292.1
1989	228.8	124.0	213.2	209.3	347.1	312.8
1990	236.8	129.3	219.2	215.0	364.8	329.4
1991	253.7	129.8	234.3	233.9	296.6	357.7
1992	291.2	130.3	274.6	275.3	319.4	400.6
1993	335.2	126.8	320.5	321.8	363.5	455.5
1994	383.8	130.5	366.0	367.5	414.8	529.3
1995	438.7	138.9	420.2	420.1	518.5	601.8
1996	496.2	145.8	466.8	463.8	647.6	710.7
1997	559.7	151.9	516.3	511.1	757.0	837.9
1998	617.3	155.2	558.6	551.0	869.0	961.9
1999	681.5	158.5	608.9	603.9	863.8	1 090.8
2000	756.5	163.9	668.6	665.5	889.7	1 238.1
2001	835.9	168.8	748.8	746.0	986.7	1 354.5
2002	930.4	173.9	839.4	840.7	1 049.8	1 502.1
2003	1 044.8	177.9	974.5	988.7	1 063.4	1 637.3
2004	1 193.2	169.0	1 119.7	1 147.9	1 071.9	1 868.2
2005	1 329.2	152.6	1 237.3	1 268.4	1 181.2	2 107.3
2006	1 498.0	153.8	1 385.8	1 418.1	1 352.5	2 393.9
2007	1 725.7	156.9	1 545.2	1 591.1	1 406.6	2 844.0
2008	1 893.1	158.0	1 661.1	1 712.0	1 486.8	3 176.7
2009	2 048.3	156.3	1 719.2	1 761.6	1 660.8	3 564.3
2010	2 259.3	146.0	2 008.0	2 069.9	1 793.7	3 767.5

表3.3 上海市生产总值比上年增长(1978~2010)
GROWTH RATE OF GROSS DOMESTIC PRODUCT RAISED PRECEDING YEAR

单位:%

年 份 Year	上海市生产总 值 Gross Domestic Product	其 中 of which				
		第一产业 Primary Industry	第二产业 Secondary Industry	其 中 of which		第三产业 Tertiary Industry
				工 业 Industry	建筑业 Construction	
1978	15.8	27.0	16.6	15.8	89.8	10.6
1979	7.4	-0.7	8.6	8.8	-2.2	3.1
1980	8.4	-0.6	6.0	6.1	1.6	22.2
1981	5.6	0.3	4.9	4.1	39.2	8.9
1982	7.2	26.2	4.6	4.2	18.7	13.4
1983	7.8	平	7.5	7.5	8.9	9.8
1984	11.6	25.2	10.0	9.7	19.3	14.7
1985	13.4	-22.2	14.9	15.0	11.1	14.7
1986	4.4	-0.2	4.0	3.7	11.7	6.0
1987	7.5	-2.7	7.4	6.8	22.3	8.9
1988	10.1	4.6	9.4	9.3	12.1	12.6
1989	3.0	0.3	1.6	1.9	-4.4	7.1
1990	3.5	4.3	2.8	2.7	5.1	5.3
1991	7.1	0.4	6.9	8.8	-18.7	8.6
1992	14.8	0.4	17.2	17.7	7.7	12.0
1993	15.1	-2.7	16.7	16.9	13.8	13.7
1994	14.5	2.9	14.2	14.2	14.1	16.2
1995	14.3	6.4	14.8	14.3	25.0	13.7
1996	13.1	5.0	11.1	10.4	24.9	18.1
1997	12.8	4.2	10.6	10.2	16.9	17.9
1998	10.3	2.2	8.2	7.8	14.8	14.8
1999	10.4	2.1	9.0	9.6	-0.6	13.4
2000	11.0	3.4	9.8	10.2	3.0	13.5
2001	10.5	3.0	12.0	12.1	10.9	9.4
2002	11.3	3.0	12.1	12.7	6.4	10.9
2003	12.3	2.3	16.1	17.6	1.3	9.0
2004	14.2	-5.0	14.9	16.1	0.8	14.1
2005	11.4	-9.7	10.5	10.5	10.2	12.8
2006	12.7	0.8	12.0	11.8	14.5	13.6
2007	15.2	2.0	11.5	12.2	4.0	18.8
2008	9.7	0.7	7.5	7.6	5.7	11.7
2009	8.2	-1.1	3.5	2.9	11.7	12.2
2010	10.3	-6.6	16.8	17.5	8.0	5.7

表3.4 上海市生产总值构成(1978~2010)
STRUCTURE OF GROSS DOMESTIC PRODUCT

单位:%

年 份 Year	上海市生产总值 Gross Domestic Product	其中 of which				
		第一产业 Primary Industry	第二产业 Secondary Industry	其中 of which		第三产业 Tertiary Industry
				工业 Industry	建筑业 Construction	
1978	100	4.0	77.4	76.1	1.3	18.6
1979	100	4.0	77.2	75.6	1.6	18.8
1980	100	3.2	75.7	74.0	1.7	21.1
1981	100	3.3	75.2	73.0	2.2	21.5
1982	100	3.9	74.0	71.4	2.6	22.1
1983	100	3.8	72.6	70.0	2.6	23.6
1984	100	4.4	70.5	67.4	3.1	25.1
1985	100	4.2	69.8	66.7	3.1	26.0
1986	100	4.0	68.5	65.0	3.5	27.5
1987	100	4.0	66.8	61.7	5.1	29.2
1988	100	4.2	66.8	61.6	5.2	29.0
1989	100	4.3	66.9	62.1	4.8	28.8
1990	100	4.4	64.7	60.1	4.6	30.9
1991	100	3.8	61.6	57.6	4.0	34.6
1992	100	3.1	60.8	57.1	3.7	36.1
1993	100	2.5	59.4	55.7	3.7	38.1
1994	100	2.4	57.7	54.0	3.7	39.9
1995	100	2.4	56.8	52.3	4.5	40.8
1996	100	2.3	54.0	49.1	4.9	43.7
1997	100	2.1	51.6	46.5	5.1	46.3
1998	100	1.9	49.3	44.0	5.3	48.8
1999	100	1.8	47.4	42.7	4.7	50.8
2000	100	1.6	46.3	41.9	4.4	52.1
2001	100	1.5	46.1	41.6	4.5	52.4
2002	100	1.4	45.7	41.3	4.4	52.9
2003	100	1.2	47.9	43.9	4.0	50.9
2004	100	1.0	48.2	44.5	3.7	50.8
2005	100	1.0	47.4	43.7	3.7	51.6
2006	100	0.9	47.0	43.3	3.7	52.1
2007	100	0.8	44.6	41.3	3.3	54.6
2008	100	0.8	43.2	39.6	3.6	56.0
2009	100	0.7	39.9	36.0	3.9	59.4
2010	100	0.7	42.0	38.0	4.0	57.3

表3.5 上海市人均生产总值(1978～2010)
PER CAPITA GROSS DOMESTIC PRODUCT

年份 Year	上海市生产总值(亿元) Gross Domestic Product (100 million yuan)	人均生产总值(按人民币计算)(元) Per Capita Gross Domestic Product (yuan)	人均生产总值指数 Per Capita Gross Domestic Product Index		人均生产总值(按美元计算)(美元) Per Capita Gross Domestic Product (USD)
			以1978年为100 (1978＝100)	以上年为100 (preceding year＝100)	
1978	272.81	2 485	100.0	114.9	1 445
1979	286.43	2 556	105.3	105.3	1 787
1980	311.89	2 725	111.8	106.2	1 829
1981	324.76	2 800	116.5	104.2	1 642
1982	337.07	2 864	123.0	105.6	1 513
1983	351.81	2 947	130.7	106.3	1 492
1984	390.85	3 232	144.0	110.2	1 389
1985	466.75	3 811	161.3	112.0	1 298
1986	490.83	3 956	166.1	103.0	1 146
1987	545.46	4 340	176.2	106.1	1 166
1988	648.30	5 080	191.0	108.4	1 365
1989	696.54	5 362	193.3	101.2	1 424
1990	781.66	5 911	196.6	101.7	1 236
1991	893.77	6 661	207.6	105.6	1 251
1992	1 114.32	8 208	235.6	113.5	1 488
1993	1 519.23	1 1061	268.1	113.8	1 920
1994	1 990.86	14 328	303.2	113.1	1 662
1995	2 499.43	17 779	342.3	112.9	2 129
1996	2 957.55	20 647	380.0	111.0	2 483
1997	3 438.79	23 397	417.6	109.9	2 822
1998	3 801.09	25 206	448.9	107.5	3 045
1999	4 188.73	27 071	483.0	107.6	3 270
2000	4 771.17	30 047	522.6	108.2	3 630
2001	5 210.12	31 799	559.7	107.1	3 842
2002	5 741.03	33 958	603.9	107.9	4 103
2003	6 694.23	38 486	658.9	109.1	4 650
2004	8 072.83	44 839	727.4	110.4	5 417
2005	9 247.66	49 649	781.2	107.4	6 061
2006	10 572.24	54 858	851.5	109.0	6 882
2007	12 494.01	62 041	939.2	110.3	8 159
2008	14 069.87	66 932	987.1	105.1	9 637
2009	15 046.45	69 164	1 032.5	104.6	10 125
2010	17 165.98	76 074	1 098.6	106.4	11 238

①1978年～1992年的人均生产总值按户籍人口计算，1993年以后按半年以上常住人口计算。
②2001～2009年的人均生产总值根据第六次人口普查结果调整后的年末常住人口数计算。
❶Per Capita Gross Domestic Product from 1978 to 1992 were calculated by registared population ,and resident population above half year after 1993.
❷Data of Per Capita Gross Domostic Product from 2001 to 2009 are calculated by resident popution at year-end which have been adjusted according to the result of the sixth National Population Census.

表3.6 主要年份上海市生产总值(按三次产业分)
GROSS DOMESTIC PRODUCT (CLASSIFIED BY THREE INDUSTRIES) IN MAIN YEARS

单位:亿元(100 million yuan)

指标	Indicators	2001	2009	2010
上海市生产总值	**Gross Domestic Product**	**5 210.12**	**15 046.45**	**17 165.98**
第一产业	Primary Industry	78.00	113.82	114.15
第二产业	Secondary Industry	2 403.18	6 001.78	7 218.32
工　业	Industry	2 166.74	5 408.75	6 536.21
建筑业	Construction	236.44	593.03	682.11
第三产业	Tertiary Industry	2 728.94	8 930.85	9 833.51
交通运输、仓储和邮政业	Transportation, Warehousing and Post	345.99	635.01	834.40
信息传输、计算机服务和软件业	Information Transmission, Computer Servcie and Software Industries	176.72	601.73	675.98
批发和零售业	Retail and Wholesale Industries	555.06	2 183.85	2 594.34
住宿和餐饮业	Hoteling and Catering	104.30	238.36	266.45
金融业	Financial Industry	529.26	1 804.28	1 950.96
房地产业	Real Estate Industry	328.59	1 237.56	1 002.50
租赁和商务服务业	Leasehold and Business in Services	136.97	641.97	776.13
科学研究、技术服务和地质勘查业	Scientific Research, Technology Service and Geological Prospecting	114.91	364.90	391.28
水利、环境和公共设施管理业	Water Conservancy, Environment and Public Facility Management Industries	32.59	45.06	50.19
居民服务和其他服务业	Community Service and Other Service Industries	46.16	156.83	179.98
教　育	Education	136.53	378.18	400.36
卫生、社会保障和社会福利业	Health, Social Security and Welfare Industries	72.27	227.47	250.41
文化、体育和娱乐	Culture, Sports and Entertainment	43.96	87.49	93.98
公共管理和社会组织	Public Administration and Social Organizations	105.63	328.16	366.55

表3.7 主要年份上海市生产总值指数(按三次产业分，以上年为100)
INDEX OF GROSS DOMESTIC PRODUCT IN MAIN YEARS(CLASSIFIED BY THREE INDUSTRIES, PRECEDING YEAR = 100)

指标	Indicators	2001	2009	2010
上海市生产总值	**Gross Domestic Product**	**110.5**	**108.2**	**110.3**
第一产业	Primary Industry	103.0	98.9	93.4
第二产业	Secondary Industry	112.0	103.5	116.8
工　业	Industry	112.1	102.9	117.5
建筑业	Construction	110.9	111.7	108.0
第三产业	Tertiary Industry	109.4	112.2	105.7
交通运输、仓储和邮政业	Transportation, Warehousing and Post	108.9	91.4	116.0
信息传输、计算机服务和软件业	Information Transmission, Computer Servcie and Software Industries	118.1	108.4	111.2
批发和零售业	Retail and Wholesale Industries	115.7	113.6	115.6
住宿和餐饮业	Hoteling and Catering	107.8	96.9	106.8
金融业	Financial Industry	90.9	124.9	105.1
房地产业	Real Estate Industry	91.4	127.0	70.7
租赁和商务服务业	Leasehold and Business in Services	129.5	103.7	115.7
科学研究、技术服务和地质勘查业	Scientific Research, Technological Service and Geological Prospecting	109.9	113.1	105.1
水利、环境和公共设施管理业	Water Conservancy, Environment and Public Facility Management Industries	123.9	106.8	109.2
居民服务和其他服务业	Community Service and Other Services Industries	118.8	111.8	112.5
教　育	Education	114.4	104.6	104.6
卫生、社会保障和社会福利业	Health, Social Security and Welfare Industries	114.0	106.7	106.2
文化、体育和娱乐	Culture, Sports and Entertainment	113.8	105.1	106.4
公共管理和社会组织	Public Administration and Social Organizations	114.5	105.2	109.5

表 3.8　上海市生产总值收入法项目（1978～2010）
GROSS DOMESTIC PRODUCT（BY INCOME ITEM）

单位：亿元（100 million yuan）

年　份 Year	上海市生产总　值 Gross Domestic Product	劳动者报酬 Compensation of Employees	生产税净额 Net Taxes on Production	固定资产折旧 Depreciation of Fixed Assets	营业盈余 Operating Surplus
1978	272.81	62.03	45.53	10.6	154.65
1979	286.43	68.15	45.61	11.13	161.54
1980	311.89	74.47	49.49	13.05	174.88
1981	324.76	78.99	54.52	14.7	176.55
1982	337.07	85.00	57.09	16.3	178.68
1983	351.81	90.36	57.51	18.73	185.21
1984	390.85	108.79	68.74	20.81	192.51
1985	466.75	125.99	87.36	26.16	227.24
1986	490.83	141.95	86.31	33.42	229.15
1987	545.46	163.88	98.61	40.73	242.24
1988	648.3	197.69	126.95	71.85	251.81
1989	696.54	223.35	136.01	79.79	257.39
1990	781.66	244.03	149.35	92.93	295.35
1991	893.77	302.94	170.42	126.62	293.79
1992	1 114.32	397.72	207.40	160.36	348.84
1993	1 519.23	563.59	257.30	159.93	538.41
1994	1 990.86	692.40	356.32	245.26	696.88
1995	2 499.43	901.83	430.67	339.77	827.16
1996	2 957.55	1 065.85	576.01	376.70	938.99
1997	3 438.79	1 195.63	716.02	425.04	1 102.10
1998	3 801.09	1 341.22	809.04	514.85	1 135.98
1999	4 188.73	1 518.26	902.1	615.28	1 153.09
2000	4 771.17	1 724.29	1 124.3	679.43	1 243.15
2001	5 210.12	1 934.27	1 184.62	769.59	1 321.64
2002	5 741.03	2 205.79	1 219.35	850.69	1 465.20
2003	6 694.23	2 452.32	1 265.89	975.24	2 000.78
2004	8 072.83	2 771.77	1 313.83	1 265.16	2 722.07
2005	9 247.66	3 312.31	1 459.39	1 488.54	2 987.42
2006	10 572.24	3 846.06	1 729.03	1 721.21	3 275.94
2007	12 494.01	4 481.91	2 142.97	1 931.76	3 937.37
2008	14 069.87	5 417.93	2 662.86	2 132.75	3 856.33
2009	15 046.45	5 901.84	2 916.92	2 229.19	3 998.50
2010	17 165.98	6 742.05	3 298.73	2 275.95	4 849.25

表 3.9 上海市生产总值收入法项目构成(1978~2010)
STRUCTURE OF GROSS DOMESTIC PRODUCT(BY INCOME ITEM)

单位:%

年 份 Year	上海市生产总 值 Gross Domestic Product	劳动者报酬 Compensation of Employees	生产税净额 Net Taxes on Production	固定资产折旧 Depreciation of Fixed Assets	营业盈余 Operating Surplus
1978	100	22.7	16.7	3.9	56.7
1979	100	23.8	15.9	3.9	56.4
1980	100	23.9	15.8	4.2	56.1
1981	100	24.3	16.8	4.5	54.4
1982	100	25.2	17.0	4.8	53.0
1983	100	25.7	16.4	5.3	52.6
1984	100	27.8	17.6	5.3	49.3
1985	100	27.0	18.7	5.6	48.7
1986	100	28.9	17.6	6.8	46.7
1987	100	30.0	18.1	7.5	44.4
1988	100	30.5	19.6	11.1	38.8
1989	100	32.1	19.5	11.5	36.9
1990	100	31.2	19.1	11.9	37.8
1991	100	33.9	19.1	14.1	32.9
1992	100	35.7	18.6	14.4	31.3
1993	100	37.1	16.9	10.5	35.5
1994	100	34.8	17.9	12.3	35.0
1995	100	36.1	17.2	13.6	33.1
1996	100	36.0	19.5	12.7	31.8
1997	100	34.8	20.8	12.4	32.0
1998	100	35.3	21.3	13.5	29.9
1999	100	36.3	21.5	14.7	27.5
2000	100	36.1	23.6	14.2	26.1
2001	100	37.1	22.7	14.8	25.4
2002	100	38.4	21.3	14.8	25.5
2003	100	36.6	18.9	14.6	29.9
2004	100	34.3	16.3	15.7	33.7
2005	100	35.8	15.8	16.1	32.3
2006	100	36.3	16.4	16.3	31.0
2007	100	35.9	17.1	15.5	31.5
2008	100	38.5	18.9	15.2	27.4
2009	100	39.2	19.4	14.8	26.6
2010	100	39.3	19.2	13.3	28.2

表 3.10 主要年份上海市生产总值(按所有制分)
GROSS DOMESTIC PRODUCT(BY OWNERSHIP) IN MAIN YEARS

年 份 Year	上海市生产总值 Gross Domestic Product	其 中 of which				
		公有制经济 Public-owned	其 中 of which		非公有制经济 Non-public-owned	其 中 of which
			国有经济 State-owned	集体经济 Collective-owned		#私营和个体 Private
绝对值(亿元)	**Absolute Volume(100 million yuan)**					
1990	781.66	746.03	556.87	189.16	35.63	22.39
1995	2 499.43	2 047.57	1 489.06	558.51	451.86	192.66
1996	2 957.55	2 302.16	1 677.56	624.60	655.39	273.94
1997	3 438.79	2 648.19	1 953.84	694.35	790.60	337.15
1998	3 801.09	2 860.45	2 118.64	741.81	940.64	393.10
1999	4 188.73	3 063.77	2 297.74	766.03	1 124.96	485.79
2000	4 771.17	3 409.97	2 626.33	783.64	1 361.20	623.84
2001	5 210.12	3 554.56	2 773.76	780.80	1 655.56	830.27
2002	5 741.03	3 703.46	2 888.57	814.89	2 037.57	1 055.48
2003	6 694.23	4 171.16	3 360.21	810.95	2 523.07	1 258.15
2004	8 072.83	4 810.32	4 069.95	740.37	3 262.51	1 293.56
2005	9 247.66	5 256.49	4 471.92	784.57	3 991.17	1 944.55
2006	10 572.24	5 812.87	4 994.48	818.39	4 759.37	2 281.10
2007	12 494.01	6 674.98	5 852.65	822.33	5 819.03	2 804.01
2008	14 069.87	7 341.75	6 452.92	888.83	6 728.12	3 313.18
2009	15 046.45	7 769.86	6 864.01	905.85	7 276.59	3 571.19
2010	17 165.98	8 662.92	7 755.35	907.57	8 503.06	4 139.07
构 成(%)	**Composition(%)**					
1990	100	95.4	71.2	24.2	4.6	2.9
1995	100	81.9	59.6	22.3	18.1	7.7
1996	100	77.8	56.7	21.1	22.2	9.3
1997	100	77.0	56.8	20.2	23.0	9.8
1998	100	75.2	55.7	19.5	24.8	10.3
1999	100	73.2	54.9	18.3	26.8	11.6
2000	100	71.4	55.0	16.4	28.6	13.1
2001	100	68.2	53.2	15.0	31.8	15.9
2002	100	64.5	50.3	14.2	35.5	18.4
2003	100	62.3	50.2	12.1	37.7	18.8
2004	100	59.6	50.4	9.2	40.4	19.7
2005	100	56.9	48.4	8.5	43.1	21.0
2006	100	55.0	47.3	7.7	45.0	21.6
2007	100	53.4	46.8	6.6	46.6	22.4
2008	100	52.2	45.9	6.3	47.8	23.5
2009	100	51.6	45.6	6.0	48.4	23.7
2010	100	50.5	45.2	5.3	49.5	24.1

表 3.11 主要年份非公有制经济增加值（按产业分）
ADDED VALUE OF NON-PUBLIC-OWNED (GROUPED BY INDUSTRY) IN MAIN YEARS

单位：亿元(100 million yuan)

年 份 Year	非公有制经济增加值 Added Value of Non-public-owned	其 中 of which			
		第一产业 Primary Industry	第二产业 Secondary Industry	其 中 of which 工 业 Industry	第三产业 Tertiary Industry
1990	35.63	9.01	15.22	13.74	11.40
1995	451.86	13.29	285.73	274.64	152.84
1996	655.39	14.31	424.3	407.69	216.78
1997	790.60	13.42	503.69	470.23	273.49
1998	940.64	13.25	561.66	518.25	365.72
1999	1 124.96	13.56	635.83	585.76	475.57
2000	1 361.20	14.25	773.50	715.18	573.45
2001	1 655.56	14.77	924.21	857.62	716.58
2002	2 037.57	14.34	1 085.12	1 004.78	938.11
2003	2 523.07	13.04	1 459.67	1 378.21	1 050.36
2004	3 262.51	10.44	1 921.74	1 757.96	1 330.33
2005	3 991.17	11.12	2 228.18	2 054.78	1 751.87
2006	4 759.37	11.41	2 634.01	2 438.40	2 113.95
2007	5 819.03	11.98	3 044.61	2 831.64	2 762.44
2008	6 728.12	13.35	3 294.60	3 039.51	3 420.17
2009	7 276.59	13.09	3 213.99	2 925.50	4 049.50
2010	8 503.06	13.13	3 928.43	3 575.67	4 561.50

表 3.12 主要年份上海市生产总值分配
STRUCTURE OF GROSS DOMESTIC PRODUCT BY DISTRIBUTION IN MAIN YEARS

单位：亿元(100 million yuan)

年 份 Year	上海市生产总值 Gross Domestic Product	政府所得 State-owned	企业所得 Collective-owned	个人所得 Personal-owned
1990	781.66	252.74	201.99	326.93
1995	2 499.43	590.96	872.16	1 036.31
1996	2 957.55	725.27	980.04	1 252.24
1997	3 438.79	1 000.07	1 059.09	1 379.63
1998	3 801.09	1 100.75	1 175.22	1 525.12
1999	4 188.73	1 217.92	1 286.23	1 684.58
2000	4 771.17	1 483.36	1 448.83	1 838.98
2001	5 210.12	1 625.56	1 587.93	1 996.63
2002	5 741.03	1 798.64	1 739.11	2 203.28
2003	6 694.23	2 195.62	2 008.80	2 489.81
2004	8 072.83	2 659.12	2 423.58	2 990.13
2005	9 247.66	3 059.06	2 682.19	3 506.41
2006	10 572.24	3 553.50	3 024.49	3 994.25
2007	12 494.01	4 165.64	3 697.25	4 631.12
2008	14 069.87	4 875.46	3 755.03	5 439.38
2009	15 046.45	5 290.46	3 827.42	5 928.57
2010	17 165.98	5 767.76	4 090.32	7 307.90

表3.13 上海市生产总值(支出法)(1978～2010)
GROSS DOMESTIC PRODUCT(BY EXPENDITURE APPROACH)

年 份 Year	上海市生产总值(亿元) Gross Domestic Product (100 million yuan)	其中 of which 货物和服务净流出 Net Outflows of Goods and Services	其中 of which 本市使用的生产总值 Gross Domestic Product Used	其中 of which 最终消费支出 Final Consumption	其中 of which 资本形成总额 Gross Capital Formation	上海市生产总值构成(%) Composition of GDP(%) #最终消费支出 Final Consumption	上海市生产总值构成(%) Composition of GDP(%) #资本形成总额 Gross Capital Formation	可供投资率(%) Available Investment Rate(%)
1978	272.81	165.79	107.02	59.06	47.96	21.6	17.6	78.4
1979	286.43	171.48	114.95	71.34	43.61	24.9	15.2	75.1
1980	311.89	164.13	147.76	81.24	66.52	26.0	21.3	74.0
1981	324.76	158.35	166.41	89.73	76.68	27.6	23.6	72.4
1982	337.07	153.90	183.17	92.90	90.27	27.6	26.8	72.4
1983	351.81	178.76	173.05	101.19	71.86	28.8	20.4	71.2
1984	390.85	171.97	218.88	117.25	101.63	30.0	26.0	70.0
1985	466.75	122.47	344.28	155.15	189.13	33.2	40.5	66.8
1986	490.83	80.97	409.86	181.74	228.12	37.0	46.5	63.0
1987	545.46	103.70	441.76	200.74	241.02	36.8	44.2	63.2
1988	648.30	57.32	590.98	255.42	335.56	39.4	51.8	60.6
1989	696.54	46.24	650.30	298.62	351.68	42.9	50.5	57.1
1990	781.66	91.87	689.79	358.45	331.34	45.9	42.4	54.1
1991	893.77	167.68	726.09	386.06	340.03	43.2	38.0	56.8
1992	1 114.32	150.12	964.2	476.57	487.63	42.7	43.8	57.2
1993	1 519.23	75.60	1 443.63	699.52	744.11	46.0	49.0	54.0
1994	1 990.86	-90.46	2 081.32	919.83	1 161.49	46.2	58.3	53.8
1995	2 499.43	-218.64	2 718.07	1 150.35	1 567.72	46.0	62.7	54.0
1996	2 957.55	-348.05	3 305.60	1 348.76	1 956.84	45.6	66.2	54.4
1997	3 438.79	-210.99	3 649.78	1 600.83	2 048.95	46.6	59.6	53.4
1998	3 801.09	32.25	3 768.84	1 758.09	2 010.75	46.3	52.9	53.7
1999	4 188.73	259.37	3 929.36	1 959.12	1 970.24	46.8	47.0	53.2
2000	4 771.17	356.93	4 414.24	2 244.52	2 169.72	47.0	45.5	53.0
2001	5 210.12	377.21	4 832.91	2 476.20	2 356.71	47.5	45.2	52.5
2002	5 741.03	418.68	5 322.35	2 791.06	2 531.29	48.6	44.1	51.4
2003	6 694.23	399.96	6 294.27	3 217.59	3 076.68	48.1	46.0	51.9
2004	8 072.83	457.99	7 614.84	3 832.59	3 782.25	47.5	46.9	52.5
2005	9 247.66	548.33	8 699.33	4 480.34	4 218.99	48.4	45.6	51.6
2006	10 572.24	523.75	10 048.49	5 175.15	4 873.34	49.0	46.1	51.0
2007	12 494.01	604.04	11 889.97	6 170.38	5 719.59	49.4	45.8	50.6
2008	14 069.87	753.38	13 316.49	7 172.67	6 143.82	51.0	43.7	49.0
2009	15 046.45	411.80	14 634.65	7 868.64	6 766.01	52.3	45.0	47.7
2010	17 165.98	333.91	16 832.07	9 424.29	7 407.78	54.9	43.2	45.1

注：本表至表3.16中2010年的数据根据第六次人口普查结果调整后的人口数计算，与历年数据不可比。
Note: The data of 2010 in table 3.13 to 3.16 are adjusted accordingh the sixth National Population Census, and is uncomparable to historical data.

表3.14 最终消费支出及构成(1978～2010)
FINAL CONSUMPTION AND COMPOSITION

年份 Year	最终消费支出(亿元) Final Consumption (100 million yuan)					最终消费支出构成(%) Composition of Final Consumption (%)	
	合计 Total	居民消费支出 Household Consumption	其中 of which 农村居民 Rural Residents	其中 of which 城镇居民 Urban Residents	政府消费支出 Government Consumption	居民消费支出 Household Consumption	政府消费支出 Government Consumption
1978	59.06	48.25	12.82	35.43	10.81	81.7	18.3
1979	71.34	58.80	17.02	41.78	12.54	82.4	17.6
1980	81.24	66.31	19.43	46.88	14.93	81.6	18.4
1981	89.73	73.69	23.25	50.44	16.04	82.1	17.9
1982	92.90	75.02	26.41	48.61	17.88	80.8	19.2
1983	101.19	81.64	26.91	54.73	19.55	80.7	19.3
1984	117.25	94.56	31.10	63.46	22.69	80.6	19.4
1985	155.15	124.78	38.35	86.43	30.37	80.4	19.6
1986	181.74	145.73	42.49	103.24	36.01	80.2	19.8
1987	200.74	161.09	47.23	113.86	39.65	80.2	19.8
1988	255.42	211.04	55.97	155.07	44.38	82.6	17.4
1989	298.62	244.60	61.15	183.45	54.02	81.9	18.1
1990	358.45	284.79	66.15	218.64	73.66	79.5	20.5
1991	386.06	311.09	72.17	238.92	74.97	80.6	19.4
1992	476.57	366.09	84.86	281.23	110.48	76.8	23.2
1993	699.52	555.45	110.30	445.15	144.07	79.4	20.6
1994	919.83	732.71	130.08	602.63	187.12	79.7	20.3
1995	1 150.35	926.54	152.90	773.64	223.81	80.5	19.5
1996	1 348.76	1 080.79	168.13	912.66	267.97	80.1	19.9
1997	1 600.83	1 262.12	176.50	1 085.62	338.71	78.8	21.2
1998	1 758.09	1 379.41	178.52	1 200.89	378.68	78.5	21.5
1999	1 959.12	1 528.95	176.73	1 352.22	430.17	78.0	22.0
2000	2 244.52	1 756.27	176.79	1 579.48	488.25	78.2	21.8
2001	2 476.20	1 910.44	181.22	1 729.22	565.76	77.2	22.8
2002	2 791.06	2 134.79	185.58	1 949.21	656.27	76.5	23.5
2003	3 217.59	2 437.44	187.78	2 249.66	780.15	75.8	24.2
2004	3 832.59	2 869.26	186.78	2 682.48	963.33	74.9	25.1
2005	4 480.34	3 332.99	194.59	3 138.40	1 147.35	74.4	25.6
2006	5 175.15	3 858.54	223.98	3 634.56	1 316.61	74.6	25.4
2007	6 170.38	4 609.59	245.82	4 363.77	1 560.79	74.7	25.3
2008	7 172.67	5 290.40	275.91	5 014.49	1 882.27	73.7	26.3
2009	7 868.64	5 782.88	303.57	5 479.31	2 085.76	73.5	26.5
2010	9 424.29	7 281.88	339.11	6 942.77	2 142.41	77.3	22.7

表 3.15 居民消费水平及指数(1978～2010)
HOUSEHOLD CONSUMPTION LEVEL AND INDEX

年 份 Year	居民消费水平(元) Household Consumption Level(yuan)			指数(以 1978 年为 100) Index(1978 = 100)		
	全 市 Total	其 中 of which		全 市 Total	其 中 of which	
		农村居民 Rural Households	城镇居民 Urban Households		农村居民 Rural Households	城镇居民 Urban Households
1978	442	283	555	100.0	100.0	100.0
1979	527	379	627	117.2	129.1	111.6
1980	582	437	675	123.1	141.9	114.2
1981	638	521	712	133.1	167.2	118.7
1982	640	589	672	133.5	168.9	118.6
1983	688	600	741	142.8	192.9	122.9
1984	788	697	842	160.8	219.5	137.2
1985	1 031	938	1 078	182.0	252.2	153.1
1986	1 190	1 058	1 254	197.7	266.6	167.6
1987	1 298	1 102	1 401	199.9	257.5	173.3
1988	1 680	1 316	1 867	220.3	269.9	194.3
1989	1 927	1 449	2 165	221.4	271.5	194.7
1990	2 225	1 576	2 542	216.1	249.5	193.7
1991	2 420	1 726	2 755	234.3	283.9	206.7
1992	2 842	2 042	3 222	249.5	306.0	219.1
1993	3 923	2 737	4 394	287.4	311.8	255.9
1994	5 081	3 371	5 706	325.3	357.0	286.1
1995	6 310	4 120	7 050	379.3	402.7	333.3
1996	7 228	4 680	8 033	416.5	438.1	364.0
1997	8 289	5 086	9 234	449.0	462.2	391.3
1998	8 896	5 344	9 871	480.4	480.7	417.5
1999	9 683	5 497	10 753	515.9	495.1	448.0
2000	10 922	5 705	12 168	557.7	509.0	484.3
2001	11 807	6 052	13 114	604.5	543.6	523.0
2002	13 137	6 464	14 569	673.4	580.6	582.1
2003	14 247	6 914	15 631	721.9	616.0	617.0
2004	16 470	7 715	17 883	815.0	671.4	689.8
2005	18 741	9 683	19 895	906.0	817.1	750.1
2006	21 475	11 228	22 755	1 019.2	926.5	842.4
2007	25 099	11 845	26 787	1 148.5	934.7	956.6
2008	28 242	13 166	30 140	1 245.9	993.1	1 038.1
2009	30 358	13 979	32 466	1 345.3	1 055.3	1 123.4
2010	32 271	13 609	34 588	1 478.5	1 133.4	1 233.5

注：1993 年以前为年平均户籍人口数，1993 年起为年平均常住人口数。
Note: Data in this table refer to yearly average registered population before 1993, and yearly average resident population after 1993.

表3.16 资本形成总额和指数(1978~2010)
GROSS CAPITAL FORMATION AND INDEX

年份 Year	资本形成总额(亿元) Gross Capital Formation(100 million yuan)			资本形成总额指数(以1978年为100) Index of Gross Capital Formation (1978=100)		
	合计 Total	固定资本形成总额 Fixed Capital Formation	存货增加 Inventory Change	总指数 Indices	固定资本形成总额 Fixed Capital Formation	存货增加 Inventory Change
1978	47.96	31.69	16.27	100	100	100
1979	43.61	39.05	4.56	90.3	119.7	36.9
1980	66.52	45.57	20.95	134.6	133.5	136.7
1981	76.68	55.10	21.58	156.4	164.4	138.1
1982	90.27	70.49	19.78	178.8	210.5	107.6
1983	71.86	74.51	-2.65	150.7	223.7	-12.5
1984	101.63	90.70	10.93	210.0	262.7	91.9
1985	189.13	116.70	72.43	387.6	308.1	564.0
1986	228.12	144.41	83.71	431.8	352.5	607.4
1987	241.02	183.79	57.23	380.0	415.9	298.8
1988	335.56	236.92	98.64	449.2	474.1	392.1
1989	351.68	232.22	119.46	423.1	419.6	429.7
1990	331.34	248.46	82.88	338.1	430.5	131.1
1991	340.03	276.08	63.95	334.0	447.7	109.0
1992	487.63	382.01	105.62	435.2	561.5	162.1
1993	744.11	624.31	119.80	530.1	731.0	154.5
1994	1 161.49	996.48	165.01	726.8	1 019.1	196.1
1995	1 567.72	1 380.85	186.87	950.6	1 373.7	218.8
1996	1 956.84	1 711.46	245.38	1 158.8	1 660.8	279.5
1997	2 048.95	1 795.83	253.12	1 175.0	1 700.6	268.3
1998	2 010.75	1 804.81	205.94	1 129.2	1 695.5	201.2
1999	1 970.24	1 801.59	168.65	1 098.7	1 683.7	164.0
2000	2 169.72	1 933.01	236.71	1 152.5	1 746.0	191.0
2001	2 356.71	2 099.99	256.72	1 263.2	1 906.6	216.1
2002	2 531.29	2 366.10	165.19	1 387.0	2 192.6	148.9
2003	3 076.68	2 643.07	433.61	1 588.1	2 365.8	299.4
2004	3 782.25	3 239.04	543.21	1 804.1	2 680.5	347.3
2005	4 218.99	3 775.55	443.44	1 962.0	3 024.4	279.9
2006	4 873.34	4 383.33	490.01	2 210.4	3 427.9	299.0
2007	5 719.59	5 192.50	527.09	2 575.3	4 030.2	319.5
2008	6 143.82	5 614.47	529.35	2 708.2	4 235.3	338.4
2009	6 766.01	6 447.52	318.49	2 899.7	4 741.8	119.2
2010	7 407.78	6 380.33	1 027.45	3 094.0	4 533.2	383.5

表 3.17 主要年份六大支柱产业增加值
VALUE ADDED OF SIX PILLAR INDUSTRIES IN MAIN YEARS

指 标	Indicators	2000	2009	2010
增加值(亿元)	**Value Added (100 million yuan)**	**1 919.10**	**7 846.92**	**8 902.68**
信息产业	Information Industry	338.18	1 334.76	1 672.14
金融业	Financial Industry	602.95	1 804.28	1 950.96
商贸流通业	Trading and Circulation Industry	431.43	2 183.85	2 594.34
汽车制造业	Auto Manufacturing	166.05	618.84	1 010.01
成套设备制造业	Whole-set Equipment Manufacturing Industry	129.73	701.19	727.35
房地产业	Real Estate Industry	263.35	1 237.56	1 002.50
增加值占上海市生产总值比重(%)	**Ratio of Value Added to GDP (%)**	**40.2**	**52.2**	**51.9**

①信息产业增加值含有与其他行业的交叉重复因素，本表中“六大支柱产业增加值占上海市生产总值的比重”已经扣除重复计算因素。
②商贸流通业中不包括餐饮业增加值。
❶The ratio of value added from six pillar industries to GDP has excluded some overlapping factors.
❷Trading and circulation industry does not include the catering industry.

表 3.18 主要年份旅游产业增加值
VALUE ADDED OF TOURISM INDUSTRY IN MAIN YEARS

指 标	Indicators	2005	2009	2010
增加值(亿元)	**Value Added (100 million yuan)**	**584.26**	**1 007.08**	**1 360.80**
按行业分	**Grouped by Sectors**			
#旅行社服务业	Travel Agency	9.02	13.46	17.50
旅游宾(旅)馆业	Hotel	91.78	104.17	212.34
旅游运输业	Travel Transportation	120.86	124.91	159.67
邮电通信业	Post and Telecommunication	25.21	28.26	38.60
旅游商业	Tourism Commerce	96.17	263.53	529.28
餐饮业	Catering	68.92	131.45	67.17
城市交通业	Urban Traffic		74.54	93.18
园林文化业	Gardening	92.42	148.22	169.98
旅游产业增加值占上海市生产总值比重(%)	**Ratio of Value Added of Tourism Industry to GDP (%)**	**6.3**	**6.8**	**8.1**

表 3.19 主要年份信息产业增加值
VALUE ADDED OF INFORMATION INDUSTRY IN MAIN YEARS

指 标	Indicators	2000	2009	2010
增加值(亿元)	**Value Added (100 million yuan)**	**338.18**	**1 344.76**	**1 672.14**
信息产品制造业	Information Products Manufacturing	195.82	529.00	690.76
信息产品销售业	Information Products Distribution	12.59	43.56	54.62
信息服务业	Information Services	129.77	772.20	926.76
信息产业增加值占上海市生产总值比重(%)	**Ratio of Value Added of Information Industry to GDP(%).**	**7.1**	**8.9**	**9.7**

表 3.20 经营性固定资产原价年末数(1978～2010)
ORIGINAL VALUE OF OPERATING FIXED ASSETS(YEAR-END)

单位:亿元(100 million yuan)

年 份 Year	合 计 Total	其 中 of which					
		第一产业 Primary Industry	第二产业 Secondary Industry	其 中 of which		第三产业 Tertiary Industry
				工 业 Industry	建筑业 Construction	
1978	298.53	8.03	205.17	197.68	7.49	85.33
1979	321.52	10.56	213.94	205.94	8.00	97.02
1980	355.16	11.81	225.55	216.16	9.39	117.80
1981	388.93	10.04	249.08	237.37	11.71	129.81
1982	413.23	9.56	271.76	255.57	16.19	131.91
1983	448.41	10.88	298.22	280.77	17.45	139.31
1984	493.76	11.47	327.20	309.22	17.98	155.09
1985	569.97	12.09	377.06	355.61	21.45	180.82
1986	726.95	13.25	496.56	472.68	23.88	217.14
1987	868.91	14.73	576.61	548.62	27.99	277.57
1988	975.78	15.78	656.35	629.34	27.01	303.65
1989	1 106.60	20.04	755.02	723.02	32.00	331.54
1990	1 263.17	22.80	866.64	827.01	39.63	373.73
1991	1 656.84	24.03	1 067.81	1 026.08	41.73	565.00
1992	2 011.38	26.29	1 279.04	1 236.56	42.48	706.05
1993	2 486.40	31.36	1 581.16	1 537.56	43.60	873.88
1994	3 536.83	47.58	2 330.14	2 271.38	58.76	1 159.11
1995	4 756.42	59.48	2 915.53	2 810.27	105.26	1 781.41
1996	5 827.13	69.64	3 393.66	3 263.77	129.89	2 363.83
1997	6 915.42	80.87	3 879.13	3 721.96	157.17	2 955.42
1998	8 392.45	82.93	4 573.10	4 406.50	166.60	3 736.42
1999	9 991.27	91.22	5 311.01	5 137.11	173.90	4 589.04
2000	11 684.90	104.25	5 940.30	5 749.23	191.07	5 640.35
2001	12 667.45	112.71	6 451.78	6 249.24	202.54	6 102.96
2002	13 839.09	118.78	6 937.81	6 596.13	341.68	6 782.50
2003	15 639.55	127.33	7 614.96	7 197.71	417.25	7 897.26
2004	18 896.30	152.61	9 183.79	8 717.45	466.34	9 559.90
2005	21 843.13	162.19	10 963.19	10 445.07	518.12	10 717.75
2006	24 069.59	164.44	12 335.84	11 752.39	583.45	11 569.31
2007	26 562.67	196.56	13 384.28	12 766.31	617.97	12 981.83
2008	30 395.26	210.67	14 521.97	13 947.02	574.95	15 662.62
2009	33 672.12	223.18	15 991.38	15 371.01	620.37	17 457.56
2010	36 618.30	223.50	16 364.93	15 612.46	752.47	20 029.87

表 3.21 存货年末数(1978～2010)
YEAR-END INVENTORY

单位:亿元(100 million yuan)

年份 Year	合计 Total	其中 of which				
		第一产业 Primary Industry	第二产业 Secondary Industry	其中 of which		第三产业 Tertiary Industry
				工业 Industry	建筑业 Construction	
1978	264.20	3.00	108.10	106.69	1.41	153.10
1979	267.45	2.05	112.27	107.60	4.67	153.13
1980	288.41	1.99	117.84	112.92	4.92	168.58
1981	310.09	3.22	125.21	120.27	4.94	181.66
1982	316.31	2.98	126.04	120.73	5.31	187.29
1983	305.04	2.79	129.03	123.82	5.21	173.22
1984	332.15	2.08	151.59	144.79	6.80	178.48
1985	412.20	2.87	206.32	194.62	11.70	203.01
1986	512.61	3.84	272.77	251.55	21.22	236.00
1987	577.18	4.50	299.99	281.86	18.13	272.69
1988	688.13	5.94	364.38	341.53	22.85	317.81
1989	834.92	6.84	451.30	424.89	26.41	376.78
1990	908.98	7.70	522.20	490.51	31.69	379.08
1991	994.92	8.43	632.74	602.03	30.71	353.75
1992	1 096.19	8.59	704.17	673.86	30.31	383.43
1993	1 269.30	10.46	852.01	789.73	62.28	406.83
1994	1 417.12	14.85	911.57	879.26	32.31	490.70
1995	1 528.21	21.74	1 066.51	1 029.50	37.01	439.96
1996	1 726.41	25.48	1 196.31	1 153.02	43.29	504.62
1997	1 874.05	31.98	1 276.86	1 227.71	49.15	565.21
1998	1 876.73	32.81	1 231.86	1 189.80	42.06	612.06
1999	1 965.43	33.46	1 290.14	1 244.17	45.97	641.83
2000	2 093.40	34.20	1 392.88	1 343.70	49.18	666.32
2001	2 156.65	34.53	1 425.91	1 374.52	51.39	696.21
2002	2 201.73	35.22	1 440.11	1 386.15	53.96	726.40
2003	2 512.05	35.06	1 711.72	1 654.75	56.97	765.27
2004	3 719.86	35.81	2 278.35	2 218.54	59.81	1 405.70
2005	4 032.85	36.53	2 501.82	2 441.09	60.73	1 494.50
2006	4 361.72	37.26	2 713.94	2 652.00	61.94	1 610.52
2007	5 320.30	35.79	3 333.24	3 259.64	73.60	1 951.27
2008	6 296.79	36.97	3 562.86	3 484.92	77.94	2 696.96
2009	6 524.65	37.86	3 555.19	3 470.63	84.56	2 931.60
2010	7 723.30	38.61	4 184.36	4 083.38	100.98	3 500.33

表 3.22 每百元增加值占用的资产总额(1978~2010)
TOTAL ASSETS PER 100 YUAN WORTH OF VALUE ADDED

单位:元(yuan)

年 份 Year	合 计 Total	其 中 of which				
		第一产业 Primary Industry	第二产业 Secondary Industry	其 中 of which		第三产业 Tertiary Industry
				工 业 Industry	建筑业 Construction	
1978	196.80	99.59	141.67	140.09	233.24	447.09
1979	201.05	103.78	144.54	142.62	234.97	453.82
1980	197.59	130.74	141.80	139.17	257.93	408.38
1981	206.70	127.88	146.86	144.80	214.40	428.01
1982	211.91	96.92	154.84	152.43	222.58	423.61
1983	210.77	96.93	161.57	158.55	243.71	380.69
1984	202.04	78.86	164.51	163.11	194.74	328.91
1985	193.69	72.99	163.09	161.39	199.62	295.01
1986	226.32	81.39	201.29	199.83	228.40	309.71
1987	246.19	84.08	225.85	230.99	163.83	314.58
1988	239.86	74.84	219.07	225.44	143.17	311.81
1989	258.81	82.02	238.87	244.71	162.76	331.24
1990	263.14	83.79	256.64	262.37	181.34	302.11
1991	269.86	92.43	280.52	286.11	200.50	270.41
1992	258.42	98.56	271.91	277.89	178.37	249.30
1993	225.88	101.41	244.71	250.25	160.47	204.67
1994	218.74	109.48	247.07	254.93	132.93	184.35
1995	224.82	120.07	254.46	267.17	104.91	189.72
1996	233.94	128.31	268.43	284.16	109.59	196.96
1997	237.63	144.37	274.47	292.65	108.36	200.82
1998	250.70	154.79	292.56	315.47	102.87	212.28
1999	265.30	161.37	312.56	334.94	108.95	224.91
2000	269.69	171.58	315.60	337.03	110.25	231.97
2001	274.49	183.14	316.48	339.61	104.51	240.12
2002	268.81	189.03	309.93	329.52	127.65	235.42
2003	255.39	195.25	275.86	286.18	162.42	237.52
2004	252.50	210.19	267.06	275.36	167.36	239.52
2005	262.19	214.46	284.48	295.05	160.44	242.64
2006	256.84	213.42	286.87	298.24	155.10	230.48
2007	241.38	213.11	285.11	295.19	160.45	206.07
2008	243.69	214.66	285.93	299.97	132.05	211.45
2009	255.50	223.46	313.50	335.32	114.48	216.94
2010	246.24	229.15	277.74	294.80	114.23	223.31

表 3.23 每百元增加值占用的固定资产(1978~2010)
FIXED ASSETS PER 100 YUAN WORTH OF VALUE ADDED

单位:元(yuan)

年份 Year	合计 Total	其中 of which				
		第一产业 Primary Industry	第二产业 Secondary Industry	其中 of which		第三产业 Tertiary Industry
				工业 Industry	建筑业 Construction	
1978	102.95	72.41	90.97	89.05	202.51	159.39
1979	108.24	81.61	94.73	93.16	168.74	169.38
1980	108.48	110.74	93.07	91.42	166.25	163.51
1981	114.56	103.26	97.12	95.63	146.12	177.27
1982	118.99	73.63	104.45	102.38	162.78	175.79
1983	122.46	75.59	111.62	108.90	185.65	163.44
1984	120.53	64.75	113.56	112.08	145.44	149.87
1985	113.95	60.32	108.14	106.84	135.87	138.13
1986	132.11	64.35	130.00	129.87	132.31	147.26
1987	146.29	64.77	147.26	151.74	93.16	155.10
1988	142.27	55.76	142.36	147.42	82.04	154.67
1989	149.48	60.45	151.38	156.19	88.71	158.22
1990	151.59	62.56	160.37	164.96	100.13	145.83
1991	163.35	68.75	175.65	179.99	113.47	151.86
1992	164.59	73.65	173.23	177.69	103.43	157.79
1993	148.03	76.22	158.48	163.82	77.31	136.43
1994	151.27	82.90	170.29	177.26	69.06	127.89
1995	165.90	89.49	184.78	194.22	73.74	144.11
1996	178.92	93.95	197.57	209.05	81.69	160.41
1997	185.28	104.48	204.76	218.20	81.97	167.24
1998	201.36	110.92	225.55	243.10	80.26	180.55
1999	219.44	116.89	249.02	266.88	86.57	195.47
2000	227.16	127.46	254.83	272.30	87.45	205.67
2001	233.70	139.08	257.83	276.88	83.24	215.16
2002	230.85	145.26	255.29	271.23	106.95	212.01
2003	220.18	151.88	226.75	234.49	141.71	215.61
2004	213.90	167.73	215.80	221.46	147.82	213.03
2005	220.27	174.39	229.93	237.34	142.94	212.28
2006	217.14	174.09	234.40	242.58	139.56	202.30
2007	202.63	177.24	230.84	237.84	144.18	179.96
2008	202.41	182.12	229.27	239.50	117.17	181.93
2009	212.90	190.59	254.20	271.02	100.78	185.43
2010	204.74	195.65	224.13	237.01	100.63	190.61

表 3.24 每百元增加值占用的存货(1978～2010)
INVENTORY PER 100 YUAN WORTH OF VALUE ADDED

单位:元(yuan)

年 份 Year	合 计 Total	其 中 of which				
		第一产业 Primary Industry	第二产业 Secondary Industry	其 中 of which		第三产业 Tertiary Industry
				工 业 Industry	建筑业 Construction	
1978	93.85	27.18	50.70	51.04	30.73	287.71
1979	92.81	22.17	49.81	49.46	66.23	284.44
1980	89.11	20.00	48.73	47.76	91.68	244.87
1981	92.14	24.62	49.74	49.17	68.28	250.74
1982	92.92	23.29	50.39	50.05	59.80	247.82
1983	88.31	21.34	49.95	49.65	58.06	217.25
1984	81.51	14.11	50.95	51.03	49.30	179.04
1985	79.74	12.67	54.96	54.55	63.75	156.88
1986	94.21	17.04	71.29	69.96	96.09	162.45
1987	99.90	19.31	78.59	79.25	70.67	159.48
1988	97.59	19.08	76.71	78.02	61.13	157.14
1989	109.33	21.57	87.49	88.52	74.05	173.02
1990	111.55	21.23	96.27	97.42	81.21	156.29
1991	106.51	23.68	104.87	106.12	87.03	118.55
1992	93.83	24.91	98.68	100.20	74.94	91.51
1993	77.85	25.19	86.23	86.43	83.16	68.24
1994	67.47	26.58	76.78	77.67	63.84	56.46
1995	58.92	30.58	69.68	72.95	31.17	45.61
1996	55.02	34.36	70.86	75.11	27.90	36.55
1997	52.35	39.89	69.71	74.45	26.39	33.58
1998	49.34	43.87	67.01	72.37	22.61	31.73
1999	45.86	44.48	63.54	68.06	22.38	29.44
2000	42.53	44.12	60.77	64.73	22.80	26.30
2001	40.79	44.06	58.65	62.73	21.27	24.96
2002	37.96	43.77	54.64	58.29	20.70	23.41
2003	35.21	43.37	49.11	51.69	20.71	21.91
2004	38.60	42.46	51.26	53.90	19.54	26.49
2005	41.92	40.07	54.55	57.71	17.50	30.36
2006	39.70	39.33	52.47	55.66	15.54	28.18
2007	38.75	35.87	54.27	57.35	16.27	26.11
2008	41.28	32.54	56.66	60.47	14.88	29.52
2009	42.61	32.87	59.30	64.30	13.70	31.51
2010	41.50	33.50	53.61	57.79	13.60	32.70

表3.25 全员劳动生产率(1978~2010)
OVERALL LABOUR PRODUCTIVITY

单位:元/人

年 份 Year	合 计 Total	第一产业 Primary Industry	第二产业 Secondary Industry	第三产业 Tertiary Industry
1978	3 960	455	7 001	3 488
1979	4 060	490	6 931	3 500
1980	4 322	462	6 886	4 096
1981	4 386	508	6 697	4 177
1982	4 452	667	6 532	4 234
1983	4 590	729	6 431	4 510
1984	5 080	1 055	6 641	5 140
1985	6 041	1 408	7 493	6 098
1986	6 299	1 653	7 444	6 473
1987	6 944	2 019	7 913	7 314
1988	8 205	2 796	9 301	8 288
1989	8 833	3 258	10 011	8 655
1990	9 940	3 892	10 863	10 382
1991	11 272	4 011	11 737	12 940
1992	13 885	4 270	14 382	16 013
1993	19 060	4 957	19 485	22 473
1994	25 308	6 327	25 626	30 192
1995	31 634	7 791	32 503	36 878
1996	37 269	8 717	37 813	44 181
1997	43 497	8 895	44 461	51 279
1998	47 816	9 071	49 227	55 670
1999	52 130	9 191	52 397	61 961
2000	58 443	9 754	59 909	67 345
2001	64 298	8 843	70 375	71 696
2002	70 790	9 295	81 306	75 456
2003	79 488	10 257	94 726	80 210
2004	88 087	11 836	98 278	91 065
2005	94 967	14 069	102 494	99 058
2006	107 089	16 125	119 732	107 174
2007	123 120	18 679	132 409	126 429
2008	135 445	21 690	143 753	139 607
2009	142 104	23 250	141 687	152 331
2010	159 300	26 664	166 557	163 512

上/海/统/计/年/鉴

主要统计指标解释

■ 生产总值(原国内生产总值)

指按市场价格计算的一个地区所有常住单位在一定时期内生产活动的最终成果。生产总值有三种表现形态,即价值形态、收入形态和产品形态。从价值形态看,它是所有常住单位在一定时期内所生产的全部货物和服务价值超过同期投入的全部非固定资产货物和服务价值的差额,即所有常住单位的增加值之和;从收入形态看,它是所有常住单位在一定时期内所创造并分配给常住单位和非常住单位的初次收入之和;从产品形态看,它是所有常住单位在一定时期内最终使用的货物和服务减去货物和服务的进口价值。在实际核算中,生产总值有三种计算方法,即生产法、收入法和支出法。三种方法分别从不同的方面反映生产总值及其构成。根据国务院和国家统计局有关我国 GDP 核算和数据发布制度的规定,上海国内生产总值自 2004 年起更名为"上海市生产总值",简称"上海市 GDP"。

■ 三次产业

三次产业的划分是国际上常用的产业结构分类。第一产业是指产品直接取自自然界的部门,第二产业是指对初级产品进行再加工的部门,第三产业是指为生产和消费提供各种服务的部门。

第一产业包括农业、林业、畜牧业、渔业和农林牧渔服务业。

第二产业包括采矿业、制造业、电力、燃气及水的生产和供应业、建筑业。

第三产业是除第一、第二产业以外的其他行业。

■ 劳动者报酬

指劳动者因从事生产活动所获得的全部报酬。包括劳动者获得的各种形式的工资、奖金和津贴,既包括货币形式的,也包括实物形式的,还包括劳动者所享受的公费医疗和医药卫生费、上下班交通补贴、单位支付的社会保险费、住房公积金等。对于个体经济来说,其所有者所获得的劳动报酬和经营利润不易区分,这两部分统一作为劳动者报酬处理。

■ 生产税净额

指生产税减生产补贴后的余额。生产税指政府对生产单位从事生产、销售和经营活动以及因从事生产活动使用某些生产要素(如固定资产、土地、劳动力)所征收的各种税、附加费和规费。生产补贴与生产税相反,指政府对生产单位的单方面转移支出,因此视为负生产税,包括政策亏损补贴、价格补贴等。

■ 固定资产折旧

指一定时期内为弥补固定资产损耗按照规定的固定资产折旧率提取的固定资产折旧,或按国民经济核算统一规定的折旧率虚拟计算的固定资产折旧。它反映了固定资产在当期生产中的转移价值。各类企业和企业化管理的事业单位的固定资产折旧是指实际计提的折旧费;不计提折旧的政府机关、非企业化管理的事业单位和居民住房的固定资产折旧是按照统一规定的折旧率和固定资产原值计算的虚拟折旧。原则上,固定资产折旧应按固定资产当期的重置价值计算,但是目前我国尚不具备对全社会固定资产进行重估价的基础,所以暂时只能采用上述办法。

■ 营业盈余

指常住单位创造的增加值扣除劳动者报酬、生产税净额和固定资产折旧后的余额。它相当于企业的营业利润加上生产补贴,但要扣除从利润中开支的工资和福利等。

■ 支出法生产总值

是从最终使用的角度反映一个国家(或地区)一定时期内生产活动最终成果的一种方法,包括最终消费支出、资本形成总额及货物和服务净出口三部分。计算公式为:

支出法生产总值 = 最终消费支出 + 资本形成总额 + 货物和服务净出口

■ 最终消费支出

指常住单位在一定时期内对于货物和服务的全部最终消费支出,也就是常住单位为满足物质、文化和精神生活的需要,从本国经济领土和国外购买的货物和服务的支出;不包括非常住单位在本国经济领土内的消费支出。最终消费分为居民消费和政府消费。

主要统计指标解释

■ 居民消费支出

指常住住户在一定时期内对货物和服务的全部最终消费支出。居民消费按市场价格计算，即按居民支付的购买者价格计算。购买者价格是购买者取得货物所支付的价格，包括购买者支付的运输和商业费用。居民消费除了直接以货币形式购买货物和服务的消费之外，还包括以其他方式获得的货物和服务的消费支出，即所谓的虚拟消费支出。居民虚拟消费支出包括以下几种类型：单位以实物报酬及实物转移的形式提供给劳动者的货物和服务；住户生产并由本住户消费了的货物和服务，其中的服务仅指住户的自有住房服务；金融机构提供的金融媒介服务；保险公司提供的保险服务。

■ 政府消费支出

指常住住户在一定时期内对货物和服务的全部最终消费支出。居民消费按市场价格计算，即按居民支付的购买者价格计算。购买者价格是购买者取得货物所支付的价格，包括购买者支付的运输和商业费用。居民消费除了直接以货币形式购买货物和服务的消费之外，还包括以其他方式获得的货物和服务的消费支出，即所谓的虚拟消费支出。居民虚拟消费支出包括以下几种类型：单位以实物报酬及实物转移的形式提供给劳动者的货物和服务；住户生产并由本住户消费了的货物和服务，其中的服务仅指住户的自有住房服务；金融机构提供的金融媒介服务；保险公司提供的保险服务。

■ 资本形成总额

指常住单位在一定时期内获得的，并减去处置的固定资产，加上存货的变动，包括固定资本形成总额和存货增加。

■ 固定资本形成总额

指生产者在一定时期内获得的固定资产减处置的固定资产的价值总额。固定资产是通过生产活动生产出来的，且其使用年限在一年以上、单位价值在规定标准以上的资产，不包括自然资产。可分为有形固定资本形成总额和无形固定资本形成总额。有形固定资本形成总额包括一定时期内完成的建筑工程、安装工程和设备工器具购置(减处置)价值，以及土地改良、新增役、种、奶、毛、娱乐用牲畜和新增经济林木价值。无形固定资本形成总额包括矿藏的勘探、计算机软件等获得减处置。

■ 存货增加

指常住单位在一定时期内存货实物量变动的市场价值，即期末价值减期初价值的差额，再扣除当期由于价格变动而产生的持有收益。存货增加可以是正值，也可以是负值，正值表示存货上升，负值表示存货下降。存货包括生产单位购进的原材料、燃料和储备物资等存货，以及生产单位生产的产成品、在制品和半成品等存货。

■ 货物和服务净流出

指货物和服务流出减货物和服务流入的差额。流出包括常住单位向非常住单位出售或无偿转让的各种货物和服务的价值；流入包括常住单位从非常住单位购买或无偿得到的各种货物和服务的价值。地区核算净流出，除包括本地区对外贸易及国外非贸易往来的净出口额，还包括地区间货物和服务流出减流入后的净额。

■ 信息产业

是指与电子信息相关联的各种活动的集合，包括信息产品的制造、销售和信息服务等活动。由于信息产业增加值是依据若干行业的有关资料进行跨行业核算的，因此不宜将其与上海市生产总值中其他行业的增加值进行加总，否则会造成重复计算。

■ 旅游产业

指本市与旅游相关的各行业，为境内外旅游者提供旅游服务的产业。这些服务包括：旅行社服务、交通运输服务、住宿服务、电讯服务、娱乐服务、餐饮服务、商品零售服务等。由于旅游产业增加值是依据相关行业的有关资料进行跨行业核算的，因此不宜将其与上海市生产总值中其他行业的增加值进行加总，否则会造成重复计算。

SHANGHAI STATISTICAL YEARBOOK

EXPLANATORY NOTES TO MAJOR STATISTICAL INDICATORS

□ Gross Regional Product(former Gross Domestic Product)

Gross Regional Product refers to the final products at market prices by (of) all resident units of a region during a certain period of time. Gross product is expressed in three different forms, i.e value, income, and products respectively. The form of value added refers to the total value of all products and services produced by all resident units during a certain period of time minus the total value of inputs of non-fixed-assets products and services or the summation of the value added of all resident units; the form of income includes all the income items produced by all resident units and distributed primarily to all resident and non-resident units; the form of product refers to all final goods and services minus the value of imports of goods and services. In the practice of national accounting, it is calculated by three approaches, i.e. product approach, income approach, and expenditure approach, respectively, to reflect Gross Product and its composition of different aspects. According to the regulations of GDP national accounting and data release issued by the State Council and National Bureau of Statistics, since 2004 Shanghai Gross Domestic Product has been renamed as Shanghai Gross Product Value, for short Shanghai GDP.

□ Three Industries

Classification of economic activities into three strata of industry is a common practice in the world. Primary industry refers to extraction of natural resources; secondary industry involves processing of primary products; and tertiary industry provides services of various kinds for production and consumption.

Primary industry includes farming, forestry, animal husbandry, fishery industry and service industry for farming, forestry, animal husbandry and fishery.

Secondary industry includes mining, manufacturing, power, steam and water production and supply and construction.

Tertiary industry refers to all other industries not included in primary or secondary industries.

□ Labourers Remuneration

Labourers Remuneration refers to the whole payment of various forms earned by the labourers from the productive activities they are engaged in. It includes wages, bonuses and allowances the labourers earned in monetary form and in kind. It also includes the free medical services provided to the labourers and the medicine expenses, traffic subsidies and social insurance, housing fund paid by the employers. As the individual economy is concerned, since the labourers remuneration is not easily distinguished from the operating profit, both are treated as labourers remuneration.

□ Net Taxes on Production

Net Taxes on Production refers to the difference of the taxes on production minus the subsidies on production. The taxes on production refers to the various taxes, extra charges and fees levied on the production units on their production, sale and business activities as well as on the use of some factors of production, such as fixed assets, land and labour force in the production activities they are engaged in. In contrast to the taxes on production, the subsidies on production refer to the unilateral government transfer to the production units and are therefore regarded as negative taxes on production. They include subsidies on the loss due to implementation of government policies, price subsidies, etc.

□ Depreciation of Fixed Assets

Depreciation of Fixed Assets refers to the depreciation of fixed assets of a given period, drawn in accordance with the stipulated depreciation rate for the purpose of compensating the wear loss of the fixed assets or the depreciation of fixed assets calculated in a fictitious way in accordance with the stipulated unified depreciation rate in the national economic accounting system. It reflects the value of transfer of the fixed assets in the production of the current period. The depreciation of fixed assets in various enterprises and institutions managed as enterprises refers to the depreciation expenses actually drawn. In government agencies and institutions not managed as enterprises which do not draw the depreciation expenses, as well as for the houses of residents, the depreciation of fixed assets is the imputed depreciation, which is calculated in accordance with the stipulated unified depreciation rate. In principle, the depreciation of fixed assets should be calculated on the basis of the re-purchased value of the fixed assets. However, there is no actual condition to re-evaluate all the fixed assets in China. Therefore, the above-mentioned methods are

EXPLANATORY NOTES TO MAJOR STATISTICAL INDICATORS

temporarily adopted at present.

□ Operating Surplus

Operating Surplus refers to the balance of the value added created by the resident units deducting the labourers remuneration, net taxes on production and the depreciation of fixed assets. It is equivalent to the business profit of the enterprises plus subsidies on production, but the wages and welfare expenses paid from the profits should be deducted.

□ GDP by Expenditure Approach

GDP by Expenditure Approach refers to the method of measuring the final results of production activities of a country (region) during a given period from the perspective of final use. It includes final consumption, total capital formation and net export of goods and services, i.e.:

GDP by expenditure approach = final consumption + total capital formation + net export of goods and services

□ Final Consumption

Final Consumption refers to the total expenditure of resident units on final consumption of goods and services in a certain period, namely the expenditure of the resident units for purchases of goods and services from domestic economic territory and abroad to meet the requirements of material, cultural and spiritual life. It excludes the expenditure of non-resident units on consumption in the economic territory of the country. The final consumption is classified into household consumption and government consumption.

□ Household Consumption

Household Consumption refers to the total expenditure of resident households on the final consumption of goods and services in a certain period of time. The households consumption is calculated at market prices, namely the purchasers prices which the households pay; the purchasers prices of goods are the prices the households pay when they obtain the goods, including the transport and commercial expenses paid by the households. In addition to the consumption of goods and services bought by the households directly with money, the expenditure on goods and services obtained by the households in other ways, i.e. the so-called imputed expenditure on consumption, is also included in the households consumption. The imputation expenditure of the households on consumption includes the following types: (a) the goods and services provided to the households by the units in the form of payment in kind and transfer in kind; (b) the goods and services produced and consumed by the households themselves, in which the services refer only to the services provided by the residential buildings owned by the households; (c) the services of financial intermediary provided by the financial institutions; (d) the insurance services provided by the insurance companies.

□ Government Consumption

Government Consumption refers to the expenditure on the consumption of the public services provided by the government to the whole society and the net expenditure on the goods and services provided by the government to the households at free charge or lower prices in a certain period of time. The former equals to the output value of the government services minus the value of operating income obtained by the government departments. (The output value of the government services equals to its current operating expenditure plus depreciation of fixed assets). The latter equals to the market value of the goods and services provided by the government free of charge or at low prices to the households minus the value received by the government from the households.

□ Total Capital Formation

Total Capital Formation refers to the fixed assets acquired minus those disposed and the change in inventory, including the total fixed capital assets formation and the increase in inventory.

□ Total Fixed Capital Formation

Total Fixed Capital Formation refers to the value of fixed assets acquired minus those disposed of during a given period. Fixed assets are the assets produced through production activities with specified unit value which could be used for over one year, excluding natural assets. Total fixed capital formation can be categorized into total tangible capital formation and total intangible capital formation. The total tangible capital formation include the value of the construction projects, installation projects completed and the equipment, apparatus and instruments purchased as well as the value of land improved, the value of draught animals, breeding stock, animals for milk, wool and for recreational purpose, and the newly increased forest with economic value during a given period. The total intangible capital formation includes the prospecting of minerals, the acquisition of computer software minus the disposal of them.

EXPLANATORY NOTES TO MAJOR STATISTICAL INDICATORS

□ Increase in Inventory

Increase in Inventory refers to the market value of the change in inventory of resident units during a given period, i.e. the difference of value between the beginning and the end of the period minus the current gains due to the change in prices. The increase in inventory can be positive or negative. A positive value indicates the increase in inventory while a negative value indicates the decrease in stock. The inventory includes the raw materials, fuels and reserve materials purchased by the production units as well as the inventory of finished products, semi-finished products, work-in-progress, etc.

□ Net Outflow of Goods and Services

Net Outflow of Goods and Service refers to difference of outflow of goods and service minus inflow of goods and service. The outflow includes the value of various goods and service sold or gratuitously transferred by resident unit to non-resident unit, and the inflow includes the value of various goods and service sold or gratuitously transferred by non-resident unit to resident unit. The net outflow of district, include the net outflow of foreign trade or non-trade of local district, and also the difference of outflow minus inflow of goods and service between domestic districts.

□ Information Industry

Information Industry refers to the aggregation of all kinds of activities related to electronic information, including manufactory and distribution of information-related products and information service. As accounted by referring to relevant documents of several industries, the value added of the information industry shall not be counted together with that of other industries in the Shanghai GDP to avoid repetitive computation.

□ Tourism Industry

Tourism Industry refers to those tourism-related industries that provide tourism services to domestic and overseas tourists, including: travel agency service, transportation service, hostelling service, telecommunication service, entertainment service, catering service and retailing service, etc.. As accounted by referring to relevant cross-industry data of several industries, the value added of the tourism industry shall not be counted together with that of other industries in the Shanghai GDP to avoid repetitive computation.

第四篇

CHAPTER 4

财政收支

FISCAL REVENUE AND EXPENDITURE

表4.1 财政收支(1978~2010)
FISCAL REVENUES AND EXPENDITURES

单位:亿元 (100 million yuan)

年份 Year	地方财政收入 Local Fiscal Revenue	其中 of which		地方财政支出 Local Fiscal Expenditure
		#税收收入 Taxes	非税收入 Non-taxes	
1978	169.22	51.51	117.71	26.01
1979	172.69	53.73	118.96	27.06
1980	174.73	57.59	117.14	19.18
1981	174.35	62.93	111.42	19.06
1982	167.99	65.79	102.20	20.68
1983	156.39	110.05	46.34	22.39
1984	163.96	137.67	26.29	30.32
1985	184.23	185.76	-1.53	46.07
1986	179.46	177.90	1.56	59.08
1987	168.97	167.26	1.71	53.85
1988	161.62	182.42	-20.80	65.88
1989	166.88	190.21	-23.33	73.31
1990	166.99	183.31	-16.32	75.56
1991	175.53	182.88	-7.35	86.05
1992	185.56	188.61	-3.05	94.99
1993	242.34	252.99	-10.65	129.26
1994	175.33	196.60	-21.27	196.98
1995	227.30	240.06	-12.76	267.89
1996	288.49	308.26	-19.77	342.66
1997	352.33	369.23	-16.90	428.92
1998	392.22	406.73	-14.51	480.70
1999	431.85	427.23	4.62	546.38
2000	497.96	484.00	13.96	622.84
2001	620.24	589.91	30.33	726.38
2002	719.79	657.70	62.09	877.84
2003	899.29	796.87	102.42	1 102.64
2004	1 119.72	1 036.23	83.49	1 395.69
2005	1 433.90	1 238.40	195.50	1 660.32
2006	1 600.37	1 393.97	206.40	1 813.80
2007	2 102.63	1 975.48	127.15	2 201.92
2008	2 382.34	2 223.43	158.91	2 617.68
2009	2 540.30	2 368.45	171.85	2 989.65
2010	2 873.58	2 707.80	165.78	3 302.89

注：本表数据由上海市财政局提供。
Note: Data in the table are provided by Shanghai Municipal Financical Bureau.

表4.2 主要年份地方财政收入
LOCAL FISCAL REVENUE IN MAIN YEARS

	指 标 Indicators	2000	2009	2010
地方财政收入(亿元)	**Local Fiscal Revenue (100 million yuan)**	**497.96**	**2 540.30**	**2 873.58**
#增值税	Value-added Tax	93.55	372.47	388.62
营业税	Business Tax	153.81	839.68	933.91
企业所得税	Enterprise Income Tax	103.03	481.69	606.05
个人所得税	Personal Income Tax	60.24	230.44	261.20
契　税	Deed	14.37	162.01	173.58
#市级财政收入	Fiscal Revenue at Municipal Level	215.81	1 257.06	1 393.23
区县级财政收入	Fiscal Revenue at District (County) Level	282.15	1 283.24	1 480.35
地方财政收入构成(%)	**Compostion of Local Fiscal Revenue (%)**	**100**	**100**	**100**
#增值税	Value-added Tax	18.8	14.7	13.5
营业税	Business Tax	30.9	33.1	32.5
企业所得税	Enterprise Income Tax	20.7	19.0	21.1
个人所得税	Personal Income Tax	12.1	9.1	9.1
契　税	Deed	2.9	6.4	6.0
#市级财政收入	Fiscal Revenue at Municipal Level	43.3	49.5	48.5
区县级财政收入	Fiscal Revenue at District (County) Level	56.7	50.5	51.5

注：本表数据由上海市财政局提供。
Note: Data in the table are provided by Shanghai Municipal Financical Bureau.

表 4.3 主要年份区县级财政收支
FISICAL REVENUE AND EXPENDITURES OF DISTRICTS AND COUNTIES IN MAIN YEARS

单位:亿元 (100 million yuan)

地 区	District	区县级财政收入 Local Fiscal Revenue of Districts and Counties			区县级财政支出 Local Fiscal Expenditure of Districts and Counties		
		2000	2009	2010	2000	2009	2010
总 计	**Total**	**282.15**	**1 283.24**	**1 480.35**	**331.15**	**1 792.37**	**2 024.13**
浦东新区	Pudong New Area	64.53	379.99	425.40	79.45	475.58	524.06
黄 浦 区	Huangpu	21.91	55.85	64.36	22.80	73.13	80.73
卢 湾 区	Luwan	11.37	46.62	51.30	11.32	55.03	56.69
徐 汇 区	Xuhui	15.40	78.56	90.43	19.10	89.51	99.29
长 宁 区	Changning	13.74	62.95	72.08	14.80	74.31	85.50
静 安 区	Jing'an	11.00	56.33	65.96	11.27	66.78	71.43
普 陀 区	Putuo	12.70	44.26	51.97	14.56	71.55	78.57
闸 北 区	Zhabei	11.89	36.26	46.30	13.95	56.86	68.55
虹 口 区	Hongkou	14.20	42.05	48.36	16.35	63.95	74.52
杨 浦 区	Yangpu	11.52	44.05	50.07	14.70	71.49	82.65
宝 山 区	Baoshan	16.17	62.70	70.35	17.60	96.44	114.43
闵 行 区	Minhang	18.98	110.35	125.30	20.65	138.49	156.60
嘉 定 区	Jiading	13.33	67.98	82.96	16.12	94.99	112.84
金 山 区	Jinshan	8.16	23.95	30.75	13.61	60.00	70.98
松 江 区	Songjiang	12.12	67.30	77.33	13.34	91.01	103.55
青 浦 区	Qingpu	13.24	48.68	58.95	15.36	78.38	88.40
奉 贤 区	Fengxian	6.53	31.96	40.43	8.04	65.03	77.12
崇 明 县	Chongming	5.36	23.41	28.04	8.13	69.84	78.21

①本表数据由上海市财政局提供。
②2000 年浦东新区的数据为原浦东新区和原南汇区的合计数。
❶Data in the table are provided by Shanghai Municipal Financical Bureau.
❷The data of Pudong New Area in 2000 include former Pudong New Area district and former Nanhui district.

表 4.4 地方财政支出(2008～2010) LOCAL FISCAL EXPENDITURES

	指 标 Indicators	2008	2009	2010
地方财政支出（亿元）	**Local Fiscal Expenditure(100 million yuan)**	**2 617.68**	**2 989.65**	**3 302.89**
#一般公共服务	General Public Services	198.71	206.68	226.02
公共安全	Public Security	149.57	163.41	187.25
教 育	Education	326.06	346.95	417.28
社会保障和就业	Social Security and Jobs	334.97	336.08	362.56
医疗卫生	Medical and Health Care	122.28	132.85	160.07
城乡社区事务	Urban and Country Community Affairs	492.46	602.36	475.47
#市级财政支出	Fiscal Expenditure at Municipal Level	984.15	1 197.28	1 278.76
区县级财政支出	Fiscal Expenditure at District (County) Level	1 633.53	1 792.37	20 24.13
地方财政支出比重（%）	**Percentage of the Local Fiscal Expenditure(%)**	**100**	**100**	**100**
#一般公共服务	General Public Services	7.6	6.9	6.8
公共安全	Public Security	5.7	5.5	5.7
教 育	Education	12.5	11.6	12.6
社会保障和就业	Social Security and Jobs	12.8	11.2	11.0
医疗卫生	Medical and Health Care	4.7	4.4	4.8
城乡社区事务	Urban and Country Community Affairs	18.8	20.1	14.4
#市级财政支出	Fiscal Expenditure at Municipal Level	37.6	40.0	38.7
区县级财政支出	Fiscal Expenditure at District (County) Level	62.4	60.0	61.3

注：本表数据由上海市财政局提供。
Note: Data in the table are provided by Shanghai Municipal Financial Bureau.

表 4.5 主要年份全市税收收入 TAXATION (TAX SCOPE) IN MAIN YEARS

单位:亿元(100 million yuan)

	指 标 Indicators	2000	2009	2010
全市税收收入	**Taxation**	**1 479.21**	**6 675.17**	**8 003.43**
#证券交易印花税	Stamp Tax of Stock Transaction	245.49	332.69	305.26
海关代征	Custom Taxation	313.04	1 555.10	2 082.92
国内增值税	Domestic Value Added Tax	380.21	1 507.49	1 575.00
国内消费税	Domestic Excise	69.71	343.11	499.58
营业税	Business Tax	171.42	839.72	933.93
企业所得税	Enterprise Income Tax	186.36	1 231.11	1 567.31
个人所得税	Personal Income Tax	67.79	561.72	653.01

注：本表数据由上海市国家税务局、上海市地方税务局提供。
Note: Data in this table are provided by Shanghai Minicipal Office ,SAT and Shanghai Local Taxation Bureau.

上/海/统/计/年/鉴

主要统计指标解释

■ 地方财政收入

地方财政收入是指根据现行财政管理体制规定，划归地方财政的税收收入和非税收入。

■ 税收收入

地方财政收入中的税收收入主要包括营业税、房产税、城镇土地使用税、车船税、土地增值税、耕地占用税、契税等固定收入，以及增值税、企业所得税、个人所得税等共享收入部分。

■ 地方财政支出

地方财政支出是指按照现行中央政府与地方政府事权的划分，经地方人大批准，用于保障地方经济社会发展的各项财政支出。主要包括一般公共服务，公共安全，教育，科学技术，文化体育与传媒，社会保障和就业，医疗卫生，环境保护，城乡社区事务，农林水事务，交通运输等支出。

SHANGHAI STATISTICAL YEARBOOK

EXPLANATORY NOTES TO MAJOR STATISTICAL INDICATORS

□ Local Fiscal Revenue

Local Fiscal Revenue refers to the tax revenue and non-tax revenue collected by the local government as defined by the finance management system.

□ Tax Revenue

Tax Revenue of local fiscal revenue mainly includes business tax, house property tax, urban land use tax, tax on vehicles and boat operation, land appreciation tax, farm land occupation tax, deed tax, etc and the share part of value added tax, corporate income tax, individual income tax, etc.

□ Local Fiscal Expenditure

Local Fiscal Expenditure refers to the fiscal expenditure demarcated on the basis of the classification of the affairs administration rights between the central government and local government. It is approved by the local people's congress and used for the development of local economy and society. Local fiscal expenditure mainly includes the expenditure for general public services, public security, education, science and technology, culture, sport and media, social safety and employment, medical and health care, environment protection, urban and rural community affairs, agriculture, forestry and water conservancy and transportation, etc.

第五篇

CHAPTER 5

能源生产和消费

ENERGY PRODUCTION AND CONSUMPTION

表5.1 主要年份能源消耗基本情况
ENERGY CONSUMPTION IN MAIN YEARS

单位:亿元(100 million yuan)

年份 Year	能源消费量 (万吨标准煤) Energy Consumption (10 000 tons SCE)	其中 of which #工业 Industry	电力消耗 (亿千瓦时) Electricity Power Consumption (100 million kwh)	其中 of which #工业 Industry
1985	2 553.21	2 015.10	203.77	179.91
1990	3 191.06	2 462.21	264.74	220.97
1995	4 465.87	3 512.49	403.27	307.01
1996	4 626.21	3 484.47	430.40	318.18
1997	4 758.82	3 498.83	454.26	333.79
1998	4 874.11	3 452.96	482.94	343.60
1999	5 119.19	3 608.67	501.20	358.31
2000	5 499.48	3 778.76	559.42	393.13
2001	5 894.78	3 931.58	592.99	413.33
2002	6 249.34	3 988.13	645.71	447.46
2003	6 796.34	4 304.81	745.97	507.00
2004	7 405.64	4 518.82	821.44	555.12
2005	8 225.05	5 105.04	921.97	617.59
2006	8 875.70	5 371.06	990.15	656.10
2007	9 670.45	5 722.05	1 072.38	705.90
2008	10 207.36	5 886.83	1 138.22	727.13
2009	10 367.38	5 763.27	1 153.38	701.59
2010	11 160.87	6 265.87	1 295.87	786.61

表5.1 续表1 continued

年份 Year	单位生产总值能耗 (吨标准煤/万元) Energy Consumption of GDP (ton SCE/10 000 yuan)	单位生产总值电耗 (千瓦时/万元) Electricity Power Consumption of GDP (kwh/10 000 yuan)	单位工业增加值能耗 (吨标准煤/万元) Energy Consumption of Value Added in Industry (ton SCE/10 000 yuan)	单位工业增加值电耗 (千瓦时/万元) Electricity Power Consumption of Value Added in Industry (kwh/10 000 yuan)
1985	5.470	4 365.72	6.477	5 782.66
1990	4.082	3 386.89	5.241	4 703.19
1995	1.787	1 613.45	2.685	2 346.81
1996	1.564	1 455.26	2.398	2 190.13
1997	1.384	1 320.99	2.188	2 087.61
1998	1.282	1 270.53	2.067	2 057.25
1999	1.222	1 196.54	2.018	2 003.99
2000	1.153	1 172.50	1.890	1 966.67
2001	1.131	1 138.15	1.815	1 907.61
2002	1.089	1 124.73	1.684	1 889.60
2003	1.015	1 114.35	1.464	1 723.76
2004	0.917	1 017.55	1.258	1 544.90
2005	0.889	996.98	1.261	1 529.88
2006	0.851	949.69	1.187	1 453.81
2007	0.805	892.62	1.127	1 394.24
2008	0.775	863.64	1.080	1 334.46
2009	0.727	808.50	1.028	1 251.81
2010	0.712	826.20	0.953	1 194.05

注:2005 年起单位生产总值能耗、工业增加值能耗和增加值电耗按 2005 年可比价计算。
Note: Since 2005, Energy intensity and Electricity intensity by GDP or value added is calculated by comparable prices of 2005.

表5.2 能源消费弹性系数(1978～2010)
ELASTICITY OF ENERGY CONSUMPTION

年 份 Year	能源消费 比上年增长 (%) Growth Rate of Energy Consumption over Preceding Year(%)	电力消费 比上年增长 (%) Growth Rate of Electric Power Consumption over Preceding Year(%)	生产总值 比上年增长 (%) Growth Rate of GDP Over Preceding Year(%)	能源消费 弹性系数 Elasticity of Energy Consumption	电力消费 弹性系数 Elasticity of Electric Power Consumption
1978	6.6	10.8	15.8	0.42	0.68
1979	1.5	3.0	7.4	0.20	0.41
1980	-0.6	3.4	8.4		0.40
1981	1.0	6.4	5.6	0.18	1.14
1982	2.6	4.4	7.2	0.36	0.61
1983	2.5	4.2	7.8	0.32	0.54
1984	2.5	4.1	11.6	0.22	0.35
1985	4.9	3.9	13.4	0.37	0.74
1986	9.0	6.8	4.4	2.05	1.34
1987	5.7	4.1	7.5	0.77	0.81
1988	1.3	2.5	10.1	0.13	0.51
1989	4.4	1.3	3.0	1.46	0.83
1990	2.6	5.8	3.5	0.73	2.09
1991	8.6	9.0	7.1	1.22	1.28
1992	5.5	10.0	14.8	0.37	0.67
1993	7.9	9.0	15.1	0.52	0.59
1994	5.8	9.1	14.5	0.40	0.63
1995	6.9	6.9	14.3	0.48	0.48
1996	3.6	6.7	13.1	0.27	0.51
1997	2.9	5.5	12.8	0.22	0.43
1998	2.4	6.3	10.3	0.24	0.61
1999	5.0	3.8	10.4	0.48	0.36
2000	7.4	11.6	11.0	0.68	1.06
2001	7.2	6.0	10.5	0.68	0.57
2002	6.0	8.9	11.3	0.53	0.79
2003	8.8	15.5	12.3	0.71	1.26
2004	9.0	10.1	14.2	0.63	0.71
2005	11.1	12.2	11.4	0.97	1.07
2006	7.9	7.4	12.7	0.62	0.58
2007	9.0	8.3	15.2	0.59	0.55
2008	5.6	6.1	9.7	0.57	0.63
2009	1.6	1.3	8.2	0.19	0.16
2010	7.7	12.4	9.9	0.77	1.24

表5.3 主要年份能源消费总量
FINAL CONSUMPTION OF ENERGY IN MAIN YEARS

单位:万吨标准煤(10 000 tons SCE)

年份 Year	能源消费总量 Energy Consumption	能源终端消费量 Final Consumption of Energy	加工转换投入(－)产出(＋)量 Processing Conversion Input (－) and Output (＋)	损失量 Loss Volume
1985	2 553.21	2 416.44	－70.29	66.48
1990	3 191.06	3 098.82	－52.20	40.04
1995	4 465.87	4 250.45	－74.67	140.75
1996	4 626.21	4 376.37	－98.48	151.36
1997	4 758.82	4 505.70	－117.53	135.59
1998	4 874.11	4 608.13	－108.22	157.76
1999	5 119.19	4 899.60	－83.98	135.60
2000	5 499.48	5 226.79	－89.20	183.49
2001	5 894.78	5 549.69	－133.94	211.16
2002	6 249.34	5 898.56	－132.17	218.62
2003	6 796.34	6 394.49	－158.30	243.55
2004	7 405.64	7 055.08	－131.85	218.71
2005	8 225.05	7 895.17	－140.59	189.29
2006	8 875.70	8 514.40	－167.58	193.73
2007	9 670.45	9 314.77	－147.01	208.67
2008	10 207.36	9 750.47	－227.60	229.28
2009	10 367.38	9 951.81	－181.67	233.90
2010	11 160.87	10 802.03	－108.68	250.17

表5.4 主要年份平均每人生活用能源
ANNUAL RESIDENT ENERGY CONSUMPTION PER CAPITA IN MAIN YEARS

	品名 Items	2000	2005	2009	2010
生活消费能源总计（千克标准煤）	**Total Resident Energy Consumption (kg of SCE)**	**290.49**	**345.95**	**436.50**	**446.28**
煤炭（千克）	Coal (kg)	87.85	36.14	22.88	20.67
天然气（立方米）	Natural Gas (cu. m)	4.53	15.52	29.60	34.52
液化石油气（千克）	Liquefied Petroleum Gas (kg)	13.31	11.98	15.62	14.65
煤气（立方米）	Gas (cu. m)	97.49	60.29	34.29	27.88
电力（千瓦时）	Electric Power (kwh)	335.05	586.27	701.09	748.74

注：本表按年平均人口数计算。
Note: This table is calculated by annual average population.

表5.5 平均每天各种能源消费量(2007～2010)
AVERAGE DAILY ENERGY CONSUMPTION BY VARIETY

	能源品种 Items	2007	2008	2009	2010
能源消费量合计(万吨标准煤)	**Total(10 000 tons of SCE)**	**26.49**	**27.97**	**28.40**	**30.58**
煤炭(万吨)	Coal(10 000 tons)	11.00	11.70	11.47	13.05
焦炭(万吨)	Coke(10 000 tons)	2.00	1.96	1.86	1.96
燃料油(万吨)	Fuel Oil(10 000 tons)	2.32	2.16	2.04	2.04
汽油(万吨)	Gasoline(10 000 tons)	0.83	0.93	1.06	1.13
煤油(万吨)	Kerosene(10 000 tons)	0.81	0.88	0.97	1.09
柴油(万吨)	Diesel Oil(10 000 tons)	1.04	1.17	1.32	1.37
天然气(亿立方米)	Natural Gas(100 million cu. m)	0.08	0.08	0.09	0.12
电力(亿千瓦时)	Electricity(100 million kwh)	2.94	3.12	3.16	3.55

表5.6　主要年份能源终端消费量
FINAL CONSUMPTION OF ENERGY IN MAIN YEARS

单位:万吨标准煤(10 000 tons SCE)

年 份 Year	能源终端消费量 Final Consumption of Energy	其 中 of which 第一产业 Primary Industry	第二产业 Secondary Industry	第三产业 Tertiary Industry	生活消费 Living Consumption
1980	2 130.56	71.04	1 655.92	194.64	208.96
1990	3 098.82	58.49	2 387.88	403.47	248.98
1995	4 250.45	77.12	3 339.73	517.05	316.53
1996	4 376.37	102.18	3 291.05	626.39	356.78
1997	4 505.70	90.53	3 312.18	715.31	387.72
1998	4 608.13	91.06	3 261.21	828.84	427.02
1999	4 899.60	98.01	3 467.49	915.48	418.62
2000	5 226.79	103.37	3 592.86	1 069.32	461.24
2001	5 549.69	113.84	3 698.28	1 282.08	455.49
2002	5 898.56	109.13	3 802.12	1 508.46	478.85
2003	6 394.49	111.83	4 063.76	1 690.50	528.40
2004	7 055.08	108.35	4 339.27	2 016.48	590.98
2005	7 895.17	61.44	4 940.24	2 249.12	644.37
2006	8 514.40	59.16	5 183.29	2 555.08	716.87
2007	9 314.77	60.70	5 547.36	2 902.64	804.07
2008	9 750.47	62.81	5 636.03	3 153.79	897.85
2009	9 951.81	62.71	5 587.85	3 351.64	949.60
2010	10 802.03	63.49	6 154.82	3 576.70	1 007.02

表5.7　主要年份工业能源终端消费量
FINAL CONSUMPTION OF ENERGY INDUSTRY IN MAIN YEARS

年 份 Year	工业能源终端消费量(万吨标准煤) Final Consumption Energy of Industry (10 000 tons SCE)	原煤(万吨) Coal (10 000 tons)	焦炭(万吨) Coke (10 000 tons)	燃料油(万吨) Fuel Oil (10 000 tons)	电 力(亿千瓦时) Electric power (100 million kwh)
1978	1 630.24	490.54	206.45	158.01	128.51
1980	1 645.20	535.03	211.52	122.41	136.85
1990	2 369.99	596.14	419.24	136.09	209.21
1991	2 591.11	641.71	516.28	140.06	226.69
1992	2 731.13	630.83	651.49	112.47	247.75
1993	2 988.03	700.97	617.24	170.97	262.75
1994	3 053.73	661.10	625.62	165.55	270.54
1995	3 297.07	694.31	687.98	154.76	282.87
1996	3 234.63	726.24	637.73	149.69	293.04
1997	3 245.71	698.14	653.75	147.70	309.74
1998	3 186.98	723.59	660.40	132.93	318.12
1999	3 389.09	792.14	658.28	120.21	335.01
2000	3 506.06	733.65	676.06	139.67	362.94
2001	3 586.48	790.51	654.79	136.93	381.64
2002	3 637.35	676.60	571.92	112.19	413.61
2003	3 902.97	675.58	573.94	117.11	464.74
2004	4 168.27	731.30	552.68	118.77	510.63
2005	4 775.16	843.73	603.16	130.94	568.29
2006	5 009.75	869.58	617.92	118.85	604.59
2007	5 366.37	790.10	691.38	91.99	649.82
2008	5 449.51	787.01	684.92	74.98	667.59
2009	5 376.05	825.59	658.32	71.92	641.58
2010	5 936.45	823.18	705.21	63.12	718.63

表5.8 主要年份能源平衡表(标准量)
BALANCE SHEET OF ENERGY IN MAIN YEARS (STANDARD EQUIVALENT)

单位:万吨标准煤(10 000 tons SCE)

指标	Indicators	2000	2005	2009	2010
可供本地区消费的能源量	**Volume of Energy Available for Local Consumption**	**5 462.45**	**8 223.01**	**10 368.82**	**11 161.94**
库存差	Inventory Change	-69.09	86.91	32.68	-54.92
一次能源生产量	Primary Energy Production	103.4	126.83	78.64	72.39
回收能	Recovery of Energy	62.06	150.52	211.10	186.77
外省(市)调入量	Inflow from Other Provinces(Autonomous Region and Municipalities)	8 533.76	11 437.33	11 937.34	13 802.64
进口量	Imports	1 475.48	3 168.27	3 440.64	3 335.53
我轮、机在外国加油量	China Airplanes&ships Refueling in Abroad	40.15	694.14	887.50	860.33
本市调出量	Outflow from Shanghai(Autonomous Region of Municipality)	-4 438.19	-7 160.56	-5 876.62	-6 668.81
出口量	Exports	-179.95	-138.64	-163.62	-175.45
外轮、机在我国加油量(-)	Foreign Airplanes&ships Refueling in China	-65.14	-141.80	-178.83	-196.53
加工转换投入(-)产出(+)量	**Processing Conversion Input (-) and Output (+)**	**-89.20**	**-140.59**	**-181.67**	**-108.68**
#火力发电	Fuel Power Generation	-0.49			
供热	Heating Supply				-37.11
炼焦	Coke Making	-57.93	-39.35	-39.45	-34.77
炼油	Oil Refining	-20.63	-96.84	-129.39	-26.33
制气	Gas Making	-9.79	-4.41	-12.83	-10.46
损失量	**Loss Volume**	**183.49**	**189.29**	**233.90**	**250.17**
#运输和输配损失	Loss in Transportation and Distribution	183.49	189.29	233.90	250.17
终端消费量	**Final Consumption**	**5 226.79**	**7 895.17**	**9 951.81**	**10 802.03**
第一产业	Primary Industry	103.37	61.44	62.71	63.49
第二产业	Secondary Industry	3 592.87	4 940.24	5 587.85	6 154.82
工业	Industry	3 506.07	4 775.16	5 376.05	5 936.45
建筑业	Construction	86.80	165.07	211.80	218.37
第三产业	Tertiary Industry	1 069.32	2 249.12	3 351.64	3 576.70
#交通运输、仓储及邮电通信业	Transportation, Warehousing, Post and Communications	598.09	1 407.10	1 934.52	2 062.90
批发和零售贸易业、餐饮业	Wholesale, Retail Sales and Catering	130.08	321.15	479.36	491.36
生活消费	Living Consumption	461.24	644.37	949.60	1 007.02
城镇	Urban	345.20	549.18	794.39	842.91
乡村	Rural	116.03	95.19	155.21	164.11
平衡差额	**Balance**	**-37.03**	**-2.04**	**1.44**	**1.07**
能源消费总量	**Total Energy Consumption**	**5 499.48**	**8 225.05**	**10 367.38**	**11 160.87**

表5.9 能源终端消费量(2010)
FINAL CONSUMPTION OF ENERGY

单位:万吨(10 000 tons)

行业	Sectors	原煤 Coal	焦炭 Coke	燃料油 Fuel Oil
总计	**Total**	**975.53**	**705.21**	**724.35**
生产消费	**Production Consumption**	**928.88**	**705.21**	**724.35**
第一产业	Primary Industry	2.22		
第二产业	Secondary Industry	833.71	705.21	72.74
#工业	Industry	823.18	705.21	63.12
第三产业	Tertiary Industry	92.95		651.61
#交通运输、仓储及邮电通信业	Transportation, Warehousing, Post and Communications	4.81		643.36
批发和零售贸易业、餐饮业	Wholesale, Retail Sales and Catering Trade	40.36		6.82
生活消费	**Living Consumption**	**46.65**		

表5.9 续表1 continued

单位:万吨(10 000 tons)

行业	Sectors	汽油 Gasoline	煤油 Kerosene	柴油 Diesel Oil
总计	**Total**	**412.37**	**399.07**	**499.81**
生产消费	**Production Consumption**	**293.14**	**399.08**	**457.93**
第一产业	Primary Industry	16.34	0.01	13.24
第二产业	Secondary Industry	58.42	4.28	113.22
#工业	Industry	32.88	4.28	73.62
第三产业	Tertiary Industry	218.38	394.79	331.47
#交通运输、仓储及邮电通信业	Transportation, Warehousing, Post and Communications	95.11	394.75	166.79
批发和零售贸易业、餐饮业	Wholesale, Retail Sales and Catering Trade	49.65	0.01	70.9
生活消费	**Living Consumption**	**119.23**		**41.88**

表5.9 续表2 continued

行业	Sectors	其他石油制品(万吨) Other Petroleum Products (10 000 tons)	热力(万百万千焦) Thermopower (10 000 million K.J)	电力(亿千瓦时) Electric Power (100 million kwh)
总计	**Total**	**178.37**	**7 176.88**	**1 227.89**
生产消费	**Production Consumption**	**178.37**	**7 171.16**	**1 058.93**
第一产业	Primary Industry			6.07
第二产业	Secondary Industry	178.31	6945.23	744.31
#工业	Industry	178.22	6942.52	718.63
第三产业	Tertiary Industry	0.06	225.93	308.55
#交通运输、仓储及邮电通信业	Transportation, Warehousing, Post and Communications	0.05	86.56	34.11
批发和零售贸易业、餐饮业	Wholesale, Retail Sales and Catering Trade	0.01	50.53	69.44
生活消费	**Living Consumption**		**5.71**	**168.95**

表5.10 煤炭、石油、电力平衡表(2010)
COAL,PETROLEUM,ELECTRICITY BALANCE SHEEET

	指 标 Indicators	煤 炭 (万吨) Coal (10 000 tons)	石 油 (万吨) Crude oil (10 000 tons)	电 力 (亿千瓦时) Electricity (100 million kwh)
可供本地区消费的能源量	**Total Energy Available for Consumption**	**5 842.97**	**3 287.24**	**1 295.87**
库存差	Inventory Changes in the Year	-40.09	-19.85	
生产量	Energy Production		13.68	943.89
外省(市)调入量	Inflow from Other Provinces	7 720.43	4 287.90	399.20
进口量	Imports	30.03	2 172.41	
我轮、机在外国加油量	China Airplanes&ships Refueling in Abroad		597.98	
本市调出量(-)	Outflow from Shanghai	-1 867.12	-3 512.22	-47.22
出口量(-)	Exports	-0.27	-119.09	
外轮、机在我国加油量(-)	Foreign Airplanes&ships Refueling in China		-133.57	
消费量	**Total Energy Consumption**	**5 843.81**	**3 286.72**	**1 295.87**
按行业分	Consumption by Sectors			
农、林、牧、渔业	Farming,Forestry,Animal Husbandry,Fishery and Water Conservancy	2.22	29.61	6.07
工 业	Industry	5 691.46	1 230.34	786.61
建筑业	Construction	10.53	92.07	25.68
交通运输、仓储和邮政业	Transport,Storage and Post	4.81	1 345.34	34.11
批发、零售业和住宿、餐饮业	Wholesale,Retail Trade and Hotel, Restaurants	40.36	148.47	69.44
其 他	Others	47.78	219.22	205.00
生活消费	Residential Consumption	46.65	221.69	168.95
按用途分	Consumption by Usage			
终端消费	Final Consumption	1 105.04	3 255.58	1 227.89
#工 业	Industry	952.69	1 199.20	718.63
用于加工转换	Processing and Conversion	4 726.77	31.14	
损失量	Others Losses	12.00		67.98
平衡差额	**Balanced Difference**	**-0.83**	**0.52**	

表5.11　电力建设情况(2007~2010)
STATISTICS OF ELECTRIC POWER COUSTRUCTION

指　标	Indicators	2007	2008	2009	2010
发电量(亿千瓦时)	**Electric Power Generated(100 million kwh)**	**740.97**	**794.16**	**781.79**	**943.89**
线损率(%)	Electricity Loss Rate on Lines(%)	6.05	6.05	6.05	6.05
年末发电设备容量(万千瓦)	**Power Generating Equipment Capacity (year-end)(10 000kw)**	**1 439.74**	**1 679.74**	**1 654.94**	**1 855.38**
架空线长度(公里)	**Length of Overhead Lines(km)**	**7 684.41**	**8 020.58**	**8 558.49**	**8 549.50**
500KV(公里)	500KV(km)	608.41	608.41	798.24	992.91
220KV(公里)	220KV(km)	2 770.63	2 886.58	2 928.84	2 956.08
110KV(公里)	110KV(km)	710.63	721.94	738.13	702.60
35KV(公里)	35KV(km)	3 594.74	3 803.65	3 986.70	3 791.78
电缆长度(公里)	**Length of Cable(km)**	**6 699.68**	**7 341.13**	**14 965.05**	**7 846.98**
220KV(万千伏安)	220KV(10000kva)	516.89	517.41	636.00	516.44
110KV(万千伏安)	110KV(10000kva)	793.87	893.84	1 161.00	962.54
35KV(万千伏安)	35KV(10000kva)	5 388.92	5 929.88	13 168.05	6 336.76
公用变电容量(万千伏安)	**Public Transformer Capacity(10 000kva)**	**8 684.29**	**9 544.27**	**10 418.65**	**11 657.19**
500KV(万千伏安)	500KV(10 000kva)	2 241.40	2 441.40	2 841.40	3 116.40
220KV~35KV(万千伏安)	220KV~35KV(10 000kva)	6 442.89	7 102.87	7 102.87	7 827.75
用电最高负荷(万千瓦)	**Peak Electric Power Consumption Load (10 000kw)**	**2 120.80**	**2 243.20**	**2 379.90**	**2 621.20**

注：本表数据由市电力公司提供。
Note: Data in this table is provided by Shanghai Electric Power Corporation.

上 / 海 / 统 / 计 / 年 / 鉴

主要统计指标解释

能源消费总量

能源消费总量指一定时期内全国(地区)物质生产部门、非物质生产部门和生活消费的各种能源的总和,是观察能源消费水平、构成和增长速度的总量指标。能源消费总量包括原煤和原油及其制品、天然气、电力,但不包括低热值燃料、生物质能和太阳能等的利用。能源消费总量分为三部分,即终端能源消费量、能源加工转换损失量和能源损失量。

(1)终端能源消费量指一定时期内全国(地区)物质生产部门、非物质生产部门和生活消费的各种能源在扣除了用于加工转换二次能源消费量和损失量以后的数量。

(2)能源加工转换损失量指一定时期内全国(地区)投入加工转换的各种能源数量之和与产出各种能源产品之和的差额。它是观察能源在加工转换过程中损失量变化的指标。

(3)能源损失量指一定时期内能源在输送、分配、储存过程中发生的损失和由客观原因造成的各种损失量。不包括各种气体能源放空、放散量。

能源生产弹性系数

能源生产弹性系数反映能源生产量的增长与国民经济增长之间的比值。计算公式:

$$能源生产弹性系数=\frac{能源生产总量年平均增长速度}{国民经济年平均增长速度}$$

电力生产弹性系数

电力生产弹性系数反映电力生产量的增长与国民经济增长之间的比值。计算公式:

$$电力生产弹性系数=\frac{电力生产总量年平均增长速度}{国民经济年平均增长速度}$$

能源消费弹性系数

能源消费弹性系数反映能源消费增长速度与国民经济增长速度之间比例关系的指标:

$$能源消费弹性系数=\frac{能源消费量年平均增长速度}{国民经济年平均增长速度}$$

电力消费弹性系数

电力消费弹性系数反映电力消费增长速度与国民经济增长速度之间比例关系的指标。计算公式为:

$$电力消费弹性系数=\frac{电力消费量年平均增长速度}{国民经济年平均增长速度}$$

能源加工转换效率

能源加工转换效率指一定时期内能源经过加工转换后,产出的各种能源产品的数量与投入加工转换的各种能源数量的比率。它是观察能源加工转换装置和生产工艺先进与落后、管理水平高低等的重要指标。计算公式为:

$$能源加工转换效率=\frac{加工转换产出量}{加工转换投入量}\times 100\%$$

SHANGHAI STATISTICAL YEARBOOK

EXPLANATORY NOTES TO MAJOR STATISTICAL INDICATORS

□ Total Energy Consumption

Total Energy Consumption refers to the total energy consumption of various forms by material production departments, non-material production departments and households in the country (region) in a given period of time. It is a comprehensive indicator to observe the scale, composition and development of energy consumption. The total energy consumption includes raw coal, crude petroleum and their products, natural gas and electricity, but excludes fuel of low calorific value, bioenergy and solar energy. Total domestic energy consumption can be divided into three parts:

(1) Final Energy Consumption refers to the total energy consumption by material production departments, non-material production departments and households in the country (region) in a given period of time, after deducting the secondary energy consumption and loss during the process of energy conversion.

(2)Loss During the Process of Energy Conversion refers to the total input of various forms for conversion, minus the total output of energy of various forms in the country in a given period of time. It is an indicator to observe the loss that occurs during the process of energy conversion.

(3)Loss refers to the total loss of energy due to mistakes or any objective reasons during the course of energy transport, distribution and storage in a given period of time. The loss of various kinds of gas due to gas discharges and stocktaking is excluded.

□ Elasticity of Energy Production

Elasticity of Energy Production is an indicator to show the relationship between the growth rate of energy production and the growth rate of the national economy. The formula is :

$$\text{Elasticity of Energy Production} = \frac{\text{average annual growth rate of energy production}}{\text{average annual growth rate of national economy}}$$

□ Elasticity of Electricity Production

Elasticity of Electricity Production is an indicator to show the relationship between the growth rate of electricity production and the growth rate of the national economy. The formula is :

$$\text{Elasticity of Electricity Production} = \frac{\text{average annual growth rate of electrictity production}}{\text{average annual growth rate of national economy}}$$

□ Elasticity of Energy Consumption

Elasticity Ratio of Energy Consumption is an indicator to show the relationship between the growth rate of energy consumption and the growth rate of the national economy. The formula is:

$$\text{Elasticity of Energy Consumption} = \frac{\text{average annual growth rate of energy consumption}}{\text{average annual growth rate of national economy}}$$

□ Elasticity of Electricity Consumption

Elasticity Ratio of Electricity Consumption is an indicator to show the relationship between the growth rate of electricity consumption and the growth rate of the national economy. The formula is:

$$\text{Elasticity of Electricity Consumption} = \frac{\text{average annual growth rate of electricity consumption}}{\text{average annual growth rate of national economy}}$$

□ Efficiency of Energy Transformation

Efficiency of Energy Transformation refers to the ratio of the total output of energy products after transformation and the total input of energy for transformation in the same reference period .It is an indicator to show the current conditions of energy processing and conversion equipment, production technique and management. The formula is:

$$\text{Efficiency of Energy Transformation} = \frac{\text{output of enery from transformation}}{\text{Input of energy for transformation}}$$

第六篇

CHAPTER 6

固定资产投资

INVESTMENT IN FIXED ASSETS

表6.1 全社会固定资产投资总额(按管理渠道分)(1978~2010)
TOTAL INVESTMENT IN FIXED ASSETS(GROUPED BY ADMINISTRATIVE CHANNELS)

单位:亿元(100 million yuan)

年 份 Year	合 计 Total	其 中 of which						
		基本建设 Capital Construction	更新改造 Technical Update and Transformation	其他投资 Other Investment	房地产开发 Investment in Real Estate	农村集体 Rural Collective	城镇私人建房 Urban Private Home Construction	农村私人建房 Rural Private Home Construction
1978	27.91	14.46	5.60	3.77		2.96	0.09	0.79
1979	35.58	21.13	7.69	3.26		2.17	0.14	0.94
1980	45.43	25.73	11.30	3.24		3.01	0.17	1.41
1981	54.60	30.80	11.18	3.02		4.65	0.20	3.97
1982	71.34	43.63	14.41	3.58		4.06	0.29	4.32
1983	75.94	43.01	17.44	4.56		4.95	0.25	4.48
1984	92.30	47.42	22.56	5.82		7.07	0.24	7.28
1985	118.56	57.05	35.61	3.26		7.04	0.20	12.00
1986	146.93	71.37	46.83	4.26		9.80	0.18	10.30
1987	186.30	92.10	57.39	4.02	0.97	13.84	0.53	12.66
1988	245.27	115.55	76.95	4.55	1.68	22.19	0.66	16.90
1989	214.76	111.76	61.88	3.42	1.85	16.94	0.64	14.32
1990	227.08	108.54	71.77	3.77	8.16	14.38	0.59	15.96
1991	258.30	108.90	95.21	3.91	7.59	23.62	0.70	14.17
1992	357.38	129.60	126.84	6.52	12.71	55.42	0.55	17.00
1993	653.91	273.64	220.30	9.91	22.04	104.82	2.13	5.33
1994	1 123.29	511.24	304.01	13.99	117.43	141.23	1.21	10.40
1995	1 601.79	551.86	389.20	16.33	466.20	139.57	0.72	13.10
1996	1 952.05	651.28	415.73	12.43	657.79	158.32	1.09	20.00
1997	1 977.59	762.00	386.24	7.43	614.23	166.16	1.09	16.80
1998	1 964.83	844.15	365.01	13.44	577.12	137.40	1.41	12.76
1999	1 856.72	786.81	393.59	9.88	514.83	134.33	1.23	5.54
2000	1 869.67	703.50	396.26	21.21	566.17	161.61	1.50	10.36
2001	1 994.73	712.49	436.84	30.70	630.73	173.13	1.06	9.28
2002	2 187.06	784.13	422.58	54.93	748.89	167.92	1.13	6.87
2003	2 452.11	927.29	388.01	57.01	901.24	170.00	2.07	6.49
2004	3 084.66	1 721.56			1 175.46	180.82	0.95	5.86
2005	3 542.55	1 984.61			1 246.86	304.00		7.08
2006	3 925.09	2 246.93			1 275.59	396.60		5.96
2007	4 458.61	2 775.81			1 307.53	370.06		5.21
2008	4 829.45	3 044.46			1 366.87	414.92		3.20
2009	5 273.33	3 384.31			1 464.18	423.31		1.53
2010	5 317.67	2 858.56			1 980.68	476.39		2.03

注：2004年起，全社会投资由城镇投资和农村投资两部分组成。其中城镇投资包括建设改造投资和房地产开发投资，农村投资包括农村集体和农村私人建房。

Note: Since 2004, total investment in fixed assets was composed of urban investment and rural investment. Urban investment includes construction rebuild investment and real estate investment, and rural investment includes rural collective investment and rural private home construction.

表6.2 全社会固定资产投资总额(按经济类型分)(1978～2010)
TOTAL INVESTMENT IN FIXED ASSETS (GROUPED BY ECONOMIC TYPES)

单位:亿元(100 million yuan)

年 份 Year	合 计 Total	其 中 of which			
		#国有经济 State-owned	#集体经济 Collective-owned	#股份制经济 Shareholding	#外商、港澳台经济 Hong Kong, Macao, Taiwan and Foreign Funded
1978	27.91	23.83	3.20		
1979	35.58	32.08	2.42		
1980	45.43	40.27	3.58		
1981	54.60	45.00	5.43		
1982	71.34	61.62	5.11		
1983	75.94	65.01	6.20		
1984	92.30	75.80	8.98		
1985	118.56	95.92	10.44		
1986	146.93	122.46	13.99		
1987	186.30	154.45	18.65		
1988	245.27	198.68	29.03		
1989	214.76	178.81	21.00		
1990	227.08	192.24	18.29		
1991	258.30	215.61	27.82		
1992	357.38	275.67	64.16		
1993	653.91	419.22	124.18	32.83	61.61
1994	1 123.29	721.37	189.75	76.99	101.78
1995	1 601.79	935.92	247.11	150.17	208.30
1996	1 952.05	1 048.27	239.47	165.57	340.18
1997	1 977.59	1 148.69	257.10	118.80	367.50
1998	1 964.83	1 087.94	208.84	203.81	405.17
1999	1 856.72	986.82	227.19	268.68	325.58
2000	1 869.67	829.98	156.34	421.53	319.05
2001	1 994.73	760.58	136.81	580.75	362.25
2002	2 187.06	742.72	101.33	631.70	369.96
2003	2 452.11	811.85	116.63	647.27	468.20
2004	3 084.66	955.12	146.58	667.52	851.39
2005	3 542.55	1 240.27	131.07	916.27	640.31
2006	3 925.09	1 460.09	159.31	910.31	725.85
2007	4 458.61	1 779.43	121.51	1 169.49	711.35
2008	4 829.45	2 295.74	104.86	1 026.67	748.14
2009	5 273.33	2 618.61	132.30	1 174.81	617.90
2010	5 317.67	2 234.12	183.07	1 200.26	686.95

表6.3 主要年份全社会固定资产投资主要指标
MAJOR INDICATORS OF TOTAL INVESTMENT IN FIXED ASSETS IN MAIN YEARS

单位:亿元(100 million yuan)

指 标	Indicators	2000	2009	2010
投资总额	**Total Investment**	**1 869.67**	**5 273.33**	**5 317.67**
按隶属关系分	**Grouped by Administrative Relationship**			
中央项目	Central Government Projects	257.67	797.81	761.06
地方项目	Local Projects	1 612.00	4 475.52	4 556.61
按构成分	**Grouped by Use of Funds**			
建筑安装工程	Construction and Installation	882.91	3 000.14	2 820.17
设备、工具、器具购置	Purchase of Equipment and Instruments	482.47	876.89	991.10
其他费用	Others	504.29	1 396.30	1 506.40
按建设性质分	**Grouped by Type of Construction**			
#新 建	New Construction	730.76	2 557.99	2 052.69
改建和技改	Reconstruction and Technical Transformation	216.40	574.63	513.80
扩 建	Expansion	216.71	423.89	368.07
单纯购置	Simply Purchase	39.02	216.46	373.43
按产业分	**Grouped by Type of Industry**			
第一产业	Primary Industry	7.87	11.41	16.40
第二产业	Secondary Industry	615.94	1 427.50	1435.37
第三产业	Tertiary Industry	1 245.86	3 834.42	3 865.90
#住 宅	Residential Housing	443.90	922.81	1 232.96
按经济类型分	**Grouped by Economic Types**			
国有经济	State-owned	829.98	2 618.61	2 234.12
非国有经济	Non-state-owned	1 039.69	2 654.72	3 083.55
集体经济	Collective-owned	156.34	132.30	183.07
私营经济	Private	83.29	701.93	992.16
联营经济	Joint Owned	41.20	14.93	11.52
股份制经济	Shareholding	421.53	1 174.81	1 200.26
外商经济	Foreign Funded	222.86	423.69	439.28
港澳台经济	Hong Kong, Macao and Taiwan Funded	96.19	194.21	247.67
其他经济	Others	18.28	12.85	9.58
新增固定资产	**Newly Increased Fixed Assets**	**1 493.35**	**2 686.43**	**3 179.40**
固定资产交付使用率(%)	Rate of Fixed Assets Transfered and in Use(%)	79.9	50.9	59.8
房屋建筑面积(万平方米)	**Floor Space of Buildings (10 000 sq. m)**			
施工面积	Floor Space Under Construction	8 636.31	13 553.64	15 020.76
#住 宅	Residential Housing	4 804.12	6 581.16	7 344.07
竣工面积	Floor Space Completed	3 266.52	2 970.92	2 776.21
#住 宅	Residential Housing	1 724.02	1 522.07	1 415.44

注:从2000年起,固定资产投资统计起点为50万元以上(含50万元)项目,按建设性质分中不包括房地产开发投资。

Note: Since 2000, the statistics that have been collected are about projects of fixed assets investment each involving 500 000 yuan and above. In "Type of Construction" the investment in real estate development is excluded.

表6.4 建设改造投资主要指标(2010)
MAJOR INDICATORS OF INVESTMENT FOR CONSTRUCTION AND TRANSFORMATION

单位:亿元(100 million yuan)

指标	Indicators	全市 Total	#地方 Local Projects
投资总额	**Total Investment**	**2 858.56**	**2 142.53**
按建设性质分	**Grouped by Type of Construction**		
#新　建	New Construction	1 775.51	1 465.87
改建和技改	Reconstruction and Technical Transformation	461.71	323.01
扩　建	Expansion	294.71	167.52
单纯购置	Simply Purchase	307.09	168.09
按产业分	**Grouped by Type of Industry**		
第一产业	Primary Industry	5.55	5.55
第二产业	Secondary Industry	1 143.41	835.53
第三产业	Tertiary Industry	1 709.61	1 301.45
#住　宅	Residential Housing	1.01	1.01
按行业分	**Grouped by Economic Sectors**		
#工　业	Industry	1 132.75	832.55
交通运输、仓储和邮政业	Transportation, Storage and Post Industries	774.62	497.17
信息传输、计算机服务和软件业	Information Transmission,Computer Servcie and Software Industries	115.69	11.29
批发和零售业	Retail and Wholesale	28.05	28.05
住宿和餐饮业	Hotel and Eateries	32.26	32.08
金融业	Financial Industry	28.98	21.96
房地产业	Real Estate Industry	109.24	109.20
租赁和商务服务业	Leasing and Business Service	39.00	39.00
科学研究、技术服务和地质勘查业	Scientific Research,Technology Service and Geological Prospecting	25.44	15.38
水利、环境和公共设施管理业	Water Conservancy,Environment and Public Facility Management	422.23	422.02
居民服务和其他服务业	Residents Service and Other Service	1.88	1.88
教　育	Education	45.11	37.14
卫生、社会保障和社会福利业	Health,Social Security and Welfare	36.14	36.14
文化、体育和娱乐业	Culture,Sports and Entertainment	35.26	34.56
公共管理和社会组织	Public Administration and Social Organizations	15.72	15.57
新增固定资产	**Newly Increased Fixed Assets**	**1 926.24**	**1 373.89**
固定资产交付使用率(%)	Rate of Fixed Assets Transfered and in Use(%)	67.4	64.1
房屋建筑面积(万平方米)	**Floor Space of Buildings (10 000 sq. m)**		
施工面积	Floor Space Under Construction	2 398.48	2 182.09
#住　宅	Residential Housing	11.12	11.12
竣工面积	Floor Space Completed	461.14	421.97

注:本表不包括农村投资。
Note: Data of this table exclude rural investment.

表6.5 地方固定资产投资主要指标(2008~2010)
MAJOR INDICATORS OF LOCAL INVESTMENT IN FIXED ASSETS

单位:亿元(100 million yuan)

指 标	Indicators	2008	2009	2010
投资总额	**Total Investment**	**4 016.98**	**4 475.52**	**4 556.61**
按构成分	**Grouped by Use of Funds**			
建筑安装工程	Construction and Installation	2 297.71	2 662.23	2 590.17
设备、工具、器具购置	Purchase of Equipment and Instruments	509.89	522.13	629.75
其他费用	Others	1 209.38	1 291.16	1 336.68
按建设性质分	**Grouped by Type of Construction**			
#新 建	New Construction	1 965.98	2 178.33	1 741.31
改建和技改	Reconstruction	237.26	374.75	375.10
扩 建	Expansion	283.77	263.66	240.89
单纯购置	Simply Purchase	137.27	185.48	233.97
按产业分	**Grouped by Type of Industry**			
第一产业	Primary Industry	8.40	10.53	16.40
第二产业	Secondary Industry	964.81	1 016.15	1 127.04
第三产业	Tertiary Industry	3 043.77	3 448.84	3 413.17
#住 宅	Residential Housing	866.28	903.45	1 204.30
按行业分	**Grouped by Sectors**			
#工 业	Industry	962.16	1 009.03	1 121.43
交通运输、仓储和邮政业	Transportation, Storage, Postal and Telecommunications	641.39	806.39	512.05
信息传输、计算机服务和软件业	Information Transmission, Computer Servcie and Software Industries	7.87	5.49	12.33
批发和零售业	Wholesale and Retail	44.48	43.22	73.15
住宿和餐饮业	Hotel and Eateries	37.31	48.20	45.34
金融业	Finance	17.27	11.33	23.08
房地产业	Real Estate	1 506.54	1 600.74	2 076.60
租赁和商务服务业	Leasing and Business Service	74.29	118.29	53.71
科学研究、技术服务和地质勘查业	Scientific Research, Technology Service and Geological Prospecting	17.31	19.47	20.76
水利、环境和公共设施管理业	Water Conservancy, Environment and Public Facility Management	592.14	661.48	449.77
居民服务和其他服务业	Residents Service and Other Service	3.19	3.07	2.38
教 育	Education	40.79	36.77	42.19
卫生、社会保障和社会福利业	Health, Social Security and Welfare	16.92	19.32	37.97
文化、体育和娱乐业	Culture, Sports and Entertainment	27.82	55.85	44.80
公共管理和社会组织	Public Administration and Social Organizations	16.45	19.21	19.06
新增固定资产	**Newly Increased Fixed Assets**	**2 195.44**	**2 180.36**	**2 597.99**
固定资产交付使用率(%)	Rate of Fixed Assets Transfered and in Use(%)	54.7	48.7	57.0
房屋建筑面积(万平方米)	**Floor Space of Buildings (10 000 sq. m)**			
施工面积	Floor Space Under Construction	13 804.05	13 139.78	14 561.90
#住 宅	Residential Housing	6 994.52	6 499.45	7 164.39
竣工面积	Floor Space Completed	3 767.70	2 905.16	2 686.62
#住 宅	Residential Housing	1 884.53	1 502.30	1 381.30

表6.6 工业各行业建设改造投资主要指标(2010)
MAIN INDICATORS OF INVESTMENT FOR CONSTRUCTION AND TRANSFORMATION BY INDUSTRIAL SECTORS

行业	Sectors	施工项目(个) Projects Under Construction (unit)	全部建成投产项目(个) Projects Completed and Put into Production (unit)	建成投产率(%) Rate of Projects Completed and Put into Use(%)	建设改造投资额(万元) Construction and Transformation Investment (10 000 yuan)
总计	**Total**	**1 918**	**804**	**41.9**	**11 327 511**
采矿业	**Excavation**	**21**	**10**	**47.6**	**24 591**
石油和天然气开采业	Petroleum and Natural Gas Exploiting	1			3 280
黑色金属矿采选业	Nonmetal Minerals Mining	20	10	50.0	21 311
非金属矿采选业	Other Excavation				
制造业	**Manufacturing**	**1 510**	**521**	**34.5**	**8 958 560**
农副食品加工业	Farm and Sideline Products Processing	27	16	59.3	69 609
食品制造业	Food Manufacturing	21	5	23.8	76 937
饮料制造业	Beverage Manufacturing	11	3	27.3	102 572
烟草制品业	Tabacco Manufacturing	27	11	40.7	306 006
纺织业	Textile	28	21	75.0	77 325
纺织服装、鞋、帽制造业	Garments, Shoes and Accessories Manufacturing	13	2	15.4	23 605
皮革、毛皮、羽毛(绒)及其他制品业	Leather, Fur, and Wool Products Manufacturing	2			2 496
木材加工及木、竹、藤、棕、草制品业	Timber Processing and Timber, Bamboo, Rattan, Coir and Straw Products Manufacturing	10	5	50.0	56 258
家具制造业	Furniture Manufacturing	6	3	50.0	20 015
造纸及纸制品业	Paper-making and Paper Products Manufacturing	4	4	100.0	23 343
印刷业和记录媒介的复制	Printing and Record Duplicating	8	5	62.5	86 915
文教体育用品制造业	Stationary, Education and Sports Goods Manufacturing	7	4	57.1	14 172
石油加工、炼焦及核燃料加工业	Oil Processing, Coking and Nuclear Fuel Processing	40	33	82.5	247 980
化学原料及化学制品制造业	Raw Chemical Materials and Chemical Products Manufacturing	138	51	37.0	753 358
医药制造业	Medicine Manufacturing	76	43	56.6	155 861
化学纤维制造业	Chemical Fiber Manufacturing	11	5	45.5	11 541
橡胶制品业	Rubber Products Manufacturing	7	4	57.1	26 108
塑料制品业	Plastic Products Manufacturing	25	11	44.0	126 037
非金属矿物制品业	Nonmetal Mineral Products	21	8	38.1	66 056
黑色金属冶炼及压延加工业	Smelting and Pressing of Ferrous Metals	335	97	29.0	1 064 576
有色金属冶炼及压延加工业	Smelting and Pressing of Nonferrous Metals	5	2	40.0	100 303
金属制品业	Metal Products Manufacturing	44	12	27.3	201 639
通用设备制造业	General Equipment Manufacturing	98	31	31.6	367 871
专用设备制造业	Special Purpose Equipment Manufacturing	75	16	21.3	513 357
交通运输设备制造业	Transportation Equipment Manufacturing	189	44	23.3	1 534 021
电气机械及器材制造业	Electric Machinery Equipments and Manufacturing	74	18	24.3	442 037
通信设备、计算机及其他电子设备制造业	Communications Equipment, Computer and Other Electronic Equipment Manufacturing	92	28	30.4	1 642 449
仪器仪表及文化、办公用机械制造业	Instruments, Meters, Culture and Office Equipments Manufacturing	20	7	35.0	49 569
工艺品及其他制造业	Artworks and Other Manufacturing	85	31	36.5	774 262
废弃资源和废旧材料回收加工业	Waste Resources and Materials Recycling and Processing	11	1	9.1	22 282
电力、燃气及水的生产和供应业	**Power, Gas, Water Production and Supply**	**387**	**273**	**70.5**	**2 344 360**
电力、热力的生产和供应业	Power and Heat Production and Supply	279	215	77.1	1 484 977
燃气生产和供应业	Gas Production and Supply	35	30	85.7	249 491
水的生产和供应业	Water Production and Supply	73	28	38.4	609 892

表6.7　六大重点发展工业行业固定资产投资额(2008～2010)
FIXED ASSETS INVESTMENT IN SIX KEY INDUSTRIES

单位:亿元(100 million yuan)

指　标	Indicators	2008	2009	2010
工业六大重点行业	**Six Key Industries**	**808.76**	**626.37**	**730.68**
电子信息产品制造业	Electronic Information Product Manufacturing	167.58	91.55	219.65
汽车制造业	Automobile Manufacturing	85.78	98.58	109.68
石油化工及精细化工制造业	Petrochemical and Fine Chemical Products Manufacturing	116.26	103.42	85.03
精品钢材制造业	Fine Steel Manufacturing	266.46	160.76	113.79
成套设备制造业	Equipment Complex Manufacturing	156.25	141.86	176.31
生物医药制造业	Bio-medicine Manufacturing	16.44	30.21	26.21

表6.8　主要年份新增固定资产
NEWLY INCREASED FIXED ASSETS IN MAIN YEARS

年　份 Year	新增固定资产(亿元) Newly Increased Fixed Assets (100 million yuan)	其　中 of which #房地产开发 Investment in Real Estate Development	固定资产交付使用率(%) Rate of Fixed Assets Transferred and in Use(%)
1990	222.99	4.97	98.2
1995	826.94	127.08	51.6
2000	1 493.35	477.39	79.9
2005	2 547.02	1 054.02	71.9
2006	2 680.85	1 058.94	68.3
2007	2 466.68	1 048.47	55.3
2008	2 773.14	994.10	57.4
2009	2 686.43	932.24	50.9
2010	3 179.40	964.27	59.8

表6.9　主要年份固定资产投资资金来源
CAPITAL SOURCES OF INVESTMENT IN FIXED ASSETS IN MAIN YEARS

单位:亿元(100 million yuan)

指　标	Indicators	2000	2009	2010
资金来源合计	**Total Capital Sources**	**2 061.66**	**7 586.02**	**7 997.62**
上年末结余资金	Balance at End of Previous Year	241.05	927.51	1 440.57
本年资金来源小计	Sub-total Capital Source of this Year	1 820.61	6 658.51	6 557.05
国家预算内资金	State Budgetary Funds	48.30	90.26	116.71
国内贷款	Domestic Loans	379.21	1 522.44	1 568.79
债　券	Bonds	4.85	65.35	10.06
利用外资	Foreign Investment	161.83	176.15	239.18
#外商直接投资	Foreign Direct Investment	73.71	107.21	139.72
自筹资金	Self-Financed Capital	905.46	3 003.22	3 273.11
#市自筹	Self-Financed by Municipal Government	72.63	231.34	129.95
企、事业单位自筹	Self-Financed by Enterprises and Institutions	509.93	1 648.91	2 764.91
其他资金	Other Capital	320.96	1 801.09	1 349.21
本年各项应付投资款	Investment Due to Pay of this Year	310.42	913.76	997.93
#工程款	Project Funds	76.52	458.77	438.19

上/海/统/计/年/鉴

主要统计指标解释

全社会固定资产投资

固定资产投资是国民经济再生产活动的一个重要部分。固定资产投资额是以货币形式表现的在一定时期内建造和购置固定资产的工作量以及与此有关的费用总称。它是反映固定资产投资规模、结构和发展速度的综合性指标。按照现行国家统计制度，全社会固定资产投资包括建设改造、房地产开发、城乡集体经济单位、城乡私人建房和其他经济单位投资。

自 1997 年起，固定资产投资统计起点为 50 万元(含 50 万元)以上项目；自 2011 年起，固定资产投资统计起点为 500 万元(含 500 万元)以上项目。

房地产开发投资

指各种登记注册类型的房地产开发公司、商品房建设公司及其他房地产开发法人单位和附属于其他法人单位实际从事房地产开发或经营活动的单位统一开发的包括统代建、拆迁还建的住宅、厂房、仓库、饭店、宾馆、度假村、写字楼、办公楼等房屋建筑物和配套的服务设施，土地开发工程(如道路、给水、排水、供电、供热、通讯、平整场地等基础设施工程)的投资；不包括单纯的土地交易活动。

固定资产投资按国民经济行业分

固定资产投资按国民经济行业分是根据建设项目建成投产后的主要产品或主要用途及社会经济活动性质来确定国民经济行业。一般情况下，一个建设项目或一个企业、事业单位只能属于一种国民经济行业。

固定资产投资按隶属关系分

固定资产投资按隶属关系分是按建设单位或企业、事业、行政单位的主管上级机关确定的。

(1)中央：是指中共中央、人大常委会和国务院各部、委、局、总公司以及直属机构直接领导的建设项目和企业、事业、行政单位。这些单位的固定资产投资计划由国务院各部门直接编制和下达，建设中所需物资、主要设备以及建设中的问题都由中央有关部门安排和解决。

(2)地方：是由省(自治区、直辖市)、地区(州、盟、省辖市)、县(旗、县级市)三级政府及业务主管部门直接领导和管理的建设项目、企业、事业、行政单位。地方项目还包括不隶属以上各级政府及主管部门的建设项目和企业、事业单位，如外商投资企业和无主管部门的企业等。

固定资产投资按构成分

固定资产投资按构成分是按其工作内容和实现方式来划分的，主要分为建筑安装工程，设备、工具、器具购置，其他费用三个部分。

(1)建筑安装工程(建筑安装工作量)：指各种房屋、建筑物的建造工程和各种设备、装置的安装工程。包括各种房屋建造工程；各种用途设备基础和各种工业窑炉的砌筑工程及金属结构工程；为施工而进行的各种准备工作和临时工程以及完工后的清理工作等；铁路、道路的铺设，矿井的开凿及石油管道的架设等；水利工程；防空地下建筑等特殊工程；列入房屋工程预算内的暖气、卫生、通风、照明、煤气等设备的价值及装设油饰工程；列入建筑工程预算内的各种管道(蒸汽、压缩空气、石油、给排水等管道)、电力、电讯电缆导线等的敷设工程；以及各种机械设备的安装工程；为测定安装工程质量，对设备进行的试运工作；房地产开发单位进行的商品房屋开发建设工程、土地开发工程。

在安装工程中，不包括被安装设备本身的价值。

(2)设备、工具、器具购置：指建设单位或企、事业单位购置或自制的，达到固定资产标准的设备、工具、器具的价值。新建单位及扩建单位的新建车间，按照设计或计划要求购置或自制的全部设备、工具、器具，不论是否达到固定资产标准均计入“设备、工具、器具购置”中。

(3)其他费用：指在固定资产建造和购置过程中发生的，除上述几项内容以外的各种应分摊计入固定资产的费用。

固定资产投资的资金来源

固定资产投资的资金来源是根据固定资产投资的资金来源不同，分为国家预算内资金、国内贷款、债券、利用外资、自筹资金和其他资金来源。

(1)国家预算内资金：指中央财政和地方财政中由国家统筹安排的基本建设拨款和更新改造拨款，以及中央财政安排的专项拨款中用于基本建设的资金和基本建设拨款改贷款的资金等。

(2)国内贷款：指报告期内企、事业单位向银行及非银行金融机构借入的用于固定资产投资的各种国内借

主要统计指标解释

款。包括银行利用自有资金及吸收的存款发放的贷款、上级主管部门拨入的国内贷款、国家专项贷款(包括煤代油贷款、劳改煤矿专项贷款等)、地方财政专项资金安排的贷款、国内储备贷款、周转贷款等。

(3)债券:是企业(公司)或金融机构通过发行各种债券,筹集用于固定资产投资的资金。包括由银行代理国家专业投资公司发行的重点企业债券和基本建设债券。

(4)利用外资:指报告期内收到的用于固定资产投资的国外资金,包括统借统还、自借自还的国外贷款,中外合资项目中的外资,以及对外发行债券和股票等。国家统借统还的外资指由我国政府出面同外国政府、团体或金融组织签订贷款协议、并负责偿还本息的国外贷款。

(5)自筹资金:指建设单位报告期内收到的,用于进行固定资产投资的上级主管部门、地方和企、事业单位自筹资金。

(6)其他资金来源:指报告期内收到的除以上各种拨款、借款、自筹资金以外其他用于固定资产投资的资金。

固定资产投资按建设性质分

建设项目的性质一般分为新建、改建和技改、扩建和单纯建造生活设施。

(1)新建:一般指从无到有"平地起家"开始建设的企业、事业和行政单位或独立的工程。现有企业、事业、行政单位一般不属于新建。但如有的单位原有基础很小,经过建设后新增的固定资产价值超过该企、事业、行政单位原有固定资产价值(原值)三倍以上的也应作为新建。

(2)改建和技改:指现有企业、事业单位,对原有设施进行技术改造或更新(包括相应配套的辅助性生产、生活福利设施)的建设项目。现有企业、事业单位为适应市场变化的需要,而改变企业的主要产品种类(如军工企业转产民用品等)的建设项目,应作为改建和技改。原有产品生产作业线由于各工序(车间)之间能力不平衡,为填平补齐充分发挥原有生产能力而增建不增加本企业主要产品设计能力的车间,也应作为改建和技改。

(3)扩建:指在厂内或其他地点,为扩大原有产品的生产能力(或效益)或增加新的产品生产能力,而增建主要的生产车间(或主要工程)、分厂、独立的生产线。行政、事业单位在原单位增建业务用房(如学校增建教学用房、医院增建门诊部、病房等)也作为扩建。

现有企、事业单位为扩大原有主要产品生产能力或增加新的产品生产能力,增建一个或几个主要生产车间(或主要工程)、分厂,同时进行一些更新改造工程的,也应作为扩建。

(4)单纯建造生活设施:是指企(事)业及行政单位在不扩建、改建生产性工程和业务用房的情况下,单纯建造职工住宅、托儿所、子弟学校、医务室、浴室、食堂等生活福利设施。

新增固定资产

新增固定资产又称交付使用的固定资产,是指已经完成建造和购置过程,并已交付生产或使用单位的固定资产价值。新增固定资产是表示固定资产投资成果的价值量指标,也是反映建设进度、计算固定资产投资效果的必要数据。

固定资产交付使用率

指一定时期新增固定资产与同期完成投资额的比率。该指标是反映固定资产动用速度,衡量建设过程中宏观投资效果的综合指标。由于新增固定资产是较长时期内形成的结果,而投资额则是当年完成的,因此,该指标一般适宜于反映较长时期内固定资产的动用情况。

施工项目

指报告期内进行过建筑或安装施工活动的项目。凡是报告期内施过工的建设项目,不论施工时间长短,均作为施工项目统计。施工项目个数可以反映一定时期固定资产投资的实际规模,与同期建成投产的建设项目个数相比,可以从建设速度的角度反映固定资产投资的效果。根据建设项目施工活动的不同性质,施工项目又分为:本年正式施工项目、本年收尾项目和以前年度全部停缓建项目。

全部建成投产项目

工业项目指设计文件规定形成生产能力的主体工程及其相应配套的辅助设施全部建成,经负荷试运转,证明具备生产设计规定合格产品的条件,并经过验收鉴定合格或达到竣工验收标准,与生产性工程配套的生活福利设施可以满足近期正常生产的需要,正式移交生产的建设项目。非工业项目指设计文件规定的主体工程和相应的配套工程全部建成,能够发挥设计规定的全部效益,经验收鉴定合格或达到竣工验收标准,正式移交使用的建设项目。

建成投产率

指一定时期内全部建成投产项目个数与同期施工项目个数的比率。该指标是从建设单位建设速度的角度反映投资效果的指标。

SHANGHAI STATISTICAL YEARBOOK

EXPLANATORY NOTES TO MAJOR STATISTICAL INDICATORS

□ Total Investment in Fixed Assets

Investment in Fixed Assets constitutes an important portion of the national economic reproduction. Fixed assets investment is a general term for both the work volume of production and purchase of fixed assets and relevant expenditure, in the form of currency, during a certain period. It is a comprehensive indicator of scale, structure and development speed of fixed assets investment. As stipulated in the current national statistics regulations, the social fixed assets investment includes the investment into infrastructure and reformation, real estate development, urban and rural collective economic bodies, private house construction in urban and rural areas and other economic bodies.

From 1997, the fixed assets items only include those with investment of 0.5 million yuan and above. From 2011, the fixed assets items only include those with investment of 5 million yuan and above.

□ Investment in Real Estate Development

Investment in Real Estate Development refers to the investment by the real estate development companies, commercial buildings construction companies and other real estate development units of various types of ownership in the construction of house buildings, such as residential buildings, factory buildings, warehouses, hotels, guesthouses, holiday villages, office buildings, and the complementary service facilities and land development projects, such as roads, water supply, water drainage, power supply, heating, telecommunications, land leveling and other projects of infrastructure. It excludes the activities in pure land transactions.

□ Investment in Fixed Assets by Sector

Investment in Fixed Assets by Sector refers to determining the classification of construction projects by the major products or the purpose of the projects when they are put into production or use, and by the nature of their social economic activities. In general, one project or one enterprise or institution can only be classified into one sector.

□ Investment in Fixed Assets by Jurisdiction of Management

Investment in Fixed Assets by Jurisdiction of Management refers to the classification of investment by the competent authorities under which investment is made by construction units, enterprises, institutions or administrative units.

(1) Central investment refers to the investment in projects or by enterprises, institutions or administrative units which are under the direct leadership and management of the CPC Central Committee, the NPC Standing Committee, the State Council and of the national commissions, ministries, agencies and state-owned large corporations. Various ministries and departments of the State Council prepare and implement plans for investment in fixed assets by those departments, and arrange and ensure the supply of materials and key equipment required for the projects.

(2) Local investment refers to the investment in projects or by enterprises, institutions or administrative units which are under the direct leadership and management of departments under the provincial, prefecture and county governments. Also included are projects by foreign-invested enterprises and enterprises without competent managing authorities.

□ Investment in Fixed Assets by Structure

Investment in Fixed Assets by Structure is classified by their contents. It is mainly classified into 3 categories, i.e. construction and installation, purchase of equipment and instrument, and other expenses.

(1) Construction and installation (work volume of construction and installation) refers to the construction of various houses and buildings and installation of various kinds of equipment and instruments. They include construction of various houses; equipment foundations, industrial kilns and stoves, and metal structure work; preparation works for project construction, and clearing up works post project construction; pavement of railways and roads, drilling of mines and putting up of oil pipes; construction of projects of water conservancy; construction of underground air-raid shelters and construction of other special projects; value of equipment for heating, sanitation, ventilation, lighting, gas, painting, etc. that are covered by the budget of housing projects; laying out of various pipelines (for steam, compressed air, petroleum, tap water and sewage) and lines for electric power and for communications; installation of various machinery equipment, testing operation for pre-testing the quality of installation projects, and land

EXPLANATORY NOTES TO MAJOR STATISTICAL INDICATORS

and other development work conducted by real estate developers for commercial housing. The value of equipment installed is not included in the value of installation projects.

(2) Purchase of equipment and instruments refers to the total value of equipment, tools, and instruments purchased or self-produced which come up to standards for fixed assets by the construction units or investing enterprises or institutions. Equipment, tools and instruments purchased or self-produced for new workshops by newly established or expanded units are categorized as "purchase of equipment and instruments" no matter whether they come up to the standards for fixed assets.

(3) Other expenses refer to expenses occurring during the construction or purchase of fixed assets other than those mentioned above.

□ Sources of Capital for Investment in Fixed Assets

Sources of capital for Investment in Fixed Assets include state budgetary appropriation, domestic loans, bond, foreign investment, self-raised funds, and others.

(1)State budgetary appropriation refers to appropriation in the budget of the central and local governments earmarked for capital construction and for innovation projects, and the special appropriation from the budget of the central government for capital construction and for the transfer fund to banks to be issued as loans for capital construction projects.

(2)Domestic loans refers to various funds borrowed by enterprises and institutions from banks and non-bank financial institutions during the reference period for the purpose of investment in fixed assets, including loans issued by banks from their self-owned funds and deposit, loans appropriated by higher responsible authorities, special loans by government (including loan for replacing petroleum with coal, special loan for reform-through-labour coal mines), loans arranged by local government from special funds, domestic reserve loan, and working loan, etc..

(3) Bond refers to company and finance institutions raising funds for investment in fixed assets by issuing various bond, including keystone enterprise bond and infrastructure bond issued by banks as agency of national professional investment company.

(4) Foreign Investment refers to foreign funds received during the reference period for the purpose of investment in fixed assets, including foreign funds borrowed and managed by the government, by individual units, foreign fund in joint venture program, and issue of bonds and stocks at the international financial markets. The foreign funds borrowed and managed by the government refer to foreign loans borrowed by the government from foreign governments, organizations, or financial institutions under official agreements signed by both parties, under which government is responsible for the repayment of both the principal and interests of the foreign loans.

(5)Self-raised funds refers to funds received by construction enterprises from their higher responsible authorities, local governments, or raised by enterprises or institutions themselves for the purpose of investment in fixed assets during the reference period.

(6) Others refer to funds received during the reference period which are not included in the above-mentioned sources.

□ Investment in Fixed Assets by Type of Construction

The construction projects in general can be classified, by the type of construction, into new construction, reconstruction and technical transformation and simply constructing establishment for life.

(1) New construction in general refers to newly constructed enterprises, institutions, administrative agencies or independent projects from scratch. Construction in the existing enterprises, institutions or agencies is not considered as new construction. In case the asset of the existing unit is quite small, and the value of newly added fixed assets exceeds the original value of assets by three times, the expansion will be considered as new construction.

(2)Reconstruction and technical transformation refers to construction projects by existing enterprises or institutions in innovation or technical transformation of the old facilities (including auxiliary production equipment and welfare facilities). Also considered as Reconstruction and Technical Transformation is the construction of new workshops by the existing enterprises or institutions to change the variety of products to meet the market demand (such as the production of civil products by defense industries), or to bring the designed production capacity into full play through a more balanced production process on production lines.

(3) Expansion refers to construction of new major production workshop, branch factory or independent production line within a factory or in other locations, for the purpose of increasing the production capacity (or improving efficiency) of the original products. Newly constructed houses for the operation of institutions and administrative organizations (such as the newly constructed buildings for teaching in schools, buildings for clinics or wards in hospitals, etc.) are also classified as expansion.

EXPLANATORY NOTES TO MAJOR STATISTICAL INDICATORS

Also included in the expansion are investments by existing enterprises or institutions in building major production line (s) or branch factory (ies) along with some work on innovation, for the purpose of expending the production capacity of original products or producing new products.

(4) Simply constructing establishment for life refers to enterprises and administrative unit simply construct the employee's residence, nursery, children school, infirmary, bathroom and eatery, without expanding or rebuilding the productive engineering and operation houses.

□ Newly Increased Fixed Assets

Newly Increased Fixed Assets, also called fixed assets put into operation, refers to the value of fixed assets that has been put into production or handed over to the production units after the completion of the process of construction and purchase. The newly increased fixed asset is an value indicator of the result of investment. It is also the necessary data for reflecting the construction process and the result of investment in fixed assets.

□ Rate of Projects of Fixed Assets Completed and Put into Operation

Rate of Projects of Fixed Assets Completed and Put into Operation refers to the ratio of the newly increased fixed assets to the total investment made in the same period. This is a comprehensive indicator reflecting the speed of the employment of fixed assets and the investment efficiency at the macro-level. As the newly increase fixed assets is the result of a long period while the investment is completed in the current year, this indicator is expected to be used to reflect the employment of fixed assets over a long period of time.

□ Projects under Construction

Projects under Construction refer to projects with construction and installation activities undertaken in the reference period. All projects that have construction activities undertaken during the reference period are reported as projects under construction irrespective of the length of construction work. The number of projects under construction can reflect the actual size of investment in fixed assets during a given period, and when compared with the number of projects completed and put into use during the same period, it demonstrates the results of investment in fixed assets. Depending on the nature of construction activities, projects under construction can also be classified into projects under construction in current year, winding-up projects in current year and stopped or suspended projects in previous years (with preservation work in current year).

□ Projects Completed and Put into Use

Projects Completed and Put into Use Industrial projects refer to the major projects and accessory facilities completed which result in forming production capacity and have been checked and accepted while the living and welfare facilities have been completed and can ensure normal production and formally put into production. Non-industrial projects refer to the major projects and accessory facilities completed which possess the designed capacity and have been checked, accepted and formally put into production.

□ Rate of Construction Projects Completed and Put into Use

Rate of Construction Projects Completed and Put into Use refers to the ratio of the number of construction projects completed and put into use in certain period of time to the number of projects under construction in the same period. This reflects the investment efficiency from the perspective of the speed of projects construction.

第七篇

CHAPTER 7

对外经济贸易和旅游

FOREIGN ECONOMIC RELATIONS, TRADE AND TOURISM

表7.1 主要年份上海关区出口总额
TOTAL EXPORT TRADE VOLUME THROUGH CUSTOMS IN MAIN YEARS

单位:亿美元 (100 million USD)

年份 Year	关区出口总额 Export Trade Volume Through Customs	其中 of which				
		#一般贸易 Ordinary Trade	#来料加工装配贸易 Processing and Assembly Trade with Customers' Materials	#进料加工贸易 Processing Trade with Imported Materials	#对外承包工程货物 Construction Projects in Foreign Countries	#出料加工贸易 Outward Processing Trade
1990	86.62	51.39	3.20	30.67	0.41	0.45
1995	256.07	149.16	14.31	90.12	0.63	0.06
1996	272.13	146.05	25.42	97.69	1.01	
1997	334.51	178.93	37.17	115.17	0.71	
1998	374.58	199.24	44.13	127.55	0.79	
1999	442.88	234.43	55.08	149.68	0.59	
2000	615.72	341.02	64.21	205.13	1.25	
2001	680.07	380.43	61.09	228.43	1.26	0.13
2002	818.03	473.13	66.88	266.72	1.44	0.13
2003	1 123.06	618.90	78.81	408.79	1.18	0.12
2004	1 612.68	824.92	126.99	623.27	3.18	0.14
2005	2 124.30	1 057.68	195.83	813.26	6.37	0.16
2006	2 665.65	1 319.56	212.77	1 058.07	9.45	0.14
2007	3 284.80	1 659.44	228.77	1 273.71	20.55	0.17
2008	3 936.50	2 050.49	240.91	1 467.78	53.92	0.23
2009	3 251.28	1 647.82	175.38	1 252.87	69.78	0.13
2010	4 233.40	2 183.98	178.52	1 639.70	60.55	0.09

表7.2 主要年份上海关区进口总额
TOTAL IMPORT TRADE VOLUME THROUGH CUSTOMS IN MAIN YEARS

单位:亿美元 (100 million USD)

年份 Year	关区进口总额 Import Trade Volume Through Customs	其中 of which				
		#一般贸易 Oridinary Trade	#来料加工装配贸易 Processing and Assembly Trade with Customers' Materials	#进料加工贸易 Processing Trade with Imported Materials	#外商投资企业进口设备 Imported Equipment of Foreign Funded Enterprise	#租赁贸易 Leasing Trade
1990	86.27	51.79	2.40	19.70	6.11	
1995	225.30	93.79	13.49	65.96	45.16	0.11
1996	256.57	85.64	20.48	69.33	70.09	3.10
1997	252.32	83.02	27.64	79.79	45.86	3.65
1998	261.80	93.24	29.63	80.37	40.52	2.63
1999	318.63	137.56	35.72	82.84	30.36	4.55
2000	477.39	212.65	44.87	125.13	40.26	2.47
2001	524.81	245.94	47.38	123.39	47.46	2.45
2002	606.98	267.66	48.12	160.91	54.95	1.89
2003	888.95	377.21	54.47	243.24	66.32	2.36
2004	1 213.07	472.16	89.47	338.57	99.72	4.70
2005	1 382.48	502.49	133.69	409.30	74.76	7.85
2006	1 621.89	574.40	122.52	497.41	73.72	23.74
2007	1 924.29	719.30	154.88	528.03	75.22	24.46
2008	2 129.07	848.23	174.86	525.68	76.91	22.21
2009	1 903.61	883.20	121.40	428.62	38.92	4.36
2010	2 613.05	1 209.42	169.36	552.83	43.81	18.56

①本页数据由上海海关提供。
②自2008年起，原口岸进出口商品总额改为上海关区进出口总额。
❶Data on this page are provided by Shanghai Custom.
❷Since 2008, Total Volume of Port Imports and Exports have been changed to Total Trade Volume through Customs.

表7.3 主要年份按国别(地区)分的上海关区出口总额
TOTAL EXPORT TRADE VOLUME THROUGH CUSTOMS BY COUNTRIES AND REGIONS

单位:亿美元 (100 million USD)

国别(地区)	Country (Region)	2005	2009	2010
总计	**Total**	**2 124.30**	**3 251.28**	**4 233.40**
#亚洲	**Asia**	**898.90**	**1 303.43**	**1 653.96**
#中国香港	Hong Kong, China	160.72	169.74	210.46
中国台湾	Taiwan, China	59.81	80.79	112.52
日本	Japan	298.78	362.86	442.82
韩国	Republic of Korea	78.66	110.54	138.83
新加坡	Singapore	48.69	78.64	94.80
马来西亚	Malaysia	38.27	52.70	73.08
泰国	Thailand	22.39	41.53	61.18
菲律宾	Philippines	16.58	22.03	29.43
巴基斯坦	Pakistan	8.07	14.07	16.12
科威特	Kuwait	1.40	3.65	4.05
沙特阿拉伯	Saudi Arabia	8.84	18.65	19.22
阿拉伯联合酋长国	United Arab Emirates	23.24	39.26	44.97
非洲	**Africa**	**53.42**	**109.65**	**130.79**
#埃及	Egypt	5.89	10.59	12.11
苏丹	Sudan	2.35	4.22	4.39
欧洲	**Europe**	**505.52**	**819.17**	**1 095.67**
#德国	Germany	99.69	163.15	214.67
法国	France	44.84	89.37	110.42
意大利	Italy	42.81	70.87	118.34
荷兰	Netherlands	75.62	103.38	154.89
英国	United Kingdoms	59.10	94.92	117.88
瑞典	Sweden	9.42	13.49	20.26
俄罗斯	Russia	18.60	31.10	59.95
美洲	**America**	**618.05**	**932.43**	**1 234.11**
#美国	United States	501.11	711.71	910.54
加拿大	Canada	42.58	59.24	74.81
巴西	Brazil	14.61	45.19	75.44
智利	Chile	7.26	12.86	20.47
大洋洲及太平洋岛屿	**Oceanic and Pacific Island**	**48.41**	**86.60**	**118.87**
#澳大利亚	Australia	41.94	72.44	95.45
新西兰	New Zealand	5.50	7.81	9.87

注：本表数据由上海海关提供。
Note: Data in this table are provided by Shanghai Custom.

表 7.4 主要年份按国别(地区)分的上海关区进口总额
TOTAL IMPORT TRADE VOLUME THROUGH CUSTOMS BY COUNTRIES AND REGIONS IN MAIN YEARS

单位:亿美元(100 million USD)

国别(地区)	Country (Region)	2005	2009	2010
总 计	**Total**	**1 382.48**	**1 903.61**	**2 613.05**
亚 洲	**Asia**	**873.45**	**1 054.13**	**1 477.09**
#中国香港	Hong Kong, China	17.41	13.30	17.05
中国台湾	Taiwan, China	155.56	155.05	210.86
日 本	Japan	267.91	352.04	473.84
韩 国	Republic of Korea	163.95	177.53	279.87
新加坡	Singapore	44.30	35.25	51.61
马来西亚	Malaysia	43.88	53.06	117.63
泰 国	Thailand	36.53	50.75	63.19
菲律宾	Philippines	36.08	26.06	36.47
巴基斯坦	Pakistan	2.15	1.98	3.24
科威特	Kuwait	0.23	0.37	0.71
沙特阿拉伯	Saudi Arabia	4.01	5.68	8.28
阿拉伯联合酋长国	United Arab Emirates	0.95	1.27	1.85
非 洲	**Africa**	**13.76**	**26.92**	**41.85**
#埃 及	Egypt	0.44	1.12	1.31
南 非	South Africa	6.62	12.36	16.60
欧 洲	**Europe**	**264.89**	**461.14**	**619.42**
#德 国	Germany	103.93	173.95	248.28
法 国	France	28.81	45.92	53.72
意大利	Italy	23.91	36.07	51.07
荷 兰	Netherlands	8.17	11.74	15.19
英 国	United Kingdoms	15.62	24.56	37.69
瑞 典	Sweden	11.94	26.74	28.75
俄罗斯	Russia	8.30	18.23	22.93
美 洲	**America**	**202.70**	**319.04**	**420.66**
#美 国	United States	139.52	197.46	268.76
加拿大	Canada	14.89	18.80	27.89
巴 西	Brazil	13.08	18.99	19.03
智 利	Chile	18.42	54.97	63.82
大洋洲及太平洋岛屿	**Oceanic and Pacific Island**	**27.50**	**42.28**	**53.73**
#澳大利亚	Australia	23.79	35.61	45.35
新西兰	New Zealand	3.04	6.34	8.33
其 他	**Others**	**0.18**	**0.10**	**0.30**

注：本页数据由上海海关提供。
Note: Data on this page are provided by Shanghai Custom.

表7.5 主要年份上海市进出口总额
TOTAL VALUE OF FOREIGN TRADE IMPORTS AND EXPORTS IN MAIN YEARS

年 份 Year	上海市进出口总额（亿美元） Total Value of Foreign Trade Imports and Exports (100 million USD)	上海市进口总额（亿美元） Total Value of Foreign Trade Imports (100 million USD)	上海市出口总额（亿美元） Total Value of Foreign Trade Exports (100 million USD)	进出口差额（亿美元） Balance (100 million USD)	进出口总额相当于生产总值的比例(%) Foreign Trade Imports and Export as Percentage of Gross Domestic Product(%)	出口总额相当于生产总值的比例(%) Foreign Trade Export as Percentage of Gross Domestic Product(%)
1990	74.31	21.10	53.21	32.11	47.0	33.6
1995	190.25	74.48	115.77	41.29	63.6	38.7
1996	222.63	90.25	132.38	42.13	62.6	37.2
1997	247.64	100.40	147.24	46.84	59.7	35.5
1998	313.44	153.88	159.56	5.68	68.3	34.8
1999	386.04	198.19	187.85	-10.34	76.3	37.1
2000	547.10	293.56	253.54	-40.02	94.9	44.0
2001	608.98	332.70	276.28	-56.42	96.7	43.9
2002	726.64	406.09	320.55	-85.54	104.8	46.2
2003	1 123.97	639.15	484.82	-154.33	139.0	59.9
2004	1 600.26	865.06	735.20	-129.86	164.1	75.4
2005	1 863.65	956.23	907.42	-48.81	166.6	81.1
2006	2 274.89	1 139.16	1 135.73	-3.43	174.9	87.3
2007	2 829.73	1 390.45	1 439.28	48.83	179.3	91.2
2008	3 221.38	1 527.88	1 693.50	165.62	163.3	85.9
2009	2 777.31	1 358.17	1 419.14	60.97	127.3	65.1
2010	3 688.69	1 880.85	1 807.84	-73.01	148.0	72.5

注：1999年以前外贸进口、出口商品总额为外经贸委统计口径，1999年以后为海关统计的上海企业进口、出口总额(以下同)。
Note: Before 1999, the figures of Shanghai's foreign trade imports and exports were based on statistics from Shanghai Foreign Trade and Economic Cooperation Commission. Since 1999, the figures representing imports and exports are made by Shanghai enterprises through Shanghai Custom(Same as follows).

表7.6 主要年份上海市出口总额
TOTAL VALUE OF FOREIGN TRADE EXPORTS IN MAIN YEARS

单位:亿美元 (100 million USD)

指 标	Indicators	2000	2009	2010
出口总额	**Total Value of Exports**	**253.54**	**1 419.14**	**1 807.84**
按企业性质分	**Grouped by Different Enterprises**			
#国有企业	State-owned Enterprises	106.78	264.59	307.67
外商投资企业	Foreign-funded Enterprises	142.61	970.92	1 259.74
按贸易方式分	**Grouped by Trade**			
#一般贸易	Original Trade	101.72	488.62	632.74
加工贸易	Processing Trade	147.83	814.63	1 003.74
按产品类别分	**Grouped by Different Products**			
#机电产品	Electrical and Mechanical Products	121.43	1 025.63	1 311.14
#高新技术产品	High-tech Products		636.16	841.11

注：本页数据由上海海关提供。
Note: Data on this page are provided by Shanghai Custom.

表7.7 主要年份按国别(地区)分的上海市出口总额
TOTAL VALUE OF FOREIGN TRADE EXPORTS BY COUNTRIES AND REGIONS IN MAIN YEARS

单位:亿美元 (100 million USD)

国别(地区)	Country (Region)	2000	2009	2010
总　计	**Total**	**253.54**	**1 419.14**	**1 807.84**
亚　洲	**Asia**	**129.10**	**573.95**	**725.93**
#中国香港	Hong Kong, China	23.02	109.86	134.09
中国台湾	Taiwan, China	5.67	40.69	56.54
日　本	Japan	60.81	160.84	196.46
韩　国	Republic of Korea	10.59	46.90	58.92
新加坡	Singapore	7.88	48.43	59.01
马来西亚	Malaysia	2.59	30.04	42.52
泰　国	Thailand	2.48	14.51	24.14
巴基斯坦	Pakistan	0.55	2.39	3.08
科威特	Kuwait	0.20	1.18	1.53
沙特阿拉伯	Saudi Arabia	1.14	6.16	5.72
阿拉伯联合酋长国	United Arab Emirates	1.79	19.50	20.67
非　洲	**Africa**	**5.63**	**32.18**	**40.98**
#埃　及	Egypt	0.44	2.75	3.28
苏　丹	Sudan	0.22	0.50	1.21
阿尔及利亚	Algeria	0.09	1.21	1.29
摩洛哥	Morocco	0.20	0.94	0.97
欧　洲	**Europe**	**45.62**	**370.76**	**450.72**
#德　国	Germany	9.48	71.32	86.05
法　国	France	4.50	50.39	60.97
意大利	Italy	4.98	23.56	36.99
荷　兰	Netherlands	6.16	51.16	77.61
比利时	Belgium	2.95	13.67	16.70
英　国	United Kingdoms	7.07	35.17	43.11
俄罗斯	Russia	0.37	10.34	21.15
美　洲	**America**	**67.82**	**402.33**	**532.30**
#美　国	United States	56.25	320.94	409.91
加拿大	Canada	4.04	22.74	27.80
巴　西	Brazil	1.06	14.92	26.95
古　巴	Cuba	0.07	0.88	0.90
大洋洲及太平洋岛屿	**Oceanic and Pacific Island**	**5.37**	**39.92**	**57.91**
#澳大利亚	Australia	4.74	34.15	45.59

注：本表数据由上海海关提供。
Note: Data in this table are provided by Shanghai Custom.

表 7.8 主要年份按国别(地区)分的上海市进口总额
TOTAL VALUE OF FOREIGN TRADE IMPORTS BY COUNTRIES AND REGIONS IN MAIN YEARS

单位:亿美元 (100 million USD)

国别(地区)	Country (Region)	2000	2009	2010
总　计	**Total**	**293.56**	**1 358.17**	**1 880.85**
亚　洲	**Asia**	**161.59**	**746.55**	**1 041.98**
#中国香港	Hong Kong, China	16.68	9.91	12.61
中国台湾	Taiwan, China	19.44	111.23	150.05
日　本	Japan	70.43	225.96	308.71
韩　国	Republic of Korea	20.63	92.52	146.41
新加坡	Singapore	9.39	26.75	39.42
马来西亚	Malaysia	6.49	48.20	107.75
泰　国	Thailand	4.35	43.42	53.09
菲律宾	Philippines	1.83	23.19	33.44
科威特	Kuwait	0.22	0.40	0.94
沙特阿拉伯	Saudi Arabia	0.78	4.86	7.23
阿拉伯联合酋长国	United Arab Emirates	0.40	1.41	2.11
非　洲	**Africa**	**1.89**	**15.16**	**28.19**
欧　洲	**Europe**	**63.36**	**297.75**	**400.75**
#德　国	Germany	26.59	96.70	140.61
法　国	France	7.95	36.29	42.54
意大利	Italy	4.81	23.93	36.46
荷　兰	Netherlands	2.43	7.89	11.06
比利时	Belgium	2.83	17.49	25.08
英　国	United Kingdoms	3.76	16.45	23.43
瑞　士	Switzerland	2.22	21.89	29.87
瑞　典	Sweden	4.53	12.92	15.77
美　洲	**America**	**58.60**	**255.31**	**344.63**
#美　国	United States	40.11	150.91	202.75
加拿大	Canada	7.03	15.92	20.90
巴　西	Brazil	4.11	31.94	40.89
大洋洲及太平洋岛屿	**Oceanic and Pacific Island**	**8.07**	**43.37**	**65.13**
#澳大利亚	Australia	6.68	36.99	56.25
新西兰	New Zealand	1.25	5.00	7.48
其　他	**Others**	**0.05**	**0.03**	**0.17**

注：本表数据由上海海关提供。
Note: Data on this page are provided by Shanghai Custom.

表 7.9 主要年份进出口商品检验情况
IMPORTS AND EXPORTS INSPECTION IN MAIN YEARS

指 标	Indicators	2000	2009	2010
进口商品检验	**Imports Inspection**			
检验批数(批)	Groups of Inspection(group)	51 940	935 279	1 205 446
检验金额(亿美元)	Values of Inspection(100 million USD)	76.16	922.02	1 326.68
不合格批数(批)	Unqualified Groups (group)	1 539	3 339	5 562
占检验批数比重(%)	Percentage in Total (%)	3.0	0.4	0.5
不合格金额(亿美元)	Unqualified Values (100 million USD)	0.99	6.67	9.75
占检验金额比重(%)	Percentage in Total (%)	1.3	0.7	0.7
出口商品检验	**Exports Inspection**			
检验批数(批)	Groups of Inspection(group)	344 138	657 649	728 946
检验金额(亿美元)	Values of Inspection(100 million USD)	100.86	197.17	238.8
不合格批数(批)	Unqualified Groups (group)	564	182	202
不合格金额(亿美元)	Unqualified Values (100 million USD)	0.11	0.05	0.06

注：本表数据由市出入境检验检疫局提供。
Note: Data in this table are provided by Shanghai Entry-Exit Inspection and Quarantine Bureau.

表 7.10 主要年份直接吸收外资情况
FOREIGN DIRECT INVESTMENT IN MAIN YEARS

指 标	Indicators	2000	2009	2010
签订合同项目(个)	**Number of Signed Contracts (item)**	**1 814**	**3 090**	**3 906**
#合资经营	Joint Ventures	441	361	445
合作经营	Cooperative Ventures	226	7	14
独资经营	Sole-foreign Funded Enterprises	1 146	2 721	3 443
签订合同金额(亿美元)	**Contracted Foreign Capital (100 million USD)**	**63.90**	**133.01**	**153.07**
#合资经营	Joint Ventures	13.86	17.40	21.54
合作经营	Cooperative Ventures	5.86	3.73	1.11
独资经营	Sole-oreign Funded Enterprises	44.14	109.23	128.17
实际吸收外资金额(亿美元)	**Foreign Investment Actually Absorbed(100 million USD)**	**31.60**	**105.38**	**111.21**
#合资经营	Joint Ventures	12.94	16.16	17.84
合作经营	Cooperative Ventures	2.99	2.04	1.69
独资经营	Sole-foreign Funded Enterprises	15.67	87.18	90.71

注：本表部分数据由市商务委员会提供。
Note: Data in this table are provided by Shanghai Municipal Commission of Commerce.

表 7.11 外商直接投资合同项目和金额（2010）
NUMBER OF CONTRACTS SIGNED AND VALUES OF FOREIGN DIRECT INVESTMENT PROJECTS

类别	Types	签订合同项目(个) Number of Contracts Signed(item) 2010	至2010年底累计 Total by the End of 2010	签订合同金额(亿美元) Contracted Foreign Capital (100 million USD) 2010	至2010年底累计 Total by the End of 2010	实际吸收外资金额(亿美元) Foreign Investment Actually Absorbed (100 million USD) 2010	至2010年底累计 Total by the End of 2010
总　计	**Total**	**3 906**	**59 497**	**153.07**	**1 751.23**	**111.21**	**1 064.27**
#1 000 万美元以上项目	**Projects of Over 10 Million USD**	**203**		**125.65**			
#工　业	Industry	52		23.31			
按投资方式分	**Grouped by Investment Mode**						
#合资经营	Joint Ventures	445	16 583	21.54	415.16	17.84	315.92
合作经营	Cooperative Ventures	14	5 091	1.11	136.33	1.69	91.83
独资经营	Sole-foreign Funded Enterprises	3 443	37 744	128.17	1 157.30	90.71	627.80
按产业分	**Grouped by Industry**						
第一产业	Primary Industry	26	290	0.15	4.65	0.89	3.39
第二产业	Secondary Industry	372	25 644	28.85	802.59	22.01	445.24
#工　业	Industry	337	24 766	27.75	784.39	21.59	439.47
第三产业	Tertiary Industry	3 508	33 563	124.07	944.00	88.31	615.64
按主要国别（地区）分	**Grouped by Country and Region**						
#中国香港	Hong Kong, China	1 335	17 734	68.08	608.25	46.35	311.18
中国澳门	Macao, China	8	246	-0.06	4.01	0.08	1.59
中国台湾	Taiwan, China	399	6 564	1.56	53.33	1.00	37.65
日　本	Japan	566	8 155	12.98	178.5	10.10	131.91
韩　国	Republic of Korea	187	2 075	2.09	23.62	1.46	13.45
新加坡	Singapore	200	3 071	22.52	103.54	12.62	52.35
泰　国	Thailand	11	229	0.24	2.76	0.08	2.58
德　国	Germany	100	1 367	1.91	68.47	3.80	49.72
英　国	United Kingdoms	71	973	0.95	26.51	1.41	20.88
法　国	France	54	609	3.14	25.27	2.83	14.46
意大利	Italy	62	653	0.45	7.22	0.32	3.72
美　国	United States	297	6 622	3.59	129.21	4.47	89.33
加拿大	Canada	46	998	0.17	9.46	0.67	4.84
澳大利亚	Australia	44	1 079	0.54	11.52	0.43	5.94

注：本表数据由市商务委员会提供。
Note: Data in this table are provided by Shanghai Municipal Commission of Commerce.

表 7.12 主要年份引进技术设备实际到货金额
ARRIVED CAPITAL THROUGH IMPORTED TECHNOLOGY AND EQUIPMENT IN MAIN YEARS

单位:万美元(10 000 USD)

国 别(地区)	Country(Region)	2000	2009	2010
总 计	**Total**	**104 558**	**2 675 848**	**3 903 807**
#中国香港	Hong Kong, China	10 746	12 594	17 414
日 本	Japan	10 069	577 492	886 132
德 国	Germany	16 314	513 089	814 006
意大利	Italy	622	82 829	123 823
美 国	United States	49 431	356 433	427 275
瑞 士	Switzerland	1 862	84 424	126 605
英 国	United Kingdoms	712	59 876	85 649
瑞 典	Sweden	639	55 573	72 594
奥地利	Austria	1 162	19 897	31 804
法 国	France	1 926	111 585	98 172

注：本表数据由上海海关提供。
Note: Data in this table are provided by Shanghai Custom.

表 7.13 主要年份对外经济合作情况
ECONOMIC COOPERATION WITH FOREIGN COUNTRIES OR REGIONS IN MAIN YEARS

指 标	Indicators	2000	2009	2010
签订合同项目（个）	**Number of Contracted Projects (item)**	**1 076**	**7 480**	**7 532**
#对外承包工程	Overseas Contracted Projects	143	2 638	3 397
对外劳务合作	Overseas Labor Services Cooperation	836	4 842	4 135
签订合同金额（万美元）	**Value of Contract (10 000 USD)**	**98 050**	**1 240 205**	**1 066 977**
#对外承包工程	Overseas Contracted Projects	76 058	1 193 790	1 010 276
对外劳务合作	Overseas Labor Services Cooperation	20 837	46 415	56 701
实际营业额（万美元）	**Actual Business Volume (10 000 USD)**	**83 790**	**734 105**	**754 163**
#对外承包工程	Overseas Contracted Projects	61 906	665 664	689 616
对外劳务合作	Overseas Labor Services Cooperation	21 049	68 441	64 547
年末在外人员（人）	**Persons Abroad (year-end) (person)**	**30 052**	**26 250**	**26 847**
#对外承包工程	Overseas Contracted Projects	1 327	8 178	9 430
对外劳务合作	Overseas Labor Services Cooperation	28 710	18 072	17 417

注：本表数据由市商务委员会提供。
Note: Data in this table are provided by Shanghai Municipal Commission of Commerce.

表 7.14 海外企业情况(2009～2010)
ENTERPRISES ABROAD

指　标	Indicators	2009 年新增 Established in 2009	至 2009 年底累计 Total by the end of 2009	2010 年新增 Established in 2010	至 2010 年底累计 Total by the end of 2010
企业数(个)	Number of Enterprises (unit)	166	1 329	179	1 508
投资额(万美元)	Investment Value (10 000 USD)	153 644	526 266	242 029	768 295

表 7.15 国际会展(2009～2010)
INTERNATIONAL CONFERENCE AND EXHIBITION

指　标	Indicators	2009	2010
举办国际会展次数(次)	International Exhibit(time)	243	232
国际会展展出总面积(万平方米)	Total Square of International Exhibit(10 000 sq. m)	560.44	577.50

表 7.16 主要年份旅行社接待经营情况
TOURISTS RECEIVED BY TOUR AGENCIES IN MAIN YEARS

指　标	Indicators	2005	2009	2010
接待境内外来沪旅游者(万人次)	**Overseas and Domestic Tourists (10 000 person-times)**	**750.89**	**885.92**	**1 239.28**
境外旅游者	Overseas Tourists	95.11	88.44	158.25
#外国人	Foreigners	90.01	86.52	147.79
中国香港	Tourists from Hong Kong, China	1.48	0.66	4.47
中国澳门	Tourists from Macao, China	0.01	0.01	0.08
中国台湾	Tourists from Taiwan,China	3.51	1.25	5.91
境内旅游者	Domestic Tourists	655.88	797.48	1 081.03
出境旅游者(万人次)	**Tourists Going Abroad (10 000 person-times)**	**51.71**	**86.04**	**116.86**
经营和财务状况	**Operation and Financial Status**			
营业收入(亿元)	Operational Revenues(100 million yuan)	132.43	247.57	341.88
利润总额(亿元)	Total Profits(100 million yuan)	1.61	1.95	4.02

注：本表数据由市旅游局提供。
Note: Data in this table are provided by Shanghai Municipal Tourism Bureau.

表 7.17 主要年份旅游景点基本情况
BASIC STATISTICS OF SCENIC SPOTS IN MAIN YEARS

指 标	Indicators	2005	2009	2010
A 级旅游景点数(家)	Scenic Spots of A Level and above(unit)	18	50	61
#5A 级景点	AAAAA-Level		2	3
4A 级景点	AAAA-Level	17	25	28
红色旅游基地数(个)	Red Travelling Base(unit)		27	30
#全国红色旅游基地	National Red Travelling Base		4	8

注：本表数据由市旅游局提供。
Note: Data in this table are provided by Shanghai Municipal Tourism Bureau.

表 7.18 主要年份国内旅游者来沪人数和人均消费支出
NUMBER OF DOMESTIC TOURISTS VISITING SHANGHAI AND PER CAPITA CONSUMPTION EXPENDITURES IN MAIN YEARS

指 标	Indicators	2005	2009	2010
国内旅游者来沪人数(万人次)	**Number of Domestic Tourists Visiting Shanghai(10 000 person-times)**	**9 012**	**12 361**	**21 463**
外省市来沪旅游人数	Number of Tourists from other Provinces Visiting Shanghai	6 805	8 484	11 255
本市市民在本地旅游人数	Number of Local Tourists	2 207	3 877	10 208
国内旅游者人均消费支出（元）	**Consumption Expenditure Per Person（yuan）**	**1 452**	**1 548**	**1 175**
#长途交通费	Long-distance Traffic Expenditure	176	168	139
住宿费	Accommodation Expenditure	219	224	168
餐饮费	Food Expenditure	220	235	153
购物费	Shopping Expenditure	553	596	453
门票费	Ticket Expenditure	96	112	131
娱乐费	Entertainment Expenditure	30	57	42
市内交通费	Local Traffic Expenditure	88	81	53
邮电通信费	Post and Telecommunications Expenditure	37	27	14

注：本表为抽样调查资料。
Note: Data in this table are from the sampling survey.

表 7.19 旅游星级饭店基本情况(2010)
BASIC STATISTICS OF STAR-RATED TOURISM HOTELS

	指　标 Indicators	合　计 Total	五星级 Five-Star	四星级 Four-Star	三星级 Three-Star	二星级 Two-Star	一星级 One-Star
饭店数(个)	Number of Hotels(unit)	298	44	64	123	65	2
客房数(万间)	Number of Rooms (10 000 rooms)	6.51	1.96	2.04	1.97	0.53	0.01
床位数(万张)	Number of Beds (10 000 beds)	10.10	2.69	3.08	3.37	0.94	0.02
客房平均出租率(%)	Average Occupancy Rate (%)	65.7	68.0	66.5	63.1	63.9	52.0
营业收入(亿元)	Business Revenues (100 million yuan)	190.52	98.28	54.71	31.58	5.87	0.08
平均房价 (元/间天)	Average Room Rates (yuan/room. day)	686.30	1 136.25	607.52	371.83	269.28	178.06

注：本表数据由市旅游局提供。
Note: Data in this table are provided by Shanghai Municipal Tourism Bureau.

表 7.20 主要年份国际旅游入境人数
NUMBER OF OVERSEAS TOURISTS IN MAIN YEARS

	指　标 Indicators	2000	2009	2010
国际旅游入境人数(万人次)	**Number of Overseas Tourists Through Shanghai Custom(10 000 person-times)**	**181.40**	**628.92**	**851.12**
#外国人	Foreigner	139.14	489.74	665.63
#日　本	Japanese	53.76	124.38	152.47
新加坡	Singaporean	5.29	18.43	23.50
德　国	German	7.11	23.11	29.52
法　国	French	5.39	16.41	24.86
英　国	Briton	1.69	17.54	20.94
意大利	Italian	1.88	8.23	11.49
加拿大	Canadian	2.25	12.37	20.97
美　国	American	13.78	59.17	80.79
澳大利亚	Australian	3.23	14.08	21.33
港澳同胞	Hong Kong and Macao Chinese	17.62	54.05	77.47
台湾同胞	Taiwanese	19.88	85.13	108.02
平均每天来沪旅游人数(人次/天)	**Average Number of Tourists Visiting Shanghai Everyday (person-time/day)**	**4 970**	**17 231**	**23 382**
来沪旅游者平均逗留天数(天/人)	**Average Time Tourists Staying in Shanghai (day/person)**	**3.92**	**3.60**	**3.51**
国际旅游(外汇)收入(亿美元)	**Foreign Exchange Earnings from International Tourism(100 million USD)**	**16.13**	**47.96**	**64.05**

注：本表数据由市旅游局、市出入境边防检查总站等提供。
Note: Data in this table are provided by Shanghai Municipal Tourism Bureau, Shanghai Entry-Exit Inspection and Quarantine Bureau and ect.

上 / 海 / 统 / 计 / 年 / 鉴

主要统计指标解释

■ 关区进出口总额

指由海关统计的进出口商品总额。统计方法依据联合国的国际贸易统计原则，反映进出上海而引起物质资源储备增加或减少的商品运动。按上述原则应具备条件：实际进出上海（海关关境），不仅包括经商业交易行为的进出口货品，也包括援助、捐赠等未发生买卖关系的货品价值。出口按离岸价（FOB）统计，进口按到岸价（CIF）统计。

■ 上海市进出口总额

指海关统计中按经营单位即进出口企业在海关注册地的行政区域口径统计的数据，它反映的是上海行政辖区内各类具有进出口经营权企业（外贸企业）的进出口。它不包含外省市外贸企业途经上海口岸由上海海关结关放行及统计的进出口商品，但包含上海外贸企业经由非上海口岸进出口结关放行及统计的商品。

■ 外商直接投资

指外国企业和经济组织或个人（包括华侨、港澳台胞以及我国在境外注册的企业）按我国有关政策、法规，用现汇、实物、技术等在我国境内开办外商独资企业、与我国境内的企业或经济组织共同举办中外合资经营企业、合作经营企业或合作开发资源的投资（包括外商投资收益的再投资）以及企业投资总额内直接投资者对企业的贷款，即外方股东贷款（需在报告期内将相应合同及贷款协议报商务部备案核查）。

■ 引进技术

指通过贸易途径从国外获得发展我国国民经济和提高技术水平所需要的技术装备。引进方式有：许可证贸易（技术贸易）、生产线（包括成套设备）、单机（包括关键设备）、软硬件结合（同时引进技术和设备）和其他。

■ 对外承包工程

对外承包工程包括各对外承包公司以招标议标承包方式承揽的下列业务：(1) 承包国外工程建设项目。(2) 承包我国对外经济援助项目。(3) 承包我国驻外机构的工程建设项目。(4) 承包我国境内利用外资进行建设的工程项目。(5) 与外国承包公司合营或联合承包工程项目时我国公司分包部分。(6) 以服务成果向业主收费的技术服务项目（包括承担地形地貌测绘；地质资源勘探与普查；建设区域规划；提供设计文件、图纸、生产工艺技术资料和工程技术经济咨询；工程项目的可行性考察、研究和评估；进行技术指导和培训人员等）。(7) 对外承包兼营的房屋开发业务。对外承包工程的营业额是以货币表现的本期内完成的对外承包工程的工作量，包括以前年度签订的合同和本年度新签订的合同在报告期完成的工作量。

■ 对外劳务合作

指以收取工资的形式向业主或承包商提供技术和劳动服务的活动。上海对外承包公司在境外开办的合营企业，上海公司同时又提供劳务的，其劳务部分也纳入劳务合作统计。劳务合作营业额按报告期内向雇主提交的结算数（包括工资、加班费和奖金等）统计。

■ 国际旅游入境人数

指来上海参观、访问、旅行、探亲、访友、休养、考察、参加会议和从事经济、科技、文化、教育、体育、宗教等活动的外国人、华侨、港澳和台湾同胞的人数。不包括来上海常住1年以上的外国专家、留学生等。上海入境的境外旅游人数包括从上海口岸入境的境外旅游人数和从我国其他口岸入境的境外旅游人数。

■ 国际旅游（外汇）收入

指入境旅游的外国人、华侨、港澳台同胞在上海旅游过程中发生的一切旅游支出。

SHANGHAI STATISTICAL YEARBOOK

EXPLANATORY NOTES TO MAJOR STATISTICAL INDICATORS

□ Total Trade Volume Through Customs

Total Trade Volume through Customes refers to the aggregate volume of commodities that are imported or exported through Shanghai's ports. The statistics method follows the international trade statistics principles set by the United Nations. It reflects the fluctuation of Shanghai's material reserves caused by export or import. Requirements involved in the principle is: the commodities refer to those enter or leave Shanghai's ports, including not only the business trading activities but also the commodities value of the aid and donations that haven't been involved in sales . Exports are calculated according to FOB price, and imports are calculated according to CIF.

□ The Value of Foreign Trade Imports and Exports of Shanghai

Total Value of Foreign Trade Imports and Exports of Shanghai is offered by Customs authorities, covering the operation units, or the enterprises involved in import and export, that have registered in the administrative regions where the Customs operate. It reflects the import and export of all the enterprises with import and export rights (foreign trade enterprises) under the administration of Shanghai Municipality. It excludes those commodities of foreign trade enterprises from out of town that underwent customs clearance at Shanghai ports but includes commodities of foreign trade enterprises of Shanghai that underwent customs clearance in non-Shanghai ports.

□ Foreign Direct Investment

Foreign Direct Investment refers to the investments made inside China by foreign enterprises and economic organizations or individuals (including overseas Chinese, compatriots in Hong Kong, Macao and Chinese enterprises registered abroad), in line with the relevant policies and laws of China, for the establishment of wholly foreign-owned enterprises, and joint ventures or development projects launched in China (including re-investment of profits from foreign businesses), and the funds that enterprises borrow from abroad in the total investment of projects which are approved by the relevant departments of the governments and the loans from the direct investors within the total investment of the projects, i.e., foreign shareholders' loans. (The related contracts and loans agreements in the report period should be filed with the Ministry of Commerce)

□ Import of Technology

Import of Technology refers to technology and equipments obtained through the trade channel from other countries which are needed for advancing China's national economy and improving its technological level. The import form includes: licensing (technological trade), production lines (including complete plant), single machine (including key equipments), combination of hardware and software (importing technology and equipments simultaneously) and others.

□ Overseas Contracted Projects

Overseas Contracted Projects refer to projects undertaken by Chinese contractors (project contracting companies) through bidding process. They include: (1) overseas civil engineering construction projects financed by foreign investors. (2) overseas projects financed by the Chinese government through its foreign-aid programs. (3) construction projects of Chinese diplomatic missions, trade offices and other institutions stationed abroad. (4) construction projects in China financed by foreign investment. (5) sub-contracted projects to be taken by Chinese contractors through a joint umbrella project with foreign contractor (s). (6) technical assistance projects in the form of service results and chargeable to the owners (such as topographic surveying, geological prospecting, development zone programming, provision of documents, blueprint, materials on production process, technical consultation, project feasibility studies and evaluation, personnel training, etc.). and (7) housing development projects. The business turnover from international contracting is the work of contracted projects completed during the reporting period, expressed in monetary terms, including completed work on project contracts signed in previous years.

□ Overseas Labor Service Cooperation

Overseas Labor Service Cooperation refers to activities of providing technology and labor services to employers or contractors by collecting salaries and wages. Labor services provided by Shanghai's international contrasting corporations to their overseas

EXPLANATORY NOTES TO MAJOR STATISTICAL INDICATORS

joint ventures shall be included into the statistics of overseas services. The business turn over of overseas labor services is the settlement price (including salaries, overtime pay and bonuses) submitted to the employers during the reporting period.

□ Number of Overseas Tourists to Shanghai

Number of Overseas Tourists to Shanghai refers to the number of foreigners, overseas Chinese, and compatriots from Hong Kong, Macao and Taiwan coming to Shanghai for sightseeing, visits, tours, family reunions, meeting friends, vacations, study tours, attending meetings and other activities of an economic, scientific and technological, cultural, physical culture and religious nature. This does not include foreign experts and students residing in Shanghai for over 1 year. The number of overseas tourists to Shanghai includes those overseas tourists entering China through Shanghai customs and through customs other than Shanghai.

□ Foreign Exchange Earnings from International Tourism

Foreign Exchange Earnings from International Tourism refer to the total expenditures of foreigners, overseas Chinese, Chinese compatriots from Hong Kong, Macao and Taiwan during their stay in Shanghai.

第八篇

CHAPTER 8

价 格 水 平

PRICES

表 8.1　居民消费价格和商品零售价格指数（1978～2010）
OVERALL RESIDENTS CONSUMER PRICE INDEX AND RETAIL PRICE INDEX

年　份 Year	居民消费价格指数 Overall Residents Consumer Price Index		年　份 Year	商品零售价格指数 Retail Price Index	
	以上年价格为 100 preceding year = 100	以 1978 年价格为 100 1978 = 100		以上年价格为 100 preceding year = 100	以 1978 年价格为 100 1978 = 100
1978	100.5	100.0	1978	100.1	100.0
1979	100.9	100.9	1979	101.0	101.0
1980	105.9	106.9	1980	106.5	107.6
1981	101.4	108.3	1981	101.5	109.2
1982	100.3	108.7	1982	100.3	109.5
1983	100.2	108.9	1983	100.1	109.6
1984	102.2	111.3	1984	102.2	112.0
1985	115.2	128.2	1985	116.4	130.4
1986	106.3	136.3	1986	106.7	139.1
1987	108.1	147.3	1987	108.8	151.4
1988	120.1	176.9	1988	121.3	183.6
1989	115.9	205.1	1989	116.7	214.3
1990	106.3	218.0	1990	104.8	224.6
1991	110.5	240.9	1991	109.5	245.9
1992	110.0	265.0	1992	109.7	269.8
1993	120.2	318.5	1993	117.5	317.0
1994	123.9	394.6	1994	117.5	372.4
1995	118.7	468.4	1995	113.0	420.9
1996	109.2	511.5	1996	105.0	441.9
1997	102.8	525.8	1997	98.8	436.6
1998	100.0	525.8	1998	95.1	415.2
1999	101.5	533.7	1999	97.3	404.0
2000	102.5	547.0	2000	96.4	389.5
2001	100.0	547.0	2001	98.6	384.0
2002	100.5	549.8	2002	98.7	379.0
2003	100.1	550.3	2003	99.0	375.4
2004	102.2	562.2	2004	100.9	378.8
2005	101.0	567.6	2005	99.4	376.7
2006	101.2	574.5	2006	100.2	377.4
2007	103.2	592.6	2007	102.4	386.5
2008	105.8	626.8	2008	105.3	407.1
2009	99.6	624.3	2009	99.4	404.8
2010	103.1	643.6	2010	101.7	411.7

注：本表数据由国家统计局上海调查总队提供。
Note: Data on this table are provided by Survey Office of the National Bureau of Statistics in Shanghai.

表 8.2 居民消费价格指数(1991～2010, 以 1990 年价格为 100)
OVERALL RESIDENTS CONSUMER PRICE INDEX (1990 = 100)

年 份 Year	居民消费价格指数 Overall Residents Consumer Price Index	食 品 Food	烟酒及用品 Cigarettes, Liquors and Related Items	衣 着 Clothing
1991	110.5	113.5	103.0	105.7
1992	121.6	128.7	113.0	115.7
1993	146.1	157.2	124.5	137.3
1994	181.0	207.1	139.5	158.8
1995	214.9	261.2	149.1	172.8
1996	234.6	288.6	149.1	187.8
1997	241.2	288.6	134.6	189.9
1998	241.2	282.3	129.2	178.5
1999	244.8	274.9	129.8	175.5
2000	250.9	270.0	126.1	167.2
2001	250.9	270.8	124.7	165.4
2002	252.2	278.6	123.4	161.2
2003	252.5	282.3	123.1	157.2
2004	257.8	305.6	121.0	148.1
2005	260.3	319.4	120.6	136.4
2006	263.4	327.5	120.9	145.2
2007	271.7	358.3	121.7	147.1
2008	287.4	413.1	123.7	149.5
2009	286.3	421.6	124.7	148.5
2010	295.2	454.1	126.1	146.4

注：本表数据由国家统计局上海调查总队提供。
Note: Data on this table are provided by Survey Office of the National Bureau of Statistics in Shanghai.

表 8.2 续表 continued

年 份 Year	家庭设备用品及维修服务 Home Appliances and Repair Service	医疗保健和个人用品 Medicine, Medical Services and Personal Aricles	交通和通信 Transportation and Communication	娱乐教育文化用品及服务 Recreation, Education and Culture Articles	居 住 Residence
1991	112.5	113.1	108.5	96.9	129.3
1992	115.4	132.7	108.9	93.8	153.9
1993	126.4	151.8	127.5	115.7	206.8
1994	140.2	180.9	149.5	136.1	249.4
1995	145.5	199.0	171.5	158.2	300.0
1996	144.2	210.9	181.9	187.6	329.1
1997	131.8	215.4	210.3	205.6	396.9
1998	121.9	219.5	218.1	218.6	450.9
1999	117.5	223.6	245.1	244.1	477.5
2000	112.5	223.4	271.9	296.6	493.3
2001	109.3	217.6	266.7	302.8	504.6
2002	106.8	212.4	258.4	305.3	504.6
2003	105.1	212.4	248.9	306.2	510.2
2004	102.8	212.2	240.4	306.0	518.5
2005	103.6	212.9	234.3	300.8	533.7
2006	106.4	215.2	227.8	295.5	549.2
2007	109.9	215.7	220.8	287.4	573.9
2008	119.0	222.5	215.3	282.3	588.4
2009	120.8	221.3	210.0	276.5	568.1
2010	122.1	229.5	204.5	279.0	587.9

表8.3 居民消费价格指数(1991～2010，以上年价格为100)
OVERALL RESIDENTS CONSUMER PRICE INDEX (PRECEDING YEAR＝100)

年 份 Year	居民消费价格指数 Overall Residents Consumer Price Index	食 品 Food	烟酒及用品 Cigarettes, Liquors and Related Items	衣 着 Clothing
1991	110.5	113.5	103.0	105.7
1992	110.0	113.4	109.7	109.5
1993	120.2	122.1	110.2	118.6
1994	123.9	131.8	112.0	115.7
1995	118.7	126.1	106.9	108.8
1996	109.2	110.5	100.0	108.7
1997	102.8	100.0	90.3	101.1
1998	100.0	97.8	96.0	94.0
1999	101.5	97.4	100.4	98.3
2000	102.5	98.2	97.2	95.3
2001	100.0	100.3	98.9	98.9
2002	100.5	102.9	98.9	97.5
2003	100.1	101.3	99.8	97.5
2004	102.2	108.3	98.3	94.2
2005	101.0	104.5	99.7	92.1
2006	101.2	102.5	100.2	106.4
2007	103.2	109.4	100.7	101.3
2008	105.8	115.3	101.7	101.6
2009	99.6	102.1	100.8	99.3
2010	103.1	107.7	101.1	98.6

注：本表数据由国家统计局上海调查总队提供。
Note: Data on this table are provided by Survey Office of the National Bureau of Statistics in Shanghai.

表8.3 续表 continued

年 份 Year	家庭设备用品及维修服务 Home Appliances and Repair Service	医疗保健和个人用品 Medicine, Medical Services and Personal Aricles	交通和通信 Transportation and Communication	娱乐教育文化用品及服务 Recreation, Education and Culture Articles	居 住 Residence
1991	112.5	113.1	108.5	96.9	129.3
1992	102.6	117.3	100.4	96.8	119.0
1993	109.5	114.4	117.0	123.4	134.4
1994	110.9	119.2	117.3	117.6	120.6
1995	103.8	110.0	114.7	116.2	120.3
1996	99.1	106.0	106.1	118.6	109.7
1997	91.4	102.1	115.6	109.6	120.6
1998	92.5	101.9	103.7	106.3	113.6
1999	96.4	101.9	112.4	111.7	105.9
2000	95.7	99.9	110.9	121.5	103.3
2001	97.2	97.4	98.1	102.1	102.3
2002	97.7	97.6	96.9	100.8	100.0
2003	98.4	100.0	96.3	100.3	101.1
2004	97.8	100.0	96.5	99.9	101.6
2005	100.8	100.3	97.5	98.3	102.9
2006	102.7	101.1	97.3	98.2	102.9
2007	103.3	100.2	96.9	97.3	104.5
2008	108.3	103.1	97.5	98.2	102.5
2009	101.5	99.4	97.5	98.0	96.6
2010	101.1	103.7	97.4	100.9	103.5

表8.4 主要年份居民消费价格指数(以上年价格为100)
CLASSIFIED RESIDENTS CONSUMER PRICE INDEX IN MAIN YEARS(PRECEDING YEAR = 100)

类 别	Types	2001	2009	2010
居民消费价格指数	**Overall Residents Consumer Price Index**	**100.0**	**99.6**	**103.1**
#服务项目价格	Services Items Price	105.4	97.5	102.0
食 品	**Food**	**100.3**	**102.1**	**107.7**
粮 食	Grain	102.9	103.7	112.0
淀 粉	Starch	103.6	106.0	95.5
干豆类及豆制品	Dry Beans and Bean Products	95.6	100.2	108.7
油 脂	Oil or Fat	84.5	80.3	105.6
肉禽及其制品	Meat Poultry and Their Products	99.3	95.5	104.3
蛋	Eggs	102.4	103.0	106.1
水产品	Aquatic Products	100.1	105.4	116.4
菜	Vegetables	108.9	116.5	111.0
#鲜 菜	Fresh Vegetables	110.2	117.6	111.5
调味品	Flavoring	99.2	104.0	106.5
糖	Sugars	101.4	101.3	103.8
茶及饮料	Tea and Beverages	98.4	103.0	103.9
干鲜瓜果	Dried and Fresh Fruits	104.3	100.3	112.0
#鲜瓜果	Fresh Fruits	105.8	101.6	113.9
糕点饼干	Cakes,Biscuits and Bread	100.5	102.8	100.5
液体乳及乳制品	Milk and Its Products	100.8	100.5	102.3
在外用膳食品	Dining Out	98.0	101.8	105.6
其他食品	Other Food	99.2	99.3	105.0
烟酒及用品	**Cigarettes,Liquors and Related Items**	**98.9**	**100.8**	**101.1**
烟 草	Tobacco	99.2	100.4	101.0
酒	Liquors	98.2	100.8	101.6
吸烟饮酒用品	Cigarettes and Spirits Related Items	100.0	104.5	100.9
衣 着	**Clothing**	**98.9**	**99.3**	**98.6**
服 装	Garments	96.4	99.4	99.9
男式服装	Men'Wear	99.0	99.4	102.8
女式服装	Women's Wear	94.7	99.8	98.3
儿童服装	Children's Wear	95.4	96.2	93.6
衣着材料	Clothing Materials	98.7	102.9	102.9
鞋袜帽	Shoes, Socks and Hats	106.2	98.3	93.6
#鞋	Shoes	106.6	97.6	92.4
衣着加工服务	Garment Processing Service	100.0	103.3	107.2

注：本表数据由国家统计局上海调查总队提供。
Note: Data on this table are provided by Survey Office of the National Bureau of Statistics in Shanghai.

表8.4 续表 continued

类　别	Types	2001	2009	2010
家庭设备用品及维修服务	**Home Appliances and Repair Service**	**97.2**	**101.5**	**101.1**
耐用消费品	Durable Consumer Goods	94.7	100.0	99.6
室内装饰品	Interior Decorations	101.0	99.0	99.2
床上用品	Bed Articles	100.5	99.9	104.2
家庭日用杂品	Daily Use Household Articles	98.6	103.3	99.4
家庭服务及加工维修服务	Other Daily Use Articles	100.0	106.1	108.8
医疗保健和个人用品	**Medicine, Medical Services and Personal Aricles**	**97.4**	**99.4**	**103.7**
医疗保健	Medicine and Medical Services	96.5	101.0	100.8
#中药材及中成药	Herbs and Ready-made Traditional Chinese Medicine	105.5	101.5	105.5
西　药	Western Medicine	92.0	100.3	99.6
保健器具及用品	Healthcare Equipment	95.4	99.8	98.6
医疗保健服务	Medical and Healthcare Service	100.0	102.5	103.7
个人用品及服务	Personal Aricles and Service	99.8	97.7	107.1
交通和通信	**Transportation and Communication**	**98.1**	**97.5**	**97.4**
交　通	Transport	102.3	99.7	98.7
#交通工具	Transport Tools	97.9	99.7	99.5
通　信	Communications	94.4	94.4	95.3
通信工具	Communications Tools	69.7	64.6	71.4
通信服务	Communications Service	103.1	100.7	100.0
娱乐教育文化用品及服务	**Recreation, Education and Culture Articles**	**102.1**	**98.0**	**100.9**
文娱用耐用消费品及服务	Durable Consumer Goods for Recreational Use	91.2	82.8	89.4
教　育	Education	109.6	102.1	101.2
文化娱乐类	Recreation and Culture Articles	105.2	104.2	101.0
旅　游	Tourism	96.2	93.9	115.9
居　住	**Residence**	**102.3**	**96.6**	**103.5**
建房及装修材料	Construction and Decoration Materials	97.5	100.8	102.1
租　房	Reriting	111.0	98.1	106.8
自有住房	Self-owned House	99.8	81.3	103.0
水电燃料	Water, Electricity and Fuels	101.7	106.4	103.8
#水	Water	109.3	111.5	123.6
电	Electricity	100.0	100.0	100.0
液化石油气	LPG	118.4	89.3	117.2
管道煤气	Gas	100.0	117.2	100.0

表8.5 主要年份商品零售价格指数 (以上年价格为 100)
CLASSIFIED RETAIL PRICE INDEX IN MAIN YEARS (PRECEDING YEAR = 100)

类别	Types	2001	2009	2010
商品零售价格指数	**Overall Retail Price Index**	**98.6**	**99.4**	**101.7**
食　品	Food	98.4	102.0	107.6
粮　食	Grain	100.1	103.7	112.0
淀　粉	Starch	100.4	106.0	95.5
干豆类及豆制品	Dry Beans and Bean Products	111.3	100.2	108.7
油　脂	Oil or Fat	81.4	80.3	105.6
肉禽及其制品	Meat Poultry and Their Products	100.4	95.6	104.2
蛋	Eggs	110.7	103.0	106.1
水产品	Aquatic Products	90.1	105.2	116.1
菜	Vegetables	107.1	116.5	111.0
调味品	Flavoring	99.5	104.0	106.5
糖	Sugars	104.4	101.3	103.8
干鲜瓜果	Dried and Fresh Fruits	107.3	100.3	112.1
糕点饼干面包	Cakes, Biscuits and Bread	99.8	102.8	100.5
液体乳及乳制品	Milk and Its Products	99.8	100.4	102.3
在外用膳食品	Dining Out	100.7	101.8	105.6
其他食品	Other Food	99.5	99.3	105.0
饮料、烟酒	Beverages, Tobacco and Liquor	98.4	101.2	101.9
服装、鞋帽	Garments, Shoes and Hats	107.7	99.2	98.4
纺织品	Textiles	98.8	100.5	103.9
家用电器及音像器材	Household Appliances and Audio-video Appliances	95.0	90.8	92.4
文化办公用品	Cultural Office Articles	98.7	93.9	97.7
日用品	Daily Use Articles	99.0	102.4	100.3
体育娱乐用品	Sports and Recreation Goods	99.1	92.1	95.9
交通、通信用品	Transportation and Communication Goods	97.4	91.1	94.0
家　具	Furniture	90.4	99.9	101.1
化妆品	Cosmetics	100.7	100.5	101.0
金银珠宝	Jewelry	87.2	98.6	111.7
中西药品及医疗保健用品	Traditional Chinese and Western Medicines	98.7	100.6	99.8
书报杂志及电子出版物	Newspapers and Magazines and Electronic Publications	99.5	111.4	103.2
燃　料	Fuels	111.4	102.1	112.8
建筑材料及五金电料	Building Materials and Hardwares	101.8	97.9	103.3

注：本表数据由国家统计局上海调查总队提供。
Note: Data on this table are provided by Survey Office of the National Bureau of Statistics in Shanghai.

表8.6 工业品出厂价格指数（2001～2010,以2000年价格为100）
PRODUCER PRICE INDEX OF INDUSTRIAL PRODUCTS(2000＝100)

类别	Types	2001	2002	2003	2004	2005
工业品出厂价格指数	**Producer Price Index of Industrial Products**	**96.7**	**93.2**	**94.5**	**97.9**	**99.6**
按轻重工业分	**Grouped by Light or Heavy Industries**					
轻工业	Light Industry	97.8	94.9	94.1	95.0	95.6
以农产品为原料	Using Farm Products as Raw Materials	99.8	98.7	99.7	102.9	103.3
以非农产品为原料	Using Non-farm Products as Raw Materials	95.4	90.5	89.0	88.8	89.4
重工业	Heavy Industry	96.1	92.4	95.1	99.9	102.2
采掘	Mining and Guarrying	100.0	100.4	113.1	134.9	168.0
原料	Raw Material	98.7	96.8	104.5	118.2	129.7
加工	Manufacturing	94.7	90.0	90.8	92.9	92.8
按用途分	**Grouped by Use**					
生产资料	Means of Production	96.3	92.3	95.2	101.0	104.2
生活资料	Consumer Goods	97.3	94.7	92.9	91.7	90.5
#食品	Food	102.6	105.3	105.4	106.8	107.4
衣着	Clothing	99.6	99.4	99.1	101.6	103.0
一般日用品	Non-Durable Consumer Goods	97.2	94.4	93.7	94.9	95.6
耐用消费品	Durable Consumer Goods	95.1	90.1	86.6	81.9	78.4
按工业部门分	**Grouped by Sector**					
冶金工业	Metallurgy Industry	98.4	95.2	107.1	126.8	138.6
电力工业	Electric Power Industry	100.2	99.8	99.1	101.0	102.3
煤碳及炼焦工业	Coal and Coling Industry	103.8	108.7	126.5	142.1	143.4
石油工业	Petroleum Industry	99.8	97.5	113.4	131.9	159.2
化学工业	Chemical Industry	96.2	92.6	95.7	103.5	110.6
机械工业	Machinery Industry	93.6	88.2	85.2	82.9	80.5
建筑材料工业	Building Material Industry	102.2	98.5	98.7	104.5	99.1
森林工业	Forest Industry	97.6	94.0	92.3	90.9	91.9
食品工业	Food Industry	102.8	105.2	107.0	111.4	113.1
纺织工业	Textile Industry	96.2	91.2	94.1	97.6	97.2
缝纫工业	Sewing Industry	99.1	98.9	98.7	101.3	102.8
皮革工业	Leather Industry	100.7	99.5	98.9	99.2	99.1
造纸工业	Paper Making Industry	97.8	92.6	90.8	90.1	88.7
文教艺术用品工业	Cultural Educational and Art Goods	96.9	95.9	95.1	94.1	93.8
其他工业	Others Industry	100.5	105.5	107.1	112.6	114.4

①采掘业工业品出厂价格指数以2001年价格为100计算。
②本表数据由国家统计局上海调查总队提供。
❶The prices of minging and quarrying industry in 2001 are set at 100.
❷Date in this table are provided by Survey Office of the National Bureau of Statistics in Shanghai.

表 8.6 续表 continued

	类 别 Types	2006	2007	2008	2009	2010
工业品出厂价格指数	**Producer Price Index of Industrial Products**	**100.2**	**101.4**	**103.6**	**97.2**	**99.4**
按轻重工业分	**Grouped by Light or Heavy Industries**					
轻工业	Light Industry	94.5	94.5	93.6	88.7	86.1
以农产品为原料	Using Farm Products as Raw Materials	103.9	107.1	111.0	112.2	115.1
以非农产品为原料	Using Non-farm Products as Raw Materials	87.8	87.0	85.2	79.3	75.8
重工业	Heavy Industry	104.7	107.1	112.7	104.7	111.9
采 掘	Mining and Guarrying	192.7	195.6	246.1	203.0	237.3
原 料	Raw Material	140.3	145.9	161.5	148.3	173.2
加 工	Manufacturing	93.1	94.7	97.4	91.1	93.7
按用途分	**Grouped by Use**					
生产资料	Means of Production	105.5	107.0	109.7	101.0	103.7
生活资料	Consumer Goods	89.5	89.7	90.9	91.4	92.0
#食 品	Food	107.9	113.1	119.1	121.5	126.8
衣 着	Clothing	103.4	105.2	107.5	107.8	108.4
一般日用品	Non-Durable Consumer Goods	96.5	97.5	99.6	101.5	103.2
耐用消费品	Durable Consumer Goods	74.8	71.5	69.5	68.5	66.9
按工业部门分	**Grouped by Sector**					
冶金工业	Metallurgy Industry	144.3	156.0	168.5	141.4	161.9
电力工业	Electric Power Industry	103.1	103.6	105.7	109.4	111.0
煤碳及炼焦工业	Coal and Coling Industry	144.8	163.3	226.3	212.5	229.1
石油工业	Petroleum Industry	182.3	188.9	226.5	217.2	262.4
化学工业	Chemical Industry	112.8	116.2	121.2	110.0	122.4
机械工业	Machinery Industry	79.0	77.3	75.7	71.3	68.6
建筑材料工业	Building Material Industry	95.5	97.0	102.5	99.9	102.9
森林工业	Forest Industry	92.8	95.2	97.8	98.2	93.7
食品工业	Food Industry	114.2	120.7	127.8	129.5	135.7
纺织工业	Textile Industry	97.8	98.3	97.9	99.4	102.8
缝纫工业	Sewing Industry	103.0	105.0	107.3	107.6	108.4
皮革工业	Leather Industry	99.9	100.0	100.5	99.7	99.5
造纸工业	Paper Making Industry	88.3	88.5	91.9	97.1	97.6
文教艺术用品工业	Cultural Educational and Art Goods	92.1	91.3	92.3	91.7	92.2
其他工业	Others Industry	120.2	122.8	131.9	135.7	148.3

表8.7 工业品出厂价格指数(2002～2010，以上年价格为100)
PRODUCER PRICE INDEX OF INDUSTRIAL PRODUCTS IN MAIN YEARS (PRECEDING YEAR = 100)

类 别	Types	2002	2003	2004	2005
工业品出厂价格指数	**Producer Price Index of Industrial Products**	**96.4**	**101.4**	**103.6**	**101.7**
按轻重工业分	**Grouped by Light or Heavy Industries**				
轻工业	Light Industry	97.0	99.2	101.0	100.6
以农产品为原料	Using Farm Products as Raw Materials	98.9	101.0	103.2	100.4
以非农产品为原料	Using Non-farm Products as Raw Materials	94.9	98.3	99.8	100.7
重工业	Heavy Industry	96.1	102.9	105.0	102.3
采 掘	Mining and Guarrying	100.4	112.6	119.3	124.5
原 料	Raw Material	98.1	108.0	113.1	109.7
加 工	Manufacturing	95.0	100.9	102.3	99.9
按用途分	**Grouped by Use**				
生产资料	Means of Production	95.8	103.1	106.1	103.2
生活资料	Consumer Goods	97.3	98.1	98.7	98.7
#食 品	Food	102.6	100.1	101.3	100.6
衣 着	Clothing	99.8	99.7	102.5	101.4
一般日用品	Non-Durable Consumer Goods	97.1	99.3	101.3	100.7
耐用消费品	Durable Consumer Goods	94.7	96.1	94.6	95.7
按工业部门分	**Grouped by Sector**				
冶金工业	Metallurgy Industry	96.7	112.5	118.4	109.3
电力工业	Electric Power Industry	99.6	99.3	101.9	101.3
煤碳及炼焦工业	Coal and Coking Industry	104.7	116.4	112.3	100.9
石油工业	Petroleum Industry	97.7	116.3	116.3	120.7
化学工业	Chemical Industry	96.3	103.4	108.2	106.9
机械工业	Machinery Industry	94.2	96.6	97.3	97.1
建筑材料工业	Building Material Industry	96.4	100.2	105.9	94.8
森林工业	Forest Industry	96.3	98.2	98.5	101.1
食品工业	Food Industry	102.3	101.7	104.1	101.5
纺织工业	Textile Industry	94.8	103.2	103.7	99.6
缝纫工业	Sewing Industry	99.8	99.8	102.6	101.5
皮革工业	Leather Industry	98.8	99.4	100.3	99.9
造纸工业	Paper Making Industry	94.7	98.1	99.2	98.5
文教艺术用品工业	Cultural Educational and Art Goods	99.0	99.2	99.0	99.7
其他工业	Other Industry	105.0	101.5	105.1	101.6

注：本表数据由国家统计局上海调查总队提供。
Note: Data on this table are provided by Survey Office of the National Bureau of Statistics in Shanghai.

表8.7 续表 continued

	类别 Types	2006	2007	2008	2009	2010
工业品出厂价格指数	**Producer Price Index of Industrial Products**	**100.6**	**101.2**	**102.2**	**93.8**	**102.3**
按轻重工业分	**Grouped by Light or Heavy Industries**					
轻工业	Light Industry	98.8	100.0	99.1	94.8	97.1
以农产品为原料	Using Farm Products as Raw Materials	100.6	103.1	103.6	101.1	102.6
以非农产品为原料	Using Non-farm Products as Raw Materials	98.2	99.1	97.9	93.1	95.6
重工业	Heavy Industry	102.4	102.3	105.2	92.9	106.9
采　掘	Mining and Guarrying	114.7	101.5	125.8	82.5	116.9
原　料	Raw Material	108.2	104.0	110.7	91.8	116.8
加　工	Manufacturing	100.3	101.7	102.8	93.5	102.9
按用途分	**Grouped by Use**					
生产资料	Means of Production	101.2	101.4	102.5	92.1	102.7
生活资料	Consumer Goods	98.9	100.2	101.3	100.6	100.7
#食　品	Food	100.5	104.8	105.3	102.0	104.4
衣　着	Clothing	100.4	101.7	102.2	100.3	100.6
一般日用品	Non-Durable Consumer Goods	100.9	101.0	102.2	101.9	101.7
耐用消费品	Durable Consumer Goods	95.4	95.6	97.2	98.5	97.6
按工业部门分	**Grouped by Sector**					
冶金工业	Metallurgy Industry	104.1	108.1	108.0	83.9	114.5
电力工业	Electric Power Industry	100.8	100.5	102.0	103.5	101.5
煤碳及炼焦工业	Coal and Coking Industry	101.0	112.8	138.6	93.9	107.8
石油工业	Petroleum Industry	114.5	103.6	119.9	95.9	120.8
化学工业	Chemical Industry	102.0	103.0	104.3	90.8	111.3
机械工业	Machinery Industry	98.1	97.8	97.9	94.2	96.2
建筑材料工业	Building Material Industry	96.4	101.6	105.7	97.5	103.0
森林工业	Forest Industry	101.0	102.6	102.7	100.4	95.4
食品工业	Food Industry	101.0	105.7	105.9	101.3	104.8
纺织工业	Textile Industry	100.6	100.5	99.6	101.5	103.4
缝纫工业	Sewing Industry	100.2	101.9	102.2	100.3	100.7
皮革工业	Leather Industry	100.8	100.1	100.5	99.2	99.8
造纸工业	Paper Making Industry	99.6	100.2	103.8	105.7	100.5
文教艺术用品工业	Cultural Educational and Art Goods	98.2	99.1	101.1	99.4	100.5
其他工业	Other Industry	105.1	102.2	107.4	102.9	109.3

表8.8 原材料、燃料、动力购进价格指数（2001～2010，以2000年价格为100）
PURCHASING PRICE INDEX OF RAW MATERIALS, FUELS AND POWER (2000 = 100)

	类 别 Types	2001	2002	2003	2004	2005
原材料、燃料、动力购进价格指数	**Purchasing Price Index of Raw Materials, Fuels and Power**	**98.7**	**96.4**	**102.6**	**119.4**	**127.5**
燃料、动力类	Fuel and Power	99.9	101.5	109.3	136.4	169.3
黑色金属材料类	Ferrous Metals	104.5	104.6	118.9	160.0	165.1
#钢 材	Rolled-steel	99.7	96.6	105.2	129.6	142.4
有色金属材料和电线类	Nonferrous Metals and Electric Wire	93.2	88.6	90.8	108.9	122.2
化工原料类	Chemical Raw Materials	90.4	83.8	89.9	102.8	114.2
木材及纸浆类	Wood and Paper Pulps	94.9	92.6	92.0	92.8	94.2
建筑材料及非金属矿类	Building Materials and Nonmetal Minerals	101.6	97.8	100.7	115.9	103.0
其他工业原材料及半成品类	Other Industrial Raw and Processed Materials	100.9	98.6	97.5	100.4	99.7
农副产品类	Farm and Sideline Products	99.3	98.8	107.9	119.1	116.8
纺织原料类	Textile Raw Material	96.8	91.5	93.3	97.9	99.7

注：本表数据由国家统计局上海调查总队提供。
Note: Date in this table are provided by Survey Office of the National Bureau of Statistics in Shanghai.

表8.8 续表 continued

	类 别 Types	2006	2007	2008	2009	2010
原材料、燃料、动力购进价格指数	**Purchasing Price Index of Raw Materials, Fuels and Power**	**133.6**	**139.1**	**153.4**	**137.8**	**153.2**
燃料、动力类	Fuel and Power	187.8	195.9	265.6	201.9	260.5
黑色金属材料类	Ferrous Metals	153.0	163.1	190.8	165.4	188.4
#钢 材	Rolled-steel	136.6	142.6	162.7	142.9	150.0
有色金属材料和电线类	Nonferrous Metals and Electric Wire	170.0	182.2	175.6	151.5	196.0
化工原料类	Chemical Raw Materials	117.9	124.0	131.3	114.9	133.3
木材及纸浆类	Wood and Paper Pulps	94.5	96.4	98.9	95.2	98.4
建筑材料及非金属矿类	Building Materials and Nonmetal Minerals	102.8	105.6	115.1	113.5	119.6
其他工业原材料及半成品类	Other Industrial Raw and Processed Materials	103.0	105.3	107.7	104.1	106.5
农副产品类	Farm and Sideline Products	122.8	131.0	141.0	141.0	152.6
纺织原料类	Textile Raw Material	100.2	102.0	105.3	104.5	111.2

表 8.9 原材料、燃料、动力购进价格指数（2002 ~ 2010，以上年价格为 100）
PURCHASING PRICE INDEX OF RAW MATERIALS ,FUELS AND POWER IN MAIN YEARS (PRECEDING YEAR = 100)

	类 别 Types	2002	2003	2004	2005
原材料、燃料、动力购进价格指数	**Purchasing Price Index of Raw Materials Fuels and Power**	**97.7**	**106.4**	**116.4**	**106.8**
燃料、动力类	Fuels and Power	101.6	107.7	124.8	124.1
黑色金属材料类	Ferrous Metals	100.1	113.7	134.6	103.2
#钢 材	Rolled-steel	96.9	108.9	123.2	109.9
有色金属材料和电线类	Nonferrous Metals and Electric Wire	95.1	102.5	119.9	112.2
化工原料类	Chemical Raw Materials	92.7	107.3	114.3	111.1
木材及纸浆类	Wood and Paper Pulps	97.6	99.3	100.9	101.5
建筑材料及非金属矿类	Building Materials and Nonmetal Minerals	96.3	103.0	115.1	88.9
其他工业原材料及半成品类	Other Industrial Raw and Processed Materials	97.7	98.9	103.0	99.3
农副产品类	Farm and Sideline Products	99.5	109.2	110.4	98.1
纺织原料类	Textile Raw Material	94.5	102.0	104.9	101.8

注：本表数据由国家统计局上海调查总队提供。
Note: Data on this table are provided by Survey Office of the National Bureau of Statistics in Shanghai.

表 8.9 续表 continued

	类 别 Types	2006	2007	2008	2009	2010
原材料、燃料、动力购进价格指数	**Purchasing Price Index of Raw Materials, Fuels and Power**	**104.8**	**104.1**	**110.3**	**89.8**	**111.2**
燃料、动力类	Fuels and Power	110.9	104.3	135.6	76.0	129.0
黑色金属材料类	Ferrous Metals	92.7	106.6	117.0	86.7	113.9
#钢 材	Rolled-steel	95.9	104.4	114.1	87.8	105.0
有色金属材料和电线类	Nonferrous Metals and Electric Wire	139.1	107.2	96.4	86.3	129.4
化工原料类	Chemical Raw Materials	103.2	105.2	105.9	87.5	116.0
木材及纸浆类	Wood and Paper Pulps	100.3	102.0	102.6	96.3	103.4
建筑材料及非金属矿类	Building Materials and Nonmetal Minerals	99.8	102.7	109.0	98.6	105.4
其他工业原材料及半成品类	Other Industrial Raw and Processed Materials	103.3	102.2	102.3	96.7	102.3
农副产品类	Farm and Sideline Products	105.1	106.7	107.6	100.0	108.2
纺织原料类	Textile Raw Material	100.5	101.8	103.2	99.2	106.4

表8.10 固定资产投资价格指数（1996～2010，以1995年价格为100）
PRICE INDEX OF INVESTMENT IN FIXED ASSETS (1995 =100)

年份 Year	固定资产投资价格指数 Price Index of Fixed Asset Investment	建筑安装、装饰工程 Building Project Price Index	#人工费 Manpower Cost Price Index	#材料费 Material Price Index	#机械使用费 Machinery Used Price Index	设备、工器具购置 Equipment and Instrument Price Index	其他费用投资 Other Investment Price Index
1996	107.0	108.9	114.2	97.4	118.5	101.7	107.7
1997	107.5	110.4	124.5	96.1	123.8	99.5	108.6
1998	105.8	109.2	119.5	94.5	123.5	95.6	108.1
1999	103.8	106.8	123.6	90.8	124.1	92.6	107.9
2000	103.8	108.4	124.3	92.4	123.8	89.8	107.8
2001	104.5	111.0	135.5	93.6	123.5	86.7	109.2
2002	104.8	113.1	149.7	93.4	126.9	83.8	109.5
2003	107.4	119.0	156.5	98.5	133.1	81.7	111.1
2004	114.6	131.6	165.4	110.3	144.7	81.3	116.3
2005	115.5	132.8	173.3	109.7	152.8	79.1	120.0
2006	115.6	132.9	181.6	108.1	157.3	77.0	122.4
2007	119.6	139.0	194.9	112.7	161.1	76.5	127.4
2008	129.0	155.8	212.1	128.4	169.0	76.1	134.3
2009	125.1	147.7	225.3	117.0	172.0	73.1	137.3
2010	129.9	156.7	240.8	124.6	176.1	72.1	140.6

表8.11 固定资产投资价格指数(1995～2010，以上年价格为100)
PRICE INDEX OF INVESTMENT IN FIXED ASSETS (PRECEDING YEAR =100)

年份 Year	固定资产投资价格指数 Price Index of Fixed Asset Investment	建筑安装、装饰工程 Building Project Price Index	#人工费 Manpower Cost Price Index	#材料费 Material Price Index	#机械使用费 Machinery Used Price Index	设备、工器具购置 Equipment and Instrument Price Index	其他费用投资 Other Investment Price Index
1995	103.1	101.9	108.7	99.5		104.8	107.0
1996	107.0	108.9	114.2	97.4	118.5	101.7	107.7
1997	100.5	101.4	109.0	98.7	104.5	97.8	100.8
1998	98.4	98.9	96.0	98.3	99.7	96.1	99.6
1999	98.1	97.8	103.4	96.1	100.5	96.9	99.8
2000	100.0	101.5	100.6	101.8	99.8	97.0	99.9
2001	100.7	102.4	109.0	101.2	99.7	96.5	101.3
2002	100.3	101.9	110.5	99.8	102.8	96.7	100.3
2003	102.4	105.2	104.5	105.5	104.9	97.5	101.4
2004	106.7	110.6	105.7	112.0	108.7	99.4	104.7
2005	100.8	100.9	104.8	99.4	105.6	97.4	103.2
2006	100.1	100.1	104.8	98.6	102.9	97.3	102.0
2007	103.5	104.6	107.3	104.3	102.4	99.4	104.1
2008	107.9	112.1	108.8	113.9	104.9	99.5	105.4
2009	97.0	94.8	106.2	91.1	101.8	96.1	102.2
2010	103.8	106.1	106.9	106.5	102.4	98.6	102.4

注：本页数据由国家统计局上海调查总队提供。
Note: Data on this table are provided by Survey Office of the National Bureau of Statistics in Shanghai.

表 8.12 房屋租赁和土地交易价格指数(2001～2010，以 2000 年价格为 100)
REAL ESTATE LEASING AND LAND EXCHANGE PRICE INDEX

	类 别 Types	2001	2002	2003	2004	2005
房屋租赁价格指数	**Price Index of Real Estate Leasing**	**104.9**	**103.9**	**106.0**	**111.9**	**115.9**
#住 宅	Residence	107.4	107.4	108.7	110.1	113.7
办公楼	Offices	98.6	97.9	103.0	110.1	117.2
商业营业用房	Commercial and Business Housing	107.2	104.0	102.8	110.4	111.4
土地交易价格指数	**Price Index of Land Exchange**	**97.2**	**103.3**	**118.9**	**143.1**	**153.0**
#居住用地	Residential	92.2	102.3	125.1	161.8	170.6
工业用地	Workshops	91.6	82.7	84.0	85.1	88.3

表 8.12 续表 continued

	类 别 Types	2006	2007	2008	2009	2010
房屋租赁价格指数	**Price Index of Real Estate Leasing**	**120.6**	**126.7**	**132.6**	**133.4**	**139.3**
#住 宅	Residence	116.4	123.9	129.2	129.6	135.9
办公楼	Offices	121.6	127.1	134.2	135.5	137.3
商业营业用房	Commercial and Business Housing	118.2	125.1	131.3	132.2	143.9
土地交易价格指数	**Price Index of Land Exchange**	**154.8**	**166.9**	**180.0**	**184.0**	**218.7**
#居住用地	Residential	169.7	177.2	189.5	195.0	246.5
工业用地	Workshops	90.8	103.4	110.9	112.8	129.8

①本表数据由国家统计局上海调查总队提供。
②按照国家统计局新的调查制度规定，从 2008 年开始，房屋租赁价格指数中商业娱乐用房改为“商业营业用房”，土地交易价格指数中工业仓储用地改为“工业用地”。(下表同)
❶Date in this table are provided by Survey Office of the National Bureau of Statistics in Shanghai.
❷According to the new investigation system regulation of NBS, since year of 2008, Commercial and Entertainment Housing had been changed into Commercial and Business Housing in the price index of real estats leasing, Land for Workshops and Warehouses had been changed into Land for Workshops in the price index of land exchange(same as follows).

表 8.13 房屋租赁和土地交易价格指数(2003～2010，以上年价格为 100)
REAL ESTATE LEASING AND LAND EXCHANGE PRICE INDEX (PRECEDING YEAR = 100)

	类 别 Types	2003	2004	2005	2006
房屋租赁价格指数	**Price Index of Real Estate Leasing**	**102.1**	**105.5**	**103.6**	**104.0**
#住 宅	Residence	101.2	101.3	103.3	102.3
办公楼	Offices	105.2	106.9	106.4	103.8
商业营业用房	Commercial and Business Housing	98.9	107.3	101.0	106.1
土地交易价格指数	**Price Index of Land Exchange**	**115.1**	**120.3**	**106.9**	**101.2**
#居住用地	Residential	122.2	129.4	105.4	99.5
工业用地	Workshops	101.5	101.4	103.7	102.9

注：本表数据由国家统计局上海调查总队提供。
Note: Data on this table are provided by Survey Office of the National Bureau of Statistics in Shanghai.

表 8.13 续表 continued

	类 别 Types	2007	2008	2009	2010
房屋租赁价格指数	**Price Index of Real Estate Leasing**	**105.1**	**104.6**	**100.6**	**104.4**
#住 宅	Residence	106.5	104.2	100.3	104.9
办公楼	Offices	104.5	105.6	101.0	101.3
商业营业用房	Commercial and Business Housing	105.8	104.9	100.7	108.8
土地交易价格指数	**Price Index of Land Exchange**	**107.8**	**107.9**	**102.2**	**118.9**
#居住用地	Residential	104.4	106.9	102.9	126.4
工业用地	Workshops	113.8	107.3	101.7	115.1

上/海/统/计/年/鉴

主要统计指标解释

居民消费价格指数

居民消费价格指数是度量一组代表性消费商品及服务项目价格水平随着时间而变动的相对数，反映居民家庭购买的消费品及服务价格水平的变动情况。它是宏观经济分析和决策、价格总水平监测和调控以及国民经济核算的重要指标。其按年度计算的变动率通常被用来作为反映通货膨胀或紧缩程度的指标。

现行的居民消费价格指数按用途分为八个大类，包括食品、烟酒及用品、衣着、家庭设备用品及维修服务、医疗保健和个人用品、交通和通信、娱乐教育文化用品及服务、居住。

商品零售价格指数

商品零售价格指数是反映一定时期内城乡商品零售价格变动趋势和程度的相对数。商品零售价格的变动直接影响城乡居民的生活支出和国家的财政收入，影响居民购买力和市场供需的平衡，影响消费与积累的比例关系。因此，该指数可以从一个侧面对上述经济活动进行观察和分析。

工业品出厂价格指数

工业品出厂价格指数是反映一定时期内全部工业产品出厂价格总水平的变动趋势和程度的相对数，包括工业企业售给本企业以外所有单位的各种产品和直接售给居民用于生活消费的产品。该指数可以观察出厂价格变动对工业总产值及增加值的影响。

原材料燃料和动力购进价格指数

原材料燃料和动力购进价格指数是反映工业企业作为生产投入，从物资交易市场和能源、原材料生产企业购买原材料、燃料和动力产品时，所支付的价格水平变动趋势和程度的统计指标，是扣除工业企业物质消耗成本中的价格变动影响的重要依据。

目前，我国编制的原材料燃料和动力购进价格指数所调查的产品包括燃料动力、黑色金属、有色金属、化工、建材等九大类的近 1800 种产品。

固定资产投资价格指数

固定资产投资价格指数是反映一定时期内固定资产投资品及项目的价格变动趋势和程度的相对数。固定资产投资额是由建筑安装工程投资完成额、设备工器具购置投资完成额和其他费用投资完成额三部分组成的。编制固定资产投资价格指数应首先分别编制上述三部分投资的价格指数，然后采用加权算术平均法求出固定资产投资价格总指数。

该指数可以准确地反映固定资产投资中涉及的各类投资品和收费项目价格变动趋势和变动幅度，消除按现价计算的固定资产投资指标中的价格变动因素，真实地反映固定资产投资的规模、速度、结构和效益，为国家科学地制定、检查固定资产投资计划并提高宏观调控水平，为完善国民经济核算体系提供科学的、可靠的依据。

房屋租赁价格指数

房屋租赁指以支付租金形式取得房屋使用权。它包括住宅租赁、办公用房租赁 、商业用房租赁租赁部分。房屋租赁价格指数是指房屋租赁价格总水平变动趋势和程度的相对数。

土地交易价格指数

指房地产开发商或其他建设单位在进行商品房开发之前，为取得土地使用权而实际支付的价格的变动趋势和程度的相对数。

SHANGHAI STATISTICAL YEARBOOK

EXPLANATORY NOTES TO MAJOR STATISTICAL INDICATORS

□ Consumer Price Index

The Consumer Price Index is an index that reflects the time-based change of prices of a group of representative consumption commodities and services. It is an important reference factor for macro-economic analysis and strategy, monitoring and adjustment of overall price level and the national economic budgeting. The year-on-year change of the index is often a norm reflecting the inflation or deflation.

The current CPI covers eight categories of goods and services: food; tobacco, liquor and related articles; garments; household facilities, articles and repair services; medical and health care and personal items; traffic and telecommunications; education, culture and recreation articles and services and residence.

□ Retail Price Index

Retail Price Indices reflect the trend and degree of change in retail prices of commodities during a given period. The change in retail prices of commodities directly affect the living expenditure of urban and rural residents, government revenue, purchasing power of residents and the equilibrium of market supply and demand, and the ratio of consumption to accumulation. Therefore, the retail price indices are useful to analyze the changes of the above economic activities.

□ Ex-factory Price Indices of Industrial Products

Ex-factory Price Indices of Industrial Products reflect the trend and degree of changes in general ex-factory prices of all industrial products during a given period, including sales of industrial products by an industrial enterprise to all units outside the enterprise, as well as sales of consumer goods to residents. It can be used to analyze the impact of ex-factory prices on gross output value and value-added of the industrial sector.

□ Indices of Purchasing Prices of Raw Materials, Fuels and Power

Indices of Purchasing Prices of Raw Materials, Fuels and Power reflect changes in the level and degree of prices paid by industrial enterprises when they purchase production input such as raw materials, fuels and power from the market or from other energy or raw materials producing enterprises. These indices provide important basis for measuring the material consumption of industrial enterprises after removing influence of price changes.

At present, close to 1,800 products in 9 categories, including fuels and power, ferrous metals, non-ferrous metals, chemicals, building materials, are covered in China for the survey to produce indices of purchasing prices of raw materials, fuels and power.

□ Price Indices of Investment in Fixed Assets

Price Indices of Investment in Fixed Assets reflect the trend and degree of changes in prices of investment goods and projects in fixed assets during a given period. The investment in fixed assets consists of three components, namely the investment in construction and installation, the investment in purchases of equipment and instrument, and the investment in other items. Price indices of investment in fixed assets are calculated as the weighted arithmetic mean of the price indices of the three components of investment in fixed assets.

Removing the factor of price change in the aggregates of investment at current prices, this indicator shows the changes in the prices of commodities and fees involved in the investment of fixed assets, and can be used to observe the actual size, growth, structure, and efficiency of investment in fixed assets and provides reliable and scientific data for government planning, management, decision-making, and further improving the current national accounting system.

□ Price Index of Real Estate Leasing

Real estate leasing refers to the acquisition of the real estate ownership by means of paying rent. Included are the leasing of residential houses, office building, workshop and warehouse, and hotel and restaurant. The Price Index of Real Estate leasing is an indicator of general trend and variation of the leasing price of real estate.

EXPLANATORY NOTES TO MAJOR STATISTICAL INDICATORS

□ Price Index of Land Exchange

Price Index of Land Exchange is an indicator of the general trend and variation of the paid price in order to obtain the ownership of the land by the real estate developer or other construction organizations before the development.

第九篇
CHAPTER 9

人民生活
LIVING STANDARDS

表9.1 从业人员报酬(1978~2010)
COMPENSATION OF EMPLOYEES

年 份 Year	从业人员报酬(亿元) Compensation of Employees (100 million yuan)	按产业分 Grouped by Industry			按登记注册类型分 Classified According to the Categories of Registration		
		第一产业 Primary Industry	第二产业 Secondary Industry	第三产业 Tertiary Industry	国有单位 State-owned Units	集体单位 Collective-owned Units	其他单位 Other Ownership Units
1978	28.18	1.31	17.18	9.69	23.88	4.30	
1979	32.90	1.44	20.43	11.03	27.77	5.13	
1980	38.26	1.66	23.42	13.18	31.71	6.55	
1981	39.76	1.61	24.40	13.75	32.55	7.21	
1982	41.55	1.59	25.15	14.81	33.83	7.72	
1983	43.21	1.48	26.07	15.66	35.07	8.14	
1984	54.13	1.63	33.29	19.21	43.39	10.29	0.45
1985	69.63	2.10	42.86	24.67	55.96	13.18	0.49
1986	84.89	2.45	51.70	30.74	68.32	15.84	0.73
1987	96.36	2.64	58.18	35.54	78.15	17.46	0.75
1988	117.04	3.18	70.35	43.51	94.78	20.91	1.35
1989	134.04	3.60	81.41	49.03	106.57	25.17	2.30
1990	150.48	4.02	89.48	56.98	121.56	25.64	3.28
1991	177.55	4.64	105.25	67.66	142.00	30.24	5.31
1992	223.36	2.47	135.49	85.40	179.43	35.40	8.53
1993	290.42	2.57	157.10	130.75	212.10	39.56	38.76
1994	374.44	3.11	186.81	184.52	268.19	48.59	57.66
1995	465.67	3.53	232.10	230.04	324.72	56.99	83.96
1996	521.63	3.72	250.94	266.97	359.56	60.18	101.89
1997	547.87	3.69	245.59	298.59	366.61	60.11	121.15
1998	535.51	3.47	255.43	276.61	330.70	45.11	159.70
1999	612.85	3.35	277.11	332.39	366.55	43.62	202.68
2000	647.55	3.32	283.20	361.03	369.65	38.88	239.02
2001	716.95	3.25	301.93	411.77	389.26	36.91	290.78
2002	788.55	3.76	333.64	451.15	404.89	34.18	349.48
2003	873.06	2.53	373.19	497.34	434.93	32.43	405.70
2004	925.33	2.69	383.84	538.80	435.30	31.00	459.03
2005	1 245.44	3.21	478.97	763.26	474.39	30.28	740.77
2006	1 598.09	3.92	656.41	937.76	559.02	31.15	1 007.92
2007	1 976.54	4.35	796.03	1 176.16	704.35	35.94	1 236.25
2008	2 399.63	4.68	934.34	1 460.61	797.29	36.40	1 565.94
2009	2 902.66	5.28	1 060.30	1 837.08	938.66	38.70	1 925.30
2010	3 320.86	5.76	1 224.97	2 090.13	1 055.50	38.39	2 226.97

①2009 年起，本表从业人员报酬指城镇、街道级及以上法人单位以及城镇私营企业从业人员报酬(下表同)。
②本表“其他单位”包括港澳台及外商企业。
❶Compensation of employees in this table has been included compensation from legal entity above town or street commintee level and urban private enterprises since 2009(same as follows).
❷“Other Ownership Units” in this table includes foreign invested and HongKong, Macau and Taiwan funded enterprises.

表9.2 从业人员平均报酬(2010)
AVERAGE ANNUAL COMPENSATION OF EMPLOYEES

单位:元 (yuan)

行业	Sectors	合计 Total	国有单位 State-owned Units	集体单位 Collective-owned Units	港澳台及外商投资单位 Units with Investment from Hong Kong, Macao, Taiwan and Foreign Countries	其他单位 Other Ownership Units
全　市	**Total**	**47 478**	**71 885**	**41 106**	**57 245**	**35 141**
一、按产业分	**Grouped by Industry**					
第一产业	Primary Industry	31 836	45 146	35 066	22 955	25 250
第二产业	Secondary Industry	39 471	72 325	29 791	48 706	29 991
第三产业	Tertiary Industry	53 968	71 931	43 933	84 443	39 353
二、按行业分	**Grouped by Sector**					
农、林、牧、渔业	Farming, Forestry, Animal Husbandry and Fishery	31 836	45 146	35 066	22 955	25 250
工　业	Industry	40 473	73 375	31 123	48 442	29 650
采矿业	Mining	62 356	97 531			27 819
制造业	Manufacturing	39 321	65 813	29 267	48 331	29 216
电力、燃气及水的生产和供应业	Power, Gas and Water Production and Supply	91 409	97 810	57 729	99 447	72 621
建筑业	Construction	34 457	67 626	25 042	87 392	30 953
交通运输、仓储和邮政业	Transportation, Warehousing and Post	50 413	58 631	27 433	74 312	44 892
#交通运输	Transportation	49 356	57 335	26 405	77 713	44 844
邮政业	Postal	64 780	66 106			35 250
信息传输、计算机服务和软件业	Information Transmission, Computer Servcies and Software Industries	74 028	115 411	65 312	99 783	53 011
#信息传输	Information Transmission	113 489	120 843	78 944	104 424	109 173
批发和零售业	Wholesale and Retail	32 790	70 047	38 714	79 539	24 753
批发业	Wholesale	34 828	81 168	47 872	104 927	24 203
零售业	Retail	29 133	54 325	34 068	41 334	25 793
住宿和餐饮业	Hoteling and Catering	27 056	40 773	30 315	24 962	26 538
#餐饮业	Catering	23 135	48 868	30 294	22 824	22 779
金融业	Financial Industries	153 603	171 849	85 182	240 182	137 436
房地产业	Real Estate	37 394	54 415	35 152	43 388	33 038
租赁和商务服务业	Leasing and Business Services	40 109	41 913	32 803	144 441	27 993
科学研究、技术服务和地质勘查业	Scientific Research, Technological Service and Geological Prospecting	70 992	76 884	75 730	142 070	49 734
水利、环境和公共设施管理业	Water Conservancies, Environment and Public Facilities Management	40 641	45 302	28 211	70 698	30 774
居民服务和其他服务业	Resident Service and Other Services	22 581	41 256	30 677	28 555	20 468
教　育	Education	67 909	71 138	48 941	81 093	36 161
卫生、社会保障和社会福利业	Healthcare, Social Security and Social Welfare	70 943	74 940	63 423	86 533	30 564
卫　生	Healthcare	73 074	77 239	66 736	86 533	30 283
社会保障	Social Security	51 844	49 285	58 797		159 406
社会福利业	Social Welfare	36 086	40 521	17 700		18 598
文化、体育和娱乐业	Culture, Sports and Entertainment	57 762	72 515	51 772	39 946	32 855
文　化	Culture	75 955	78 828	50 618	59 401	71 884
体　育	Sports	49 667	50 801	77 226		25 971
娱乐业	Entertainment	23 821	54 430	69 571	32 453	20 502
公共管理和社会组织	Public Administration and Social Organizations	73 073	73 660	33 472		46 493

表9.3 职工工资总额和平均工资(1978～2010)
TOTAL WAGES AND AVERAGE ANNUAL WAGES OF STAFF AND WORKERS

年 份 Year	职工工资总额 (亿元) Total Wages of Staff and Workers (100 million yuan)	其 中 of which 国有单位 State-owned Units	集体单位 Collective-owned Units	其他单位 Other Ownership Units	职工平均工资 (元) Average Annual Wages of Staff and Workers (yuan)	其 中 of which 国有单位 State-owned Units	集体单位 Collective-owned Units	其他单位 Other Ownership Units
1978	28.12	23.82	4.30		672	716	500	
1979	32.73	27.63	5.10		784	834	590	
1980	38.10	31.59	6.51		873	918	702	
1981	39.59	32.42	7.17		870	910	727	
1982	41.34	33.71	7.63		883	920	750	
1983	42.91	34.93	7.98		897	935	763	
1984	53.72	43.19	10.08	0.45	1 110	1 160	938	1 149
1985	68.99	55.50	13.00	0.49	1 416	1 467	1 227	1 628
1986	83.35	67.49	15.15	0.71	1 689	1 752	1 443	2 029
1987	94.78	77.19	16.87	0.72	1 893	1 960	1 623	2 510
1988	114.47	93.62	19.55	1.30	2 277	2 354	1 951	2 715
1989	131.10	105.08	23.77	2.25	2 608	2 691	2 259	3 235
1990	146.78	119.26	24.30	3.22	2 917	3 037	2 394	3 611
1991	172.84	139.12	28.51	5.21	3 375	3 487	2 817	4 363
1992	217.21	175.95	32.89	8.37	4 273	4 451	3 363	5 486
1993	279.33	206.12	36.60	36.61	5 650	5 784	4 253	7 043
1994	357.89	259.78	44.73	53.38	7 401	7 529	5 389	9 617
1995	440.75	314.69	51.61	74.45	9 279	9 578	6 309	11 518
1996	492.70	348.96	54.92	88.82	10 663	11 015	7 051	13 186
1997	510.10	353.69	53.69	102.72	11 425	11 733	7 329	14 313
1998	510.35	330.10	44.13	136.12	12 059	12 361	7 138	14 430
1999	583.54	366.21	43.22	174.11	14 147	14 419	7 935	16 736
2000	614.53	371.39	39.35	203.79	15 420	15 737	8 041	17 942
2001	678.29	389.91	35.79	252.59	17 764	17 820	8 525	20 865
2002	733.31	404.44	31.54	297.33	19 473	19 777	8 707	21 886
2003	803.84	430.92	30.52	342.40	22 160	22 541	9 844	24 359
2004	837.39	428.49	29.36	379.53	24 398	24 726	11 539	26 270
2005	1 146.97	463.24	28.44	655.29	26 823	28 803	12 819	26 792
2006	1 475.93	539.88	28.41	907.64	29 569	36 010	15 209	27 459
2007	1 802.17	673.20	32.75	1 096.22	34 707	46 426	19 244	30 687
2008	2 184.20	753.44	31.72	1 399.04	39 502	53 554	21 787	35 180
2009	2 594.20	889.50	34.24	1 670.46	42 789	62 390	25 390	37 104
2010	3 018.55	994.05	33.62	1 990.88	46 757	70 585	28 225	40 397

①2009 年起，职工工资总额和平均工资包括城镇私营企业职工工资。
② 本表"其他单位"包括港澳台及外商企业。
❶Total and average wages of staff and workers has been included urban private enterprises since 2009.
❷"Other Ownership Units" in this table inoludes foreign invested and HongKong, Macan and Taiwan funded enterprises.

表 9.4 职工工资总额（2010）
TOTAL WAGES OF STAFF AND WORKERS

单位：亿元（100 million yuan）

行业	Sectors	合计 Total	国有单位 State-owned Units	集体单位 Collective-owned Units	港澳台及外商投资单位 Units with Investment from Hong Kong, Macao, Taiwan and Foreign Countries	其他单位 Other Ownership Units
全　市	**Total**	**3 018.55**	**994.05**	**33.62**	**682.15**	**1 308.73**
一、按产业分	**Grouped by Industry**					
第一产业	Primary Industry	4.65	2.30	0.22	0.05	2.08
第二产业	Secondary Industry	1 104.17	149.33	4.71	447.75	502.38
第三产业	Tertiary Industry	1 909.73	842.42	28.69	234.35	804.27
二、按行业分	**Grouped by Sector**					
农、林、牧、渔业	Farming, Forestry, Animal Husbandry and Fishery	4.65	2.30	0.22	0.05	2.08
工　业	Industry	939.00	125.40	3.90	443.30	366.41
采矿业	Mining	0.50	0.38			0.12
制造业	Manufacturing	887.02	85.84	3.37	440.98	356.84
电力、燃气及水的生产和供应业	Power, Gas and Water Production and Supply	51.47	39.18	0.53	2.32	9.45
建筑业	Construction	165.17	23.94	0.81	4.45	135.97
交通运输、仓储和邮政业	Transportation, Warehousing and Post	210.41	75.43	1.25	14.73	119.00
#交通运输	Transportation	193.20	63.63	1.12	11.47	116.98
邮政业	Postal	9.92	9.88			0.04
信息传输、计算机服务和软件业	Information Transmission, Computer Servcies and Software Industries	98.16	21.15	0.22	33.69	43.10
#信息传输	Information Transmission	30.62	18.83	0.20	7.74	3.86
批发和零售业	Retail and Wholesale	270.05	22.81	4.03	68.73	174.48
批发业	Wholesale	185.95	15.15	1.64	54.22	114.94
零售业	Retail	84.10	7.67	2.39	14.51	59.53
住宿和餐饮业	Hoteling and Catering	56.28	5.25	0.28	11.77	38.97
#餐饮业	Catering	34.30	0.65	0.22	9.62	23.81
金融业	Financial Industries	342.58	82.07		39.71	220.80
房地产业	Real Estate	69.39	12.86	0.88	10.99	44.66
租赁和商务服务业	Leasing and Business Services	149.62	33.29	4.75	35.58	76.00
科学研究、技术服务和地质勘查业	Scientific Research, Technological Service and Geological Prospecting	204.63	142.94	1.46	15.69	44.54
水利、环境和公共设施管理业	Water Conservancies Environment and Public Facilities Management	24.63	18.59	1.20	0.12	4.72
居民服务和其他服务业	Resident Service and Other Services	27.79	3.10	0.66	1.64	22.38
教　育	Education	178.71	170.57	1.08	0.16	6.90
卫生、社会保障和社会福利业	Healthcare, Social Security and Social Welfare	110.84	96.12	11.30	0.30	3.12
卫　生	Healthcare	105.71	92.03	10.33	0.30	3.06
社会保障	Social Security	3.12	2.27	0.80		0.05
社会福利业	Social Welfare	2.01	1.82	0.18		0.01
文化、体育和娱乐业	Culture, Sports and Entertainment	31.13	23.55	0.79	1.25	5.55
文　化	Culture	23.97	19.61	0.74	0.74	2.87
体　育	Sports	3.63	3.60	0.02		
娱乐业	Entertainment	3.53	0.33	0.02	0.51	2.67
公共管理和社会组织	Public Administration and Social Organizations	135.52	134.67	0.80		0.05

表9.5 职工平均工资(2010)
AVERAGE ANNUAL WAGES OF STAFF AND WORKERS

单位:元(yuan)

行业	Sectors	合计 Total	国有单位 State-owned Units	集体单位 Collective-owned Units	港澳台及外商投资单位 Units with Investment from Hong Kong, Macao, Taiwan and Foreign Countries	其他单位 Other Ownership Units
全市	**Total**	**46 757**	**70 585**	**28 225**	**56 296**	**35 213**
一、按产业分	**Grouped by Industry**					
第一产业	Primary Industry	30 387	43 285	44 359	21 582	22 466
第二产业	Secondary Industry	37 839	60 172	15 513	47 600	29 571
第三产业	Tertiary Industry	54 217	72 948	32 512	86 528	40 044
二、按行业分	**Grouped by Sector**					
农、林、牧、渔业	Farming, Forestry, Animal Husbandry and Fishery	30 387	43 285	44 359	21 582	22 466
工业	Industry	38 593	59 108	14 231	47 444	29 099
采矿业	Mining	63 139	106 997			27 309
制造业	Manufacturing	37 331	50 001	12 767	47 315	28 639
电力、燃气及水的生产和供应业	Power, Gas and Water Production and Supply	91 619	97 642	53 452	98 601	74 289
建筑业	Construction	34 054	66 436	27 326	70 760	30 922
交通运输、仓储和邮政业	Transportation, Warehousing and Post	52 408	60 606	13 355	72 833	48 090
#交通运输	Transportation	51 380	58 609	12 404	74 768	48 125
邮政业	Postal	80 301	82 934			9 800
信息传输、计算机服务和软件业	Information Transmission, Computer Servcies and Software Industries	74 049	119 059	67 433	99 727	53 417
#信息传输	Information Transmission	125 863	125 674	77 475	140 711	107 403
批发和零售业	Retail and Wholesale	31 469	45 055	24 547	78 055	24 819
批发业	Wholesale	33 145	54 435	30 214	102 432	24 211
零售业	Retail	28 304	33 610	21 744	41 336	26 084
住宿和餐饮业	Hoteling and Catering	28 405	40 565	21 329	35 817	25 809
#餐饮业	Catering	24 955	57 402	20 819	33 929	22 273
金融业	Financial Industries	161 126	175 793	48 333	229 903	148 534
房地产业	Real Estate	38 530	63 562	35 131	40 034	34 379
租赁和商务服务业	Leasing and Business Services	33 648	31 260	21 120	124 044	26 480
科学研究、技术服务和地质勘查业	Scientific Research, Technological Service and Geological Prospecting	71 206	77 397	78 868	127 083	50 331
水利、环境和公共设施管理业	Water Conservancies Environment and Public Facilities Management	46 280	54 556	29 180	70 784	31 760
居民服务和其他服务业	Resident Service and Other Services	20 893	34 826	8 781	27 376	20 248
教育	Education	72 778	76 466	48 247	38 973	34 783
卫生、社会保障和社会福利业	Healthcare, Social Security and Social Welfare	76 506	81 620	69 032	57 231	30 510
卫生	Healthcare	78 320	83 558	72 871	57 231	30 150
社会保障	Social Security	57 556	55 824	60 518		169 964
社会福利业	Social Welfare	44 787	51 124	20 300		24 244
文化、体育和娱乐业	Culture, Sports and Entertainment	57 553	72 023	49 279	41 185	33 133
文化	Culture	75 713	77 499	54 581	56 457	78 075
体育	Sports	51 918	53 245	112 250		34 286
娱乐业	Entertainment	22 889	53 382	10 139	32 906	20 459
公共管理和社会组织	Public Administration and Social Organizations	76 723	77 230	37 089		49 689

表9.6 在岗职工工资总额(2010)
TOTAL WAGES OF WORKING STAFF AND WORKERS

单位:亿元(100 million yuan)

行业	Sectors	合计 Total	国有单位 State-owned Units	集体单位 Collective-owned Units	港澳台及外商投资单位 Units with Investment from Hong Kong, Macao,Taiwan and Foreign Countries	其他单位 Other Ownership Units
全　市	**Total**	**2 984.14**	**976.30**	**31.95**	**679.37**	**1 296.52**
一、按产业分	**Grouped by Industry**					
第一产业	Primary Industry	4.50	2.23	0.22	0.05	2.00
第二产业	Secondary Industry	1 090.77	143.30	4.16	445.24	498.07
第三产业	Tertiary Industry	1 888.87	830.77	27.57	234.08	796.45
二、按行业分	**Grouped by Sector**					
农、林、牧、渔业	Farming, Forestry, Animal Husbandry and Fishery	4.50	2.24	0.21	0.05	2.00
工　业	Industry	926.82	119.97	3.40	440.79	362.66
采矿业	Mining	0.50	0.38			0.12
制造业	Manufacturing	875.07	80.52	2.89	438.48	353.18
电力、燃气及水的生产和供应业	Power, Gas and Water Production and Supply	51.25	39.07	0.51	2.31	9.36
建筑业	Construction	163.95	23.33	0.76	4.45	135.41
交通运输、仓储和邮政业	Transportation, Warehousing and Post	205.74	73.60	1.09	14.69	116.36
#交通运输	Transportation	188.69	61.93	0.97	11.43	114.36
邮政业	Postal	9.86	9.81			0.04
信息传输、计算机服务和软件业	Information Transmission, Computer Servcies and Software Industries	97.96	21.03	0.21	33.63	43.09
#信息传输	Information Transmission	30.45	18.71	0.20	7.70	3.84
批发和零售业	Retail and Wholesale	267.26	21.26	3.62	68.66	173.72
批发业	Wholesale	184.86	14.50	1.53	54.16	114.67
零售业	Retail	82.40	6.77	2.09	14.50	59.05
住宿和餐饮业	Hoteling and Catering	55.69	5.06	0.24	11.77	38.63
#餐饮业	Catering	34.07	0.62	0.19	9.61	23.64
金融业	Financial Industries	340.91	80.86		39.69	220.35
房地产业	Real Estate	68.53	12.35	0.87	10.98	44.33
租赁和商务服务业	Leasing and Business Services	144.25	30.92	4.52	35.52	73.30
科学研究、技术服务和地质勘查业	Scientific Research, Technological Service and Geological Prospecting	204.09	142.46	1.45	15.68	44.50
水利、环境和公共设施管理业	Water Conservancies, Environment and Public Facilities Management	24.28	18.32	1.19	0.12	4.65
居民服务和其他服务业	Resident Service and Other Services	27.10	2.96	0.57	1.64	21.93
教　育	Education	177.38	169.27	1.07	0.16	6.89
卫生、社会保障和社会福利业	Healthcare, Social Security and Social Welfare	110.12	95.52	11.18	0.30	3.11
卫　生	Healthcare	105.01	91.44	10.21	0.30	3.06
社会保障	Social Security	3.11	2.27	0.79		0.05
社会福利业	Social Welfare	2.00	1.81	0.18		0.01
文化、体育和娱乐业	Culture, Sports and Entertainment	30.22	22.67	0.77	1.25	5.53
文　化	Culture	23.12	18.79	0.73	0.74	2.86
体　育	Sports	3.58	3.56	0.02		
娱乐业	Entertainment	3.52	0.33	0.02	0.51	2.67
公共管理和社会组织	Public Administration and Social Organizations	135.33	134.48	0.79		0.05

表9.7 在岗职工平均工资(2010)
AVERAGE ANNUAL WAGES OF STAFF AND WORKERS

单位:元 (yuan)

行业	Sectors	合计 Total	国有单位 State-owned Units	集体单位 Collective-owned Units	港澳台及外商投资单位 Units with Investment from Hong Kong, Macao,Taiwan and Foreign Countries	其他单位 Other Ownership Units
全　市	**Total**	**48 867**	**78 651**	**45 395**	**57 106**	**35 962**
一、按产业分	**Grouped by Industry**					
第一产业	Primary Industry	33 573	50 107	46 032	23 145	24 211
第二产业	Secondary Industry	39 346	77 013	31 800	48 369	30 139
第三产业	Tertiary Industry	56 877	79 062	48 520	87 039	40 960
二、按行业分	**Grouped by Sector**					
农、林、牧、渔业	Farming, Forestry, Animal Husbandry and Fishery	33 573	50 107	46 032	23 145	24 211
工　业	Industry	40 333	77 247	32 338	48 212	29 780
采矿业	Mining	66 796	123 003			27 309
制造业	Manufacturing	39 033	69 750	29 995	48 081	29 314
电力、燃气及水的生产和供应业	Power, Gas and Water Production and Supply	92 736	98 770	58 137	99 855	74 775
建筑业	Construction	34 563	75 834	29 608	71 542	31 144
交通运输、仓储和邮政业	Transportation, Warehousing and Post	55 491	64 646	27 524	73 405	49 952
#交通运输	Transportation	54 365	62 523	25 980	75 521	49 903
邮政业	Postal	85 502	85 831			45 800
信息传输、计算机服务和软件业	Information Transmission, Computer Servcies and Software Industries	74 298	119 880	68 706	100 617	53 477
#信息传输	Information Transmission	126 945	126 193	78 944	142 618	109 443
批发和零售业	Retail and Wholesale	32 691	77 156	43 277	78 633	25 024
批发业	Wholesale	33 973	89 352	56 088	102 967	24 269
零售业	Retail	30 141	59 699	37 068	41 779	26 633
住宿和餐饮业	Hoteling and Catering	29 024	45 681	33 510	35 838	26 230
#餐饮业	Catering	25 293	73 341	32 918	33 939	22 528
金融业	Financial Industries	162 942	180 471	48 333	229 985	149 747
房地产业	Real Estate	40 175	79 077	43 467	40 192	35 285
租赁和商务服务业	Leasing and Business Services	39 542	48 971	35 548	124 467	28 146
科学研究、技术服务和地质勘查业	Scientific Research, Technological Service and Geological Prospecting	71 776	78 178	81 743	129 847	50 414
水利、环境和公共设施管理业	Water Conservancies, Environment and Public Facilities Management	47 695	56 760	29 267	70 784	32 319
居民服务和其他服务业	Resident Service and Other Services	22 533	53 048	36 790	27 376	20 464
教　育	Education	73 820	77 498	53 334	38 973	35 385
卫生、社会保障和社会福利业	Healthcare, Social Security and Social Welfare	77 674	82 943	70 455	57 231	30 499
卫　生	Healthcare	79 570	85 010	74 312	57 231	30 139
社会保障	Social Security	57 755	55 869	61 268		169 964
社会福利业	Social Welfare	45 309	51 242	21 214		24 244
文化、体育和娱乐业	Culture, Sports and Entertainment	59 249	75 690	56 535	41 185	33 262
文　化	Culture	79 688	82 434	55 520	56 457	79 632
体　育	Sports	52 688	54 119	122 929		34 286
娱乐业	Entertainment	23 192	55 585	71 778	32 906	20 472
公共管理和社会组织	Public Administration and Social Organizations	76 974	77 480	37 042		51 569

表9.8 主要年份离退休、退职人员养老金
PENSION FOR RETIRED STAFF IN MAIN YEARS

	指 标 Indicators	2000	2009	2010
离退休、退职人员养老金(亿元)	**Pension for Nonworking Staff and Workers (100 million yuan)**	**205.14**	**689.35**	**783.42**
离休职工的离休费	Pensions for Retired Veteran Cadres	7.32	13.34	11.41
退休职工的退休费	Pensions for Retired	195.90	668.13	763.44
退职人员的退职生活费	Living Expenses for the Resigned	1.92	7.88	8.57

表9.9 离退休、退职人员养老金(2010)
PENSION FOR RETIRED STAFF

	指 标 Indicators	合 计 Total	国有单位 State-owned Units	集体单位 Collective-owned Units	其他单位 Other Ownership Units
离退休、退职人员养老金(亿元)	**Labour Insurance and Welfare Funds for Nonworking Staff and Workers (100 million yuan)**	**783.42**	**398.61**	**93.80**	**291.01**
离休职工的离休费	Pensions for Retired Veteran Cadres	11.41	8.25	0.19	2.97
退休职工的退休费	Pensions for Retired	763.44	386.66	91.87	284.91
退职人员的退职生活费	Living Expenses for Resigned	8.57	3.70	1.74	3.13

注：本表"其他单位"包括港澳台及外商企业。
Note: "Other Ownership Unit" in this table includes foreign invested and HongKong, Macao and Taiwan funded enterprises.

表9.10 储蓄存款年末余额(1997～2010)
SAVINGS DEPOSITS AT YEAR－END

年 份 Year	储蓄存款余额(亿元) Savings Deposits (100 million yuan)	其中 of which 定期储蓄 Time Account	活期储蓄 Current Account	人均储蓄存款(元) Average Deposits (yuan)
1997	2 109.18	1 843.25	265.93	14 169
1998	2 372.94	2 017.16	355.78	15 536
1999	2 597.12	2 119.82	477.30	16 572
2000	2 627.07	2 084.21	542.86	16 331
2001	3 109.50	2 301.33	808.17	19 264
2002	4 915.54	3 603.05	1 312.49	30 245
2003	6 054.60	4 260.87	1 793.73	35 385
2004	6 960.99	4 904.93	2 056.06	39 956
2005	8 432.49	6 071.83	2 360.66	47 416
2006	9 480.28	6 701.87	2 778.31	52 231
2007	9 326.45	6 185.85	3 140.60	50 194
2008	12 083.66	8 555.64	3 528.02	63 987
2009	14 357.65	9 733.13	4 624.53	75 373
2010	16 249.29	10 853.11	5 396.19	76 933

注：本表数据由中国人民银行上海总部提供。2000年起储蓄存款为中外资金融机构本外币存款余额。
Note: Data in this table are provided by Shanghai Headquarters of the People's Bank of China. Since 2000, the Savings deposits refered to all deposits in foreign and domestic currency of foreign and domestic funded financial institutions.

表9.11　城市居民家庭生活基本情况(1980～2010)
BASIC STATISTICS OF URBAN HOUSEHOLDS

年　份 Year	调查户数 (户) Number of Households Surveyed (household)	平均每户家庭人口 (人) Average Number Persons per Household (person)	平均每户就业人口 (人) Average Number of Employees per Household (person)	平均每户就业面 (%) Percentage of Emplyment per Household (%)	平均每一就业者负担人数 (人) Persons Supported by Each Employee (person)	平均每人可支配收入 (元) Average per Capita Disposable Income (yuan)
1980	500	4.06	2.41	59.4	1.68	637
1981	500	4.06	2.47	60.8	1.64	637
1982	500	4.03	2.48	61.5	1.63	659
1983	500	4.00	2.52	63.0	1.59	686
1984	500	3.94	2.53	64.2	1.56	834
1985	500	3.72	2.27	61.0	1.64	1 075
1986	500	3.66	2.30	62.8	1.59	1 293
1987	500	3.55	2.20	62.0	1.61	1 437
1988	500	3.38	2.08	61.5	1.63	1 723
1989	500	3.27	2.00	61.2	1.64	1 976
1990	500	3.25	1.98	60.9	1.64	2 183
1991	500	3.18	1.91	60.1	1.66	2 486
1992	500	3.11	1.84	59.2	1.69	3 009
1993	500	3.03	1.77	58.4	1.71	4 277
1994	500	3.07	1.69	55.0	1.82	5 868
1995	500	3.11	1.65	53.1	1.88	7 172
1996	500	3.07	1.58	51.5	1.94	8 159
1997	500	3.08	1.59	51.6	1.94	8 439
1998	500	3.09	1.58	51.1	1.96	8 773
1999	500	3.08	1.73	56.2	1.78	10 932
2000	500	3.04	1.64	53.9	1.85	11 718
2001	500	3.00	1.55	51.7	1.94	12 883
2002	500	2.90	1.52	52.4	1.91	13 250
2003	500	2.99	1.55	51.8	1.93	14 867
2004	1 000	3.04	1.53	50.3	1.99	16 683
2005	1 000	3.01	1.55	51.5	1.94	18 645
2006	1 000	3.02	1.60	53.0	1.89	20 668
2007	1 000	3.01	1.64	54.5	1.84	23 623
2008	1 000	2.97	1.63	54.9	1.82	26 675
2009	1 000	2.93	1.60	54.6	1.83	28 838
2010	1 000	2.90	1.60	55.2	1.81	31 838

①本表数据为城市居民家庭收支抽样调查资料，由国家统计局上海调查总队提供。
②2002 年起，人均可支配收入不包括出售财物收入和个人交纳的社会保障支出。其他年份按原口径计算。
❶Data in this table are obtained from the sample survey of urban households and provided by Survey Office of the National Bureau of Statistics in Shanghai.
❷Incomes from selling properties and social security expenditure are excluded from disposable income since 2002.

表 9.11 续表 continued

年 份 Year	平均每人消费支出(元) Average per Capita Consumption Expenditures (yuan)	其中 of which #服务性消费支出 Service Consumption Expenditures	服务性消费支出占消费支出比重(%) Percentage of Service Consumption Expenditures to the Total Expenditure (%)	可支配收入比上年增长(%)(按当年价格) Growth Rate of Disposable Income on Preceding Year (at current Price)(%)	消费支出比上年增长(%)(按当年价格) Growth Rate of Consumption Expenditure on Preceding Year (at current Price)(%)	恩格尔系数(%) Engel Coefficient(%)
1980	553	75	13.6	32.5	28.8	56.0
1981	585	79	13.5	持平	5.7	56.8
1982	576	82	14.2	3.5	-1.5	58.9
1983	615	87	14.1	4.0	6.9	58.5
1984	726	101	13.9	21.6	18.0	56.5
1985	992	121	12.2	28.9	36.6	52.1
1986	1 170	136	11.6	20.3	18.0	52.7
1987	1 282	161	12.6	11.1	9.6	54.4
1988	1 648	171	10.4	19.9	28.6	52.7
1989	1 812	190	10.5	14.6	9.9	55.8
1990	1 937	233	12.0	10.5	6.9	56.5
1991	2 167	294	13.6	13.9	11.9	56.9
1992	2 509	365	14.5	21.1	15.8	55.9
1993	3 530	568	16.1	42.2	40.7	53.1
1994	4 669	732	15.7	37.2	32.3	53.5
1995	5 868	889	15.1	22.2	25.7	53.4
1996	6 763	1 205	17.8	13.8	15.3	50.7
1997	6 820	1 173	17.2	3.4	0.8	51.7
1998	6 866	1 344	19.6	4.0	0.7	50.6
1999	8 248	1 781	21.6	24.6	20.1	45.2
2000	8 868	2 154	24.3	7.2	7.5	44.5
2001	9 336	2 393	25.6	9.9	5.3	43.4
2002	10 464	3 033	29.0	11.5	11.4	39.4
2003	11 040	3 369	30.5	12.2	5.5	37.2
2004	12 631	4 084	32.3	12.2	14.4	36.4
2005	13 773	4 447	32.3	11.8	9.0	35.9
2006	14 762	4 841	32.8	10.8	7.2	35.6
2007	17 255	5 595	32.4	14.3	16.9	35.5
2008	19 398	6 287	32.4	12.9	12.4	36.6
2009	20 992	6 656	31.7	8.1	8.2	35.0
2010	23 200	6 955	30.0	10.4	10.5	33.5

注：平均每人可支配收入增长和平均每人消费支出增长是按同口径计算的。
Note: Growth of per Caspita Disposable Income and growth of per Capita Consumption Expenditures are calculated by the same caliber.

表 9.12 城市居民家庭生活基本情况(2010，按收入水平分组)
BASIC STATISTICS OF URBAN HOUSEHOLD INCOME AND EXPENDITURES (2010,GROUPED BY INCOME LEVEL)

指 标	Indicators	总平均 Total Average	低收入户 Low Income	中低收入户 Medium-low Income
调查户数（户）	Number of Households Surveyed (household)	1 000	200	200
平均每户家庭人口（人）	Average Number of Persons per Household (person)	2.90	3.08	2.95
平均每户就业人口（人）	Average Number of Employees per Household (person)	1.60	1.49	1.46
平均每户就业面（%）	Percentage of Employment per Household (%)	55.2	48.4	49.5
平均每一就业者负担人数（人）	Persons Supported by Each Employee (person)	1.81	2.07	2.02
可支配收入（元）	Average per Capita Disposable Income (yuan)	31 838	14 996	21 780
工资性收入	Salaries	21 745	9 814	12 760
经营净收入	Net Income from Household Business	1 628	627	744
财产性收入	Property Income	511	92	228
转移性收入	Transferred Income	7 954	4 463	8 048
#养老金或离退休金	Pensions and Retirement Pay	6 794	3 503	7 433
出售财物收入（元）	Income from Selling Properties(yuan)	3 721	2 386	…
借贷收入（元）	Borrowings and other Credit Items(yuan)	6 329	2 232	2 116
#住房贷款	Morgage Loans	465		
提取储蓄存款	Drawings of Saving Deposits	5 650	1 574	2 114
消费支出(元)	Average Per Capita Consumption Expenditures (yuan)	23 200	12 555	15 970
#服务性消费支出	Service Consumption Expenditure	6 955	3 651	4 512
购房与建房支出（元）	Buying and Building House Expenditure (yuan)	2 644	2 469	160
转移性支出（元）	Transferred Expenditure (yuan)	3 244	1 113	1 343
社会保障支出(元)	Social Security Expenditure (yuan)	3 015	1 614	1 958
借贷支出（元）	Lendings and other Debit Items (yuan)	8 729	1 155	2 738

注：本表数据为城市居民家庭收支抽样调查资料，由国家统计局上海调查总队提供。
Note: Data in this table are obtained from the sample survey of urban households and provided by Survey Office of the National Bureau of Statistics in Shanghai.

表9.12 续表 continued

指 标	Indicators	中等收入户 Medium Income	中高收入户 Medium-high Income	高收入户 High Income
调查户数（户）	Number of Households Surveyed (household)	200	200	200
平均每户家庭人口（人）	Average Number of Persons per Household (person)	2.90	2.82	2.75
平均每户就业人口（人）	Average Number of Employees per Household (person)	1.63	1.59	1.82
平均每户就业面（%）	Percentage of Employment per Household (%)	56.2	56.4	66.2
平均每一就业者负担人数（人）	Persons Supported by Each Employee (person)	1.78	1.77	1.51
可支配收入（元）	Average per Capita Disposable Income (yuan)	27 484	35 120	62 465
工资性收入	Salaries	17 811	22 989	47 454
经营净收入	Net Income from Household Business	1 559	860	4 544
财产性收入	Property Income	210	609	1 494
转移性收入	Transferred Income	7 904	10 662	8 973
#养老金或离退休金	Pensions and Retirement Pay	6 919	9 589	6 730
出售财物收入（元）	Income from Selling Properties(yuan)	3 446	44	13 267
借贷收入（元）	Borrowings and other Credit Items(yuan)	3 953	7 132	17 067
#住房贷款	Morgage Loans			2 447
提取储蓄存款	Drawings of Saving Deposits	3 613	7 120	14 592
消费支出(元)	Average per Capita Consumption Expenditures (yuan)	21 611	26 773	40 744
#服务性消费支出	Service Consumption Expenditure	6 649	7 883	12 604
购房与建房支出（元）	Buying and Building House Expenditure(yuan)	2 432		8 452
转移性支出（元）	Transferred Expenditure(yuan)	1 890	4 071	8 222
社会保障支出(元)	Social Security Expenditure(yuan)	2 756	3 183	5 799
借贷支出（元）	Lendings and other Debit Items (yuan)	5 026	6 838	29 375

表9.13 主要年份城市居民家庭人均可支配收入
PER CAPITA DISPOSABLE INCOME OF URBAN HOUSEHOLDS IN MAIN YEARS

单位:元(yuan)

年份 Year	人均可支配收入 Average per Capita Disposable Income	工资性收入 Salaries	经营净收入 Net Income from Household Business	财产性收入 Property Income	转移性收入 Transferred Income
1980	637	551			86
1985	1 075	794	1		280
1990	2 183	1 548	1	21	613
1991	2 486	1 780		29	677
1992	3 009	2 138	3	44	824
1993	4 277	3 099	4	37	1 137
1994	5 868	4 224	28	54	1 562
1995	7 172	5 002	69	92	2 009
1996	8 159	5 889	87	61	2 122
1997	8 439	5 969	150	69	2 251
1998	8 773	6 004	98	57	2 614
1999	10 932	7 326	156	68	3 382
2000	11 718	7 832	120	65	3 701
2001	12 883	7 975	119	39	4 750
2002	13 250	7 915	436	94	4 805
2003	14 867	10 097	377	130	4 263
2004	16 683	11 422	507	215	4 539
2005	18 645	12 409	798	292	5 146
2006	20 668	13 962	959	300	5 447
2007	23 623	16 598	1 158	369	5 498
2008	26 675	18 909	1 399	369	5 998
2009	28 838	19 811	1 435	474	7 118
2010	31 838	21 745	1 628	511	7 954

表9.14 主要年份城市居民家庭人均可支配收入与消费支出
PER CAPITA ANNUAL DISPOSABLE INCOME AND CONSUMPTION EXPENDITURES OF URBAN HOUSEHOLDS IN MAIN YEARS

单位:元(yuan)

指标	Indicators	2000	2009	2010
人均可支配收入	**Average per Capita Disposable Income**	**11 718**	**28 838**	**31 838**
低收入户	Low Income	6 840	13 205	14 996
中低收入户	Medium-low Income	8 815	19 320	21 780
中等收入户	Medium Income	10 529	24 717	27 484
中高收入户	Medium-high Income	12 892	32 212	35 120
高收入户	High Income	19 959	57 726	62 465
人均消费支出	**Average per Capita Consumption Expenditures**	**8 868**	**20 992**	**23 200**
低收入户	Low Income	6 272	11 654	12 555
中低收入户	Medium-low Income	7 516	16 155	15 970
中等收入户	Medium Income	8 555	18 487	21 611
中高收入户	Medium-high Income	9 445	24 253	26 773
高收入户	High Income	12 763	36 063	40 744

注：本页数据为城市居民家庭收支抽样调查资料，由国家统计局上海调查总队提供。
Note: Data on this page are obtained from the sample survey of urban households and provided by Survey Office of the National Bureau of Statistics in Shanghai.

表9.15 主要年份城市居民家庭人均消费支出
PER CAPITA CONSUMPTION EXPENDITURES OF URBAN HOUSEHOLDS IN MAIN YEARS

单位:元(yuan)

年份 Year	消费支出 Total Consumption Expenditures	食品 Food	衣着 Clothing	家庭设备用品及服务 Household Facilities, Articles and Services	医疗保健 Medicines and Medical Services	交通和通信 Traffic and Communi-cations	教育文化娱乐服务 Education, Culture and Recreation Services	居住 Residence	其他商品和服务 Other Commodities and Services
1980	553	310	79	50	7	20	49	26	12
1985	992	517	148	131	5	30	91	43	27
1990	1 937	1 095	208	196	11	58	231	90	48
1995	5 868	3 131	561	637	113	321	508	401	196
1996	6 763	3 429	590	614	148	496	827	416	243
1997	6 820	3 526	552	525	197	397	828	605	190
1998	6 866	3 477	472	453	261	406	893	674	230
1999	8 248	3 731	551	772	347	583	1 094	842	328
2000	8 868	3 947	567	683	501	759	1 287	794	330
2001	9 336	4 056	577	579	558	958	1 422	796	390
2002	10 464	4 120	613	653	734	1 115	1 668	1 189	372
2003	11 040	4 102	751	792	603	1 259	1 834	1 280	419
2004	12 631	4 593	797	780	762	1 703	2 195	1 327	474
2005	13 773	4 940	940	800	797	1 984	2 273	1 412	627
2006	14 762	5 249	1 027	877	763	2 333	2 432	1 436	645
2007	17 255	6 125	1 330	959	857	3 154	2 654	1 412	764
2008	19 398	7 109	1 521	1 182	755	3 373	2 875	1 646	937
2009	20 992	7 345	1 593	1 365	1 002	3 499	3 139	1 913	1 136
2010	23 200	7 777	1 794	1 800	1 006	4 076	3 363	2 166	1 218

表9.16 主要年份城市居民家庭人均消费支出构成
COMPOSITION OF PER CAPITA CONSUMPTION EXPENDITURES OF URBAN HOUSEHOLDS IN MAIN YEARS

单位:%

年份 Year	消费支出 Total Consumption Expenditures	食品 Food	衣着 Clothing	家庭设备用品及服务 Household Facilities Articles and Services	医疗保健 Medicine and Medical Services	交通和通信 Traffic and Communi cations	教育文化娱乐服务 Education, Cultural and Recreation Services	居住 Residence	其他商品和服务 Other Commodities and Services
1980	100	56.0	14.3	9.0	1.3	3.6	8.9	4.7	2.2
1985	100	52.1	14.9	13.2	0.5	3.0	9.2	4.4	2.7
1990	100	56.5	10.7	10.1	0.6	3.0	11.9	4.7	2.5
1995	100	53.4	9.6	10.8	1.9	5.5	8.7	6.8	3.3
1996	100	50.7	8.7	9.1	2.2	7.3	12.2	6.2	3.6
1997	100	51.7	8.1	7.7	2.9	5.8	12.1	8.9	2.8
1998	100	50.6	6.9	6.6	3.8	5.9	13.0	9.8	3.4
1999	100	45.2	6.7	9.3	4.2	7.1	13.3	10.2	4.0
2000	100	44.5	6.4	7.7	5.6	8.6	14.5	9.0	3.7
2001	100	43.4	6.2	6.2	6.0	10.3	15.2	8.5	4.2
2002	100	39.4	5.9	6.2	7.0	10.7	15.9	11.4	3.5
2003	100	37.2	6.8	7.2	5.4	11.4	16.6	11.6	3.8
2004	100	36.4	6.3	6.2	6.0	13.5	17.4	10.5	3.7
2005	100	35.9	6.8	5.8	5.8	14.4	16.5	10.2	4.6
2006	100	35.6	6.9	5.9	5.2	15.8	16.5	9.7	4.4
2007	100	35.5	7.7	5.5	5.0	18.3	15.4	8.2	4.4
2008	100	36.6	7.9	6.1	3.9	17.4	14.8	8.5	4.8
2009	100	35.0	7.6	6.5	4.8	16.7	14.9	9.1	5.4
2010	100	33.5	7.7	7.8	4.3	17.6	14.5	9.3	5.3

注：本页数据为城市居民家庭收支抽样调查资料，由国家统计局上海调查总队提供。
Note: Data on this page are obtained from the sample survey of households and provided by Survey Office of the National Bureau of Statistics in Shanghai.

表9.17 主要年份城市居民家庭人均消费支出
PER CAPITA CONSUMPTION EXPENDITURES OF URBAN HOUSEHOLD IN MAIN YEARS

单位:元(yuan)

类别	Types	2000	2009	2010
消费支出	**Total Consumption Expenditures**	**8 868**	**20 992**	**23 200**
食品	Food	3 947	7 345	7 777
#粮油	Grain and Oil	396	653	885
肉禽蛋水产品	Meat, Poultry, Eggs and Aquatic Products	1 324	1 905	2 071
蔬菜	Vegetables	305	550	622
干鲜瓜果	Dry and Fresh Fruits	293	522	594
糕点、奶及奶制品	Cake, Milk and Dairy Products	315	563	615
在外饮食	Dining Out	710	2 191	1 925
衣着	Clothing	567	1 593	1 794
#服装	Garments	387	1 190	1 352
家庭设备用品及服务	Household Facilities, Articles and Services	683	1 365	1 800
#耐用消费品	Durable Consumer Goods	340	684	816
医疗保健	Medicines and Medical Services	501	1 002	1 006
#药品费	Medicines	244	400	430
医疗费	Medical Services	69	284	239
交通和通信	Traffic and Communications	759	3 499	4 076
交通	Traffic	375	2 426	2 891
#交通费	Traffic Fees	335	759	749
通信	Communications	384	1 073	1 185
#电信费	Telecommunication Fees	272	878	969
教育文化娱乐服务	Education, Culture and Recreation Articles and Services	1 287	3 139	3 363
教育	Education	585	1 191	1 168
#学杂费	Tuition	365	449	456
家教及培训班	Family Education and Training		315	410
成人教育费	Adult Education Fee	78	193	124
文化娱乐服务	Culture and Recreation Services	147	990	1 139
文化娱乐用品	Culture and Recreation Articles	555	958	1 056
#家用电脑	Computers	197	305	289
书报杂志	Books, Newspapers and Magazines	73	76	76
居住	Residence	794	1 913	2 166
#水费	Water	72	107	119
电费	Electricity	258	398	452
燃料费	Fuels	157	194	201
租赁房房租	Rent	142	235	265
物业管理费	Estate Management Fee	20	162	161
其他商品和服务	Miscellanecus Commodities and Services	330	1 136	1 218

注：本表数据为城市居民家庭收支抽样调查资料，由国家统计局上海调查总队提供。
Note: Data in this table are obtained from the sample survey of urban households and provided by Survey Office of the National Bureau of Statistics in Shanghai.

表9.18 城市居民家庭人均消费支出（2010，按收入水平分组）
PER CAPITA CONSUMPTION EXPENDITURES OF URBAN HOUSEHOLD (2010,GROUPED BY INCOME LEVEL)

单位:元(yuan)

类别	Types	总平均 Total Average	低收入户 Low Income	中低收入户 Medium-low Income
消费支出	**Total Consumer Expenditures**	**23 200**	**12 555**	**15 970**
食品	Food	7 777	5 578	6 821
#粮油	Grain and Oil	885	740	854
肉禽蛋水产品	Meat,Poultry,Eggs and Aquatic Products	2 071	1 737	2 020
蔬菜	Vegetables	622	536	614
干鲜瓜果	Dry and Fresh Fruit	594	417	552
糕点、奶及奶制品	Cake,Milk and Dairy Products	615	448	537
在外饮食	Dining Out	1 925	913	1 302
衣着	Clothing	1 794	803	1 113
#服装	Garments	1 352	584	813
家庭设备用品及服务	Household Facilities Articles and Services	1 800	690	1 022
#耐用消费品	Durable Consumer Goods	816	255	431
医疗保健	Medicine and Medical Services	1 006	712	878
#药品费	Medicines	430	402	418
医疗费	Medical Services	239	155	248
交通和通信	Traffic and Communications	4 076	1 657	1 806
交通	Traffic	2 891	864	785
#交通费	Traffic Fees	749	416	567
通信	Telecommunications	1 185	793	1 021
#电信费	Communication Fees	969	705	855
教育文化娱乐服务	Education, Culture and Recreation Articles and Services	3 363	1 921	2 331
教育	Education	1 168	1 170	906
#学杂费	Tuition	456	548	433
家教及培训班	Family Education and Training	410	331	270
成人教育费	Adult Education Fee	124	82	71
文化娱乐服务	Culture and Recreation Services	1 139	339	640
文化娱乐用品	Culture and Recreation Articles	1 056	412	785
#家用电脑	Computers	289	139	282
书报杂志	Books, Newspapers and Magazines	76	33	50
居住	Residence	2 166	907	1 194
#水费	Water	119	102	115
电费	Electricity	452	355	416
燃料费	Fuels	201	163	195
租赁房房租	Rent	265	113	250
物业管理费	Estate Management Fee	161	67	83
其他商品和服务	Miscellanecus Commodities and Services	1 218	287	805

注：本表数据为城市居民家庭收支抽样调查资料，由国家统计局上海调查总队提供。
Note: Data in this table are obtained from the sample survey of urban households and provided by Survey Office of the National Bureau of Statistics in Shanghai.

表9.18 续表 continued

单位:元(yuan)

类别	Types	中等收入户 Medium Income	中高收入户 Medium-high Income	高收入户 High Income
消费支出	**Total Consumer Expenditures**	**21 611**	**26 773**	**40 744**
食品	Food	7 590	8 598	10 586
#粮油	Grain and Oil	888	985	974
肉禽蛋水产品	Meat,Poultry,Eggs and Aquatic Products	2 088	2 212	2 333
蔬菜	Vegetables	642	656	670
干鲜瓜果	Dry and Fresh Fruit	603	677	737
糕点、奶及奶制品	Cake,Milk and Dairy Products	612	706	795
在外饮食	Dining Out	1 730	2 092	3 746
衣着	Clothing	1 516	2 239	3 457
#服装	Garments	1 116	1 690	2 680
家庭设备用品及服务	Household Facilities Articles and Services	1 543	2 140	3 786
#耐用消费品	Durable Consumer Goods	790	1 029	1 658
医疗保健	Medicine and Medical Services	999	1 010	1 470
#药品费	Medicines	402	442	492
医疗费	Medical Services	268	240	291
交通和通信	Traffic and Communications	3 675	4 941	8 731
交通	Traffic	2 531	3 623	7 027
#交通费	Traffic Fees	768	784	1 255
通信	Telecommunications	1 144	1 318	1 704
#电信费	Communication Fees	949	1 054	1 316
教育文化娱乐服务	Education, Culture and Recreation Articles and Services	3 010	3 853	5 936
教育	Education	1 170	947	1 673
#学杂费	Tuition	465	327	504
家教及培训班	Family Education and Training	382	364	727
成人教育费	Adult Education Fee	129	131	216
文化娱乐服务	Culture and Recreation Services	935	1 602	2 301
文化娱乐用品	Culture and Recreation Articles	905	1 304	1 962
#家用电脑	Computers	235	333	473
书报杂志	Books, Newspapers and Magazines	71	89	143
居住	Residence	2 339	2 515	4 064
#水费	Water	118	124	139
电费	Electricity	442	471	587
燃料费	Fuels	202	202	246
租赁房房租	Rent	499	267	198
物业管理费	Estate Management Fee	129	177	367
其他商品和服务	Miscellanecus Commodities and Services	939	1 477	2 714

表9.19 城市居民家庭平均每人主要消费品消费量(2008～2010)
PER CAPITA CONSUMPTION OF MAJOR CONSUMER GOODS OF URBAN HOUSEHOLDS

商品名称	Name of Commodities	2008	2009	2010
大米(千克)	Grain(kg)	42.5	41.6	39.9
食用植物油(千克)	Edible Vegetable Oil(kg)	10.2	9.4	8.0
猪　肉(千克)	Pork(kg)	18.3	18.5	18.6
牛羊肉(千克)	Beef and Mutton(kg)	2.6	2.6	2.8
鸡(千克)	Poultry(kg)	7.4	6.6	6.9
鸭(千克)	Duck(kg)	2.8	2.6	2.5
鲜　蛋(千克)	Eggs(kg)	9.6	9.8	9.6
鱼(千克)	Fish(kg)	15.4	14.9	14.2
虾(千克)	Shrimp(kg)	4.9	5.3	4.4
鲜　菜(千克)	Vegetables(kg)	103.4	102.1	102.7
啤 酒(千克)	Beer(kg)	6.9	6.5	5.6
糕点类(千克)	Cake(kg)	5.9	5.9	5.5
鲜瓜果(千克)	Fresh Melon and Fruit(kg)	67.1	67.2	65.5
鲜乳品和酸奶(千克)	Fresh Milk and Yogurt (kg)	29.4	29.9	28.8
服　装(件)	Clothing (unit)	11.1	10.2	10.4
生活用水(立方米)	Household Water Consumption (cubic meters)	54.7	53.7	52.2
生活用电(千瓦时)	Household Power Consumption (kwh)	687.0	716.9	814.9
液化石油气(千克)	Liquified Petroleum Gas (kg)	0.7	1.0	0.8
管道煤气(立方米)	Pipeline Gas (cubic meters)	137.3	120.9	113.3

注：管道燃气包括管道煤气和管道天然气。
Note: Pipline Gas includes pipeline coal gas and pipeline natural gas.

表9.20 主要年份平均每百户城市居民家庭年末耐用消费品拥有量
PER 100 URBAN HOUSEHOLDS YEAR-END POSSESSION OF DURABLE CONSUMER GOODS IN MAIN YEARS

商品名称	Name of Commodities	2000	2009	2010
彩色电视机(台)	Color TV Set (unit)	147	185	188
照相机(架)	Camera (unit)	71	91	95
摄像机(架)	Video Camera (unit)	3	16	17
家用电脑(台)	Personal Computer (unit)	26	123	129
移动电话(部)	Mobile Phone (unit)	29	223	230
组合音响(台)	Music Center (unit)	32	50	52
家用空调器(台)	Household Air Conditioner (unit)	96	196	200
洗衣机(台)	Washing Machine (unit)	93	99	99
电冰箱(台)	Household Refrigerator (unit)	102	104	104
热水淋浴器(台)	Water Heater (unit)	64	98	98
微波炉(台)	Microwave Oven (unit)	78	97	98
消毒碗柜(台)	Dish-sterilization Boxes(unit)		15	16
家用轿车(辆)	Family Car(unit)		14	17

注：本页数据为城市居民家庭收支抽样调查资料，由国家统计局上海调查总队提供。
Note: Data on this page are obtained from the sample survey of urban households and provided by Survey Office of the National Bureau of Statistics in Shanghai.

表 9.21 农村居民家庭生活基本情况（1990～2010）
BASIC STATISTICS OF RURAL HOUSEHOLDS

年 份 Year	调查户数 （户） Number of Households Surveyed (household)	平均每户人口 （人） Average Number of Person per Household (person)	平均每户劳动力 （人） Average Number of Labours per Household (person)	平均每一劳动力负担人数 （人） Persons Supported by Each Labourer (person)	平均每人总收入 （元） Average Gross Income per Capita (yuan)	平均每人可支配收入 （元） Average Disposable Income per Capita (yuan)
1990	1 000	3.68	2.46	1.49	1 990	1 665
1991	600	3.49	2.36	1.48	2 376	2 003
1992	600	3.43	2.36	1.46	2 581	2 226
1993	600	3.41	2.45	1.39	3 149	2 727
1994	600	3.41	2.51	1.36	3 940	3 437
1995	600	3.47	2.54	1.37	4 861	4 246
1996	600	3.40	2.54	1.34	5 506	4 846
1997	600	3.35	2.48	1.35	5 933	5 277
1998	600	3.33	2.50	1.33	5 965	5 407
1999	600	3.31	2.54	1.30	5 924	5 481
2000	600	3.31	2.53	1.31	6 400	5 565
2001	600	3.29	2.48	1.33	6 827	5 850
2002	600	3.33	2.52	1.32	7 080	6 212
2003	600	3.34	2.59	1.29	7 260	6 658
2004	600	3.33	2.54	1.31	7 994	7 337
2005	600	3.21	2.19	1.47	9 234	8 342
2006	600	3.20	2.24	1.43	10 225	9 213
2007	600	3.18	2.17	1.47	11 382	10 222
2008	600	3.15	2.15	1.46	12 662	11 385
2009	600	3.15	2.11	1.50	13 404	12 324
2010	600	3.11	2.11	1.48	15 346	13 746

注：本表数据为农村居民家庭收支抽样调查资料，由国家统计局上海调查总队提供。
Note: Data in this table are obtained from the sample survey of households and provided by Survey office of the National Bureau of Statistics in Shanghai.

表 9.21 续表 continued

年 份 Year	平均每人总支出（元） Average Expenditures Per Capita (yuan)	平均每人生活消费支出（元） per Capita Consumpition Expenditures (yuan)	平均每人可支配收入指数（以 1990 年为 100） Index of per Capita Disposable Income (1990 = 100)	平均每人生活消费支出指数（以 1990 年为 100） Index of Per Capita Consumption Expenditures (1990 = 100)	平均每人年底居住房屋面积（平方米） Average per Capita Living Space Year-end (sq. m)
1990	1 592	1 262	100.0	100.0	37.08
1991	1 893	1 540	120.3	122.0	39.60
1992	2 322	1 967	133.7	155.7	42.07
1993	2 660	2 200	163.8	174.3	44.22
1994	3 320	2 715	206.4	215.1	44.15
1995	4 041	3 368	255.0	266.9	43.08
1996	4 581	3 868	291.1	306.5	45.47
1997	4 953	4 228	316.9	335.0	46.44
1998	4 924	4 207	324.7	333.4	47.24
1999	4 431	3 867	329.2	306.4	49.00
2000	5 578	4 138	334.2	327.9	53.58
2001	6 353	4 753	351.3	376.6	54.70
2002	6 988	5 311	373.1	420.8	57.08
2003	6 931	5 670	399.9	449.3	59.03
2004	7 580	6 329	440.7	502.0	59.84
2005	8 663	7 265	501.0	575.7	56.56
2006	9 344	8 006	553.3	634.4	59.99
2007	10 429	8 845	613.9	700.9	61.22
2008	10 840	9 115	683.8	722.3	62.30
2009	11 436	9 804	740.2	776.9	60.18
2010	11 988	10 225	825.6	810.2	59.68

注：2000 年前平均每人可支配收入按纯收入口径计算，平均每人总收入不包括内部亲友赠送。
Note: The per Capita Disposable income before 2000 refers to the Net Income. The Gross Income excludes the donations from relatives and friends.

表9.22 主要年份农村居民家庭人均可支配收入
PER CAPITA DISPOSABLE INCOME OF RURAL HOUSEHOLDS IN MAIN YEARS

年 份 Year	人均可支配收入(元) Average Disposable Income per Capita (yuan)	工资性收入 Wages	家庭经营纯收入 Household Business Income	转移性和财产性收入 Property and Transferred Income	比重(以人均可支配收入为100) Proportion(Average Disposable Income Per Capita = 100)		
					工资性收入 Wages	家庭经营纯收入 Household Business Income	转移性和财产性收入 Property and Transferred Income
1990	1 665	1 066	539	60	64.0	32.4	3.6
1995	4 246	2 734	1 183	329	64.4	27.9	7.7
2000	5 565	4 310	934	321	77.4	16.8	5.8
2001	5 850	4 491	967	392	76.8	16.5	6.7
2002	6 212	4 920	774	518	79.2	12.5	8.3
2003	6 658	5 284	813	561	79.4	12.2	8.4
2004	7 337	5 757	886	694	78.5	12.1	9.4
2005	8 342	6 364	811	1 167	76.3	9.7	14.0
2006	9 213	6 892	766	1 555	74.8	8.4	16.8
2007	10 222	7 498	754	1 970	73.3	7.4	19.3
2008	11 385	8 182	711	2 492	71.9	6.2	21.9
2009	12 324	8 721	590	3 013	70.8	4.8	24.4
2010	13 746	9 606	589	3 551	69.9	4.3	25.8

注：2000 年前平均每人可支配收入按纯收入口径计算。
Note: The per Capita Annual Disposable Income before 2000 refers to the Net Income.

表9.23 农村居民家庭人均可支配收入和人均生活消费支出(2000～2010)
PER CAPITA DISPOSABLE INCOME AND LIVING EXPENDITURES FOR CONSUMPTION OF RURAL HOUSEHOLDS

单位:元(yuan)

年 份 Year	总平均 Average	低收入户 Low Income	中低收入户 Medium-low Income	中等收入户 Medium Income	中高收入户 Medium-high Income	高收入户 High Income
人均可支配收入	**Average per Capita Disposable Income**					
2000	5 565	2 330	3 906	5 264	6 725	10 405
2001	5 850	2 351	4 078	5 649	7 122	10 930
2002	6 212	2 429	4 266	5 701	7 513	11 989
2003	6 658	2 761	4 621	6 213	7 972	12 777
2004	7 337	3 122	5 148	7 006	8 775	13 652
2005	8 342	3 347	5 594	7 612	9 755	15 309
2006	9 213	3 830	6 194	8 412	10 714	16 843
2007	10 222	4 321	7 098	9 442	11 807	18 443
2008	11 385	4 690	8 065	10 487	13 094	20 748
2009	12 324	5 279	8 785	11 184	14 039	22 465
2010	13 746	5 968	10 107	12 929	16 327	24 536
人均生活消费支出	**Average per Capitor Consumption Expenditures**					
2000	4 138	2 390	3 387	3 887	5 487	5 880
2001	4 753	2 921	3 250	4 334	5 356	8 449
2002	5 311	2 350	4 341	4 834	5 873	9 683
2003	5 670	2 886	3 681	5 363	6 286	10 769
2004	6 329	4 076	4 914	5 309	6 992	10 971
2005	7 265	4 618	5 690	6 317	7 059	12 975
2006	8 006	4 788	6 001	6 951	8 015	15 058
2007	8 845	4 890	6 077	7 305	9 541	17 317
2008	9 115	5 024	6 280	9 555	10 700	14 517
2009	9 804	5 472	6 266	9 026	12 843	16 035
2010	10 225	5 026	7 881	8 739	15 103	15 187

注：本页数据为农村居民家庭收支抽样调查资料，由国家统计局上海调查总队提供。
Note: Data on this page are obtained from the sample survey of households and provided by Survey office of the National Bureau of Statistics in Shanghai.

表 9.24 主要年份农村居民家庭人均生活消费支出
PER CAPITA CONSUMPTION EXPENDITURES OF RURAL HOUSEHOLDS IN MAIN YEARS

单位：元(yuan)

年份 Year	生活消费支出 Total Consumption Expenditures	食品 Food	衣着 Clothing	居住 Residence	家庭设备用品及服务 Household Facilities, Articles and Services	交通和通信 Traffic and Communi-cations	文教娱乐用品及服务 Education, Culture and Recreation Articles and Services	医疗保健 Medicines and Medical Services	其他商品和服务 Other Commodities and Services
1990	1 262	586	107	272	129	6	59	33	70
1995	3 368	1 491	233	761	284	159	256	73	111
2000	4 138	1 823	201	724	225	279	559	209	118
2001	4 753	1 915	226	890	294	340	673	265	150
2002	5 311	1 872	226	1 392	281	462	661	280	137
2003	5 670	2 004	250	1 437	297	587	676	333	86
2004	6 329	2 191	280	1 446	344	720	806	425	117
2005	7 265	2 676	367	1 323	458	739	936	562	204
2006	8 006	3 024	418	1 658	481	780	920	549	176
2007	8 845	3 259	476	2 097	452	884	857	571	249
2008	9 115	3 732	467	1 806	504	880	850	697	179
2009	9 804	3 639	496	2 103	481	1 212	943	739	191
2010	10 225	3 807	554	2 070	528	1 459	1 012	585	210

表 9.25 主要年份农村居民家庭人均生活消费支出构成
COMPOSITION OF PER CAPITA CONSUMER EXPENDITURES OF RURAL HOUSEHOLDS IN MAIN YEARS

单位：%

年份 Year	生活消费支出 Total Consumption Expenditures	食品 Food	衣着 Clothing	居住 Residence	家庭设备用品及服务 Household Facilities, Articles and Services	交通和通信 Traffic and Communi-cations	文教娱乐用品及服务 Education, Culture and Recreation Articles and Services	医疗保健 Medicines and Medical Services	其他商品和服务 Other Commodities and Services
1990	100	46.4	8.5	21.6	10.2	0.5	4.7	2.6	5.5
1995	100	44.3	6.9	22.6	8.4	4.7	7.6	2.2	3.3
1996	100	42.8	6.6	21.1	9.4	5.2	9.0	2.8	3.1
1997	100	41.5	6.3	21.8	8.0	5.7	9.8	4.1	2.8
1998	100	42.2	5.7	20.8	8.8	5.4	11.0	4.0	2.1
1999	100	43.1	5.2	17.6	10.1	5.1	12.3	4.1	2.5
2000	100	44.0	4.9	17.5	5.4	6.7	13.5	5.1	2.9
2001	100	40.3	4.7	18.7	6.2	7.1	14.2	5.6	3.2
2002	100	35.2	4.3	26.2	5.3	8.7	12.4	5.3	2.6
2003	100	35.4	4.4	25.3	5.2	10.4	11.9	5.9	1.5
2004	100	34.6	4.4	22.9	5.4	11.4	12.7	6.7	1.9
2005	100	36.8	5.1	18.2	6.3	10.2	12.9	7.7	2.8
2006	100	37.8	5.2	20.7	6.0	9.7	11.5	6.9	2.2
2007	100	36.8	5.4	23.7	5.1	10.0	9.7	6.5	2.8
2008	100	40.9	5.1	19.8	5.5	9.7	9.3	7.7	2.0
2009	100	37.1	5.1	21.5	4.9	12.4	9.6	7.5	1.9
2010	100	37.2	5.4	20.2	5.2	14.3	9.9	5.7	2.1

注：本页数据为农村居民家庭收支抽样调查资料，由国家统计局上海调查总队提供。
Note: Data on this page are obtained from the sample survey of households and provided by Survey office of the National Bureau of Statistics in Shanghai.

表9.26 农村居民家庭人均可支配收入(2010,按收入水平分组)
AVERAGE PER CAPITA DISPOSABLE INCOME OF RURAL HOUSEHOLDS (2010,GROUPED BY INCOME LEVEL)

单位:元(yuan)

指 标	Indicators	总平均 Total Average	低收入户 Low Income	中低收入户 Medium-low Income
平均每人可支配收入	**Average per Capita Disposable Income**	**13 746**	**5 968**	**10 107**
工资性收入	Wage	9 606	4 179	7 107
家庭经营纯收入	Household Business Income	589	371	399
#农业纯收入	Agricultural Income	364	272	315
财产性收入	Property Income	970	239	563
#利息收入	Interest Income	34	15	10
租金收入	Rental Income	602	76	301
土地征用补偿	Compensation for Land Requisition	75	9	2
转移性收入	Transferred Income	2 581	1 179	2 038
#离退休金、养老金	Pension	2 855	1 643	2 239

注：本表数据为农村居民家庭收支抽样调查资料，由国家统计局上海调查总队提供。
Note: Data in this table are obtained from the sample survey of households and provided by Survey office of the National Bureau of Statistics in Shanghai.

表9.26 续表 continued

单位:元(yuan)

指 标	Indicators	中等收入户 Medium Income	中高收入户 Medium-high Income	高收入户 High Income
平均每人可支配收入	**Average per Capita Disposable Income**	**12 929**	**16 327**	**24 536**
工资性收入	Wage	9 268	11 539	17 458
家庭经营纯收入	Household Business Net Income	293	819	1 172
#农业纯收入	Agricultural Income	163	721	383
财产性收入	Property Net Income	860	1 073	2 281
#利息收入	Interest Income	14	37	104
租金收入	Rental Income	498	750	1 501
土地征用补偿	Compensation for Land Requisition		1	412
转移性收入	Transferred Income	2 508	2 896	3 625
#离退休金、养老金	Pension	2 673	3 313	3 542

表 9.27 农村居民家庭人均生活消费支出（2010,按收入水平分组）
PER CAPITA EXPENDITURES OF RURAL HOUSEHOLDS (2010, GROUPED BY INCOME LEVEL)

单位:元(yuan)

指 标	Indicators	总平均 Total Average	低收入户 Low Income	中低收入户 Medium-low Income
生活消费支出	**Consumption Expenditures**	**10 225**	**5 026**	**7 881**
食 品	Food	3 807	2 384	3 352
衣 着	Clothing	554	232	358
居 住	Residence	2 070	554	1 327
家庭设备用品及服务	Household Faclities, Articles and Services	528	237	364
交通通信	Traffic and Communications	1 459	496	930
文教娱乐用品及服务	Education, Culture and Recreation Articles and Services	1 012	545	894
医疗保健	Medicine and Medical Services	585	407	523
其 他	Others	210	171	133

注：本表数据为农村居民家庭收支抽样调查资料，由国家统计局上海调查总队提供。
Note: Data in this table are obtained from the sample survey of households and provided by Survey office of the National Bureau of Statistics in Shanghai.

表 9.27 续表 continued

单位:元(yuan)

指 标	Indicators	中等收入户 Medium Income	中高收入户 Medium-high Income	高收入户 High Income
生活消费支出	**Consumption Expenditures**	**8 739**	**15 103**	**15 187**
食 品	Food	3 764	4 091	5 649
衣 着	Clothing	551	601	1 091
居 住	Residence	951	5 766	1 938
家庭设备用品及服务	Household Faclities, Articles and Services	504	716	864
交通通信	Traffic and Communications	1 385	2 131	2 495
文教娱乐用品及服务	Education, Culture and Recreation Articles and Services	1 029	1 013	1 644
医疗保健	Medicine and Medical Services	423	546	1 099
其 他	Others	132	239	407

表9.28 主要年份农村居民家庭平均每人主要消费品消费量
PER CAPITA CONSUMPTION OF MAJOR CONSUMER GOODS OF RURAL HOUSEHOLDS IN MAIN YEARS

商品名称	Name of Commodities	2000	2009	2010
粮　食（千克）	Grain (kg)	222.27	138.82	135.82
#稻　谷	Rice	205.25	133.54	130.52
油脂类（千克）	Edible Oil (kg)	7.99	8.06	7.46
蔬菜及菜制品(千克)	Vegetables and Their Products(kg)	92.41	64.76	65.01
肉禽及其制品（千克）	Meat, Poultry and Their Products (kg)	29.68	35.41	34.98
蛋类及蛋制品（千克）	Eggs and Their Products (kg)	10.71	8.45	8.07
奶及奶制品（千克）	Milk and Dairy Products(kg)	2.07	7.02	7.03
水产品（千克）	Aquatic Products (kg)	14.51	18.46	17.21
#鱼　类	Fish	10.11	11.72	11.29
虾、贝、蟹类	Shrimp, Testacean, Crab	2.61	4.79	4.34
水果及水果制品(千克)	Fruits and Their Products(kg)	36.94	29.56	29.04
食　糖（千克）	Suger (kg)	2.47	1.68	1.90
卷　烟（盒）	Cigarette (case)	44.49	45.53	46.70
酒（千克）	Liquor (kg)	15.68	16.07	15.07

表9.29 主要年份平均每百户农村居民家庭年末耐用消费品拥有量
PER 100 RURAL HOUSEHOLD YEAR-END POSSESSION OF DURABLE CONSUMER GOODS IN MAIN YEARS

商品名称	Name of Commodities	2000	2009	2010
彩色电视机（台）	Color TV Set (unit)	97	190	198
电冰箱（台）	Household Refrigerator (unit)	74	101	103
洗衣机（台）	Washing Machine (unit)	69	93	95
影碟机（台）	VCD Player (unit)	27	26	22
生活用汽车（辆）	Moped and Motorcycle (vehicle)		4	6
家用空调器（台）	Household Air Conditioner (unit)	14	135	147
抽油烟机（台）	Cooking Soat Inducer (unit)	35	71	74
微波炉（台）	Microwave Oven (unit)	14	82	84
吸尘器（台）	Vacuam Cleaner (unit)	9	28	28
热水器（台）	Water Heater (unit)	44	94	96
移动电话（部）	Mobile Phone (unit)	19	174	194
家用电脑（台）	Personal Computer (unit)	5	54	60

注：本页数据为农村居民家庭收支抽样调查资料，由国家统计局上海调查总队提供。
Note: Data on this page are obtained from the sample survey of households and provided by Survey office of the National Bureau of Statistics in Shanghai.

上 / 海 / 统 / 计 / 年 / 鉴

主要统计指标解释

从业人员报酬

指各单位在一定时期内直接支付给本单位全部从业人员的劳动报酬总额。包括在岗职工工资总额和本单位其他从业人员劳动报酬两部分。

职工工资总额

指在报告期内直接支付给本单位职工的劳动报酬或生活费。职工工资总额包括在岗职工工资和离岗职工生活费两部分。

职工平均工资

指企业、事业、机关单位的职工在一定时期内平均每人所得的货币工资额。它表明一定时期职工工资收入的高低程度,是反映职工工资水平的主要指标。计算公式为:

职工平均工资 = 报告期实际支付的全部职工工资总额 / 报告期全部职工平均人数

城市居民可支配收入

指居民可用于最终消费支出和其他非义务性支出以及储蓄的总和,即居民家庭可以用来自由支配的收入。它是家庭总收入扣除交纳的所得税、个人交纳的社会保障费以及调查户的记账补贴后的收入。不包括出售财物和借贷收入。

城市居民家庭消费支出

指城市居民家庭用于日常生活的全部支出。包括食品、衣着、家庭设备用品及服务、医疗保健、交通和通信、教育文化娱乐服务、居住、杂项商品和服务等八大类。

城市居民家庭服务性消费支出

指调查户用于本家庭支付社会提供的各种文化和生活方面的非商品性服务费用。服务性消费的特点在于其劳动过程和消费过程在时间与空间上的统一。在居民家庭八大类消费中,服务性消费支出包括:1、食品类中加工服务费和部分在外饮食费用;2、衣着类中衣着加工服务费;3、家庭设备用品及服务类中家庭服务(如家政服务费用);4、医疗保健类中医疗费(如诊疗费、上门出诊费、护工费用);5、交通和通信类中交通工具服务费(如汽车使用、维修费用)、交通费中使用飞机、轮船、火车等交通工具费用、通信服务费(如电信费、邮费);6、教育文化娱乐服务类中文化娱乐服务费(如参观、游览费用、健身活动费、团体旅游、其他文娱活动费)、文娱用品修理服务费、教育费(如义务、非义务教育支出)、成人教育支出、家教费、培训班费用、择校费;7、居住类中租赁费用、部分房屋装潢费用(人工费用)、居住服务费(如物业管理、维修费用);8、杂项商品和服务(如美容、洗澡、理发费用,旅馆住宿等费用)

储蓄存款余额

指个人客户在其他存款性公司开立账户并存入资金或货币,由其他存款性公司出具存款凭证,个人客户凭存款凭证可以支取本金或利息的存款。

农村居民可支配收入

指农村居民获得的经过初次分配与再分配后的收入。可支配收入可用于住户的最终消费、非义务性支出以及储蓄。

农村居民可支配收入 = 总收入 - 家庭经营费用支出 - 税费支出 - 生产性固定资产折旧 - 财产性支出 - 转移性支出。

农村居民家庭生活消费支出

指农村住户用于物质生活和精神生活方面的支出。包括食品,衣着,居住,家庭设备用品及服务,医疗保健,交通和通信,文化教育娱乐用品及服务,其他商品和服务等消费支出。

财产性收入

指金融资产或有形非生产性资产的所有者向其他机构单位提供资金或将有形非生产性资产供其支配,作为回报而从中获得的收入。

转移性收入

指农村住户和住户成员无须付出任何对应物而获得的货物、服务、资金或资产所有权等,不包括无偿提供的用于固定资本形成的资金。一般情况下,是指农村住户在二次分配中的所有收入。

SHANGHAI STATISTICAL YEARBOOK

EXPLANATORY NOTES TO MAJOR STATISTICAL INDICATORS

□ Labor Compensation

Labor Compensation refers to total payment by various units to their employees during a certain period of time, including wages to permanent staff and workers and payment to other employees.

□ Total Wages of Staff and Workers

Total Wages of Staff and Workers refer to the compensation for services of living cost a unit pays to its employees on the payroll, including the living cost paid to those not on duty.

□ Average Wages of Staff and Workers

Average Wages of Staff and Workers refers to the average wage in money terms per person during a certain period of time for staff and workers in enterprises, institutions, and government agencies, which reflects the general level of wage income during a certain period of time and is calculated as follows:

Average Wages of Staff and Workers = Total Wages of Staff and Workers at Reference Time /Average Number of Staff and Workers at Reference Time.

□ Disposable Income of Urban Households

Disposable Income of Urban Households refers to the actual income at the disposal of members of the households which can be used for final consumption, other non-compulsory expenditure and savings, which is part of the urban households' income that can be disposed by the urban households themselves. It is the income after deducting personal income tax, social insurance paid by individuals and investigation allowance from the total income of the households. The income from selling properties and borrowing are not included.

□ Consumption Expenditures of Urban Households

Consumption Expenditures of Urban Households refer to all the expenditures paid by urban households for consumption in daily life, including 8 categories as follows: food; clothing; household facilities, articles and services; medical care; traffic and telecommunication; education, culture and recreation services; housing; miscellaneous commodities and services.

□ Urbanities' Spending on Services

Urbanities'spending on services refers to urbanites pay for services rather than commodities. Services are offered and consumed at the same time and place. The service spending for an urban family falls into the following eight types: 1. Money paid for food processing and money spent while eating out; 2. Money paid for clothing processing; 3. Domestic services and services for home amenities; 4. Medical cost (including medical diagnosis and treatment, in-home medical services and nursing cost); 5. Transport tool service fees (such as for the use of a car and maintenance fee thereby arising), transport tools (plane, ship, train) fees, post and telecommunications fees; 6. Fees for culture and entertainment services (such as tour and fitness building), fees for repair of sports and entertainment items, education cost (spending on obligatory and non-obligatory education), adult education cost, tutor fees, training courses fees and extra money paid as sponsorship fee to a school a student outside his or her education community; 7. Housing rents, some interior decoration cost (for labor), residence service fees (such as for property management and repairs); 8. Fees for other services (such as at a beauty salon, bathhouse, hairdresser's and hotels).

□ Savings Deposits

Savings Deposits refers to the amount of the personal deposit account opened in other deposit-taking companies. The other deposit-taking companies issue the certificate of Savings Deposits to individual customers, by which the individual customers can withdraw principal or interest.

□ Disposable Income of Rural Households

Disposable Income of Rural Households refers to the actual income at the disposal of rural households after initial distribution and reallocation. Disposal Income can be used for final consumption, non-compulsory expenditure and savings.

Disposal Income of Rural Households=total household income-expenditure for household operations-taxes and fees- depreciation of productive fixed assets-expenses on properties-expenses on transfers.

EXPLANATORY NOTES TO MAJOR STATISTICAL INDICATORS

□ Living Expenditures for Consumption of Rural Households

Living Expenditures for Consumption of Rural Households refer to expenditures of material and culture life of rural household, including expenses on food, clothing, housing, household appliances and service, medical and health care, traffic and communication items, cultural, education and recreation items and service and other commodities and service.

□ Income from Properties

Income from Properties refers to the income received as returns by owners of financial assets or tangible non-productive assets by providing capitals or tangible non-productive assets to other institutional units.

□ Income from Transfers

Income from Transfers refers to the receipt by rural households and their members of goods, services, capitals or rights of assets without giving or repaying accordingly, excluding capitals provided to them for the formation of fixed assets. In general, it refers to all income received by rural households through redistribution.

第十篇

CHAPTER 10

城 市 建 设

URBAN CONSTRUCTION

表 10.1 主要年份城市基础设施投资额
URBAN INFRASTRUCTURE INVESTMENT IN MAIN YEARS

单位:亿元(100 million yuan)

年 份 Year	合 计 Total	其 中 of which						
		电力建设 Power Generation	运 输 邮 电 Transportation, Postal and Telecommunications	其 中 of which		公 用 设 施 Facilities for Public Use	其 中 of which	
				交通运输 Transportation	邮电通信 Postal and Telecommunications		公用事业 Public Utilities	市政建设 Civil Construction
1950 ~ 1978	60.08	19.71	23.25	19.41	3.84	17.12	6.85	10.27
1980	9.55	5.31	2.91	2.31	0.60	1.33	0.64	0.69
1985	23.49	3.97	6.75	5.52	1.23	12.77	7.88	4.89
1986	24.78	5.68	8.40	6.56	1.84	10.70	5.67	5.03
1987	32.64	9.31	12.39	10.02	2.37	10.94	5.36	5.58
1988	37.08	14.18	12.35	8.80	3.55	10.55	4.01	6.54
1989	36.09	11.69	9.96	6.16	3.80	14.44	6.84	7.60
1990	47.22	17.53	10.06	7.17	2.90	19.63	10.83	8.80
1991	61.38	19.79	19.07	14.49	4.58	22.52	9.15	13.37
1992	84.35	19.70	21.44	15.01	6.43	43.21	12.58	30.63
1993	167.94	25.77	46.44	31.75	14.69	95.73	37.91	57.82
1994	238.16	41.57	72.68	36.83	35.85	123.91	26.77	97.14
1995	273.78	57.33	79.36	25.94	53.42	137.09	35.03	102.06
1996	378.78	77.61	147.21	69.66	77.55	153.96	48.31	105.65
1997	412.85	80.24	146.10	85.06	61.04	186.51	52.24	134.27
1998	531.38	89.58	181.46	108.79	72.67	260.34	58.37	201.97
1999	501.39	83.05	166.16	102.24	63.92	252.18	64.20	187.98
2000	449.90	64.61	117.52	48.83	68.69	267.77	104.43	163.34
2001	510.78	72.22	168.42	60.72	107.70	270.14	92.25	177.89
2002	583.49	62.14	171.24	63.01	108.23	350.11	148.42	201.69
2003	604.62	66.00	350.35	273.77	76.58	188.28	36.91	151.36
2004	672.58	89.52	371.35	316.96	54.39	211.71	26.92	184.80
2005	885.74	124.22	443.90	385.58	58.32	317.62	41.33	276.28
2006	1 125.54	116.23	703.24	589.52	113.72	306.07	56.23	249.84
2007	1 466.33	163.30	942.03	840.46	101.57	361.01	60.90	300.11
2008	1 733.18	129.53	947.49	838.91	108.59	656.15	112.81	543.34
2009	2 113.45	253.39	1 100.90	978.24	122.66	759.16	135.95	623.21
2010	1 497.46	148.50	866.20	754.66	111.54	482.76	86.58	396.18

注：本表各项投资额均不包括住宅建设投资。 从2003年起，交通运输投资包括公用设施中市内公共交通投资(下表同)。

Note: All items in this table exclude investment in residential housing. Since 2003, public traffic investment, which is belong to facilities for public use has been included in transportation investment(same as follows).

表 10.2 用于公用事业和市政建设的投资额 (1985～2010)
INVESTMENT IN PUBLIC UTILITIES AND CIVIL CONSTRUCTION

单位:亿元(100 million yuan)

年份 Year	公用事业 Public Utilities	其中 of which 自来水 Tap Water	煤气 Gas	市政建设 Civil Construction	其中 of which 园林绿化 Parks and Green Areas	环境卫生 Environmental Sanitation	市政工程管理 Administration of Civil Utilities	其他 Others
1985	7.88			4.89				
1986	5.67	2.74	1.78	5.03	0.43	0.71	3.84	0.05
1987	5.36	2.53	1.79	5.58	0.30	0.34	4.94	…
1988	4.01	0.72	1.25	6.54	0.24	0.58	5.72	…
1989	6.84	1.52	0.90	7.60	0.01	0.52	7.02	0.05
1990	10.83	1.06	1.81	8.80	0.11	0.37	8.31	0.01
1991	9.15	2.34	2.35	13.37	0.15	0.45	12.77	…
1992	12.58	3.20	3.24	30.63	0.32	0.79	28.45	1.07
1993	37.91	6.90	16.72	57.82	0.52	1.06	56.24	…
1994	26.77	11.49	7.80	97.14	2.42	1.01	93.47	0.24
1995	35.03	13.12	12.97	102.06	4.27	1.26	96.21	0.32
1996	48.31	22.12	14.61	105.65	2.66	1.14	101.80	0.05
1997	52.24	27.08	10.03	134.27	5.11	1.62	127.41	0.13
1998	58.37	14.59	13.15	201.97	9.10	3.35	189.41	0.11
1999	64.20	6.41	9.89	187.98	28.62	2.97	155.73	0.66
2000	104.43	5.35	6.88	163.34	38.76	19.34	102.36	2.88
2001	92.25	5.97	5.83	177.89	32.92	2.97	140.63	1.37
2002	148.42	8.62	6.83	201.69	38.83	1.47	160.64	0.75
2003	36.91	22.89	14.02	151.36	33.85	9.25	107.73	0.53
2004	26.92	16.66	10.26	184.80	16.69	7.01	160.22	0.88
2005	41.33	29.66	11.67	276.28	13.88	15.36	246.58	0.46
2006	56.23	43.79	12.44	249.84	26.41	10.17	213.26	
2007	60.90	50.12	10.78	300.11	34.66	11.26	254.19	
2008	112.81	93.24	19.57	543.34	29.01	20.04	494.29	
2009	135.95	109.79	26.16	623.21	27.96	21.91	573.19	0.15
2010	86.58	61.63	24.95	396.18	35.87	10.80	349.27	0.25

表 10.3 主要年份各类房屋构成情况
COMPOSITION OF BUILDINGS IN MAIN YEARS

单位：万平方米(10 000 sq. m)

指 标	Indicators	2000	2009	2010
总 计	**Total**	**34 206**	**87 327**	**93 591**
居住房屋	Residential Buildings	20 865	50 211	52 640
花园住宅	Villas	250	1 935	2 064
公 寓	Apartments	206	501	492
职工住宅	Staff Dwellings	17 939	45 644	47 951
新式里弄	Improved Residential Blocks	428	528	528
旧式里弄	Old Residential Blocks	1 896	1 276	1 237
简 屋	Simple Housings	84	28	29
其 他	Others	62	299	339
非居住房屋	Non-Residential Buildings	13 341	37 116	40 952
工 厂	Plants	5 739	16 801	18 524
学 校	Schools	1 417	2 808	3 172
仓库堆栈	Warehouses	650	1 354	1 654
办公楼	Offices	2 416	5 971	6 365
商场店铺	Stores	1 191	5 089	5 497
医 院	Hospitals	367	658	754
旅 馆	Hotels	376	863	931
影剧院	Theatres and Cinemas	47	73	75
其 他	Others	1 138	3 500	3 979

表 10.4 主要年份八层以上房屋情况
BUILDINGS OVER EIGHT STOREYS IN MAIN YEARS

类 别	Types	单 位 Unit	2000	2009	2010
总 计	**Total**	**幢 (building)**	**3 529**	**19 183**	**20 579**
		万平方米 (10 000 sq. m)	6 180	20 464	21 911
8～10 层	8～10 Storeys	幢 (building)	536	2 369	2 744
		万平方米 (10 000 sq. m)	451	2 196	2 430
11～15 层	11～15 Storeys	幢 (building)	684	8 992	9 672
		万平方米 (10000 sq. m)	875	5 783	6 320
16～19 层	16～19 Storeys	幢 (building)	831	3 995	4 247
		万平方米 (10 000 sq. m)	1 100	4 199	4 449
20～29 层	20～29 Storeys	幢 (building)	1 266	2 852	2 936
		万平方米 (10000 sq. m)	2 695	5 203	5 504
30 层以上	Over 30 Storeys	幢 (building)	212	975	980
		万平方米 (10 000 sq. m)	1 059	3 083	3 208

①本页数据由市住房保障和房屋管理局提供。
②本页数据按建筑面积计算。
❶Data on this page are provided by Shanghai Municipal Housing Security and Building Administration Bureau.
❷Data on this page are calculated according to floor space of builings.

表 10.5 各区、县房屋建筑分布情况(2010)
DISTRIBUTION OF BUILDINGS IN DIFFERENT DISTRICTS AND COUNTIES

单位：万平方米(10 000 sq. m)

地 区 District		建筑面积合计 Total	其中 of which #年内新增 Newly Constructed	居住房屋 Residential	其中 of which #年内新增 Newly Constructed	非居住房屋 Non-Residential	其中 of which #年内新增 Newly Constructed
总 计	**Total**	**93 591**	**6 264**	**52 640**	**2 429**	**40 952**	**3 835**
浦东新区	Pudong New Area	18 270	99	11 709	182	6 562	-83
黄 浦 区	Huangpu	1 942		838		1 103	
卢 湾 区	Luwan	1 328	47	759	11	569	36
徐 汇 区	Xuhui	6 332	1 336	3 670	546	2 662	790
长 宁 区	Changning	3 419	141	2 086	49	1 333	92
静 安 区	Jing'an	1 593	12	836	-6	757	18
普 陀 区	Putuo	5 146	115	3 341	47	1 805	67
闸 北 区	Zhabei	2 797	28	1 608	20	1 190	8
虹 口 区	Hongkou	3 192	50	1 937	6	1 256	45
杨 浦 区	Yangpu	4 730	125	3 072	90	1 657	35
闵 行 区	Minhang	12 221	2 557	6 535	250	5 686	2 306
宝 山 区	Baoshan	7 248	61	4 581	248	2 668	-187
嘉 定 区	Jiading	7 073	765	2 858	477	4 216	288
金 山 区	Jinshan	2 526	220	1 328	90	1 198	130
松 江 区	Songjiang	8 109	255	3 613	217	4 496	38
青 浦 区	Qingpu	4 169	251	1 638	98	2 531	153
奉 贤 区	Fengxian	1 866	108	1 083	86	783	22
崇 明 县	Chongming	1 628	95	1 146	17	482	78

①本表数据由市住房保障和房屋管理局提供。
②原南汇区划并入浦东新区。(以下同)
❶Data in this table are provided by Shanghai Municipal Housing Security and Building Administration Bureau.
❷Former Nanhui district has been merged into Pudong New Area. (same as follows)

表 10.6 各区、县各类房屋分布情况（2010）
DISTRIBUTION OF BUILDINGS IN DIFFERENT DISTRICTS AND COUNTIES

单位：万平方米（10 000 sq. m）

地 区 District		居住房屋 Residential Buildings	其 中 of which				
			花园住宅 Villas	公 寓 Apartments	一类职工住宅 Staff Dwellings of 1st Class	二类职工住宅 Staff Dwellings of 2nd Class	三类职工住宅 Staff Dwellings of 3rd Class
总 计	**Total**	**52 639.61**	**2 064.14**	**491.96**	**17 961.11**	**29 135.02**	**855.30**
浦东新区	Pudong New Area	11 708.79	450.12		4 220.20	6 490.70	89.80
黄 浦 区	Huangpu	838.35	1.29	2.58	536.51	125.14	5.41
卢 湾 区	Luwan	759.28	15.62	297.31	155.88	138.25	6.99
徐 汇 区	Xuhui	3 670.42	85.26	77.80	1 666.80	1 692.70	9.02
长 宁 区	Changning	2 086.44	56.44	17.59	936.19	1 030.91	7.53
静 安 区	Jing'an	835.92	20.86	35.82	519.25	129.60	3.41
普 陀 区	Putuo	3 341.25	32.76	17.52	1 543.05	1 648.12	22.03
闸 北 区	Zhabei	1 607.63	0.54	0.19	746.89	704.73	27.28
虹 口 区	Hongkou	1 936.87	9.59	15.60	933.02	760.57	15.51
杨 浦 区	Yangpu	3 072.38	3.67	0.90	1 068.29	1 833.40	13.46
闵 行 区	Minhang	6 535.30	298.21	3.23	2 823.29	2 813.87	435.22
宝 山 区	Baoshan	4 580.52	29.47		990.17	3 548.32	
嘉 定 区	Jiading	2 857.62	82.70		144.92	2 571.18	29.06
金 山 区	Jinshan	1 327.68	6.57	2.05	265.68	899.69	68.42
松 江 区	Songjiang	3 613.00	641.05		1 024.84	1 793.83	30.10
青 浦 区	Qingpu	1 638.26	278.49	21.37	203.44	1 004.16	83.64
奉 贤 区	Fengxian	1 083.48	51.52		158.56	866.56	2.09
崇 明 县	Chongming	1 146.43			24.10	1 083.30	6.34

注：本表数据由市住房保障和房屋管理局提供。
Note: Data in this table are provided by Shanghai Municipal Housing Security and Building Administration Bureau.

表10.6 续表1 continued

单位：万平方米(10 000 sq. m)

地区 District		其中 of which				
		新式里弄 Improved Residential Blocks	旧式里弄 Old Residential Blocks		简屋 Simple Housings	其他 Others
			一等 1st Class	二等 2 nd Class		
总计	**Total**	**527.78**	**469.75**	**767.19**	**28.74**	**338.63**
浦东新区	Pudong New Area	165.90	64.30	77.90	8.30	141.60
黄浦区	Huangpu	29.20	89.43	13.00	0.36	35.42
卢湾区	Luwan	70.77	61.29	10.51	0.28	2.39
徐汇区	Xuhui	72.33	18.88	27.19	2.49	17.88
长宁区	Changning	21.52	1.18	12.74	0.53	1.83
静安区	Jing'an	86.90	22.58	12.58		4.92
普陀区	Putuo	5.02	9.21	55.24	2.08	6.22
闸北区	Zhabei	0.72	57.69	66.62	2.18	0.81
虹口区	Hongkou	63.67	82.60	46.08	3.24	6.99
杨浦区	Yangpu	7.21	40.17	96.01	8.30	0.96
闵行区	Minhang	2.04		89.20		70.30
宝山区	Baoshan		10.07	2.48		
嘉定区	Jiading	0.71	1.01	27.88	0.09	0.08
金山区	Jinshan		2.02	34.20	0.04	49.00
松江区	Songjiang			123.19		
青浦区	Qingpu	1.53	6.50	38.15	0.74	0.25
奉贤区	Fengxian	0.28	0.74	3.74		
崇明县	Chongming		2.09	30.49	0.11	

表 10.6 续表 2 continued

单位：万平方米(10 000 sq. m)

地区 District		非居住房屋 Non-Residential Buildings	其中 of which			
			工厂 Plants	学校 Schools	仓库堆栈 Warehouses	办公楼 Offices
总 计	**Total**	**40 951.67**	**18 524.09**	**3 171.95**	**1 653.65**	**6 364.93**
浦东新区	Pudong New Area	6 561.69	1 540.30	532.40	78.00	1 855.20
黄 浦 区	Huangpu	1 103.47	68.87	48.75	16.38	574.87
卢 湾 区	Luwan	568.95	79.10	40.46	7.27	239.26
徐 汇 区	Xuhui	2 661.63	626.55	344.79	94.85	751.68
长 宁 区	Changning	1 332.87	259.32	144.63	31.55	422.25
静 安 区	Jing'an	756.87	108.68	42.32	4.52	344.45
普 陀 区	Putuo	1 805.12	471.72	155.23	272.73	357.18
闸 北 区	Zhabei	1 189.70	470.39	110.85	68.76	157.84
虹 口 区	Hongkou	1 255.62	361.52	152.84	76.55	222.33
杨 浦 区	Yangpu	1 657.32	863.28	247.37	71.93	166.75
闵 行 区	Minhang	5 685.51	3 285.60	326.36	370.62	218.78
宝 山 区	Baoshan	2 667.94	1 067.20	177.87	235.76	332.67
嘉 定 区	Jiading	4 215.63	3 011.47	211.97	38.08	220.48
金 山 区	Jinshan	1 197.98	707.22	68.99	27.43	75.8
松 江 区	Songjiang	4 495.96	3 233.27	325.98	147.02	137.95
青 浦 区	Qingpu	2 530.85	1 854.80	149.18	72.87	153.44
奉 贤 区	Fengxian	782.70	377.74	48.35	18.06	89.26
崇 明 县	Chongming	481.85	137.07	43.60	21.29	44.75

表 10.6 续表 3 continued

单位：万平方米(10 000 sq. m)

地区 District		其中 of which 商场店铺 Stores	医院 Hospitals	旅馆 Hotels	影剧院 Theatres and Cinemas	其他 Others
总计	**Total**	**5 497.47**	**754.15**	**930.63**	**75.43**	**3 979.36**
浦东新区	Pudong New Area	1 738.40	128.90	166.70	18.50	503.29
黄浦区	Huangpu	192.43	32.70	83.62	10.00	75.86
卢湾区	Luwan	103.72	19.72	37.48	2.05	39.90
徐汇区	Xuhui	306.93	96.46	83.24	3.35	353.78
长宁区	Changning	113.77	42.50	109.91	2.40	206.55
静安区	Jing'an	96.57	33.23	77.09	3.29	46.72
普陀区	Putuo	269.97	27.42	41.78	2.36	206.75
闸北区	Zhabei	231.04	38.72	19.07	1.11	91.92
虹口区	Hongkou	194.98	37.96	42.28	2.36	164.81
杨浦区	Yangpu	135.64	35.45	23.36	3.34	110.20
闵行区	Minhang	501.21	48.69	19.84	6.29	908.12
宝山区	Baoshan	262.51	40.02	34.07	5.15	512.69
嘉定区	Jiading	391.73	35.53	42.74	0.62	263.02
金山区	Jinshan	219.35	21.50	14.85	2.17	60.67
松江区	Songjiang	365.38	29.79	37.71	6.93	211.93
青浦区	Qingpu	167.07	21.89	18.94	3.35	89.32
奉贤区	Fengxian	166.98	45.05	8.65	1.38	27.22
崇明县	Chongming	39.81	18.62	69.31	0.79	106.60

表 10.7 各区、县八层以上房屋分布(2010)
DISTRIBUTION OF BUILDINGS OVER EIGHT STOREYS BY DISTRICTS AND COUNTIES

单位：万平方米(10 000 sq. m)

地 区 District		合 计 Total		8～10 层 8～10 Storeys		11～15 层 11～15 Storeys	
		幢 Building	面 积 Floor Space	幢 Building	面 积 Floor Space	幢 Building	面 积 Floor Space
总 计	**Total**	**20 579**	**21 911**	**2 744**	**2 430**	**9 672**	**6 320**
浦东新区	Pudong New Area	4 480	4 632	543	295	2 474	1 575
黄 浦 区	Huangpu	541	1 216	84	98	65	96
卢 湾 区	Luwan	345	728	30	20	55	66
徐 汇 区	Xuhui	2 221	2 086	333	184	774	373
长 宁 区	Changning	1 194	1 716	183	107	325	322
静 安 区	Jing'an	504	1 096	61	44	47	52
普 陀 区	Putuo	1 708	1 723	157	80	571	358
闸 北 区	Zhabei	424	526	34	19	164	100
虹 口 区	Hongkou	784	1 260	94	77	187	183
杨 浦 区	Yangpu	1 362	1 358	140	61	596	441
闵 行 区	Minhang	3 350	2 912	691	1 252	1 939	1 139
宝 山 区	Baoshan	1 592	958	210	88	1 135	643
嘉 定 区	Jiading	568	523	39	23	396	346
金 山 区	Jinshan	385	249	48	24	258	152
松 江 区	Songjiang	634	533	39	24	388	280
青 浦 区	Qingpu	271	193	32	21	169	82
奉 贤 区	Fengxian	170	169	8	7	102	88
崇 明 县	Chongming	46	34	18	8	27	23

注：本表数据由市住房保障和房屋管理局提供。
Note: Data in this table are provided by Shanghai Municipal Housing Security and Building Administration Bureau.

表 10.7 续表 continued

单位：万平方米(10 000 sq. m)

地　区 District		16～19 层 16～19 Storeys		20～29 层 20～29 Storeys		30 层以上 Over 30 Storeys	
		幢 Building	面　积 Floor Space	幢 Building	面　积 Floor Space	幢 Building	面　积 Floor Space
总　计	**Total**	**4 247**	**4 449**	**2 936**	**5 504**	**980**	**3 208**
浦东新区	Pudong New Area	820	903	508	1 101	135	759
黄 浦 区	Huangpu	100	170	188	464	104	388
卢 湾 区	Luwan	58	88	126	285	76	269
徐 汇 区	Xuhui	518	458	437	761	159	309
长 宁 区	Changning	223	265	342	615	121	407
静 安 区	Jing'an	80	111	220	524	96	365
普 陀 区	Putuo	428	379	422	601	130	305
闸 北 区	Zhabei	97	259	76	97	53	52
虹 口 区	Hongkou	230	302	199	411	74	287
杨 浦 区	Yangpu	370	387	232	414	24	55
闵 行 区	Minhang	641	445	73	69	6	7
宝 山 区	Baoshan	226	202	21	26		
嘉 定 区	Jiading	100	120	32	30	1	4
金 山 区	Jinshan	70	54	9	19		
松 江 区	Songjiang	172	179	34	49	1	2
青 浦 区	Qingpu	66	76	4	14		
奉 贤 区	Fengxian	48	53	12	21		
崇 明 县	Chongming			1	3		

表 10.8 主要年份市政工程设施情况 CIVIL FACILITIES IN MAIN YEARS

指 标	Indicators	2000	2009	2010
道路长度(公里)	Length of Roads(km)	6 641	16 071	16 687
道路面积(万平方米)	Area of Roads (10 000 sq. m)	8 147	24 566	25 607
城市桥梁(座)	Bridges (bridge)	4 432	11 466	11 849
防洪堤长度(公里)	Length of Floodwalls (km)	335	1 013	1 009
城市排水管道长度(公里)	Length of Sewage Pipelines (km)	3 920	9 732	11 483
污水处理厂污水处理能力(万吨/日)	Capacity of Sewage Treatment(10 000 tons/day)	463	687	684
防汛泵站(座)	Pumping Stations of Flood Prevention (bridge)	160	188	186

①本表数据由市城乡建设和交通委员会、市水务局提供。
②2008 年起，道路中包括公路中的村道。
❶Data in this table are provided by Shanghai Municipal Urban and Rural Construction and Transportation Commission and Shanghai Water Authority.
❷Village roads hava been included in that of roads since 2008 .

表 10.9 主要年份自来水情况 TAP WATER SUPPLY IN MAIN YEARS

指 标	Indicators	2000	2009	2010
水厂个数(个)	Quantity of Water Works (unit)	218	113	105
水厂生产能力(万立方米/日)	Production Capacity (10000 cu. m/day)	1 048	1 096	1 131
供水管道长度(公里)	Length of Water Supply Pipelines (km)	15 943	29 464	31 182
供水总量(亿立方米)	Volume of Water Supply (100 million cu. m)	24.00	30.47	30.90
售水总量(亿立方米)	Sales Volume of Tap Water (100 million cu. m)	19.75	24.06	24.44
#工业用水	Industrial Use	5.49	5.59	5.80
生活用水	Living Use	14.26	18.47	18.64
#居民生活用水	Living Use for Residents	6.82	9.73	9.80
人均日居民生活用水量(升)	Per Capita Daily Consumption of Water (liter)	114	139	117

注：本表数据由市水务局提供。
Note: Data in this table are provided by Shanghai Water Authority.

表 10.10 主要年份用电量
ELECTRICITY POWER CONSUMPTION IN MAIN YEARS

指 标	Indicators	2000	2009	2010
用电量（亿千瓦小时）	Power Consumption (100 million kwh)	559.51	1 153.38	1 295.87
#农业用电	Agricultural Consumption	9.10	5.39	6.07
工业用电	Industrial Consumption	392.97	701.58	786.61
交通运输、仓储、邮政业	Transportation, Storage and Post Industry	5.94	25.89	34.11
商业、住宿和餐饮业	Commercial, Hotel and Eateries	41.81	64.75	69.44
金融、房地产、商务及居民服务业	Finance, Real Estate, Commerce and Residential Service	25.0	112.24	130.82
公共事业及管理组织	Public Affairs and Administrative Organization	23.18	70.39	76.64
城市居民生活用电	Urban Residential Consumption	53.20	152.52	168.95

表 10.11 主要年份电力建设情况
ELECTRICITY POWER CONSTRUCTION IN MAIN YEARS

指 标	Indicators	2001	2009	2010
年末发电设备容量(万千瓦)	Year-end Capacity of Electricity Generating Equipment (10 000 KW)	1 121.09	1 654.74	1 855.38
架空线长度(公里)	Length of Trolly Wire(k. m.)	6 480.72	8 451.91	8 549.50
#220KV	220KV	1 756.74	2 928.84	2 956.08
电缆长度(公里)	Length of Cable(k. m.)	3 397.80	7 677.24	7 846.98
#220KV	220KV	144.00	636.00	516.44
公用变电容量(万千伏安)	Public Power Transformation Capacity(10 000 KVA)	4 601.08	10 418.65	11 657.19
#220KB－35KV	220KB－35KV	3 716.68	7 577.25	7 827.75

注：本页数据由市电力公司提供。
Note: Data on this page are provided by Shanghai Electric Power Corporation.

表 10.12 主要年份煤气、液化石油气、天然气情况
GAS, LIQUEFIED PETROLEUM GAS AND NATURAL GAS IN MAIN YEARS

指 标	Indicators	2000	2009	2010
煤 气	**Gas**			
煤气生产能力(万立方米/日)	Production Capacity (10 000 cu. m/day)	984	867	817
煤气管线长度(公里)	Length of Gas Pipelines (km)	6 606	6 156	5 517
煤气销售总量(亿立方米)	Total Sales Volume (100 million cu. m)	18.40	14.19	12.85
#家庭用量	Household Consumption	11.50	7.46	6.28
家庭煤气用户数(万户)	Households Users (10 000 households)	255.89	151.48	132.89
液化石油气	**Liquefied Petroleum Gas (LPG)**			
液化石油气销售总量(万吨)	Sales of LPG (10 000 tons)	45.94	40.11	40.05
#家庭用量	Household Consumption	20.47	24.11	23.62
家庭液化石油气用户数(万户)	Household Users (10 000 households)	239.30	310.16	316.37
天然气	**Natural Gas**			
天然气销售总量(亿立方米)	Sales of Natural Gas (100 million cu. m)	2.16	31.33	42.66
#家庭用量	Household Consumption	0.45	6.43	7.79
天然气管线长度(公里)	Length of Natural Gas Pipelines (km)	1 742	14 997	17 316
家庭天然气用户数(万户)	Household Users of Natural Gas (10 000 households)	38.10	366.78	405.89

注：本表数据由市城乡建设和交通委员会提供。
Note: Data in this table are provided by Shanghai Urban Construction & Communications Committee.

表 10.13 主要年份公共交通和轮渡情况
PUBLIC TRANSPORTATION AND FERRY IN MAIN YEARS

指 标	Indicators	2000	2009	2010
公共汽电车	**Buses and Trolley Buses**			
公交线路长度(公里)	Length of Public Bus Lines (km)	23 260	23 033	23 131
公交线路条数(条)	Number of Public Bus Lines (line)	978	1 129	1 165
运营公交车辆数(辆)	Operating Public Transportation Vehicles (vehicle)	17 939	16 272	17 455
#公共汽车	Buses	17 358	16 039	17 038
客运总量(亿人次)	Passenger Volume (100million person-times)	26.49	27.06	28.08
出租汽车	**Taxi**			
运营车辆(辆)	Operating Vehicles (vehicle)	42 943	49 111	50 007
#小客车	Small Passenger Car	40 806	47 457	49 016
载客车次(万次)	Number of Carryings(10 000 times)	37 599	60 926	63 307
运营里程(亿公里)	Operation Length (100 million km)	46.48	61.99	64.85
#营业里程	Operation Lengths	24.35	37.73	39.79
运营收入(亿元)	Operation Revenues(100 million yuan)	76.68	135.75	154.72
运营单位(个)	Operation Unit (unit)	1 178	3 306	3 301
轮 渡	**Ferry**			
年末轮渡船数(艘)	Year-end Number of Ferry Boats (ship)	95	42	42
乘客人数(亿人次)	Passenger Volume (100 million person-times)	1.85	0.94	0.89

注：本表数据由市交通运输和港口管理局提供。
Note: Data in this table are provided by Shanghai Municipal Transport and Port Authority.

表 10.14 轨道交通、高架道路、黄浦江大桥和隧道基本情况 (2008～2010)
BASIC FACTS OF URBAN RAILWAY COMMUNICATION,ELEVATED ROADS,BRIDGES ACROSS HUANGPU RIVER AND TUNNELS

指 标	Indicators	2008	2009	2010
轨道交通	**Urban Metro**			
运营车辆(节)	Operating Vehicles(car)	1 431	1 833	2 842
轨道交通线路条数(条)	Number of Operation Lines(line)	9	11	12
运营线路长度(公里)	Length of Operation Lines(km)	264.30	355.05	452.57
行驶里程(万列・公里)	Mileage(10000 vehicle-km)	2 516	2 871	4 778
客运总量(万人次)	Volume of Passenger Traffic(10 000 person-times)	112 798	131 837	188 407
年末从业人数(人)	Year-end Number of Staff and Workers (person)	11 985	20 349	39 785
高架、大桥和隧道	**Elevated Roads, Bridges and Tunnels**			
高架道路长度(公里)	Length of Elevated Roads (km)	114	114	196
越江大桥数(座)	Number of Bridges Across Huangpu River (bridge)	7	8	10
越江隧道数(条)	Tunnels Across Huangpu River (tunnel)	6	9	12

注：本表数据由市交通运输和港口管理局、市城乡建设和交通委员会提供。
Note: Data in this table are provided by Shanghai Municipal Transport and Port Authority and Shanghai Municipal Urban and Rural Construction and and Transportation Commission.

表 10.15 主要年份城市设施水平
LEVEL OF URBAN FACILITIES IN MAIN YEARS

指 标	Indicators	2000	2009	2010
人均日综合生活用水量(升)	Per Capita Daily Consumption of Water for Life (liter)	241	264	223
人均日居民生活用水量(升)	Per Capita Daily Consumption of Water (liter)	114	139	117
自来水普及率(%)	Percentage of Population with Access to Tap Water (%)	99.97	99.99	99.99
拥有道路长度(公里/万人)	Per Capita Length of Roads (km/10 000 persons)	5.84	11.47	11.82
人均拥有道路面积(平方米)	Per Capita Area of Roads (sq・m)	7.17	17.54	18.13
每万人拥有城市排水管道长度(公里)	Length of Sewage Pipelines Per 10 000 Persons (km)	2.86	7.05	8.13
每万人拥有公共交通车辆(辆)	Number of Public Transportation Vehicles Per 10 000 Persons (vehicle)	12.08	11.09	12.46
每万人拥有出租汽车(辆)	Number of Taxi Per 10 000 Persons (vehicle)	25.61	22.22	21.72
人均拥有公共绿地面积(平方米)	Per Capita Public Green Areas (sq・m)	4.60	12.80	13.00
每万人拥有公共厕所(座)	Number of Public Lavatories Per 10 000 Persons (unit)	1.38	2.55	2.62

①本表数据由市城乡建设和交通委员会、市水务局、市绿化和市容管理局等单位提供。
②每万人拥有供交通车辆数包括轨道交通车辆数。
❶Data in this table are provided by Shanghai Municipal Urban and Rural Construction and Transportation Commission, Shanghai Water Authority and Shanghai Municipal Virescence and Appearance Adimistration Bureau, and etc.
❷Number of Public Transportation Vehicles per 10000 Persons includes the number of urban railway vehicles

表 10.16 主要年份城市绿地情况
URBAN GREEN SPACE IN MAIN YEARS

单位:公顷(hectare)

年 份 Year	城市绿地面积 Urban Green Space	其 中 of which				
		#公园绿地 Public Green Area	其 中 of which		#附属绿地 Sub Green	#生产绿地 Production Green
			公园面积 Area of Parks	街道绿地 Roadside Green Area		
1990	3 570	983	712	271	2 255	294
1995	6 561	1 793	920	873	4 429	309
1996	7 231	2 008	933	1 076	4 889	305
1997	7 849	2 484	961	1 523	5 083	253
1998	8 855	3 117	976	2 141	5 456	253
1999	11 117	3 856	993	2 863	6 888	318
2000	1 2601	4 812	1 153	3 658	7 346	388
2001	14 771	5 820	1 291	4 529	8 624	248
2002	18 758	7 810	1 411	6 399	9 591	267
2003	24 426	9 450	1 473	7 977	10 218	335
2004	26 689	10 979	1 481	9 498	10 921	335
2005	28 865	12 038	1 521	10 516	11 591	335
2006	30 609	13 307	1 525	11 782	12 202	331
2007	31 795	13 899	1 675	12 224	13 590	204
2008	34 256	14 777	1 686	13 091	14 739	189
2009	116 929	15 406	1 687	13 119	17 376	230
2010	120 148	16 053	1 915	13 418	18 589	230

注:根据《城市和村镇建设统计报表制度》,2009 年对绿地分类进行了调整。城市绿地由公园绿地、生产绿地、防护绿地、附属绿地和其他绿地五大类构成。

Note: The Categories of Urban Green are included Production Green Area, Protection Green Area, Sub Green Area and Other Green Area, Which have been adjusted by the Statistical Reporting Rgulation of City and Town Construction since 2009.

表 10.16 续表 continued

年 份 Year	公园数 (个) Parks (unit)	游园人数 (万人次) Visitors to Parks and Zooes (10 000 person-times)	行道树实有数 (万株) Roadside Trees (10 000 trees)	新辟绿地面积(公顷) Greenlands Newly Created (hectare)	绿化覆盖率 (%) Coverage Rate of Urban Green Areas(%)
1990	83	8 474	23	186	12.4
1995	100	9 064	33	516	16.0
1996	105	9 797	41	587	17.0
1997	108	9 757	43	728	17.8
1998	111	9 285	48	1 077	19.1
1999	115	9 601	54	1 315	20.3
2000	122	8 184	57	1 458	22.2
2001	125	8 561	65	1 374	23.8
2002	133	8 796	68	2 600	30.0
2003	136	9 629	74	4 904	35.2
2004	136	13 381	80	2 434	36.0
2005	144	13 656	83	2 116	37.0
2006	144	16 652	86	1 691	37.3
2007	146	18 342	69	1 629	37.6
2008	147	22 119	73	1 190	38.0
2009	147	21 671	76	1 096	38.1
2010	148	21 794	81	1 223	38.2

注:本页数据由市绿化和市容管理局提供。

Note: Data on this page are provided by Shanghai Municipal Virescence and Appearance Adimistration Bureau.

表 10.17 各区、县绿化面积(2010)
URBAN GREEN AREA IN DIFFERENT DISTRICTS AND COUNTIES

地 区	District	城市绿地面积（公顷）Urban Green Space (hectare)	其中 of which #公园绿地面积 Park Green Areas	公园数（个）Quantity of Parks (unit)	公园游园人数（万人次）Visitors to Parks and Zoos (10 000 person-times)
总 计	**Total**	**120 148.20**	**16 053.05**	**148**	**21 794.06**
浦东新区	Pudong New Area	25 796.53	5 524.98	20	1 909.55
黄 浦 区	Huangpu	135.94	96.82	7	2 690.78
卢 湾 区	Luwan	123.77	64.02	5	380.18
徐 汇 区	Xuhui	1 230.96	487.68	11	2 362.41
长 宁 区	Changning	1 014.94	438.57	13	1 435.90
静 安 区	Jing'an	101.07	45.11	3	312.40
普 陀 区	Putuo	1 141.43	518.39	16	2 105.23
闸 北 区	Zhabei	601.94	223.92	7	1 216.76
虹 口 区	Hongkou	405.14	152.05	9	2 019.82
杨 浦 区	Yangpu	1 361.04	441.00	14	2 762.39
闵 行 区	Minhang	7 950.44	2 053.01	10	1 596.23
宝 山 区	Baoshan	6 179.16	1 849.17	10	1 981.20
嘉 定 区	Jiading	7 339.46	1 197.41	5	229.25
金 山 区	Jinshan	8 471.83	563.67	7	149.15
松 江 区	Songjiang	12 519.22	710.87	5	302.44
青 浦 区	Qingpu	10 136.55	1 071.31	3	90.59
奉 贤 区	Fengxian	9 679.64	476.59	1	223.92
崇 明 县	Chongming	25 959.14	138.48	2	25.86

注：本表数据由市绿化和市容管理局提供。
Note: Data on this page are provided by Shanghai Municipal Virescence and Appearance Adimistration Bureau.

上/海/统/计/年/鉴

主要统计指标解释

城市基础设施

城市基础设施包括电力建设、交通运输、邮电通信、公用事业和市政建设等。

道路长度

指道路长度和与道路相通的桥梁、隧道的长度，按车行道中心线计算。

城市绿地

指以自然植被和人工植被为主要存在形态的城市用地。它包含两个层次的内容：一是城市建设用地范围内用于绿化的土地；二是城市建设用地之外，对城市生态、景观和居民休闲生活具有积极作用、绿化环境较好的区域。

绿地面积

指报告期末用作园林和绿化的各种绿地面积。包括公园绿地、生产绿地、防护绿地、附属绿地和其他绿地面积。

其中，公园绿地指向公众开放的、以游憩为主要功能，有一定的游憩设施和服务设施，同时兼有健全生态、美化景观、防灾减灾等综合作用的绿化用地。它是城市建设用地、城市绿地系统和城市市政公用设施的重要组成部分。

供水管道长度

指从送水泵至用户水表之间所有管道的长度。不包括新安装尚未使用的管道。

供水总量

指报告期供水企业(单位)供出的全部水量。包括有效供水量和漏损水量。

生活用水

生活用水包括城市公共用水和居民家庭用水。城市公共用水包括建筑业用水、公共服务用水及生态环境用水。建筑业用水指土木工程建筑业、线路管道和设备安装业、建筑安装业、建筑装饰业和其他建筑业用水。生态环境用水主要包括城镇绿化、环卫用水及深井回灌用水。公共服务用水指为城市社会公共生活服务的用水。包括行政事业单位、部队营区和公共设施服务、社会服务业、批发零售贸易业、旅馆饮食业以及其他公共服务业等单位的用水。居民家庭用水指城市范围内所有居民家庭的日常生活用水。包括城市居民、农民家庭、公共供水站用水。

煤气生产能力

指报告期末煤气生产厂制气、净化、输送等环节的综合生产能力，不包括备用设备能力。一般按设计能力计算，如果实际生产能力大于设计能力时，应按实际测定的生产能力计算。测定时应以制气、净化、输送三个环节中最薄弱的环节为主。

排水管道长度

指所有排水总管、干管、支管、检查井及连接井进出口等长度之和。

运营公交车辆数

指年末公交企业(单位)用于运营业务的全部车辆数。以企业(单位)固定资产台帐中已投入运营的车辆数为准。

污水日处理能力

指污水处理厂(或处理装置)每昼夜处理污水量的设计能力。

SHANGHAI STATISTICAL YEARBOOK

EXPLANATORY NOTES TO MAJOR STATISTICAL INDICATORS

□ Urban Infrastructure Facilities

Urban Infrastructure Facilities include facilities for power generating, transportation, post and telecommunication, public utilities, development of municipal engineering.

□ Length of Roads

The length of roads refers to the length of roads and of the bridges and tunnels connected to the roads, calculated by the center line of the roads.

□ Urban Green

Urban Green refers the urban land mainly used as natural vegetation and artificial vegetation. First, it includes the area of urban construction land for greening. Except the urban construction land, the green area which is beneficial for urban ecology, landscape and residents leisure is also included.

□ Green Space

Green Space includes all kinds of gardens and green at the end of reporting period. Park green area, production green area, protection green area, sub green area and other green area are all included.

Park green area refers to green areas open to the public for amusement and rest with the facilities of amusement, rest and services. Its function includes perfecting ecology, beautifying landscape, and preventing and reducing disaster. It is an important part of urban construction land, urban green and municipal public infrastructure in city

□ Length of Water Supply Pipelines

Length of Water Supply Pipelines refers to the total length of all the pipelines between the water pumps and the user's water meters, excluding pipelines newly installed but not used yet

□ Volume of Water Supply

Volume of Water Supply refers to the total volume of water supplied by water-works (units) during the reference period, including both the effective water supply and loss during the water supply.

□ Consumption of Water for Living Use

Consumption of Water for Linving Use refers to the water consumption for city public and the water consumption of households for daily life. The water consumption for city public includes the water consumption of construction, the water consumption of public service facilities and the water consumption of city ecology. The water consumption of construction refers to the water consumption of civil engineering, line pipe and equipment installation, construction installation, construction decoration and other construction. The water consumption of city ecology mainly includes the consumption of urban green, urban Sanitation and deep well re-irrigation. The water consumption of public service facilities refers to the water consumption for urban public services, including the consumption of government agencies and public institutions, military barracks, public facilities, wholesale and retail outlets, restaurants, hotels, and other units providing public services. Household water consumption refers to consumption of water for daily life of all households in the boundary of cities, including households of urban residents and farmers, and public water supply stations.

□ Production Capacity of Gas

Production Capacity of Gas refers to the comprehensive production capacity of the urban gasworks in gas generation, purification and delivery at the end of the reference period, excluding capacity of the reserved facilities. In general, it is determined by the designed capacity, and when actual production capacity is larger than the designed capacity, the capacity is determined by the actual measurement on the weakest link in the production, purification and delivery.

□ Length of Sewage Pipes

Length of Sewage Pipes refers to the total length of general drainage, trunks, branch and inspection wells, connection wells, inlets and outlets, etc.

EXPLANATORY NOTES TO MAJOR STATISTICAL INDICATORS

□ Number of Operating Public Transportation Vehicles

Number of Operating Public Transportation Vehicles refers to the total number of vehicles under operation by public transport enterprises (units) at the end of the year, based on the records of operational vehicles by the enterprises (units).

□ Daily Disposal Capacity of Urban Sewage

Daily Disposal Capacity of Urban Sewage refers to the designed 24 hour capacity of sewage disposal by the sewage treatment works or facilities.

第十一篇

CHAPTER 11

农　　业

AGRICULTURE

表 11.1 农业总产值(1978～2010)
GROSS OUTPUT VALUE OF AGRICULTURE

单位:亿元(100 million yuan)

年 份 Year	农业总产值 Gross Output Value of Agriculture	其 中 of which 种植业 Planting	林 业 Forestry	畜牧业 Animal Husbandry	渔 业 Fishery	农林牧渔服务业 Service Industry for Agriculture
1978	18.26	13.49	0.06	3.67	0.86	
1979	20.41	15.10	0.04	4.22	0.90	
1980	18.90	11.40	0.06	6.27	0.97	
1981	20.33	11.91	0.21	6.38	1.23	
1982	23.97	13.80	0.23	7.81	1.56	
1983	22.68	12.59	0.20	7.80	1.29	
1984	26.59	16.41	0.21	8.06	1.40	
1985	31.38	15.63	0.21	12.25	2.82	
1986	33.76	16.83	0.24	12.75	3.45	
1987	38.84	17.69	0.34	15.48	4.79	
1988	53.07	22.47	0.45	22.18	7.43	
1989	60.63	25.53	0.39	26.41	7.88	
1990	68.16	29.09	0.37	30.25	8.04	
1991	73.65	30.51	0.39	33.38	8.97	
1992	80.01	32.80	0.43	37.19	9.18	
1993	96.20	40.52	0.41	42.95	12.31	
1994	140.24	60.19	0.49	62.04	17.52	
1995	182.47	77.71	0.45	81.48	22.83	
1996	200.95	87.64	0.67	85.46	27.18	
1997	204.41	85.20	0.47	88.37	30.37	
1998	206.75	89.10	0.84	87.27	29.54	
1999	206.90	87.86	0.98	86.35	31.71	
2000	216.50	89.81	1.41	87.35	37.92	
2001	227.61	95.53	3.52	88.43	40.13	
2002	233.57	97.21	7.75	83.48	45.13	
2003	247.29	98.17	13.05	81.13	49.21	5.73
2004	248.89	109.32	13.14	70.77	49.90	5.76
2005	233.39	111.25	11.11	54.34	51.64	5.05
2006	237.01	119.99	10.43	46.29	55.25	5.05
2007	255.98	126.74	10.05	58.00	54.19	7.00
2008	280.35	137.52	9.12	68.40	57.11	8.20
2009	283.15	147.53	8.99	64.61	53.53	8.49
2010	287.03	155.27	7.53	62.90	52.62	8.71

注：2003 年以前，农业总产值不包括农林牧渔服务业。
Note：The Gross Output Value of Agriculture did not include the output value of service industry for planting, forestry, animal husbandary and fishery before 2003.

表 11.2　农业总产值指数(以 1978 年为 100，1978～2010)
GROSS OUTPUT VALUE INDEXS OF AGRICULTURE (1978 = 100)

年　份 Year	农业总产值指数 Indexs of Gross Output Value of Agriculture	其　中　of which				
		种植业 Planting	林　业 Forestry	畜牧业 Animal Husbandry	渔　业 Fishery	农林牧渔服务业 Service Industry for Agriculture
1978	100.0	100.0	100.0	100.0	100.0	
1979	101.4	92.9	121.9	128.1	101.6	
1980	92.1	78.6	152.9	115.8	104.1	
1981	100.0	83.9	144.0	140.2	97.3	
1982	117.4	97.4	161.1	170.1	107.3	
1983	109.9	86.0	116.1	167.3	123.6	
1984	124.5	109.0	98.4	167.5	114.7	
1985	113.0	88.2	107.2	181.4	127.6	
1986	119.7	89.5	134.5	201.2	149.5	
1987	122.5	90.6	138.9	206.7	158.1	
1988	130.3	95.3	166.0	227.0	160.0	
1989	132.0	92.3	134.9	245.6	171.8	
1990	139.5	96.3	139.7	271.2	164.3	
1991	146.2	95.6	153.7	299.0	172.7	
1992	154.7	101.3	144.0	322.9	168.8	
1993	147.9	94.1	129.4	313.8	166.8	
1994	159.4	96.0	130.5	336.7	215.0	
1995	177.0	104.0	125.2	363.0	252.4	
1996	191.6	114.5	168.6	389.1	269.6	
1997	202.5	123.1	133.0	404.3	288.4	
1998	207.3	129.4	185.2	412.1	278.6	
1999	212.6	133.2	258.3	418.0	289.2	
2000	220.9	141.2	414.9	414.6	321.9	
2001	236.5	145.2	629.7	433.7	392.0	
2002	243.6	145.7	1 546.0	416.4	442.6	100.0
2003	246.3	135.3	2 062.4	395.5	544.4	102.6
2004	229.6	144.0	2 070.6	306.5	526.4	103.2
2005	205.5	136.7	1 613.0	221.6	555.4	91.4
2006	206.9	141.1	1 514.6	205.0	587.6	90.3
2007	210.0	142.9	1 458.6	214.2	573.5	121.6
2008	210.2	147.2	1 185.8	223.6	520.2	134.6
2009	209.1	145.1	1 147.9	238.6	481.7	140.0
2010	198.4	138.3	960.8	231.9	443.2	139.2

注：根据国家统计局方法制度规定，从 2006 年起，农业总产值指数按可比价计算，2006 年以前按不变价计算。

Note：According to the regulation of National Bureau of Statistics, since 2006, index of gross output value of agriculture has been calculated by comparable price. and before 2006, it was calculated by constant price.

表 11.3 耕地面积(1978～2010)
AREAS UNDER CULTIVATION

年 份 Year	耕地面积 (万公顷) Cultivated Area (10 000 hectares)	其 中 of which 水 田 Paddy Fields	 旱 田 Dry Fields	平均每个农村人口 占有耕地(平方米) Cultivated Area Per Rural Person (sq·m)	平均每个农村从业人员 占有耕地(平方米) Cultivated Area Per Rural Employee (sq·m)
1978	36.01	31.88	4.14	800	1 240
1979	35.58	31.49	4.08	793	1 220
1980	35.41	31.26	4.15	787	1 193
1981	35.27	31.02	4.25	773	1 173
1982	35.17	30.96	4.21	767	1 173
1983	34.99	31.00	4.00	760	1 193
1984	34.58	30.89	3.69	760	1 207
1985	33.96	30.45	3.51	753	1 200
1986	33.30	29.75	3.56	740	1 200
1987	33.09	29.67	3.42	740	1 207
1988	32.72	29.28	3.44	740	1 213
1989	32.40	28.95	3.45	733	1 227
1990	32.32	28.54	3.78	773	1 293
1991	32.10	28.38	3.72	731	1 236
1992	31.78	28.03	3.75	718	1 303
1993	30.20	26.42	3.78	712	1 215
1994	29.38	25.81	3.58	735	1 262
1995	29.00	25.39	3.61	740	1 189
1996	30.06	27.16	2.89	753	1 051
1997	29.80	26.93	2.87	762	1 052
1998	29.38	26.67	2.71	758	1 087
1999	29.09	26.15	2.94	732	1 058
2000	28.59	25.74	2.85	731	1 048
2001	28.06	26.02	2.04	722	1 029
2002	27.04	25.06	1.98	693	986
2003	25.73	24.19	1.54	668	951
2004	24.57	22.88	1.69	654	918
2005	23.73	22.34	1.39	647	899
2006	20.80	18.83	1.97	583	901
2007	20.60	18.65	1.95	580	942
2008	20.50	17.51	2.99	550	884
2009	20.23	16.98	3.25	553	895
2010	20.10	15.32	4.78	598	969

表 11.4　主要年份农村户数、人口和从业人员
RURAL HOUSEHOLDS, POPULATION AND EMPLOYEES IN MAIN YEARS

指　标	Indicators	2000	2009	2010
户数(万户)	**Households (10 000 households)**	**115.17**	**95.20**	**114.22**
人口(万人)	**Population (10 000 persons)**	**360.71**	**332.78**	**305.68**
从业人员(万人)	**Employees (10 000 persons)**	**253.45**	**205.72**	**188.70**
#农　业	Agriculture	81.45	45.55	34.06
工　业	ndustry	108.75	104.89	100.85
建筑业	Construction	11.14	9.23	8.99
交通运输、仓储及邮政业	Transportation, Storage and Post	7.07	7.91	7.85
批发和零售业	Wholesale and Retail	13.49	6.01	6.16

注：从业人员包括农村国有经济的机关、团体、学校、企事业单位的集体户和户口在家而领取工资的国家职工。
Note: Employees have included salary taking state staff and workers who had local residential papers or registered in the collective residential papers of stateowned economic departments, organizations, schools, enterprises and institutions in rural areas.

表 11.5　主要年份农作物总播种面积
TOTAL SOWN AREA OF PLANTING IN MAIN YEARS

年　份 Year	总播种面积(万公顷) Total Sown Area (10 000 hectare)	粮食作物 Grain Crops		经济作物 Cash Crops		其他作物 Others	
		播种面积 Sown Area	占总播种面积(%) Percentage (%)	播种面积 Sown Area	占总播种面积(%) Percentage (%)	播种面积 Sown Area	占总播种面积(%) Percentage (%)
1990	63.11	41.71	66.1	11.16	17.7	10.24	16.2
1995	54.22	34.40	63.5	8.88	16.4	10.94	20.1
1996	57.01	35.38	62.1	8.33	14.6	13.30	23.3
1997	55.23	36.58	66.2	6.91	12.5	11.74	21.3
1998	55.64	35.25	63.4	7.42	13.3	12.97	23.3
1999	55.17	33.50	60.7	7.97	14.5	13.70	24.8
2000	52.15	25.88	49.6	8.84	17.0	17.43	33.4
2001	49.09	21.12	43.0	8.08	16.5	19.89	40.5
2002	47.67	18.77	39.4	8.07	16.9	20.83	43.7
2003	41.92	14.83	35.4	6.07	14.5	21.02	50.1
2004	40.44	15.47	38.3	4.90	12.1	20.07	49.6
2005	40.36	16.61	41.1	4.75	11.8	19.00	47.1
2006	40.14	16.55	41.2	3.73	9.3	19.86	49.5
2007	39.07	16.96	43.4	2.77	7.1	19.34	49.5
2008	38.84	17.45	44.9	2.81	7.2	18.58	47.9
2009	39.61	19.33	48.8	2.53	6.4	17.75	44.8
2010	40.12	17.92	44.7	2.07	5.2	20.13	50.1

表 11.6 主要年份农副产品产量
OUTPUT OF MAJOR FARM AND SIDELINE PRODUCTS IN MAIN YEARS

指 标	Indicators	2000	2009	2010
农副产品	**Farm and Sideline Products**			
粮 食(万吨)(包括大豆)	Grain(10 000 tons)(Including Soybean)	174.00	121.68	118.40
棉 花(万吨)	Cotton(10 000 tons)	0.12	0.26	0.35
油 料(万吨)	Oil Plants(10 000 tons)	16.37	3.39	2.29
#油菜籽	Rapeseed	15.71	3.09	2.04
蔬 菜(万吨)	Vegetables(10 000 tons)	377.00	394.08	398.08
西甜瓜(万吨)	Watermelons and Muskmelons(10 000 tons)	49.88	57.57	55.44
水 果(万吨)	Fruits(10 000 tons)	22.54	45.16	44.16
#生 梨	Pear	1.74	3.27	3.84
柑 桔	Citrus Fruits	10.18	23.58	20.16
畜禽产品	**Livestock and Poultry**			
生猪出栏量 (万头)	Quantity of Sold Hogs(10 000 heads)	471.46	269.74	265.98
生猪年末圈存量 (万头)	Hogs In Pens By Year-end(10 000 heads)	241.60	175.16	171.87
奶牛年末头数 (万头)	Cows In Pens By Year-end(10 000 heads)	5.83	6.39	6.72
羊年末头数 (万头)	Sheep In Pens By Year-end(10 000 heads)	55.44	25.08	24.46
兔年末圈存量 (万头)	Rabbits In Pens By Year-end(10 000 heads)	88.90	21.00	12.17
猪 肉(万吨)	Pork(10 000 tons)	25.96	17.55	17.87
牛羊肉(万吨)	Beef and Mutton(10 000 tons)	0.79	0.57	0.54
家禽出栏量 (万羽)	Quantity of Poultry Sold Birds(10 000 fowls)	17 213	4 098	4 084
牛 奶(万吨)	Milk(10 000 tons)	25.95	21.25	24.71
鲜 蛋(万吨)	Fresh Egg(10 000 tons)	16.64	6.17	6.28
水产品	**Aquatic Products**			
海水产品(万吨)	Seawater Aquatic Products (10 000 tons)	12.23	16.85	12.15
淡水产品(万吨)	Freshwater Aquatic Products (10 000 tons)	16.64	15.27	16.82

表 11.7 农牧业特色种养产品产量(2009～2010)
OUTPUT OF SPECIAL PRODUCTS IN FARMING AND ANIMAL HUSBANDRY

指 标	Indicators	2009	2010	指 标	Indicators	2009	2010
桃 子 (万吨)	Peach (10 000 tons)	9.51	10.14	野 鸡(万只)	Pheasant (10 000 fowls)	21.42	22.47
葡 萄 (万吨)	Graper (10 000 tons)	7.71	9.08	野 鸭(万只)	mallard (10 000 fowls)	228.44	229.64
草 莓 (万吨)	Strawberry (10 000 tons)	1.93	2.28	肉 鸽 (万只)	Meat Dove (10 000 fowls)	594	705
枣(吨)	Date(ton)	1 721	1 214	甲 鱼 (吨)	Soft-shelled Turtle (ton)	754	642
猕猴桃 (吨)	Kiwi (ton)	352	411	河 蟹 (万吨)	Hairy Crab (10 000 tons)	1.64	1.67

表 11.8　主要农副产品产量与建国以来最高年产量的比较 (2010)
OUTPUT OF MAJOR FARM AND SIDELINE PRODUCTS
IN COMPARISON WITH THE PEAK YEAR SINCE 1949

指　标	Indicators	2010	建国以来最高年 Peak Year Since 1949		2010 年为建国以来最高年份(%) 2010/Peak Year Since 1949
			年　份 Year	产　量 Output	
农产品	**Farm products**				
粮　食(万吨)	Grain(10 000 tons)	118.40	1978	260.88	45.4
棉　花(万吨)	Cotton(10 000 tons)	0.35	1978	12.10	2.9
油菜籽(万吨)	Rapeseed(10 000 tons)	2.04	1992	21.84	9.3
蔬　菜(万吨)	Vegetables(10 000 tons)	398.08	2002	476.60	83.5
西甜瓜(万吨)	Watermelons and Muskmelons(10 000 tons)	55.44	2003	76.50	72.5
水　果(万吨)	Fruits(10 000 tons)	44.16	2008	46.12	95.8
畜产品	**Animal Husbandry Products**				
猪年末圈存数(万头)	Quantity of Hogs in Pens(year-end)(10 000 heads)	171.87	1978	365.74	47.0
猪　肉(万吨)	Pork(10 000 tons)	17.87	2001	26.40	67.7
奶牛年末头数(万头)	Quantity of Milk Cow(year-end)(10 000 heads)	6.72	1991	7.31	91.9
牛　奶(万吨)	Milk(10 000 tons)	24.71	2002	27.98	88.3
家禽出栏量(万羽)	Quantity of Poultry Sold(10 000 fowls)	4084	1997	17 851	22.9
鲜　蛋(万吨)	Fresh Eggs(10 000 tons)	6.28	2001	16.87	37.2
水产品	**Aquatic Products**				
海水产品(万吨)	Seawater Aquatic Products(10 000 tons)	12.15	2006	19.44	62.5
淡水产品(万吨)	Freshwater Aquatic Products(10 000 tons)	16.82	2003	22.13	76.0

注：建国以来最高年年份和产量均是指 2009 年及以前的年份和产量，不包括 2010 年在内。
Note: Peak year and output of peak year since 1949 refer to the years before 2009, excluding 2010.

表 11.9 主要年份农业商品产值和商品率
OUTPUT VALUE OF AGRICULTURAL COMMODITY AND COMMODITY RATE IN MAIN YEARS

指 标	Indicators	2000	2009	2010
农业商品产值(亿元)	**Output Value of Agricultural Commodity (100 million yuan)**	**179.79**	**237.04**	**236.15**
#种植业	Planting	61.84	114.29	120.22
#粮食作物	Grain Crops	10.15	14.71	16.43
牧 业	Animal Husbandry	80.75	60.04	58.01
#猪	Hogs	29.82	33.61	30.38
禽	Poultry	33.41	9.12	8.95
蛋	Eggs	7.94	4.67	5.10
渔 业	Fishery	36.53	51.39	50.42
#淡水产品	Freshwater Aquatic Products	25.14	35.97	36.62
农业商品率(%)	**Agricultural Commodity Rate (%)**	**83.0**	**83.7**	**83.7**
#种植业	Planting	68.8	77.5	77.8
#粮食作物	Grain Crops	45.4	56.1	53.8
牧 业	Animal Husbandry	92.4	92.9	92.2
#猪	Hogs	95.8	95.4	94.7
禽	Poultry	91.9	88.1	86.5
蛋	Eggs	82.3	91.5	93.3
渔 业	Fishery	96.3	96.0	95.8
#淡水产品	Freshwater Aquatic Products	95.9	95.0	95.0

表 11.10 主要年份农产品出口情况
EXPORTS OF AGRICULTURAL PRODUCTS IN MAIN YEARS

单位:亿元(100 million yuan)

指 标	Indicators	2000	2009	2010
农产品出口总额	**Output Value of Exports of Agricultural Products**	**7.88**	**12.91**	**11.28**
#农业产品	Farm Products	0.63	2.76	2.30
牧业产品	Animal Husbardry Products	1.71	0.19	0.16
渔业产品	Fishery Products	5.55	9.59	8.41
农产品直接出口总额	**Output Value of Direct Exports of Agricultural Products**	**6.82**	**10.24**	**9.50**
#农业产品	Farm Products	0.47	1.47	1.27
牧业产品	Animal Husbardry Products	0.99	0.08	0.07
渔业产品	Fishery Products	5.37	8.34	7.79
主要出口产品	**Main Products of Exports**			
蔬 菜	Vegetables	0.19	2.16	2.03
活 猪	Hogs	0.63	0.19	0.16
水产品	Aquatic Products	5.55	9.59	8.41
海水产品	Seawater Aquatic Products	5.29	7.90	7.37
淡水产品	Freshwater Aquatic Products	0.26	1.69	1.04

表 11.11 主要年份农田水利工程投资
INVESTMENT IN FARM WATER CONSERVANCY PROJECTS IN MAIN YEARS

单位:万元(10 000 yuan)

年 份 Year	合 计 Total	国家投资 State Investment	其 中 of which 海 塘 Seadike	农田水利 Farm Water Conservancy	基本建设 Capital Construction	乡、镇自筹 Funds Raised by Township and Town	企事业和区县自筹 Funds Raised by Enterprises and Public Affairs Departments
1990	26 143	15 959	907	10 877	1 506	10 184	
1995	62 474	44 651	6 103	10 583	21 800	17 823	
1996	76 467	56 421	6 470	16 159	20 693	20 046	
1997	83 097	60 497	14 467	27 153	22 447	22 600	
1998	108 565	83 596	9 660	25 712	37 780	24 969	
1999	150 324	119 193	18 580	32 882	53 660	31 131	
2000	184 102	151 539	22 063	31 282	53 532	32 563	
2001	244 337	188 477	10 598	42 406	120 575	32 178	23 682
2002	382 935	264 370	23 548	59 869	140 875	28 140	90 425
2003	516 075	375 688	13 083	78 515	199 341	27 568	112 819
2004	576 050	219 506	7 317	71 920	97 328	57 676	298 868
2005	543 780	176 215	7 010	34 973	55 290	66 421	301 145
2006	467 449	202 815	2 603	85 161	30 423	37 330	227 304
2007	577 116	379 071	4 138	131 779	193 886	56 843	141 202
2008	623 627	443 344	14 774	217 776	175 652	70 429	109 854
2009	619 579	497 583	7 299	240 471	128 160	106 142	15 854
2010	534 195	433 825	11 455	232 469	17 623	52 836	47 534

表 11.12 主要年份农村用电量
RURAL ELECTRICITY POWER CONSUMPTION IN MAIN YEARS

年 份 Year	农村用电量 (亿千瓦小时) Rural Electricity Power Consumption (100 million kwh)	其 中 of which 机电排灌 Motorized Drainage and Irrigation	农、副业加工 Farming and Sideline Products Processing	乡村办工业 Rural Enterprises
1990	32.16	1.75	4.00	22.85
1995	58.19	2.00	7.26	41.24
1996	62.07	2.01	7.79	44.16
1997	64.98	1.94	6.92	47.55
1998	67.91	2.09	6.79	49.55
1999	70.89	2.09	6.34	52.67
2000	73.19	2.34	6.12	49.71
2001	79.66	1.51	3.57	62.51
2002	81.79	1.24	3.62	57.56
2003	89.70	1.12	3.24	61.53
2004	114.35	1.17	2.41	79.01
2005	124.53	0.99	2.70	99.72
2006	143.54	1.03	2.84	97.98
2007	171.68	0.85	2.44	108.11
2008	178.05	0.94	2.94	117.22
2009	191.80	0.86	2.94	141.97
2010	195.48	0.61	4.41	

注：因统计口径调整,2010 年起,乡村办工业用电量不再单独统计。
Note：Sine 2010,the Electricity Power Consumption of Rural Enterprises is ho longer retained according to new statistilal standard.

表 11.13 主要年份农业机械拥有量
POSSESSION OF AGRICULTURAL MACHINERY IN MAIN YEARS

机械名称	Name of Machinery	2000	2009	2010
农业机械总动力(万千瓦)	**Total Power of Agricultural Machinery(10 000 kw)**	**142.50**	**99.23**	**104.15**
耕作机械动力合计(万千瓦)	Total Power of Farming Machinery(10 000 kw)	37.60	27.44	29.55
#大、中型拖拉机(台)	Large and Medium Tractors(set)	7 844	5 394	5 796
(万千瓦)	(10 000 kw)	29.30	21.76	24.21
小型拖拉机(台)	Small Tractors(set)	9 253	6 105	5 788
(万千瓦)	(10 000 kw)	8.30	5.68	5.34
排灌机械动力合计(万千瓦)	Total Power of Drainage and Irrigation Machinery (10 000 kw)	25.92	21.96	21.80
收获机械动力合计(万千瓦)	Total Power of Harvest Machinery(10 000 kw)	33.30	11.69	12.18
#联合收割机(台)	Combined Harvesters(set)	4 991	2 113	2 230
(万千瓦)	(10 000 kw)	2.70	7.82	8.52
机动脱粒机(万台)	Motorized Threshers(10 000 sets)	11.34	1.05	0.75
(万千瓦)	(10 000 kw)	30.05	3.61	2.96
植物保护机械动力合计(万千瓦)	Total Power of Plant Protecting Machine(10 000 kw)	3.07	4.25	5.34
#机动喷雾器(万台)	Motorized Nebulizers(10 000 sets)	2.07	1.83	2.11
(万千瓦)	(10 000 kw)	3.07	4.16	4.72
渔业机械动力合计(万千瓦)	Total Power of Fishery Machinery(10 000 kw)	23.40	22.72	23.23
#机动渔船(艘)	Motorized Fishing Boats(ship)	2905	1 869	1 788
(万千瓦)	(10 000 kw)	20.50	18.60	18.74
运输机械动力合计(万千瓦)	**Total Power of Transport Machinery(10 000 kw)**	**8.11**	**1.20**	**0.83**
#农用载重汽车(万千瓦)	Agricultural Camions(10 000 kw)	5.89	1.20	0.83
(辆)	(automobile)	953	254	186
其他农业机械动力合计(万千瓦)	Total Power of Other Agricultural Machine(10 000 kw)	11.13	9.83	11.05
#推土机(万千瓦)	Bulldozers(10 000 kw)	0.25	0.24	0.24
(辆)	(automobile)	45	41	41

表 11.14 主要年份农业技术应用和综合开发情况
TECHNOLOGY APPLICATIONS AND INTEGRATIVE EXPLOITATION IN AGRICULTURE IN MAIN YEARS

指 标	Indicators	2000	2009	2010
机耕面积(万公顷)	Areas of Motorized Cultivation (10 000 hectares)	23.46	38.90	39.47
机电排灌总控制面积(万公顷)	Total Area with Motorized Drainage and Irrigation Facilities (10 000 hectares)	28.59	18.34	18.55
机种面积(万公顷)	Areas of Motorized Planting (10 000 hectares)	6.08	5.04	5.30
占粮食播种面积(%)	Percentage in Total Planting Area of Grain (%)	23.5	26.1	29.6
机收面积(万公顷)	Areas of Motorized Harvesting (10 000 hectares)	16.42	18.33	16.57
占粮食收获面积(%)	Percentage in Total Harvesting Area of Grain (%)	63.4	94.8	92.5
喷、滴管灌面积(万公顷)	Areas of Irrigating by Insufflantion and Dripping Pipeline (10 000 hectares)	0.43	0.22	0.80
机械植保面积(万公顷)	Areas of Mechancial Protecting (10 000 hectares)	41.10	28.79	30.41
化肥施用面积(万公顷)	Areas of Chemical Fertilizing (10 000 hectares)	32.10	24.23	22.66
化肥施用量(实物量)(万吨)	Chemical Fertilizer Consumption (real)(10 000 tons)	82.54	47.96	44.89
化肥施用量(折纯量)(万吨)	Chemical Fertilizer Consumption (convert to pure amount) (10 000 tons)	19.33	12.56	11.84
农药施用面积(万公顷)	Areas of Farm Pesticides (10 000 hectares)	31.02	23.59	22.78
农药施用量(万吨)	Farm Pesticides Consumption (10 000 tons)	1.10	0.73	0.70
农用塑料薄膜使用量(万吨)	Agricultural Plastic Film Consumption (10 000 tons)	2.13	2.04	2.11
地膜覆盖面积(万公顷)	Areas Covered by Plastic Film (10 000 hectares)	2.05	2.99	2.62
蔬菜大棚面积(万公顷)	Areas of Trellis of Vegetables (10 000 hectares)	0.15	0.66	0.81
温室面积(公顷)	Areas of Greenhouse (hectares)	88.15	237.70	244.80
科技兴农项目数(个)	Quantity of Scientific and Technological Agriculiural Promotion Projects (unit)		83	64
科技兴农项目资金(市级财政)(亿元)	Capital of Scientific and Technological Agricultiral Promotion Projects(from municipal fiscal expenditure(100 million yuan)		1.47	1.53
常年菜田面积(万公顷)	Areas of Perennial Vegetable Farmland (10 000 hectares)	1.25	2.75	3.29
#设施菜田	Established Vegetable Farmland	0.27	1.53	1.15
精养渔塘面积(万公顷)	Areas of Find-breed Ponds(10 000 hectares)	1.05	0.58	0.54
粮食良种使用面积(万公顷)	Areas of Well-bred Provision Farmland(10 000 hectares)	23.56	17.94	15.41

表 11.15 市级农业园区基本情况(2010)
MAJOR INDICATORS OF MUNICIPAL AGRICULTURAL ZONE

项 目	Item	园区规划面积(公顷) Planning Area of Zone (hectare)	已开发利用面积(公顷) Developed Area (hectare)	引进投资项目(个) Introduction of Investment Item (unit)	引进投资金额(万元) Value of Investment Item (10 000 yuan)	基础设施投资(万元) Infrastruture Investment (10 000 yuan)
总 计	**Total**	**33 798**	**20 287**	**755**	**1 109 898**	**366 968**
闵 行	Minhang	2 163	1 173	132	27 641	13 348
宝 山	Baoshan	2 000	947	8	13 300	8 951
嘉 定	Jiading	2 200	1 302	17	2 286	28 715
孙 桥	Sunqiao	932	346	76	67 939	17 746
临 空	Linkong	1 038	222	33	46 184	4 223
金 山	Jinshan	4 800	1 579	46	99 944	90 065
松 江	Songjiang	4 000	2 957	255	151 182	32 404
青 浦	Qingpu	1 707	583	56	36 743	22 823
南 汇	Nanhui	1 030	349	22	249 831	20 943
奉 贤	Fengxian	1 849	1 641	69	363 367	78 386
崇 明	Chongming	2 600	1 483	8	12 286	18 180
上 实	Shangshi	8 467	7 388	8	19 783	16 990
农工商	Nonggongshang	1 012	317	25	19 412	14 193

上 / 海 / 统 / 计 / 年 / 鉴

主要统计指标解释

农村从业人员

指乡村人口中16岁以上实际参加生产经营活动并取得实物或货币收入的人员，既包括劳动年龄内实际参加劳动人员，也包括超过劳动年龄但实际参加劳动的人员，但不包括户口在家的在外学生、现役军人和丧失劳动能力的人，也不包括待业人员和家务劳动者。劳动者年龄为16岁以上。

农业总产值

农业总产值是以货币表现的农、林、牧、渔业全部产品的总量和对农林牧渔生产活动进行的各种支持性服务活动的价值。它反映一定时期内农业生产的总规模和总成果。

农、林、牧、渔业的统计范围是：

(1)种植业　包括农作物种植业和其他农业。

农作物种植业包括谷物、豆类、薯类、棉、油料、糖料、麻类、烟叶、蔬菜、药材、瓜类和其他农作物的种植，以及茶园、桑园、果园的生产经营。

其他农业包括采集野生植物的果实、纤维、树胶、树脂、油料以及柴草、野生药材、菌类等及农民家庭兼营的商品性工业。

(2)林业　包括林木的栽培(不包括茶园、桑园和果园的栽培、管理和收获等活动)、林产品的采集和村及村以下合作经济组织和农户的竹木采伐。

(3)牧业　包括除渔业养殖以外的一切动物饲养和放牧，以及野生动物的捕猎和饲养。

(4)渔业　包括水生动物和海藻类植物的养殖和捕捞。

(5)农林牧渔服务业　包括农林牧渔业生产活动进行的各种支持性服务活动。但不包括各种科学技术和专业技术服务活动。

从所有制看，包括国有经济的各种专业农(农、林、牧、渔)场以及国家各级机关团体学校、科研机构、部队经营的农业；集体所有制的乡镇村各级办农场；农村各种经济组织经营的农、林、牧、渔业以及工矿企业家属集体经营的农业；农民家庭自营的农林牧渔业及兼营商品性工业等。

农业总产值的计算方法通常是按农林牧渔业产品及其副产品的产量分别乘以各自单位产品价格求得，少数生产周期较长、当年没有产品或产品产量不易统计的，则采用间接方法匡算其产值，然后将四业产品产值和服务业产值相加即为农业总产值。

1957年以前的农业总产值中包括了厩肥和农民自给性手工业(如农民自制衣服、鞋、袜，自己从事粮食初步加工等)。1958年及以后的农业总产值，林业中增加了村及村以下竹木采伐产值；牧业中取消了厩肥产值；副业中取消了农民自给性手工业产值，增加了村及村以下办的工业产值；渔业中增加了海洋捕捞水产品产值。1980年及以后的农业总产值，在副业中增加了农民家庭兼营工业商品部分的产值。从1984年起村及村以下办工业产值划归工业。从1993年起，取消副业。将野生动物的捕猎划入牧业，野生植物采集和农民家庭兼营商品性工业划归农业。从2003年起，农业总产值中包括了农林牧渔服务业产值。

农业机械总动力

指用于农、林、牧、渔业生产的各种动力机械的动力总和。动力机械包括耕作、排灌、种植、植物保护、收获、农产品加工、运输、畜牧、渔业、农田水利等各种机械。不包括专门用于乡办工业、基本建设、非农业运输、科学试验和教学等非农业生产方面用的动力机械与作业机械的数量。

农作物播种面积

指报告期内收获农产品的作物的实际播种或移植有农作物的面积。凡是实际种植农作物的面积，不论种植在耕地上还是种植在非耕地上，均包括在农作物播种面积中。在播种季节基本结束后，因遭灾而重新改种和补种的农作物面积，也包括在内。

粮食产量

指全社会的产量。包括国有经济经营的、集体统一经营的和农民家庭经营的粮食产量，还包括工矿企业办的农场和其他生产单位的产量。粮食除包括稻谷、小麦、玉米、高粱、谷子及其他杂粮外，还包括薯类和豆类。其产量计算方法，豆类按去豆荚后的干豆计算；薯类(包括甘薯和马铃薯，不包括芋头和木薯)1963年以前按每4公斤鲜薯折1公斤粮食计算，从1964年开始改为按5公斤鲜

主要统计指标解释

薯折1公斤粮食计算。城市郊区作为蔬菜的薯类(如马铃薯等)按鲜品计算,并且不作粮食统计。其他粮食一律按脱粒后的原粮计算。1989年以前粮食产量数据主要靠全面报表取得,1989年开始使用抽样调查数据。

■ 棉花产量

指全社会的产量。包括春播棉和夏播棉。产量按皮棉计算。3公斤籽棉折1公斤皮棉,不包括木棉。

■ 油料产量

指全部油料作物的生产量。包括花生、油菜籽、芝麻、向日葵籽、胡麻籽(亚麻籽)和其他油料。不包括大豆、木本油料和野生油料。花生以带壳干花生计算。

■ 水产品产量

指人工养殖的水产品和天然生长的水产品的捕捞量。包括海水的鱼类、虾蟹类、贝类和藻类以及内陆水域的鱼类、虾蟹类和贝类,不包括淡水生植物。水产品产量是通过各级水产和统计部门逐级上报取得数据。1995年及以前,贝类中牡蛎按鲜肉计算;蚶、蛤、蛙按5斤鲜品折1斤计算。1996年以后则统一按鲜品计算。

■ 猪、牛、羊肉产量

指当年出栏并已屠宰、除去头蹄下水后带骨肉(即胴体重)的重量。包括全社会范围内的产量。1996年前为各级逐级上报数据。1996年第一次农业普查以后,由于畜牧业产品年报数据与普查数据之间存在一定的差距,国家统计局农调总队对畜牧业年报数据与普查数据进行衔接。1999年以后,国家统计局开展了猪、牛、羊、禽等主要畜禽品种的抽样调查,并用抽样数据作为国家定案数据使用。未开展抽样调查的品种,仍使用各级统计部门逐级上报数据。

SHANGHAI STATISTICAL YEARBOOK

EXPLANATORY NOTES TO MAJOR STATISTICAL INDICATORS

□ Employees in Rural Areas

Employees in Rural Areas refers to people in rural areas who are older than 16 years and engaged in production and business activities that generate incomes in cash or in practicality. It includes all working laborers, no matter whether they are within the working age or not, whereas students studying outside but with their registered residence at home, active serviceman, people who lost their ability to work, unemployed people, and those engaged in housework are not included. The working age is defined as older than 16 years.

□ Gross Output Value of Agriculture

Gross Output Value of Agriculture refers to the total volume of products of farming, forestry, animal husbandry and fishery expressed in the monetary terms and output value of all kinds of service activities that support farming, forestry, animal husbandry and fishery production. It reflects the overall scale and achievements of agricultural production during a given period of time.

The scope of statistics on farming, forestry, animal husbandry, and fishery are as follows:

(1) Farming includes cultivation of farm crops and other agricultural activities.

Cultivation of farm crops include cultivation of grain crops, legume crops, tuber-crops, cotton, oil-bearing crops, sugar crops, bastfiber plants, tobacco, vegetables, medicinal herbs, melon crops, and cultivation and management of tea plantations, mulberry fields and orchards.

Other agricultural activities include harvesting wild fruits, fiber, tree gum, resin, oil-bearing plants, firewood, wild medicinal herbs, fungus, and rural-household commodity industries.

(2) Forestry refers to planting trees of various kinds (excluding tea plantations, mulberry fields and orchards), collection of forestry products and cutting and felling of bamboo and trees by villages and other cooperative organizations under village level.

(3) Animal husbandry refers to raising and grazing of all kinds of farm animals except fishing and aquatic cultivating, and hunting and rising of wild animals.

(4) Fishery refers to cultivation and catching of fish and other aquatic products and cultivation and collection of seaweed and other aquatic plants.

(5) Service Industry for Farming, Forestry, Animal Husbandry and Fishery refers to all kinds of service activities that support farming, forestry, animal husbandry and fishery production, whereas activities of science, technology and professional service are not included.

In terms of ownership, China's agriculture includes specialized state farms (for farming, forestry, animal husbandry, fishery), farms managed by various government agencies, organizations, schools, research institutions, and army; farms managed by rural collective organizations at levels of the township, town, and village; farming, forestry, animal husbandry, fishery run by various rural collective organizations and farming run by collective family members' organizations of mining and industrial enterprises; farming, forestry, animal husbandry and fishery and some commodity industries run by individual farmers.

Gross output value of agriculture is obtained by first multiplying the output of products or by-products by their unit price. For a small number of products, annual output of which is not available or difficult to get due to the long production/growing process involved, the output value will be estimated through an indirect approach. The sum of output value of all products of farming, forestry, animal husbandry and fishery and output value of service activities will then and together to form gross output value of agriculture.

Before 1957, China's gross agricultural output value included the value of barnyard manure and handicraft products for self-consumption (clothes, shoes, stockings, and initial grain processing under-taken by peasants). After 1958, the output value of cutting and felling of bamboo and trees by villages and other cooperative organizations under villages have been included in forestry; value of barnyard manure has been excluded from animal husbandry; the value of self-consumed handicrafts has been excluded from sideline occupations, while output value of industries run by villages and cooperative organizations under village level has been included in sideline occupations and output value of fish catches by motor fishing boats has been added to fishery. Since 1980, the output value of handicraft products made for sale by farmer households has been added to sideline occupations, From 1984, industries run by villages and cooperative organizations under village level have been included in the sector of industry. Af-

EXPLANATORY NOTES TO MAJOR STATISTICAL INDICATORS

ter 1993, the category of sideline occupations has been canceled and hunting of wild animals has been classified into husbandry, and harvesting of wild vegetation and commodity industry run by rural households have been grouped into the category of agriculture. Since 2003, the output value of service industry for farming, forestry, animal husbandry and fishery is included in the gross output value of agriculture.

□ Total Power of Agricultural Machinery

Total Power of Agricultural Machinery refers to the total mechanical power of machinery used in farming, forestry animal husbandry and fishery, including machines used for ploughing, irrigation and drainage, crop growing, plant protection, harvesting, farm product processing, transport, stock breeding, fishery and water conservancy. Machinery employed for non-agricultural purposes such as township industry, capital construction, non-agricultural transport, scientific experiments and for teaching is excluded.

□ Sown Area of Planting

Sown Area of Planting refers to area of land sown or transplanted with crops that have been harvested during report period, regardless of being in cultivated area or non-cultivated area. Area of land re-sown due to natural disasters is also included.

□ Grain Output

Grain Output refers to the total output in the whole country including grains produced by state farms, collective units, rural households, as well as by farms affiliated to industrial and mining enterprises and other production units. Grain includes rice, wheat, corn, sorghum, millet and other miscellaneous grains as well as tubers and bean. Output of beans refers to dry beans without pods. The output of tubers (sweet potatoes and potatoes, not including taros and cassava) was converted into that of grain at the ratio 4 : 1, i.e. 4 kilograms of fresh tubers was equivalent to 1 kilogram of grain up to 1963. Since 1964 the ratio for conversion has been 5 : 1. Tubers supplied as vegetables (such as potatoes) in cities and suburbs are calculated as fresh vegetables and their output is not included in the output of grain. Output of all other grains refers to husked grain. Data on grain production before 1989 were obtained through Comprehensive Statistical Reporting System. Since 1989, data from sample surveys are used.

□ Cotton Output

Cotton Output refers to the cotton production in the whole country including cotton sown in spring and in autumn. Output is measured as the weight of ginned cotton. Three kilograms of seed-cotton are equivalent to 1 kilogram of ginned cotton, excluding ceiba.

□ Output of Oil-bearing Crops

Output of Oil-bearing Crops refers to the total production of oil-bearing crops of various kinds, including peanuts, (dry, in shell) rapeseeds, sesame, sunflower seeds, flax seeds, and other oil-bearing crops. Soybeans, oil-bearing woody plants, and wild oil-bearing crops are not included.

□ Output of Aquatic Products

Output of Aquatic Products refers to catches of both artificially cultured and naturally grown aquatic products, including fish, shrimps, crabs and shellfish in sea and inland water as well as seaweed. Freshwater plants are not included. Data on output of aquatic products are reported by aquatic product and statistical agencies level by level. Before 1995, among the shellfish, the oyster was counted as fresh meat; 5 kilograms of ark shell, clams and frogs are equivalent to 1 kilogram of fresh aquatic products; they are all counted as fresh aquatic products since 1996.

□ Output of Pork, Beef, and Mutton

Output of Pork, Beef, and Mutton refers to the meat of slaughtered hogs, cattle, sheep and goats with head, feet, and offal taken away. Data refers to the production of the whole country. The first agriculture census of China in 1996 revealed some discrepancy between the production of animal products from the annual reports and that from the census. Efforts were made by the Rural Socio-economic Survey Organization of NBS to adjust the output value of animal husbandry to make the figures from the annual reports consistent with the census data. Since 1999, NBS conducted sample survey for the major animal husbandry products, such as hogs, cattle, sheep and goats and fowls, and the data from sample surveys are used as national finalized data. Those products, which are not covered by the sample survey, are still reported by statistical agencies level by level.

第十二篇

CHAPTER 12

工　　业

INDUSTRY

表 12.1 工业总产值及指数(1978～2010)
GROSS OUTPUT VALUE AND INDEX OF INDUSTRY

年 份 Year	工业总产值(亿元) Gross Output Value of Industry(100 million yuan)			工业总产值指数(以 1978 年为 100) Indices of Gross Output Value of Industry(1978 = 100)		
	合 计 Total	轻工业 Light Industry	重工业 Heavy Industry	总指数 Index	轻工业 Light Industry	重工业 Heavy Industry
1978	514.01	266.02	247.99	100.0	100.0	100.0
1979	556.30	290.78	265.52	108.6	109.7	107.6
1980	598.75	331.13	267.62	115.7	123.4	108.3
1981	620.12	360.12	260.00	120.0	135.9	104.6
1982	634.65	359.62	275.03	125.6	139.9	111.9
1983	663.53	363.92	299.61	134.4	147.6	121.8
1984	728.12	395.60	332.52	147.7	163.3	132.7
1985	862.73	456.59	406.14	167.7	184.3	151.9
1986	952.21	493.09	459.12	177.0	192.2	162.6
1987	1 073.84	556.96	516.88	188.9	206.3	172.4
1988	1 304.66	679.17	625.49	208.8	227.2	191.4
1989	1 524.67	789.57	735.10	215.0	233.6	197.3
1990	1 642.75	846.63	796.12	223.6	241.8	206.7
1991	1 947.18	976.34	970.84	255.2	269.2	241.9
1992	2 429.96	1 132.75	1 297.21	306.7	306.4	306.6
1993	3 327.04	1 401.33	1 925.71	368.2	352.7	380.1
1994	4 255.19	1 890.12	2 365.06	435.3	429.9	437.6
1995	5 349.53	2 432.67	2 916.86	510.9	504.2	513.9
(1995)	(4 547.47)	(2 092.89)	(2 454.57)			
1996	5 126.22	2 334.29	2 791.73	590.1	568.7	606.4
1997	5 649.93	2 528.19	3 121.74	675.7	640.4	704.1
1998	5 763.67	2 527.56	3 236.11	728.5	657.7	788.7
1999	6 213.24	2 679.71	3 533.53	805.1	709.1	887.5
2000	7 022.98	2 903.40	4 119.59	913.7	782.2	1 027.7
2001	7 806.18	2 986.59	4 819.59	1 063.8	865.2	1 234.8
2002	8 730.00	3 169.30	5 560.70	1 219.1	934.7	1 463.2
2003	11 708.49	3 550.80	8 157.68	1 601.9	1 064.0	2 061.3
2004	14 595.29	3 871.33	10 723.97	1 927.1	1 268.2	2 492.2
2005	16 876.78	4 299.31	12 577.48	2 195.0	1 395.0	2 873.5
2006	19 631.23	4 747.28	14 883.94	2 500.1	1 494.0	3 341.9
2007	23 108.63	5 318.85	17 789.78	2 892.6	1 641.9	3 926.7
2008	25 968.38	5 839.41	20 128.96	3 126.9	1 770.0	4 244.8
2009	24 888.08	5 663.34	19 224.74	3 227.0	1 716.9	4 457.0
2010	31 038.57	6 692.35	24 346.22	3 966.0	2 025.9	5 540.1

注：从 1996 年开始，工业总产值按新规定计算，括号内数为 1995 年新规定数。以下同。

Note: Since 1996, new regulations have been adopted in calculating total industrial gross output value of industry. The figures of 1995 in brackets are calculated in line with the new regulations. same as follows.

表 12.2 各区、县工业企业主要指标(2010)
MAJOR INDICATIORS OF INDUSTRIAL ENTERPRISES IN DISTRICTS AND COUNTIES

地 区 District		单位数(个) Number of Enterprises (unit)	从业人员(万人) Employees (10 000 persons)	工业总产值(亿元) Gross Output Value of Industry (100 million yuan)	年末资产总计(亿元) Total Assets (year-end) (100 million yuan)	主营业务收入(亿元) Prime Operating Revenue (100 million yuan)	利润总额(亿元) Total Pre-tax Profits (100 million yuan)
总 计	**Total**	**16 684**	**293.23**	**30 114.41**	**27 555.88**	**32 084.08**	**2 299.66**
浦东新区	Pudong New Area	3 711	68.38	8 481.78	8 735.86	9 403.47	784.71
黄 浦 区	Huangpu	39	1.19	95.57	142.01	175.59	5.70
卢 湾 区	Luwan	30	0.84	73.06	81.20	84.52	4.88
徐 汇 区	Xuhui	306	5.48	633.20	516.47	697.35	51.76
长 宁 区	Changning	85	1.19	85.82	103.52	98.24	10.47
静 安 区	Jing'an	24	0.29	16.72	44.54	18.56	3.73
普 陀 区	Putuo	281	4.64	249.30	291.44	286.84	28.06
闸 北 区	Zhabei	127	2.59	160.09	244.76	166.75	6.41
虹 口 区	Hongkou	88	1.23	60.74	88.53	67.68	6.31
杨 浦 区	Yangpu	194	3.71	829.50	1 131.32	844.15	152.48
闵 行 区	Minhang	2 039	39.34	3 592.57	3 036.42	3 678.11	248.63
宝 山 区	Baoshan	1 059	16.11	2 477.54	2 807.52	2 865.77	212.00
嘉 定 区	Jiading	2 291	37.87	3 373.05	2 493.55	3 637.63	313.56
金 山 区	Jinshan	1 012	15.47	1 472.76	984.39	1 482.93	82.02
松 江 区	Songjiang	1 775	41.72	4 252.10	2 503.69	4 244.97	151.97
青 浦 区	Qingpu	1 494	24.65	1 322.87	1 182.03	1 307.03	78.64
奉 贤 区	Fengxian	1 780	20.96	1 295.28	1 211.60	1 320.18	84.93
崇 明 县	Chongming	301	6.00	383.73	564.10	390.04	8.85
其 他	others	48	1.58	1 258.72	1 392.96	1 314.28	64.56

注：本表统计范围为主营业务收入在500万元及以上工业企业。
Note: Data in this table are collected from enterprises with revenue of prime operating revenue of 5 million yuan and above.

表 12.3　工业企业主要指标(2010)
MAJOR INDICATORS OF THE CITY'S INDUSTRIAL ENTERPRISES

类别	Types	单位数(个) Quantity of Enterprises (unit)	从业人员(万人) Employees (10 000 persons)
总　计	**Total**	**16 684**	**293.23**
按隶属关系分	**Grouped by Subordination**		
#中央工业	Central Government	178	15.09
市(局)属工业	Municipality	825	37.89
区属工业	District	775	13.30
县属工业	County	20	0.22
街道属工业	Subdistrict	104	1.42
镇属工业	Town	1 428	25.70
乡属工业	Township	134	3.74
村属工业	Village	768	8.14
按登记注册类型分	**Grouped by Registration Categories**		
内　资	Domestic	10 556	131.23
国　有	State-owned	265	9.67
集　体	Collective-owned	525	5.76
股份合作	Share-holding Coorperation	322	2.92
联　营	Joint Owned	102	1.39
有限责任公司	Companies with Limited Liabilities	1 081	26.13
股份有限公司	Share-holding Companies with Limited Liabilities	151	10.10
私　营	Private	8 065	74.63
其　他	Others	45	0.63
港澳台商投资	Hong Kong, Macao and Taiwan Funded	1 823	45.41
外商投资	Foreign Funded	4 305	116.59
按轻、重工业分	**Grouped by Light and Heavy Industry**		
轻工业	Light Industry	6 418	106.01
重工业	Heavy Industry	10 266	187.22
按企业规模分	**Grouped by Size of Enterprises**		
大型企业	Large	112	52.53
中型企业	Medium	1 638	107.99
小型企业	Small	14 934	132.72
按工业行业分	**Grouped by Sectors**		
采矿业	Mining Industry	1	0.02
#石油和天然气开采业	Petroleum and Natural Gas Exploiting	1	0.02
制造业	Manufacture Industry	16 593	289.04
农副食品加工业	Farm and Sideline Products Processing	202	3.16
食品制造业	Food Manufacturing	296	6.55

注：本表为主营业务收入在500万元及以上企业。
Note: Data in this table are collected from enterprises with revenue of prime operating revenue of 5 million yuan and above.

工业总产值 (亿元) Gross Output Value of Industry (100 million yuan)	年末资产总计 (亿元) Total Assets (year-end) (100 million yuan)	固定资产净值 (亿元) Net Value of Fixed Assets (100 million yuan)	流动资产合计 (亿元) Current Assets (100 million yuan)
30 114.41	**27 555.88**	**8 070.95**	**15 728.25**
6 381.61	7 492.37	3 424.04	2 884.77
6 273.17	6 610.43	1 475.57	3 809.06
975.02	875.28	197.48	576.27
9.63	8.53	2.04	5.41
74.98	71.06	12.15	47.56
1 316.31	1 203.07	252.60	828.39
206.80	138.03	28.63	98.25
388.23	287.65	52.56	218.51
11 706.73	13 794.15	4 549.09	6 873.18
1 752.99	2 842.97	1 419.63	1 040.69
244.53	167.73	28.06	126.83
111.63	93.56	20.01	67.01
80.38	57.92	12.72	39.67
3 220.90	3 910.03	1 239.01	2 115.79
2 765.60	3 719.33	1 214.34	1 427.83
3 483.32	2 960.21	607.14	2 024.53
47.36	42.39	8.19	30.83
5 347.54	3 328.29	793.98	2 075.43
13 060.13	10 433.44	2 727.88	6 779.65
6 315.13	6 098.95	1 364.17	3 934.83
23 799.27	21 456.93	6 706.78	11 793.42
12 864.20	11 233.08	3 539.76	5 827.34
9 279.55	8 550.34	2 529.29	4 925.49
7 970.65	7 772.46	2 001.90	4 975.43
10.67	37.63	0.10	27.02
10.67	37.63	0.10	27.02
28 465.57	24 875.64	6 109.04	15 437.80
262.07	183.89	29.31	122.99
442.28	391.62	112.34	226.86

表 12.3 续表 1 continued

类 别	Types	单位数（个）Quantity of Enterprises (unit)	从业人员（万人）Employees (10 000 persons)
饮料制造业	Beverage Manufacturing	63	1.40
烟草制品业	Tabacco Manufacturing	2	0.40
纺织业	Textile	853	12.84
纺织服装、鞋、帽制造业	Garments, Shoes and Accessories Manufacturing	957	17.16
皮革、毛皮、羽毛(绒)及其制品业	Leather, Fur, and Wool Products Manufacturing	222	4.75
木材加工及木、竹、藤、棕、草制品业	Timber Processing and Timber, Bamboo, Rattan, Coir and Straw Products Manufacturing	178	1.88
家具制造业	Furniture Manufacturing	285	4.90
造纸及纸制品业	Paper-making and Paper Products Manufacturing	370	4.12
印刷业和记录媒介的复制	Printing and Record Duplicating	420	4.81
文教体育用品制造业	Stationary, Education and Sports Goods Manufacturing	256	5.07
石油加工、炼焦及核燃料加工业	Oil Processing, Coking and Nuclear Fuel Processing	53	2.34
化学原料及化学制品制造业	Raw Chemical Materials and Chemical Products Manufacturing	1 142	12.23
医药制造业	Medicine Manufacturing	237	5.55
化学纤维制造业	Chemical Fiber Manufacturing	48	0.45
橡胶制品业	Rubber Products Manufacturing	254	4.12
塑料制品业	Plastic Products Manufacturing	1 079	13.63
非金属矿物制品业	Nonmetal Mineral Products	654	7.95
黑色金属冶炼及压延加工业	Smelting and Pressing of Ferrous Metals	125	4.04
有色金属冶炼及压延加工业	Smelting and Pressing of Nonferrous Metals	247	3.01
金属制品业	Metal Products Manufacturing	1 560	17.46
通用设备制造业	General Equipment Manufacturing	2 156	29.67
专用设备制造业	Special Purpose Equipment Manufacturing	1 129	15.71
交通运输设备制造业	Transportation Equipment Manufacturing	999	29.69
电气机械及器材制造业	Electric Machinery Equipments and Manufacturing	1 476	26.59
通信设备、计算机及其他电子设备制造业	Communications Equipment, Computer and Other Electronic Equipment Manufacturing	719	40.73
仪器仪表及文化、办公用机械制造业	Instruments, Meters, Culture and Office Equipments Manufacturing	357	5.94
工艺品及其他制造业	Artworks and Other Manufacturing	212	2.59
废弃资源和废旧材料回收加工业	Waste Resources and Materials Recycling and Processing	42	0.30
电力、燃气及水的生产和供应业	Production and Supply of Power, Gas and Water	90	4.17
电力、热力的生产和供应业	Production and Supply of Electricity and Thermal Power	37	2.09
燃气生产和供应业	Production and Supply of Gas	18	1.00
水的生产和供应业	Production and Supply of Water	35	1.08

工业总产值 (亿元) Gross Output Value of Industry (100 million yuan)	年末资产总计 (亿元) Total Assets (year-end) (100 million yuan)	固定资产净值 (亿元) Net Value of Fixed Assets (100 million yuan)	流动资产合计 (亿元) Current Assets (100 million yuan)
169.37	165.22	56.78	94.38
538.70	756.76	33.69	591.95
414.21	422.90	89.31	265.73
463.41	413.31	61.58	307.34
138.90	129.44	16.29	105.38
85.94	84.54	18.73	57.15
258.52	170.12	28.09	124.77
262.12	247.32	88.73	135.62
202.62	235.92	83.50	127.22
151.15	128.88	28.42	88.46
1 359.92	532.56	235.14	171.24
2 284.33	2 060.35	763.11	1 048.96
410.76	487.35	107.56	299.96
41.48	44.30	17.15	22.29
182.97	201.26	48.44	123.92
642.27	622.81	179.26	366.99
514.86	606.31	138.61	398.55
1 722.87	2 048.15	1 019.81	655.84
444.19	276.67	69.83	176.16
905.96	809.61	184.45	542.98
2 395.11	2 749.92	530.68	1 942.23
1 077.19	1 264.28	232.91	913.79
4 475.48	4 696.26	842.22	2 854.65
1 962.26	1 664.99	290.27	1 212.14
6 026.91	3 004.65	717.98	2 104.10
354.57	310.63	43.70	244.54
235.76	142.39	33.06	98.31
39.38	23.24	8.12	13.31
1 638.17	2 642.61	1 961.81	263.43
1 454.75	2 113.78	1 696.46	157.92
139.56	233.79	68.23	68.23
43.86	295.03	197.12	37.27

表 12.3 续表 2 continued

类 别	Types	年末负债合计 Total Liabilities (year-end)	年末所有者权益 Owners' Equity (year-end)
总 计	**Total**	**14 500.46**	**13 055.42**
按隶属关系分	**Grouped by Subordination**		
#中央工业	Central Government	3 368.35	4 124.02
市(局)属工业	Municipality	3 490.07	3 120.36
区属工业	District	491.17	384.11
县属工业	County	4.80	3.72
街道属工业	Subdistrict	37.11	33.95
镇属工业	Town	664.36	538.71
乡属工业	Township	82.26	55.77
村属工业	Village	158.17	129.48
按登记注册类型分	**Grouped by Registration Categories**		
内 资	Domestic	6 720.19	7 073.96
国 有	State-owned	800.35	2 042.62
集 体	Collective-owned	91.94	75.79
股份合作	Share-holding Coorperation	52.02	41.54
联 营	Joint Owned	35.76	22.16
有限责任公司	Companies with Limited Liabilities	2 457.07	1 452.96
股份有限公司	Share-holding Companies with Limited Liabilities	1 519.83	2 199.50
私 营	Private	1 737.32	1 222.89
其 他	Others	25.90	16.50
港澳台商投资	Hong Kong, Macao and Taiwan Funded	1 937.10	1 391.19
外商投资	Foreign Funded	5 843.17	4 590.27
按轻、重工业分	**Grouped by Light and Heavy Industry**		
轻工业	Light Industry	2 851.02	3 247.93
重工业	Heavy Industry	11 649.44	9 807.49
按企业规模分	**Grouped by Size of Enterprises**		
大型企业	Large	5 735.42	5 497.65
中型企业	Medium	4 626.81	3 923.53
小型企业	Small	4 138.22	3 634.24
按工业行业分	**Grouped by Sectors**		
采矿业	Mining Industry	7.34	30.28
#石油和天然气开采业	Petroleum and Natural Gas Exploiting	7.34	30.28
制造业	Manufacture Industry	13 435.39	11 440.26
农副食品加工业	Farm and Sideline Products Processing	98.90	84.99
食品制造业	Food Manufacturing	233.31	158.31

单位：亿元(100 million yuan)

主营业务收入 Prime Operating Revenue	利润总额 Total After-tax Profits	税金总额 Total Tax and Duties	成本费用总额 Total Cost and Expenses
32 084.08	**2 299.66**	**1 395.01**	**29 670.94**
6 711.05	474.70	685.98	5 889.80
7 458.65	772.22	351.34	6 803.39
1 051.75	60.54	24.09	1 007.15
9.37	0.93	0.33	8.60
76.99	4.25	2.35	73.34
1 340.47	92.25	33.27	1 259.53
244.21	7.56	5.63	238.28
407.17	21.59	9.25	387.68
12 465.24	928.73	806.97	11 461.12
1 822.53	171.75	441.23	1 367.74
252.07	8.16	7.87	247.76
113.61	5.58	4.61	109.79
81.20	3.23	2.17	79.52
3 407.90	163.58	97.80	3 310.45
3 228.40	382.31	159.03	2 959.84
3 516.10	191.57	93.09	3 344.96
43.43	2.55	1.17	41.06
5 363.35	240.84	136.91	5 101.58
14 255.49	1 130.09	451.13	13 108.25
6 548.73	565.87	593.37	5 721.30
25 535.36	1 733.79	801.63	23 949.64
14 198.13	1 049.72	910.12	12 824.59
9 619.98	700.79	251.68	9 057.95
8 265.98	549.15	233.22	7 788.41
11.79	3.44	1.32	7.39
11.79	3.44	1.32	7.39
30 383.78	2 265.53	1 341.82	27 945.39
279.28	11.44	3.45	272.48
484.58	32.22	25.73	450.83

表 12.3 续表 3　continued

类　别	Types	年末负债合　计 Total Liabilities (Year-end)	年末所有者权　益 Owners Equity (Year-end)
饮料制造业	Beverage Manufacturing	90.74	74.48
烟草制品业	Tabacco Manufacturing	51.86	704.90
纺织业	Textile	204.76	218.14
纺织服装、鞋、帽制造业	Garments, Shoes and Accessories Manufacturing	232.10	181.21
皮革、毛皮、羽毛(绒)及其制品业	Leather, Fur, and Wool Products Manufacturing	54.87	74.57
木材加工及木、竹、藤、棕、草制品业	Timber Processing and Timber, Bamboo, Rattan, Coir and Straw Products Manufacturing	47.51	37.04
家具制造业	Furniture Manufacturing	104.43	65.69
造纸及纸制品业	Paper-making and Paper Products Manufacturing	136.77	110.54
印刷业和记录媒介的复制	Printing and Record Duplicating	103.11	132.82
文教体育用品制造业	Stationary, Education and Sports Goods Manufacturing	69.78	59.10
石油加工、炼焦及核燃料加工业	Oil Processing, Coking and Nuclear Fuel Processing	231.69	300.87
化学原料及化学制品制造业	Raw Chemical Materials and Chemical Products Manufacturing	1 051.53	1 008.82
医药制造业	Medicine Manufacturing	210.62	276.73
化学纤维制造业	Chemical Fiber Manufacturing	18.08	26.22
橡胶制品业	Rubber Products Manufacturing	112.57	88.69
塑料制品业	Plastic Products Manufacturing	312.97	309.85
非金属矿物制品业	Nonmetal Mineral Products	341.09	265.22
黑色金属冶炼及压延加工业	Smelting and Pressing of Ferrous Metals	959.51	1 088.64
有色金属冶炼及压延加工业	Smelting and Pressing of Nonferrous Metals	164.15	112.52
金属制品业	Metal Products Manufacturing	437.74	371.87
通用设备制造业	General Equipment Manufacturing	1 648.80	1 101.12
专用设备制造业	Special Purpose Equipment Manufacturing	751.03	513.25
交通运输设备制造业	Transportation Equipment Manufacturing	2 652.69	2 043.57
电气机械及器材制造业	Electric Machinery Equipments and Manufacturing	905.81	759.17
通信设备、计算机及其他电子设备制造业	Communications Equipment, Computer and Other Electronic Equipment Manufacturing	1 971.27	1 033.38
仪器仪表及文化、办公用机械制造业	Instruments, Meters, Culture and Office Equipments Manufacturing	149.81	160.82
工艺品及其他制造业	Artworks and Other Manufacturing	74.00	68.39
废弃资源和废旧材料回收加工业	Waste Resources and Materials Recycling and Processing	13.90	9.34
电力、燃气及水的生产和供应业	Production and Supply of Power, Gas and Water	1 057.73	1 584.88
电力、热力的生产和供应业	Production and Supply of Electricity and Thermal Power	800.73	1 313.05
燃气生产和供应业	Production and Supply of Gas	82.57	151.22
水的生产和供应业	Production and Supply of Water	174.43	120.60

单位:亿元(100 million yuan)

主营业务收入 Prime Operating Revenue	利润总额 Total After-tax Profits	税金总额 Total Tax and Duties	成本费用总额 Total Cost and Expenses
170.59	7.49	14.56	159.92
538.16	141.76	397.16	92.47
434.43	25.01	10.24	415.05
470.64	38.87	18.04	433.70
137.47	13.94	5.00	124.75
88.65	4.20	2.41	84.35
264.13	20.29	6.49	247.60
269.01	15.08	8.28	256.80
206.08	18.34	8.06	190.13
154.68	8.17	2.37	147.73
1 389.42	70.16	173.12	1 206.09
2 386.91	180.10	72.72	2 219.37
409.89	57.08	25.99	362.88
40.83	3.11	1.12	38.52
233.18	13.10	5.52	222.59
649.32	44.54	16.00	609.16
535.19	31.65	19.21	508.12
2 086.98	154.93	40.85	1 945.92
440.64	12.10	3.76	430.33
922.05	58.95	23.16	871.52
2 409.32	174.69	78.58	2 241.60
1 103.38	106.83	32.12	1 022.28
5 440.37	675.79	277.56	4 850.47
2 013.26	148.63	37.73	1 878.80
6 132.25	142.68	18.29	6 014.46
372.79	39.25	8.68	340.28
278.04	12.76	4.74	266.82
42.25	2.38	0.85	40.38
1 688.51	30.69	51.87	1 718.16
1 454.05	32.05	47.18	1 475.97
182.58	-0.06	1.99	186.14
51.87	-1.31	2.71	56.05

表 12.4 工业企业销售产值(2010)
SALES VALUE OF INDUSTRIAL ENTERPRISES

单位：亿元(100 million yuan)

类别	Types	工业销售产值 Sales Value of Industry	其中 of which #出口交货值 Delivery Value of Industry Export
总 计	**Total**	**29 838.11**	**8 204.27**
按隶属关系分	**Grouped by Subordination**		
#中央工业	Central Government	6 372.05	839.11
市(局)属工业	Municipality	6 188.10	734.18
区属工业	District	966.70	151.76
县属工业	County	9.33	1.27
街道属工业	Subdistrict	76.25	8.89
镇属工业	Town	1 302.39	232.74
乡属工业	Township	203.11	46.68
村属工业	Village	389.23	63.41
按登记注册类型分	**Grouped by Registration Categories**		
内 资	Domestic	11 622.73	1 081.68
国 有	State-owned	1 755.02	32.39
集 体	Collective-owned	243.49	3.67
股份合作	Share-holding Coorperation	112.27	6.41
联 营	Joint Owned	79.35	1.57
有限责任公司	Companies with Limited Liabilities	3 209.55	525.38
股份有限公司	Share-holding Companies with Limited Liabilities	2 755.07	236.93
私 营	Private	3 424.18	267.05
其 他	Others	43.80	8.27
港澳台商投资	Hong Kong, Macao and Taiwan Funded	5 286.09	2 925.40
外商投资	Foreign Funded	12 929.30	4 197.19
按轻、重工业分	**Grouped by Light and Heavy Industry**		
轻工业	Light Industry	6 206.51	1 308.32
重工业	Heavy Industry	23 631.60	6 895.96
按企业规模分	**Grouped by Size of Enterprises**		
大型企业	Large	12 776.78	4 929.88
中型企业	Medium	9 146.95	2 168.78
小型企业	Small	7 914.38	1 105.61
按工业行业分	**Grouped by Sectors**		
采矿业	Mining Industry	11.79	
石油和天然气开采业	Petroleum and Natural Gas Exploiting	11.79	
制造业	Manufacture Industry	28 190.22	8 204.26
农副食品加工业	Farm and Sideline Products Processing	259.86	12.06
食品制造业	Food Manufacturing	437.28	18.06

注：本表为主营业务收入在500万元及以上企业。
Note: Data in this table are collected from enterprises with revenue of Prime Operating Revenue of 5 million yuan and above.

表 12.4 续表 continued

单位:亿元(100 million yuan)

类 别	Types	工业销售产值 Sales Value of Industry	其中 of which #出口交货值 Delivery Value of Industry Export
饮料制造业	Beverage Manufacturing	159.76	5.35
烟草制品业	Tabacco Manufacturing	539.69	7.82
纺织业	Textile	410.15	115.88
纺织服装、鞋、帽制造业	Garments, Shoes and Accessories Manufacturing	452.07	126.46
皮革、毛皮、羽毛(绒)及其制品业	Leather, Fur, and Wool Products Manufacturing	136.58	44.37
木材加工及木、竹、藤、棕、草制品业	Timber Processing and Timber, Bamboo, Rattan, Coir and Straw Products Manufacturing	85.96	19.83
家具制造业	Furniture Manufacturing	253.71	72.47
造纸及纸制品业	Paper-making and Paper Products Manufacturing	257.19	19.84
印刷业和记录媒介的复制	Printing and Record Duplicating	200.45	19.99
文教体育用品制造业	Stationary, Education and Sports Goods Manufacturing	150.15	84.31
石油加工、炼焦及核燃料加工业	Oil Processing, Coking and Nuclear Fuel Processing	1 358.26	47.15
化学原料及化学制品制造业	Raw Chemical Materials and Chemical Products Manufacturing	2 290.54	223.84
医药制造业	Medicine Manufacturing	385.89	33.94
化学纤维制造业	Chemical Fiber Manufacturing	40.79	8.30
橡胶制品业	Rubber Products Manufacturing	184.13	48.72
塑料制品业	Plastic Products Manufacturing	636.72	130.50
非金属矿物制品业	Nonmetal Mineral Products	520.79	58.21
黑色金属冶炼及压延加工业	Smelting and Pressing of Ferrous Metals	1 711.90	145.78
有色金属冶炼及压延加工业	Smelting and Pressing of Nonferrous Metals	434.97	47.77
金属制品业	Metal Products Manufacturing	891.69	200.76
通用设备制造业	General Equipment Manufacturing	2 353.13	422.03
专用设备制造业	Special Purpose Equipment Manufacturing	1 067.13	201.78
交通运输设备制造业	Transportation Equipment Manufacturing	4 443.50	646.38
电气机械及器材制造业	Electric Machinery Equipments and Manufacturing	1 935.83	510.13
通信设备、计算机及其他电子设备制造业	Communcations Equipment, Computer and Other Electronic Equipment Manufacturing	5 961.72	4 763.57
仪器仪表及文化、办公用机械制造业	Instruments, Meters, Culture and Office Equipments Manufacturing	355.63	155.49
工艺品及其他制造业	Artworks and Other Manufacturing	235.29	11.70
废弃资源和废旧材料回收加工业	Waste Resources and Materials Recycling and Processing	39.48	1.77
电力、燃气及水的生产和供应业	Production and Supply of Power, Gas and Water	1 636.10	0.01
电力、热力的生产和供应业	Production and Supply of Electricity and Thermal Power	1 454.74	
燃气生产和供应业	Production and Supply of Gas	139.55	0.01
水的生产和供应业	Production and Supply of Water	41.81	

表 12.5 工业企业经济效益指标(2010)
ECONOMIC EFFICIENCY INDICATORS OF INDUSTRIAL ENTERPRISES

类 别	Types	工业经济效益综合指数 Industrial Economic Benefit Synthetic Index	总资产贡献率(%) Total Assets Contribution Ratio (%)	资产保值增值率(%) Ratio of Capital Hold and Rise (%)	资产负债率(%) Asset-debt Ratio (%)
总 计	**Total**	**250.70**	**14.68**	**114.17**	**52.62**
#国有控股企业	Enterprises with the State Holding Major Shares	518.46	18.02	112.28	48.78
#大中型企业	Large and Medium Enterprises	578.36	19.14	112.53	48.29
按隶属关系分	**Grouped by Subordination**				
中央工业	Central Government	828.07	16.29	106.57	44.96
地方工业	Municipality	217.96	14.05	118.07	55.48
按轻、重工业分	**Grouped by Light and Heavy Industry**				
轻工业	Light Industry	240.83	20.55	111.38	46.75
重工业	Heavy Industry	261.08	13.01	115.13	54.29
按企业规模分	**Grouped by Size of Enterprise**				
大型企业	Large	442.68	18.70	112.04	51.06
中型企业	Medium	225.35	12.55	116.84	54.11
小型企业	Small	182.42	11.21	114.64	53.24

注：本表为主营业务收入在500万元以上企业。
Note: Data in this table are collected from enterprises with revenue of prime operating revenue more than 5 million yuan.

表 12.5 续表 continued

类 别	Types	工业全员劳动生产率(元/人) Overall Industrial Labor Productivity (yuan/person)	流动资产周转次数(次) Turnover of Current Assets (time)	成本费用利润率(%) Ratio of pre-tax Profits to Cost and Expenses(%)	工业产品销售率(%) Sales Rate of Industrial Products(%)
总 计	**Total**	**216 404.49**	**2.25**	**7.75**	**99.08**
#国有控股企业	Enterprises with the State Holding Major Shares	631 550.78	2.44	9.94	99.44
#大中型企业	Large and Medium Enterprises	723 322.04	2.48	10.42	99.43
按隶属关系分	**Grouped by Subordination**				
中央工业	Central Government	1 159 591.60	2.50	8.06	99.85
地方工业	Municipality	164 956.16	2.19	7.67	98.88
按轻、重工业分	**Grouped by Light and Heavy Industry**				
轻工业	Light Industry	176 414.82	1.83	9.89	98.28
重工业	Heavy Industry	239 282.53	2.39	7.24	99.30
按企业规模分	**Grouped by Size of Enterprise**				
大型企业	Large	511 237.34	2.70	8.19	99.32
中型企业	Medium	182 068.74	2.17	7.74	98.57
小型企业	Small	125 766.74	1.81	7.05	99.29

表 12.6 国有控股企业主要指标占全市比重(2010)
PROPORTION OF THE MAJOR INDICATORS OF ENTERPRISES WITH THE STATE HOLDING MAJOR SHARES

指　标	Indicators	合　计 Total	国有控股企业 Enterprises with the State Holding Major Shares	占全市比重(%) Proportion(%)
企业单位数（个）	Number of Enterprises (unit)	16 684	1 013	6.1
从业人员（万人）	Year-end Employees (10 000 persons)	293.23	46.63	15.9
工业总产值(亿元)	Gross Output Value of Industry (100 million yuan)	30 114.41	11 190.55	37.2
年末资产总计(亿元)	Total Assets (year-end) (100 million yuan)	27 555.88	12 770.58	46.3
流动资产合计(亿元)	Current Assets(100 million yuan)	15 728.25	5 851.16	37.2
固定资产净值(亿元)	Net Value of Fixed Assets(100 million yuan)	8 070.95	4 522.66	56.0
年末负债合计(亿元)	Total Liabilities (year-end) (100 million yuan)	14 500.46	6 230.11	43.0
年末所有者权益(亿元)	Owners Equity (year-end) (100 million yuan)	13 055.42	6 540.47	50.1
主营业务收入(亿元)	Prime Operating Revenue(100 million yuan)	32 084.08	12 743.02	39.7
主营业务税金及附加(亿元)	Product Sales Tax and Addition (100 million yuan)	578.04	558.02	96.5
利润总额(亿元)	Total Pre-Tax Profits (100 million yuan)	2 299.66	1 130.68	49.2
税金总额(亿元)	Total Tax and Duty (100 million yuan)	1 395.01	1 007.38	72.2
亏损企业数（个）	Number of Loss-making Enterprises (unit)	2 838	196	6.9
亏损企业亏损额(亿元)	Total Losses Made by Enterprises-in-red (100 million yuan)	143.59	37.46	26.1

注：本表为主营业务收入在500万元及以上企业。
Note: Data in this table are collected from enterprises with revenue of prime operating revenue of 5 million yuan and above.

表 12.7 六个重点发展工业行业主要指标(2010)
MAJOR INDICATORS OF SIX KEY INDUSTRIES ABOVE THE SET SCALE

行业	Sectors	单位数(个) Quantity of Enterprises (unit)	从业人员平均人数(万人) Average Employees (10 000 persons)	工业总产值(亿元) Gross Output Value of Industry (100 million yuan)
总计	**Total**	**6 066**	**138.09**	**19 891.08**
电子信息产品制造业	Electronic Information Product Manufacturing	1 717	55.33	7 022.46
汽车制造业	Automobile Manufacturing	659	20.77	3 626.46
石油化工及精细化工制造业	Petrochemical and Fine Chemical Products Manufacturing	995	12.88	3 442.44
精品钢材制造业	Fine Steel Manufacturing	125	3.99	1 722.87
成套设备制造业	Equipment Complex Manufacturing	2 106	35.96	3 485.65
生物医药制造业	Bio-medicine Manufacturing	464	9.15	591.20
六个重点发展工业行业占全市比重(%)	Percentage of the Six Key Industries in Shanghai (%)	36.4	47.4	66.1

注：本表为主营业务收入在500万元及以上企业。
Note: Data in this table are collected from enterprises with revenue of Prime Operating Revenue of 5 million yuan and above.

表 12.7 续表 1 continued

行业	Sectors	工业销售产值(亿元) Sales Value of Industry (100 million yuan)	年末资产总计(亿元) Total Property (year-end) (100 million yuan)
总计	**Total**	**19 727.73**	**16 858.38**
电子信息产品制造业	Electronic Information Product Manufacturing	6 953.06	3 902.88
汽车制造业	Automobile Manufacturing	3 604.18	3 366.28
石油化工及精细化工制造业	Petrochemical and Fine Chemical Products Manufacturing	3 445.52	2 362.88
精品钢材制造业	Fine Steel Manufacturing	1 711.90	2 048.15
成套设备制造业	Equipment Complex Manufacturing	3 453.69	4 498.95
生物医药制造业	Bio-medicine Manufacturing	559.38	679.23
六个重点发展工业行业占全市比重(%)	Percentage of the Six Key Industries in Shanghai (%)	66.1	61.2

表 12.7 续表 2 continued

行业	Sectors	主营业务收入(亿元) Prime Operating Revenue (100 million yuan)	利润总额(亿元) Total Pre-tax Profits (100 million yuan)	税金总额(亿元) Total Tax and Duties (100 million yuan)
总计	**Total**	**21 498.84**	**1 587.94**	**689.05**
电子信息产品制造业	Electronic Information Product Manufacturing	7 168.66	209.22	28.25
汽车制造业	Automobile Manufacturing	4 603.17	634.42	259.66
石油化工及精细化工制造业	Petrochemical and Fine Chemical Products Manufacturing	3 564.36	238.42	238.14
精品钢材制造业	Fine Steel Manufacturing	2 086.98	154.93	40.85
成套设备制造业	Equipment Complex Manufacturing	3 485.2	271.31	90.07
生物医药制造业	Bio-medicine Manufacturing	590.48	79.64	32.08
六个重点发展工业行业占全市比重(%)	Percentage of the Six Key Industries in Shanghai (%)	67.0	69.1	50.7

表 12.8 信息产品制造业主要指标(2010)
MAJOR INDICATORS OF INFORMATION PRODUCTS MANUFACTURING INDUSTRY

单位:亿元(100 million yuan)

指 标	Indicators	工业总产值 Gross Output Value of Industry	工业销售产值 Sales Value of Industry	年末资产总计 Total Assets (year-end)
总 计	**Total**	**7 022.46**	**6 953.06**	**3 902.88**
通信设备制造	Communications Equipment	757.60	749.83	574.61
雷达及配套产品制造	Radar ane Supported Product	0.67	0.91	1.06
广播电视设备制造	Broadcast and Television Equipment	13.27	12.98	10.59
电子计算机制造	Computer	3 868.91	3 834.38	1 077.11
家用视听设备制造	Household Seeing and Hearing Equipment	236.40	233.96	108.92
电子测量仪器制造	Geodesic Equipment of Electron	140.87	140.55	121.56
电子专用设备制造	Special Equipment of Electron	169.38	165.70	190.60
电子元件制造	Electronic Component	612.37	605.87	527.98
电子器件制造	Electronic Equipment	604.55	591.01	756.80
#集成电路制造	Integrated Circuit	347.57	342.62	513.73
电子机电产品制造	Machinery and Electronic Products of Electron	578.66	576.88	485.51
电子专用材料制造	Special Materials of Electron	39.79	40.99	48.15

表 12.8 续表 continued

单位:亿元(100 million yuan)

指 标	Indicators	主营业务收入 Prime Operating Revenue	利润总额 Total Pre-tax Profits	税金总额 Total Tax and Duty
总 计	**Total**	**7 168.66**	**209.22**	**28.25**
通信设备制造	Communications Equipment	770.69	26.80	1.07
雷达及配套产品制造	Radar ane Supported Product	0.90	0.09	0.10
广播电视设备制造	Broadcast and Television Equipment	13.29	1.33	0.15
电子计算机制造	Computer	3 965.21	28.45	1.48
家用视听设备制造	Household Seeing and Hearing Equipment	241.66	2.98	0.34
电子测量仪器制造	Geodesic Equipment of Electron	145.59	18.59	3.67
电子专用设备制造	Special Equipment of Electron	178.63	15.62	5.10
电子元件制造	Electronic Component	614.16	53.25	5.79
电子器件制造	Electronic Equipment	593.30	35.69	3.75
#集成电路制造	Integrated Circuit	344.75	26.67	3.58
电子机电产品制造	Machinery and Electronic Products of Electron	605.77	21.09	6.34
电子专用材料制造	Special Materials of Electron	39.46	5.32	0.45

表 12.9 高技术产业主要指标(2009～2010)
MAIN FACT ABOUT HIGH TECHNOLOGY INDUSTRY

类别	Types	工业总产值(亿元) Gross Output Value of Industry (100 million yuan) 2009	2010
总　计	**Total**	**5 560.65**	**6 958.01**
占全市比重(%)	**Proportion (%)**	**23.3**	**23.2**
按登记注册类型分	**Grouped by Registration Categories**		
国　有	State-owned	64.11	79.79
集　体	Collective-owned	1.38	2.61
股份合作企业	Cooperative	6.75	8.87
股份制企业	Share Holding	299.57	390.37
外商投资企业	Foreign Funded	5 151.15	6 436.45
其　他	Others	37.69	39.92
按技术领域分	**Grouped by Technology Areas**		
信息化学品制造	Information Chemical Product	10.45	39.66
医药制造业	Medical and Pharmaceutical Product	351.74	413.16
航空航天器制造	Aviation and Aircraft Manufaturing	22.1	35.94
电子及通信设备制造业	Electron and Communicate Equipments	1 691.42	2 176.04
电子计算机及办公设备制造业	Electronic Computers and Office Equipments	3 194.02	3 922.95
医疗设备及仪器仪表制造业	Medical Treatment Instrument and Meter	290.93	370.25

表 12.9 续表 1　continued

类别	Types	工业销售产值(亿元) Sales Value of Industry (100 million yuan) 2009	2010	年末资产总计(亿元) Total Property(year-end) (100 million yuan) 2009	2010
总　计	**Total**	**5 466.77**	**6 832.61**	**3 648.33**	**4 036.79**
占全市比重(%)	**Proportion(%)**	**23.1**	**23.0**	**15.0**	**14.7**
按登记注册类型分	**Grouped by Registration Categories**				
国　有	State-owned	63.02	83.57	113.55	142.13
集　体	Collective-owned	1.36	2.57	4.55	6.77
股份合作企业	Cooperative	6.57	9.40	5.67	11.12
股份制企业	Share Holding	295.2	377.25	475.08	592.90
外商投资企业	Foreign Funded	5 068.28	6 321.99	3 021.17	3 248.82
其　他	Others	32.34	37.83	28.31	35.05
按技术领域分	**Grouped by Technology Areas**				
信息化学品制造	Information Chemical Product	10.49	40.68	30.32	52.44
医药制造业	Medical and Pharmaceutical Product	336.26	388.25	427.34	496.81
航空航天器制造	Aviation and Aircraft Manufaturing	22.63	36.03	73.89	117.63
电子及通信设备制造业	Electron and Communicate Equipments	1 673.77	2 117.23	1 821.62	1 920.90
电子计算机及办公设备制造业	Electronic Computers and Office Equipments	3 136.94	3 883.76	1 002.06	1 107.18
医疗设备及仪器仪表制造业	Medical Treatment Instrument and Meter	286.68	366.66	293.10	341.82

表 12.9 续表 2 continued

类 别	Types	主营业务收入(亿元) Prime Operating Revenue (100 million yuan)		利润总额(亿元) Total Pre-tax Profits (100 million yuan)	
		2009	2010	2009	2010
总 计	**Total**	**5 768.**	**7 035.68**	**72.94**	**246.74**
占全市比重(%)	**Proportion (%)**	**22.9**	**22.0**	**5.2**	**11.1**
按登记注册类型分	**Grouped by Registration Categories**				
国 有	State-owned	64.40	87.16	5.50	13.21
集 体	Collective-owned	2.22	3.18	0.76	0.21
股份合作企业	Cooperative	6.73	10.01		1.14
股份制企业	Share Holding	330.99	405.54	23.80	34.02
外商投资企业	Foreign Funded	5 331.36	6 491.66	41.50	195.64
其 他	Others	32.3	38.12	1.38	2.51
按技术领域分	**Grouped by Technology Areas**				
信息化学品制造	Information Chemical Product	13.88	38.85	1.14	5.53
医药制造业	Medical and Pharmaceutical Product	357.75	413.48	47.08	56.70
航空航天器制造	Aviation and Aircraft Manufaturing	24.34	37.32	1.69	1.53
电子及通信设备制造业	Electron and Communicate Equipments	1 696.44	2 157.66	-30.80	111.77
电子计算机及办公设备制造业	Electronic Computers and Office Equipments	3 376.87	4 006.76	21.19	26.98
医疗设备及仪器仪表制造业	Medical Treatment Instrument and Meter	298.72	381.60	32.65	44.23

表 12.9 续表 3 continued

类 别	Types	税金总额(亿元) Total Tax and Duties (100 million yuan)		产品销售率(%) Sales Rate of Industrial Products(%)	
		2009	2010	2009	2010
总 计	**Total**	**48.95**	**56.11**	**98.3**	**98.2**
占全市比重(%)	**Proportion (%)**	**4.4**	**4.1**		
按登记注册类型分	**Grouped by Registration Categories**				
国 有	State-owned	2.75	4.20	98.3	104.7
集 体	Collective-owned	0.08	0.19	99.1	98.6
股份合作企业	Cooperative	0.34	1.08	97.2	106.0
股份制企业	Share Holding	15.08	15.31	98.5	96.6
外商投资企业	Foreign Funded	29.50	34.24	98.4	98.2
其 他	Others	1.20	1.09	85.8	94.8
按技术领域分	**Grouped by Technology Areas**				
信息化学品制造	Information Chemical Product	0.87	0.34	100.3	102.6
医药制造业	Medical and Pharmaceutical Product	21.79	26.28	95.6	94.0
航空航天器制造	Aviation and Aircraft Manufaturing	0.46	0.58	102.4	100.2
电子及通信设备制造业	Electron and Communicate Equipments	14.43	15.43	99.0	97.3
电子计算机及办公设备制造业	Electronic Computers and Office Equipments	2.69	3.10	98.2	99.0
医疗设备及仪器仪表制造业	Medical Treatment Instrument and Meter	8.72	10.38	98.5	99.0

表 12.10 都市型工业主要指标(2009～2010)
MAIN STATISTICS OF URBAN INDUSTRIES

类别	Types	单位数(个) Quantity of Enterprises (unit)		从业人员(万人) Employees (10 000 persons)		工业总产值(亿元) Gross Output Value of Industry(100 million yuan)	
		2009	2010	2009	2010	2009	2010
总计	**Total**	**4 356**	**3 916**	**72.74**	**68.04**	**2 809.48**	**3 294.97**
按企业规模分	**Grouped by Size of Enterprises**						
大型	Large	19	23	5.57	6.60	277.02	481.47
中型	Medium	411	403	26.90	25.72	1 285.57	1 491.90
小型	Small	3 926	3 490	40.27	35.71	1 246.89	1 321.61
按登记注册类型分	**Grouped by Registration Categories**						
内资	Domestic Investment	2 567	2 300	29.04	27.48	947.74	1 205.57
国有	State-owned	64	53	0.94	0.80	50.87	32.79
集体	Collective-owned	112	87	0.96	0.72	19.59	16.69
股份合作	Share-holding Coorperative	60	56	0.70	0.53	12.44	12.67
联营	Joint Owned	26	19	0.34	0.21	8.13	8.86
有限责任公司	Companies with Limited Liabilities	226	196	3.87	3.75	224.06	350.41
股份有限公司	Share-holding Companies with Limited Liabilities	35	38	1.50	2.08	103.15	189.60
私营	Private	2 039	1 842	20.68	19.27	527.27	590.20
其他	Others	5	9	0.06	0.12	2.23	4.34
港澳台商投资	Hong Kong, Macao and Taiwan Funded	613	540	14.19	13.31	527.13	633.51
外商投资	Foreign Funded	1 176	1 076	29.51	27.24	1 334.61	1 455.89
按行业分	**Grouped by Sectors**						
服装服饰业	Garment and Trappings	1 480	1 247	27.55	22.26	582.81	593.08
食品加工制造业	Food Processing	535	507	10.10	10.42	733.81	819.80
包装、印刷业	Packaging and Printing	614	577	6.48	6.49	250.75	284.22
室内装饰用品制造业	Indoor Decoration Materials and Equipments Manufacturing	778	696	10.35	10.01	395.83	483.96
化妆品及清洁洗涤用品制造业	Cosmetics and Cleaning Manufacturing	225	225	2.71	2.80	256.05	288.43
工艺美术品、旅游用品制造业	Art Crafts and Tourism Equipments Manufacturing	463	413	8.06	7.90	320.47	391.12
小型电子信息产品制造业	Small Electronic Information Products Manufacturing	261	251	7.49	8.14	269.76	434.36

表 12.10 续表 1 continued

单位:亿元(100 million yuan)

类别	Types	工业销售产值 Sales Value of Industry		年末资产总计 Total Assets (year-end)		主营业务收入 Prime Operating Revenue	
		2009	2010	2009	2010	2009	2010
总 计	**Total**	**2 769.76**	**3 254.42**	**2 582.51**	**2 845.03**	**2 900.98**	**3 463.85**
按企业规模分	**Grouped by Size of Enterprises**						
大 型	Large	277.94	480.25	247.05	407.99	310.3	534.94
中 型	Medium	1 256.31	1 463.09	1 130.57	1 227.39	1 313.24	1 543.98
小 型	Small	1 235.51	1 311.09	1 204.9	1 209.65	1 277.45	1 384.93
按登记注册类型分	**Grouped by Registration Categories**						
内 资	Domestic Investment	936.51	1 194.90	912.60	1 042.47	1 008.28	1 309.09
国 有	State-owned	50.59	32.36	56.86	49.30	55.70	39.18
集 体	Collective-owned	18.75	16.84	19.91	15.61	19.39	16.79
股份合作	Share-holding Coorperative	12.60	12.72	15.36	13.34	12.56	12.69
联 营	Joint Owned	8.08	8.66	9.74	8.61	8.21	9.11
有限责任公司	Companies with Limited Liabilities Liabilities	221.83	349.41	184.33	225.64	258.52	379.65
股份有限公司	Share-holding Companies with Limited Liabilities	101.83	186.16	191.86	271.79	135.46	253.41
私 营	Private	520.62	584.44	432.27	454.99	516.27	593.91
其 他	Others	2.20	4.31	2.26	3.20	2.18	4.35
港澳台商投资	Hong Kong, Macao and Taiwan Funded	517.01	619.81	492.99	533.00	545.83	637.31
外商投资	Foreign Funded	1 316.24	1 439.71	1 176.92	1 269.55	1 346.86	1 517.45
按行业分	**Grouped by Sectors**						
服装服饰业	Garment and Trappings	567.01	579.16	479.88	522.07	574.69	600.82
食品加工制造业	Food Processing	721.77	804.33	630.77	687.33	779.17	879.03
包装、印刷业	Packaging and Printing	246.19	282.01	295.30	319.14	251.26	293.58
室内装饰用品制造业	Indoor Decoration Materials and Equipments Manufacturing	393.19	476.38	336.86	373.88	398.49	501.52
化妆品及清洁洗涤用品制造业	Cosmetics and Cleaning Manufacturing	254.35	292.43	251.86	293.72	262.63	315.57
工艺美术品、旅游用品制造业	Art Crafts and Tourism Equipments Manufacturing	317.08	390.11	273.58	281.09	363.99	439.50
小型电子信息产品制造业	Small Electronic Information Products Manufacturing	270.17	430.00	314.27	367.81	270.75	433.82

表 12.10 续表 2 continued

单位：亿元（100 million yuan）

类 别	Types	利润总额 Total Pre-tax Profits 2009	2010	税金总额 Total Tax and Duties 2009	2010
总 计	**Total**	**181.14**	**239.50**	**98.20**	**113.59**
按企业规模分	**Grouped by Size of Enterprises**				
大 型	Large	18.21	49.68	12.14	15.46
中 型	Medium	96.25	118.62	46.44	60.43
小 型	Small	66.69	71.21	39.62	37.70
按登记注册类型分	**Grouped by Registration Categories**				
内 资	Domestic Investment	49.52	82.06	30.74	39.85
国 有	State-owned	2.75	3.14	2.04	1.53
集 体	Collective-owned	0.37	0.53	0.86	0.75
股份合作	Share-holding Coorperative	0.36	0.30	0.61	0.53
联 营	Joint Owned	-0.55	0.25	0.37	0.30
有限责任公司	Companies with Limited Liabilities	15.40	19.80	7.35	8.81
股份有限公司	Share-holding Companies with Limited Liabilities	9.46	29.06	4.09	11.02
私 营	Private	21.68	28.39	15.34	16.84
其 他	Others	0.04	0.59	0.08	0.06
港澳台商投资	Hong Kong, Macao and Taiwan Funded	44.17	54.09	19.66	18.60
外商投资	Foreign Funded	87.45	103.35	47.80	55.14
按行业分	**Grouped by Sectors**				
服装服饰业	Garment and Trappings	32.30	44.88	16.07	20.65
食品加工制造业	Food Processing	51.75	46.84	33.22	41.66
包装、印刷业	Packaging and Printing	21.61	22.66	10.81	10.73
室内装饰用品制造业	Indoor Decoration Materials and Equipments Manufacturing	22.40	34.53	10.67	11.47
化妆品及清洁洗涤用品制造业	Cosmetics and Cleaning Manufacturing	23.45	27.90	16.36	16.41
工艺美术品、旅游用品制造业	Art Crafts and Tourism Equipments Manufacturing	17.47	22.32	6.31	6.93
小型电子信息产品制造业	Small Electronic Information Products Manufacturing	12.16	40.38	4.75	5.74

表 12.11 主要年份工业产品产量
OUTPUT OF INDUSTRIAL PRODUCTS IN MAIN YEARS

年 份 Year	化学纤维 (万吨) Chemical Fibers (10 000 tons)	食用植物油 (万吨) Vegetatble Oil (10 000 tons)	啤 酒 (亿升) Beer (100 million litres)	罐 头 (万吨) Can (10 000 tons)	彩色电视机 (万部) Color TV Set (10 000 units)
1978	11.59	7. 32	0.50	4.75	0.24
1980	15.15	6. 77	0.66	5.46	0.55
1985	22.49	11. 13	0.83	6.84	71.75
1990	25.74	13. 42	1.66	4.97	81.48
1995	37.83	39.94	2.16	3.50	111.77
1996	38.61	17. 38	2.00	3.43	42.59
1997	39.26	12. 35	2.61	3.72	70.42
1998	40.93	19. 46	2.69	3.70	107.80
1999	37.38	8. 03	2.65	3.49	152.05
2000	47.15	11.55	3.04	3.26	147.97
2001	45.46	10.32	3.33	3.70	108.30
2002	51.67	9.65	3.62	3.79	137.02
2003	54.17	8.64	3.99	4.02	158.15
2004	48.45	3.51	5.92	4.51	135.08
2005	49.78	45.11	7.05	4.99	145.46
2006	50.60	72.86	7.17	5.78	251.67
2007	51.48	85.24	7.30	7.20	158.37
2008	43.00	96.88	7.27	4.96	185.78
2009	37.91	92.27	6.74	3.71	195.51
2010	49.00	85.31	6.54	4.06	254.03

表 12.11 续表 1 continued

年 份 Year	家用洗衣机 (万台) Household Washing Machines (10 000 units)	家用电冰箱 (万台) Household Refrigerators (10 000 units)	房间空气调节器 (万台) Household Airconditioners (10 000 units)	燃气热水器 (万台) Water Heaters (10 000 units)	服 装 (亿件) Garments (10 000 million cases)
1980	0.81	0.42	0.10		1.19
1985	113.85	20.49	0.74		2.33
1990	101.29	53.36	1.83		2.43
1995	144.80	128.72	62.46		6.3
1996	141.52	93.12	86.75	37.90	7.14
1997	124.81	30.72	88.20	36.25	5.63
1998	72.55	38.61	113.98	36.52	5.50
1999	57.03	43.03	180.70	35.07	5.26
2000	62.11	43.12	186.08	32.27	4.45
2001	70.79	43.44	223.57	27.86	4.35
2002	95.92	35.97	217.57	36.32	4.84
2003	134.27	34.46	239.72	37.24	4.91
2004	165.67	33.14	399.16	51.86	4.63
2005	183.26	42.68	358.57	65.64	6.72
2006	288.74	101.08	410.60	69.89	6.73
2007	289.68	100.66	395.21	80.46	6.60
2008	234.63	123.21	387.12	67.89	6.10
2009	207.79	189.15	317.78	59.35	3.91
2010	216.57	218.55	400.41	103.70	5.72

表 12.11 续表 2 continued

年 份 Year	机制纸及纸板(万吨) Machine-Made Paper and Paperboards (10 000 tons)	粗 钢 (万吨) Steel (10 000 tons)	成品钢材 (万吨) Rolled-Steel Products (10 000 tons)	生 铁 (万吨) Pig Iron (10 000 tons)	塑 料 (万吨) Plastic (10 000 tons)
1978	27.34	476.52	360.08	149.86	12.86
1980	29.57	521.61	412.63	171.12	14.57
1985	41.29	570.16	451.18	215.37	17.46
1990	46.49	914.62	609.59	526.90	25.35
1995	47.08	1 006.92	738.08	664.04	33.91
1996	38.85	1 441.92	1 175.74	964.03	65.46
1997	40.00	1 532.42	1 296.48	1 054.56	64.56
1998	45.46	1 603.75	1 417.58	1 208.57	77.42
1999	45.42	1 668.62	1 486.08	1 337.75	89.67
2000	43.54	1 778.70	1 544.46	1 473.00	95.47
2001	41.35	1 874.71	1 641.11	1 468.91	104.19
2002	42.61	1 719.42	1 626.98	1 276.12	129.57
2003	44.40	1 726.65	1 710.80	1 300.24	158.26
2004	35.96	1 823.65	1 818.41	1 356.47	163.44
2005	35.73	1 927.96	1 964.16	1 582.89	61.93
2006	85.87	1 902.82	2 129.78	1 639.13	66.21
2007	83.76	2 081.58	2 144.16	1 790.00	72.46
2008	80.46	1 992.09	2 074.95	1 735.87	83.82
2009	71.03	2 032.24	2 181.37	1 787.48	116.94
2010	86.94	2 214.27	2 475.95	1 901.39	204.44

表 12.11 续表 3 continued

年 份 Year	轮胎外胎 (万条) Tires (10 000tires)	水 泥 (万吨) Cement (10 000 tons)	乙 烯 (万吨) Ethylene (10 000 tons)	发电设备 (万千瓦) Power Generating Equipments (10 000 kw)	金属切削机床(台) Metal-cutting Machines (unit)
1978	149.59	139.47	12.69	109.80	17 384
1980	174.85	161.28	13.59	58.20	16 949
1985	219.00	219.31	14.02	133.00	19 408
1990	318.78	230.30	21.95	210.20	13 796
1995	375.31	433.22	8.20	496.50	15 833
1996	942.69	443.77	46.51	494.30	15 379
1997	829.57	338.47	45.44	541.60	18 700
1998	957.75	330.95	50.36	403.85	11 916
1999	804.43	251.14	59.26	314.55	17 822
2000	830.66	311.69	59.05	179.00	22 346
2001	545.97	334.75	63.10	336.20	21 839
2002	704.80	351.58	80.00	461.90	27 252
2003	846.92	568.24	94.83	1 013.70	33 497
2004	927.17	665.01	95.60	1 520.30	13 975
2005	932.27	719.97	160.44	2 138.05	13 158
2006	1 055.47	818.28	193.83	2 944.71	13 372
2007	932.54	786.24	187.24	2 845.59	14 440
2008	866.65	765.46	182.03	2 831.10	16 430
2009	849.07	754.19	180.30	2 440.70	5 641
2010	915.22	670.80	226.72	2 555.60	13 386

表 12.11 续表 4 continued

年 份 Year	发电量（亿千瓦时）Electric Power Generation (100 million kwh)	硫 酸（万吨）Sulfuric (10 000 tons)	程控交换机（万线）Program Controlled Exchanges (10 000 lines)	微型计算机设备（万部）Personal Computers (10 000 units)
1978	199.32	34.49		
1980	206.41	38.76		
1985	256.25	35.22		
1990	284.10	40.04	95.23	0.77
1995	403.42	31.03	476.60	4.07
1996	428.64	36.24	580.93	6.20
1997	458.48	36.79	631.62	40.39
1998	482.16	32.59	794.96	21.16
1999	498.01	38.38	915.46	40.09
2000	553.09	34.22	1 091.64	42.04
2001	572.86	36.15	1 752.90	47.13
2002	608.92	30.41	1 227.25	75.25
2003	684.99	31.41	1 883.47	734.68
2004	766.15	33.67	2 054.28	996.09
2005	728.74	33.32	796.59	2 176.17
2006	710.96	30.37	553.53	2 670.09
2007	737.80	30.46	447.54	4 478.78
2008	773.54	26.06	465.14	5 767.97
2009	778.20	27.02	387.00	7 320.15
2010	876.19	28.66	247.03	9 388.44

表 12.11 续表 5 continued

年 份 Year	移动通信基站设备（万信道）Mobile Communication Facilities (10 000 channels)	集 成 电路（万块）Semi-conduct IC (10 000 units)	汽 车（万辆）Motor Vehicles (10 000 vehicles)	其 中 of which #轿 车 Cars
1978			1.04	0.26
1980			1.47	0.53
1985			1.22	0.86
1990		1 167	2.81	2.46
1995		15 290	16.27	16.07
1996		11 624	20.17	20.02
1997		88 098	23.30	23.15
1998		92 908	23.64	23.50
1999		170 001	25.58	25.42
2000	1.60	239 330	25.29	25.15
2001	39.49	225 315	29.00	28.88
2002	24.82	339 494	39.19	39.05
2003	28.20	397 313	59.58	58.84
2004	57.67	548 727	55.96	54.99
2005	115.03	677 003	48.45	48.09
2006	174.16	640 483	65.28	64.47
2007	307.46	891 138	82.12	81.15
2008	343.58	830 487	80.65	80.00
2009	198.76	722 883	125.03	122.46
2010	299.44	1 134 629	169.89	159.77

注：2000 年开始移动通信基站设备不包括手机。
Note: The figure of mobile communication facilities has excluded mobile phones since 2000.

表 12.12 主要工业产品生产、销售总量(2010)
OUTPUT AND SALES OF MAIN INDUSTRIAL PRODUCTS

产品名称	Product	单 位 Unit	生产量 Output	销售量 Sales
发电量	Electric Power Generation	亿千瓦时 (100 million kwh)	876.19	699.13
啤 酒	Beer	亿升 (100 million liters)	6.54	6.40
无酒精饮料 (软饮料)	Non-alcoholic Beverage	万吨 (10 000 tons)	260.98	259.55
卷 烟	Cigarettes	亿支(100 million pieces)	882.59	878.53
化学纤维	Chemical Fibers	万吨 (10 000 tons)	49.00	49.70
纱	Yarn	万吨 (10 000 tons)	4.66	3.96
布	Cloth	亿米 (100 million m)	1.70	1.69
蚕丝及交织机织物	Silk Products	万米 (10 000 m)	70.44	72.40
服 装	Garments	亿件 (100 million cases)	5.72	5.81
皮革鞋靴	Leather Shoes	万双 (10 000 pairs)	2 269.57	2 207.86
机制纸及纸版	Paperboard	万吨 (10 000 tons)	86.94	82.30
汽 油	Gasoline	万吨 (10 000 tons)	259.67	233.93
柴 油	Diesel Oil	万吨 (10 000 tons)	773.61	741.13
焦 炭	Coke	万吨 (10000 tons)	630.75	83.76
硫 酸	Sulphuric Acid	万吨 (10 000 tons)	28.66	23.77
烧 碱	Caustic Soda	万吨 (10 000 tons)	72.63	75.34
化学农药原药	Chemical Pesticides	万吨 (10 000 tons)	5.28	5.16
乙 烯	Ethylene	万吨 (10 000 tons)	226.72	53.82
合成橡胶	Synthetic Rubber	万吨 (10 000 tons)	26.98	26.19
合成洗涤剂	Synthetic Detergents	万吨 (10 000 tons)	23.21	22.72
轮胎外胎	Tires	万条 (10 000 tires)	915.22	892.16
水 泥	Cement	万吨 (10 000 tons)	670.80	674.93
铜 材	Copper Materials	万吨 (10 000 tons)	39.31	38.30
生 铁	Pig Iron	万吨 (10 000 tons)	1 901.39	1.49
粗 钢	Steel	万吨 (10 000 tons)	2 214.27	39.68
金属切削机床	Metal-cutting Machines	台(unit)	13 386.00	13 520.00
#数控机床	Digital Machine Tools	台(unit)	6 136.00	6 031.00
金属集装箱	Metal Container	万立方米 (10 000 cu. m)	1 155.48	1 063.85
卫生陶瓷	Sanitary Ceramics	万件 (10 000 pieces)	258.46	255.69
涂 料	Coating	万吨 (10 000 tons)	132.80	131.38
#建筑涂料	Construction Coating	万吨 (10 000 tons)	75.29	74.04
集成电路	Integrated Circuits	亿块 (100 million units)	113.46	111.58
乳制品	Dairy Product	万吨 (10 000 tons)	42.30	42.19

表 12.12 续表 continued

产品名称	Product	单位 Unit	生产量 Output	销售量 Sales
成品钢材	Rolled-steel Products	万吨（10 000tons）	2 475.95	2 461.81
内燃机	Internal Combustion Engines	万千瓦（10 000kw）	14 330.35	6 635.98
缝纫机	Sewing Machines	万架（10 000units）	77.52	79.38
汽　车	Motor Vehicles	万辆（10 000vehicles）	169.89	168.94
#轿　车	Cars	万辆（10 000vehicles）	159.77	158.75
摩托车	Motorcycles	万辆（10 000vehicles）	86.74	83.75
自行车	Bicycles	万辆（10 000vehicles）	512.83	513.22
民用钢质船舶	Civil Steel Ships	万载重吨（10 000 syn-tons）	1 111.82	1 111.82
发电设备	Power Generating Equipments	万千瓦（10 000kw）	2 555.60	2 193.42
电力电缆	Electric Cable	万公里（10 000km）	119.11	118.90
家用洗衣机	Household Washing Machines	万台（10 000units）	216.57	215.97
家用电冰箱	Household Refrigerators	万台（10 000units）	218.55	213.54
房间空气调节器	Household Air-conditioners	万台（10 000units）	400.41	395.74
家用吸排油烟机	Range Hoods	万台（10 000units）	4.82	4.87
微波炉	Microware Oven	万台（10 000units）	554.84	545.46
电饭锅	Electric Rice Cookers	万个（10 000units）	632.85	615.59
家用吸尘器	Vacuum Cleaners	万台（10 000units）	5.77	5.66
燃气热水器	Water Heaters	万台（10 000units）	103.70	102.56
程控交换机	Program-controlled Exchanges	万线（10 000lines）	247.03	247.84
集成电路圆片	Wafer	万片（10 000units）	288.79	282.36
微型计算机设备	Personal Computers	万部（10 000units）	9 388.44	9 284.45
彩色电视机	Color Television Sets	万部（10 000units）	254.03	253.23
移动通信基站设备	Mobile Communication Base Station Facilities	万信道（10 000channels）	299.44	300.19
糖　果	Candy	万吨（10 000tons）	13.37	14.32
实木地板	Solid Wood Flooring	万平方米（10 000sq. m）	486.69	483.74
复合地板	Flooring	万平方米（10 000sq. m）	3 074.70	3 037.86

表 12.13 国有工业企业主要指标(2010)
MAJOR INDICATORS OF STATE-OWNED INDUSTRIAL ENTERPRISES

类 别	Types	单位数 (个) Quantity of Enterprises (unit)	从业人员 (万人) Employees (10 000 persons)
总 计	**Total**	**265**	**9.67**
按隶属关系分	**Grouped by Subordination**		
#中央工业	Central Government	57	4.20
市（局）属工业	Municipality	122	4.30
区属工业	District	51	0.62
县属工业	County	1	0.02
按轻、重工业分	**Grouped by Light and Heavy Industry**		
轻工业	Light Industry	98	2.97
重工业	Heavy Industry	167	6.69
按企业规模分	**Grouped by Size of Enterprises**		
大型企业	Large	6	2.85
中型企业	Medium	57	4.56
小型企业	Small	202	2.26
按工业行业分	**Grouped by Sectors**		
#制造业	Manufacture Industry	243	7.70
农副食品加工业	Farm and Sideline Products Processing	4	0.14
食品制造业	Food Manufacturing	8	0.12
饮料制造业	Beverage Manufacturing	1	…
烟草制品业	Tabacco Manufacture	1	0.36
纺织业	Textile	3	0.20
纺织服装、鞋、帽制造业	Garments, Shoes and Accessories Manufacturing	6	0.04
皮革、毛皮、羽毛(绒)及其制品业	Leather, Fur, and Wool Products Manufacturing	2	0.04
木材加工及木、竹、藤、棕、草制品业	Timber Processing and Timber, Bamboo, Rattan, Coir and Straw Products Manufacturing	1	…

工业总产值（亿元）Gross Output Value of Industry (100 million yuan)	年末资产总计（亿元）Total Assets (year-end) (100 million yuan)	固定资产净值（亿元）Net Value of Fixed Assets (100 million yuan)	流动资产合计（亿元）Current Assets (100 million yuan)
1 752.99	**2 842.97**	**1 419.63**	**1 040.69**
1 377.97	2 221.26	1 200.65	742.80
308.97	476.03	142.51	247.82
26.38	76.29	33.52	28.10
0.20	0.49	0.25	0.24
647.95	1 026.14	148.66	686.94
1 105.05	1 816.83	1 270.97	353.75
1 349.08	2 191.75	1 215.88	702.11
263.86	435.00	127.75	232.66
140.05	216.22	76.00	105.93
1 038.67	1 443.28	207.72	977.61
5.76	4.17	0.90	2.69
8.93	7.96	2.56	4.87
0.24	0.35	0.09	0.07
536.23	751.82	32.17	589.13
5.99	11.96	3.45	7.13
1.31	1.16	0.15	0.99
0.38	0.83	0.04	0.70
0.07	0.04	0.01	0.04

表 12.13 续表 1　continued

类　别	Types	单位数（个） Quantity of Enterprises (unit)	从业人员（万人） Employees (10 000 persons)
家具制造业	Furniture Manufacturing	1	…
造纸及纸制品业	Paper-making and Paper Products Manufacturing	1	…
印刷业和记录媒介的复制	Printing and Record Duplicating	16	0.25
文教体育用品制造业	Stationary, Education and Sports Goods Manufacturing	4	0.04
化学原料及化学制品制造业	Raw Chemical Materials and Chemical Products Manufacturing	23	0.65
医药制造业	Medicine Manufacturing	12	0.63
橡胶制品业	Rubber Products Manufacturing	4	0.11
塑料制品业	Plastic Products Manufacturing	10	0.10
非金属矿物制品业	Nonmetal Mineral Products	13	0.18
黑色金属冶炼及压延加工业	Smelting and Pressing of Ferrous Metals	3	0.04
有色金属冶炼及压延加工业	Smelting and Pressing of Nonferrous Metals	3	0.06
金属制品业	Metal Products Manufacturing	9	0.12
通用设备制造业	General Equipment Manufacturing	36	0.91
专用设备制造业	Special Purpose Equipment Manufacturing	16	0.49
交通运输设备制造业	Transportation Equipment Manufacturing	35	2.41
电气机械及器材制造业	Electric Machinery Equipments and Manufacturing	10	0.17
通信设备、计算机及其他电子设备制造业	Communcations Equipment, Computer and Other Electronic Equipment Manufacturing	7	0.39
仪器仪表及文化、办公用机械制造业	Instruments, Meters, Culture and Office Equipments Manufacturing	8	0.18
工艺品及其他制造业	Artworks and Other Manufacturing	4	0.04
废弃资源和废旧材料回收加工业	Recycling and Disposal of Waste	2	0.01
电力、燃气及水的生产和供应业	Production and Supply of Power, Gas and Water	22	1.97
电力、热力的生产和供应业	Production and Supply of Electricity and Thermal Power	9	1.48
燃气生产和供应业	Production and Supply of Gas	1	0.02
水的生产和供应业	Production and Supply of Water	12	0.47

工业总产值（亿元）Gross Output Value of Industry (100 million yuan)	年末资产总计（亿元）Total Assets (year-end) (100 million yuan)	固定资产净值（亿元）Net Value of Fixed Assets (100 million yuan)	流动资产合计（亿元）Current Assets (100 million yuan)
0.22	0.05	0.01	0.04
0.07	0.06	0.01	0.03
11.24	22.94	5.62	10.73
0.83	2.23	0.29	1.81
63.47	96.18	30.47	34.88
31.87	52.32	12.21	26.51
3.38	3.08	0.62	1.56
3.80	4.83	1.86	2.64
17.77	13.23	3.67	9.11
7.69	7.29	1.26	4.42
6.52	4.13	1.90	2.12
17.93	23.75	4.71	9.16
45.68	63.83	12.44	42.88
21.74	26.03	4.08	19.19
185.55	240.15	60.89	139.65
31.20	40.01	0.80	37.66
22.14	43.99	25.28	14.04
7.50	13.15	1.24	10.62
0.69	7.33	0.97	4.58
0.45	0.38	0.02	0.36
714.33	1 399.69	1 211.91	63.08
695.75	1 267.29	1 121.22	46.37
0.57	0.90	0.27	0.63
18.00	131.50	90.42	16.08

表 12.13 续表 2 continued

类别	Types	年末负债合计 Total Liabilities (year-end)	年末所有者权益 Owners' Equity (year-end)
总　计	**Total**	**800.35**	**2 042.62**
按隶属关系分	**Grouped by Subordination**		
#中央工业	Central Government	437.25	1 784.01
市（局）属工业	Municipality	279.55	196.48
区属工业	District	35.19	41.11
县属工业	County	0.14	0.35
按轻、重工业分	**Grouped by Light and Heavy Industry**		
轻工业	Light Industry	180.02	846.12
重工业	Heavy Industry	620.33	1 196.50
按企业规模分	**Grouped by Size of Enterprises**		
大型企业	Large	451.91	1 739.84
中型企业	Medium	217.34	217.66
小型企业	Small	131.10	85.12
按工业行业分	**Grouped by Sectors**		
#制造业	Manufacture Industry	437.89	1 005.39
农副食品加工业	Farm and Sideline Products Processing	2.01	2.16
食品制造业	Food Manufacturing	5.08	2.87
饮料制造业	Beverage Manufacturing	0.20	0.15
烟草制品业	Tabacco Manufacture	50.81	701.01
纺织业	Textile	6.20	5.77
纺织服装、鞋、帽制造业	Garments, Shoes and Accessories Manufacturing	0.49	0.67
皮革、毛皮、羽毛(绒)及其制品业	Leather, Fur, and Wool Products Manufacturing	1.11	-0.27
木材加工及木、竹、藤、棕、草制品业	Timber Processing and Timber, Bamboo, Rattan, Coir and Straw Products Manufacturing	0.04	0.01

单位:亿元(100 million yuan)

主营业务收入 Prime Operating Revenue	利润总额 Total Pre-tax Profits	税金总额 Total Tax and Duties	成本费用总额 Total Cost and Expenses
1 822.53	**171.75**	**441.23**	**1 367.74**
1 387.74	151.86	425.58	938.16
368.89	17.30	13.39	364.04
28.89	1.61	1.19	28.83
0.24	…	0.02	0.25
664.90	155.17	403.40	211.36
1 157.63	16.59	37.83	1 156.37
1 351.01	150.52	423.48	905.01
317.87	20.63	12.41	306.54
153.64	0.60	5.34	156.18
1 106.94	171.23	414.76	650.46
6.00	0.31	0.06	5.70
8.80	0.89	0.28	8.09
0.24	0.03	…	0.20
535.69	141.18	396.79	90.56
10.46	0.20	0.42	10.42
1.38	0.18	0.11	1.21
0.41	-0.01	0.02	0.47
0.07		…	0.07

表 12.13 续表 3 continued

类别	Types	年末负债合计 Total Liabilities (year-end)	年末所有者权益 Owners' Equity (year-end)
家具制造业	Furniture Manufacturing	0.02	0.03
造纸及纸制品业	Paper-making and Paper Products Manufacturing	0.15	-0.09
印刷业和记录媒介的复制	Printing and Record Duplicating	7.06	15.88
文教体育用品制造业	Stationary, Education and Sports Goods Manufacturing	1.89	0.34
化学原料及化学制品制造业	Raw Chemical Materials and Chemical Products Manufacturing	40.17	56.01
医药制造业	Medicine Manufacturing	15.73	36.59
橡胶制品业	Rubber Products Manufacturing	1.68	1.40
塑料制品业	Plastic Products Manufacturing	2.45	2.37
非金属矿物制品业	Nonmetal Mineral Products	6.37	6.87
黑色金属冶炼及压延加工业	Smelting and Pressing of Ferrous Metals	3.84	3.45
有色金属冶炼及压延加工业	Smelting and Pressing of Nonferrous Metals	1.08	3.06
金属制品业	Metal Products Manufacturing	14.29	9.46
通用设备制造业	General Equipment Manufacturing	44.56	19.26
专用设备制造业	Special Purpose Equipment Manufacturing	18.14	7.89
交通运输设备制造业	Transportation Equipment Manufacturing	140.63	99.52
电气机械及器材制造业	Electric Machinery Equipments and Manufacturing	30.37	9.64
通信设备、计算机及其他电子设备制造业	Communcations Equipment, Computer and Other Electronic Equipment Manufacturing	32.92	11.07
仪器仪表及文化、办公用机械制造业	Instruments, Meters, Culture and Office Equipments Manufacturing	7.71	5.44
工艺品及其他制造业	Artworks and Other Manufacturing	2.73	4.60
废弃资源和废旧材料回收加工业	Recycling and Disposal of Waste	0.16	0.21
电力、燃气及水的生产和供应业	Production and Supply of Power, Gas and Water	362.46	1 037.23
电力、热力的生产和供应业	Production and Supply of Electricity and Thermal Power	294.32	972.97
燃气生产和供应业	Production and Supply of Gas	0.06	0.84
水的生产和供应业	Production and Supply of Water	68.07	63.42

单位:亿元(100 million yuan)

主营业务收入 Prime Operating Revenue	利 润 总 额 Total Pre-tax Profits	税 金 总 额 Total Tax and Duties	成本费用 总 额 Total Cost and Expenses
0.22	0.01	0.01	0.22
0.08	-0.13	0.01	0.21
15.29	1.26	0.74	14.25
0.88	0.08	0.07	0.82
64.26	4.16	1.38	69.53
34.00	8.85	2.34	27.12
3.33	0.05	0.14	3.31
3.89	0.05	0.19	4.17
18.37	1.04	0.71	17.50
14.38	-0.04	0.31	14.34
6.56	0.08	0.03	6.45
22.24	-3.25	0.70	22.72
49.31	0.88	1.60	50.95
20.70	0.95	1.02	19.90
219.04	10.17	5.49	212.36
34.42	0.42	1.39	34.27
23.59	2.03	0.22	23.71
10.19	1.31	0.60	9.07
2.67	0.35	0.08	2.54
0.46	0.16	0.04	0.32
715.59	0.53	26.47	717.28
691.99	1.38	25.26	691.86
0.59	…	0.03	0.60
23.01	-0.86	1.18	24.83

表 12.14 股份制、港澳台商和外商投资企业主要指标(2010)
MAJOR INDICATORS OF SHARE-HOLDING ENTERPRISES AND ENTERPRISES WITH INVESTMENT FROM OTHER COUNTRIES OR FROM HONG KONG, MACAO AND TAIWAN

指标	Indicators	股份有限公司 Stock-holding Companies with Limited Liabilities	港澳台商投资企业 Enterprises with Investment from Hong kong, Macao and Taiwan
单位数(个)	Number of Enterprises (unit)	151	1 823
从业人员(万人)	Employees (10 000 persons)	10.10	45.41
工业总产值(亿元)	Gross Output Value of Industry (100 million yuan)	2 765.60	5 347.54
出口交货值(亿元)	Delivery Value of Exports(100 million yuan)	236.93	2 925.40
实收资本(股本)(亿元)	Paid-up Capital(Stock Capital) (100 million yuan)	564.22	895.58
#国家资本(国家股)	State Capital (State Stock)	177.07	6.03
年末资产总计(亿元)	Total Assets (year-end) (100 million yuan)	3 719.33	3 328.29
流动资产合计(亿元)	Total Current Assets (100 million yuan)	1 427.83	2 075.43
固定资产合计(亿元)	Total Fixed Assets (100 million yuan)	1 260.43	829.42
固定资产原价(亿元)	Original Value of Fixed Assets (100 million yuan)	2 766.23	1 643.23
固定资产净值(亿元)	Net Value of Fixed Assets (100 million yuan)	1 214.34	793.98
年末负债合计(亿元)	Total Liabilities (year-end) (100 million yuan)	1 519.83	1 937.10
流动负债合计(亿元)	Total Current Liabilities (100 million yuan)	1 078.02	1 766.29
长期负债合计(亿元)	Long-Term Liabilities (100 million yuan)	438.62	160.21
年末所有者权益(亿元)	Owners' Equity (year-end) (100 million yuan)	2 199.50	1 391.19
主营业务收入(亿元)	Prime Operating Revenue(100 million yuan)	3 228.40	5 363.35
利润总额(亿元)	Total Pre-tax Profits (100 million yuan)	382.31	240.84
税金总额(亿元)	Total Tax and Duties (100 million yuan)	159.03	136.91

其中 of which				其中 of which		
与港澳台商合资合作经营 Joint and Cooperation Enterprises with Investment from Hong Kong, Macao and Taiwan	港澳台商独资 Ventures Solely Invested by Business from Hong kong, Macao and Taiwan	港澳台商投资股份有限公司 Stock-holding Companies with Limited Liabilities with Investment from Hong Kong, Macao and Taiwan	外商投资企业 Foreign-invested Enterprises	中外合资合作企业 Sino-foreign Joint and Cooperation Enterprises	外商独资 Solely Foreign-invested Ventures	外商投资股份有限公司 Stock-holding Companies with Limited Liabilities with Foreign Investment
656	1 129	38	4 305	1 377	2 869	59
14.60	27.70	3.11	116.59	39.72	74.33	2.54
820.50	3 670.83	856.21	13 060.13	6 317.87	6 390.47	351.79
249.73	2 582.79	92.88	4 197.19	906.01	3 116.66	174.53
236.03	507.08	152.47	3 194.29	1 358.8	1 735.91	99.58
5.73		0.30	59.62	48.65	0.61	10.36
798.02	1 908.79	621.48	10 433.44	4 970.33	4 806.59	656.52
493.15	1 390.84	191.44	6 779.65	3 359.57	3 058.63	361.44
232.21	393.65	203.56	2 749.67	1 133.11	1 443.99	172.57
403.29	766.11	473.84	5 194.64	2 268.86	2 669.04	256.74
219.23	383.72	191.03	2 727.88	1 117.20	1 437.62	173.06
442.14	1230.02	264.95	5 843.17	2 780.88	2 670.16	392.13
402.52	1 146.32	217.44	5 208.31	2 523.25	2 382.37	302.70
37.33	75.73	47.15	584.56	226.25	269.74	88.56
355.89	678.77	356.53	4 590.27	2 189.45	2 136.42	264.39
833.09	3 663.98	866.28	14 255.49	7 221.67	6 691.57	342.25
57.91	129.61	53.32	1 130.09	721.58	409.54	-1.03
20.46	28.98	87.47	451.13	322.35	123.77	5.01

表 12.15 大中型工业企业主要指标(2010)
MAJOR INDICATORS OF LARGE AND MEDIUM SIZED INDUSTRIAL ENTERPRISES

类 别	Types	单位数（个）Quantity of Enterprises (unit)	从业人员（万人）Employees (10 000 persons)	工业总产值（亿元）Gross Output Value of Industry (100 million yuan)	工业销售产值（亿元）Sales Value of Industry Products(100 million yuan)
总 计	**Total**	**1 750**	**160.51**	**22 143.75**	**21 923.73**
按轻、重工业分	**Grouped by Light and Heavy Industry**				
大型企业	Large Enterprises	112	52.53	12 864.20	12 776.78
轻工业	Light Industry	29	8.19	1 139.74	1 139.31
重工业	Heavy Industry	83	44.33	11 724.46	11 637.48
中型企业	Medium Enterprises	1 638	107.99	9 279.55	9 146.95
轻工业	Light Industry	666	42.10	2 856.19	2 776.67
重工业	Heavy Industry	972	65.89	6 423.36	6 370.27
按隶属关系分	**Grouped by Subordination**				
大型企业	Large Enterprises	112	52.53	12 864.20	12 776.78
中央工业	Central Government	16	9.30	4 609.72	4 599.75
地方工业	Local Government	96	43.23	8 254.49	8 177.03
中型企业	Medium Enterprises	1 638	107.99	9 279.55	9 146.95
中央工业	Central Government	51	4.48	1 512.71	1 512.15
地方工业	Local Government	1 587	103.50	7 766.84	7 634.80
按从业人员分	**Grouped by Number of Employees**				
1 万人及以上	10 000 persons and above	10	17.07	6 481.40	6 444.46
5000～9999 人	5 000～9 999 persons	21	13.66	2 474.12	2 446.93
3000～4999 人	3 000～4 999 persons	33	12.30	2 104.01	2 102.16
1000～2999 人	1 000～2 999 persons	303	48.64	4 947.86	4 903.14
1000 人以下	Below 1 000 persons	1 383	68.85	6 136.37	6 027.04
按工业总产值分	**Grouped by Gross Output Value of Industry**				
10 亿元及以上	1 000 million yuan and above	296	67.05	17 949.00	17 776.56
5～9.99 亿元	500～999 million yuan	265	26.27	1 846.57	1 831.02
1～4.99 亿元	100～499 million yuan	881	54.23	2 127.72	2 092.00
5000～9999 万元	50～99.99 million yuan	259	11.02	200.56	204.22
1000～4999 万元	10～49.99 million yuan	49	1.94	19.90	19.93
1000 万元以下	Below 10 million yuan				
按固定资产原价分	**Grouped by Original Value of Fixed Assets**				
10 亿元及以上	1000 million yuan and above	123	43.68	13 607.42	13 499.80
1～9.99 亿元	100～999 million yuan	722	68.58	6 377.67	6 311.82
5000～9999 万元	50～99.99 million yuan	397	22.51	1 090.15	1 057.97
1000～4999 万元	10～49.99 million yuan	422	20.36	893.43	880.51
1000 万元以下	Below 10 million yuan	86	5.37	175.09	173.63

实收资本（股本）（亿元）Paid-in Capital (fixed capital stock) (100 million yuan)	年末资产总计（亿元）Total Assets (year-end) (100 million yuan)	年末负债合计（亿元）Total Liabilities (year-end) (100 million yuan)	主营业务收入（亿元）Prime Operation Revenue (100 million yuan)	利润总额（亿元）Total Pre-tax Profits (100 million yuan)	税金总额（亿元）Total Tax and Duties (100 million yuan)	成本费用总额（亿元）Total Costs and Expenses (100 million yuan)
4 237.94	**19 783.42**	**10 362.24**	**23 818.11**	**1 750.51**	**1 161.79**	**21 882.53**
1 605.50	11 233.08	5 735.42	14 198.13	1 049.72	910.12	12 824.59
138.13	1 345.77	368.82	1 232.57	213.06	422.65	714.74
1 467.37	9 887.31	5 366.60	12 965.56	836.66	487.46	12 109.85
2 632.44	8 550.34	4 626.81	9 619.98	700.79	251.68	9 057.95
749.83	2 558.67	1 298.84	2 913.04	216.88	103.55	2 718.62
1 882.61	5 991.67	3 327.98	6 706.94	483.91	148.13	6 339.33
1 605.50	11 233.08	5 735.42	14 198.13	1 049.72	910.12	12 824.59
622.93	5 752.58	2 415.05	4 834.75	373.24	629.23	4 059.67
982.57	5 480.49	3 320.37	9 363.37	676.48	280.89	8 764.92
2 632.44	8 550.34	4 626.81	9 619.98	700.79	251.68	9 057.95
395.13	1 441.73	778.88	1 541.06	88.89	46.59	1 507.37
2 237.31	7 108.62	3 847.93	8 078.92	611.90	205.08	7 550.57
484.16	4 686.18	2 220.45	6 913.77	327.88	236.68	6 496.63
474.96	2 486.57	1 372.33	3 236.35	333.38	123.31	3 012.18
291.68	1861.60	668.10	2 172.93	271.71	508.43	1 552.25
1 436.01	5311.26	3 170.80	5 171.83	370.40	140.13	4 851.49
1 551.13	5437.81	2 930.55	6 323.23	447.14	153.25	5 969.99
2 761.02	15 127.65	7 966.39	19 417.75	1 403.68	1 040.44	17 761.47
578.15	1 924.53	1 035.44	1 941.30	167.26	53.21	1 802.53
761.46	2 373.02	1 184.78	2 211.76	166.84	61.66	2 077.78
107.58	297.07	143.58	220.38	13.35	5.91	210.80
29.73	61.15	32.04	26.92	-0.62	0.57	29.96
2 488.74	12 640.53	6 380.00	14 874.75	1 060.06	939.83	13 540.89
1 394.48	5 474.38	3 035.60	6 716.93	533.23	166.16	6 253.33
203.76	931.02	492.45	1 138.28	94.74	26.46	1 059.52
138.84	646.42	396.26	914.59	53.17	21.92	864.35
12.11	91.06	57.92	173.56	9.31	7.41	164.44

表 12.15 续表 continued

类别	Types	单位数（个）Quantity of Enterprises (unit)	从业人员（万人）Employees (10 000 persons)	工业总产值（亿元）Gross Output Value of Industry (100 million yuan)
按工业行业分	**Grouped by Sectors**			
制造业	**Manufacture Industry**	**1 721**	**156.85**	**20 762.88**
农副食品加工业	Farm and Sideline Products Processing	19	1.61	113.78
食品制造业	Food Manufacturing	53	4.11	302.08
饮料制造业	Beverage Manufacturing	16	0.97	142.26
烟草制品业	Tabacco Manufacturing	2	0.40	538.70
纺织业	Textile	77	4.83	167.90
纺织服装、鞋、帽制造业	Garments, Shoes and Accessories Manufacturing	77	5.68	241.16
皮革、毛皮、羽毛(绒)及其制品业	Leather, Fur, and Wool Products Manufacturing	28	2.41	88.54
木材加工及木、竹、藤、棕、草制品业	Timber Processing and Timber, Bamboo, Rattan, Coir and Straw Products Manufacturing	13	0.64	28.17
家具制造业	Furniture Manufacturing	27	2.40	178.09
造纸及纸制品业	Paper-making and Paper Products Manufacturing	28	1.45	115.86
印刷业和记录媒介的复制	Printing and Record Duplicating	28	1.53	82.95
文教体育用品制造业	Stationary, Education and Sports Goods Manufacturing	43	2.85	97.76
石油加工、炼焦及核燃料加工业	Oil Processing, Coking and Nuclear Fuel Processing	4	2.06	1 270.19
化学原料及化学制品制造业	Raw Chemical Materials and Chemical Products Manufacturing	64	4.63	1 172.30
医药制造业	Medicine Manufacturing	44	3.43	263.20
化学纤维制造业	Chemical Fiber Manufacturing	2	0.07	2.39
橡胶制品业	Rubber Products Manufacturing	27	1.87	98.28
塑料制品业	Plastic Products Manufacturing	91	5.49	231.49
非金属矿物制品业	Nonmetal Mineral Products	46	3.09	198.76
黑色金属冶炼及压延加工业	Smelting and Pressing of Ferrous Metals	9	3.05	1 574.26
有色金属冶炼及压延加工业	Smelting and Pressing of Nonferrous Metals	26	1.60	234.99
金属制品业	Metal Products Manufacturing	90	5.96	351.18
通用设备制造业	General Equipment Manufacturing	162	13.64	1 479.43
专用设备制造业	Special Purpose Equipment Manufacturing	113	7.42	588.67
交通运输设备制造业	Transportation Equipment Manufacturing	190	20.18	3 909.42
电气机械及器材制造业	Electric Machinery Equipments and Manufacturing	192	15.81	1 249.87
通信设备、计算机及其他电子设备制造业	Communications Equipment, Computer and Other Electronic Equipment Manufacturing	198	35.37	5 701.52
仪器仪表及文化、办公用机械制造业	Instruments, Meters, Culture and Office Equipments Manufacturing	35	3.22	204.03
工艺品及其他制造业	Artworks and Other Manufacturing	17	1.09	135.65
电力、燃气及水的生产和供应业	**Production and Supply of Power, Gas and Water**	**29**	**3.66**	**1 380.88**
电力、热力的生产和供应业	Production and Supply of Electricity and Thermal Power	11	1.88	1 285.28
燃气生产和供应业	Production and Supply of Gas	9	0.94	63.33
水的生产和供应业	Production and Supply of Water	9	0.84	32.27

工业销售产值（亿元） Sales Value of Industry Products(100 million yuan)	实收资本（股本）（亿元） Paid-in Capital (fixed capital stock)(100 million yuan)	年末资产总计（亿元） Total Assets (year-end) (100 million yuan)	年末负债合计（亿元） Total Liabilities (year-end) (100 million yuan)	主营业务收入（亿元） Prime Operation Revenue (100 million yuan)	利润总额（亿元） Total Pre-tax Profits (100 million yuan)	税金总额（亿元） Total Tax and Duties (100 million yuan)	成本费用总额（亿元） Total Costs and Expenses (100 million yuan)
20 544.25	**3 888.91**	**17 677.17**	**9 572.24**	**22 387.98**	**1 742.55**	**1 120.18**	**20 407.88**
111.83	22.43	69.99	37.77	126.83	3.71	1.81	123.86
301.36	75.50	258.35	140.73	346.58	25.04	20.39	319.14
132.20	41.00	129.08	71.79	141.52	5.94	12.97	134.01
539.69	20.30	756.76	51.86	538.16	141.76	397.16	92.47
165.61	64.75	213.49	88.08	181.59	14.73	4.44	170.88
232.12	49.13	246.11	130.55	241.77	33.17	12.08	208.92
87.36	9.32	88.15	28.02	87.87	13.02	3.97	75.52
28.57	8.92	30.57	14.43	28.96	2.11	0.86	26.79
174.97	18.22	105.36	64.52	183.25	16.57	3.92	169.16
111.52	29.54	95.90	49.91	119.96	10.08	4.48	110.58
81.40	24.28	100.73	38.91	86.09	9.83	3.96	77.98
97.15	24.81	79.41	42.91	98.35	6.42	1.25	92.74
1 268.47	163.00	496.03	211.97	1 285.06	63.81	170.79	1 108.11
1 180.68	408.87	1 037.05	544.96	1 239.80	84.45	39.64	1 163.65
242.43	90.24	299.50	130.55	261.19	38.64	18.79	231.15
2.38	4.34	5.30	0.36	2.42	0.47	0.12	2.43
99.35	34.88	129.01	77.20	147.08	6.78	2.56	142.23
226.28	70.75	257.97	126.79	231.61	20.70	6.20	211.89
204.53	69.77	250.48	137.68	210.27	16.63	6.46	195.94
1 562.67	242.60	1 931.10	888.77	1867.81	151.05	37.83	1 730.06
226.69	56.70	167.25	97.83	231.02	7.42	1.47	224.47
342.54	62.47	288.04	156.36	349.66	29.38	6.87	326.60
1 451.37	314.00	1 821.66	1 147.13	1 480.46	104.55	50.01	1 370.27
585.22	156.78	714.87	448.65	605.36	64.54	15.01	559.52
3 877.37	730.21	4 189.87	2 365.01	4 846.86	628.11	259.47	4 297.92
1 232.37	221.86	971.84	543.52	1 289.07	96.65	20.22	1 203.44
5 635.18	820.93	2 704.87	1 818.32	5 793.80	116.78	10.24	5 697.70
204.93	38.88	168.70	85.13	217.53	21.39	4.22	200.29
138.02	14.44	69.71	32.51	148.04	8.81	2.99	140.16
1 379.48	**349.03**	**2 106.25**	**789.99**	**1 430.13**	**7.96**	**41.61**	**1 474.66**
1 285.28	191.74	1 754.31	580.76	1 283.69	12.23	37.55	1 322.15
63.40	65.72	107.20	59.64	105.99	-1.85	1.84	107.87
30.81	91.57	244.74	149.60	40.45	-2.42	2.22	44.63

表 12.16 国家级、市级工业园区主要经济指标(2010)
MAJOR ECONOMIC INDICATORS OF MUNICIPAL AND NATIONAL INDUSTRIAL ZONE

指标	Indicators	国家级开发区 National Level Develop Zone	其中 of which	
			外高桥保税区 Waigaoqiao Free Trade Zone	金桥出口加工区 Jinqiao Export Processing Zone
单位数(个)	Qiantity of Enterprises (unit)	941	190	245
从业人员(万人)	Employees (10 000 persons)	45.30	4.83	10.98
工业总产值(亿元)	Gross Output Value of Industry(100 million yuan)	7 549.93	701.00	2 099.45
出口交货值(亿元)	Delivery Value of Industry Exports(100 million yuan)	4 157.38	159.53	393.85
实收资本(股本)(亿元)	Paid-in Capital(Fixed capital stock)(100 million yuan)	1 325.96	90.18	470.78
年末资产总计(亿元)	Total Assets (year-end)(100 million yuan)	5 319.87	420.67	1 777.28
流动资产合计(亿元)	Total Current Assets(100 million yuan)	3 565.51	320.59	1 317.42
固定资产合计(亿元)	Total Fixed Assets(100 million yuan)	907.79	89.25	259.07
固定资产原价(亿元)	Original Value of Fixed Assets(100 million yuan)	2 093.97	163.38	682.23
年末负债合计(亿元)	Total Liabilities (year-end)(100 million yuan)	3 014.21	255.60	1 078.79
年末流动负债合计(亿元)	Total Current Liabilities (year-end)(100 million yuan)	2746.90	236.33	1 014.47
长期负债合计(亿元)	Total Long-term Liabilities(100 million yuan)	257.42	18.54	58.10
年末所有者权益(亿元)	Owners' Equity (year-end)(100 million yuan)	2 305.66	165.08	698.49
主营业务收入(亿元)	Prime Operating Revenue(100 million yuan)	8 425.53	738.06	2 858.46
利润总额(亿元)	Total Pre-tax Profits(100 million yuan)	631.53	43.23	289.17
税金总额(亿元)	Total Tax and Duties(100 million yuan)	206.62	11.17	133.69
亏损总额(亿元)	Total Loss(100 million yuan)	14.91	2.26	4.19

其 中 of which						
张江高科技园区 Zhangjiang Hi-Tec Park	漕河泾新兴技术开发区 Caohejing Hi-tec Park	漕河泾出口加工区 Caohejing Export Processing Zone	闵行经济技术开发区 Minhang Hi-tec Park	松江出口加工区 Songjiang Export Processing Zone	闵行出口加工区 Minhang Export Processing Zone	青浦出口加工区 Qingpu Export Processing Zone
114	196	14	75	56	5	11
5.42	3.93	3.42	3.69	11.09	0.08	0.31
591.44	367.14	793.54	403.17	2 404.57	11.46	32.89
242.09	131.64	741.30	76.21	2 374.24	3.15	31.36
409.10	116.11	19.43	98.65	72.58	3.58	11.89
1 303.95	358.71	150.31	359.28	784.22	13.62	31.89
569.41	226.08	109.79	274.64	649.68	6.32	18.08
208.21	68.64	37.72	70.68	124.33	6.72	12.71
579.80	167.30	69.39	146.54	198.91	7.66	15.82
424.09	169.32	124.42	192.74	660.83	9.14	20.39
293.58	156.05	123.12	185.66	648.98	6.18	11.85
129.99	12.93	1.30	6.09	10.76	2.96	8.53
879.86	189.39	25.89	166.54	123.39	4.48	11.50
638.31	397.72	791.74	433.65	2 379.63	12.94	31.26
173.06	39.64	6.07	47.00	25.13	1.64	2.01
27.20	9.06	…	21.12	…		…
0.81	1.06	0.09	3.32	0.81	0.09	1.17

表 12.16 续表 1 continued

指 标 Indicators		其 中 of which		
		陆家嘴金融贸易区 Lujiazui Financial Trade Zone	虹桥经济技术开发区 Hongqiao Economic and Technological Development Zone	佘山国家旅游度假区 Sheshan State Holiday Resort
单位数(个)	Qiantity of Enterprises (unit)	27	2	6
从业人员(万人)	Employees (10 000 persons)	1.45	0.06	0.04
工业总产值(亿元)	Gross Output Value of Industry(100 million yuan)	142.03	0.44	2.80
出口交货值(亿元)	Delivery Value of Industry Exports(100 million yuan)	3.64	0.22	0.15
实收资本(股本)(亿元)	Paid-in Capital(Fixed capital stock)(100 million yuan)	33.23	0.11	0.31
年末资产总计(亿元)	Total Assets (year-end)(100 million yuan)	116.17	1.42	2.35
流动资产合计(亿元)	Total Current Assets(100 million yuan)	71.21	0.51	1.80
固定资产合计(亿元)	Total Fixed Assets(100 million yuan)	29.49	0.43	0.53
固定资产原价(亿元)	Original Value of Fixed Assets(100 million yuan)	61.42	0.70	0.82
年末负债合计(亿元)	Total Liabilities (year-end)(100 million yuan)	76.11	1.08	1.72
年末流动负债合计(亿元)	Total Current Liabilities (year-end)(100 million yuan)	67.89	1.08	1.71
长期负债合计(亿元)	Total Long-term Liabilities(100 million yuan)	8.21		0.01
年末所有者权益(亿元)	Owners' Equity (year-end)(100 million yuan)	40.06	0.34	0.63
主营业务收入(亿元)	Prime Operating Revenue(100 million yuan)	140.54	0.51	2.70
利润总额(亿元)	Total Pre-tax Profits(100 million yuan)	4.33	0.02	0.21
税金总额(亿元)	Total Tax and Duties(100 million yuan)	4.31	0.02	0.04
亏损总额(亿元)	Total Loss(100 million yuan)	1.10		

市级开发区 Municipal Level Development Zone	其中 of which					
	上海宝山工业园区 Haibaoshan Industrial Park	上海月杨工业园区 Yueyang Industrial Park	上海富盛经济开发区 Fusheng Economic Development Zone	上海浦东空港工业园区 Pudong Konggang Industrial Park	上海嘉定工业园区 Jiading Industrial Park	上海嘉定汽车产业园区 Jiading Automobile Industrial Park
4 792	283	135	7	187	696	373
94.94	4.50	2.21	0.09	3.09	13.31	7.21
7 941.33	269.36	167.17	1.18	179.88	945.01	536.67
2 127.85	48.49	10.43	0.51	22.77	246.85	54.05
2 097.05	80.96	46.68	0.16	31.32	248.29	105.48
7 083.73	282.15	158.90	1.31	159.60	798.17	444.18
4 345.29	176.84	106.93	0.78	103.34	522.02	308.12
2 102.78	66.77	36.95	0.51	40.68	198.75	101.52
3 275.02	94.92	56.66	0.66	53.04	340.30	162.72
3 957.53	154.75	85.26	0.92	92.39	407.36	259.52
3 434.79	143.89	76.41	0.92	87.61	356.79	244.98
459.73	10.02	8.01		4.44	39.40	12.29
3 126.20	127.40	73.64	0.39	67.20	390.81	184.66
8 189.66	282.15	229.82	1.27	176.52	987.88	553.97
618.05	19.63	9.52	0.17	12.82	76.75	53.03
187.81	7.02	3.99	0.03	4.87	15.91	12.22
49.38	2.36	0.50		0.49	5.10	1.18

表 12.16 续表 2 continued

指 标	Indicators	其 中 of which 上海市莘庄工业园区 Xinzhuang Industrial Paek	上海青浦工业园区 Qingpu Industrial Park	上海西郊工业园区 Xijiao Economic Development Zone
单位数(个)	Qiantity of Enterprises (unit)	322	439	231
从业人员(万人)	Employees (10 000 persons)	7.05	9.24	4.75
工业总产值(亿元)	Gross Output Value of Industry(100 million yuan)	673.29	585.83	227.12
出口交货值(亿元)	Delivery Value of Industry Exports(100 million yuan)	210.90	129.85	70.66
实收资本(股本)(亿元)	Paid-in Capital(Fixed capital stock)(100 million yuan)	157.25	186.97	75.99
年末资产总计(亿元)	Total Assets (year-end)(100 million yuan)	696.41	546.08	216.51
流动资产合计(亿元)	Total Current Assets(100 million yuan)	481.44	349.39	135.31
固定资产合计(亿元)	Total Fixed Assets(100 million yuan)	164.90	157.10	64.37
固定资产原价(亿元)	Original Value of Fixed Assets(100 million yuan)	249.94	243.80	112.82
年末负债合计(亿元)	Total Liabilities (year-end)(100 million yuan)	393.03	273.59	111.28
年末流动负债合计(亿元)	Total Current Liabilities (year-end)(100 million yuan)	360.25	249.95	104.11
长期负债合计(亿元)	Total Long-term Liabilities(100 million yuan)	31.62	17.97	4.85
年末所有者权益(亿元)	Owners' Equity (year-end)(100 million yuan)	303.38	272.49	105.23
主营业务收入(亿元)	Prime Operating Revenue(100 million yuan)	669.84	567.96	232.32
利润总额(亿元)	Total Pre-tax Profits(100 million yuan)	75.31	45.88	10.55
税金总额(亿元)	Total Tax and Duties(100 million yuan)	17.47	19.37	6.12
亏损总额(亿元)	Total Loss(100 million yuan)	4.87	7.29	2.35

其 中 of which						
上海松江工业园区 Songjiang Industrial Park	上海松江经济开发区 Songjiang Economic Development Zone	上海奉贤经济开发区 Fengxian Economic Development Zone	上海金山工业园区 Jinshan Industrial Park	上海枫泾工业园区 Fengjing Industrial Park	上海朱泾工业园区 Zhujing Industrial Park	上海市北工业园区 Shibei Industrial Park
693	165	211	258	130	67	31
16.63	2.41	4.46	3.63	2.01	0.92	0.43
1 178.63	131.81	325.35	261.11	161.41	44.75	21.58
337.34	29.72	132.82	29.14	9.76	9.21	4.07
358.87	32.40	88.87	70.39	30.73	7.97	8.81
1 076.67	110.88	297.31	234.29	128.47	34.04	21.77
698.04	74.66	197.00	127.68	78.21	22.45	17.74
298.86	26.29	68.34	82.49	29.97	10.02	3.64
526.23	43.49	96.84	104.35	44.63	15.73	8.99
585.52	55.30	169.91	142.04	68.84	21.58	11.23
520.82	49.90	157.33	114.43	65.52	20.89	11.07
59.14	4.54	8.82	25.01	2.95	0.69	0.16
491.15	55.57	127.40	92.24	59.63	12.46	10.54
1 198.68	128.69	365.25	265.38	156.04	46.27	21.67
85.73	10.47	25.10	10.47	12.11	0.80	1.31
23.23	3.26	6.72	6.26	4.92	0.53	0.93
7.06	0.61	4.37	2.61	0.22	0.35	0.03

表 12.16 续表 3 continued

指 标	Indicators	其 中 of which 上海崇明工业园区 Congming Industrial Park	上海星火工业园区 Xinghuo Industrial Park	上海紫竹高新技术产业园区 Zizhu High and New Technical Industrial Park
单位数(个)	Qiantity of Enterprises (unit)	26	38	8
从业人员(万人)	Employees (10000 persons)	0.30	0.94	0.39
工业总产值(亿元)	Gross Output Value of Industry(100 million yuan)	10.15	180.47	111.22
出口交货值(亿元)	Delivery Value of Industry Exports(100 million yuan)	0.53	29.31	3.24
实收资本(股本)(亿元)	Paid-in Capital(Fixed capital stock)(100 million yuan)	2.61	61.72	20.74
年末资产总计(亿元)	Total Assets (year-end)(100 million yuan)	11.37	166.76	109.91
流动资产合计(亿元)	Total Current Assets(100 million yuan)	6.73	88.12	79.27
固定资产合计(亿元)	Total Fixed Assets(100 million yuan)	3.78	70.52	21.29
固定资产原价(亿元)	Original Value of Fixed Assets(100 million yuan)	5.34	111.40	38.74
年末负债合计(亿元)	Total Liabilities (year-end)(100 million yuan)	5.15	96.69	71.57
年末流动负债合计(亿元)	Total Current Liabilities (year-end)(100 million yuan)	4.83	83.04	71.00
长期负债合计(亿元)	Total Long-term Liabilities(100 million yuan)	0.13	4.97	0.57
年末所有者权益(亿元)	Owners' Equity (year-end)(100 million yuan)	6.22	70.07	38.34
主营业务收入(亿元)	Prime Operating Revenue(100 million yuan)	9.72	186.15	107.02
利润总额(亿元)	Total Pre-tax Profits(100 million yuan)	0.95	10.22	6.02
税金总额(亿元)	Total Tax and Duties(100 million yuan)	0.49	2.14	9.01
亏损总额(亿元)	Total Loss(100 million yuan)	0.03	2.16	0.14

其 中 of which						
上海浦东康桥工业园区 Pudong Kangqiao Industial Park	上海化学工业园区 Chemicao Industrial Park	上海新杨工业园区 Xinyang Industrial Psrk	上海浦东合庆工业园区 Pudong Heqing Industrial Park	上海南汇工业园区 Nanhui Industrial Park	上海奉城工业园区 Fengcheng Industrial Park	上海未来岛高新技术产业园区 Weilai Island High and New Technical Industrial Park
224	25	13	83	92	46	9
6.21	0.52	0.19	1.95	1.53	0.74	0.22
991.09	643.03	16.00	129.67	92.17	24.08	33.33
618.95	57.50	0.47	37.64	25.39	3.45	4.78
130.81	276.56	2.90	35.64	26.00	5.07	3.86
584.76	683.96	17.05	158.37	99.17	21.64	24.01
406.67	165.81	10.81	95.61	58.66	14.74	18.92
127.46	440.24	3.74	45.65	30.34	5.42	3.17
205.66	631.04	5.57	66.60	40.24	8.91	6.40
356.22	407.24	8.50	101.51	54.87	10.93	12.34
336.09	216.86	8.41	77.93	48.97	10.45	12.34
19.61	175.11	…	23.39	5.71	0.31	
228.54	276.72	8.55	56.86	44.31	10.72	11.67
1 028.97	674.89	17.19	135.13	86.52	25.91	34.47
62.54	58.24	2.30	10.46	8.83	1.68	7.18
15.30	21.59	0.66	2.26	1.53	0.47	1.51
4.26	2.15	…	0.49	0.52	0.20	0.05

上/海/统/计/年/鉴

主要统计指标解释

工　业

指从事自然资源的开采，对采掘品和农产品进行加工和再加工的物质生产部门。具体包括：(1)对自然资源的开采，如采矿、晒盐等(但不包括禽兽捕猎和水产捕捞)；(2)对农副产品的加工、再加工，如粮油加工、食品加工、缫丝、纺织、制革等；(3)对采掘品的加工、再加工，如炼铁、炼钢、化工生产、石油加工、机器制造、木材加工等，以及电力、自来水、煤气的生产和供应等；(4)对工业品的修理、翻新，如机器设备的修理、交通运输工具(包括小卧车)的修理等。

1984年以前农村的村及村以下办工业归属农业，1984年以后划归工业。

工业统计调查单位为独立核算法人工业企业。

独立核算法人工业企业指从事工业生产经营活动的单位。独立核算法人工业企业应同时具备以下条件：①依法成立，有自己的名称、组织机构和场所，能够承担民事责任；②独立拥有和使用资产，承担负债，有权与其他单位签订合同；③独立核算盈亏，并能够编制资产负债表。

轻工业

指主要提供生活消费品和制作手工工具的工业。按其所使用的原料不同，可分为两大类：(1)以农产品为原料的轻工业，是指直接或间接以农产品为基本原料的轻工业。主要包括食品制造、饮料制造、烟草加工、纺织、缝纫、皮革和毛皮制作、造纸以及印刷等工业；(2)以非农产品为原料的轻工业，是指以工业品为原料的轻工业。主要包括文教体育用品、化学药品制造、合成纤维制造、日用化学制品、日用玻璃制品、日用金属制品、手工工具制造、医疗器械制造、文化和办公用机械制造等工业。

重工业

指为国民经济各部门提供物质技术基础的主要生产资料的工业。按其生产性质和产品用途，可以分为下列三类：(1)采掘(伐)工业，是指对自然资源的开采，包括石油开采、煤炭开采、金属矿开采、非金属矿开采等工业；(2) 原材料工业，指向国民经济各部门提供基本材料、动力和燃料的工业。包括金属冶炼及加工、炼焦及焦炭、化学、化工原料、水泥、人造板以及电力、石油和煤炭加工等工业；(3)加工工业，是指对工业原材料进行再加工制造的工业。包括装备国民经济各部门的机械设备制造工业、金属结构、水泥制品等工业，以及为农业提供的生产资料如化肥、农药等工业。

根据上述划分原则，修理业中以重工业产品为修理作业对象的划为重工业，反之划为轻工业。

工业总产值

(1)定义：工业总产值是以货币形式表现的，工业企业在一定时期内生产的工业最终产品或提供工业性劳务活动的总价值量。它反映一定时间内工业生产的总规模和总水平。

(2)计算原则：

工业生产的原则，即凡是企业在报告期生产的经检验合格的产品，不管是否在报告期销售，均包括在内。

最终产品的原则，即凡是计入工业总产值的产品，必须是本企业生产的经检验合格的，不需要再进行任何加工的最终产品。如果企业有中间产品(半成品)对外销售，则对外销售的中间产品应视为企业的最终产品。

工厂法原则，即工业总产值是以工业企业作为基本计算(核算)单位，即按企业的最终产品计算工业总产值。按这种方法计算的工业总产值，不允许同一产品价值在企业内部重复计算，不能把企业内部各个车间(分厂)生产的成果相加，但允许企业间的重复计算。

(3)内容及计算方法：1995年全国工业普查对工业总产值(原规定)的内容及计算原则和方法做了某些修订，修订后的工业总产值(新规定)包括三项内容：即本期生产成品价值、对外加工费收入、在制品半成品期末期初差额价值三部分。

本期生产成品价值：指企业本期生产，并在报告期内不再进行加工，经检验、包装入库的全部工业成品(半产品)价值合计，包括企业生产的自制设备及提供给本企业在建工程、其他非工业部门和福利部门等单位使用的成品价值。本期生产成品价值为按自备原材料生产的产品的数量乘以本期不含增值税(销项税额)的产品实际销售平均单价计算；会计核算中按成本价格转帐的自制设备和自产自用的成品，按成本价格计算生产成品价值。生产成品价值中不包括用定货者来料加工的成品 (半产品)价值。

对外加工费收入：指企业在报告期内完成的对外承

主要统计指标解释

接的工业品加工(包括用定货者来料加工产品)的加工费收入和对外工业修理作业所取得的加工费收入。对外加工费收入按不含增值税(销项税额)的价格计算,可根据会计"产品销售收入"科目的有关资料取得。

对于本企业对内非工业部门提供的加工修理、设备安装的劳务收入,如果企业会计核算基础较好,能取得这部分资料,而且这部分价值所占比重较大,应包括在对外加工费收入中。

自制半成品在制品期末期初差额价值:指企业报告期在制品期末减期初的差额价值,本指标一般可以从会计核算资料中取得。如果会计产品成本核算中不计算半成品、在制品的成本,则总产值中也不包括这部分价值,反之则包括。

(4)工业总产值统计范围变化和计算方法修订情况:

1984 年以前工业总产值不包括村办工业,村办工业总产值划归农业。1984 年以后工业总产值包括村办工业。

1995 年工业普查对工业总产值计算方法做了修订,即从 1995 年始按新修订(新规定)方法计算工业总产值。新规定与原规定的区别如下:

全价与加工费的计算原则不同:新规定为凡自备原材料,不论其生产繁简程度如何,一律按全价计算工业总产值;凡来料加工,允许按加工费计算工业总产值。原规定则视生产加工的繁简程度不同,规定哪些行业按全价,哪些行业按加工费计算工业总产值。

自制半成品、在产品期末期初差额价值的计算原则不同:新规定要求,凡会计产品成本核算时计算了成本的差额价值,总产值中就应包括,否则可不包括;原规定则按生产周期六个月的界限区分,凡生产周期六个月以上的企业,总产值计算中应包括这部分差额价值,否则可不包括。

计算价格不同:新规定按不含增值税(销项税额)的价格计算;原规定则按含增值税(销项税额)的价格计算。

大、中、小型企业

大中小型企业划分标准:自 2003 年年报起,大中小型企业划分标准执行"统计上大中小型企业划分办法(暂行)"(国统字[2003]17 号)。即大型企业必须同时达到从业人员数≥2000 人、销售收入≥30000 万元、资产总额≥40000 万元;中型企业必须同时达到 2000 人 > 从业人员数≥300 人、30000 万元 > 销售收入 > 3000 万元、40000 万元 > 资产总额≥4000 万元;其余的均为小型企业。

资产总计

资产是指企业拥有或者控制的能以货币计量的经济资源,包括各种财产、债权和其他权利。资产按其流动性(即资产的变现能力和支付能力)划分为:流动资产、长期投资、固定资产、无形资产、递延资产和其他资产。该指标根据企业会计"资产负债表"中"资产总计"项目的期末数增列。

流动资产

指企业可以在一年内或者超过一年的一个生产周期内变现或者耗用的资产,包括现金及各种存款、短期投资,应收及预付款项、存货等。根据会计"资产负债表"中"流动资产合计"项的期末数填列。

固定资产净值

固定资产净值指固定资产原价减去累计折旧后的净额。该指标根据"资产负债表"中"固定资产原价"、"累计折旧"指标的期初、期末数计算填列。

计算公式为:

固定资产净值 = 固定资产原价 - 累计折旧

负债合计

指企业所承担的能以货币计量,将以资产或劳务偿付的债务总计。负债一般按偿还期长短分为流动负债和长期负债。流动负债合计是指企业在一年内或超过一年的一个营业周期内偿还的债务;长期负债合计是指偿还期在一年以上或者超过一年的一个营业周期内偿还债务。

所有者权益

指企业投资人对企业净资产的所有权。企业净资产等于企业全部资产减去全部负债后的余额,包括企业投资人对企业的最初投入的实际到位的资产及资本公积金、盈余公积金和未分配利润。所有者权益合计数小于零,表示企业资不抵债。

利润总额

指企业生产经营活动的最终成果,是企业在一定时期内实现的盈亏相抵后的利润总额(亏损以"-"号表示),它等于营业利润加上补贴收入加上投资收益加上营业外净收入再加上以前年度损益调整。

总资产贡献率

反映企业全部资产的获利能力,是企业经营业绩和

主要统计指标解释

管理水平的集中体现，是评价和考核企业盈利能力的核心指标。计算公式为：

总资产贡献率(%)= 利润总额 + 税金总额 + 利息支出 / 平均资金总额 × 100%

公式中：税金总额为产品销售税金及附加与应缴增值税之和；平均资产总额为期初期末资产之和的算术平均值。

资产负债率

该指标既反映企业经营风险的大小，也反映企业利用债权人提供的资金从事经营活动的能力。计算公式为：

资产负债率(%)= 负债总额 / 资产总额 × 100%

资产与负债均为报告期期末数。

流动资产周转次数

指一定时期内流动资产完成的周转次数，反映投入工业企业流动资金的周转速度。计算公式为：

流动资产周转次数 = 产品销售收入 / 全部流动资产平均余额

公式中：全部流动资产平均余额为期初和期末的流动资产之和的算术平均值。

成本费用利润率

反映企业投入的生产成本及费用的经济效益，同时也反映企业降低成本所取得的经济效益。计算公式为：

成本费用利润 (%)= 利润总额 / 成本费用总额 × 100%

公式中：成本费用总额为产品销售成本、销售费用、管理费用、财务费用之和。

产品销售率

该指标反映工业产品已实现销售的程度，是分析工业产销衔接情况、研究工业产品满足社会需求的指标。计算公式为：

产品销售率 (%)= 工业销售产值 / 工业总产值 (现价) × 100%

资产保值增值率

该指标反映企业净资产的变动状况，是企业发展能力的集中体现。计算公式为：

资本保值增值率＝报告期期末所有者权益 / 上年同期期末所有者权益

所有者权益等于资产总计减负债总计。

全员劳动生产率

该指标反映企业的生产效率和劳动投入的经济效益。计算公式为：

$$全员劳动生产率(元/人)= \frac{工业增加值}{全部从业人员平均人数}$$

SHANGHAI STATISTICAL YEARBOOK

EXPLANATORY NOTES TO MAJOR STATISTICAL INDICATORS

□ Industry

Industry refers to the material production sector which is engaged in extraction of natural resources and processing and reprocessing of minerals and agricultural products, including (1) extraction of natural resources, such as mining, salt production (but not including hunting and fishing); (2) processing and reprocessing of farm and sideline produces, such as rice husking, flour milling, wine making, oil pressing, silk reeling, spinning and weaving, and leather making; (3) manufacture of industrial products, such as steel making, iron smelting, chemicals manufacturing, petroleum processing, machine building, timber processing; water and gas production and electricity generation and supply; (4)repairing of industrial products such as the repairing of machinery and means of transport (including cars).

Prior to 1984, the rural industry run by villages and cooperative organizations under village was classified into agriculture. Since 1984, it has been grouped into industry.

Units of industrial statistics survey corporate industrial enterprises with independent accounting system.

Corporate industrial enterprises with independent accounting system refer to enterprises engaging in industrial production activities, which meet the following requirements: ①They are established legally, having their own names, organizations, location, able to take civil liability; ②They possess and use their assets independently, assume liabilities, and are entitled to sign contracts with other units; ③They are financially independent and compile their own balance sheets.

□ Light Industry

Light Industry refers to the industry that produces consumer goods and hand tools. It consists of two categories, depending on the materials used:

(1) Industries using farm products as raw materials. These are branches of light industry which directly or indirectly use farm products as basic raw materials, including the manufacture of food and beverages, tobacco processing, textile, clothing, fur and leather manufacturing, paper making, printing, etc.

(2) Industries using non farm products as raw materials. These are branches of light industry which use manufactured goods as raw materials, including the manufacture of cultural, educational articles and sports goods, chemicals, synthetic fiber, chemical products for daily use, glass products for daily use, metal products for daily use, hand tools, medical apparatus and instruments, and the manufacture of cultural and clerical machinery.

□ Heavy Industry

Heavy Industry refers to the industry which produces capital goods, and provides various sectors of the national economy with necessary material and technical basis. It consists of the following three branches according to the purpose of production or the use of products:

(1) Mining, quarrying and logging industry refers to the industry that extracts natural resources, including extraction of petroleum, coal, metal and non-metal ores.

(2) Raw materials industry refers to the industry that provides various sectors of the national economy with raw materials, fuels and power. It includes smelting and processing of metals, coking and coke chemistry, chemical materials and building materials such as cement, plywood, and power, petroleum refining and coal dressing.

(3) Manufacturing industry refers to the industry that processes raw materials. It includes machine building industry which equips sectors of the national economy, industries of metal structure and cement products, industries producing means of agricultural production, such as chemical fertilizers and pesticides. According to the above principle of classification, the repairing trades which are engaged primarily in repairing products of heavy industry are classified into heavy industry while these engaged in repairing products of light industry are classified into light industry.

□ Gross Output Value of Industry

(1) Definition: Gross industrial output value is the total volume of final industrial products produced and industrial services provided during a given period. It reflects the total achievements and overall scale of industrial production during a given period.

(2) Principles for calculation:

Statistics on industrial production follow the principle that all products produced by the enterprises and accepted during the reference period are to be included no matter whether they are

EXPLANATORY NOTES TO MAJOR STATISTICAL INDICATORS

sold or not during the reference period.

Determination of final products follow the principle that all products that are included in the calculation of grow industrial output value are the final products of the enterprise which have been accepted through quality check and require no further processing. If an enterprise has intermediate (semi-finished) products to sell, these intermediate products are considered as the final products of the enterprise.

Gross industrial output value is calculated following the principle of factory approach, i.e. industrial enterprise is used as the basic accounting unit in calculating the gross industrial output value. By this approach, value of the same product is not to be double counted, and the output value of different workshops (branch factories) should not be added. However, this approach does not exclude the possibility of double counting between enterprises.

(3) Content and calculation method: The old definition of gross industrial output value was modified during the national industrial census in 1995. The revised (new) definition of gross industrial output value consists of 3 components: value of the finished products during the reference period, income from external processing, and value of change in semi-finished products at the end and at the beginning of the reference period.

Value of the finished products during the reference period: refers to the value of all finished (semi-finished) industrial products that are produced during the reference period without the need for further processing, checked for acceptance, packed and put into the warehouse of the enterprise, including the value of own-produced equipment and the value of products provided to the projects under construction of the enterprise, and to other non-industrial or welfare units. Value of finished products during the reference period is calculated by the quantity of products produced using own materials multiplied by the average unit prices at which products are sold (excluding value-added tax). Own-produced equipment and products produced for own use are value at cost prices as in the case of enterprise accounting. Value of finished products does not include the value of finished products (semi-finished products) that are produced using the materials from the clients who make the orders.

Income from external processing: refers to income from contracted external processing of industrial products (including processing of industrial products using materials from the clients), and the income from industrial repairing work provided to other units. Income from external processing is calculated using information from the item "products sales income" in the enterprise accounting at the prices excluding value-added tax.

For income from services such as processing, repairing and installation of equipment provided to non-industrial units within the enterprise, if the accounting work of the enterprise is good enough to separate it from other records, and the share of such services is significant, it should also be included in the income from external processing.

Value of change in semi-finished products at the end and at the beginning of the reference period: refers to the value of change in semi-finished products at the end and at the beginning of the reference period, which generally can be obtained from accounting records of enterprises. If the enterprise accounting excludes the cost of semi-finished products, then it should not be included in the gross industrial output value, and vice versa.

(4) Changes in the coverage and method of calculation of gross industrial output value

Prior to 1984, the value of rural industry run by villages was classified into agriculture instead of industry. Since 1984, it has been included in the gross industrial output value.

Method of calculation for the gross industrial output value was modified in the industrial census in 1995. The difference in the new method as compared with the old one is outlined below: Principle in using full value vs. processing fee: The new method stipulates that all products produced using own materials are to be calculated with full value in reporting the gross industrial output value irrespective of sophistication of production, and for external processing, it allows calculation using processing fee. In the old method, however, the use of full value or processing fee was determined by the degree of sophistication of production in different branches of industries.

Principle in determining the value of change in semi-finished products: The new method requires that value of the change in semi-finished products should be included in the gross industrial output value if it is included in the accounting record of the enterprise, otherwise it should not be included. By the old method, it is determined by the type of enterprises in terms of production cycle. If the production cycle is over 6 months, the value of change in semi-finished products is included in the gross industrial output value, otherwise it is excluded.

Difference in prices: The new method uses prices excluding value-added tax in the calculation of gross industrial output value, while the old method used prices including value-added tax.

EXPLANATORY NOTES TO
MAJOR STATISTICAL INDICATORS

□ Large, Medium and Small Enterprises

Since 2003 annual report enforcement, the criteria for classifying large, medium and small enterprises has been based on The Method for Classifying Large, Medium and Small Enterprises (Provisional) (State Statistics Bureau [2003] No.17). That is, an enterprise could be entitled Large Enterprise only when it has more than 2000 employees, its sales revenue exceeds 300 million yuan and total property exceeds 400 million yuan , simultaneously. An enterprise could be entitled Medium Enterprise when its employee number ranges from 300 to 2000, its sales revenue ranges from 30 million to 300 million yuan and its total property ranges from 40 million to 400 million yuan, simultaneously. All other enterprises should be entitled Small Enterprises.

□ Aggregate Assets

Total Assets refer to all economic resources, in monetary terms, that is owned or controlled by enterprises, including properties, creditors equity and other economic rights of all forms. Classified by the degree of equitability, total assets include circulating assets, long-term investment, fixed assets, intangible assets and deferred assets, and other assets. Data on this indicator can be obtained by the year-end figures of total assets in the Assets and Liability Table of accounting records of enterprises.

□ Working Capital

Working Capital refers to capital that an enterprise can cash or use during one year or one production cycle that may exceed one year, including cash and savings deposits of various forms, short-term investment, money receivable and prepaid money, inventories, etc. Data on this indicator can be obtained by the year-end figures of working capitak in the Asset and Liability Table of accounting records of enterprise.

□ Net Value of Fixed Assets

Net value of fixed assets refers to the original value of fixed assets minus depreciation over years, i.e.:

Net value of fixed assets=original value of fixed assets- cumulative depreciation. Information on this indicator can be obtained from the beginning and ending figures of the original value of fixed assets and cumulative depreciation from the Assets and Liability Table of enterprise.

□ Aggregate Liabilities

Aggregate liabilities refer to the total debts of an enterprise which can be calculated in monetary term and will be repaid in the forms of assets or service. Usually, the debts are divided into liquid liability and long-term debt according to the length of the payback period. The liquid liability is the debt that an enterprise will pay back during an operation cycle which is either shorter or longer than a year. The long-term debt refers to a debt whose payback period is longer than a year or which will be repaid during an operation cycle that is longer than a year.

□ Creditors' Equity

Creditors' Equity refers to investors ownership of net assets of the enterprise, which is equal to the total assets of the enterprise minus its total liabilities, including the primary input actually received at the enterprise from investors, capital accumulation fund, surplus accumulation fund and undistributed profit. When the total of creditors' equity is less than zero, that indicates the liability of the enterprise is larger that its assets.

□ Total Profits

Total Profits refer to the final achievements of production and operation of the enterprises, represented by the total profits after deducting losses (loss is expressed by the negative figure). It is the sum of profits from operation, income from subsidies, investment earnings, net income from activities other than operation, and adjustment of profits and losses of previous years.

□ Ratio of Profits, Taxes and Interests to Average Assets

Ratio of Profits, Taxes and Interests to Average Assets reflects the profit-making capability of all assets of the enterprise and is a key indicator manifesting the performance and management and evaluating the profit-making potential of the enterprise. It is calculated as follows:

Ratio of Profits, Taxes and Interests to Average Assets (%) = [(total profits + total taxes + interest payment) / average assets] × 100%

In the above formula, total taxes is the sum of tax and extra charges on the sales of products and value-added tax payable; and average assets is the arithmetic mean of the sum of beginning assets and ending assets.

□ Ratio of Debts to Assets

Ratio of Debts to Assets reflect both the operation risk and the capability of the enterprise in making use of the capital from

EXPLANATORY NOTES TO MAJOR STATISTICAL INDICATORS

the creditors. It is calculated as follows:

Ratio of Debts to Assets (%) = (total debts / total assets) × 100%

Both assets and debts are figures at the end of the reference period.

□ Turnover of Working Capital

Turnover of Working Capital refers to the number of times of turnover of working capital in a given period of time, which reflects the speed of the turnover of working capital of industrial enterprises, and is calculated as follows:

Turnover of Working Capital= (sales revenue of products) / (average balance of total working capital)

In the above formula, average balance of total working capital refers to the arithmetic mean of the sum of working capital at the beginning and at the end of the reference period.

□ Ratio of Profits to Total Industrial Costs

Ratio of Profits to Total Industrial Costs refers to the ratio of profits realized in a given period to the total costs in the same period, which reflects the economic efficiency of input cost and is calculated as follows:

Ratio of Profits to Total Industrial Cost(%)=(total profits/ total costs) × 100%

Total costs in the above formula is the sum of cost of products sold, marketing cost, management cost and financial cost.

□ Ratio of Sales to Gross Output Value

Ratio of Sales to Gross Output Value reflects the degree at which industrial products are sold. It helps to analyze the linkage between production and sales and the extent of the needs of the society that has been met by the supply of industrial products. It is calculated as follows:

Ratio of Sales to Gross Output Value= (Industrial sales / Gross industrial output value at current prices) × 100%

□ Capital Maintenance and Appreciation Rate

Capital Maintenance and Appreciation Rate reflects the changes of an enterprise's net assets. It epitomizes the growth capability of an enterprise. Its calculating formula is:

Capital maintenance and appreciation rate = Ownership equity at the end of the reporting period/Ownership equity at the same period of the previous year. Ownership equity is the result of total assets minus total liabilities.

□ Overall Labour Productivity

Overall Labour Productivity is an indicator reflecting the production efficiency of an enterprise and the economic efficiency of its labour input, calculated by the formula:

Overall Labour Productivity (yuan/person)=industrial value-added/average of all persons engaged.

第十三篇

CHAPTER 13

建 筑 业

CONSTRUCTION

表 13.1 建筑业主要指标(1978 ~ 2010)
MAJOR INDICATORS OF CONSTRUCTION INDUSTRY

年 份 Year	年末从业人员 (万人) Year-end Employees (10 000 persons)	总产值 (亿元) Output Value (100 million yuan)	房屋竣工面积 (万平方米) Floor Space of Building Completed (10 000 sq. m)	平均每个职工房屋竣工面积 (平方米/人) Area of Completed Building for Every Staff and Worker (sq. m/person)	全员劳动生产率 (按总产值计算) (元/人) Overall Labor Productivity (In Term of Output Value) (yuan/person)
1978	10.07	5.55	234.03	26.32	6 005
1979	23.35	13.98	564.62	26.10	6 226
1980	27.27	17.07	607.91	24.13	6 513
1981	30.21	18.03	649.93	22.28	5 941
1982	30.73	21.56	684.61	22.90	6 928
1983	33.35	24.64	736.34	22.46	7 189
1984	32.94	30.62	799.40	23.10	8 402
1985	33.35	36.73	819.24	23.78	10 070
1986	35.53	49.91	867.08	22.87	12 147
1987	35.83	59.45	872.25	22.66	14 455
1988	36.70	68.83	836.73	21.26	16 251
1989	34.43	74.75	758.34	19.70	18 053
1990	34.01	75.62	747.88	20.01	18 569
1991	34.62	84.30	775.63	20.14	21 022
1992	36.33	117.68	860.49	19.92	26 221
1993	36.90	193.00	1 144.16	26.10	44 020
1994	39.95	309.68	1 557.87	29.33	58 305
1995	41.10	391.42	1 485.87	25.44	67 023
1996	36.19	450.41	1 514.58	26.95	80 161
1997	37.40	564.37	1 777.41	29.60	93 995
1998	40.88	593.11	1 913.55	33.08	102 531
1999	39.01	573.06	1 950.76	33.86	99 473
2000	35.91	631.64	1 909.11	33.02	109 244
2001	35.52	730.33	2 434.73	39.55	118 641
2002	41.97	822.27	2 596.95	42.23	133 698
2003	50.52	1 195.80	3 609.20	71.44	153 910
2004	74.26	1 724.40	4 672.53	62.92	168 719
2005	72.23	1 889.25	5 648.85	78.21	182 299
2006	73.44	2 285.38	6 506.41	88.59	208 368
2007	69.33	2 524.18	6 090.22	87.84	228 710
2008	80.79	3 245.77	5723.90	70.85	293 520
2009	88.88	3 830.53	5 719.93	64.36	312 360
2010	96.09	4 300.19	6 217.15	64.70	344 720

表 13.2 建筑业主要指标（2010）
MAJOR INDICATORS OF CONSTRUCTION INDUSTRY

类 别	Types	企业数（个）Quantity of Enterprises (unit)	年末从业人员（万人）Year-end Employees (10 000 persons)	竣工产值（亿元）Output Value of Construction Completed (100 million yuan)
总 计	**Total**	**3 094**	**96.09**	**2 672.73**
按登记注册类型分	**By Registration Categories**			
内 资	Domestic Funded	2 941	93.97	2 556.57
国 有	State-owned	123	5.08	267.43
集 体	Collective Owned	83	2.63	38.90
股份合作	Stock-holding Cooperation	14	0.12	2.22
联 营	Joint Owned	15	0.35	9.55
有限责任公司	Companies with Limited Liabilition	536	30.28	1 089.71
股份有限公司	Stock-holding Companies Liabilities	60	6.24	416.82
私 营	Private	2 110	49.26	731.95
港澳台商投资	Hong Kong, Macao and Taiwan Funded	82	1.07	36.82
外商投资	Foreign Funded	71	1.06	79.34
按行业分	**By Sectors**			
房屋和土木工程建筑业	Housing Construction and Civil Engineering Industry	1 402	75.47	2 097.95
建筑安装业	Construction and Installation Industry	888	12.05	378.56
建筑装饰业	Construction and Decoration Industry	660	7.39	171.04
其他建筑业	Other Construction Industries	144	1.18	25.19
按资质标准分	**By Qualification Standard**			
施工总承包	Chief Construction Contract	1 431	79.25	2 287.23
专业承包	Professional Contract	1 663	16.84	385.51

表 13.2 续表 1 continued

类 别	Types	总产值（亿元）Output Value (100 million yuan)	其中 of which	
			#建筑工程 Construction	#安装工程 Installation
总 计	**Total**	**4 300.19**	**3 519.02**	**622.44**
按登记注册类型分	**By Registration Categories**			
内 资	Domestic Funded	4 079.03	3 390.97	545.48
国 有	State-owned	392.41	330.77	38.79
集 体	Collective Owned	63.11	52.36	7.43
股份合作	Stock-holding Cooperation	10.54	10.26	0.23
联 营	Joint Owned	16.02	12.02	1.36
有限责任公司	Companies with Limited Liabilition	1 888.59	1 655.92	189.91
股份有限公司	Stock-holding Companies Liabilities	464.94	361.37	96.84
私 营	Private	1 243.43	968.27	210.93
港澳台商投资	Hong Kong, Macao and Taiwan Funded	122.57	64.55	51.78
外商投资	Foreign Funded	98.58	63.50	25.18
按行业分	**By Sectors**			
房屋和土木工程建筑业	Housing Construction and Civil Engineering Industry	3 427.77	3 080.05	254.39
建筑安装业	Construction and Installation Industry	519.87	155.81	327.65
建筑装饰业	Construction and Decoration Industry	314.21	257.56	35.86
其他建筑业	Other Construction Industries	38.35	25.60	4.54
按资质标准分	**By Qualification Standard**			
施工总承包	Chief Construction Contract	3 635.55	3 122.64	413.36
专业承包	Professional Contract	664.64	396.38	209.08

表 13.2 续表 2 continued

类 别	Types	房屋建筑面积(万平方米) Floor Space of Buildings (10 000 sq. m)	
		施工面积 Under Construction	竣工面积 Completed
总 计	**Total**	**22 996.81**	**6 217.15**
按登记注册类型分	**By Registration Categories**		
内 资	Domestic Investment	22 602.21	6 036.02
国 有	State-owned	797.94	134.11
集 体	Collective Owned	393.43	196.87
股份合作	Stock-holding Cooperation	191.89	11.92
联 营	Joint Owned	31.80	4.94
有限责任公司	Companies with Limited Liabilition	10 159.91	2 296.22
股份有限公司	Stock-holding Companies Liabilities	3 350.56	926.56
私 营	Private	7 676.68	2 465.40
港澳台商投资	Hong Kong, Macao and Taiwan Funded	30.45	24.18
外商投资	Foreign Funded	364.16	156.94
按行业分	**By Sectors**		
房屋和土木工程建筑业	Housing Construction and Civil Engineering Industry	22 671.47	6 067.78
建筑安装业	Construction and Installation Industry	321.23	145.53
建筑装饰业	Construction and Decoration Industry		
其他建筑业	Other Construction Industries	4.11	3.84
按资质标准分	**By Qualification Standard**		
施工总承包	Chief Construction Contract	22 555.60	6 024.86
专业承包	Professional Contract	441.21	192.29

表 13.3 各区、县建筑业主要指标(2010)
MAIN CONSTRUCTION INDICATORS OF DISTRICTS AND COUNTIES

地区	District	企业数(个) Quantity of Enterprises (unit)	年末从业人员(万人) Year-end Employees (10 000 persons)	总产值(亿元) Output Value (100 million yuan)
总计	**Total**	**3 094**	**96.09**	**4 300.19**
浦东新区	Pudong New Area	608	21.13	940.94
黄浦区	Huangpu	133	4.56	200.93
卢湾区	Luwan	72	1.30	44.64
徐汇区	Xuhui	217	6.27	429.53
长宁区	Changning	179	4.30	200.62
静安区	Jing'an	92	0.86	67.49
普陀区	Putuo	212	7.52	293.18
闸北区	Zhabei	91	3.69	346.67
虹口区	Hongkou	192	7.85	347.78
杨浦区	Yangpu	247	4.96	216.99
闵行区	Minhang	146	7.51	187.00
宝山区	Baoshan	197	7.90	514.89
嘉定区	Jiading	147	3.71	92.89
金山区	Jinshan	107	2.74	69.62
松江区	Songjiang	124	4.05	128.81
青浦区	Qingpu	89	2.39	65.00
奉贤区	Fengxian	196	3.90	114.64
崇明县	Chongming	45	1.44	38.58

注：原南汇区划并入浦东新区。
Note: Former Nanhui district has been merged into pudong New Area.

表 13.3 续表 Continued

地 区 District		房屋建筑施工面积(万平方米) Floor Space of Buildings Under Construction (10 000 sq. m)	房屋建筑竣工面积(万平方米) Floor Space of Buildings Completed (10 000 sq. m)	其中 of which #住 宅 Residence
总 计	**Total**	**22 996.81**	**6 217.15**	**2 735.90**
浦东新区	Pudong New Area	6 468.08	1 554.24	654.44
黄 浦 区	Huangpu	1 145.33	282.80	219.64
卢 湾 区	Luwan	45.33	11.63	8.85
徐 汇 区	Xuhui	1 105.37	302.49	151.77
长 宁 区	Changning	1 943.64	456.36	174.51
静 安 区	Jing'an	142.26	29.59	13.38
普 陀 区	Putuo	1 722.16	468.94	283.70
闸 北 区	Zhabei	292.02	82.08	44.94
虹 口 区	Hongkou	2 227.49	504.44	236.59
杨 浦 区	Yangpu	598.47	241.09	90.82
闵 行 区	Minhang	1 433.01	477.55	168.84
宝 山 区	Baoshan	2 593.75	516.05	169.58
嘉 定 区	Jiading	883.71	281.05	156.50
金 山 区	Jinshan	235.76	123.33	21.79
松 江 区	Songjiang	1 009.95	517.69	207.56
青 浦 区	Qingpu	351.00	175.74	56.30
奉 贤 区	Fengxian	602.30	141.17	60.88
崇 明 县	Chongming	197.17	50.91	15.80

表 13.4 建筑业主要财务指标(2010)
MAJOR ACCOUNTING INDICATORS OF CONSTRUCTION ENTERPRISES

指 标	Indicators	合 计 Total	内 资 Domestic Investment
施工企业单位数(个)	Quantity of Construction Enterprises(unit)	3 094	2 941
固定资产原价(亿元)	Fixed Assets(Original Value)(100 million yuan)	538.23	521.28
固定资产净值(亿元)	Fixed Assets(Net Value)(100 million yuan)	296.17	286.91
自有机械设备台数(万台)	Machinery and Equipment(10 000 units)	17.32	16.82
自有机械设备净值(亿元)	Machinery and Equipment(Net Value)(100 million yuan)	144.54	143.32
自有机械设备总功率(万千瓦)	Capacity of Machinery and Equipment(10 000 kw)	362.82	358.47
总产值(亿元)	Output Value(100 million yuan)	4 300.19	4 079.03
资产合计(亿元)	Assets at Year-end(100 million yuan)	4 886.75	4 649.26
#流动资产	Current Assets	4 048.14	3 826.02
固定资产	Fixed Assets	334.33	324.27
无形及递延资产	Intangible and Defered Assets	43.80	43.01
负债合计(亿元)	Total Liabilities at Year-end(100 million yuan)	3 668.84	3 486.44
流动负债	Current Liabilities	3 483.62	3 306.01
长期负债	Long-term Liabilities	185.22	180.42
所有者权益(亿元)	Total OwnersEquity(100 million yuan)	1 217.90	1 162.82
企业总收入(亿元)	Total Revenue of Enterprises(100 million yuan)	4 944.99	4 693.28
工程结算收入	Revenue of Engineering Settlement Accounts	4 880.76	4 633.84
其他业务收入	Other Revenue	64.24	59.44
施工面积(万平方米)	Floor Space of Building Under Construction(10 000 sq. m)	22 996.81	22 602.21
竣工面积(万平方米)	Floor Space of Building Completed(10 000 sq. m)	6 217.15	6 036.02
利润总额(亿元)	Total Profits(100 million yuan)	160.27	147.95
全员劳动生产率(元/人)(按总产值计算)	Overall Labor Productivity(yuan/person)(In Term of Output Value)	344 720	340 569
技术装备率(元/人)	Per Capita Machinery Value(yuan/person)	15 042	15 252
动力装备率(千瓦/人)	Per Capita Machinery Capacity(kw/person)	3.8	3.8
房屋建筑面积竣工率(%)	Rate of Buiding Completed(%)	27.0	26.7
产值利润率(%)	Ratio of Profit/Gross Output Value(%)	3.7	3.6
产值利税率(%)	Ratio of Profit and Taxes/Gross Output Value(%)	7.0	6.9

其 中 of which						
国 有 Stateowned	集 体 Collective Owned	股份合作 Stock-holding Cooperation	联 营 Joint Owned	有限责任公司 Companies With Limited Liabilition	股份有限公司 Stock-holding Companies Liabilities	私 营 Private
123	83	14	15	536	60	2 110
68.70	4.61	0.51	3.18	257.11	56.97	130.20
36.71	2.43	0.24	1.77	141.47	27.27	77.01
1.33	0.43	0.04	0.16	5.79	0.91	8.16
24.13	0.96	0.06	0.14	79.18	13.28	25.56
54.31	5.55	0.26	4.79	172.15	24.74	96.68
392.41	63.11	10.54	16.02	1 888.59	464.94	1 243.43
556.12	63.76	19.14	12.41	2 200.73	505.03	1 292.07
399.41	58.65	14.94	10.03	1 811.46	396.41	1 135.12
40.30	2.92	0.26	1.90	158.46	30.78	89.65
6.66	0.15	…	0.01	28.01	3.80	4.38
401.67	47.75	17.16	8.16	1 820.70	382.26	808.74
365.88	46.86	17.12	8.12	1 738.77	339.54	789.74
35.80	0.90	0.04	0.04	81.93	42.72	19.00
154.44	16.01	1.99	4.26	380.03	122.77	483.33
478.35	73.77	12.27	17.28	2 172.90	651.62	1 287.10
468.21	71.79	12.25	16.63	2 142.92	649.25	1 272.80
10.14	1.98	0.02	0.64	29.98	2.37	14.30
797.94	393.43	191.89	31.80	10 159.91	3 350.56	7 676.68
134.11	196.87	11.92	4.94	2 296.22	926.56	2 465.40
23.58	1.18	0.04	0.68	60.92	15.57	45.99
438 976	232 361	416 616	290 936	484 528	310 029	233 124
47 476	3 664	5 149	3 960	26 151	21 301	5 188
10.7	2.1	2.1	13.5	5.7	4.0	2.0
16.8	50.0	6.2	15.5	22.6	27.7	32.1
6.0	1.9	0.4	4.2	3.2	3.3	3.7
8.8	5.4	3.3	7.2	6.4	7.5	6.9

表 13.4 续表 Continued

	指 标 Indicators	港澳台商投资 Hong Kong, Macao and Taiwan Funded	外商投资 Foreign Funded
施工企业单位数(个)	Quantity of Construction Enterprises(unit)	82	71
固定资产原价(亿元)	Fixed Assets(Original Value)(100 million yuan)	7.52	9.43
固定资产净值(亿元)	Fixed Assets(Net Value)(100 million yuan)	4.18	5.07
自有机械设备台数(万台)	Machinery and Equipment(10 000 units)	0.18	0.32
自有机械设备净值(亿元)	Machinery and Equipment(Net Value)(100 million yuan)	0.37	0.86
自有机械设备总功率(万千瓦)	Capacity of Machinery and Equipment(10 000 kw)	1.07	3.28
总产值(亿元)	Output Value(100 million yuan)	122.57	98.58
资产合计(亿元)	Assets at Year-end(100 million yuan)	133.30	104.19
#流动资产	Current Assets	125.44	96.68
固定资产	Fixed Assets	4.89	5.17
无形及递延资产	Intangible and Defered Assets	0.56	0.22
负债合计(亿元)	Total Liabilities at Year-end(100 million yuan)	102.32	80.08
流动负债	Current Liabilities	99.39	78.22
长期负债	Long-term Liabilities	2.94	1.86
所有者权益(亿元)	Total Owners,Equity(100 million yuan)	30.97	24.11
企业总收入(亿元)	Total Revenue of Enterprises(100 million yuan)	140.92	110.80
工程结算收入	Revenue of Engineering Settlement Accounts	140.61	106.31
其他业务收入	Other Revenue	0.30	4.49
施工面积(万平方米)	Floor Space of Building Under Construction(10 000 sq. m)	30.45	364.16
竣工面积(万平方米)	Floor Space of Building Completed(10 000 sq. m)	24.18	156.94
利润总额(亿元)	Total Profits(100 million yuan)	8.66	3.67
全员劳动生产率(元/人)(按总产值计算)	Overall Labor Productivity(yuan/person) (In Term of Output Value)	520 046	376 798
技术装备率(元/人)	Per Capita Machinery Value(yuan/person)	3 465	8 129
动力装备率(千瓦/人)	Per Capita Machinery Capacity(kw/person)	1.0	3.1
房屋建筑面积竣工率(%)	Rate of Buiding Completed(%)	79.4	43.1
产值利润率(%)	Ratio of Profit/Gross Output Value(%)	7.1	3.7
产值利税率(%)	Ratio of Profit and Taxes/Gross Output Value(%)	9.6	6.3

表 13.5 建筑业签订合同情况(2010)
SIGNED CONTRACT OF CONSTRUCTION INDUSTRY

类别	Types	签订合同额(亿元) Signed Contract Value (100 million yuan)	上年结转合同额(亿元) Value from Contracts Signed in 2008 (100 million yuan)	本年新签合同额(亿元) Value from New Contracts Signed in 2009 (100 million yuan)
总　计	**Total**	**8 791.73**	**3 564.10**	**5 227.63**
按经济类型分	**Grouped by Registration Categories**			
内　资	Domestic Funded	8 411.23	3 356.63	5 054.59
国　有	State-owned	815.07	392.04	423.03
集　体	Collective Owned	76.07	22.12	53.95
股份合作	Stock-holding Cooperation	31.12	25.31	5.81
联　营	Joint Owned	16.19	5.65	10.54
有限责任公司	Companies with Limited Liabilition	3 974.31	1 495.86	2 478.45
股份有限公司	Stock-holding Companies Liabilities	1 577.52	703.93	873.59
私　营	Private	1 920.93	711.73	1 209.21
港澳台商投资	Hong Kong, Macao and Taiwan Funded	200.43	130.50	69.93
外商投资	Foreign Funded	180.07	76.97	103.10
按隶属关系分	**Grouped by Subordination**			
#中央属	Central Government	3 138.72	1 169.83	1 968.88
市　属	Municipality	2 034.98	947.06	1 087.92
区(县)属	District and County	469.55	220.79	248.76
按资质等級分	**Grouped by Quarlification Level**			
#特　级	Special Grade	3 651.45	1 479.85	2 171.60
一　级	First Grade	3 321.22	1 410.55	1 910.67
二　级	Second Grade	1 274.86	490.27	784.59
三　级	Third Grade	521.78	173.73	348.06
按行业类别分	**Grouped by Sector**			
房屋和土木工程建筑业	Housing Construction and Civil Engineering Industry	7 521.80	3 129.78	4 392.02
建筑安装业	Construction and Installation Industry	798.76	300.05	498.71
建筑装饰业	Construction and Decoration Industry	428.49	124.00	304.49
其他建筑业	Other Construction Industry	42.66	10.26	32.41
按资质标准分	**Grouped by Qualification Standard**			
施工总承包	Chief Construction Contract	7 864.36	3 269.96	4 594.40
专业承包	Professional Contract	927.37	294.13	633.23

表 13.6 建筑业承包工程完成情况(2010) COMPLETION OF CONTRACTED PROJECTS BY CONSTRUCTION ENTERPRISES

类别	Types	直接从建设单位承揽工程完成产值(亿元) Completed Output Value of Projects Contracted Directly form Investors (100 million yuan)	其中 of Which: 自行完成施工产值 Own-completed Output Value	分包出去工程的产值 Output Value of Out-sourced Projects	从建设单位外承揽工程完成产值(亿元) Completed Output Value of Projects Contracted from Non-investors (100 million yuan)
总 计	**Total**	**4 360.10**	**3 858.60**	**501.51**	**441.59**
按经济类型分	**Grouped by Registration Categories**				
内 资	Domestic Funded	4 137.09	3 663.92	473.16	415.11
国 有	State-owned	409.78	344.50	65.28	47.91
集 体	Collective Owned	62.68	61.63	1.05	1.48
股份合作	Stock-holding Cooperation	9.68	9.56	0.12	0.98
联 营	Joint Owned	11.42	11.41	0.00	4.61
有限责任公司	Companies with Limited Liabilition	1 943.26	1 793.84	149.42	94.75
股份有限公司	Stock-holding Companies Liabilities	534.63	312.12	222.51	152.82
私 营	Private	1 165.65	1 130.86	34.79	112.57
港澳台商投资	Hong Kong, Macao and Taiwan Funded	125.73	110.36	15.37	12.22
外商投资	Foreign Funded	97.29	84.32	12.97	14.26
按隶属关系分	**Grouped by Subordination**				
#中央属	Central Government	1 375.38	1 289.75	85.64	65.27
市 属	Municipality	780.46	458.02	322.44	195.14
区(县)属	District and County	251.25	240.03	11.22	25.35
按资质等级分	**Grouped by Quarlification Level**				
#特 级	SpecialGrade	1 453.29	1 169.93	283.36	80.92
一 级	First Grade	1 683.23	1 521.77	161.46	236.85
二 级	Second Grade	812.71	769.98	42.74	87.53
三 级	Third Grade	399.88	386.66	13.22	35.65
按行业类别分	**Grouped by Sector**				
房屋和土木工程建筑业	Housing Construction and Civil Engineering Industry	3 593.97	3 136.95	457.02	290.82
建筑安装业	Construction and Installation Industry	450.01	412.22	37.79	107.65
建筑装饰业	Construction and Decoration Industry	279.86	274.05	5.81	40.16
其他建筑业	Other Construction Industry	36.27	35.38	0.89	2.97
按资质标准分	**Grouped by Qualification Standard**				
施工总承包	Chief Construction Contract	3 762.44	3 292.52	469.92	343.04
专业承包	Professional Contract	597.67	566.08	31.59	98.56

上/海/统/计/年/鉴

主要统计指标解释

建筑业总产值

建筑业总产值是以货币表现的建筑业企业在一定时期内生产的建筑业产品和服务的总和。建筑业总产值包括:

(1)建筑工程产值:指列入建筑工程预算内的各种工程价值。

(2)安装工程产值:指设备安装工程价值,不包括被安装设备本身价值。

(3)其他产值:建筑业总产值中除建筑工程、安装工程以外的产值。包括房屋构筑物修理产值、非标准设备制造产值、总包企业向分包企业收取的管理费以及不能明确划分的施工活动所完成的产值。

a.房屋构筑物修理产值:指房屋和构筑物修理所完成的产值,但不包括被修理房屋、构筑物本身价值和生产设备的修理产值。

b.非标准设备制造产值:指加工制造没有定型的非标准生产设备的加工费和原材料价值(如化工厂、炼油厂用的各种罐、槽,矿井生产统一使用的各种漏斗、三角槽、阀门等) 以及附属加工厂为本企业承建工程制作的非标准设备的价值。

按建筑业总产值计算的全员劳动生产率

即平均每个从事建筑业生产活动的人员的建筑业总产值,计算公式为:

按建筑业总产值计算的全员劳动生产率 = 建筑业总产值 / 计算建筑业劳动生产率的平均人数

计算建筑业劳动生产率的平均人数指建筑业企业报告期实际拥有的、与建筑施工活动有关的人员的平均人数,包括参加本企业建筑施工活动的非本企业人员,但不包括企业内部社会服务性机构的人员以及由本企业支付工资但所从事的工作与本企业生产基本无关的人员。

房屋建筑面积

指房屋全部平面面积的总和。它从房屋的外墙线算起,包括可供使用的有效面积和墙柱等结构占用面积。多层房屋按各层(包括地下室)面积总和计算。旧房加层或改造,只计算增加的建筑面积;旧房拆除重建,计算其全部面积;临时房屋不计算建筑面积。

房屋建筑施工面积

指报告期内施过工的全部房屋建筑面积,包括本期新开工的房屋面积、上期跨入本期继续施工的房屋面积、上期停缓建在本期恢复施工的房屋面积、本期竣工的房屋面积及本期施工后又停缓建的房屋面积。

房屋建筑竣工面积

指在报告期内房屋建筑按照设计要求已全部完工,达到了使用条件,经检查验收鉴定合格,正式移交使用单位的房屋建筑面积。

SHANGHAI STATISTICAL YEARBOOK

EXPLANATORY NOTES TO MAJOR STATISTICAL INDICATORS

□ Gross Output Value of Construction

Gross Output Value of Construction refers to total of construction products and services, expressed in money terms, produced of rendered by construction and installation enterprises during a given period of time. It includes:

(1) Output value of construction projects: the value of projects covered by the project budgets;

(2) Output value of installation projects: the value of the installation of equipments, (excluding the value of the equipment to be installed);

(3) Other output values: the output value of construction industry apart from that of construction projects and installation projects. It includes: output value of repair of buildings and structures; output value of non-standard equipment manufacturing; overhead expenses received by contracted enterprises from the sub-contracted enterprises and the complete output value of construction activities for which there is no clear definition.

a. Output value of repair of buildings and structures: the value created through the repair of buildings and structures. It doesn't include the value of buildings or structures being repaired and the value of the repair of production equipment;

b. Output value of manufactured non-standard equipment: the value of non-standard production equipment, including raw materials and manufacturing cost, made for the project (i.e., chemical plant; kettles or tanks used by refineries; various fillers, triangle tanks, valves used by mines). It also includes the output value of equipment manufactured by subsidiary workshops.

□ All-personnel Labor Productivity Calculated by Gross Output Value of Construction Industry

All-personnel labor productivity calculated by gross output value of construction industry refers to the average gross output value of construction industry by every personnel engaged in production activities in the construction industry.

All-personnel labor Productivity Calculated by Gross Output Value of Construction Industry = Gross Output Value of Construction Industry / Average Number of Construction Industry

Average Number of Construction Industry refers to average number of personals that construction enterprises actually have and related to construction activities, includes those engaged in the construction activities of the enterprises but belong to other enterprises, and excludes those work for the social service institutions inside the enterprise and those paid by the enterprise but whose work has nothing to with the construction.

□ Floor Space of Buildings

Floor Space of Buildings under Construction refers to total floor space of the horizontal section of outer walls above the plinth of the building, including the effective area and the area occupied by the structure. Multi-storey building refers to the sum of each storey, including the basement. The old buildings with storey added or rebuild only calculate the floor space added. The old buildings after dismantling and reconstruction calculate the total floor space. The tabernacle calculates no floor space.

□ Floor Space of Buildings Under Construction

Floor Space of Buildings under Construction refers to floor space of buildings under construction during the reference period, including newly started buildings, buildings started earlier and continued during the reference period, and buildings suspended earlier but restarted during the reference period, buildings completed during the reference period, and buildings under construction and then suspended during the reference period.

□ Floor Space of Buildings Completed

Floor Space of Buildings Completed refers to the floor space of buildings that are completed in the reference period in accordance with the requirements of the design, up to the standard for putting them into use, and have been checked and accepted by concerned departments as qualified ones.

第十四篇

CHAPTER 14

交通运输、邮政和信息传输

TRANSPORTATION, POSTS AND INFORMATION TRANSMISSION

表 14.1 主要年份运输线路长度
LENGTHS OF TRAFFIC LINES IN MAIN YEARS

指 标	Indicators	2000	2009	2010
铁路运输	**Railway**			
运营里程(公里)	Operation Mileage (km)	257	309	414
正线延展里程(公里)	Mainline Railway Length Extended (km)	397	457	697
公路运输	**Highway**			
通车里程(公里)	Operation Mileage(km)	5 970	11 671	11 974
#高速公路	High Speed Highways	98	768	775
内河航道	**Navigable Inland Waterways**			
航道里程(公里)	Length of Navigable Inland Waterways (km)	2 100	2 138	2 110

表 14.2 主要年份交通运输主要指标
MAJOR INDICATORS OF TRANSPORTATION IN MAIN YEARS

指 标	Indicators	2000	2009	2010
公路运输	**Highway Transportation**			
货运汽车每车吨年产量（万吨·公里）	Annual Tonnage of Each Ton-wagon (10 000 tons · km)	1.50	1.93	2.01
汽油车耗油（升/百吨·公里）	Oil Consumption of Gasoline Trucks (litre/100 tons · km)	6.87	5.23	5.5
柴油车耗油（升/百吨·公里）	Oil Consumption of Diesel Trucks (litre/100 tons · km)	4.77	6.04	6.07
港 口	**Harbor**			
船舶平均在港停泊时间（天）	Average Days of Vessel Berthed at Harbor (day)	0.9	0.4	0.4
机 场	**Aviation**			
起降航班数(万架次)	Aircraft Movements(sortie)		47.67	55.11
进出港旅客人次(万人次)	Passenger Turnover(10000 person-times)		5 699.96	7 187.74
#国内航线	Domestic Flight		4 089.65	5 106.96
国际及地区航线	International and Regional Flight		1 610.31	2 080.78

注：本页数据由上海铁路局、市城市交通和港口管理局、上海机场集团等单位提供。
Note: Data on this page are provided by Shanghai Railway Bureau, Shanghai Municipal Transport and Port Authority , Shanghai Airport Group.

表 14.3 主要年份旅客发送量
PASSENGER DEPARTING IN MAIN YEARS

单位:万人次(10 000 person-times)

年 份 Year	旅客发送量 Passenger Departures	其 中 of which			
		铁 路 Railway	公 路 Highway	港 口 Harbor	民用航空 Civil Aviation
1990	3 835	2 476	605	555	199
1995	5 265	2 929	1 257	512	567
1996	5 822	2 804	1 974	422	622
1997	6 057	2 779	2 277	328	673
1998	6 139	2 760	2 006	678	695
1999	6 406	2 906	2 178	581	741
2000	6 893	2 980	2 482	539	892
2001	6 324	3 231	1 508	543	1 042
2002	7 326	3 518	2 046	526	1 236
2003	7 212	3 391	2 052	528	1 241
2004	8 968	4 076	2 465	621	1 806
2005	9 487	4 313	2 468	626	2 080
2006	9 619	4 458	2 784	68	2 309
2007	10 371	4 795	2 872	95	2 609
2008	10 927	5 339	2 934	89	2 565
2009	11 136	5 161	2 995	90	2 890
2010	13 432	6 095	3 634	90	3 613

①2000 年前旅客发送量是专业运输部门的数字，2001 年开始改为跨省市旅客运输的行业统计数字。
②港口旅客发送量从 2006 年起口径不包含海港到内河部分。
❶The passenger departures volume before 2000 is based on the figures for special traffic departments and the volume since 2001 is based on the figures for the inter-provincial passenger transport industries.
❷The volume of passenger departures excludes those from seaports to freshwater since 2006.

表 14.4 主要年份旅客周转量
TURNOVER VOLUME OF PASSENGER TRAFFIC IN MAIN YEARS

单位:亿人・公里 (100 million persons・km)

年 份 Year	旅客周转量 Turnover Volume of Passenger Traffic	其 中 of which			
		铁 路 Railway	公 路 Highway	水 运 Waterway	民用航空 Civil Aviation
1990	113.94	26.85	8.42	40.84	37.84
1995	170.98	34.18	8.23	31.71	96.86
1996	171.81	31.49	8.83	24.13	107.36
1997	181.99	31.44	12.61	16.52	121.42
1998	199.15	30.68	12.07	9.97	146.43
1999	217.95	34.18	15.81	7.94	160.02
2000	234.72	35.40	16.44	6.77	176.11
2001	286.93	37.81	42.31	5.48	201.30
2002	332.12	39.48	50.43	4.41	237.80
2003	353.62	38.10	58.00	4.65	252.88
2004	599.62	46.35	72.09	4.49	476.70
2005	663.93	48.86	75.06	4.52	535.48
2006	742.87	51.23	86.85	4.52	600.28
2007	883.25	51.34	94.02	6.10	731.79
2008	869.07	53.18	94.07	6.73	715.09
2009	1 002.59	51.12	99.57	6.38	845.52
2010	1 214.25	60.16	115.44	3.69	1 034.96

注：本页数据由上海铁路局、市交通运输和港口管理局、上海机场集团等单位提供。
Note: Data on this page are provided by Shanghai Railway Bureau, Shanghai Municipal Transport and Port Authority, Shanghai Airport Group.

表 14.5 主要年份货物运输量
FREIGHT TRAFFIC VOLUME IN MAIN YEARS

单位:万吨(10 000 tons)

年 份 Year	货物运输量 Freight Traffic Volume	其 中 of which				
		铁 路 Railway	公 路 Highway	水 运 Waterway	其 中 of which #远洋运输 Ocean Shipping	民用航空 Civil Aviation
1990	22 848	1 257	8 714	12 864	2 246	13
1995	22 531	1 376	6 273	14 845	2 778	37
1996	40 928	1 320	25 023	14 544	3 594	41
1997	41 373	1 252	25 991	14 082	4 201	48
1998	42 090	1 152	26 352	14 529	4 844	57
1999	44 485	997	27 171	16 241	5 783	76
2000	47 954	1 055	28 369	18 442	7 022	88
2001	49 545	1 080	28 869	19 496	7 129	100
2002	54 196	1 131	29 759	23 174	7 210	132
2003	58 669	1 208	30 678	26 621	7 832	162
2004	63 180	1 284	31 554	30 148	8 603	194
2005	68 741	1 278	32 684	34 557	10 091	222
2006	72 617	1 223	33 799	37 342	11 766	253
2007	78 108	1 143	35 634	41 041	12 575	290
2008	84 347	985	40 328	42 729	12 197	305
2009	76 967	941	37 745	37 983	11 916	298
2010	81 024	959	40 890	38 803	15 172	372

①2005 年起民航货物吞吐量不包括旅客行李。
②2008 年，公路货运量为交通部公路运输专项调查数据。
❶The Freight Traffic Volume of civil aviation in 2005 doesn't include the freight transportation volume.
❷The Highway Freight Traffic Volume of 2008 refers to the result of highway transportation special investigation hold by Ministry of Communications.

表 14.6 主要年份货物周转量
TURNOVER VOLUME OF FREIGHT TRAFFIC IN MAIN YEARS

单位:亿吨·公里(100 million tons·km)

年 份 Year	货物周转量 Turnover Volume of Freight Traffic	其 中 of which				
		铁 路 Railway	公 路 Highway	水 运 Waterway	其 中 of which #远洋运输 Ocean Shipping	民用航空 Civil Aviation
1990	3 359	111	11	3 236	1 957	1
1995	4 187	143	9	4 030	2 259	5
1996	3 814	133	49	3 627	2 721	5
1997	4 016	123	47	3 840	3 049	6
1998	4 838	117	49	4 665	3 794	7
1999	5 606	113	51	5 432	4 020	10
2000	6 620	122	56	6 430	5 285	12
2001	6 992	113	60	6 808	5 511	11
2002	7 472	100	65	7 295	5 674	12
2003	8 587	118	69	8 385	6 376	15
2004	10 036	42	71	9 899	7 486	24
2005	12 132	47	73	11 986	9 285	27
2006	13 837	55	80	13 683	10 817	19
2007	15 949	35	85	15 789	12 039	40
2008	16 031	29	253	15 712	11 529	37
2009	14 436	25	244	14 118	10 596	49
2010	16 173	26	266	15 818	14 535	63

①2004 年起，上海铁路分局改为上海铁路局，货物周转量数据有所调整。
②2006 年民航货物周转量未包括中国货运航空公司的数据。
③2008 年，公路货物周转量为交通部公路运输专项调查数据。
④本页数据由上海铁路局、市交通运输和港口管理局、上海机场集团等单位提供。
❶Since 2004, Shanghai Railway Branch Bureau has been change into Shanghai Railway Bureau ,the turnover volume of freight has been adjusted accordingly.
❷In 2006,the date of China Cargo Airlines wasn't included in the turnover volume of freight of aviation .
❸The highway freight turnover volume of 2008 refers to the result of highway transportation special investigation hold by Ministry of Communications.
❹Data on this page are provided by Shanghai Railway Bureau, Shanghai Municipal Transport and Port Authority, Shanghai Airport Group.

表 14.7 主要年份港口码头情况
PORTS IN MAIN YEARS

年份 Year	沿海码头长度（万米）Length of Harbor (10 000 m)	沿海泊位（个）Berths (unit)	其中 of which #万吨级 10 000 Tonnage	其中 of which #集装箱泊位 Container Berths
1990	1.77	122	64	7
1995	1.90	140	68	12
1996	1.90	138	69	12
1997	1.96	142	71	12
1998	7.58	1 108	109	13
1999	7.69	1 110	113	18
2000	7.64	1 098	111	18
2001	7.67	1 087	112	18
2002	7.92	1 096	115	20
2003	8.76	1 202	125	24
2004	8.90	1 198	123	24
2005	8.95	1 181	124	28
2006	9.16	1 140	131	32
2007	10.15	1 155	133	37
2008	11.49	1 203	137	42
2009	11.68	1 145	148	38
2010	11.92	1 218	157	45

注：1997 年以前，码头长度、泊位为原港务局数据，从 1998 年后，为全港数据。
Note: Before 1997, the figures of length of harbor and berths were from the ports belonged Port Administration Bureau, and after 1998, they have been collected from all types of ports.

表 14.8 主要年份港口货物吞吐量
PORT FREIGHT THROUGHPUT IN MAIN YEARS

单位：万吨（10 000 tons）

年份 Year	港口货物吞吐量 Port freight Throughput	其中 of which 内贸 Internal Trade	外贸 Foreign Trade	进港 Arrival	其中 of which 内贸 Internal Trade	外贸 Foreign Trade	出港 Departure	其中 of which 内贸 Internal Trade	外贸 Foreign Trade
1990	13 959	11 366	2 593	9 461	7 592	1 869	4 498	3 774	724
1995	16 567	12 481	4 086	12 097	9 492	2 605	4 470	2 989	1 481
1996	16 401	12 265	4 136	11 947	9 266	2 681	4 454	3 000	1 454
1997	16 397	11 684	4 713	11 852	8 921	2 931	4 545	2 763	1 782
1998	16 387	11 483	4 904	11 839	8 815	3 024	4 548	2 669	1 879
1999	18 641	12 356	6 285	12 936	9 037	3 899	5 705	3 319	2 386
2000	20 440	12 807	7 633	13 791	9 242	4 549	6 649	3 565	3 084
2001	22 099	13 446	8 653	14 922	9 706	5 216	7 177	3 740	3 437
2002	26 384	15 776	10 609	17 444	11 096	6 349	8 940	4 680	4 260
2003	31 621	18 653	12 968	20 606	12 999	7 607	11 015	5 654	5 361
2004	37 897	22 061	15 836	24 113	15 022	9 091	13 784	7 039	6 745
2005	44 317	25 825	18 492	27 539	17 441	10 098	16 778	8 384	8 394
2006	53 748	32 480	21 268	34 600	23 613	10 987	19 148	8 867	10 281
2007	56 144	30 574	25 570	35 479	22 619	12 860	20 665	7 956	12 709
2008	58 170	30 793	27 377	36 481	22 782	13 699	21 689	8 012	13 677
2009	59 205	33 394	25 811	39 000	24 920	14 080	20 205	8 474	11 731
2010	65 339	35 114	30 225	41 549	25 083	16 466	23 791	10 032	13 759

注：本表数据由上海港务集团提供。
Note: Data in this table is provided by Shanghai International Port Group.

表 14.9 主要年份国际集装箱吞吐量(按进出港分)
INTERNATIONAL CONTAINERS AND CARGO THROUGHPUT OF FOREIGN TRADE IN MAIN YEARS

年 份 Year	国际标准集装箱吞吐量重量(万吨) Weight of International Containers (10 000 tons)	国际标准集装箱吞吐量(万 TEU) International Containers (10 000 TEU)	其 中 of which	
			进 港 Input	出 港 Output
1990	446	45.6	22.4	23.2
1995	1 389	152.6	69.3	83.3
1996	1 785	197.1	92.4	104.7
1997	2 304	252.8	114.7	138.1
1998	2 766	306.6	141.1	165.5
1999	3 949	421.6	196.7	224.9
2000	5 170	561.2	266.1	295.1
2001	5 911	634.0	305.4	328.6
2002	7 822	861.2	414.1	447.1
2003	10 225	1 128.3	544.4	583.8
2004	13 294	1 455.4	699.6	755.8
2005	16 250	1 808.4	887.2	921.3
2006	19 595	2 171.9	1 064.4	1 107.5
2007	23 850	2 615.2	1 276.3	1 338.9
2008	25 992	2 800.6	1 397.8	1 402.8
2009	24 619	2 500.2	1 222.9	1 277.3
2010	27 992	2 906.9	1 436.1	1 470.8

①TEU 是"折合 20 英尺标准箱"英文缩写语。
②本表数据由市交通运输和港口管理局提供。
❶TEU is the abbreviation, which refers to 20 – foot equivalent unit.
❷Data in this table are provided by Shanghai Municipal Transport and Port Authority.

表 14.10 集装箱吞吐量(按内外贸航线分)(2010)
CONTAINER THROUGHPUT OF INTERNAL AND FOREIGN TRADE FLIGHT COURSES

指 标	Indicators	合 计(万 TEU) Total (10 000 TEU)	其 中 of which		重 量(万吨) Werght (10 000 tons)	其 中 of which
			空 箱 Empty Van	重 箱 Loaded Van		#货 重 Weight of Goods
国际标准集装箱吞吐量	International Standard Container Throughput	2 907	786	2 121	27 992	22 261
#洋山深水港区	Yangshan Deep Water Port	1 011	275	736	8 888	6 931
进 港	Arrival	1 436	631	805	13 163	10 305
国际航线	International Flight	1 079	563	517	8 346	6 211
内支线	Domestic Lateral Flight	170	13	156	2 030	1 696
内贸线	Internal Trade Flight	187	55	132	2 787	2 398
出 港	Departure	1 471	154	1 316	14 829	11 956
国际航线	International Flight	1 121	26	1 094	10 759	8 600
内支线	Domestic Lateral Flight	160	51	109	1 766	1 452
内贸线	Internal Trade Flight	190	77	113	2 304	1 904

注：本表数据由上海港码头管理中心提供。
Note: Data in this table are provided by Shanghai Port Management Center.

表 14.11 经营性停车场(库)营运情况(2008～2010)
STATISTICS OF PARKING LOTS (GARAGES) OPERATION

指 标	Indicators	2008	2009	2010
计时停放(万辆次)	Time Parking (10 000 vehicletimes)	6 596	7 532	8 585
包停放(万辆次)	Monthly Parking (10 000 vehicletimes)	2 586	2 520	2 913
车辆停放车次合计(万辆次)	Quantity of Parking Times (10 000 vehicletimes)	9 181	10 052	11 498
经营车辆停放收入(亿元)	Revenue of Parking Lots (100 million yuan)	9.07	9.81	10.81

注：本表数据由市交通运输和港口管理局提供。
Note: Data on this table are provided by Shanghai Municipal Transport and Port Authority.

表 14.12 民用车辆拥有量(2008～2010)
CIVIL MOTOR VEHICLES

单位:万辆(10 000 vehicles)

指 标	Indicators	2008	2009	2010
总 计	**Total**	**261.50**	**285.00**	**309.70**
#汽 车	Civil Automobile	132.31	147.30	170.25
载客汽车	Passenger Vehicles	110.73	124.90	146.24
#轿 车	Cars	82.96	95.10	111.52
载货汽车	Freight Trucks	21.39	22.19	23.81
其他汽车	Other Automobile	0.19	0.20	0.20
摩托车	Motorcycle	127.37	128.64	129.12
拖拉机	Tractors	1.13	1.15	1.16

注：本表不包括军用车辆和码头、机场等专用特种车辆。
Note: Data in this table doesn't include the quantity of military vehicles and special vehicles for port and airport.

表 14.13 个人民用车辆拥有量(2008～2010)
INDIVIDUAL CIVIL MOTOR VEHICLES

单位:万辆(10 000 vehicles)

指 标	Indicators	2008	2009	2010
总 计	**Total**	**196.03**	**210.42**	**229.83**
#汽 车	Civil Automobile	72.21	85.19	103.85
载客汽车	Passenger Vehicles	71.99	84.95	103.57
#轿 车	Cars	59.69	71.06	86.54
载货汽车	Freight Trucks	0.05	0.08	0.11
其它汽车	Other Automobile	0.17	0.16	0.17
摩托车	Motorcycle	123.82	125.22	125.95

注：本页数据由上海市公安局车管所提供，拖拉机数据由市农机办提供。
Note: Data on this page are provided by Shanghai Land-carriage Administration and the data of tractors are provided by Civil Agricultural Engineering Office.

表 14.14 邮政电信主要指标(2008～2010)
MAIN INDICATORS OF POST AND TELECOMMUNICATION

	指 标 Indicators	2008	2009	2010
邮电局、所(个)	Post Office (unit)	661	631	593
报刊图书销售点(个)	Publications Sales Outlet (unit)	2 175	2 128	1 868
邮政信筒信箱(个)	Mail Boxe (unit)	3 756	3 673	3 568
集邮品销售点(个)	Stamps Sales Outlet (unit)	358	356	376
邮政储蓄网点(个)	Postal Savings Office (unit)	447	368	371
邮路条数(条)	Number of Mail Route (route)	942	998	521
邮路总长度(万公里)	Total Length of Mail Routes (10 000 km)	26.18	27.82	5.23
农村投递路线总长度(万公里)	Length of Rural Delivery Routes (10 000 km)	2.62	3.28	2.36
长途电话业务电路(2M)	Long Distance Call Line (2M)	184 522	259 156	272 645
长途光缆线路长度(公里)	Long-distance Cable (km)	4 333	4 297	4 670

①本表数据由上海市邮政公司提供。
②由于邮政速递物流公司成立，邮政公司的部分基础设施被拨出。
❶Data in this table are provided by Shanghai Post Corporation.
❷The part of post infrastructure are transferred from Shanghai Post Corporation to newly established Shanghai Post Express and Logistics Corporation.

表 14.15 主要年份邮政业务主要指标
MAJOR INDICATORS OF POSTAL BUSINESS IN MAIN YEARS

	指 标 Indicators	2000	2009	2010
邮政业务总量(亿元)	Volume of Postal Business (100 million yuan)	22.40	68.60	49.48
函 件(亿件)	Mails (100 million units)	4.61	12.98	11.66
国内特快专递(万件)	Domestic Express Mails (10 000 pieces)	709.90	3 588.30	56 198.07
国际特快专递(万件)	International Express Mails (10 000 pieces)	52.10	513.60	507.20
邮政储蓄期末余额(亿元)	Postal Saving Deposit Balance (100 million yuan)	153.50	709.70	545.64
报纸、杂志累计订销数(亿份)	Total Copies of Newspapers and Magazines Subscribed and Sold (100 million pieces)	11.30	11.83	11.57
集邮业务(万枚)	Stamp Collection Business (10 000 stamps)	9 467	3 839	5 156

①本表数据由上海市邮政公司、上海市邮政局提供。
②2010 年起，"国内特快专递"和"国际特快专递"数据包括邮政业企业和年业务收入 200 万元以上的快递企业。
❶Data in this table are provided by Shanghai Post Corporation and Shanghai Municipal Post Bureau.
❷Since 2010, data of Domestic Express Mails and International Express Mails are included post interprise and express corporation of annual revenue above 2 million yuan.

表 14.16 主要年份电信业务主要指标
MAJOR INDICATORS OF TELECOM BUSINESS IN MAIN YEARS

指标	Indicators	2005	2009	2010
电信业务总量(亿元)	Volume of Telecom Business (100 million yuan)	375.77	806.86	966.96
年末固定电话用户 (万户)	Year-end Installed Telephones (10 000 households)	966.70	935.48	935.91
#住宅电话	Household Phones Installed	685.00	616.24	574.52
移动电话用户 (万户)	Mobile Phone Subscribers Users (10 000 households)	1 444.20	2 106.32	2 361.55
长途通话时长 (亿分钟)	Long-distance Call Lasting Time (100 million minutes)	110.10	190.86	205.77
固定电话长途通话时长	Installed Telephone Domestic Long-distance Call Lasting Time	31.20	27.07	38.84
国内长途电话通话时长	Domestic Trunk Calls	29.90	26.29	36.67
国际及港澳台电话通话时长	Overseas Calls	1.30	0.78	2.17
移动电话长途通话时长	Mobile Telephone Long-distance Call Lasting Time	19.60	32.28	37.37
国内长途电话通话时长	Domestic Trunk Calls	18.70	30.11	36.00
国际及港澳台电话通话时长	Overseas Calls	0.90	2.17	1.37
IP 电话通话时长	IP Telephone Long-distance Call Lasting Time	59.2	131.51	129.56
国内长途电话通话时长	Domestic Trunk Calls	55.8	127.81	127.11
国际及港澳台电话通话时长	Overseas Calls	3.4	3.7	2.45
移动电话通话时长 (亿分钟)	Mobile Calls (100 million minutes)	290.10	877.89	1 012.39
本地通话时长	Local Calls	270.50	845.58	975.02
长途通话时长	Long-listanve	19.60	32.31	37.37
移动短信业务量(亿条)	Volume of Mobile Short Messages (100 million pieces)	180.60	328.97	371.54
局用交换机容量 (含接入网设备容量) (万门)	Capacity of Office Telephone Exchanges(Including Access Network Capacity) (10 000 units)	1 357.00	1 386.35	1 338.61
移动电话交换机容量(万户)	Mobile Phone Exchange Capacity (10 000 households)	1 991	3 488	3 995

注：本表数据由市通信管理局提供。
Note: Data in this table are provided by Shanghai Municipal Communications Administration.

表 14.17 主要年份邮电通信水平
POSTAL AND TELECOM LEVEL IN MAIN YEARS

指 标	Indicators	2005	2009	2010
固定电话普及率（%）	Popularity Rate of Telephone Line（%）	56.1	48.7	40.8
住宅电话普及率（%）	Popularity Rate of Household Telephone（%）	137.9	120.9	110.6
移动电话普及率(%)	Popularity Rate of Mobile Telephone（%）	81.0	109.6	103.1
平均每一邮政局所服务面积(平方公里)	Average Area Served by One Post Office（sq. km）	10.00	10.05	10.69
平均每一邮政局所服务人口(万人)	Average Population Served by Every Post Office (10 000 persons)	2.99	3.04	3.86
人均每年发函件数(件)	Average Number of Letters Mailed（piece）	48	59	51
人均每年购报刊数(份)	Average Number of Newspaper and Magazine Purchased（piece）	61	54	52

表 14.18 主要年份信息化基础设施情况
INFRASTRUCTURE OF INFORMATIZATION IN MAIN YEARS

指 标	Indicators	2005	2009	2010
长途光缆线路长度(公里)	Long-distance Cable（km）	5 141	4 297	4 670
信息通信管线长度(沟公里)	Length of Information Communication Pielines（channel km）	1 621	5 354	5 821
卫星站点(个)	Satellite Station（unit）	925	772	770
本地信息交互流量(万亿字节)	Local Information Exchange Flow（TB）	1 300	2 950	2 900
国际互联网用户(万人)	Users of Internet（10 000 persons）	803	1 250	1 560
互联网用户普及率(%)	Users of Internet per Hundred People（%）	45.2	65.1	68.1
宽带接入用户(万户)	Broadband Access Users（10 000 households）	247.40	470.32	517.4
#家庭宽带	Household Users of broadband access	222.66	423.28	440
家庭宽带接入用户普及率(%)	Household Users of broadband access per hundred household（%）	33.8	60.6	61.8
IPTV 用户(万户)	IPTV Users（10 000 households）		101	130
有线数字电视用户(万户)	Digital Cable TV Users（10 000 households）		84.36	220

注：本表数据由市经济和信息化委员会提供。
Note：Data in this table are provided by Shanghai Municipal Economic and Information Commissiom.

表 14.19 主要年份信息服务业经营情况
OPERATION OF INFORMATION SERVICE INDUSTRY IN MAIN YEARS

指标	Indicators	2005	2009	2010
信息服务业经营收入(亿元)	Operating Revenue of Information Service Industry (100 million yuan)	905.06	1 700.03	1 978.51
#计算机服务及软件业	Computer Service & Software Industry	390.09	965.77	1 145.10
信息服务业从业人员(万人)	Employees of Information Service Industry (10 000 persons)	18.81	29.42	31.20
#计算机服务及软件业	Computer Service & Software Industry	12.70	21.84	23.25

表 14.20 信息技术应用(2008～2010)
APPLICATION OF INFORMATION TECHNOLOGY

指标	Indicators	2008	2009	2010
社会公共服务领域信息化	**Informatization of Public Service**			
"市民信箱"累计注册用户(万人)	Accumulative Registered Users of Citizen Mail Box(10 000 persons)	361.20	385.46	399.00
"付费通"业务平台交易量(万笔)	All-year Exchange Volum of FFT(10 000 units)	3 801.50	4 649.81	7 483.10
"付费通"业务平台交易额(亿元)	All-year Exchange Value of FFT(100 million yuan)	35.48	46.53	62.40
交通卡累计销售量(万张)	Accumulative Volum of Traffic Card (10 000 pieces)	4 161.49	4 944.28	6 486.28
交通卡销售额(亿元)	All-year Sales Value of Traffic Card (100 million yuan)	13.41	11.94	26.00
银行卡累计发卡量(万张)	Accumulative Volum of Bank Card (10 000 pieces)	7 915.22	10 009.93	11 427.54
银行卡交易额(亿元)	All-year Exchange Value of Bank Card (100 million yuan)	6 918.92	9 517.10	11 306.30
#持卡消费金额	Consumption Value with Bank Card	2 486.72	4 200.08	4 963.76
社会信用体系	**Social Credit System**			
个人信用信息入库量(万条)	Newly Recorded Individual Credit Information (10 000 pieces)	1 047	1 110	1 138
个人信用报告累计出具数量(万份)	Accumulative Provided Volum of Individual Credit Information Report (10 000 pieces)	862	911	1 461
企业信用信息入库量(万家)	Newly Recorded Enterprise Credit Information (10 000 units)	98	98	98

注：本表数据由市经济和信息化委员会提供。
Note: Data in this table are provided by Shanghai Municipal Economic and Informution Commissiom.

上/海/统/计/年/鉴

主要统计指标解释

■ 铁路运营里程

铁路运营里程又称营业长度（包括正式营业和临时营业里程），指办理客货运输业务的铁路正线总长度。凡是全线或部分建成双线及以上的线路，以第一线的实际长度计算；复线、站线、段管线、岔线和特殊用途线以及不计算运费的联络线都不计算营业里程。铁路营业里程是反映铁路运输业基础设施发展水平的重要指标，也是计算客货周转量、运输密度和机车车辆运用效率等指标的基础资料。

■ 内河航道里程

内河航道里程也称内河通航里程，指在一定时期内，能通航运输船舶及排筏的天然河流、湖泊水库、运河及通航渠道的长度。包括全年季节性通航累计三个月以上的航道，不包括仅供零散流放竹、木排的河道。该指标可以反映内河水运网的规模、水平和发展情况。

■ 货物（旅客）周转量

指在一定时期内，由各种运输工具运送的货物（旅客）数量与其相应运输距离的乘积之总和，是反映运输业生产总成果的重要指标，也是编制和检查运输生产计划，计算运输效益、劳动生产率以及核算运输单位成本的主要基础资料。通常以吨公里和人公里为计算单位。计算货物周转量通常按发出站与到达站之间的最短距离，也就是计费距离计算。

■ 货（客）运量

指在一定时期内，各种运输工具实际运送的货物（旅客）数量。它是反映运输业为国民经济和人民生活服务的数量指标，也是制定和检查运输生产计划、研究运输发展规模和速度的重要指标。货运按吨计算，客运按人计算。货物不论运输距离长短、货物类别，均按实际重量统计。旅客不论行程远近或票价多少，均按一人一次客运量统计；半价票、小孩票也按一人统计。

■ 港口货物吞吐量

指经水运进出港区范围，并经过装卸的货物数量，包括邮件及办理托运手续的行李、包裹以及补给运输船舶的燃、物料和淡水。货物吞吐量按货物流向分为进口、出口吞吐量，按货物交流性质分为外贸货物吞吐量和国内贸易货物吞吐量。货物吞吐量的货类构成及其流向，是衡量港口生产能力大小的重要指标。

■ 国际标准集装箱吞吐量

凡经过水运进、出港区范围，并经过装卸的集装箱箱数和重量（含集装箱自重），通常是按进港和出港分别统计。

TEU 是“折合 20 英尺标准箱”的英文缩写。它是指各种尺寸的国际标准集装箱的自然箱数，按各自的换算比例，折算为 20 英尺标准箱的换算箱数。其换算比例为：40 英尺箱 1：2；35 英尺箱 1：1.75；20 英尺箱 1：1；10 英尺箱 1：0.5。

■ 民用车辆拥有量

指报告期末，在公安交通管理部门按照《机动车注册登记工作规范》，已注册登记领有民用车辆牌照的全部汽车数量。汽车拥有量统计的主要分类：根据汽车结构分为载客汽车、载货汽车及其他汽车；根据汽车所有者不同分为个人（私人）汽车、单位汽车；根据汽车的使用性质分为营运汽车、非营运汽车和特种汽车；根据汽车大小规格不同载客汽车分为大型、中型、小型和微型，载货汽车分为重型、中型、轻型和微型。

■ 邮政业务总量

指以货币表现的邮政部门用于邮政服务的总数量。它综合反映了一定时期邮政工作的总成果，是研究邮政业务量构成和发展趋势的重要指标。它用各种邮政分类业务量，如函件件数、电报份数、订销报刊累计份数等，分别乘以相应的平均单位（不变价），加总后再加上其他业务收入求得。

■ 住宅电话用户

指安装在居民住宅或农民家里并按照住宅电话用户登记注册和收费的电话用户。包括私人付费、单位付费和按规定免费安装的住宅电话用户。

■ 移动电话用户

指通过移动电话交换机进入移动电话网、占用移动电话号码的电话用户。用户数量以报告期末在移动电话

主要统计指标解释

营业部门实际办理登记手续进入移动电话网的户数进行计算,一部移动电话统计为一户。

分组交换用户

指在公用交换数据网上接通的，在邮电部门办理登记手续的数据传输用户，不论其使用终端设备型号和传输速率,均按户统计。

局用交换机容量

指安装在电信企业用于接续本地固定电话的电话交换机容量。

SHANGHAI STATISTICAL YEARBOOK

EXPLANATORY NOTES TO MAJOR STATISTICAL INDICATORS

□ Operation Mileage of Railways

Operation Mileage of Railways refers to the total length of the trunk line under passenger and freight transportation (including both full operation and temporary operation). The calculation is based on the actual length of the first line even if this line has a full or partial double track or more tracks, excluding double tracks, station sidings, tracks under the charge of stations, branch lines, special-purpose lines and the non-payable connecting lines. The length of railways in operation is an important indicator to show the development of the infrastructure for the railway transport, and also the essential data to calculate volume of passenger freight transport, traffic density and utilization efficiency of the locomotives and carriages.

□ Length of Navigable Inland Waterways

Length of Navigable Inland Waterways it is an indicator reflecting the size and development of inland water network, it refers to the length of the natural rivers, lakes, reservoirs, canals, and ditches open to navigation during a given period, which enables the transport by ships and rafts. It includes the channels open to navigation for over an accumulative 3 months in a year, yet this does not include the river courses, which are only used to float odd logs and bamboo rafts. This indicator can reflect the scale, level and development situation of the inland waterway network.

□ Freight (Passenger) Turnover Volume

Freight (Passenger) Turnover Volume refers to the total of the product of the physical volume of transported cargo (passenger) by the transport distance, usually using ton/kilometer and person/kilometer as calculating units. Normally, the shortest distance between the departure point and the destination is the basis to calculate the freight turnover volume, that is to say, the payable distance. This is an important indicator to show the total results of the transport industry, to prepare and examine the transport plan and to measure the efficiency, the labor productivity and the unit cost of transport.

□ Freight (Passenger) Traffic

Freight (Passenger) Traffic refers to the volume of freight (passenger) transported with various means. The freight (passenger) traffic provides a quantitative measure to show how the transport industry serves the national economy and people, and is also an important indicator for planning the transport industry and for studying the development scale and speed of the transport industry. Freight transport is calculated in tons and passenger traffic is calculated in the number of persons. Despite the type of freight and travelling distance, the freight transport is calculated in the actual weight of the goods: and despite the travelling distance and ticket price, the passenger traffic is calculated by the principle that one person can be counted only once in one travel. The passenger who travels with a half price ticket or a child ticket is also calculated as one person.

□ Volume of Freight Handled in Ports

Volume of Freight Handled in Ports refers to the volume of cargo passing in and out the harbor area of the ports and having been loaded and unloaded. The volume includes that of the postal matters, registered luggage and fuels, materials and fresh water as supplies of the ships. The volume of freight handled may be classified by direction of flow as freight for import and freight for export, or by nature of cargo as freight for domestic trade and freight for foreign trade. As an important indicator, the volume of freight handled by type of cargo and by main flow direction reflects the production capacity of ports.

□ International Container Throughput Capacity

International Container Throughput Capacity refers to number and weight of containers which are loaded or unloaded within port area via water carriage. It is often calculated by entering and leaving port, respectively. TEU was the abbreviation of twenty foot equivalent unit, which refers to converted number of all kinds of containers. The conversion method is based on respective conversion ratio and the number of all kinds of container is converted to the standard number of twenty foot equivalent unit. The conversion ratio is: 40 feet container 1 : 2, 35 feet container 1 : 1.75, 20 feet container 1 : 1, 10 feet container 1 : 0.5.

□ Individual Civil Motor Vehicles

Individual Civil Motor Vehicles refers to the total numbers of vehicles that are registered and received vehicles' license tags ac-

EXPLANATORY NOTES TO MAJOR STATISTICAL INDICATORS

cording to the Work Standard for Motor Vehicles Registration formulated by transport management office under department of public security at the end of reference period. They are divided into following categories according to the structure of motor vehicles: passenger vehicles, trucks and others; and private vehicles and vehicles for units use according to ownerships; working vehicles, non-working vehicles and special motor vehicles according to kind of usage; large passenger vehicles, medium passenger vehicles and small passenger vehicles, heavy trucks, light -heavy trucks and light trucks according to sizes of vehicles.

□ Volume of Post Business

Volume of Post Business refers to the total amount of post services provided by the post department, which reflects the total achievements by the post departments during a given period of time in a comprehensive way, and is an important indicator to study the composition and development of the post business. It is arrived by first multiplying the business volume of different types, such as number of letters, telegrams and accumulated number of newspaper and journals subscribed and sold, etc. by their respective average unit price (fixed price) and then adding these products together, plus the income from other business revenues.

□ Household Telephone Subscribers

Household Telephone Subscribers refer to telephone sets installed in the dwelling units of urban or rural residents, and registered as residence subscribers for payment, including 3 types of payment for the service: private payment, public payment and free service.

□ Mobile Phone Subscribers

Mobile Phone Subscribers refer to the persons who own mobile telephone numbers and are connected with the mobile telephone communication network through the mobile telephone switchboards. The number of subscribers is calculated by the subscribers who have completed registration at mobile communication business centers and entered into the mobile telephone network. One mobile telephone is taken as a user.

□ Group Exchange Users

Group Exchange Users refer to the data transmission users who log on to the public exchange data network and have registered with the post and telecommunications authority. They are counted as a subscriber whatever the size of the terminal equipment or the transmission rate.

□ Capacity of Office Telephone Exchanges

Capacity of Office Telephone Exchanges refers to the capacity of telephone exchanges installed in the office of telecommunication service providers for communication between fixed telephones.

第十五篇

CHAPTER 15

批发和零售

WHOLESALE AND RETAIL

表 15.1 批发零售贸易业、餐饮业从业人员(1978～2010)
EMPLOYEES OF WHOLESALES, RETAILERS AND CATERING

年 份 Year	从业人员 (万人) Employees (10 000 persons)	其 中 of which			
		批发零售贸易业 Wholesale and Retail	其 中 of which		餐饮业 Catering
			批发业 Wholesale	零售业 Retail	
1978	39.62	30.70	5.46	25.24	5.57
1979	44.70	32.94	7.87	25.07	5.82
1980	45.78	33.94	7.91	26.03	5.66
1981	48.47	35.31	8.41	26.90	6.25
1982	50.24	36.70	9.05	27.65	6.51
1983	51.30	37.64	8.86	28.78	6.51
1984	55.24	40.57	8.81	31.76	6.86
1985	62.64	45.41	8.99	36.42	7.66
1986	63.76	44.98	8.96	36.02	7.97
1987	66.13	45.98	8.85	37.13	8.18
1988	72.80	50.89	9.42	41.47	8.67
1989	77.31	52.20	9.67	42.53	9.35
1990	74.75	50.48	8.19	42.29	9.33
1991	75.41	52.47	8.53	43.94	10.71
1992	87.27	63.71	13.74	49.97	10.98
1993	109.98	98.44	29.68	68.76	11.54
1994	88.51	77.49	27.58	49.91	11.02
1995	111.24	94.78	34.31	60.47	16.46
1996	145.67	122.21	50.79	71.42	23.46
1997	149.97	125.64	53.68	71.96	24.33
1998	150.96	126.56	53.67	72.89	24.40
1999	153.90	128.18	53.93	74.25	25.72
2000	154.32	128.41	53.79	74.62	25.91
2001	165.68	138.73	56.33	82.40	26.95
2002	179.34	152.19	65.40	86.79	27.15
2003	174.93	147.91	59.31	88.60	27.02
2004	181.25	156.21	74.77	81.44	25.04
2005	195.92	169.60	84.71	84.89	26.32
2006	203.51	174.49	86.32	88.17	29.02
2007	204.46	175.50	86.23	89.27	28.96
2008	202.84	172.72	87.98	84.74	30.12
2009	205.49	175.32	90.36	84.96	30.17
2010	207.94	176.69	91.58	85.21	31.25

注：本表从业人员是指本行业的全部从业人员。
Note: Employees in this table refer to all the employees in the sector.

表 15.2 限额以上批发贸易业产业活动单位和从业人员(2010)
QUANTITY OF BUSINESS UNITS AND EMPLOYEES OF WHOLESALE TRADE ABOVE THE SET SCALE

类 别	Types	法人企业(个) Quantity of Corporations (unit)	产业活动单位数(个) Quantity of Business Units (unit)	从业人员(人) Quantity of Employees (person)
总 计	**Total**	**4 144**	**6 093**	**261 171**
按登记注册类型分	**Grouped by Registration Categories**			
内资企业	Domestic Enterprises	3 181	4 853	153 370
国 有	State-owned	226	459	16 555
集 体	Collective-owned	66	96	4 834
私 营	Private	2 269	2 476	69 896
股份制	Share Holding	580	1 774	58 548
其他内资	Others	40	48	3 537
港澳台商投资	Hong Kong, Macao and Taiwan Funded	265	379	31 083
外商投资	Foreign Funded	698	861	76 718
按行业分	**Grouped By Sectors**			
农畜产品批发	Primary and Livestock Products	31	60	1 583
食品、饮料及烟草制品批发	Food, Beverage and Tabacco	260	829	32 852
#米、面制品及食用油批发	Rice, Flour and Cooking Oil	35	43	1 600
烟草制品批发	Tabacco	23	509	8 892
纺织、服装及日用品批发	Textile Products, Garments and Commodity	530	702	61 371
#服装批发	Garments	185	257	24 551
文化、体育用品及器材批发	Culture & Sports Articles and Equipments	106	129	7 132
医药及医疗器材批发	Medicines and Special Appliances of Medicines	154	178	20 886
矿产品、建材及化工产品批发	Mineral Products, Materials of Construction and Chemical Products	1 697	2 595	53 069
#煤炭及制品批发	Coal	77	87	2 258
石油及制品批发	Petroleum	121	751	14 240
金属及金属矿批发	Metal Products and Metal Minerals	834	887	16 494
建材批发	Building Materials	104	117	3 554
机械设备、五金交电及电子产品批发	Mechinery Equipments, Hardwares, Electric Appliances and Eletronic Products	1 035	1 226	65 321
#汽车、摩托车及零配件批发	Spare and Component Parts for Automobiles and Motorcycles	105	109	7 687
家用电器批发	Household Electrical Equipment	56	67	5 878
计算机、软件及辅助设备批发	Computers, Softwares and Accessorial Equipments	106	139	8 577
贸易经济与代理	Economic Trade and Agency	130	139	7 525
其他批发	Others	201	235	11 432

表 15.3 限额以上零售贸易业产业活动单位和从业人员（2010）
QUANTITY OF BUSINESS UNITS AND EMPLOYEES OF RETAIL TRADE ABOVE THE SET SCALE

类 别	Types	法人企业（个）Quantity of Corporations (unit)	产业活动单位数（个）Quantity of Business Units (unit)	从业人员（人）Quantity of Employees (person)
总 计	**Total**	**1 386**	**10 861**	**275 295**
按登记注册类型分	**Grouped by Registration Categories**			
内资企业	Domestic Investment Enterprises	1 231	9 330	206 583
国 有	State-owned	148	1 346	14 454
集 体	Collective-owned	65	266	3 176
私 营	Private	548	1 427	49 824
股份制	Share Holding	426	6 168	136 786
其他内资	Others	44	123	2 343
港澳台商投资	Hong Kong, Macao and Taiwan Funded	80	396	19 208
外商投资	Foreign Funded	75	1 135	49 504
按行业分	**Grouped By Sectors**			
综合零售业	Comprehensive Retail Sale	235	5 902	151 281
#百货零售	Articles For Daily Use	97	270	22 227
超级市场零售	Retail Sale of Supermarket	95	1 845	98 468
食品、饮料及烟草制品专门零售	Food, Beverage and Tabacco	88	996	9 231
纺织、服装及日用品专门零售	Textile, Garments and Articles for Daily Use	132	717	28 347
#服装零售	Garments	78	484	21 233
文化、体育用品及器材专门零售	Culture & Sports Articles and Equipments	98	311	11 668
#体育用品零售	Sports Articles	6	26	1 508
图书零售	Books	17	136	3 238
医药及医疗器材专门零售	Medicines and Special Appliances of Medicines	78	1 337	14 342
#药品零售	Medicine	72	1 231	13 857
汽车、摩托车、燃料及零配件专门零售	Automobiles, Motocycles, Fuels and Their Parts	519	897	28 847
#汽车零售	Automobiles	320	337	23 234
家用电器及电子产品专门零售	Household Electrical Appliances and Electronic Products	90	393	18 150
#家用电器零售	Household Electrical Appliances and Electronic Products	36	196	13 290
计算机、软件及辅助设备零售	Computers, Softwares and Accessorial Equipments	38	91	3 278
通信设备零售	Telecommunication Appliances	12	64	1 467
五金、家具及室内装修材料专门零售	Hardwares, Furnitures and Materials of Decoration	72	140	7 415
无店铺及其他零售	No-Shop and Others	74	168	6 014
#邮购及电子销售	Mail Orders and Electronic Sales	12	12	2 671

表 15.4 社会消费品零售总额(1978 ~ 2010)
TOTAL RETAIL SALES OF CONSUMER GOODS

单位:亿元(100 million yuan)

年 份 Year	社会消费品零售总额 Total Retail Sales of Consumer Goods	按商品用途分 by Use			
		食品类 Foods	衣着类 Clothing	用品类 Articles	燃料类 Fuels
1978	54.10	26.51	11.60	15.16	0.83
1979	68.28	30.05	16.07	21.28	0.88
1980	80.43	34.30	19.75	25.44	0.94
1981	88.73	38.78	21.27	27.73	0.95
1982	89.80	40.72	19.57	28.52	0.99
1983	100.68	44.20	22.31	33.18	0.99
1984	123.72	50.18	27.71	44.81	1.02
1985	173.39	64.08	35.51	72.70	1.10
1986	196.84	76.99	39.38	79.31	1.16
1987	225.25	91.01	42.52	90.41	1.31
1988	295.83	119.36	53.66	121.17	1.64
1989	331.38	140.03	51.95	137.70	1.70
1990	333.86	142.15	52.33	137.23	2.15
1991	382.06	162.82	52.91	163.30	3.03
1992	464.82	190.70	67.04	202.83	4.25
1993	675.92	259.93	101.30	309.26	5.43
1994	834.76	325.44	123.89	378.86	6.57
1995	1 050.96	407.44	153.74	481.96	7.82
1996	1 258.00	490.97	178.80	579.12	9.11
1997	1 435.38	564.62	200.62	659.61	10.53
1998	1 593.27	640.84	212.85	728.22	11.36
1999	1 722.33	694.03	228.18	787.62	12.50
2000	1 865.28	743.31	248.94	858.33	14.70
2001	2 016.37	802.53	266.31	931.02	16.51
2002	2 203.89	874.76	289.43	1 021.84	17.85
2003	2 404.45	939.29	309.70	1 135.27	20.19
2004	2 656.91	1 043.26	341.28	1 247.39	24.98
2005	2 979.50	1 026.70	335.30	1 563.15	54.35
2006	3 375.20	1 119.77	379.83	1 770.75	104.85
2007	3 873.30	1 204.70	435.88	2 032.07	200.65
2008	4 577.23	1 383.63	515.09	2 401.39	277.12
2009	5 173.24	1 609.01	582.17	2 714.06	268.00
2010	6 070.50	1 830.64	686.15	3 197.85	355.86

注：2005 年 ~ 2009 年社会消费品零售总额及分组依二经普数据，按国家统计局规定进行了修订。
Note: From 2005 to 2009, the total value of retail sales of cosumer goods are from second economic census, and has been revised according to the regulations of NBS.

表 15.4 续表 1　continued

单位：亿元(100 million yuan)

年　份 Year	按经济类型分 by Type of Ownership				
	国有经济 State-owned	集体经济 Collective-owned	私营经济 Private-owned	个　体 Individual	其　他 Others
1978	39.50	14.41		0.19	
1979	46.47	21.32		0.20	0.29
1980	54.01	25.31		0.24	0.87
1981	56.57	30.28	0.04	0.29	1.55
1982	56.48	31.39	0.03	0.32	1.58
1983	63.17	34.55	0.02	0.70	2.24
1984	75.63	43.80	0.02	1.68	2.59
1985	102.59	59.49	0.18	6.42	4.71
1986	111.73	69.06	0.67	8.47	6.91
1987	123.05	80.38	0.88	11.46	9.48
1988	161.65	103.84	1.72	14.56	14.06
1989	176.07	119.97	1.76	16.16	17.42
1990	179.37	115.59	2.05	16.17	20.68
1991	200.25	135.30	2.72	18.70	25.09
1992	247.68	157.56	5.75	22.88	30.95
1993	250.97	202.05	0.51	41.45	180.94
1994	249.27	198.56	0.64	65.00	321.29
1995	247.10	193.03	0.86	76.44	533.54
1996	238.54	183.50	30.10	92.64	713.22
1997	225.35	173.85	21.83	114.88	899.47
1998	210.92	161.70	59.48	126.94	1034.23
1999	180.33	141.83	62.77	141.16	1196.24
2000	150.09	118.26	496.86	153.57	946.50
2001	135.69	105.90	596.21	172.66	1 005.91
2002	131.91	102.19	699.75	190.66	1 079.38
2003	133.36	102.68	803.74	208.45	1 156.22
2004	134.44	102.78	935.44	233.01	1 251.24
2005	157.98	51.63	814.31	443.31	1 512.28
2006	178.96	58.48	922.46	502.18	1 713.12
2007	205.37	67.11	1 058.59	576.29	1 965.93
2008	242.69	79.31	1 250.98	681.03	2 323.22
2009	263.80	87.08	1 438.99	776.37	2 607.00
2010	306.34	98.29	1 739.44	927.42	2 999.01

注：1997 年以前私营经济为合营。
Note: The figures of Private Owned before 1997 refer to these of Joint Owned.

表 15.4 续表 2　continued　　单位：亿元(100 million yuan)

年　份 Year	社会消费品零售总额 Total Retail Sales of Consumer Goods	按行业分　by Sectors			
		批发零售贸易业 Wholesale and Retail Trade	住宿餐饮业 Hotels and Catering Trade	制造业 Manufacturing	其他行业 Others
1978	54.10	47.55	2.39	1.65	2.51
1979	68.28	59.02	2.82	2.54	3.90
1980	80.43	70.28	3.41	4.24	2.50
1981	88.73	77.53	3.68	4.61	2.91
1982	89.80	77.31	3.76	5.44	3.29
1983	100.68	84.93	4.26	7.72	3.77
1984	123.72	103.27	4.90	10.60	4.95
1985	173.39	150.03	7.58	8.41	7.37
1986	196.84	170.12	9.54	8.79	8.39
1987	225.25	193.50	11.09	10.47	10.19
1988	295.83	254.99	14.48	11.90	14.46
1989	331.38	265.87	15.66	16.84	33.01
1990	333.86	265.67	17.08	15.15	35.96
1991	382.06	300.26	20.91	17.70	43.19
1992	464.82	362.03	25.92	20.25	56.62
1993	675.92	559.56	35.47	29.24	51.65
1994	834.76	684.81	42.74	32.75	74.46
1995	1 050.96	864.01	52.61	38.05	96.29
1996	1 258.00	1 032.78	78.50	39.84	106.88
1997	1 435.38	1 173.94	93.49	44.38	123.57
1998	1 593.27	1 298.40	96.58	45.41	152.88
1999	1 722.33	1 391.08	114.93	47.22	169.10
2000	1 865.28	1 493.13	134.12	49.16	188.87
2001	2 016.37	1 619.13	148.88	50.78	197.58
2002	2 203.89	1 756.77	193.68	52.66	200.78
2003	2 404.45	1920.20	225.83	53.87	204.55
2004	2 656.91	2 108.59	279.44	56.29	212.59
2005	2 979.50	2 637.29	342.21		
2006	3 375.20	2 987.54	387.66		
2007	3 873.30	3 428.43	444.87		
2008	4 577.23	4 051.51	525.72		
2009	5 173.24	4 575.50	597.74		
2010	6 070.50	5 391.59	678.91		

表 15.4 续表 3 continued

单位:亿元(100 million yuan)

年 份 Year	按销售地区分 by Regions		按类别分 by Sectors		
	区 Districts	县 Counties	#家居类 Home Appliances	#通讯类 Communications	#轿车类 Cars
1978	41.42	12.68			
1979	51.60	16.68			
1980	61.08	19.35			
1981	66.66	22.07			
1982	67.49	22.31			
1983	75.62	25.06			
1984	93.71	30.01			
1985	133.59	39.80			
1986	149.64	47.20			
1987	167.61	57.64			
1988	227.12	68.71			
1989	253.51	77.87			
1990	265.83	68.03			
1991	302.54	79.52			
1992	361.64	103.18			
1993	530.97	144.95			
1994	660.00	174.76			
1995	832.92	218.04			
1996	1 006.16	251.84			
1997	1 156.08	279.30			
1998	1 289.03	304.24			
1999	1 398.60	323.73			
2000	1 521.68	343.60			
2001	1 665.46	350.91			
2002	1 884.77	319.12			
2003	2 063.71	340.74			
2004	2 292.63	364.28	278.44	62.20	196.85
2005	2 595.39	384.11	341.13	78.02	200.03
2006	2 953.52	421.68	393.20	92.00	209.31
2007	3 405.35	467.95	467.96	112.73	230.01
2008	4 044.59	532.64	569.67	118.94	287.84
2009	4 574.27	598.97	615.25	120.56	324.44
2010	5 398.34	672.16	689.08	123.69	405.55

注：县的零售额包括崇明县全部及宝山区、嘉定区、闵行区、浦东新区、松江区、金山区、青浦区和奉贤区镇以下地区零售额。

Note: The retail sales of consumer goods of counties include Chongming County and those at town level and below from Baoshan, Jiading, Pudong New Area, Songjiang, Jinshan, Qingpu and Fengxian Districts.

表 15.5 主要年份批发零售贸易业销售、库存总额
PURCHASE, SALES AND INVENTORY OF WHOLESALE AND RETAIL TRADE IN MAIN YEARS

单位:亿元(100 million yuan)

指 标	Indicators	2000	2009	2010
商品销售总额	**Sales of Commodities**	**7 474.81**	**31 974.39**	**37 383.25**
零 售	Retail	1 723.31	4 405.65	5 199.12
批 发	Wholesale	5 751.50	27 568.74	32 184.13
年末库存总额	**Year-end Inventory**	**262.50**	**1 221.90**	**1 913.49**

注：本表为国内批发零售贸易业、物资供销业、对外贸易业统计口径。
Note: The figures in this table are based on the scope of wholesale, retail trade, purchase and sales of commodities and foreign trade.

表 15.6 批发零售贸易业商品销售、库存总额(2010)
PURCHASE, SALES AND INVENTORY OF WHOLESALE AND RETAIL TRADE

单位:亿元(100 million yuan)

类 别	Types	商品销售总额 Sales of Commodities	商品库存总额 Year-end Inventory
总 计	**Total**	**37 383.25**	**1 913.49**
限额以上单位	Above the Set Scale	29 130.87	1 712.23
限额以下单位	Below the Set Scale	8 252.38	201.26

表 15.7 汽车交易情况(2008～2010)
DISTRIBUTION OF AUTOMOBILE

类 别	Types	2008	2009	2010
国产小型客车(万辆)	Domestic Small Passenger Cars(10 000 vehicles)	15.63	18.72	24.11
#国产轿车	Domestic Cars	13.25	16.03	19.73
进口小型客车(含轿车)(万辆)	Small Passenger Cars Imported(induding cars)(10 000 Vehicles)	1.51	1.64	3.02
二手车交易量(万辆)	Dealing Number of Secondhand Cars(10 000 vehicles)	21.59	25.61	31.12
#轿 车	Saloon Cars	11.81	14.30	18.30

表 15.8 限额以上批发贸易业商品购、销、存总额(2010)
PURCHASE, SALES AND INVENTORY OF WHOLESALE TRADE ABOVE THE SET SCALE

单位:亿元(100 million yuan)

类 别	Types	商品购进总额 Purchase of Commodities	商品销售总额 Sales of Commodities	商品库存总额 Year-end Inventory
总 计	**Total**	**22 800.03**	**25 208.19**	**1 432.06**
按登记注册类型分	**Grouped by Type of Registration**			
内资企业	Domestic Fund Enterprises	15 949.02	17 012.27	891.57
国有企业	State-Owned Enterprises	5 035.87	5 145.06	209.38
集体企业	Collective-Owned Enterprises	143.26	162.15	2.88
股份合作企业	Share Holding Cooperative Enterprises	103.63	105.47	6.05
联营企业	Joint-Owned Enterprises	103.30	109.39	7.74
有限责任公司	Companies with Limited Liabilities	3 784.03	4 160.49	210.12
股份有限公司	Share Holding Companies with Limited Liabilities	1 682.34	1 809.41	119.25
私营企业	Private Enterprises	4 980.75	5 402.45	330.06
其他企业	Others	115.83	117.84	6.09
港澳台商投资企业	Hong Kong, Macao and Taiwan Funded Enterprises	1 485.36	1 806.52	145.94
外商投资企业	Foreign Funded Enterprises	5 365.65	6 389.40	394.56
按行业分	**Grouped by Sector**			
农畜产品批发	Primary and Livestock Products	114.09	117.59	34.55
食品、饮料及烟草制品批发	Food, Beverage and Tabacco	1 166.20	1 355.02	105.60
#米、面制品及食用油批发	Rice, Flour and Cooking Oil	179.40	193.75	39.22
烟草制品批发	Tabacco	367.43	404.89	9.85

表 15.8 续表 continued

单位:亿元(100 million yuan)

类　别	Types	商品购进总额 Purchase of Commodities	商品销售总额 Sales of Commodities	商品库存总额 Year-end Inventory
纺织、服装及日用品批发	Textile Products, Gaments and Commodity	1 274.97	1 749.56	161.40
#服装批发	Garments	393.39	560.23	54.23
文化、体育用品及器材批发	Culture & Sports Articles and Equipments	451.59	478.84	43.94
医药及医疗器材批发	Medicines and Special Appliances of Medicines	612.98	710.43	68.40
矿产品、建材及化工产品批发	Mineral Products, Materials of Construction and Chemical Products	12 843.54	13 511.77	593.62
#煤炭及制品批发	Coal	855.60	868.16	10.61
石油及制品批发	Petroleum	3 897.76	4 037.65	73.81
金属及金属矿批发	Metal Products and Metal Minerals	5 837.42	6 272.85	360.19
建材批发	Building Materials	267.18	268.07	25.75
化肥批发	Chemical Fertilizer	44.71	51.00	3.29
机械设备、五金交电及电子产品批发	Mechinery Equipments, Hardwares, Electric Appliances and Eletronic Products	5 056.67	5 813.48	314.60
#汽车、摩托车及零配件批发	Spare and Component Parts for Automobiles and Motorcycles	1 720.37	1 879.31	73.30
家用电器批发	Household Electrical Equipment	677.38	703.01	21.26
计算机、软件及辅助设备批发	Computers, Softwares and Accessorial Equipments	645.31	820.63	38.46
贸易经纪与代理	Economic Trade and Agency	481.91	577.45	43.30
其他批发	Others	798.07	894.05	66.64

表 15.9 限额以上零售贸易业商品购、销、存总额(2010)
PURCHASE, SALES AND INVENTORY OF RETAIL TRADE ABOVE THE SET SCALE

单位:亿元(100 million yuan)

类别	Types	商品购进总额 Purchase of Commodities	商品销售总额 Sales of Commodities	商品库存总额 Year-end Inventory
总计	**Total**	**3 301.60**	**3 922.68**	**280.17**
按登记注册类型分	**Grouped by Type of Registration**			
内资企业	Domestic Enterprises	2 424.75	2 762.95	202.83
国有企业	State-Owned Enterprises	255.01	244.66	49.26
集体企业	Collective-Owned Enterprises	53.46	32.12	14.53
股份合作企业	Share Holding Cooperative Enterprises	2.89	3.56	0.09
联营企业	Joint-Owned Enterprises	24.93	32.07	1.02
有限责任公司	Companies with Limited Liabilities	968.88	1 218.61	56.85
股份有限公司	Share Holding Companies with Limited Liabilities	362.20	399.17	35.75
私营企业	Private Enterprises	736.66	808.90	44.66
其他企业	Others	20.71	23.86	0.66
港澳台商投资企业	Hong Kong, Macao and Taiwan Funded	477.44	514.44	36.48
外商投资企业	Foreign Funded Enterprises	399.41	645.29	40.87
按行业分	**Grouped by Sector**			
#综合零售业	Comprehensive Retail Sale	1 355.58	1 702.43	98.51
食品、饮料及烟草制品专门零售	Food, Beverage and Tabacco	37.05	47.94	2.80
纺织、服装及日用品专门零售	Textile Products, Gaments and Commodity	195.08	283.64	33.70
文化、体育用品及器材专门零售	Culture & Sports Articles and Equipments	97.56	176.10	23.39
医药及医疗器材专门零售	Medicines and Special Appliances of Medicines	267.29	266.65	17.77
汽车、摩托车、燃料及零配件专门零售	Automobiles, Motocycles, Fuels and Their Parts	926.76	961.03	82.63
家用电器及电子产品专门零售	Household Electrical Appliances and Electronic Products	277.37	295.92	14.81
五金、家具及室内装修材料专门零售	Hardwares, Furnitures and Materials of Decoration	44.62	71.62	3.37

表 15.10 主要年份限额以上批发零售贸易业主要生产资料销售量
SALES OF MAJOR PRODUCT MATERIAL OF WHOLESALE AND RETAIL SALES TRADE ABOVE THE SET SCALE IN MAIN YEARS

单位:万吨(10 000 tons)

生产资料名称	Names of Product Material	2005	2009	2010
钢材	Steels	1 807.99	4 893.93	5 579.00
铜	Cuprum	57.38	45.27	202.95
铝	Aluminium	21.34	35.89	152.32
煤炭	Coal	3 016.67	6 705.54	8180.34
汽油	Gasoline	1 213.18	1 516.60	1 609.10
煤油	Coal Oil	502.88	842.20	870.56
柴油	Diesel Oil	2 961.25	2 930.65	3 896.15
水泥	Concrete	118.73	428.55	362.00

表 15.11 限额以上批发零售贸易业主要商品分类销售额(2010)
TOTAL SALES OF ENTERPRISES ABOVE THE SET SCALE IN WHOLESALE AND RETAIL TRADE BY CATEGORY OF MAIN COMMODITIES

单位:亿元(100 million yuan)

类别	Types	合计 Total	批发 Wholesale	零售 Retail
食品、饮料、烟酒类	Food, Beverages, Tobacco and Liquor	2 288.40	1 580.45	707.95
#食品类	Foods	1 300.47	830.78	469.69
#粮油类	Grain and Oil	429.54	332.55	96.99
肉禽蛋类	Meat, Poultry and Eggs	143.55	68.49	75.06
饮料类	Beverages	146.94	82.51	64.42
烟酒类	Tobacco and Liquor	840.98	667.15	173.83
服装、鞋帽、针纺织品类	Clothing, Shoes, Hats and Textiles	1 512.27	1 040.88	471.39
#服装类	Clothing	1 012.00	635.61	376.39
鞋帽类	Shoes and Hat	146.60	89.32	57.28
针、纺织品类	Knitwear and Textiles	353.67	315.95	37.72
化妆品类	Cosmetics	402.84	276.13	126.72
金银珠宝类	Gold, Silver and Jewelry	456.54	265.96	190.59
日用品类	Articles for Daily Use	780.25	512.64	267.61
#洗涤用品类	Washing Articles	49.36	28.04	21.31
儿童玩具类	Toys for Children	18.89	12.16	6.73
五金、电料类	Hardware and Electrical Materials	252.27	232.33	19.95
体育、娱乐用品类	Sports and Recreation Articles	61.14	27.96	33.18
书报杂志类	Newspapers and Magazines	32.74	17.23	15.51
电子出版物及音像制品类	E-journal and Video Products	18.91	16.62	2.29
家用电器和音像器材类	Household Appliances and Video Appliances	887.91	536.00	351.91
中西药品类	Traditional Chinese and Western Medicines	763.39	465.80	297.60
#西药类	Western Medicines	567.27	329.03	238.24
中草药及中成药类	Traditional Chinese Medicines	99.05	61.39	37.67
文化办公用品类	Cultural and Official Goods	1 137.68	1 010.25	127.43
家具类	Furniture	55.14	34.10	21.04
通讯器材类	Communication Appliances	304.87	251.37	53.49
煤炭及制品类	Coal and Related Product	781.20	778.27	2.93
木材及制品类	Lumber and Related Product	95.85	95.85	
石油及制品类	Oil and Related Product	4 489.97	4 139.00	350.97
化工材料及制品类	Chemical Material and Related Product	1 684.31	1 684.31	
#化肥类	Fertilizer	31.67	31.67	
金属材料类	Metal Material	6 416.17	6 416.17	
建筑及装潢材料类	Building and Decoration Materials	190.23	160.12	30.11
机电产品及设备类	Mechanical and Electrical Products	2 424.76	2 415.56	9.20
#农机类	Agriculture Machinery	12.84	12.84	
汽车类	Automobile	2 771.48	1 979.26	792.21
种子饲料类	Seed and Feedstuff	50.57	50.57	
棉麻类	Cotton and Hemp	27.14	27.13	
其他类	Others	1 244.83	1 154.56	90.27

表 15.12 主要年份限额以上批发零售贸易业主要财务指标
MAIN FINANCIAL INDICATORS OF WHOLESALE AND RETAIL SALES ABOVE THE SET SCALE IN MAIN YEARS

单位:亿元(100 million yuan)

指 标	Indicators	2005	2009	2010
流动资产	Current Assets	2 929.27	6 442.63	7 608.03
#存 货	Inventory	722.78	1 374.06	1 655.36
固定资产原价	Fixed Assets Original Value	546.78	771.12	790.06
累计折旧	Accumulative Depreciation	169.94	266.18	291.58
#本年折旧	Depreciation	31.20	91.22	55.82
资产总计	Total Assets	3 926.22	8 254.42	9 608.53
负债合计	Total Liabilities	2 727.25	5 695.63	6 710.76
所有者权益合计	Total Owner's Equities	1 198.97	2 558.79	2 897.78
实收资本	Paid-up Capital	862.49	1 385.61	1 464.26
#国家资本	State Capital	132.19	415.86	379.67
港澳台资本	Hongkong, Macao and Taiwan Capital	38.17	108.75	137.69
外商资本	Foreign Capital	242.71	339.89	376.04
主营业务收入	Prime Operating Revenues	11 236.19	21 203.28	26 372.58
主营业务成本	Operating Costs	9 874.12	19 473.32	24 300.03
营业费用	Operating Expenses	501.98	967.55	1 135.41
主营业务税金及附加	Sales Taxes and Extra Charges	10.10	25.46	40.73
主营业务利润	Profits of Major Management	737.71	1 703.03	2 031.82
管理费用	Management Expenses	243.12	414.35	475.41
财务费用	Financial Expenses	24.09	44.37	47.93
营业利润	Operating Profits	248.71	425.95	535.95
利润总额	Total Profits	223.35	493.92	640.19
主营业务应付工资总额	Total Payable Salaries Involved in Major Business	130.25	231.39	258.66
主营业务应付福利费总额	Total Payable Welfare Involved in Major Business	21.89	11.56	17.63

表 15.13 主要年份限额以上餐饮业主要财务指标
MAIN FINANCIAL INDICATORS OF CATERING SECTOR ABOVE THE SET SCALE IN MAIN YEARS

单位:亿元(100 million yuan)

指　标	Indicators	2005	2009	2010
流动资产	Current Assets	43.60	102.09	114.24
#存　货	Inventory	5.10	13.72	8.28
固定资产原价	Fixed Assets Original Value	44.76	70.32	81.97
累计折旧	Accumulative Depreciation	15.65	31.48	31.64
#本年折旧	Depreciation	3.83	11.99	6.63
资产总计	Total Assets	94.49	185.74	214.43
负债合计	Total Liabilities	64.13	137.66	156.19
所有者权益合计	Total Owner's Equities	30.36	48.08	58.25
实收资本	Paid-up Capital	31.05	58.78	62.42
#国家资本	State Capital	0.78	2.72	5.28
港澳台资本	Hongkong, Macao and Taiwan Capital	6.95	10.84	13.36
外商资本	Foreign Capital	6.66	19.78	17.62
主营业务收入	Prime Operating Revenues	157.66	291.90	335.96
主营业务成本	Operating Costs	72.03	138.57	145.44
营业费用	Operating Expenses	53.86	105.32	123.32
主营业务税金及附加	Sales Taxes and Extra Charges	8.14	14.23	17.34
主营业务利润	Profits of Major Management	65.75	139.22	173.18
管理费用	Management Expenses	19.42	31.84	37.25
财务费用	Financial Expenses	1.15	2.89	3.47
营业利润	Operating Profits	5.49	1.58	10.96
利润总额	Total Profits	5.49	3.85	15.12
主营业务应付工资总额	Total Payable Salaries Involved in Major Business	17.54	34.78	41.08
主营业务应付福利费总额	Total Payable Welfare Involved in Major Business	2.26	1.37	2.51

表 15.14 主要年份限额以上连锁零售业、住宿和餐饮业经营情况
THE BASIC STATISTICS OF CHAIN RETAIL, ACCOMMODATION AND CATERING ABOVE SET SCALE IN MAIN YEARS

指　标	Indicators	2005	2009	2010
门店总数(个)	Quantity of Stores(unit)	15 775	18 652	20 977
营业面积(万平方米)	Operational Area(10 000 sq. m)	809.16	896.23	938.35
从业人数(万人)	Number of Persons Employed(10 000 person)	24.47	33.48	36.68
商品购进总额(亿元)	Purchase of Commodities(100 million yuan)	1 222.94	1 963.27	2 249.57
商品销售总额 (亿元)	Sales of Commodities (100 million yuan)	1 815.32	2 722.50	3 071.67
#零售额	Retail Sales	1 201.03	2 109.82	2 241.97
餐饮业营业收入(亿元)	Total Operating Revenue (100 million yuan)	35.69	72.81	106.81

表 15.15 限额以上批发零售贸易业主要财务指标(2010)
MAIN FINANCIAL INDICATORS OF WHOLESALE AND RETAIL ENTERPRISES ABOVE THE SET SCALE

类 别	Types	流动资产 Current Assets	固定资产原价 Fixed Assets Original Value	资产总计 Total Assets
总 计	**Total**	**7 608.03**	**790.06**	**9 608.53**
一、按登记注册类型分	**Grouped by Type of Registration**			
批发贸易业	**Wholesale Trade**	**6 535.45**	**414.55**	**8 032.65**
内资企业	Domestic Enterprises	4 029.73	300.90	5 143.37
国有企业	State-Owned Enterprises	887.48	53.12	1 165.48
集体企业	Collective-Owned Enterprises	32.11	8.44	42.34
股份合作企业	Share Holding Cooperative Enterprises	15.92	0.49	19.18
联营企业	Joint-Owned Enterprises	33.36	1.47	34.76
有限责任公司	Companies with Limited Liabilities	1 003.77	77.87	1 324.20
股份有限公司	Share Holding Companies with Limited Liabilities	315.74	58.05	522.33
私营企业	Private Enterprises	1 701.92	96.18	1 984.68
其他企业	Others	39.43	5.27	50.41
港澳台商投资企业	Hong Kong, Macao and Taiwan Funded	579.75	26.99	656.07
外商投资企业	Foreign Funded Enterprises	1 925.97	86.66	2 233.21
零售贸易业	**Retail Trade**	**1 072.58**	**375.51**	**1 575.88**
内资企业	Domestic Enterprises	726.96	239.42	1 112.52
国有企业	State-Owned Enterprises	55.30	21.68	85.98
集体企业	Collective-Owned Enterprises	8.12	3.31	12.06
股份合作企业	Share Holding Cooperative Enterprises	1.52	0.36	1.88
联营企业	Joint-Owned Enterprises	5.00	2.63	6.42
有限责任公司	Responsibility Co. Ltd.	283.15	107.35	393.37
股份有限公司	Share Holding Co. Ltd.	119.41	61.10	283.79
私营企业	Private Enterprises	249.02	42.20	321.69
其他企业	Others	5.45	0.79	7.32
港澳台商投资企业	Hong Kong, Macao and Taiwan Funded	164.68	40.99	209.32
外商投资企业	Foreign Funded Enterprises	180.94	95.09	254.05

单位:亿元(100 million yuan)

负债合计 Total Liabilities	所有者权益合计 Total Owner's Equity	实收资本 Paid-up Capital	主营业务收入 Prime Operating Revenues	主营业务成本 Operating Costs	主营业务利润 Profits from Major Business	利润总额 Total Profits
6 710.76	**2 897.78**	**1 464.26**	**26 372.58**	**24 300.03**	**2 031.82**	**640.19**
5 592.30	**2 440.35**	**1 157.95**	**23 067.48**	**21 444.47**	**1 593.39**	**531.77**
3 513.59	1 629.79	770.53	15 356.02	14 719.11	613.43	248.27
807.08	358.40	163.77	4 503.80	4 399.79	100.27	63.53
30.74	11.59	4.74	153.16	144.84	7.85	2.11
9.94	9.23	2.35	76.71	73.79	2.86	2.55
25.30	9.45	4.32	99.07	92.93	5.77	2.54
844.87	479.33	185.97	3 820.59	3 611.35	197.62	77.41
292.37	229.96	124.34	1 592.39	1 528.21	60.10	28.67
1 470.06	514.62	276.60	5 000.77	4 765.30	232.36	68.78
33.22	17.19	8.44	109.53	102.88	6.59	2.69
467.28	188.79	93.40	1 645.79	1416.09	228.01	69.61
1 611.44	621.77	294.03	6 065.67	5 309.27	751.95	213.90
1 118.45	**457.43**	**306.31**	**3 305.10**	**2 855.56**	**438.43**	**108.42**
751.80	360.71	173.04	2 251.68	1 989.95	252.58	62.21
55.45	30.53	12.26	220.11	193.02	26.24	6.35
7.14	4.91	3.72	29.45	27.39	1.99	0.27
0.81	1.07	0.15	3.11	2.82	0.29	0.03
3.77	2.65	1.13	29.38	27.02	2.29	1.09
290.77	102.60	56.78	1 022.20	907.02	111.03	25.18
147.44	136.35	41.88	191.63	151.55	37.72	16.11
239.31	82.38	56.05	734.25	661.91	70.76	12.56
7.11	0.21	1.06	21.54	19.23	2.26	0.63
158.58	50.74	43.31	489.25	406.32	81.83	23.51
208.07	45.98	89.96	564.16	459.29	104.02	22.70

表 15. 15 续表 continued

类别	Types	流动资产 Current Assets	固定资产原价 Fixed Assets Original Value	资产总计 Total Assets
二、按行业分	**Grouped by Sector**			
批发贸易业	**Wholesale Trade**	**6 535.45**	**414.55**	**8 032.65**
农畜产品批发	Primary and Livestock Products	95.46	9.52	158.41
食品、饮料及烟草制品批发	Food, Beverage and Tabacco	511.59	57.71	691.01
纺织、服装及日用品批发	Textile Products, Garments and Commodity	627.85	66.51	780.34
文化、体育用品及器材批发	Culture & Sports Articles and Equipments	190.05	5.49	216.22
医药及医疗器材批发	Medicines and Special Appliances of Medicines	309.24	24.33	426.62
矿产品、建材及化工产品批发	Mineral Products, Materials of Construction and Chemical Products	2 578.07	161.74	3 192.83
机械设备、五金交电及电子产品批发	Mechinery Equipments, Hardwares, Electric Appliances and Eletronic Products	1 682.79	57.69	1 949.71
贸易经济与代理	Economy on Trade and Agency	199.55	9.69	226.35
其他批发	Others	340.84	21.86	391.17
零售贸易业	**Retail Trade**	**1 072.58**	**375.51**	**1 575.88**
综合零售业	Comprehensive Retail Sale	517.04	232.58	827.12
食品、饮料及烟草制品专门零售	Food, Beverage and Tabacco	18.21	5.09	23.80
纺织、服装及日用品专门零售	Textile Products, Garments and Commodity	107.72	39.33	154.61
文化、体育用品及器材专门零售	Culture & Sports Articles and Equipments	61.43	16.94	81.34
医药及医疗器材专门零售	Medicines and Special Appliances of Medicines	20.52	5.64	28.87
汽车、摩托车、燃料及零配件专门零售	Automobiles, Motocycles, Fuels and Their Parts	184.09	34.96	235.23
家用电器及电子产品专门零售	Household Electrical Appliances and Electronic Products	111.36	12.65	135.64
五金、家具及室内装修材料专门零售	Hardwares, Furnitures and Materials of Decoration	22.30	12.88	40.39
无店铺及其他零售	No-Shop and Others	29.91	15.43	48.87

单位:亿元(100 million yuan)

负债合计 Total Liabilities	所有者权益合计 Total Owner's Equity	实收资本 Paid-up Capital	主营业务收入 Prime Operating Revenues	主营业务成本 Operating Costs	主营业务利润 Profits from Major Business	利润总额 Total Profits
5 592.30	**2 440.35**	**1 157.95**	**23 067.48**	**21 444.47**	**1 593.39**	**531.77**
98.19	60.22	30.19	115.96	113.52	2.37	2.45
453.73	237.28	96.28	1 216.23	1 040.03	164.56	51.61
478.57	301.76	151.21	1 611.26	1 230.87	377.99	101.16
158.42	57.80	37.30	428.60	398.89	28.86	11.19
252.46	174.16	53.02	635.22	564.92	69.74	20.14
2 239.95	952.88	490.75	12 218.02	1 1847.40	362.66	171.42
1 437.92	511.78	225.09	5 524.51	5 054.35	466.71	140.47
182.71	43.64	27.01	552.07	505.33	44.97	6.88
290.35	100.82	47.11	765.62	689.17	75.54	26.45
1 118.45	**457.43**	**306.31**	**3 305.10**	**2 855.56**	**438.43**	**108.42**
588.53	238.59	147.43	1 490.08	1 293.21	191.74	56.03
18.01	5.79	3.62	43.48	35.13	8.11	1.76
115.71	38.91	37.40	252.12	149.37	101.76	24.16
52.65	28.70	19.72	161.54	134.20	25.48	2.68
15.71	13.16	6.67	66.38	54.20	11.97	2.06
159.41	75.82	46.52	875.44	824.52	50.12	16.04
105.05	30.59	26.60	251.73	231.61	18.93	2.20
27.56	12.84	10.93	56.50	41.40	14.78	3.46
35.83	13.04	7.42	107.84	91.92	15.56	0.04

表 15.16 商品交易市场成交情况(2010) DEALS IN MERCHANDISE EXCHANGE MARKET

分 类	Types	年末出租摊位数(个) Quantity of Year-end booth Lent (unit)	成交额(亿元) Transaction Volume (100 million yuan)
总 计	**Total**	**168 637**	**6 657.36**
#食品、饮料、烟酒类	Foodstuff, Beverage, Tobacco and Liquor	72 532	783.00
服装、鞋帽、针纺织品类	Garments, Shoes and Hats, Textile Products	25 690	134.07
化妆品类	Cosmetics	268	0.52
金银珠宝类	Jewelry	236	0.49
日用品类	Articles for Daily Use	4 198	236.72
五金、电料类	Hardware and Electrical Appliances	4 602	17.24
体育、娱乐用品类	Recreation and Sports Articles	348	3.15
书报杂志类	Books, Newspapers and Magazines	105	1.75
电子出版物及音像制品类	Electronic Publications and Audio-video Products	282	1.20
家用电器和音像器材类	Household Appliances and Audio-video Equipments	716	10.53
中西药品类	Medicines	299	9.46
文化办公用品类	Culture and Office Articles	2 120	30.09
家具类	Furnitures	4 273	32.44
通讯器材类	Telecommunication Appliances	3 720	4.87
木材及制品类	Woods and Woods Product	1 704	30.25
石油及制品类	Oil and Oil Product	506	1 162.00
化工材料及制品类	Chemical Material and Chemical Product	1 129	89.66
金属材料类	Mental and Mental Product	6 071	3 465.85
建筑及装潢材料类	Construct and Decorate Material	18 933	320.53
机电产品及设备类	Mechanical and Electrical Product and Equipments	862	10.23
汽车类	Automobile	4 316	237.52

表 15.17 主要超市公司基本情况(2010)
BASIC STATISTICS OF MAJOR SUPERMARKET COMPANIES

名称	Name	网点(个) Outlets (unit)	其中 of which 本市 Directly-operated Stores in the City	市外 Directly-operated Stores Outside the City	销售额(亿元) Sales Volume (100 million yuan)
联华超市公司	Lianhua Supermarket Company	5 239	3 320	1 919	700.77
#上海联家超市有限公司	Shanghai Lianjia Supermarket Co., Ltd.	19	19		68.55
上海华联超市公司	Shanghai Hualian Supermarket Company	1 335	920	415	150.07
大润发超市公司	RT-Mart Supermarket Company	65	13	52	280.30
农工商超市有限公司	Nonggongshang Supermarket Company	3 205	2 125	1 080	278.13
麦德龙现购自运有限公司	Metro Cash & Carry Co Ltd	48	5	43	117.14
上海易初莲花连锁超市有限公司	Shanghai Lotus ChainSupermarket Co.,Ltd	21	21		71.34
华联集团吉买盛购物中心有限公司	Hualian GSM Shopping Center Co Ltd	22	21	1	37.14
上海家得利超市有限公司	Shanghai Homegain Supermarket Co., Ltd.	151	131	20	23.47
上海欧尚超市有限公司	Shanghai Auchan Supermarket Company Shanghai Emart Supermarket Co., Ltd.	3	3		17.55
上海捷强烟草糖酒(集团)连锁有限公司	Shanghai Jieqiang Tobacco, Sugar & Wine (Group) Chain Co., Ltd.	417	209	208	11.89
上海屈臣士日用品有限公司	Shanghai Waston Daily Articles Co.,Ltd.	82	82		11.98
上海家家乐商业发展有限公司	Jiajiale Supermarket Company	5	5		0.81
上海城市超市有限公司	Shanghai City Supermarket Co Ltd	6	6		2.44

上/海/统/计/年/鉴

主要统计指标解释

■ 社会消费品零售总额

指批发和零售业、餐饮业、新闻出版业、邮政业和其他服务业等，售予城乡居民用于生活消费的商品和社会集团用于公共消费的商品之总量。社会消费品零售总额包括：

一、批发和零售业企业(单位)：

1.售予城乡居民的各种生活消费品；

2.售予入境旅游的外国人、华侨、港澳台同胞的各类商品；

3.售予行政事业单位、社会团体、军队和武警等机构的商品，以及以零售方式售予各类企业的商品。具体包括：用于非生产和社会交往的办公用品，如通讯设备、计算器具和设备、电讯网络设备、文印设备、音像视听器材和设备、纸张、本册、文具及装订文印材料、家具、日用电器、针纺织品、清洁卫生用品、文体用品、奖品、纪念品、礼品等；供内部人员乘坐的交通工具和燃料；用于办公设施修缮的各类配件、材料、工具等；用于取暖和防暑降温的设备、燃料、材料及食品等；专用于教学的用品和设备；非营利医疗机构的中、西药品、中药材和医疗设备器材；非专用的劳动保护用品；不对外营业的内部食堂用的餐具、炊具、设备、清洁卫生工具和食品、燃料等；军队、武警用于其人员生活的衣着品和个人用品；其他各类非生产性设备和用品。

二、餐饮业出售的主食、菜肴、烟酒饮料和其他商品。

三、新闻出版业、邮政业售予城乡居民、企事业单位、军队和武警等机构的书报杂志、音像制品、邮品等。

四、其他服务业出售的食品、烟酒饮料、服装鞋帽、日常生活用品、医药保健用品、艺术品、工艺美术品、玩具、殡葬用品以及其他消费品。

■ 商品销售总额

指对本企业以外的单位和个人出售(包括对国(境)外直接出口)的商品。这个指标反映批发零售贸易业在上海市场以及上海以外市场上销售商品的总量。商品销售总额包括：(1)售给城乡居民和社会集团消费用的商品；(2)售给工业、农业、建筑业、运输邮电业、批发零售贸易业、餐饮业、服务业等作为生产、经营使用的商品；(3)售给批发零售贸易业作为转卖或加工后转卖的商品；(4)对国(境)外直接出口的商品。不包括：出售本企业自用的废旧包装用品，未通过买卖行为付出的商品，经本单位介绍，由买卖双方直接结算，本单位只收取手续费的业务，购货退出的商品以及商品损耗和损失等。

■ 主营业务收入

指企业在销售商品、提供劳务等日常活动中所产生的收入总额。

■ 主营业务成本

指企业已销商品应负担的进货原价和商品进价成本。

■ 营业费用

指批发零售贸易企业在购、销、存过程中发生的各项经营费用。包括运输费、装卸费、包装费、保险费、展览费、差旅费、广告费、商品损耗、进出口商品累计佣金、经营人员的工资及福利费等。

EXPLANATORY NOTES TO MAJOR STATISTICAL INDICATORS

□ Total Retail Sales of Consumer Goods

Total Retail Sales of Consumer Goods refer to the sum of retail sales of commodities sold by wholesale, retail, catering, publishing, post and telecommunications and other service industries to urban and rural households for private consumption and to social institutions for public consumption. Retail sales of consumer goods include:

Sales by wholesale and retail units:

of consumer goods sold to urban and rural households

of commodities sold to foreigners, overseas Chinese and Chinese compatriots from Hong Kong, Macau and Taiwan visiting in China

of commodities sold to government agencies, institutions, social organizations, military and armed police units, and commodities sold to enterprises in the form of retail sales. More specifically, they include: office facilities and articles for non-production purposes such as communications equipment, computing equipment and instruments, TV and network equipment, printing and copying equipment, audio-visual equipment and instruments, paper, notebooks, stationeries, furniture, electric appliances, knitwear, sanitation and cleaning articles, cultural and sport articles, articles for prizes, souvenirs, etc.; transport vehicles and fuels for employees; materials, spare parts and tools for the maintenance of office facilities; equipment, fuels, materials and food for winter heating or summer cooling purposes; articles and equipment for teaching purpose; Chinese and western medicines and medical equipment and facilities purchased by non profit-making medical institutes; non-specialized work safety articles; cooking utensils, tableware, equipment, cleaning articles, food and fuels purchased by internal cafeterias; clothes and personal articles purchased by military or armed police units for their officials and soldiers; and other equipment and articles for non-production purposes.

Sales of stable food, cooked dishes, beverages, tobaccos and other articles by catering units.

Sales of books, newspapers, magazines, audio-visual products and post products by publishing, post and telecommunications departments to urban and rural households and to enterprises, institutions, military and armed police units.

Sales of food, beverages, tobaccos, clothing, hats, footwear, articles for daily use, medicines, medical and health articles, work of art, handicrafts, toys, funeral articles and other articles by other service industries.

□ Total Sales of Commodities

Total Sales of Commodities refer to the selling of commodities to other establishments and individuals (including direct export). Reflecting the total value of sales of commodities at Shanghai markets and out-of-Shanghai markets, this indicator includes: (1) commodities sold to urban and rural households and institutions for their consumption; (2) commodities sold to establishments in industry, agriculture, construction, transportation, post and telecommunications, wholesale and retail trade, catering and service trade and public utility for their production and operation; (3) commodities sold to wholesale and retail establishments for re-selling, with or without further processing; and (4) commodities for direct export to other countries. Excluded are selling of waste packaging materials used by enterprises themselves commodities transferred without buying or selling procedures, commission income from brokerage in transactions whose settlement is directly handled by buyers and sellers, rejected commodities in the purchase, loss in commodities, etc.

□ Prime Operating Revenue

Prime Operating Revenue refers to the earnings a corporation receives in daily activity such as selling goods and offering labor service.

□ Operating Cost

Operating Cost refers to the cost a corporation paid to buy and deliver the commodities.

□ Operating Expenses

Operating Expenses refer to the spendings that a wholesaler or retailer pays in buying, selling or stocking goods. It includes fees incurred in transport, loading and unloading, packaging, insurance, exhibition, business trip, advertisement, commodity wastage, commissions in import and export, salaries and bonus paid to workers involved.

第十六篇

CHAPTER 16

金 融 业

FINANCE

表 16.1 年末金融业单位数(2009~2010)
QUANTITY OF FINANCIAL INSTITUTIONS

单位:家(unit)

指 标	Indicators	2009	2010
金融业单位数	Financial Institutions	794	910
#银行业	Banking Institutions	133	140
证券业	Security Institutions	98	138
保险业	Insurance Institutions	307	320
#外资金融单位数	Foreign Financial Institutions Operating in Shanghai	170	173

①金融业单位数统计中,银行业统计至市分行;证券业统计至证券公司市分公司、基金公司、期货公司、证券投资咨询公司、资信评级机构、证券市场机构和登记结算机构;保险业统计至保险公司市分公司、专业保险运营中心和保险中介机构。此外,金融单位统计包括各金融监管部门。
②本表数据分别由中国银行业监督管理委员会上海监管局、中国保险监督管理委员会上海监管局、中国证券监督管理委员会上海监管局等提供。
❶Among the statistics of financial institutions, banking institutions includes the municipal branches, security institutions include the municipal branch company, coporate fundation, futures company; security investment consultant company, credit rating agency, security market institution and registration and settlment institution; insurance institutions include insurance group, municipal branches of insurance company, specail insurance operations center and insurance agency institutions. In addition, the statistics of financial institutions includes financial regulatary institutions as well.
❷Data in this table are provided by China Banking Regulatory Commission Shanghai Bureau, China Insurance Regulatory Commission Shanghai Bureau and China Securities Regulatory Commission Shanghai Bureau, and etc.

表 16.2 主要年份原保险保费收入和赔付支出
PREMIUM OF PRIMARY INSURANCE AND PAYMENT IN MAIN YEARS

年 份 Year	原保险保费收入 (亿元) Premium of Primary Insurance (100 million yuan)	原保险赔付支出 (亿元) Payment of Primary Insurance (100 million yuan)	其 中 of which		赔付率 (%) Compensation Ratio (%)
			#人身保险 Liability Insurance	#财产保险 Property Insurance	
1990	8.99	2.22			24.7
1995	44.04	12.75			29.0
1996	58.10	15.00			25.8
1997	87.72	19.10			21.8
1998	102.92	28.67			27.9
1999	115.28	39.46			34.2
2000	127.23	36.44	20.56	15.88	28.6
2001	180.25	38.82	19.61	19.21	21.5
2002	237.61	49.97	28.38	21.59	21.0
2003	289.93	61.97	34.87	27.10	21.4
2004	307.11	70.86	36.79	34.07	23.1
2005	333.62	87.46	40.20	47.26	26.2
2006	407.04	91.31	46.14	45.17	22.4
2007	482.64	139.82	86.79	53.03	29.0
2008	600.06	184.09	104.57	79.52	30.7
2009	665.03	176.74	98.24	78.50	26.6
2010	883.86	194.54	110.28	84.26	22.0

注:本表数据由中国保险监督管理委员会上海监管局提供。
Note: Data in this table are provided by China Banking Regulatory Commission Shanghai Bureau.

表 16.3 金融机构存贷款年末余额(2009～2010)
SAVING DEPOSIT AND LOAN BALANCE OF FINANCIAL INSTITUTIONS AT YEAR-END

单位:亿元(100 million yuan)

指 标	Indicators	2009	2010
金融机构存款余额	**Saving Deposit Balance of Financial Institutions**	**44 620.27**	**52 190.04**
中资金融机构	Chinese Financial Institutions	41 486.49	48 118.64
人民币	RMB	39 935.07	46 678.13
外汇(折人民币)	Foreign Currencies(Converting into RMB)	1 551.42	1 440.51
外资金融机构	Foreign-funded Financial Institutions	3 133.78	4 071.40
人民币	RMB	2 356.39	3 168.70
外汇(折人民币)	Foreign Currencies(Converting into RMB)	777.39	902.70
金融机构贷款余额	**Loan Balance of Financial Institutions**	**29 684.10**	**34 154.17**
中资金融机构	Chinese Financial Institutions	26 086.58	29 970.80
人民币	RMB	24 108.16	27 970.18
外汇(折人民币)	Foreign Currencies(Converting into RMB)	1 978.42	2 000.62
外资金融机构	Foreign-funded Financial Institutions	3 597.52	4 183.36
人民币	RMB	2 087.91	2 603.13
外汇(折人民币)	Foreign Currencies(Converting into RMB)	1 509.61	1 580.23

表 16.4 中资金融机构人民币存款年末余额(2010)
RMB SAVING DEPOSIT OF CHINESE FINANCIAL INSTITUTIONS AT YEAR-END

单位:亿元(100 million yuan)

指 标	Indicators	2010	比 2010 年初增加 Increase from the Beginning of 2010
各项存款余额	**All Deposits**	**46 678.13**	**6 755.87**
企业存款	Enterprise Deposits	21 019.39	2 496.03
活期存款	Current Deposits	12 837.55	1 223.99
定期存款＊	Time Deposits	8 181.83	1 272.05
财政存款	Fiscal Deposits	1 903.46	657.52
机关团体存款＊	Deposits of Institutions and Organizations	3 233.88	456.66
储蓄存款	Savings Deposits	15 498.65	1 906.51
活期储蓄	Savings on Current Account	5 169.47	769.82
定期储蓄	Savings on Time Account	10 329.19	1 136.69
农业存款	Agricultural Deposits	922.67	117.05
委托存款	Entrusted Deposits	779.09	26.73
其他存款＊	Other Deposits	3 320.98	1 095.37

①本页数据由中国人民银行上海总部提供。
②因 2010 年统计口径调整，打＊指标的数据与上年不可比。
❶Data on this page are provided by Shanghai Hendquarters of People's Bank of China.
❷Data of the indicators with ＊ aren't comparable with the previous year because of the adjustment of statistical standard in 2010.

表 16.5 中资金融机构人民币贷款年末余额(2010)
RMB LOAN BALANCE OF CHINESE FINANCIAL INSTITUTIONS AT YEAR-END

单位:亿元(100 million yuan)

指 标	Indicators	2010	比 2010 年初增减
各项贷款余额	**All Loans**	**27 970.18**	**3 855.18**
境内贷款	Domestic Loans	27 952.24	3 837.36
#短期贷款	Short-term Loans	6 718.61	483.48
#个人贷款及透支 *	Personal Loans and Overdrafts	373.36	150.32
单位贷款及透支 *	Unit Loans and Overdrafts	5 858.22	97.38
贸易融资	Trade Financing	445.16	222.97
中长期贷款	Mid and Long-term Loans	19 063.43	3 537.40
#个人贷款 *	Personal Loans	5 394.10	819.87
单位贷款 *	Unit Loans	11 274.66	1 916.53
贸易融资 *	Trade Financing	190.06	17.22
融资租赁	Financing Leasing	567.55	323.02
票据融资	Bill Financing	1 151.90	-592.05
境外贷款	Foreign Loans	17.95	17.82

①本表数据由中国人民银行上海总部提供。
②因 2010 年统计口径调整,打 * 指标的数据与上年不可比。
❶Data in this table are provided by Shanghai Headquaters of People's Bank of China.
❷Data of the indicators with * arent comparable with the previous year because of the adjustment of statistical standard in 2010.

表 16.6 个人消费贷款及公积金贷款年末余额(2009~2010)
Personal Consumption Loan and Accumulation Fund Loan

单位:亿元(100 million yuan)

指 标	Indicators	2009	2010
中资商业银行人民币个人消费贷款	**Personal Consumption Loan from Domestic Funded Commercial banks**	**4 262.65**	**4 841.45**
#个人住房贷款	Housing Mortgage Loan	3 912.88	4 399.90
汽车消费贷款	Car Consumption Loan	90.89	134.29
个人住房贷款占中资商业银行人民币个人消费贷款额比重(%)	Housing Mortgage Loan Percentage of Personal Consumption Loan	91.8	90.9
公积金贷款	**Accumulation Fund Loan**	**1 026.86**	**1 127.45**

注:本表数据中的中资商业银行人民币个人消费贷款由中国人民银行上海总部提供,公积金贷款由上海市公市积金管理中心提供。
Note: Data in this table are provided by Shanghai Headquaters of People's Bank of China and Shanghai Provident Fund Administration Center.

表 16.7 主要年份中资金融机构现金收入和支出
CASH INCOME AND PAYOUT OF CHINESE FINANCIAL INSTITUTIONS IN MAIN YEARS

单位:亿元(100 million yuan)

年 份 Year	现金收入 Cash Income	其 中 of which			现金支出 Cash Payout	其 中 of which		
		#商品销售收入 Commodity Sales Income	#储蓄存款收入 Savings Income	#服务业收入 Service Income		#工资性及个人其他支出 Wage and Personal Payout	#储蓄存款支出 Savings Payout	#行政企业管理与经营费支出 Administrative Payout
1990	554.62	267.02	166.78	45.30	523.97	213.50	126.17	52.04
1995	3017.36	828.25	1 398.83	208.13	3102.50	913.91	1 201.86	342.88
1996	3469.05	938.91	1 596.81	241.53	3 650.54	932.22	1 734.95	518.44
1997	4026.57	998.75	1 877.66	279.41	4 219.72	779.27	2 404.84	606.30
1998	5681.56	1 384.74	2 866.31	439.09	5 856.38	1 023.70	3 117.37	744.89
1999	6430.00	1 506.02	3 370.06	493.27	6 612.87	949.15	3 749.12	856.16
2000	7 946.79	1 827.34	4 042.11	552.84	8 041.05	897.47	4 738.28	1 085.23
2001	10 102.34	2 085.64	5 937.10	574.42	10 305.35	977.28	6 268.39	1 426.58
2002	11 698.86	2 428.06	7 155.32	616.39	11 947.35	1 079.77	7 196.26	1 789.68
2003	15 378.63	2 918.36	10 064.82	693.09	15 730.94	1 407.72	9 836.08	2 274.99
2004	19 969.87	3 195.19	13 704.06	775.16	20 358.79	1 734.34	13 487.46	2 478.33
2005	21 195.88	3 152.31	14 838.14	745.68	21 701.53	1 919.32	14 417.49	2 615.49
2006	24 114.40	3 232.63	16 842.89	974.62	24 708.35	2 135.47	16 533.01	2 808.89
2007	30 070.03	3 637.62	22 071.51	1 271.51	30 721.55	2 488.74	21 724.99	3 162.89
2008	27 410.94	3 162.20	19 961.38	1 394.36	28 079.20	2 493.72	19 492.31	2 861.19
2009	28 079.22	3 486.53	20 903.54	1 273.93	29 033.36	2 592.88	20 705.03	2 905.51
2010	33 877.47	4 059.65	26 031.43	1 155.21	34 941.88	2 681.42	26 365.94	3 046.38

注：本表数据由中国人民银行上海总部提供。
Note: Data in this table are provided by Shanghai Headquaters of People's Bank of China.

表 16.8 主要金融市场成交概况(2008～2010)
DEAL STATISTICS OF MAIN FANANCIAL MARKET

指 标	Indicators	2008	2009	2010
上海证券交易所(亿元)	**Shanghai Stock Exchange (100 million yuan)**	**271 842.03**	**441 874.67**	**398 395.73**
上海期货交易所(亿元)	**Shanghai Future Exchange (100 million yuan)**	**288 719.90**	**737 583.45**	**1 234 794.76**
中国金融期货交易所(亿元)	**China Financial Futures Exchange(100 million yuan)**			**410 698.77**
全国银行间货币与债券市场(亿元)	**Inter-bank Lending and Bond Market(100 million yuan)**	**1 107 857.42**	**1 375 659.38**	**1 798 225.10**
同业拆借	Inter-bank Loans	150 491.81	193 504.97	278 684.03
回购交易	Bonds Repurchase.	581 205.24	702 898.67	875 935.56
现券买卖	Spot Bond Trade	371 157.71	472 699.35	640 422.08
债券远期交易	Bond Forward Transactions	5 002.66	6 556.39	3 183.43
上海黄金交易所(亿元)	**Total Gold Turnover (100 million yuan)**	**8 995.48**	**11 030.63**	**20 204.96**
上海钻石交易所(亿美元)	**Total Diamond Turnover (100 million USD)**	**13.07**	**15.21**	**28.61**

①本表数据分别由上海证券交易所、上海期货交易所、中国金融期货交易所、全国银行间同业拆借中心、上海黄金交易所和上海钻石交易所提供。
②本表数据除上海期货交易所和上海黄金交易所成交额按双向计算外,其他成交额数据均按单向计算。
❶Data in this table are provided by Shanghai Stock Exchange, Shanghai Futures Exchange, China Fanancial Futures Exchange, China Intertank Funding Center, Shanghai Gold Exchange, Shanghai Diamond Exchange and Shanghai Property Right Exchange.
❷The turnover data in the table are calculated by buy or sell except the Shanghai Futures Exchange and the Shanghai Gold Exchange turnover calculated by buy and sell.

表 16.9 金融机构人民币存款基准利率(1990～2010)
BENCHMARK INTEREST RATE OF RMB DEPOSIT FOR FINANCIAL INSTITUTIONS

单位:年利率%(annual interest rate)

调整时间 Adjust Time	活 期 Checking Deposit	定 期 fixed deposit					
		3个月 3 Months	6个月 6 Months	1年 1 Year	2年 2 Year	3年 3 Year	5年 5 Year
1990.04.15	2.88	6.30	7.74	10.08	10.98	11.88	13.68
1990.08.21	2.16	4.32	6.48	8.64	9.36	10.08	11.52
1991.04.21	1.80	3.24	5.40	7.56	7.92	8.28	9.00
1993.05.15	2.16	4.86	7.20	9.18	9.90	10.80	12.06
1993.07.11	3.15	6.66	9.00	10.98	11.70	12.24	13.86
1996.05.01	2.97	4.86	7.20	9.18	9.90	10.80	12.06
1996.08.23	1.98	3.33	5.40	7.47	7.92	8.28	9.00
1997.10.23	1.71	2.88	4.14	5.67	5.94	6.21	6.66
1998.03.25	1.71	2.88	4.14	5.22	5.58	6.21	6.66
1998.07.01	1.44	2.79	3.96	4.77	4.86	4.95	5.22
1998.12.07	1.44	2.79	3.33	3.78	3.96	4.14	4.50
1999.06.10	0.99	1.98	2.16	2.25	2.43	2.70	2.88
2002.02.21	0.72	1.71	1.89	1.98	2.25	2.52	2.79
2004.10.29	0.72	1.71	2.07	2.25	2.70	3.24	3.60
2006.08.19	0.72	1.80	2.25	2.52	3.06	3.69	4.14
2007.03.18	0.72	1.98	2.43	2.79	3.33	3.96	4.41
2007.05.19	0.72	2.07	2.61	3.06	3.69	4.41	4.95
2007.07.21	0.81	2.34	2.88	3.33	3.96	4.68	5.22
2007.08.22	0.81	2.61	3.15	3.60	4.23	4.95	5.49
2007.09.15	0.81	2.88	3.42	3.87	4.50	5.22	5.76
2007.12.21	0.72	3.33	3.78	4.14	4.68	5.40	5.85
2008.10.09	0.72	3.15	3.51	3.87	4.41	5.13	5.58
2008.10.30	0.72	2.88	3.24	3.60	4.14	4.77	5.13
2008.11.27	0.36	1.98	2.25	2.52	3.06	3.60	3.87
2008.12.23	0.36	1.71	1.98	2.25	2.79	3.33	3.60
2010.10.20	0.36	1.91	2.20	2.50	3.25	3.85	4.20
2010.12.26	0.36	2.25	2.50	2.75	3.55	4.15	4.55

注：本表数据摘自中国人民银行网站。
Note: Data in the table are from the Web of People's Bank of China.

表 16.10 金融机构人民币贷款基准利率(1991～2010)
BENCHMARK INTEREST RATE OF RMB LOAN FOR FINANCIAL INSTITUTIONS

单位:年利率%(annual interest rate)

调整时间 Adjust Time	6个月 6 Month	1年 1 Year	1～3年(含) 1～3 Years	3～5年(含) 3～5 Years	5年以上 Above 5 Years
1991.04.21	8.10	8.64	9.00	9.54	9.72
1993.05.15	8.82	9.36	10.80	12.06	12.24
1993.07.11	9.00	10.98	12.24	13.86	14.04
1995.01.01	9.00	10.98	12.96	14.58	14.76
1995.07.01	10.08	12.06	13.50	15.12	15.30
1996.05.01	9.72	10.98	13.14	14.94	15.12
1996.08.23	9.18	10.08	10.98	11.70	12.42
1997.10.23	7.65	8.64	9.36	9.90	10.53
1998.03.25	7.02	7.92	9.00	9.72	10.35
1998.07.01	6.57	6.93	7.11	7.65	8.01
1998.12.07	6.12	6.39	6.66	7.20	7.56
1999.06.10	5.58	5.85	5.94	6.03	6.21
2002.02.21	5.04	5.31	5.49	5.58	5.76
2004.10.29	5.22	5.58	5.76	5.85	6.12
2006.04.28	5.40	5.85	6.03	6.12	6.39
2006.08.19	5.58	6.12	6.30	6.48	6.84
2007.03.18	5.67	6.39	6.57	6.75	7.11
2007.05.19	5.85	6.57	6.75	6.93	7.20
2007.07.21	6.03	6.84	7.02	7.20	7.38
2007.07.21	6.03	6.84	7.02	7.20	7.38
2007.07.21	6.03	6.84	7.02	7.20	7.38
2007.08.22	6.21	7.02	7.20	7.38	7.56
2007.09.15	6.48	7.29	7.47	7.65	7.83
2007.12.21	6.57	7.47	7.56	7.74	7.83
2008.09.13	6.21	7.20	7.29	7.56	7.74
2008.10.09	6.12	6.93	7.02	7.29	7.47
2008.10.30	6.03	6.66	6.75	7.02	7.20
2008.11.27	5.04	5.58	5.67	5.94	6.12
2008.12.23	4.86	5.31	5.40	5.76	5.94
2010.10.20	5.10	5.56	5.60	5.96	6.14
2010.12.26	5.35	5.81	5.85	6.22	6.40

注：本表数据摘自中国人民银行网站。
Note: Data in the table are from the Web of People's Bank of China.

表 16.11　上海证券交易所上市公司股本结构(2008 ~ 2010)
CAPITAL STOCK STRUCTURE OF PUBLIC COMPANIES IN SHANGHAI STOCK EXCHANGE

单位:亿股(100 million Shares)

指　标	Indicators	2008	2009	2010
发行总股本	**Total**	**20 789.23**	**22 166.50**	**28 101.77**
尚未流通股份	Non-circulation Shares	10 494.34	5 081.40	5 908.20
国家拥有股份	State Shares	9 416.07	4 173.34	4 709.21
境内法人持有股份	Domestic Sponsoring Corporate Shares	562.22	310.93	235.79
外资法人持有股份	Foreign Corporate Shares	84.02	40.84	25.79
个人发起人股	Personal Sponsor Shares	34.29	15.79	20.61
募集法人股	Raised Corporate	7.65	5.19	4.53
机构配售	Transferred,Left and Others	4.73	4.86	136.38
其　他	Agencies placing	385.38	530.45	775.89
已流通股份	Circulation Shares	10 294.88	17 085.11	22 193.57
境内上市的人民币普通股	A Shares	4 794.85	11 455.02	15 901.47
境内上市外资股	B Shares	121.19	123.54	129.84
境外上市外资股	H Shares	5 378.84	5 506.55	6 162.27

表 16.12　上海证券交易所市场概况(2008 ~ 2010)
SHANGHAI STOCK EXCHANGE MARKET

指　标	Indicators	2008	2009	2010
上市公司数(个)	Quantity of Public Company (unit)	864	870	894
上市证券数(个)	Quantity of Negotiable Securities(unit)	1 184	1 351	1 500
上市股票数(个)	Quantity of Listed Stock(unit)	908	914	938
股票发行股数(亿股)	Shares of Stocks Issued (100 million shares)	15 410.39	16 659.50	21 939.51
A　股	A Shares	15 289.19	16 535.96	21 809.67
B　股	B Shares	121.19	123.54	129.84
股票市价总值(亿元)	Aggregate Value of Stocks in Market Price (100 million yuan)	97 251.91	184 655.23	179 007.24
A　股	A Shares	96 875.32	183 799.87	178 000.02
B　股	B Shares	376.59	855.35	1 007.22
流通股数(亿股)	Shares in Circulation (100 million shares)	4 916.04	11 578.56	16 031.31
A　股	A Shares	4 794.85	11 455.02	15 901.47
B　股	B Shares	121.19	123.54	129.84
流通市值(亿元)	Value in Circulation (100 million yuan)	32 305.91	114 805.00	142 337.45
A　股	A Shares	31 929.32	113 949.64	141 330.23
B　股	B Shares	376.59	855.35	1 007.22
市场筹资额(亿元)	Funds Raised from Market (100 million yuan)	3 294.91	4 817.67	7 585.14
首次发行 A 股	IPO of A Shares	733.54	1 251.25	1 891.51
再次发行 A 股	Additional A Shares Issued	1 504.62	2 091.91	3 640.62
债　券	Convertible Loan Stock	1 056.75	1 474.51	2 053.00

注：本页数据由上海证券交易所提供。
Note: Data on this page are provided by Shanghai Stock Exchange.

表16.13 主要年份上证综合指数
THE SHANGHAI COMPOSITE INDEX IN MAIN YEARS

年份 Year	开盘 Open	最高 High	日期 Date		最低 Low	日期 Date		收盘 Close
1990	96.05	127.61	12月31日	31,Dec	95.79	12月19日	19,Dec	127.61
1995	637.72	926.41	5月22日	22,May	524.43	2月7日	7,Feb	555.29
1996	550.26	1 258.69	12月11日	11,Dec	512.83	1月19日	19,Jan	917.02
1997	914.06	1 510.18	5月12日	12,May	870.80	2月20日	20,Feb	1 194.10
1998	1 200.95	1 422.95	6月4日	4,June	1 043.02	8月18日	18,Aug	1 146.70
1999	1 144.89	1 756.18	6月30日	30,June	1 047.83	5月17日	17,May	1 366.58
2000	1 368.69	2 125.72	11月23日	23,Nov	1 361.21	1月4日	4,Jan	2 073.48
2001	2 077.08	2 245.44	6月14日	14,June	1 514.86	10月22日	22,Oct	1 645.97
2002	1 643.49	1 748.89	6月25日	25,June	1 339.20	1月29日	29,Jan	1 357.65
2003	1 347.43	1 649.60	4月16日	16,Apr	1 307.40	11月13日	13,Nov	1 497.04
2004	1 492.72	1 777.52	4月6日	6,Apr	1 260.32	9月13日	13,Sep	1 266.50
2005	1 260.78	1 318.27	3月8日	8, Mar	1 011.50	7月11日	11, July	1 161.06
2006	1 163.88	2 698.90	12月29日	29,Dec	1 161.91	1月4日	4,Jan	2 675.47
2007	2 728.19	6 124.04	10月16日	16,Oct	2 541.53	2月6日	6,Feb	5 261.56
2008	5 265.00	5 522.78	1月14日	14,Jan	1 664.93	10月28日	28,Oct	1 820.81
2009	1 849.02	3 478.01	8月4日	4,Aug	1 844.09	1月5日	5,Jan	3 277.14
2010	3 289.75	3 282.18	1月5日	5,Jan	2 363.95	7月5日	5,July	2 808.08

表16.14 上证180指数和上证50指数(2006~2010)
SSE 180 INDEX AND SSE 50 INDEX

年份 Year	开盘 Open	最高 High	日期 Date		最低 Low	日期 Date		收盘 Close
上证180指数								
2006	2 174.72	4 810.86	12月29日	29, Dec	2 172.26	1月4日	4, Jan	4 780.23
2007	4 864.31	13 325.04	10月16日	16, Otc	4 750.22	1月5日	5, Jan	12 024.60
2008	12 047.40	12 884.16	1月14日	14,Jan	3 600.60	10月28日	28,Oct	4 048.00
2009	4 122.80	8 421.72	8月3日	3,Aug	4 189.17	1月13日	1,Jan	7 762.92
2010	7 799.25	7 748.25	1月5日	5,Jan	5 475.95	7月5日	5,July	6 517.60
上证50指数								
2006	801.41	1 819.04	12月29日	29, Dec	800.21	1月4日	4, Jan	1 805.31
2007	1 842.63	4 772.93	10月16日	16, Otc	1 791.64	1月5日	5, Jan	4 226.72
2008	4 230.81	4 524.29	1月14日	14,Jan	1 269.29	10月28日	28,Oct	1 384.91
2009	1 411.08	2 837.74	8月3日	3,Aug	1 414.08	1月13日	13,Jan	2 553.80
2010	2 565.11	2 543.99	1月5日	5,Jan	1 797.66	7月5日	5,July	1 977.37

注：本页数据由上海证券交易所提供。
Note: Data on this page are provided by Shanghai Stock Exchange.

表 16.15　上海证券交易所有价证券成交总额(2007～2010)
TOTAL VOLUME OF PRICED SECURITIES TRADING IN SHANGHAI STOCK EXCHANGE

单位:亿元 (100 million yuan)

指　标	Indicators	2007	2008	2009	2010
总　计	**Total**	**380 026**	**271 842**	**441 875**	**398 396**
股　票	Shocks	305 434	180 430	346 512	304 312
A 股	A Shares	301 960	179 762	345 443	303 216
B 股	B Shares	3 474	668	1 069	1 096
债　券	Bond	20 400	28 091	39 806	74 914
基　金(含 ETF)	Fund	4 298	3 700	6 549	4 772
权　证	Warrant	49 894	59 621	49 008	14 398

表 16.16　主要年份上海证券交易所股票账户开户情况
ACCOUNT-OPENING BY INVESTORS IN SHANGHAI STOCK EXCHANGE IN MAIN YEARS

单位:万户(10 000 households)

指　标	Indicators	2000	2009	2010
年末开户总数	**Total Accounts Year-end**			
总　数	Total	2 957.84	7 405.37	8 154.23
个　人	Private	2 944.89	7 370.25	8 116.45
机　构	Institution	12.95	35.12	37.78
A 股开户数	**A Shares Accounts**			
总　数	Total	2 943.32	7 255.03	8 001.44
个　人	Private	2931.20	7 221.62	7 965.48
机　构	Institution	12.12	33.41	35.96
B 股开户数	**B Shares Accounts**			
总　数	Total	14.52	150.34	152.78
个　人	Private	13.69	148.63	150.97
机　构	Institution	0.83	1.71	1.82
当年新开户总数	**Newly Opened Accounts During the Year**			
总　数	Total	676.72	862.77	748.86
个　人	Private	672.09	859.33	746.20
机　构	Institution	4.64	3.44	2.66
A 股新开户数	**Newly Opened Accounts of A Shares**			
总　数	Total	671.08	859.57	746.41
个　人	Private	666.52	856.22	743.86
机　构	Institution	4.56	3.35	2.55
B 股新开户数	**Newly Opened Accounts of B Shares**			
总　数	Total	5.64	3.20	2.45
个　人	Private	5.56	3.10	2.34
机　构	Institution	0.08	0.09	0.11

注：本页数据由上海证券交易所提供.
Note: Data on this page are provided by Shanghai Stock Exchange.

上 / 海 / 统 / 计 / 年 / 鉴

主要统计指标解释

存　款

机构或个人在保留资金或货币所有权的条件下，以不可流通的存款凭证为依据，暂时让渡或接受资金使用权所形成的债权或债务。

贷　款

机构或个人在保留资金或货币所有权的条件下，以不可流通的借款凭证或类似凭证为依据，暂时让渡或接受资金使用权所形成的债权或债务。

上证综合指数

以在上海证券交易所上市的全部股票（A股和B股）作为样本计算的股票价格指数。

市场筹资额

企业在上海证券交易所通过发行股票和债券所筹集的资金总额。

原保险保费收入

指保险人与投保人之间直接签订的原保险合同中确认的保费收入，不包括再保险保费收入。

原保险赔付支出

指保险企业根据保险人与投保人之间直接签订的原保险合同中确认的赔付款项，不包括再保险赔付支出。

SHANGHAI STATISTICAL YEARBOOK

EXPLANATORY NOTES TO MAJOR STATISTICAL INDICATORS

□ Deposits

Deposit refers to the creditor's rights or debt formed by temporary lending or receiving funds in condition of institutions or individuals to retain the ownership of funds or monetary and based on the non-negotiable certificates of deposits.

□ Loans

Loan refers to the creditor's rights or debt formed by temporary lending or receiving funds in condition of institutions or individuals to retain the ownership of funds or monetary and based on the non-negotiable certificates of loan or similar certificates.

□ SSE Composite Index

SSE Composite Index is a stock price index, which is calculated by the price of all stocks (including A stocks and B stocks) in Shanghai Stock Exchange.

□ Market Financing

Market Financing refers to the total amount of fund which enterprises raise by issuing shares or bonds in Shanghai Stock Exchange.

□ Premium of Primary Insurance

Premium of Primary Insurance includes the insurance premium which is entered into the original insurance contract signed directly between the insurer and the insured, and reinsurance premium is excluded.

□ Payment of Primary Insurance

Payment of Primary Insurance includes the insurance payment which is entered into the original insurance contract signed directly between the insurer and the insured, and reinsurance payment is excluded.

第十七篇

CHAPTER 17

房地产业

REAL ESTATE

表 17.1 全社会房屋施工面积、竣工面积(1985～2010) TOTAL FLOOR SPACE OF CONSTRUCTION AND COMPLETED BUILDINGS

年 份 Year	施工面积(万平方米) Floor Area of Construction (10 000 sq. m.)	其中 of which #住宅 Residential Housing	竣工面积(万平方米) Floor Area Completed (10 000 sq. m.)	其中 of which #住宅 Residential Housing	房屋建筑面积竣工率(%) Construction Completion Rate (%)	其中 of which #住宅 Residential Housing
1985	4 162.15	2 651.52	2 909.58	2 112.04	69.9	79.7
1986	4 874.44	2 469.27	2 493.93	1 790.01	51.2	72.5
1987	4 382.40	2 658.05	2 700.96	1 874.90	61.6	70.5
1988	4 369.20	2 667.00	2 457.34	1 758.29	56.2	65.9
1989	3 683.77	2 048.20	1 941.80	1 246.58	52.7	60.9
1990	3 801.46	2 269.06	2 138.44	1 339.02	56.3	59.0
1991	3 611.53	2 157.46	1 923.92	1 160.61	53.3	53.8
1992	4 709.52	2 463.79	2 608.20	1 379.18	55.4	56.0
1993	4 724.30	2 142.39	2 031.76	1 017.54	43.0	47.5
1994	6 720.70	3 520.27	2 519.09	1 349.24	37.5	38.3
1995	10 566.42	6 195.12	3 093.93	1 746.82	29.3	28.2
1996	10 730.85	5 874.26	3 254.57	1 872.65	30.3	31.9
1997	9 955.21	5 450.13	3 614.19	2 179.68	36.3	40.0
1998	9 364.36	5 113.52	3 364.43	1 963.51	35.9	38.4
1999	8 364.48	4 608.49	3 257.57	1 731.55	38.9	37.6
2000	8 636.31	4 804.12	3 266.52	1 724.02	37.8	35.9
2001	8 588.49	5 236.93	3 215.12	1 743.90	37.4	33.3
2002	9 425.42	5 994.70	3 102.54	1 880.50	32.9	31.4
2003	11 023.24	6 974.27	3 582.34	2 280.79	32.5	32.7
2004	12 291.81	7 873.44	4 932.57	3 270.43	40.1	41.5
2005	14 477.85	8 267.24	4 873.82	2 819.35	33.7	34.1
2006	14 596.49	8 085.28	4 901.46	2 746.80	33.6	34.0
2007	14 979.37	7 789.91	5 068.46	2 843.62	33.8	36.5
2008	14 083.52	7 060.19	3 828.79	1 899.40	27.2	26.9
2009	13 553.64	6 581.16	2 970.92	1 522.07	21.9	23.1
2010	15 020.76	7 344.07	2 776.21	1 415.44	18.5	19.3

表 17.2 住宅投资和竣工建筑面积(1978 ~ 2010)
INVESTMENT IN RESIDENTIAL HOUSING AND FLOOR SPACE OF BUILDINGS COMPLETED

年 份 Year	住宅投资额 (亿元) Investment in Residential Housing (100 million yuan)	占全社会固定资产投资总额比重(%) As Percentage of Total Investment in Fixed Asset	住宅竣工建筑面积 (万平方米) Floor Area of Residence Building Completed (10 000 sq. m.)	市区人均住房居住面积 (平方米) Dwelling Area per Capita(sq. m.)
1978	2.67	9.6	199.61	4.5
1979	3.31	9.3	215.99	4.3
1980	5.82	12.8	304.32	4.4
1981	10.02	18.4	1 380.70	4.5
1982	11.03	15.5	1 363.63	4.7
1983	11.18	14.7	1 347.79	4.9
1984	15.88	17.2	1 788.44	5.0
1985	25.47	21.5	2 112.04	5.4
1986	28.24	19.2	1 790.01	6.0
1987	36.28	19.5	1 874.90	6.2
1988	44.84	18.3	1 758.29	6.3
1989	35.82	16.7	1 246.58	6.4
1990	42.94	18.9	1 339.02	6.6
1991	48.92	18.9	1 160.61	6.7
1992	61.23	17.1	1 379.18	6.9
1993	77.14	11.8	1 017.54	7.3
1994	300.65	26.8	1 349.24	7.5
1995	433.76	27.1	1 746.82	8.0
1996	466.99	23.9	1 872.65	8.7
1997	458.22	23.2	2 179.68	9.3
1998	404.96	20.6	1 963.51	9.7
1999	378.82	20.4	1 731.55	10.9
2000	443.90	23.7	1 724.02	11.8
2001	466.71	23.4	1 743.90	12.5
2002	584.51	26.7	1 880.50	13.1
2003	694.30	28.3	2 280.79	13.8
2004	922.61	29.9	3 270.43	14.8
2005	936.36	26.4	2 819.35	15.5
2006	854.15	21.8	2 746.80	16.0
2007	853.13	19.1	2 843.62	16.5
2008	871.52	18.0	1 899.40	16.9
2009	922.81	17.5	1 522.07	17.2
2010	1 232.96	23.2	1 415.44	17.5

注：1981 年以前住宅投资额和住宅竣工建筑面积数据不包括城乡私人建房和农村投资，从 1981 年开始为全社会口径。

Note: Before 1981, investments and floor area of residential housing completed in this table dont cover private-built houses in urban and rural areas and rural investment, the whole society is covered since 1981.

表 17.3 主要年份房地产开发投资和经营情况
INVESTMENT AND OPERATION IN REAL ESTATE DEVELOPMENT IN MAIN YEARS

单位:亿元(100 million yuan)

指 标	Indicators	2000	2009	2010
投资总额	**Total Investment**	**566.17**	**1 464.18**	**1 980.68**
#土地开发投资	Investment in Land Development	25.91	89.51	97.74
在投资总额中	Of Total Investment			
住 宅	Residence	408.82	918.68	1 229.83
#别墅、高档公寓	Villas and Apartment	40.72	246.51	373.67
办公楼	Office Building	57.47	189.15	224.46
商业营业用房	Commercial Building	51.51	185.10	244.7
其 他	Others	48.38	171.25	281.69
新增固定资产	**Newly Increased Fixed Assets**	**477.39**	**932.24**	**964.27**
资金来源合计	**Total Capital Source**	**778.16**	**3 609.25**	**4 443.85**
上年末结余资金	Balance at End of Previous Year	113.48	681.86	1 214.56
本年资金来源小计	Sub-total Capital Source of this Year	664.68	2 927.39	3 229.29
国内贷款	Domestic Loans	155.37	637.14	819.57
利用外资	Foreign Capital Utilized	28.11	25.40	96.05
#外商直接投资	Foreign Direct Investment	16.24	22.71	65.52
自筹资金	Self-Financed Capital	211.86	622.21	1 070.88
其他资金	Other Capital	269.34	1 642.64	1 242.78

表 17.4 主要年份房地产开发企业房屋建筑面积和造价
CONSTRUCTION AREA AND COST OF PROPERTY DEVELOPED BY REAL ESTATE COMPANIES IN MAIN YEARS

指　标	Indicators	2000	2009	2010
房屋施工面积（万平方米）	**Floor Area of Construction（10 000 sq. m）**	**5 523.23**	**9 961.60**	**11 295.03**
住　宅	Residence	4 263.50	6 550.73	7 313.85
#别墅、高档公寓	Villas and Apartment	254.11	1 302.04	1 584.11
办公楼	Office Building	515.10	958.64	1 103.18
商业营业用房	Commercial Building	438.47	1 112.33	1 292.96
其　他	Others	306.16	1 339.90	1 585.04
房屋竣工面积（万平方米）	**Floor Area Completed（10 000 sq. m）**	**1 643.62**	**2 104.98**	**1 941.25**
住　宅	Residence	1 388.01	1 508.81	1 396.05
#别墅、高档公寓	Villas and Apartment	66.38	205.00	328.00
办公楼	Office Building	95.93	135.02	150.69
商业营业用房	Commercial Building	100.16	201.05	176.41
其　他	Others	59.52	260.10	218.09
房屋竣工价值(亿元)	**Value of Building Completed（100 million yuan）**	**355.79**	**705.80**	**779.93**
住　宅	Residence	270.29	441.11	536.66
#别墅、高档公寓	Villas and Apartment	20.66	98.49	178.27
办公楼	Office Building	45.41	81.70	74.23
商业营业用房	Commercial Building	24.29	78.35	87.13
其　他	Others	15.80	104.64	81.91
竣工房屋平均造价(元/平方米)	**Average Construction Cost（yuan/sq. m）**	**2 164**	**3 353**	**4 018**
住　宅	Residence	1 947	2 924	3 844
#别墅、高档公寓	Villas and Apartment	3 112	4 804	5 435
办公楼	Office Building	4 733	6 051	4 926
商业营业用房	Commercial Building	2 425	3 897	4 939
其　他	Others	2 654	4 023	3 756

表 17.5 主要年份商品房销售和出租情况
COMMODITY HOUSING SOLD AND LEASED IN MAIN YEARS

指 标	Indicators	2000	2009	2010
商品房销售面积(万平方米)	**Sold Area of Commodity Housing (10 000 sq. m)**	**1 557.87**	**3 372.45**	**2 055.53**
住 宅	Residence	1 445.87	2 928.04	1 685.35
#别墅、高档公寓	Villas and Apartment	53.44	450.42	341.71
办公楼	Office Building	47.76	203.00	162.89
商业营业用房	Commercial Building	54.54	126.49	125.56
其 他	Others	9.70	114.92	81.72
商品房销售额(亿元)	**Sales Volume of Commodity Housing (100 million yuan)**	**555.45**	**4 330.22**	**2 959.94**
住 宅	Residence	480.97	3 620.23	2 395.35
#别墅、高档公寓	Villas and Apartment	32.65	996.81	852.62
办公楼	Office Building	44.05	438.43	307.67
商业营业用房	Commercial Building	27.87	192.73	197.57
其 他	Others	2.56	78.84	59.34
商品房出租面积 (万平方米)	**Commodity Housing Leased (10 000 Sq. m)**	**358.38**	**1 222.91**	**1 262.47**
住 宅	Residence	59.29	102.63	85.72
#别墅、高档公寓	Villas and Apartment	37.43	74.36	76.18
办公楼	Office Building	156.15	425.55	516.18
商业营业用房	Commercial Building	62.04	349.91	373.34
其 他	Others	80.91	344.82	287.23

表 17.6 每百户城市居民家庭房屋产权构成(2008～2010)
PROPERTY RIGHT STRUCTURE OF TOWNSMAN TENEMENT PER HUNDRED HOUSEHOLDS

单位:%

类 别	Types	2008	2009	2010
每百户城市居民家庭房屋产权构成	Property Right Structure of Townsman Tenement per Hundred Households	100	100	100
租赁公房	Leasehold Public Tenement	17.4	16.3	16.4
租赁私房	Leasehold Private Tenement	4.2	3.7	3.5
原有私房	Inhere Private Tenement	0.7	0.7	0.7
房改私房	Reformed Private Tenement	37.8	37.2	37.4
商品房	Commercial Tenement	39.1	41.3	41.1
其 他	Others	0.8	0.8	0.9

表 17.7 房屋拆迁情况(1995～2010) BUILDINGS RESETTLEMENT

年份 Year	拆迁户数(户) Quantity of Resettlements (unit)	其中 of which #居民住宅 Residence	拆迁面积 (万平方米) Floor Area Resettled (10 000 sq. m.)	其中 of which #居民住宅 Residence
1995	75 777	73 695	322.77	253.90
1996	89 132	86 481	342.95	258.86
1997	79 857	77 388	479.67	363.16
1998	78 205	75 157	452.22	343.94
1999	75 185	73 709	342.50	248.17
2000	70 606	68 293	365.77	288.35
2001	73 728	71 909	515.65	386.66
2002	101 097	98 714	644.53	485.00
2003	80 858	79 077	584.93	475.47
2004	42 415	41 552	308.40	232.52
2005	75 857	74 483	1 222.53	851.85
2006	81 126	76 874	1 516.85	848.35
2007	51 354	49 092	825.00	690.00
2008	53 583	51 288	1 028.53	753.71
2009	68 286	65 439	927.63	612.56
2010	39 721	38 441	585.7	389.87

表 17.8 各区房屋拆迁情况(2010) BUILDINGS RESETTLEMENT IN DIFFERENT DISTRICTS

地区	District	拆迁户数(户) Quantity of Resettlements (unit)	其中 of which #居民住宅 Residence	拆迁面积 (万平方米) Floor Area Resettled (10 000 sq. m.)	其中 of which #居民住宅 Residence
总 计	**Total**	**39 721**	**38 441**	**585.70**	**389.87**
#浦东新区	Pudong New Area	7 331	7 173	34.81	14.06
黄 浦 区	Huangpu	1 654	1 594	20.76	5.89
卢 湾 区	Luwan	1 500	1 500	3.24	3.24
徐 汇 区	Xuhui	3 990	3 888	53.22	31.71
长 宁 区	Changning	1 340	1 294	14.57	7.68
静 安 区	Jing'an	1 118	1 041	7.62	4.27
普 陀 区	Putuo	536	536	2.15	2.15
闸 北 区	Zhabei	5 071	5 023	11.76	11.58
虹 口 区	Hongkou	1 502	1 487	7.45	5.93
杨 浦 区	Yangpu	3 546	3 520	10.35	7.02

表 17.9 土地使用权出让情况(2010) LEASE OF LAND PLOT TENURE

指 标	Indicators	出让地块（幅）Leased Plot (piece)	出让面积（万平方米）Leased Area (10 000 sq. m)
总 计	**Total**	**621**	**2 853.71**
商业服务	Commercial Service	97	423.83
住 宅	Residence	152	1 253.86
工矿仓储	Storage of Industry	362	1 170.14
公共建筑	Public Buildings	10	5.88

注：本表数据由市规划和国土资源管理局提供。
Note: Data in this table are provided by Shanghai Municipal Bureau of Planning and Land Resources.

表 17.10 存量房交易情况(1994~2010) EXCHANGE OF SECOND-HAND HOUSES

年 份 Year	成交套数（套）Houses Traded (set)	成交面积（万平方米）Areas Traded (10 000 sq. m.)	其 中 of which		
			住 宅 Residence	办公楼 Office	商业营业用房 Commerce
1994	2 821	31.76	10.59		
1995	4 176	60.87	19.70		
1996	4 689	82.29	25.09		
1997	9 180	162.40	87.68	23.95	14.95
1998	24 501	315.23	197.56	21.49	18.28
1999	44 234	510.84	336.69	37.63	14.61
2000	96 348	778.52	648.23	39.48	21.65
2001	164 598	1422.43	1 031.48	56.99	57.24
2002	204 239	1 790.50	1 341.60	65.70	91.80
2003	263 297	2 306.28	1 807.57	105.14	114.28
2004	303 291	2 726.70	2 222.24	117.12	121.39
2005	189 896	1 971.50	1 608.20	88.10	78.00
2006	184 194	1 706.81	1 375.22	67.35	46.53
2007	213 733	1 992.59	1 715.05	49.73	36.34
2008	142 224	1 413.41	1 107.17	40.61	42.04
2009	312 857	2 809.45	2 490.58	48.19	43.59
2010	202 511	1 966.86	1 522.21	68.31	70.61

注：本页数据由市住房保障和房屋管理局提供。
Note: Data on this page are provided by Shanghai Municipal Housing Security and Building Administration Bureau.

上 / 海 / 统 / 计 / 年 / 鉴

主要统计指标解释

房地产开发投资

指各种登记注册类型的房地产开发公司、商品房建设公司及其他房地产开发法人单位和附属于其他法人单位实际从事房地产开发或经营活动的单位统一开发的包括统代建、拆迁还建的住宅、厂房、仓库、饭店、宾馆、度假村、写字楼、办公楼等房屋建筑物和配套的服务设施，土地开发工程(如道路、给水、排水、供电、供热、通讯、平整场地等基础设施工程)的投资；不包括单纯的土地交易活动。

施工面积

指报告期内施工的全部房屋建筑面积。包括本期新开工的面积和上期开工跨入本期继续施工的房屋面积，以及上期已停建在本期恢复施工的房屋面积。本期竣工和本期施工后又停缓建的房屋，其建筑面积仍计入本期房屋施工面积中。

竣工面积

指在报告期内房屋建筑按照设计要求已经全部完工，达到住人和使用条件，经验收鉴定合格(或达到竣工验收标准)，正式移交使用单位的各栋房屋建筑面积的总和。

房屋建筑面积竣工率

指一定时期内房屋竣工面积占同期房屋施工面积的比率。该指标从房屋建筑施工速度的角度反映投资效果的指标。

别墅、高档公寓

指建筑造价和销售价格明显高于一般商品住宅的商品住宅。别墅一般指地处郊区，独立成栋的商品住宅；高档公寓一般指地处市内高尚社区，高层或多层的商品住宅。别墅、高档公寓的确定标准：一是经有房地产投资计划审批权的主管部门审批建设的别墅、高档公寓开发项目；二是销售价格高于当地同等地段商品住宅平均销售价格一倍以上的别墅、公寓开发项目。该指标可以分析房地产投资结构，反映高收入家庭商品住宅的供求平衡情况。

SHANGHAI STATISTICAL YEARBOOK

EXPLANATORY NOTES TO MAJOR STATISTICAL INDICATORS

□ Investment in Real Estate Development

It includes the investment by the real estate development companies, commercial buildings construction companies and other real estate development units of various types of ownership in the construction of house buildings, such as residential buildings, factory buildings, warehouses, hotels, guesthouses, holiday villages, office buildings, and the complementary service facilities and land development projects, such as roads, water supply, water drainage, power supply, heating, telecommunications, land leveling and other projects of infrastructure. It excludes the activities in simple land transactions.

□ Floor Area of Construction

Floor Area of Construction refers to total floor space of all buildings under construction during the reference period, including floor space of newly started buildings during the reference period, floor space of construction extended from the previous period to the current period, and floor space of construction suspended during the previous period and resumed in the current period. Floor space of construction completed in the current period, and floor space of construction started and then suspended in the current period are also included in the floor space under construction of the current year.

□ Floor Area Completed

Floor Area Completed refers to the floor space of all buildings completed in the reference period, which have been appraised and accepted (or come up to the designed standards) and have been transferred to the owners for use.

□ Completion Rate of Floor Space of Buildings

Completion Rate of Floor Space of Buildings refers to the ratio of the floor space of buildings completed in certain period of time to the floor space of buildings under construction in the same period. This indicator reflects the investment result from the perspective of the speed of construction.

□ Villas, High-Grade Apartments

Villas, High-Grade Apartments refers to commercial houses whose construction costs and marketing prices are significantly higher than ordinary housing. Villas are independent structures generally located in the suburbs; high-grade apartments are multi-story buildings located in elegant urban neighborhoods. Criteria for villas and high-grade apartments include: 1) projects for the construction of villas or high-grade apartments have to be approved by competent departments in charge of real estate development and investment plans, and 2) prices for projects on villas or high-grade apartments are higher by over 100% compared with the average prices of ordinary commercial housing projects in similar location. This indicator helps to analyze the investment structure of the real estate industry and the demand and supply of housing for high-income households.

第十八篇

CHAPTER 18

科学技术

SCIENCE AND TECHNOLOGY

表 18.1 主要年份科技活动主要指标
MAIN INDICATORS OF SCIENTIFIC AND TECHNOLOGICAL ACTIVITIES IN MAIN YEARS

年 份 Year	科技活动人员（万人） Personnel Engaged in Scientific and Technological Activities (10 000 persons)	研究与试验发展经费支出（亿元） Expenditures on R&D (100million yuan)	研究与试验发展经费支出相当于上海市生产总值比例（%） R&D as Percentage of Gross Domestic Product (%)	地方财政科技经费支出（亿元） Local Fiscal Expenditures on Scientific and Technological Research (100 million yuan)	科技经费支出占地方财政支出比重(%) Percentage of Expenditures on Scientific and Technological Research in Local Fiscal (%)
1990	19.34	10.13	1.30	2.44	3.2
1995	18.25	32.60	1.30	5.12	2.0
2000	20.17	76.73	1.61	10.08	1.6
2001	17.57	88.08	1.69	12.39	1.7
2002	17.89	102.36	1.78	15.25	1.7
2003	17.59	128.92	1.93	19.84	1.8
2004	18.25	170.28	2.11	39.32	2.8
2005	19.67	213.77	2.31	79.34	4.8
2006	20.07	258.84	2.45	94.89	5.2
2007	22.79	307.50	2.46	105.77	4.9
2008	23.08	362.30	2.58	120.27	4.6
2009	33.90	423.38	2.81	215.31	7.2
2010	33.39	480.18	2.80	202.03	6.1

注：本表部分数据由上海市财政局等部门提供。
Note: Data in this table are mainly provided by Shanghai Municipal Finance Bureau.

表 18.2 主要年份获得科技成果奖励情况
ACHIEVEMENTS AWARDED IN SCIENTIFIC AND TECHNOLOGICAL RESEARCH IN MAIN YEARS

单位:项(item)

指 标	Indicators	2000	2009	2010
科技成果获奖总数	**Quantity of Achievements Awarded**	**287**	**356**	**356**
获国家科技成果奖	**National Award**	**21**	**56**	**58**
#国家最高科学技术奖(人)	State Supreme Science Award		1	1
国家自然科学奖	Natural Science Award	3	47	6
国家技术发明奖	Technological Invention Award	1	3	4
国家科学技术进步奖	Science and Technology Progress Award	17	4	46
国际科学技术奖(人)	International Science and Technology Award		1	1
获上海科技进步奖	**Shanghai Award**	**266**	**300**	**298**

注：本表数据由市科学技术委员会提供。
Note: Data in this table are provided by Shanghai Science and Technology Commission.

表 18.3 主要年份研究与试验发展(R&D)活动情况
BASIC STATISTICS OF SCIENTIFIC AND TECHNOLOGICAL ACTIVITIES IN MAIN YEARS

指 标	Indicators	2000	2009	2010
一、有 R&D 活动单位数(个)	**Quantity of Science and Technology Institutions (unit)**	**1 070**	**1 986**	**1 764**
#科研机构	Research Institutions	125	112	113
高等院校	Institutions of Higher Education	41	51	68
企 业	Enterprises	820	1 667	1 444
其 他	Others	84	156	139
二、R&D 活动人员(万人年)	**R&D Personnel (10 000 persons-year)**	**6.31**	**13.29**	**13.42**
基础研究	Basic Research	0.60	1.36	1.41
应用研究	Applied Research	1.92	2.55	2.27
试验发展	Experimental Development	3.79	9.38	9.74
三、R&D 活动经费支出(亿元)	**Expenditures on R&D (100 million yuan)**	**76.73**	**423.38**	**480.18**
基础研究	Basic Research	4.98	28.81	31.03
应用研究	Applied Research	18.18	70.81	68.87
试验发展	Experimental Development	53.57	323.76	380.28
四、R&D 项目(课题)情况	**R&D project**			
项目(课题)数 (万项)	Quantity of Projects (10 000 item)	2.07	5.06	6.04
项目(课题)参加人员(万人年)	Personnell Engaged in Projects (10 000 persons year)	5.42	11.91	12.22
项目(课题)经费内部支出(亿元)	Inner Expenditure on Projects (100 million yuan)	54.31	316.48	392.60
五、科技活动产出情况	**Output of Science and Technic Activities**			
新产品产值(亿元)	Production Value of New Product(100 million yuan)	1 401.62	4 919.82	5 870.02
新产品销售收入(亿元)	Sales Revenue of New Product(100 million yuan)	1 398.54	5 442.66	6 543.07
发表科技论文数(篇)	Quantity of Science and Technic Papers Published(case)	37 216	90 147	87 449
商标申请注册数(件)	Register Applications for Trade Marks (case)	9 455	41 882	60 243
商标核准注册数(件)	Registration approved for Trade Marks (case)	6 208	35 984	70 417
科技成果登记数(项)	Quantity of Achievements Registered in Scientific and Technological Activities(item)	1 102	2 166	2 318

注：本表部分数据由市科委和市工商局提供。
Note: Data in this table are partly provided by Shanhgai? Municipal Science and Technology Commission and Shanghai Administration of Industry and Commerce.

表 18.4 国有企事业单位专业技术人员基本情况(2010)
PROFESSIONAL AND TECHNICAL PERSONNEL IN STATE-OWNED ENTERPRISES AND INSTITUTIONS

单位:项(item)

类别 Types		合计 Total	其中 of which	按学历分 by Education Background		
			#女性 Female	大学本专科以上 College and University above	中等专业 Specialized Secondary School	高中及以下 Senior Middle School and below
总计	**Total**	**82.95**	**39.78**	**71.81**	**7.23**	**3.91**
高级岗位	Senior	7.60	2.71	7.51	0.05	0.04
中级岗位	Medium	25.94	13.03	24.31	1.16	0.47
初级岗位	Junior	28.37	14.02	22.43	4.37	1.57
未聘人员	Not Appointed	21.04	10.02	17.56	1.65	1.83

表 18.4 续表 continued

单位:项(item)

类别 Types		合计 Total	其中 of which	按学历分 by Education Background		
			#女性 Female	大学本专科以上 College and University above	中等专业 Specialized Secondary School	高中及以下 Senior Middle School and below
总计	**Total**	**82.95**	**39.78**	**71.81**	**7.23**	**3.91**
工程技术人员	Engineering	21.70	4.46	18.86	1.50	1.34
农业技术人员	Agriculture	0.31	0.08	0.21	0.06	0.04
卫生技术人员	Scientific Research	1.64	0.58	1.58	0.04	0.02
科学研究人员	Medical Prlfessionals	9.49	6.56	7.15	2.20	0.14
教学人员	Teching	16.02	11.03	15.59	0.37	0.06
经济人员	Economic	21.94	10.47	18.62	1.77	1.55
财会人员	Financial Accounting	6.94	4.47	5.73	0.84	0.37
统计人员	Statistical	0.59	0.37	0.46	0.07	0.06
新闻出版、播音人员	Translator	0.13	0.07	0.13		
翻译人员	Media, Publishing & Announcer	0.81	0.43	0.76	0.03	0.02
艺术人员	Culture&Art	0.48	0.18	0.31	0.10	0.07
其他专业人员	Others	2.90	1.08	2.41	0.25	0.24

表 18.5 主要年份各类技术合同项目
VARIOUS TECHNOLOGICAL CONTRACTS IN MAIN YEARS

单位:项(item)

年份 Year	项目 Item	其中 of which 技术开发 Technological Development	技术转让 Technological Transfer	技术咨询 Technological Consulting	技术服务 Technological Service
1991	25 023	3 038	1 992	3 203	16 790
1995	21 213	1 915	775	3 672	14 851
1996	20 074	1 841	823	3 821	13 589
1997	18 863	1 643	1 037	3 569	12 614
1998	18 364	1 206	919	3 235	13 004
1999	19 721	1 158	937	3 993	13 633
2000	20 974	1 561	888	3 905	14 620
2001	23 816	2 385	1 294	5 012	15 125
2002	26 010	2 984	1 156	4 983	16 887
2003	27 292	3 512	2 112	5 306	16 362
2004	27 327	4 398	2 453	4 814	15 662
2005	30 290	5 256	2 444	4 753	17 837
2006	28 191	6 165	2 172	3 592	16 262
2007	27 742	6 425	2 133	3 086	16 098
2008	28 713	7 154	1 749	3 873	15 937
2009	27 109	8 071	1 549	3 034	14 455
2010	26 185	8 894	1 370	2 685	13 236

表 18.6 主要年份各类技术合同成交金额
TOTAL CONTRACTED VALUE IN VARIOUS TECHNOLOGICAL CONTRACTS IN MAIN YEARS

单位:亿元(100 million yuan)

年份 Year	成交金额 Contracted Value	其中 of which 技术开发 Technological Development	技术转让 Technological Transfer	技术咨询 Technological Consulting	技术服务 Technological Service
1991	9.33	2.15	1.90	0.55	4.72
1995	23.04	4.14	1.57	2.12	15.21
1996	25.65	4.38	1.50	2.81	16.97
1997	28.76	5.72	2.14	3.28	17.61
1998	31.41	4.55	2.58	2.44	21.85
1999	36.63	3.68	3.50	3.24	26.21
2000	73.90	9.96	36.44	3.51	23.99
2001	106.16	28.24	50.71	4.63	22.58
2002	120.22	45.40	46.18	4.63	24.01
2003	142.78	50.96	50.79	6.11	34.92
2004	171.70	61.31	42.32	6.00	62.07
2005	231.73	87.47	110.08	6.42	27.76
2006	344.43	142.79	165.18	7.60	28.86
2007	432.64	181.50	212.49	5.50	33.15
2008	485.75	213.24	229.53	6.41	36.57
2009	489.86	266.30	174.34	5.39	43.83
2010	525.45	264.68	213.86	4.93	41.98

注:本页数据由市技术市场管理办公室提供。
Note: Data on this page are provided by Shanghai Technology Market Administrative Office.

表 18.7 科技成果（2000 ~ 2010）
ACHIEVEMENTS IN SCIENTIFIC AND TECHNICAL RESEARCH

单位:项(item)

年 份 Year	科技成果 Achievements in Science and Technology	按成果水平分 By Level of Achievements			
		国际领先 Being First Created in the World	国际先进 Attaining Advanced World Levels	国内领先 Being First Created in China	国内先进 Attaining Advanced Domestic Levels
2000	1 102	45	462	452	117
2001	1 338	78	542	444	116
2002	1 418	65	603	463	106
2003	1 508	71	532	481	155
2004	1 629	147	669	480	155
2005	1 701	123	629	588	189
2006	1 953	250	675	655	191
2007	2 396	180	761	938	254
2008	1 866	125	664	663	226
2009	2 166	260	651	831	247
2010	2 318	188	698	724	202

表 18.7 续表 continued

单位:项(item)

年 份 Year	按成果分 By Type of Achievements				
	基础理论成果 Fundamental Theory Research Results	应用技术成果 Application of Technological Achievements	其 中 of which		软科学成果 Soft Scientific Achievements
			已推广应用 Been Populized	未应用 Not Been Populized	
2000	79	953	809	144	70
2001	81	1 196	940	256	61
2002	110	1 250	961	289	58
2003	97	1 281	1 045	236	130
2004	70	1 488	1 204	284	71
2005	61	1 555	1 261	294	85
2006	52	1 799	1 506	293	102
2007	139	2 162	1 724	438	95
2008	115	1 695	1 337	358	56
2009	94	2 009	1 747	262	63
2010	152	2 104	1 824	280	62

注：本页数据由市科学技术委员会提供。
Note： Data on this page are provided by Shanghai Science and Technology Commission.

表 18.8 主要年份专利申请量
PATENT APPLICATIONS IN MAIN YEARS

单位:件(item)

指 标	Indicators	2000	2009	2010
总 计	**Total**	**11 337**	**62 241**	**71 196**
按种类分	**By Type of Patents**			
发 明	Inventions	4 713	22 012	26 165
实用新型	Utility Models	2 760	19 650	23 188
外观设计	Designs	3 864	20 579	21 843
按对象分	**By Applicant**			
非职务发明创造	Non-position Patents	2 137	7 290	8 673
职务发明创造	Position Patents	9 200	54 951	62 523
大专院校	Universities and Colleges	618	8 699	8 173
科研单位	Research Institutions	613	1 950	2 311
工矿企业	Industrial and Mining Enterprises	7 936	41 628	45 490
机关团体	Government Agencies and Organizations	33	2 674	6 549

表 18.9 主要年份专利授权量
PATENTS CERTIFIED IN MAIN YEARS

单位:件(item)

指 标	Indicators	2000	2009	2010
总 计	**Total**	**4 050**	**34 913**	**48 215**
按种类分	**By Type of Patents**			
发 明	Inventions	304	5 997	6 867
实用新型	Utility Models	2 083	13 158	21 821
外观设计	Designs	1 663	15 758	19 527
按对象分	**By Applicant**			
非职务发明创造	Non-position Patents	1 516	3 567	4 598
职务发明创造	Position Patents	2 534	31 346	43 617
大专院校	Universities and Colleges	183	4 189	5 897
科研单位	Research Institutions	215	1 094	1 226
工矿企业	Industrial and Mining Enterprises	2 101	22 289	34 151
机关团体	Government Agencies and Organizations	35	3 774	2 343

注：本页数据由市知识产权局提供。
Note: Data on this page are provided by Shanghai Intellectual Property Bureau.

表 18.10 主要年份研究与试验发展(R&D)经费按执行部门分类
EXPENDITURES ON R&D GROUPED BY EXECUTIVE DEPARTMENT IN MAIN YEARS

单位:亿元(100 million yuan)

指 标	Indicators	2000	2009	2010
总 计	**Total**	**76.73**	**423.38**	**480.18**
科研机构	Research Institutions	25.58	86.95	105.35
高等院校	Institutions of Higher Education	7.43	40.23	45.78
企 业	Enterprises	41.44	288.49	320.23
#工业企业	Industrial Enterprises	34.78	236.51	274.05
#大中型工业企业	Large and Medium Industrial Enterprises	30.98	207.05	237.75
其 他	Others	2.28	7.71	8.82

表 18.11 主要年份自然科学研究与技术开发机构课题情况
PROJECTS OF NATURAL SCIENCE RESEARCH AND TECHNOLOGICAL DEVELOPMENT INSTITUTIONS IN MAIN YEARS

年 份 Year	机构数 (个) Quantity of Institutions (unit)	课题数 (项) Quantity of Projects (item)	投入人力 (人年) Manpower Input (person-year)	投入经费 (万元) Funds Invested (10 000 yuan)
1990	229	8 339	23 279	33 061
1995	230	6 544	17 531	80 957
1996	233	5 538	17 434	90 504
1997	232	5 481	17 507	117 199
1998	230	5 554	16 713	122 513
1999	225	5 135	16 396	125 620
2000	229	4 879	17 104	148 846
2001	221	4 468	16 972	210 910
2002	218	4 393	15 523	251 837
2003	216	4 473	17 058	282 865
2004	212	4 540	17 299	330 063
2005	206	4 416	18 924	425 266
2006	202	4 585	19 008	494 657
2007	199	5 534	20 443	542 601
2008	194	6 006	21 111	719 082
2009	195	6 653	23 773	698 690
2010	191	7 141	26 080	992 896

注：本表数据由市科学技术委员会提供。
Note: Data in this table are provided by Shanghai Science and Technology Commission.

表 18.12 自然科学研究与技术开发机构课题情况(2010)
STATISTICS OF PROJECTS OF NATURAL SCIENCE RESEARCH AND DEVELOPMENT INSTITUTIONS

类 别	Types	机构数(个) Number of Institutions (unit)	课题数(项) Number of Projects (item)	投入人力(人年) Manpower Input (person-year)	投入经费(万元) Funds Invested (10 000 yuan)
总 计	**Total**	**191**	**7 141**	**26 081**	**992 896**
按学科分	**By Subject**				
自然科学	Natural Science	17	2 881	2 979	166 077
农业科学	Agriculture Science	18	770	968	23 290
医学科学	Medical Science	17	964	1 588	55 198
工程科学与技术	Engineering Science and Technology	135	2 504	20 483	747 756
社会与人文科学	Social Science and Humanities	4	22	63	575
按行业分	**By Sector**				
#制造业	Manufacturing	98	1 340	13 863	587 370
建筑业	Construction	4	143	327	4 152
交通运输、仓储和邮政业	Transportation, Warehousing and Post	4	27	199	2 285
科学研究、技术服务和地质勘查业	Scientific Research, Technical Service and Geological Prospecting	43	4 208	8 960	341 905
水利、环境和公共设施管理业	Water Conservancy, Environment and Public Facility Management	8	255	488	5 516
卫生、社会保障和社会福利业	Health, Social Security and Welfare	13	379	809	19 008
文化、体育和娱乐业	Culture, Sports and Entertainment	2	23	345	2 986

表 18.13 自然科学研究与技术开发机构论文与著作情况(2010)
PAPERS AND WORKS OF NATURAL SCIENCE RESEARCH AND TECHNOLOGICAL DEVELOPMENT INSTITUTIONS

类 别	Types	论文(篇) Papers (piece)	其中 of which: #国外发表 Issued Abroad	科技著作(种) Scientific and Technological Works (sort)
总 计	**Total**	**8 007**	**2 865**	**120**
按学科领域分	**By Subject**			
自然科学	Natural Science	2 480	1 461	16
农业科学	Agriculture Science	793	149	7
医学科学	Medical Science	1 243	493	16
工程科学与技术	Engineering Science and Technology	3 484	762	78
社会与人文科学	Social and Humanities Science	7		3
按行业分	**By Sector**			
#农、林、牧、渔业	Farming, Forestry, Animal Husbandry and Fishery	727	156	7
制造业	Manufacturing	1 707	327	64
电力、燃气及水的生产和供应业	Electric Power, Steam and Water Production and Supply	67	4	1
建筑业	Construction	353	12	5
科学研究、技术服务和地质勘查业	Scientific Research, Technical Service and Geological Prospecting	4 067	2 121	25
卫生、社会保障和社会福利业	Health, Social Security and Welfare	755	223	11

注：本页数据由市科学技术委员会提供。
Note: Data on this page are provided by Shanghai Science and Technology Commission.

表 18.14 区县级以上国有单位独立研究与开发机构人员(2010)
PERSONNEL OF STATE-OWNED INDEPENDENT RESEARCH AND DEVELOPMENT INSTITUTIONS ABOVE DISTRICT AND COUNTY LEVEL

单位:人(person)

类 别	Types	从事科技活动人员 Personnel Engaged in Scientific and Technological Activities	其中 of which #R&D 人员 R&D Personnel	#高中级技术职称人员 Personnel with High and Medium Technic Titles	#研究生 Post-graduates	#大 学 University and College
总 计	**Total**	**40 271**	**34 582**	**22 616**	**13 514**	**16 019**
按隶属关系分	**By Subordination**					
中国科学院	The Chinese Academy of Science	12 181	6 816	6 849	3 524	5 069
国务院部门	Departments of the State Council	21 854	17 483	11 538	6 542	9 318
地 方	Local	6 236	10 283	4 229	3 448	1 632
按领域分	**By Subject**					
自然科学	Natural Science	37 951	33 849	21 029	12 594	15 170
科技情报文献	Scientific & Technological Information & Documents	1 117		660	207	577
社会与人文科学	Social Sciences and Humanities	1 203	733	927	713	272

表 18.15 主要年份区县级属研究与开发机构状况
RESEARCH AND DEVELOPMENT INSTITUTIONS AT DISTRICT AND COUNTY LEVEL IN MAIN YEARS

指 标	Indicators	2000	2009	2010
机构数(个)	Quantity of Institutions (unit)	35	20	18
从业人员(人)	Quantity of Employees (person)	1 261	1 039	1 015
#科技活动人员	Personnel for Science and Technic Activities	736	791	764
科技活动经费内部支出(万元)	Inner Expenditures on Science and Technic Activities(10 000 yuan)	7 343	15 341	15 482

注:本页数据由市科学技术委员会提供。
Note: Data on this page are provieded by Shanghai Science and Technology Commission.

表 18.16 高等学校科技活动人员（2010）
SCIENTIFIC AND TECHNOLOGICAL PERSONNEL OF INSTITUTIONS OF HIGHER EDUCATION

单位：人(person)

指 标	Indicators	合 计 Total	其中 of which 自然科学 Natural Science	工程与技术 Engineering and Technology	医学科学 Medical Science	农业科学 Agriculture Science	其 他 Others
总 计	**Total**	**44 220**	**5 197**	**13 249**	**20 247**	**403**	**5 124**
#科学家和工程师	Scientists and Engineers	41 461	5 101	12 795	18 879	390	4 296
按职称分	**By Professional Title**						
高 级	Senior	14 450	2 752	5 589	5 053	200	856
中 级	Medium	16 656	1 996	5 720	6 556	153	2 231
初 级	Junior	10 355	353	1 486	7 270	37	1 209

表 18.17 主要年份高等学校科技活动情况
SCIENTIFIC AND TECHNOLOGICAL ACTIVITIES IN MAIN YEARS

指 标	Indicators	2000	2009	2010
科技机构数（个）		**326**	**200**	**214**
科技活动人员（人）	**Technological Personnel (person)**	**49 402**	**42 563**	**44 220**
自然科学	Natural Science	5 012	5 025	5 197
工程与技术	Engineering and Technology	15 854	12 647	13 249
医学科学	Medical Science	15 817	19 126	20 247
农业科学	Agriculture Science	441	395	403
R&D 人员（人年）	**R&D Personnel (person-year)**	**13 526**	**17 048**	**17 381**
课题数（个）	**Quantity of Projects (unit)**	**12 827**	**23 180**	**26 774**
课题投入人员（万人年）	**Personnel Engaged in Projects (10 000 person-year)**	**1.71**	**2.04**	**2.12**
课题投入经费（亿元）	**Funds Financed(100 million yuan)**	**13.56**	**55.42**	**69.60**
课题经费支出（亿元）	**Inner Expenditure on Projects(100 million yuan)**	**10.64**	**41.92**	**50.37**

①本页数据由市教育委员会提供。
②本表统计范围是指高等学校中理工农医类口径。
❶Data on this page are provided by Shanghai Education Commission.
❷Figures of scientific and technological personnel in this table refer to those of science, engineering, agriculture and medicine of higher education.

表 18.18 高等学校科技机构、机构 R&D 人员和 R&D 课题情况(2010)
INSTITUTIONS OF SCIENCE AND TECHNOLOGY, PERSONNEL AND PROJECTS OF R&D OF HIGHER EDUCATION

指　标	Indicators	合　计 Total	其　中 of which			
			自然科学 Natural Science	工程与技术 Engineering and Technology	医学科学 Medical Science	农业科学 Agriculture Science
科技机构数(个)	Institutions of Science and Technology (unit)	214	44	78	83	6
机构 R&D 人员(人)	Institutions Personnel of R&D(person)	5 759	1 193	2 359	2 100	73
课题数(个)	Quantity of Projects of R&D (unit)	26 774	4 138	14 433	6 970	1 233
课题投入人员(万人年)	Personnel Engaged in Projects of R&D (10 000 person-year)	2.12	0.26	1.05	0.76	0.04
课题投入经费(亿元)	Funds Financed(100 million yuan)	69.60	10.24	44.86	12.54	1.96
课题经费支出(亿元)	Inner Expenditures on Projects of R&D (100 million yuan)	50.37	7.48	33.80	7.86	1.23

①本表数据由市教育委员会提供。
②本表统计范围是指高等学校中理工农医类口径。
❶Data in this table are provided by Shanghai Education Commission.
❷Figures of scientific and technological personnel in this table refer to those of science, engineering, agriculture and medicine of higher education.

表 18.19 各级科协机构和人员(2010)
INSTITUTIONS AND PERSONNEL OF SCIENCE AND TECHNOLOGY ASSOCIATIONS AT VARIOUS LEVELS

指　标	Indicators	市级科协 Municipal Level Associations	区级科协 District Level Associations	县级科协 County Level Associations
机构数(个)	Quantity of Institutions (unit)	1	17	1
人　员(人)	Personnel (person)	63	232	7
各级学会在册个数(个)	Quantity of Societies Registered (unit)	184	433	30

注：本表数据由市科学技术协会提供。
Note: Data in this table are provided by Shanghai Municipal Science and Technology Associations.

表 18.19 续表 continued

指　标	Indicators	机构数(个) Quantity of Institutions (unit)	个人会员(万人) Individual Members (10 000 persons)	团体会员数(个) Organization Members (unit)	所属分科学会(个) Attached Associations (unit)
市级学会	Prefectural Societies	184	20	13 838	922

表 18.20 科协系统科普活动和科技培训情况（2010）
PROMOTING SCIENCE ACTIVITIES AND TRAINING PROGRAM ORGANIZED BY SCIENCE AND TECHNOLOGY ASSOCIATIONS

指 标	Indicators	合 计 Total	其中 of which 市科协 Municipal Level Associations	区县科协 District and County Level Associations	学 会 Academies
科普活动	**Promoting Science Activities**				
科普讲座次数（次）	Lectures(time)	10 905	193	7 130	3 582
科普讲座参加人次（万人次）	Participants of Exhibition(10 000 person-times)	162	5	77	80
科普展览次数(次)	Exhibitions(time)	4 179	18	1 956	2 205
科普展览参加人次（万人次）	Participants of Lectures(10 000 person-times)	1 131	11	186	934
科技夏（冬）令营次数(次)	Technical Summer (Winter) Camps(time)	181		147	34
青少年科技竞赛次数(次)	Youth Technical Competitions(time)	935	8	883	44
培训班	**Training Classes**				
36 学时以上班数（个）	Classes of More Than 36 Learning Hours (unit)	1 845	34	625	1 186
培训人次（万人次）	Trainees (10 000 person-times)	13.9	0.2	3.3	10.4

表 18.21 科协系统出版物和科技服务情况（2010）
PUBLICATIONS AND CONSULTATIVE ACTIVITIES OF SCIENCE AND TECHNOLOGY ASSOCIATIONS

指 标	Indicators	合 计 Total	其中 of which 市科协 Municipal Level Associations	区县科协 District and County Level Associations	学 会 Academies
出版物	**Publications**				
主办科技期刊种数（种）	Academic Journals (sort)	89	1	13	75
年发行总数（万册）	Annual Issues (10 000 copies)	268	17	3	248
年发表论文(篇)	Quantity of Paper Published over the Year(piece)	12 047			12 047
编辑论文集种数（种）	Thesis Collections Edited (sort)	95	2		93
年发行总数（册）	Annual Issues (copy)	47 907	600		47 307
主办科技报纸种数（种）	Science and Technology Newspaper (sort)	4	2		2
年发行份数（万份）	Annual Circulation (10 000 pieces)	2 569	2 515		54
编著科技图书种数（种）	Science and Technology Books (sort)	124		45	79
年发行册数（万册）	Annual Issues (10 000 copies)	1 537		881	656
咨 询	**Consultation**				
完成技术咨询合同数（项）	Technical Contracts Completed (item)	1 257		600	657
咨询合同实现金额（万元）	Technical Constracts Revenue (10 000 yuan)	153 325		150 303	3 022

注：本页数据由市科学技术协会提供。
Note: Data on this page are provided by Shanghai Municipal Science and Technology Associations.

表 18.22 科协系统学术交流情况（2010）
ACADEMIC EXCHANGES OF SCIENCE AND TECHNOLOGY ASSOCIATIONS

指 标	Indicators	合 计 Total	其中 of which 市科协 Municipal Level Associations	学 会 Academies
国内学术会议	**Domestic Academic Conferences**			
举办次数（次）	Times(time)	2 721	16	1 602
参加人次（人次）	Participants (person-times)	268 117	23 630	163 232
交流论文（篇）	Papers Exchanged (piece)	31 546	2 554	28 992
国际学术会议	**International Academic Conferences**			
举办次数（次）	Times(time)	138	4	134
中方参加人次（人次）	Chinese Participants (person-time)	21 188	673	20 515
中方交流论文（篇）	Chinese Papers Exchanged (piece)	6 633	40	6 593
外方参加人次（人次）	Overseas Participants (person-time)	5 536	194	5 342
外方交流论文（篇）	Overseas Papers Exchanged (piece)	1 897	20	1 877
接待科技来访团组	**Receiving Visiting Science and Technology Delegations**			
接待海外科技团组数（个）	Foreign Science and Technology Groups (unit)	374	27	347
接待海外来访人次（人次）	Foreign Visitors (person-time)	4 139	285	3 854
接待港澳台科技团组(个)	Science and Technology Groups from Hong Kang, Macao and Taiwan (unit)	102	13	60
接待港澳台来访人次(人次)	Visitors from Hong Kang, Macao and Taiwan (person-time)	1 813	317	1 033
双边学术会议	**Bilateral Academic Conferences**			
举办次数(次数)	Quantity of Meetings(time)	14		14
参加人数(人次)	Quantity of Participants(person-times)	1 222		1 222
交流论文(篇)	Quantity of Papers Exchanged(piece)	143		143
港澳台地区学术会议	**Quantity of Academic Meetings Related with Hongkang, Macao**			
举办次数(次)	Quantity of Meetings(time)	22		22
参加人次(人次)	Quantity of Participants(person-times)	1 948		1 948
交流论文(篇)	Quantity of Papers Exchanged(piece)	745		745
海峡两岸地区学术会议	**Quantity of Academic Meetings Related with Mainland and Taiwan**			
举办次数(次)	Quantity of Meetings(time)	10		10
参加人次(人次)	Quantity of Participants(person-times)	1 160		1 160
交流论文(篇)	Quantity of Papers Exchanged(piece)	250		250
外派科技团组	**Dispatching Science and Technology Delegations Abroad**			
外派团组数（个）	Quantity of Delegations Sent Abroad (unit)	56	4	52
外派总人次（人次）	Quantity of People Sent Abroad (person-time)	269	16	253
#参加国际会议	Attending International Conferences	136		136
参加展览、技贸活动	Attending Exhibition and Technical Trade	17		17
派往港澳台地区科技团组	**Quantity of Delegations Sent to Hongkong, Macao and Taiwan**			
派出团组数(个)	Quantity of Delegations Sent Abroad (unit)	57	4	46
派出总人次(人次)	Quantity of People Sent Abroad (person-time)	491	25	451

注：本表数据由市科学技术协会提供。
Note: Data in this table are provided by Shanghai Municipal Science and Technology Associations.

表 18.23　主要年份民营科技企业状况
SCIENTIFIC AND TECHNOLOGICAL RESEARCH INSTITUTIONS RUN BY LOCAL PEOPLE IN MAIN YEARS

指标	Indicators	2000	2005	2010
机构数（个）	**Number of Institutions (unit)**	**12 316**	**16 128**	**18 008**
从业人员（万人）	**Employment (10 000 persons)**	**26.33**	**53.68**	**94.25**
#从事科技活动人员	Scientific & Technological Personnel	12.95	11.47	21.69
#高中级技术职称人员	Personnel with Medium and Senior Titles	8.9	10.91	12.12
企业内部用于科技活动的经费支出(亿元)	Inner Expenditure on Scientific and Technological Activities (100 million yuan)	–	–	473.32
当年形成用于科技活动的固定资产(亿元)	Annual Fixed Assets Formation on Scientific and Technological Activities (100 million yuan)	–	–	78.17
使用来自政府部门的科技活动资金(亿元)	Government Funds on Scientific and Technological Activities (100 million yuan)	–	–	69.80
委托外单位开展科技活动的经费支出(亿元)	External Expenditure on Scientific and Technological Activities (100 million yuan)	–	–	14.52
资产总额(亿元)	Total Assets(100 million yuan)	1 064.07	4 087.18	9 709.91
总收入(亿元)	Revenue(100 million yuan)	811.35	4 140.42	8 462.57
工业总产值(亿元)	Gross Output Value(100 million yuan)	311.22	2 949.93	5 687.91
利润总额(亿元)	Total Pre-tax Profits(100 million yuan)	47.58	193.37	601.59
税金总额(亿元)	Total Tax and Duties(100 million yuan)	28.64	166.61	417.57
出口创汇(亿美元)	Foreign Exchange Income(100 million USD)	2.83	95.63	647.36
专利申请量(件)	Patent Applications(piece)	452	8 010	31 997
#发明专利	Inventions		3 396	11 259
专利授权量(件)	Patent Certified(piece)	1 169	3 970	15 052
#发明专利	Inventions		1 085	3 912

注：本表统计范围是指经上海市科委确认的独立核算国有、集体、私营以及国有与集体联营等科技型中小企业。

Note: Private Scientific and Technological Enterprises in the table refers to the small and medium enterprises with independent accounting systems such as state-owned, collective-owned, individual, private and state-collective joint units certified by Shanghai Municipal Science and Technology Commission.

表 18.24 规模以上工业企业科技活动人员情况（2010）
PERSONNEL FOR SCIENCE AND TECHNIC ACTIVITY IN INDUSTRIAL ENTERPRISES ABOVE THE SET SCALE

类　别	Types	从事科技活动人员数(万人) Technological Development Personnel (10 000 persons)	其中 of which #R&D 人员 R&D personnel	#高中级技术职称人员 Personnel with High and Medium Technic Titles
总　计	**Total**	**15.02**	**8.21**	**4.12**
按隶属关系分	**By Subordination**			
中央单位	Central Units	2.79	1.41	1.10
地方单位	Local Units	12.23	6.80	3.02
按登记注册类型分	**By Registration Categories**			
内　资	Domestic Funded	7.37	3.81	2.28
#国　有	State-owned	0.92	0.37	0.42
有限责任公司	Companies with Limited Liabilities	1.88	1.05	0.59
股份有限公司	Share-holding Companies with Limited Liabilities	1.54	0.91	0.53
港澳台商投资	Hong Kong, Macao and Taiwan Funded	1.56	0.98	0.42
外商投资	Foreign Funded	6.09	3.42	1.42
按企业规模分	**By Size**			
大型企业	Large	5.74	3.35	1.76
中型企业	Medium	6.23	3.30	1.52
小型企业	Small	3.05	1.56	0.84
按行业分	**By Sectors**			
#高技术产业	**High Technology Industry**	**4.47**	**2.54**	**1.23**
信息化学品制造	Information Chemical Product Manufacturing	0.03	0.02	0.01
医药制造业	Medicine Manufacturing	0.58	0.36	0.20
航空航天器制造	Aviation and Aircraft Manufacturing	0.23	0.13	0.04
电子及通信设备制造业	Electronic and Communicantion Equipment Manufacturing	2.47	1.60	0.50
电子计算机及办公设备制造业	Electronic Computer and Office Equipment Manufacturing	0.55	0.16	0.28
医疗设备及仪器仪表制造业	Medical Machinery amd Measuring Instrument Manufacturing	0.61	0.27	0.20
#六个重点发展工业行业	**Six Key Industries**	**11.32**	**6.50**	**3.05**
电子信息产品制造业	Electronic Information Product Manufacturing	3.59	2.09	0.92
汽车制造业	Automobile Manufacturing	1.92	1.13	0.35
石油化工及精细化工制造业	Petrochemical and Fine Chemical Products Manufacturing	0.90	0.50	0.28
精品钢材制造业	Fine Steel Manufacturing	0.53	0.29	0.26
成套设备制造业	Equipment Complex Manufacturing	3.61	1.98	0.95
生物医药制造业	Bio-medicine Manufacturing	0.77	0.51	0.29

表 18.25 规模以上工业企业科技项目数与科技经费支出情况（2010）
SCIENCE AND TECHNICAL PROJECTS AND EXPENDITURES OF INDUSTRIAL ENTERPRISES ABOVE THE SET SCALE

类 别	Types	科技项目数（项）Quantity of Science and Tehnic Project (item)	科技活动经费内部支出（亿元）Inner Expenditures on Science and Technic Activity (100 million yuan)	其中 of which	
				#R&D 经费支出 Expenditures on R&D	#新产品开发经费支出 on New Products Development
总 计	**Total**	**16 280**	**420.21**	**274.05**	**350.88**
按隶属关系分	**By Subordination**				
中央单位	Central Units	2 655	119.30	77.75	98.47
地方单位	Local Units	13 625	300.91	196.30	252.41
按登记注册类型分	**By Registration Categories**				
内 资	Domestic Funded	8 300	208.58	131.60	165.14
#国 有	State-owned	1 036	21.61	11.96	12.47
有限责任公司	Companies with Limited Liabilities	2 037	53.10	34.77	40.13
股份有限公司	Share-holding Companies with Limited Liabilities	2 010	75.30	51.13	69.96
港澳台商投资	Hong Kong, Macao and Taiwan Funded	1 521	29.33	18.41	24.85
外商投资	Foreign Funded	6 459	182.30	124.04	160.89
按企业规模分	**By Size**				
大型企业	Large	4 072	206.84	153.23	183.23
中型企业	Medium	7 312	149.40	84.52	119.22
小型企业	Small	4 896	63.97	36.30	48.43
按行业分	**By Sectors**				
#高技术产业	**High Technology Industry**	**4 076**	**115.12**	**75.90**	**99.29**
信息化学品制造	Information Chemical Product Manufacturing	32	1.36	1.10	0.78
医药制造业	Medicine Manufacturing	871	12.81	9.02	10.17
航空航天器制造	Aviation and Aircraft Manufacturing	139	3.93	2.30	1.69
电子及通信设备制造业	Electronic and Communicantion Equipment Manufacturing	2 114	76.35	53.56	67.19
电子计算机及办公设备制造业	Electronic Computer and Office Equipment Manufacturing	122	10.83	5.07	10.43
医疗设备及仪器仪表制造业	Medical Machinery amd Measuring Instrument Manufacturing	798	9.84	4.85	9.03
#六个重点发展工业行业	**Six Key Industries**	**11 457**	**346.31**	**232.53**	**301.71**
电子信息产品制造业	Electronic Information Product Manufacturing	3 005	98.96	65.41	87.52
汽车制造业	Automobile Manufacturing	1 858	71.73	48.67	62.63
石油化工及精细化工制造业	Petrochemical and Fine Chemical Products Manufacturing	1 202	26.85	14.14	22.23
精品钢材制造业	Fine Steel Manufacturing	1 118	40.41	32.52	39.75
成套设备制造业	Equipment Complex Manufacturing	3 111	92.73	59.90	75.49
生物医药制造业	Bio-medicine Manufacturing	1 163	15.63	11.89	14.09

表 18.26 规模以上工业企业 R&D 经费内部支出来源构成 (2010)
STRUCTURE OF R&D INNER EXPENDITURE SOURCE IN INDUSTRIAL ENTERPRISES ABOVE THE SET SCALE

单位:亿元(100 million yuan)

类 别	Types	R&D 经费内部支出合计 Total of R&D Inner Expenditure	其中 of which 政府资金 Government Funds	企业资金 Enterprise Funds	境外资金 Foreign Funds
总 计	**Total**	**274.05**	**16.77**	**253.75**	**2.37**
按隶属关系分	**By Subordination**				
中央单位	Central Units	77.75	6.45	70.90	0.08
地方单位	Local Units	196.30	10.32	182.85	2.29
按登记注册类型分	**By Registration Categories**				
内 资	Domestic Funded	131.60	11.26	119.19	0.10
#国 有	State-owned	11.96	1.91	9.59	0.08
有限责任公司	Companies with Limited Liabilities	34.77	4.15	30.55	…
股份有限公司	Share-holding Companies with Limited Liabilities	51.13	3.31	47.69	…
港澳台商投资	Hong Kong, Macao and Taiwan Funded	18.41	1.45	16.36	0.54
外商投资	Foreign Funded	124.04	4.06	118.20	1.73
按企业规模分	**By Size**				
大型企业	Large	153.23	10.08	142.31	0.67
中型企业	Medium	84.52	5.42	77.40	0.99
小型企业	Small	36.30	1.27	34.04	0.71
按行业分	**By Sectors**				
#高技术产业	**High Technology Industry**	**75.90**	**6.92**	**67.40**	**1.25**
信息化学品制造	Information Chemical Product Manufacturing	1.10	…	1.10	
医药制造业	Medicine Manufacturing	9.02	0.54	8.43	0.04
航空航天器制造	Aviation and Aircraft Manufacturing	2.30	0.31	1.70	
电子及通信设备制造业	Electronic and Communicantion Equipment Manufacturing	53.56	5.70	46.84	0.99
电子计算机及办公设备制造业	Electronic Computer and Office Equipment Manufacturing	5.07	…	5.07	
医疗设备及仪器仪表制造业	Medical Machinery amd Measuring Instrument Manufacturing	4.85	0.37	4.26	0.22
#六个重点发展工业行业	**Six Key Industries**	**232.53**	**15.85**	**213.52**	**2.14**
电子信息产品制造业	Electronic Information Product Manufacturing	65.41	5.86	58.48	1.03
汽车制造业	Automobile Manufacturing	48.67	0.50	47.70	0.06
石油化工及精细化工制造业	Petrochemical and Fine Chemical Products Manufacturing	14.14	0.54	13.34	0.11
精品钢材制造业	Fine Steel Manufacturing	32.52	2.75	29.77	
成套设备制造业	Equipment Complex Manufacturing	59.90	5.44	53.42	0.62
生物医药制造业	Bio-medicine Manufacturing	11.89	0.76	10.81	0.32

表 18.27 规模以上工业企业办科技机构情况 (2010)

SCIENCE AND TECHNIC RESEARCH INSTITUTIONS FUNDED BY INDUSTRIAL ENTERPRISES ABOVE THE SET SCALE

类　别	Types	科技机构数（个）Technological Development Institutions (unit)	机构人员数（万人）Quantity of Personnel (10 000 persons)	机构经费支出（亿元）Expenditure of Institutions (100 million yuan)	机构仪器设备原价(亿元) Original Value of Equipment (100 million yuan)
总　计	**Total**	**1 085**	**7.88**	**242.52**	**206.51**
按隶属关系分	**By Subordination**				
中央单位	Central Units	54	1.30	49.08	32.88
地方单位	Local Units	1 031	6.58	193.44	173.63
按登记注册类型分	**By Registration Categories**				
内　资	Domestic Funded	567	3.26	84.56	68.81
#国　有	State-owned	38	0.22	7.10	8.03
有限责任公司	Companies with Limited Liabilities	160	0.85	21.16	20.27
股份有限公司	Share-holding Companies with Limited Liabilities	62	0.76	29.33	25.12
港澳台商投资	Hong Kong, Macao and Taiwan Funded	129	0.99	18.76	12.97
外商投资	Foreign Funded	389	3.63	139.20	124.73
按企业规模分	**By Size**				
大型企业	Large	109	3.48	137.97	105.14
中型企业	Medium	529	3.35	82.72	87.20
小型企业	Small	447	1.05	21.83	14.17
按行业分	**By Sectors**				
#高技术产业	**High Technology Industry**	**312**	**2.80**	**78.47**	**68.02**
信息化学品制造	Information Chemical Product Manufacturing	3	0.02	0.47	0.77
医药制造业	Medicine Manufacturing	78	0.35	7.58	6.52
航空航天器制造	Aviation and Aircraft Manufacturing	8	0.06	1.14	2.75
电子及通信设备制造业	Electronic and Communicantion Equipment Manufacturing	140	1.69	55.22	48.72
电子计算机及办公设备制造业	Electronic Computer and Office Equipment Manufacturing	23	0.39	9.10	7.36
医疗设备及仪器仪表制造业	Medical Machinery amd Measuring Instrument Manufacturing	60	0.29	4.96	1.90
#六个重点发展工业行业	**Six Key Industries**	**747**	**6.47**	**210.07**	**163.92**
电子信息产品制造业	Electronic Information Product Manufacturing	230	2.38	70.20	59.45
汽车制造业	Automobile Manufacturing	86	1.27	58.10	48.58
石油化工及精细化工制造业	Petrochemical and Fine Chemical Products Manufacturing	87	0.38	10.47	7.22
精品钢材制造业	Fine Steel Manufacturing	5	0.08	10.07	13.74
成套设备制造业	Equipment Complex Manufacturing	223	1.86	51.32	27.54
生物医药制造业	Bio-medicine Manufacturing	116	0.50	9.91	7.39

表 18.28 规模以上工业企业其他技术活动费用支出情况 (2010)
SPECIAL TECHNICAL PROJECT FUNDS OF INDUSTRIAL ENTERPRISES ABOVE THE SET SCALE

单位:亿元 (100 million yuan)

类别	Types	技术改造经费支出 Expenditures of Technical Transformation	技术引进经费支出 Expenditures of Technical Introduction	购买国内技术支出 Expenditures of Buying Domestic Technology
总 计	**Total**	**128.45**	**65.10**	**23.08**
按隶属关系分	**By Subordination**			
中央单位	Central Units	52.46	21.67	19.51
地方单位	Local Units	75.99	43.43	3.57
按登记注册类型分	**By Registration Categories**			
内 资	Domestic Funded	91.67	23.61	20.44
#国 有	State-owned	7.32	0.27	0.55
有限责任公司	Companies with Limited Liabilities	16.52	7.34	0.51
股份有限公司	Share-holding Companies with Limited Liabilities	47.20	14.58	17.84
港澳台商投资	Hong Kong, Macao and Taiwan Funded	2.90	1.23	0.36
外商投资	Foreign Funded	33.88	40.26	2.28
按企业规模分	**By Size**			
大型企业	Large	91.94	46.87	19.77
中型企业	Medium	31.27	14.23	2.88
小型企业	Small	5.24	4.00	0.43
按行业分	**By Sectors**			
#高技术产业	**High Technology Industry**	**10.72**	**5.07**	**1.19**
信息化学品制造	Information Chemical Product Manufacturing	0.01		
医药制造业	Medicine Manufacturing	1.67	0.78	0.34
航空航天器制造	Aviation and Aircraft Manufacturing	3.71		
电子及通信设备制造业	Electronic and Communicantion Equipment Manufacturing	4.85	3.53	0.30
电子计算机及办公设备制造业	Electronic Computer and Office Equipment Manufacturing	0.04	0.19	
医疗设备及仪器仪表制造业	Medical Machinery amd Measuring Instrument Manufacturing	0.45	0.56	0.55
#六个重点发展工业行业	**Six Key Industries**	**105.35**	**57.02**	**21.51**
电子信息产品制造业	Electronic Information Product Manufacturing	5.90	6.02	0.92
汽车制造业	Automobile Manufacturing	36.39	24.38	1.17
石油化工及精细化工制造业	Petrochemical and Fine Chemical Products Manufacturing	11.73	2.56	0.49
精品钢材制造业	Fine Steel Manufacturing	26.57	12.54	17.44
成套设备制造业	Equipment Complex Manufacturing	23.07	10.16	1.15
生物医药制造业	Bio-medicine Manufacturing	1.69	1.36	0.34

表18.29 规模以上工业企业新产品开发情况（2010）
NEW PRODUCTS DEVELOPMENT OF INDUSTRIAL ENTERPRISES ABOVE THE SET SCALE

单位：亿元（100 million yuan）

类别	Types	新产品产值 Output Value of New Products	新产品销售收入 Sales Revenue of New Products	其中 of which #新产品出口 Exports of New Products
总　计	**Total**	**5 870.20**	**6 543.07**	**1 054.05**
按隶属关系分	**By Subordination**			
中央单位	Central Units	1 316.10	1 284.74	427.42
地方单位	Local Units	4 554.10	5 258.33	626.63
按登记注册类型分	**By Registration Categories**			
内　资	Domestic Funded	2 000.76	1 998.17	485.96
#国　有	State-owned	250.55	247.69	247.69
有限责任公司	Companies with Limited Liabilities	563.72	563.66	148.36
股份有限公司	Share-holding Companies with Limited Liabilities	541.47	541.86	79.05
港澳台商投资	Hong Kong, Macao and Taiwan Funded	344.87	333.70	122.96
外商投资	Foreign Funded	3 524.57	4 211.20	445.13
按企业规模分	**By Size**			
大型企业	Large	3 721.20	4 365.20	648.20
中型企业	Medium	1 783.19	1 815.61	374.91
小型企业	Small	365.82	362.26	30.94
按行业分	**By Sectors**			
#高技术产业	**High Technology Industry**	**1 136.59**	**1 234.00**	**380.53**
信息化学品制造	Information Chemical Product Manufacturing	0.08	0.08	
医药制造业	Medicine Manufacturing	104.46	97.38	4.02
航空航天器制造	Aviation and Aircraft Manufacturing	3.95	3.86	2.65
电子及通信设备制造业	Electronic and Communicantion Equipment Manufacturing	770.92	768.79	337.84
电子计算机及办公设备制造业	Electronic Computer and Office Equipment Manufacturing	182.17	285.62	14.82
医疗设备及仪器仪表制造业	Medical Machinery amd Measuring Instrument Manufacturing	75.01	78.27	21.20
#六个重点发展工业行业	**Six Key Industries**	**5 103.09**	**5 754.15**	**898.40**
电子信息产品制造业	Electronic Information Product Manufacturing	1 076.54	1 188.33	389.34
汽车制造业	Automobile Manufacturing	2 086.71	2 639.42	27.16
石油化工及精细化工制造业	Petrochemical and Fine Chemical Products Manufacturing	261.11	263.16	22.17
精品钢材制造业	Fine Steel Manufacturing	313.43	293.30	54.20
成套设备制造业	Equipment Complex Manufacturing	1 240.37	1 250.74	400.35
生物医药制造业	Bio-medicine Manufacturing	124.93	119.20	5.18

注：新产品即包括经政府有关部门认定并在有效期内的新产品，也包括企业自行研制开发，未经政府有关部门认定，从投产之日起一年之内的新产品。

Note: New Products include new products certified by relevant government agencies within the period of certification, as well as new products designed and produced by enterprices within a year without certification by government agencies.

表 18.30 主要年份大中型工业企业科技活动情况
SCIENCE AND TECHNIC ACTIVITIES OF LARGE AND MEDIUM INDUSTRIAL ENTERPRISES IN MAIN YEARS

指 标	Indicators	2000	2009	2010
一、企业办科技机构数（个）	**Science and Technic Institutions Funded by Enterprises (unit)**	**264**	**639**	**638**
二、从事科技活动人员数（万人）	**Personnel Engaged in Science and Technic Activities (10 000 persons)**	**7.48**	**11.71**	**11.96**
#R&D 人员	R&D Personnel	2.63	7.05	6.64
#高中级技术职称人员	Personnel with High and Medium Technic Titles	3.10	3.27	3.27
三、科技活动费用情况(亿元)	**Expenditures on Science and Technic Activities (100 million yuan)**			
内部经费支出	Inner Expenditures	91.63	313.79	356.24
#R&D 经费支出	R&D Expenditures	30.98	206.99	237.75
#新产品开发经费支出	Expenditures on New Products Development	47.56	252.78	302.45
外部经费支出	External Expenditures	9.15	3.59	33.12
四、其他技术活动费用支出(亿元)	**Other Expenditures on Technic Activities (100 million yuan)**	**117.47**	**250.25**	**235.63**
技术改造经费支出	Expenditures on Technological Transformation	75.31	132.22	123.21
技术引进经费支出	Expenditures on Technological Introduction	39.00	57.08	61.09
用于消化吸收的经费	Expenditures on Technological Digesting and Absorbing	2.41	28.49	28.68
购买国内技术支出	Expenditures on Buying Domestic Technology	0.75	32.46	22.65
五、科技项目情况	**Science and Technic Project**			
项目数（项）	Quantity of Projects (item)	5 140	11 398	11 384
项目人员（人）	Personnel of Project Groups (person)	45 254	90 426	94 165
项目经费内部支出(亿元)	Intramural Expenditure on Projects(100 million yuan)	63.72	288.53	309.75
六、科技活动产出情况	**Output of Science and Technic Activities**			
新产品产值(亿元)	Taxes of New Products(100 million yuan)	1 355.19	4 567.07	5 504.38
新产品销售收入(亿元)	Prime Operating Revenue(100 million yuan)	1 351.69	5 077.08	6 180.81
#新产品出口	New Products Exported	197.41	812.65	1 023.11

上 / 海 / 统 / 计 / 年 / 鉴

主要统计指标解释

科技活动

指在自然科学、农业科学、医药科学、工程与技术科学、人文与社会科学领域(简称科学技术领域)中,与科技知识的产生、发展、传播和应用密切相关的有组织的活动。可分为研究与试验发展(R&D)、研究与试验发展成果应用及相关的科技服务三类活动。

R&D

R&D 是"科学研究与试验发展"的英文缩写。指在科学技术领域,为增加知识总量,以及运用这些知识去创造新的应用进行的系统的创造性的活动。R&D 包括基础研究、应用研究、试验发展三类活动。

基础研究

指为了获得关于现象和可观察事实的基本原理的新知识(揭示客观事物的本质、运动规律,获得新发现、新学说)而进行的实验性或理论性研究,它不以任何专门或特定的应用或使用为目的。其成果以科学论文和科学著作为主要形式。用来反映知识的原始创新能力。

应用研究

指为获得新知识而进行的创造性研究,主要针对某一特定的目的或目标。应用研究是为了确定基础研究成果可能的用途,或是为达到预定的目标探索应采取的新方法(原理性)或新途径。其成果形式以科学论文、专著、原理性模型或发明专利为主。

试验发展

指利用从基础研究、应用研究和实际经验所获得的现有知识,为产生新的产品、材料和装置,建立新的工艺、系统和服务,以及对已产生和建立的上述各项作实质性的改进而进行的系统性工作。其成果形式主要是专利、专有技术、具有新产品基本特征的产品原型或具有新装置基本特征的原始样机等。在社会科学领域,试验发展是指把通过基础研究、应用研究获得的知识转变成可以实施的计划(包括为进行检验和评估实施示范项目)的过程。人文科学领域没有对应的试验发展活动。

科技活动人员

指直接从事科技活动、以及专门从事科技活动管理和为科技活动提供直接服务,累计从事科技活动的时间占全年制度工作时间 10%及以上的人员。(1)直接从事科技活动的人员,包括:在独立核算的科学研究与技术开发机构、高等学校、各类企业及其他事业单位内设的研究室、实验室、技术开发中心及中试车间(基地)等机构中从事科技活动的研究人员、工程技术人员、技术工人及其它人员;虽不在上述机构工作,但编入科技活动项目(课题)组的人员;科技信息与文献机构中的专业技术人员;从事论文设计的研究生等。(2)专门从事科技活动管理和为科技活动提供直接服务的人员包括:独立核算的科学研究与技术开发机构、科技信息与文献机构、高等学校、各类企业及其他事业单位主管科技工作的负责人,专门从事科技活动的计划、行政、人事、财务、物资供应、设备维护、图书资料管理等工作的各类人员,但不包括保卫、医疗保健人员、司机、食堂人员、茶炉工、水暖工、清洁工等为科技活动提供间接服务的人员。

R&D 人员

R&D 人员一般用折合全时当量来表示。即参加 R&D 项目人员的全时当量及应分摊在 R&D 项目的管理和直接服务人员的全时当量两部分相加计算。一个折合全时当量是一人年。例如,一个人在 R&D 活动上花费了 30%的正常工作时间而 70%的时间用于其他工作,则其折合全时当量为 0.3。

科技活动经费支出

指企事业单位实际支出的全部科技活动费用,包括来自科研渠道的经费、教育事业费、基本建设投资、技术改造投资等实际用于科技活动支出的费用。科技活动经费支出分为内部支出和外部支出。

R&D 经费内部支出

指企事业单位用于内部开展 R&D 活动(包括基础研究、应用研究、试验发展)的实际支出。包括用于 R&D 项目(课题)活动的直接支出,以及间接用于 R&D 活动的管理费、服务费、与有关的基本建设支出以及外协加工费等。不包括生产性活动支出、归还贷款支出以

主要统计指标解释

及与外单位合作或委托外单位进行 R&D 活动而转拨给对方的经费支出。

■ 专 利

是专利权的简称，是对发明人的发明创造经审查合格后，由专利局依据专利法授予发明人和设计人对该项发明创造享有的专有权。专利包括发明、实用新型和外观设计三种类型。

■ 发 明

指对产品、方法或者其改进所提出的新的技术方案。是国际通行的反映拥有自主知识产权技术的核心指标。

■ 实用新型

指对产品的形状、构造或者其结合所提出的适于实用的新的技术方案。反映具有一定技术含量的技术成果情况。

■ 外观设计

指对产品的形状、图案、色彩或者其结合所作出的富有美感并适于工业上应用的新设计。反映拥有自主知识产权的外观设计成果情况。

■ 新产品

指采用新技术原理、新设计构思研制、生产的全新产品，或在结构、材质、工艺等某一方面比原有产品有明显改进，从而显著提高了产品性能或扩大了使用功能的产品。新产品既包括政府有关部门认定并在有效期内的新产品，也包括企业自行研制开发，未经政府有关部门认定，从投产之日起一年之内的新产品。

■ 独立研究与开发机构

指有明确的任务和研究方向，有一定学术水平的业务骨干和一定数量的研究人员，具有研究、开发、开展学术工作的基本条件，主要进行科学研究与技术开发活动，并且在行政上有独立的组织形式，财务上独立核算盈亏，有权与其他单位签订合同，在银行有单独户头的单位。

SHANGHAI STATISTICAL YEARBOOK

EXPLANATORY NOTES TO MAJOR STATISTICAL INDICATORS

□ Scientific and Technological Activities (S&TActivities)

Scientific and Technological Activities (S&T Activities) refer to organized activities which are closely related with the creation, development, dissemination and application of the scientific and technical knowledge in the fields of natural sciences, agricultural sciences, medical sciences, engineering and technological sciences, humanities and social sciences (referred to as scientific and technological fields). S&T activities can be classified into 3 categories: research and development (R&D) activities, application of R&D results, and related S&T services.

□ R&D

R&D is an abbreviation which stands for 'Science Research and Experimental Development', which means systematic and creative endeavors aimed at expanding the overall volume of knowledge and applying the knowledge in systematic creation. R&D includes basic studies, application research and experimental development.

□ Basic Research

Basic Research refers to empirical or theoretical research aiming at obtaining new knowledge on the fundamental principles of phenomena of observable facts to reveal the nature and law of movement of objects and to acquire new discoveries or new theories. Basic research takes no specific or designated application as the aim of the research. Results of basic research are mainly released or disseminated in the form of scientific papers or monographs. This indicator reflects the original innovation capacity of knowledge.

□ Applied Research

Applied Research refers to creative research aiming at obtaining new knowledge on a specific objective or target. Purpose of the applied research is to identify the possible use of results from basic research, or to explore new (fundamental) methods or new approaches. Results of applied research are expressed in the form of scientific papers, monographs, fundamental models or invention patents.

□ Experimental Development

Experimental Development refer to systematic activities aiming at using the knowledge from basic and applied researches or from practical experience to develop new products, materials and equipment, to establish new production process, systems and services, or to make substantial improvement on the existing products, process or services. Results of experiment and development activities are embodied in patents, exclusive technology, and monotype of new products or equipment. In social sciences, experiment and development activities refer to the process of converting the knowledge from basic or applied researches into feasible programmes (including conduct of demonstration projects for assessment and evaluation). There are no experiment and development activities in the science of humanities.

□ Personnel Engaged in S&T Activities

Personnel Engaged in S&T Activities refer to personnel directly engaged in S&T activities, in the management of S&T activities, and in providing direct service to S&T activities, who spend over 10% of the total working hours in a year in S&T activities.(1) Personnel directly engaged in S&T activities include researchers, engineers, technicians and other related personnel engaged in S&T activities in independent-accounting R&D institutions, institutions of higher learning, and in research institutes, laboratories, technology development centers and central experiment workshops under enterprises and institutions. Also included are people working in S&T information archiving institutes, and graduate students working on the design of their thesis.(2) Personnel engaged in the management of S&T activities and in providing direct service to S&T activities include senior management people responsible for S&T activities in independent-accounting R&D institutions, S&T information archiving institutes, institutions of higher learning, and in enterprises and institutions where S&T activities are undertaken. Also included are people responsible for the planning, administration, personnel management, financial management, logistics supply, equipment maintenance, information and library management that are related with S&T activities. People providing indirect services are excluded, such as security, medical service, drivers, plumbers, cleaners and those providing catering and related service.

EXPLANATORY NOTES TO MAJOR STATISTICAL INDICATORS

□ R&D Personnel

R&D Personnel generally amount to the full-time equivalent. It equals the full-time equivalent of personnel engaged in the R&D projects plus the full-time equivalent of personnel directly manage and service the allocated R&D projects. A full-time equivalent refers to a person year. For example, a person spent thirty percents of common working time on R&D activities and seventy percents on other jobs, then the full-time equivalent is 0.3.

□ Expenditures on Science and Technical Activities

Expenditures on Science and Technical Activities refers to the total expenditures that the enterprises actually spent on science and technical activities. It includes expenditures on scientific research, education expenses, basic construction investment, investment on technical transformation. It is divided into internal expenditure and external expenditure.

□ Internal Expenditure on R&D

Internal Expenditure on R&D refers to the actually expense on R&D activities inside enterprises. It includes the direct expense on R&D projects, and indirect expense, such as management fees, service fees, basic construction investment and processing fees, on R&D activities. But it does not include the expenditures for productive activities, expenditures on repay the loans and the expenditures pay for the R&D activities entrusted to other enterprises.

□ Patent

Patent is an abbreviation for the patent right and refers to the exclusive right of ownership by the inventors or designers for the creation or inventions, given from the patent offices after due process of assessment and approval in accordance with the Patent Law. Patents are granted for inventions, utility models and designs.

□ Invention

Inventions refer to the new technical proposals to the products or methods or their modifications. This is universal core indicator reflecting the technologies with independent intellectual property.

□ Utility Models

Utility Models refer to the practical and new technical proposals on the shape and structure of the product or the combination of both. This indicator reflects the condition of technological results with certain technical content.

□ Exterior Design

Designs refer to the aesthetics and industrially applicable new designs for the shape, pattern and color of the product, or their combinations. This indicator reflects the appearance design achievements with independent intellectual property.

□ New Products

New Products refer to new products produced with new technology and new design, or products that represent noticeable improvement in terms of structure, material, or production process so as to improve significantly the character or function of the older versions. They include new products certified by relevant government agencies within the period of certification, as well as new products that are not certified by relevant government agencies and are designed and produced by enterprises within one year since they are put into production.

□ Independent Research and Development Institutions

Independent Research and Development Institutions refer to the state-owned institutions which have direct mission and research purpose, a certain research level and quantities of personnel, favorable conditions for R&D and engaging in scientific research and technological development. The institutions also have their own independent organization, accounting system authority to sign contract with other units, and their own accounts in banks.

第十九篇

CHAPTER 19

环境保护治理

ENVIRONMENT PROTECTION AND TREATMENT

表 19.1　主要年份环保投入和"三废"综合利用
INVESTMENT ON ENVIRONMENT PROTECTION AND WASTE GAS,WASTE WATER AND SOLID WASTES UTILIZED IN MAIN YEARS

单位:亿元(100 million yuan)

年　份 Year	环境保护投资 Investment on Environment Protection	其　中　of which #城市环境基础设施建设投资 Urban Environment Infrastructure Investment	环境保护投资相当于GDP(%) Investment on Environment Protection as Percentage of Gross Domestic Product(%)	"三废"综合利用产品产值 Output Value of Products Made from Utilization of Waste Gas, Waste Water and Solid Wastes	自然保护区覆盖率(%) Coverage Rate of Natural Preservation Areas(%)
1990				2.06	
1995	46.49		1.90	6.63	
1996	68.83		2.40	7.55	
1997	82.35		2.50	12.15	
1998	102.13		2.80	8.01	
1999	111.57		2.80	8.69	
2000	141.91		3.10	9.16	7.8
2001	152.93		3.10	5.00	10.5
2002	162.39	126.99	3.00	7.25	11.8
2003	191.53	144.05	3.10	7.13	11.8
2004	225.37	166.90	3.03	13.04	11.8
2005	281.18	201.01	3.04	9.11	11.8
2006	310.85	177.81	2.94	9.72	11.8
2007	366.12	233.22	2.93	15.33	12.1
2008	422.37	284.30	3.00	16.96	12.1
2009	460.42	282.74	3.09	16.14	12.1
2010	507.54	294.73	2.96	17.04	12.1

表 19.2　主要年份工业固体废弃物防治
PREVENTION AND CURE OF INDUSTRIAL SOLID WASTES IN MAIN YEARS

指　标	Indicators	2000	2009	2010
工业固体废弃物产生量(万吨)	Volume of Industrial Solid Wastes Produced (10 000 tons)	1 354.74	2 254.59	2 448.36
#危险废物	Dangerous Wastes	28.32	47.62	51.25
工业废弃物综合利用量(万吨)	Volume of Industrial Wastes Treated and Utilized (10 000 tons)	1 515.90	2 171.60	2 366.90
#危险废物	Dangerous Wastes	27.05	30.73	28.47
工业废弃物综合利用率(%)	Ratio of Industrial Wastes Treated and Utilized (%)	93.26	95.67	96.16
工业固体废物处置量(万吨)	Volume of Industrial Solid Wastes Disposed (10 000 tons)	90.96	85.66	93.86
#危险废物	Dangerous Wastes	1.08	17.02	23.44

注：本页数据由上海市环境保护局提供。
Note: Data on this page are provided by Shanghai Environmental Protection Bureau.

表 19.3 水环境保护(1995～2010)
WATER ENVIRONMENT PROTECTION

年 份 Year	废 水 排放总量 (亿吨) Total Waste Water Discharged (100 million tons)	其 中 of which 工 业 Industrial Waste Water	 生活及其他 Residential Waste Water	废水化学需氧量 排放总量(万吨) Total Emission of Oxygen of Waste Water Needed by Chemistry (10 000 tons)	其 中 of which 工 业 Industrial Waste Water	 生活及其他 Residential Waste Water and Others
1995	22.45	11.61	10.84		12.29	
1996	22.85	11.41	11.44	27.46	12.16	15.30
1997	21.10	9.99	11.11	38.55	11.70	26.85
1998	20.81	9.00	11.81	36.55	9.63	26.92
1999	20.28	8.52	11.76	34.98	8.92	26.06
2000	19.37	7.25	12.12	31.87	6.93	24.94
2001	19.50	6.80	12.70	30.48	5.27	25.21
2002	19.21	6.49	12.72	32.96	4.78	28.18
2003	18.22	6.11	12.11	28.38	4.38	24.00
2004	19.34	5.64	13.70	29.38	3.76	25.62
2005	19.97	5.11	14.86	30.44	3.66	26.78
2006	22.37	4.83	17.54	30.20	3.53	26.67
2007	22.66	4.76	17.90	29.44	3.38	26.06
2008	22.60	4.41	18.19	26.67	2.76	23.91
2009	23.05	4.12	18.93	24.34	2.90	21.44
2010	24.82	3.67	21.15	21.98	2.16	19.82

表 19.3 续表 continued

年 份 Year	工业废水排放 达标量(万吨) Volume of Meeting Standard for Industrial Sewage Discharge (10 000 tons)	工业废水排放 达标率(%) Up-to-Standard Rate of Industrial Waste Water Discharge(%)	工业重复用水量 (万吨) Volume of Interative Used Water by Industry (10 000 tons)	污水处理厂数 (座) Quantity of Sewage Disposal Plants (unit)	污水处理厂 污水处理量 (万吨) Volume of Sewage Disposed by Sewage Disposal Plants (10 000 tons)
1995	89 365	77.0	445 391	17	14 665
1996	99 721	87.4	486 278	20	12 876
1997	86 568	86.6	495 622	22	14 790
1998	79 356	88.2	475 656	22	15 605
1999	76 664	89.9	605 772	22	17 479
2000	67 553	93.2	592 055	27	23 028
2001	64 876	95.4	709 913	26	29 487
2002	61 521	94.9	654 133	27	30 658
2003	58 020	94.9	690 068	30	39 891
2004	54 255	96.3	750 803	37	95 301
2005	49 590	97.1	886 503	42	117 833
2006	47 146	97.5	843 970	43	155 726
2007	46 492	97.7	899 098	45	152 886
2008	41 364	93.8	946 198	47	177 090
2009	40 685	98.8	1 004 672	51	171 609
2010	35 969	98.0	1 047 970	52	189 654

注：本页数据由上海市环境保护局提供。
Note: Data on this page are provided by Shanghai Environmental Protection Bureau.

表 19.4 大气环境保护(1995～2010) ATMOSPHERE ENVIRONMENT PROTECTION

年 份 Year	废 气 排放总量 (亿标立方米) Total Waste Gas Emission (100 million cu. m)	其 中 of which		烟尘排放总量(万吨) Total Emission of Smoke and Dust (10 000 tons)	其 中 of which	
		工 业 Industrial Sector	生活及其他 Residential Sector and Others		工 业 Industrial Sector	生活及其他 Residential Sector and Others
1995	5 095	4 625	471	20.78	13.33	7.45
1996	5 132	4 757	375	15.78	14.77	1.01
1997	5 249	4 755	494	17.08	13.38	3.70
1998	5 493	4 912	580	15.63	10.74	4.89
1999	5 480	4 947	533	13.57	9.00	4.57
2000	6 398	5 755	643	14.12	8.32	5.80
2001	7 620	6 964	656	13.52	6.23	7.29
2002	7 902	7 440	462	10.74	5.60	5.14
2003	8 391	7 799	592	11.54	4.97	6.57
2004	9 466	8 834	632	12.27	5.25	7.02
2005	9 103	8 482	621	11.52	4.95	6.57
2006	10 045	9 428	617	11.29	4.73	6.56
2007	10 231	9 591	640	10.60	4.04	6.56
2008	11 079	10 436	643	10.63	4.06	6.57
2009	10 709	10 059	650	10.18	3.64	6.54
2010	13 667	12 969	698	10.21	4.18	6.03

注：2008 年起工业废气排放量按新排放系数计算。
Note: The volume of industrial exhaust emission in 2008 was calculated by new emission coefficient.

表 19.4 续表 continued

年 份 Year	废气二氧化硫排放总量 (万吨) Total Emission of SO_2 (10 000 tons)	其 中 of which		工业废气二氧化硫去除量 (万吨) SO_2 Dispeled from Industrial Waste Gas (10 000 tons)	工业烟尘去除量 (万吨) Industrial Smoke and Dust Dispeled (10 000 tons)	工业粉尘去除量 (万吨) Industrial Powder and Dust Dispeled (10 000 tons)
		工 业 Industrial Sector	生活及其他 Residential Sector and Others			
1995	53.41	38.15	15.26	3.34	325.16	117.72
1996	51.00	43.30	7.70	5.58	403.95	89.11
1997	50.85	43.62	7.23	4.16	359.85	141.80
1998	48.89	39.09	9.80	3.11	273.54	151.77
1999	40.31	31.09	9.22	3.36	261.04	184.61
2000	46.49	32.68	13.81	3.77	308.35	218.08
2001	47.26	30.00	17.26	2.14	326.35	263.89
2002	44.66	32.49	12.17	5.58	366.44	301.92
2003	43.54	30.07	13.47	4.86	402.89	348.02
2004	47.31	34.95	12.36	5.53	655.27	208.07
2005	51.28	37.52	13.76	7.49	574.24	150.53
2006	50.80	37.43	13.37	9.45	520.54	146.80
2007	49.78	36.44	13.34	9.03	450.86	145.85
2008	44.61	29.80	14.81	24.03	524.42	103.36
2009	37.89	23.93	13.96	38.46	513.51	95.75
2010	35.81	22.15	13.66	34.98	472.31	138.18

注：本页数据由上海市环境保护局提供。
Note: Data on this page are provided by Shanghai Environmental Protection Bureau.

表 19.5 主要年份环境空气状况
AMBIENT AIR CONDITION IN MAIN YEARS

	指　标 Indicators	2000	2009	2010
中心城区二氧化硫年日平均值（毫克/立方米）	Annual Daily Mean Concentration of SO_2 in Urban Area（mg/m^3）	0.045	0.035	0.029
中心城区二氧化氮年日平均值（毫克/立方米）	Annual Daily Mean Concentration of NO_2 in Urban Area（mg/m^3）	0.090	0.053	0.050
中心城区可吸入颗粒平均浓度（毫克/立方米）	Mean Concentration of Inhalable Particulate in Urban Area（mg/m^3）		0.081	0.079
降水 PH 平均值	Rain PH Value	5.19	4.66	4.66
酸雨频率(%)	Frequency of Acid Rain（%）	26.0	74.9	73.9
环境空气质量优良天数(天)	Quantity of Days with Good Ambient Air Quality(day)	295	334	336
环境空气质量优良率(%)	Rate of Good Ambient Air Quality(%)	80.8	91.5	92.1

表 19.6 主要年份声环境及治理
NOISE ENVIRONMENT AND TREATMENT IN MAIN YEARS

	指　标 Indicators	2000	2009	2010
区域环境噪声平均等效声级	**Average Equivalent Sound Level of Area Ambient Noise**			
昼间时段(LeqdB(A))	Daytime（LeqdB(A)）	56.6	54.9	55.8
夜间时段(LeqdB(A))	Nighttime（LeqdB(A)）	49.2	47.8	48.3
交通环境噪声平均等效声级	**Average Equivalent Sound Level of Traffic Noise**			
昼间时段(LeqdB(A))	Daytime（LeqdB(A)）	70.5	69.8	69.8
夜间时段(LeqdB(A))	Nighttime（LeqdB(A)）	64.1	64.4	64.3

注：本页数据由上海市环境保护局提供。
Note：Data on this page are provided by Shanghai Environmental Protection Bureau.

表 19.7 城市环境卫生情况（1978～2010）
URBAN ENVIRONMENTAL SANITATION

年 份 Year	垃圾产生量 （万吨） Garbage Produced （10 000 tons）	其 中 of which		清运粪便 （万吨） Night Soil Disposal Cleared （10 000 tons）
		生活垃圾 Residential Garbage	建筑垃圾 Construction Garbage	
1978	214	108	106	418
1979	250	125	126	374
1980	272	131	141	331
1981	272	146	126	329
1982	296	169	127	325
1983	280	166	113	311
1984	308	185	123	272
1985	305	196	109	252
1986	328	226	102	263
1987	325	229	97	262
1988	329	240	89	249
1989	344	250	94	246
1990	382	279	103	243
1991	393	296	97	229
1992	428	301	127	242
1993	488	335	152	234
1994	558	358	200	240
1995	668	372	296	216
1996	736	419	317	217
1997	755	454	301	227
1998	824	470	353	218
1999	767	500	267	172
2000	858	641	217	256
2001	901	644	257	219
2002	760	467	293	238
2003	800	585	215	251
2004	802	610	192	258
2005	777	622	155	254
2006	805	658	146	247
2007	852	702	150	232
2008	841	678	153	220
2009	870	710	160	221
2010	890	732	158	201

注：本页数据由市绿化和市容管理局提供。
Note: Data on this page are provided by Shanghai Municipal Virescence and Appearance Administration Bureau.

表 19.8 环境卫生设施(1978～2010)
URBAN ENVIRONMENTAL SANITATION

年 份 Year	公共厕所 (座) Public Lavatories (unit)	生活垃圾 收集点(处) Collection Points of Residential Garbage(unit)	废物箱 (只) Trash Cans (unit)	倒粪站 (座) Excrements Stations (unit)	化粪池 (只) Septic Tanks (unit)
1978	706	13 840	2 333	3 303	25 540
1979	696	12 695	3 151	3 382	25 915
1980	713	15 707	3 402	3 445	26 754
1981	740	17 905	2 546	3 464	27 407
1982	760	18 824	2 821	3 484	28 652
1983	778	17 859	2 733	3 467	29 977
1984	798	20 384	3 890	3 481	30 943
1985	952	22 870	5 700	3 470	33 477
1986	950	31 142	5 983	3 537	39 175
1987	978	37 751	6 341	3 587	40 042
1988	992	42 802	5 117	3 342	41 171
1989	1057	46 149	5 276	3 107	41 349
1990	1 016	46 368	4 921	2 973	43 655
1991	1 033	40 309	4 980	3 006	43 089
1992	1 048	44 752	4 961	2 655	43 694
1993	1 104	46 741	5 756	2 732	43 323
1994	1 100	50 292	6 993	2 739	43 125
1995	1 100	48 563	9 019	2 532	43 151
1996	1 112	51 456	9 522	2 412	38 657
1997	1 120	53 643	12 735	2 207	44 440
1998	1 203	59 498	15 968	2 127	41 760
1999	1 311	66 067	17 326	2 192	44 694
2000	2 215	22 470	23 189	2 045	46 921
2001	2 406	17 694	24 672	1 890	47 500
2002	3 776	26 787	29 517	1 846	49 220
2003	3 468	27 814	31 272	1 709	48 831
2004	3 640	28 649	34 571	1 611	47 579
2005	3 640	28 388	39 539	1 689	47 424
2006	3 746	29 812	44 888	2 253	46 217
2007	5415	29538	47739	2158	45 841
2008	5 866	29 965	56 485	2 064	45 537
2009	5 633	30 584	67 465	2 257	43 775
2010	6 026	30 645	74 658	1 900	43 170

注：本页数据由市绿化和市容管理局提供。
Note: Data on this page are provided by Shanghai Municipal Virescence and Appearance Administration Bureau.

上/海/统/计/年/鉴

主要统计指标解释

■ “三废”综合利用产品产值

指报告期内利用“三废”作为主要原料生产的产品价值(现行价);已经销售或准备销售的应计算产品价值,留作生产自用的不应计算产品价值。

■ 自然保护区

指对有代表性的自然生态系统、珍稀濒危野生动植物物种的天然分布区、水源涵养区、有特殊意义的自然历史遗迹等保护对象所在的陆地、陆地水体或海域,依法划出一定面积进行特殊保护和管理的区域。以县及县以上各级人民政府正式批准建立的自然保护区为准(包括“六五”以前由部门或“革委会”批准且现仍存在的自然保护区)。风景名胜区、文物保护区不计在内。自然保护区分国家级、省级、地市级和县级。按主管部门分属:环保、林业、农业、地矿、海洋、水利和其他部门。

■ 工业固体废弃物产生量

指报告期内企业在生产过程中产生的固体状、半固体状和高浓度液体状废弃物的总量,包括危险废物、冶炼废渣、粉煤灰、炉渣、煤矸石、尾矿、放射性废物和其他废物等;不包括矿山开采的剥离废石和掘进废石(煤矸石和呈酸性或碱性的废石除外)。酸性或碱性废石指采掘的废石其流经水、雨淋水的pH值小于4或pH值大于10.5者。

■ 危险废物

指列入国家危险废物名录或根据国家规定的危险废物鉴别标准和鉴别方法认定的,具有爆炸性、易燃性、易氧化性、毒性、腐蚀性、易传染疾病等危险特性之一的废物。

■ 工业废弃物综合利用量

指报告期内企业通过回收、加工、循环、交换等方式,从废弃物中提取或者使其转化为可以利用的资源、能源和其他原材料的废弃物量(包括当年利用往年的工业废弃物贮存量),如用作农业肥料、生产建筑材料、筑路等。综合利用量由原产生废弃物的单位统计。

■ 工业废弃物综合利用率

指工业废弃物综合利用量占工业废弃物产生量(包括综合利用往年贮存量)的百分率。计算公式为:

$$\text{工业废弃物综合利用率} = \frac{\text{工业废弃物综合利用量}}{\text{工业废弃物产生量} + \text{综合利用往年贮存量}} \times 100\%$$

■ 工业固体废物处置量

指报告期内企业将固体废物焚烧或者最终置于符合环境保护规定要求的场所,并不再回取的工业固体废物量(包括当年处置往年的工业固体废物贮存量)。处置方式有填埋(其中危险废物应安全填埋)、焚烧、专业贮存场(库)封场处理、深层灌注、回填矿井及海洋处置(经海洋管理部门同意投海处置)等。

■ 工业废水排放量

指经过企业厂区所有排放口排到企业外部的工业废水量。包括生产废水、外排的直接冷却水、超标排放的矿井地下水和与工业废水混排的厂区生活污水,不包括外排的间接冷却水(清污不分流的间接冷却水应计算在内)。

■ 工业废水排放达标量

指报告期内废水中各项污染物指标都达到国家或地方排放标准的外排工业废水量,包括未经处理外排达标的,经废水处理设施处理后达标排放的,以及经污水处理厂处理后达标排放的。

■ 工业废水排放达标率

指工业废水排放达标量占工业废水排放量的百分率,计算公式为:

$$\text{工业废水排放达标率} = \frac{\text{工业废水排放达标量}}{\text{工业废水排放量}} \times 100\%$$

■ 工业废气排放量

指企业厂区内燃料燃烧和生产工艺过程中产生的各种排入空气的含有污染物的气体总量,按标准状态〔273K,101 325Pa〕计算。测算公式为:

$$\text{工业废气排放量} = \text{燃料燃烧过程中废气排放量} + \text{生产工艺过程中废气排放量}$$

■ 工业二氧化硫排放总量

指报告期内企业在燃料燃烧和生产工艺过程中排入

主要统计指标解释

大气的 SO_2 总量，计算公式为：

工业二氧化硫排放量 = 燃料燃烧过程中二氧化硫排放量 + 生产工艺过程中二氧化硫排放量

工业烟尘排放量

指企业厂区内燃料燃烧过程中产生的烟气中夹带的颗粒物排放量。

酸雨频率

指酸雨出现的次数占降水出现次数的比例，通常称PH值小于5.6的降水为酸雨。

SHANGHAI STATISTICAL YEARBOOK

EXPLANATORY NOTES TO MAJOR STATISTICAL INDICATORS

□ Output Value of Products Made from Waste Gas, Waste Water and Solid Wastes

Output Value of Products Made from Waste Gas, Waste Water and Solid Wastes refers current value of products with waste gas, waste water and solid wastes as main materials of production. Products sold and ready to sell shall be included while those produced for own use shall not be included.

□ Natural Preservation

Natural Reserves refer to all the land, water areas on land and sea areas are under special protection or management due to the possession of representative natural ecological system, natural distribution of rare and dying out animal zones, water-resource conservation areas, and natural historical relics. Also included are natural reserves formally approved by people's governments at various levels at and above county level (including those approved before the Sixth-five-year Program and still active natural reserves).Scenic spots and historical sites and zones for preservation of cultural relics are not included. Natural reserves are classified as national level, provincial level, prefecture level and county level ones. They are under the jurisdiction of different departments, such as: environment protection, forestry, agriculture, geological and mining, oceanic and water conservancy and so on.

□ Industrial Solid Wastes Produced

Industrial Solid Wastes Produced refers to total volume of solid, semi-solid and high concentration liquid residues produced by industrial enterprises from production process in a given period of time, including hazardous wastes, slag, coal ash, gangue, tailings, radioactive residues and other wastes, but excluding stones stripped or dug out in mining (gangue and acid or alkaline stones not included). A stone is acid or alkaline depending on the pH value of the water below 4 or above 10.5 when the stone is in, or soaked by, the water.

□ Hazardous Wastes

Hazardous Wastes refers to those included in the national hazardous wastes catalogue or specified as any one of the following properties in the national hazardous wastes identification standards: explosive, ignitable, oxidizable, toxic, corrosive or liable to cause infectious diseases or lead to other dangers.

□ Industrial Wastes Utilized

Industrial Wastes Utilized refers to volume of wastes from which useful materials can be extracted or which can be converted into usable resources, energy or other materials by means of reclamation, processing, recycling and exchange (including utilizing in the year the stocks of industrial wastes of the previous year). Examples of such utilizations include fertilizers, building materials and road materials. The information shall be collected by the producing units of the wastes.

□ Ratio of Industrial Wastes Utilized

Ratio of Industrial Wastes Utilized refers to the percentage of industrial wastes utilized over industrial wastes produced (including stocks of the previous years). It is calculated as:

$$\text{Ratio of industrial wastes utilized} = \frac{\text{volume of industrial wastes utilized}}{\text{(industrial wastes produced + stock of previous years)}} \times 100\%$$

□ Industrial Solid Wastes Disposed

Industrial Solid Wastes Disposed refers to quantity of industrial solid wastes which are burnt or placed ultimately in the sites meeting the requirements for environmental protection and not salvaged or recycled (including disposition in the year of those wastes of previous years). The disposition includes landfill (Safe landfills should be conducted for hazardous wastes), incineration, containment spaces, deep underground disposal, backfill in mining pits and disposal at sea.

□ Volume of Industrial Waste Water Discharged

Volume of Industrial Waste Water Discharged refers to the volume of industrial waste water discharged, through all outlets, to the outside of industrial enterprises, including waste water produced, direct-cooling water, underground water from mines that does not meet the standard of discharge, and the domestic sewage mixed up with industrial waste water when discharged, but excluding discharged indirect-cooling water.

EXPLANATORY NOTES TO MAJOR STATISTICAL INDICATORS

□ Industrial Waste Water Meeting Discharge Standards

Industrial Waste Water Meeting Discharge Standards refers to volume of industrial waste water discharge which, with or without treatment, reaches national or local standards with regard to all pollutants.

□ Ratio of Standard Waste Water Discharged to the Total Discharge

Ratio of Standard Waste Water Discharged to the Total Discharge refers to the share of the volume of waste water up to the standard for discharge of the total volume. The formula is as follows:

$$\text{Ratio of Standard Waste Water Discharged to the Total Discharge} = \frac{\text{Volume of Waste Water up to the Standard for Discharge}}{\text{Volume of Industrial Waste Water Discharged}} \times 100\%$$

□ Volume of Waste Industrial Gas Emission

IIndustrial Waste Air Emission refers to discharge into atmosphere of waste air containing pollutants generated from fuel burning and production process in enterprises within a given period of time. It is calculated at standard status (273K, 101325Pa) as:

Industrial waste air emission=emission through fuel burning +emission through production process

□ SO_2 Emission through Industrial Activities

SO_2 Emission through Industrial Activities refers to volume of sulphur dioxide emission from fuel burning and production process by enterprises during a given period of time. It is calculated as:

SO_2 emission through industrial activities = SO_2 emission from fuel burning + SO_2 emission from production process

□ Industrial Soot Emission

Industrial Soot Emission refers to volume of soot in smoke emitted in process of fuel burning in premises of enterprises.

□ Acid Rain Frequency

Acid Rain Frequency refers to the proportion of frequencies of acid rainfall to the total rainfall times. Rainfall is defined as acid rain when the PH value of its rainwater is small than 5.6.

第二十篇

CHAPTER 20

教　育

EDUCATION

表 20.1 主要年份教育事业基本情况
BASIC STATISTICS OF EDUCATION IN MAIN YEARS

指标	Indicators	2000	2009	2010
学校数（所）	**Quantity of Schools (unit)**	**2 225**	**1 730**	**1 730**
普通高等学校	Regular Institutions of Higher Education	37	66	66
普通中等学校	Secondary Schools	1 133	884	869
中等专业学校	Specialized Secondary Schools	84	70	65
职业中学	Vocational Secondary Schools	60	26	26
技工学校	Technical Worker Schools	115	13	10
普通中学	Regular Secondary Schools	861	762	755
工读学校	Reformatory	13	13	13
普通小学	Primary Schools	1 021	751	766
特殊教育学校	Special Education Schools	34	29	29
教职工数(万人)	**Quantity of Teachers and Staff (10 000 persons)**	**22.73**	**21.44**	**21.42**
普通高等学校	Regular Institutions of Higher Education	6.01	7.45	7.42
普通中等学校	Secondary Schools	10.43	8.35	8.26
中等专业学校	Specialized Secondary Schools	1.27	0.94	0.91
职业中学	Vocational Secondary Schools	0.66	0.44	0.43
技工学校	Technical Worker Schools	0.77	0.15	0.13
普通中学	Regular Secondary Schools	7.66	6.76	6.73
工读学校	Reformatory	0.07	0.06	0.06
普通小学	Primary Schools	6.13	5.48	5.58
特殊教育学校	Special Education Schools	0.16	0.16	0.16
专任教师(万人)	**Quantity of Full-time Teachers (10 000 persons)**	**12.83**	**14.29**	**14.52**
普通高等学校	Regular Institutions of Higher Education	2.05	3.81	3.92
普通中等学校	Secondary Schools	6.26	5.94	5.97
中等专业学校	Specialized Secondary Schools	0.53	0.49	0.50
职业中学	Vocational Secondary Schools	0.39	0.29	0.29
技工学校	Technical Worker Schools	0.30	0.07	0.07
普通中学	Regular Secondary Schools	5.01	5.05	5.07
高　中	Senior Secondary Schools	1.42	1.69	1.67
初　中	Junior Secondary Schools	3.59	3.36	3.40
工读学校	Reformatory	0.03	0.04	0.04
普通小学	Primary Schools	4.43	4.43	4.52
特殊教育学校	Special Education Schools	0.09	0.11	0.11

①本表数据由上海市教育委员会提供。
②普通中学学校数中，完全中学 130 所，高级中学 131 所，初级中学 347 所，一贯制学校 147 所。
❶Data in this table are provided by Shanghai Municipal Education Commission.
❷In regular secondary schools, there are 130 whole secondary schools , 131 senior high schools , 347 junior high schools and 147 system schools.

表 20.1 续表 continued

指　标	Indicators	2000	2009	2010
毕业生数(万人)	**Graduates (10 000 persons)**	**55.67**	**46.77**	**46.77**
普通高等学校	Regular Institutions of Higher Education	4.09	12.69	13.37
普通中等学校	Secondary Schools	32.76	22.63	22.63
中等专业学校	Specialized Secondary Schools	3.86	3.39	3.34
职业中学	Vocational Secondary Schools	3.99	1.73	1.38
技工学校	Technical Worker Schools	1.86	0.36	0.31
普通中学	Regular Secondary Schools	22.92	17.03	16.13
高　中	Senior Secondary Schools	7.18	7.04	6.24
初　中	Junior Secondary Schools	15.74	9.99	9.89
工读学校	Reformatory	0.13	0.12	0.08
普通小学	Primary Schools	18.73	11.36	12.44
特殊教育学校	Special Education Schools	0.09	0.09	0.09
招生数(万人)	**New Student Enrollment (10 000 persons)**	**52.23**	**49.49**	**50.66**
普通高等学校	Regular Institutions of Higher Education	8.13	14.35	14.46
普通中等学校	Secondary Schools	33.71	21.20	21.07
中等专业学校	Specialized Secondary Schools	3.00	2.98	2.99
职业中学	Vocational Secondary Schools	2.44	1.25	1.23
技工学校	Technical Worker Schools	1.68	0.37	0.42
普通中学	Regular Secondary Schools	26.46	16.50	16.33
高　中	Senior Secondary Schools	7.84	5.58	5.39
初　中	Junior Secondary Schools	18.62	10.92	10.94
工读学校	Reformatory	0.13	0.10	0.10
普通小学	Primary Schools	10.28	13.86	15.05
特殊教育学校	Special Education Schools	0.11	0.08	0.08
在校学生(万人)	**Student Enrollment (10 000 persons)**	**207.61**	**196.29**	**197.70**
普通高等学校	Regular Institutions of Higher Education	22.68	51.28	51.57
普通中等学校	Secondary Schools	105.53	77.39	75.47
中等专业学校	Specialized Secondary Schools	11.89	11.50	10.91
职业中学	Vocational Secondary Schools	8.48	4.14	3.77
技工学校	Technical Worker Schools	5.37	1.06	1.08
普通中学	Regular Secondary Schools	79.54	60.37	59.44
高　中	Senior Secondary Schools	23.94	17.76	16.89
初　中	Junior Secondary Schools	55.60	42.61	42.55
工读学校	Reformatory	0.25	0.32	0.27
普通小学	Primary Schools	78.86	67.12	70.16
特殊教育学校	Special Education Schools	0.54	0.50	0.50

表20.2 每万人口在校学生数、每个教师负担学生数(1978～2010)
STUDENTS ENROLLMENT PER 10 000 PERSONS AND STUDENTS TAUGHT BY EACH TEACHER

单位：人(person)

年 份 Year	平均每万人口在校学生数 Students Enrollment per 10 000 Persons				平均每个教师负担学生数 Students Taught by Each Teacher		
	大学生 College and University	中专生 Speciallized Secondary School	中学生 Secondary School	小学生 Primary School	普通高等学校 Institution of Higher Education	普通中等学校 Regular Secondary School	普通小学 Primary School
1978	46	14	908	789	3	17	18
1979	60	21	719	774	4	16	19
1980	67	24	544	742	4	13	18
1981	78	25	427	713	5	11	17
1982	71	28	451	665	4	12	16
1983	66	30	433	665	4	10	16
1984	74	37	404	686	4	11	17
1985	88	48	391	683	4	12	17
1986	94	55	387	693	5	11	17
1987	97	55	381	706	5	11	17
1988	100	51	355	764	5	11	18
1989	96	49	351	809	5	11	19
1990	90	46	362	826	5	11	19
1991	87	45	379	825	5	12	19
1992	88	47	401	830	5	13	22
1993	95	54	417	845	6	14	21
1994	100	66	468	815	6	15	21
1995	101	76	512	776	7	16	20
1996	102	68	525	734	7	16	20
1997	103	75	500	688	8	16	20
1998	108	81	483	630	8	17	19
1999	119	83	489	556	9	17	19
2000	141	74	494	490	11	17	18
2001	168	73	481	433	13	16	17
2002	194	74	461	393	14	17	17
2003	214	78	427	367	16	16	17
2004	227	77	451	293	15	17	14
2005	234	72	407	283	14	16	14
2006	237	70	362	272	14	15	14
2007	235	62	318	258	14	14	14
2008	235	56	289	276	14	13	14
2009	232	52	273	304	13	13	15
2010	224	47	258	305	13	13	16

注：本表数据由上海市教育委员会提供。
Note: Data in this table are provided by Shanghai Municipal Education Commission.

表20.3 各级各类学校在校学生数(1978～2010)
STUDENTS ENROLLMENT BY VARIOUS SCHOOLS

单位：万人 (10 000 persons)

年 份 Year	普通高等学校 Institutions of Higher Education	普通中等学校 Secondary School	其中 of which 中等专业学校 Specialized Secondary School	普通中学 Regular Secondary School	职业学校 Secondary Vocational School	技工学校 Technical Worker School	普通小学 Primary School	特殊教育学校 Special Education School
1978	5.06	101.81	1.55	100.26			87.06	0.18
1979	6.74	90.80	2.42	81.72		6.66	88.00	0.18
1980	7.67	71.68	2.81	62.71	0.29	5.87	85.47	0.18
1981	9.11	58.82	2.94	49.93	0.45	5.50	83.22	0.16
1982	8.39	61.69	3.30	53.53	0.85	4.01	78.88	0.16
1983	7.87	60.53	3.61	52.04	1.71	3.17	79.82	0.23
1984	8.99	61.01	4.48	49.18	3.07	4.28	83.47	0.21
1985	10.79	63.50	5.92	48.23	4.69	4.66	84.18	0.23
1986	11.77	64.82	6.86	48.31	4.71	4.94	86.56	0.25
1987	12.25	64.50	7.03	48.21	4.08	5.18	89.35	0.28
1988	12.82	61.20	6.52	45.68	3.69	5.31	98.39	0.30
1989	12.61	61.01	6.45	46.10	3.54	4.92	106.02	0.32
1990	12.13	62.59	6.17	48.31	3.66	4.45	110.19	0.33
1991	11.69	65.92	6.01	51.24	3.97	4.70	111.38	0.35
1992	11.95	70.84	6.41	54.77	4.90	4.76	113.37	0.38
1993	13.10	76.54	7.58	57.69	6.39	4.88	116.70	0.44
1994	14.04	87.23	9.23	65.56	7.54	4.90	113.98	0.52
1995	14.41	96.38	10.85	72.40	8.64	4.49	109.78	0.57
1996	14.79	99.97	9.95	76.23	9.12	4.67	106.46	0.62
1997	15.38	100.81	11.10	74.43	10.29	4.99	102.44	0.63
1998	16.51	102.53	12.38	73.85	10.72	5.58	96.14	0.52
1999	18.63	105.66	13.06	76.69	10.21	5.70	87.16	0.53
2000	22.68	105.28	11.89	79.54	8.48	5.37	78.86	0.54
2001	28.00	104.37	12.12	80.23	7.48	4.54	72.28	0.48
2002	33.16	103.59	12.66	78.97	7.56	4.40	67.24	0.55
2003	37.85	100.71	13.69	75.47	7.04	4.51	64.83	0.55
2004	41.57	106.94	14.05	82.78	6.43	3.68	53.74	0.54
2005	44.26	99.24	13.67	77.02	5.76	2.79	53.50	0.52
2006	46.63	92.25	13.70	71.17	5.33	2.05	53.37	0.50
2007	48.49	85.17	12.81	65.60	5.20	1.56	53.33	0.50
2008	50.29	79.97	12.08	61.77	4.80	1.32	59.06	0.51
2009	51.28	77.07	11.50	60.37	4.14	1.06	67.12	0.50
2010	51.57	75.20	10.91	59.44	3.77	1.08	70.16	0.50

①本表数据由上海市教育委员会提供。
②本表中普通中等学校在校学生数中不包括工读学校在校学生。
❶Data in this table are provided by Shanghai Municipal Education Commission.
❷Quantity of students enrollment of secondary school in this table doesn't include those of reformatory schools.

表 20.4 主要年份各阶段教育实施情况
BASIC STATISTICS OF VARIOUS PHASES EDUCATION IN MAIN YEARS

单位:%

指 标	Indicators	2000	2009	2010
小 学	**Primary School**			
小学学龄儿童净入学率	Enrollment Rate of Schoolage Children	99.9	99.9	99.9
初 中	**Junior School**			
初中学生净入学率	Enrollment Rate of Students in Junior Secondary School Phase	99.9	99.9	99.9
高 中	**Senior School**			
高中阶段新生入学率	Enrollment Rate ofStudents in Senior Secondary School Phase	97.0	97.0	96.5
普通高中招生比例	Recruit Students Rate of Regular Senior Secondary Schools	51.0	50.8	51.0
高 校	**Institutions of Higher Education**			
普通高等学校录取率	Admission Rate of Students in Regular Institution of Higher Education	67.4	84.4	85.1

表 20.5 主要年份各级民办学校基本情况
BASIC STATISTICS OF CIVIL SCHOOLS IN MAIN YEARS

类 别	Types	2000	2009	2010
民办高等学校	**Civil Institutions of Higher Education**			
学校数(所)	Schools (unit)	3	21	20
在校学生(万人)	Students Enrollment(10 000 person)	0.67	9.52	9.37
专任教师(人)	Full-time Teachers(persons)	304	3 773	3 906
民办中等专业学校	**Civil Specialized Secondary Schools**			
学校数(所)	Schools (unit)		3	3
在校学生(万人)	Students Enrollment(10 000 persons)		0.16	0.14
专任教师(人)	Full-time Teachers(person)		100	98
民办职业高中学校	**Civil Vocational Schools**			
学校数(所)	Schools (unit)	1	2	2
在校学生(万人)	Students Enrollment(10 000 persons)	0.08	0.11	0.11
专任教师(人)	Full-time Teachers(person)	30	33	25
民办中学	**Civil Secondary Schools**			
学校数(所)	Schools (unit)	155	111	109
班级数(个)	Class(unit)	1 842	2 176	2 103
在校学生(万人)	Students Enrollment(10 000 persons)	8.48	8.22	7.87
高 中	Senior	4.54	1.90	1.68
初 中	Junior	3.94	6.62	6.19
专任教师(人)	Full-time Teachers(person)	2 400	4 488	4 583
民办小学	**Civil Primary Schools**			
学校数(所)	Schools (unit)	35	171	184
班级数(个)	Class(unit)	987	3488	3747
在校学生(万人)	Students Enrollment (10 000 persons)	3.95	15.10	16.42
专任教师(人)	Full-time Teachers(person)	831	6 630	7 181
民办幼儿园	**Civil Kindergarten**			
学校数(所)	Schools (unit)	92	327	396
班级数(个)	Class(unit)	636	2 881	3 584
在校学生(万人)	Students Enrollment(10 000 persons)	1.77	7.40	9.91
专任教师(人)	Full-time Teachers(person)	1 056	5 762	7 161

注：本页数据由上海市教育委员会提供。
Note: Data on this table are provided by Shanghai Municipal Education Commission.

表 20.6 民办学校(园)基本情况(2010)
BASIC STATISTICS OF CIVIL SCHOOLS

单位:人(person)

指 标	Indicators	学校数(所) School (unit)	毕业生数 Graduate	招生数 Students Recruited	在校生数 Students Enrollment	专任教师数 Full-time Teacher
普通高等学校	Institutions of Higher Education	20	28 293	28 166	93 961	3 906
普通中等专业学校	Specialized Secondary School	3	669	513	1 390	98
职业高中学校	Secondary Vocational School	2	343	425	1 091	25
普通中学	Regular Secondary School	109	22 726	20 417	78 720	4 583
高 中	Senior School	61	7 283	4 906	16 839	1 305
初 中	Junior School	48	15 443	15 511	61 881	3 278
普通小学	Primary School	184	26 614	35 125	164 206	7 181
幼儿园	Kindergarten	396	19 120	37 386	99 099	7 161

注：根据《民办教育促进法》的新规定，民办中、小学统计口径中扣除了公立转制学校。
Note：According to new provision of Civil Education Advance Law，the scope of civil secondary and primary school excluded public schools transformed.

表 20.7 主要年份外国留学生情况
STATISTICS OF FOREIGN STUDENT IN MAIN YEARS

指 标	Indicators	2005	2009	2010
外国留学生人数(人)	**Quantity of Foreign Students(person)**	**13 691**	**15 447**	**17 340**
按费用来源分	By Tuition Resource			
#中国政府资助	Chinese Government Sustentation	934	1 989	2 585
本国政府资助	Homeland Government Sustentation	15	335	347
学校间交换	Inter-school Communion	463	1 214	1 570
自 费	Commoners	12 279	11 900	12 838
按地区来源分	By District			
亚 洲	Aisa	10 490	10 508	11 689
非 洲	Africa	289	860	969
欧 洲	Europe	1 927	2 520	3 023
北美洲	North America	766	1 102	983
南美洲	South America	129	289	477
大洋洲	Oceania	90	168	199

注：本页数据由上海市教育委员会提供。
Note：Data on this page are provided by Shanghai Municipal Education Commission.

表 20.8　主要年份研究生人数
QUANTITY OF GRADUATE STUDENTS IN MAIN YEARS

单位:人(person)

年份 Year	获博士学位人数 Quantity of Doctor's Degrees Obtained	获硕士学位人数 Quantity of Master's Degrees Obtained	研究生 Postgraduates 毕业生数 Graduates		招生数 New Students Enrollment		在读人数 Students Enrollment	
			普通高等学校 Institutions of Higher Education	研究所(院) Research Institutions (Academies)	普通高等学校 Institutions of Higher Education	研究所(院) Research Institutions (Academies)	普通高等学校 Institutions of Higher Education	研究所(院) Research Institutions (Academies)
1978			9		1 072		1 253	
1980			6		410		2 696	
1985	57	1 371	1 543	37	4 264	83	8 163	170
1990	300	2 746	2 953	369	2 803	324	8 533	1 035
1991	342	2 739	2 936	320	2 717	302	8 020	949
1992	343	2 124	2 262	264	3 323	345	8 858	997
1993	368	2 489	2 569	315	3 919	363	10 037	1 008
1994	442	2 363	2 608	251	4 665	465	11 905	1 185
1995	606	2 742	3 038	317	4 776	525	13 378	1 335
1996	627	3 233	3 537	323	5 915	592	15 307	1 528
1997	890	3 585	4 117	358	6 163	562	16 841	1 619
1998	1 090	3 552	4 253	389	7 281	593	19 499	1 663
1999	1 323	4 288	5 196	415	8 758	655	22 656	1 764
2000	1 307	4 546	5 435	433	11 796	856	28 582	2 032
2001	1 487	5 330	6 380	437	14 751	1 075	36 528	2 515
2002	1 655	6 067	7 481	445	17 848	1 363	45 713	3 183
2003	1 994	7 683	9 501	578	20 767	1 757	55 092	3 998
2004	2 678	10 580	12 788	681	23 545	1 789	64 747	4 690
2005	3 119	13 245	15 857	884	25 845	1 847	73 557	5 171
2006	3 772	15 957	18 833	1 098	28 250	1 849	81 487	5 419
2007	4 355	19 250	22 691	1 235	28 748	1 862	86 177	5 586
2008	4 483	20 734	24 431	1 322	30 195	1 947	89 778	5 720
2009	4 661	23 622	26 949	1 342	35 418	2 007	97 639	5 853
2010	4 749	23 458	26 843	1 364	36 619	2 024	105 711	6 006

①本表数据由上海市教育委员会提供。
②2001 年前的获博士学位和获硕士学位的人数为当年毕业生人数。
❶Data in this table are provided by Shanghai Municipal Education Commission .
❷Quantity of Doctor's and Master's Degrees obtained refer to quantity of graduates in this year before 2001.

表 20.9 普通高等学校基本情况（2010）
BASIC STATISTICS OF INSTITUTIONS OF HIGHER EDUCATION

类 别 Types		学校(所) Institutions (unit)	毕业生数(人) Graduates (person)	招生数(人) New Students Enrollment (person)	在校学生人数(人) Students Enrollment (person)	教职员工(人) Staff and Workers (person)	其中 of which #专任教师 Full-time Teacher	其中 of which #正、副高级 Senior and Associate Title
总 计	**Total**	**66**	**133 716**	**144 649**	**515 661**	**74 161**	**39 170**	**17 670**
#综合大学	Comprehensive Universities	3	16 318	14 457	60 900	19 871	8 402	4 751
理工院校	Science and Engineering	25	55 192	61 453	216 276	27 319	14 687	6 344
农林院校	Agriculture and Forestry	2	4 272	4 876	17 093	1 504	1 090	491
医药院校	Medical	3	2 537	2 952	9 694	1 961	1 106	329
师范院校	Teacher Training	2	8 579	9 795	38 464	6 873	3 633	1 945
语文院校	Linguistics and Literacy	3	5 700	5 464	18 165	1 991	1 248	428
财经院校	Economics and Finance	18	31 177	33 383	113 430	9 103	5 792	2 210
政法院校	Politics and Law	3	5 477	7 235	23 876	2 414	1 550	545
体育院校	Physical Culture	2	914	1 189	4 447	1 250	611	275
艺术院校	Art Schools	5	3 521	3 845	13 316	1 875	1 051	352

注：学生数中未包括在读研究生人数，在分类院校学生数中未包括成人高等学校中的普通本专科学生。
Note: Post-graduates are not included in the students enrollment. Undergraduates and junior college students in adult education schools are not included in the students.

表 20.10 普通高等学校分科专任教师数(2010)
FULL-TIME TEACHERS IN INSTITUTIONS OF HIGHER EDUCATION BY SUBJECTS

单位:人（person）

类 别 Types		专任教师数 Full-time Teachers	其中 of which 正高级 Senior Title	副高级 Associate Title	中 级 Junior Title	初 级 Primary Title	无职称 Non-Title
总 计	**Total**	**37 170**	**6 191**	**11 479**	**16 332**	**3 488**	**1 680**
哲 学	Philosophy	882	147	272	346	78	39
经济学	Economics	2 527	392	838	1 025	164	108
法 学	Law	525	337	657	1 077	282	172
教育学	Education	3 428	246	726	1 605	658	193
文 学	Literature	8 797	937	2 127	4 200	1 026	507
历史学	History	435	145	111	153	15	11
理 学	Science	3 893	962	1 289	1 404	128	110
工 学	Engineering	11 414	2 202	3 947	4 383	578	304
农 学	Agriculture	348	81	136	99	31	1
医 学	Medical	2 153	337	507	943	306	60
管理学	Administrotion	2 768	405	869	1 097	222	175

注：本页数据由上海市教育委员会提供。
Note: Data on this page are provided by Shanghai Municipal Education Commission.

表 20.11 普通高等学校分科学生数(2010)
STUDENTS IN INSTITUTIONS OF HIGHER EDUCATION BY SUBJECTS

单位:人 (person)

类别	Types	毕业生人数 Graduates 本科 Undergraduate	毕业生人数 Graduates 专科 Junior College	招生人数 New Students Enrollment 本科 Undergraduate	招生人数 New Students Enrollment 专科 Junior College	在校学生人数 Students Enrollment 本科 Undergraduate	在校学生人数 Students Enrollment 专科 Junior College
总计	**Total**	**78 331**	**55 356**	**91 154**	**53 495**	**354 940**	**160 721**
哲学	Philosophy	125		127		581	
经济学	Economics	8 238	3 544	8 377	3 624	33 068	11 878
法学	Law	5 288	1 716	5 876	2 612	22 218	6 079
教育学	Education	1 504	758	2 192	575	7 582	2 321
文学	Literature	13 170	12 283	16 108	11 518	60 672	35 451
历史学	History	208		218		913	
理学	Science	5 880		7 819		29 455	
工学	Engineering	25 333	20 985	29 799	19 047	118 277	57 162
农学	Agriculture	437	441	670	397	2 173	1 259
医学	Medical	2 262	3 692	2 124	4 829	10 419	13 076
管理学	Administrotion	15 886	11 937	17 844	10 893	69 582	33 495

表 20.12 中等专业学校基本情况(2010)
BASIC STATISTICS OF SPECIALIZED SECONDARY SCHOOLS

单位:人 (person)

类别	Types	毕业生数 Graduates	招生数 New Students Enrollment	在校学生 Students Enrollment	专业课专任教师 Full-time Teachers in Professional Course	其中 of which #正副高级 Senior and Associate Title	其中 of which #中级 Junior Title
总计	**Total**	**33 413**	**29 870**	**109 054**	**4 952**	**1 122**	**2 553**
#土木水利工程	Construction and Water Conservancy Engineering	1 613	1 887	6 248	128	40	68
加工制造	Machining and Manufacture	4 268	4 763	17 329	365	120	160
交通运输	Transport	3 787	2 800	9 767	270	46	142
信息技术	Information Technology	3 255	3 676	11 815	358	73	206
医药卫生	Health	4 891	3 670	13 838	321	98	180
财经商贸	Trade and Tour	8 673	7 004	28 854	302	69	158
旅游服务	Finance and Economics	780	531	1 968	54	9	31
文化艺术与体育	Arts and Physical Culture	1 830	1 401	5 439	467	96	246
公共管理与服务	Society Commonality Business	731	859	2 312	27	5	15

注：本页数据由上海市教育委员会提供。
Note: Data on this page are provided by Shanghai Municipal Education Commission

表20.13 各区、县普通中学基本情况(2010)
BASIC STATISTICS OF REGULAR SECONDARY SCHOOLS BY DISTRICTS AND COUNTIES

地 区 District		学校(所) Schools (unit)	毕业生数(人) Graduates (person)	招生数(人) New Students Enrollment (person)	在校学生(人) Students Enrollment (person)	教职员工(人) Staff and Workers (person)	其中 of which 专任教师 Full-time Teachers
总 计	**Total**	**755**	**161 288**	**163 277**	**594 362**	**67 277**	**50 741**
浦东新区	Pudong New Area	151	36 077	40 593	140 793	13 453	11 067
黄浦区	Huangpu	23	5 530	5 176	18 380	2 472	1 634
卢湾区	Luwan	14	2 233	2 184	7 651	1 136	826
徐汇区	Xuhui	39	10 395	10 369	37 719	4 400	3 253
长宁区	Changning	26	5 714	5 170	19 909	2 576	1 781
静安区	Jing'an	15	3 855	3 617	12 731	1 674	1 126
普陀区	Putuo	47	8 118	8 000	29 181	3 731	2 413
闸北区	Zhabei	36	8 325	6 596	25 603	3 256	2 225
虹口区	Hongkou	41	7 888	7 043	26 726	3 125	2 447
杨浦区	Yangpu	54	10 348	9 635	35 699	4 366	3 337
闵行区	Minhang	59	10 573	12 403	42 025	5 321	4 108
宝山区	Baoshan	55	9 908	11 512	39 783	3 979	3 265
嘉定区	Jiading	32	6 206	6 941	23 684	2 777	2 076
金山区	Jinshan	30	7 191	6 023	24 333	2 775	2 087
松江区	Songjiang	32	7 760	7 751	31 210	3 444	2 429
青浦区	Qingpu	25	6 238	6 419	24 812	2 452	1 980
奉贤区	Fengxian	37	6 964	8 014	29 620	2 987	2 329
崇明县	Chongming	39	7 965	5 831	24 503	3 353	2 358

注：本表数据由上海市教育委员会提供。
Note: Data in this table are provided by Shanghai Municipal Education Commission.

表20.14 各区、县普通中学初、高中学生基本情况(2010)
BASIC STATISTICS OF REGULAR JUNIOR AND SENIOR SCHOOLS' STUDENTS BY DISTRICTS AND COUNTIES

单位:人 (person)

地区	District	毕业生数 Graduates		招生数 New Students Enrollment		在校学生 Students Enrollment	
		初中 Junior	高中 Senior	初中 Junior	高中 Senior	初中 Junior	高中 Senior
总计	**Total**	**98 913**	**62 375**	**109 424**	**53 853**	**425 463**	**168 899**
浦东新区	Pudong New Area	23 234	12 843	29 105	11 488	105 681	35 112
黄浦区	Huangpu	2 857	2 673	2 675	2 501	11 099	7 281
卢湾区	Luwan	1 362	871	1 284	900	5 081	2 570
徐汇区	Xuhui	6 047	4 348	6 319	4 050	25 580	12 139
长宁区	Changning	3 369	2 345	3 362	1 808	14 106	5 803
静安区	Jing'an	2 225	1 630	2 152	1 465	8 473	4 258
普陀区	Putuo	4 698	3 420	5 297	2 703	20 387	8 794
闸北区	Zhabei	5 069	3 256	4 196	2 400	17 698	7 905
虹口区	Hongkou	4 254	3 634	4 182	2 861	17 413	9 313
杨浦区	Yangpu	5 667	4 681	5 808	3 827	23 590	12 109
闵行区	Minhang	6 627	3 946	8 879	3 524	30 775	11 250
宝山区	Baoshan	6 330	3 578	8 342	3 170	29 915	9 868
嘉定区	Jiading	4 244	1 962	4 945	1 996	17 655	6 029
金山区	Jinshan	4 697	2 494	3 787	2 236	16 920	7 413
松江区	Songjiang	5 165	2 595	5 452	2 299	23 973	7 237
青浦区	Qingpu	3 889	2 349	4 362	2 057	18 281	6 531
奉贤区	Fengxian	4 655	2 309	5 887	2 127	23 114	6 506
崇明县	Chongming	4 524	3 441	3 390	2 441	15 722	8 781

注：本表数据由上海市教育委员会提供。
Note: Data in this table are provided by Shanghai Municipal Education Commission.

表 20.15　各区、县普通小学基本情况(2010)
BASIC STATISTICS OF REGULAR PRIMARY SCHOOLS BY DISTRICTS AND COUNTIES

地　区	District	学校(所) Schools (unit)	毕业生数(人) Graduates (person)	招生数(人) New Students Enrollment (person)	在校学生(人) Students Enrollment (person)	教职员工(人) Staff and Workers (person)	其中 of which #专任教师 Full-time Teachers
总　计	**Total**	**766**	**124 353**	**150 465**	**701 578**	**55 843**	**45 239**
浦东新区	Pudong New Area	164	31 086	36 485	165 009	11 645	10 086
黄 浦 区	Huangpu	18	2 411	2 170	10 904	1 439	1 046
卢 湾 区	Luwan	13	1 320	1 314	6 690	903	642
徐 汇 区	Xuhui	42	5 993	6 197	30 395	2 653	2 231
长 宁 区	Changning	25	3 376	3 680	18 200	1 936	1 485
静 安 区	Jing'an	12	1 805	1 773	8 846	1 113	701
普 陀 区	Putuo	27	5 740	5 527	27 752	2 285	1 692
闸 北 区	Zhabei	34	4 216	4 249	20 456	2 106	1 523
虹 口 区	Hongkou	34	4 164	4 174	20 629	2 116	1 787
杨 浦 区	Yangpu	44	5 850	5 064	26 537	2 699	2 328
闵 行 区	Minhang	61	12 570	16 023	73 202	5 333	4 347
宝 山 区	Baoshan	72	11 204	12 986	60 214	4 491	3 844
嘉 定 区	Jiading	40	5 707	9 112	43 749	2 855	2 301
金 山 区	Jinshan	32	4 347	5 989	27 097	2 249	1 668
松 江 区	Songjiang	33	7 624	11 714	54 081	3 292	2 724
青 浦 区	Qingpu	45	5 864	9 730	41 848	3 127	2 350
奉 贤 区	Fengxian	33	7 317	10 199	46 884	3 123	2 631
崇 明 县	Chongming	37	3 759	4 079	19 085	2 478	1 853

注：本表数据由上海市教育委员会提供。
Note: Data in this table are provided by Shanghai Municipal Education Commission.

表 20.16 主要年份实验性示范性中学基本情况
BASIC STATISTICS OF SECONDARY CAMPUS SCHOOL IN MAIN YEARS

指 标	Indicators	2000	2009	2010
学校(所)	Schools (unit)	84	108	128
班级数(个)	Classes (unit)	2 584	3 545	4 063
在校学生(万人)	Students Enrollment (10 000 persons)	12.10	13.06	14.67
教职员工(万人)	Staff and Workers (10 000 persons)	1.40	1.65	1.88
#专任教师	Full-time Teachers	0.88	1.23	1.42

注：实验性示范性中学包括重点中学和寄宿制高级中学。
Note: Secondary campus school includs important secondary school and boarding high school.

表 20.17 主要年份幼儿园基本情况
BASIC STATISTICS OF KINDERGARTENS IN MAIN YEARS

指 标	Indicators	2000	2009	2010
幼儿园(所)	Kindergartens (unit)	958	1 111	1 252
幼儿数(万人)	Children Enrollment (10 000 persons)	24.12	35.38	40.03
教职员工(万人)	Staff and Workers (10 000 persons)	2.52	3.60	4.09
#教 师	Teachers	1.50	2.36	2.67

表 20.18 主要年份特殊教育基本情况
BASIC STATISTICS OF SPECIAL EDUCATION IN MAIN YEARS

指 标	Indicators	2000	2009	2010
学 校(所)	Schools (unit)	34	29	29
毕业生数(人)	Graduates (person)	868	901	918
招生数(人)	New Students Enrollment (person)	1 141	758	776
在校学生(人)	Students Enrollment (person)	5 407	5 044	5 036
教职员工(人)	Staff and Workers (person)	1 584	1 594	1 596
#专任教师	Full-time Teachers	943	1 121	1 143

注：本页数据由上海市教育委员会提供。
Note: Data on this page are provided by Shanghai Municipal Education Commission.

表 20.19 网络教育学生情况(2010)
BASIC STATISTICS OF NETWORK EDUCATION STUDENTS BY SUBJECT

单位:人(person)

类 别	Types	毕业生人数 Graduates		招生人数 New Students Enrollment		在校学生人数 Student Enrollment	
		本 科 Undergraduate	专 科 Junior College	本 科 Undergraduate	专 科 Junior College	本 科 Undergraduate	专 科 Junior College
总 计	**Total**	**14 873**	**35 442**	**13 735**	**39 703**	**43 727**	**107 882**
哲 学	Philosophy	62		411		411	
经济学	Economics	2 401	222	2 491	558	5 788	1 542
法 学	Law	504	82	294	115	977	218
教育学	Education	2 055	1 251	1 842	1 549	4 390	4 523
文 学	Literature	2 798	1 593	1 880	1 777	4 424	5 036
历史学	History	54					
理 学	Science	778		394		883	
工 学	Engineering	1 404	2 132	1 216	3 818	6 266	10 439
医 学	Medical	982	1 972	1 017	726	3 148	3 411
管理学	Administration	3 835	28 190	4 190	31 160	17 440	82 713

表 20.20 各级各类成人学校基本情况(2010)
BASIC STATISTICS OF ADULT SCHOOLS AT VARIOUS LEVELS

类 别	Types	学校数(所) Schools (unit)	毕业生人数(万人) Graduates (10 000 persons)	招生数(万人) New Students Enrollment (10 000 persons)	在校学生人数(万人) Students Enrollment (10 000 persons)	教职员工人数(万人) Staff and Workers (10 000 persons)	其中 of which 专任教师 Full-time Teachers
成人高等教育	**Adult Higher Education**	**17**	**6.88**	**6.54**	**19.86**	**0.20**	**0.11**
广播电视大学	Broadcasting and TV Universities	1				0.03	0.01
职工高等学校	Staff Higher Education Schools	12	0.65	0.46	1.14	0.13	0.08
管理干部学院	Institutes for Administrative Officials	4	0.12	0.05	0.27	0.04	0.02
普通高等学校办	Run by Regular High Education Institutions	(77)	6.11	6.03	18.45		
函 授	Correspondence Programs	11	0.66	0.41	1.27		
业 余	Spare Time	48	5.22	5.61	16.90		
脱 产	Full Time	18	0.23	0.01	0.28		
成人网络本、专科	**Adult Network Education**		**5.03**	**53.34**	**15.16**		
成人中等教育	**Adult Secondary Education**	**39**	**1.95**	**0.69**	**3.72**	**0.07**	**0.04**
成人中等专业学校	Specialized Secondary Schools	26	0.84	0.69	1.72	0.06	0.03
成人中学	Adult Spare-time Secondary Schools	13	1.11		2.00	0.01	0.01
成人职业技术学校	**Adult Technical Secondary Schools**	**787**	**14.57**		**18.86**	**1.45**	**0.65**

①"( )"指高等院校举办的各类成人教学点数据。成人中学学校在校学生数为在校注册学生数。
②本页数据由上海市教育委员会提供。
❶The figures with"( )" refer to the number of the adult education places conducted by higher education institutions. Students enrollment of adult spare-time secondary schools refer to the number of students registered at school.
❷Data on this page are provided by Shanghai Municipal Education Commission.

上/海/统/计/年/鉴

主要统计指标解释

学　校

指按国家规定的设置标准和审批程序批准设立的，招收适龄人口实施各级各类教育活动的教育机构。

普通高等学校

指按照国家规定的设置标准和审批程序批准举办的，通过全国普通高等学校统一招生考试，招收高中毕业生为主要培养对象，实施高等教育的全日制大学、独立设置的学院和高等专科学校、高等职业学校和其他机构。大学、独立设置的学院主要实施本科层次以上教育，高等专科学校、高等职业学校实施专科层次教育，其他机构是承担国家普通招生计划任务不计校数的机构。包括普通高等学校分校和批准筹建的普通高等学校等。

成人高等学校

指按国家规定的设置标准和审批程序举办的，通过全国成人高等教育统一招生考试，招收高中毕业或同等学历的人员为主要培养对象，利用函授、业余、脱产的多种形式对其实施高等学历教育的学校。包括：职工高等学校、农民高等学校、管理干部学院、教育学院、独立函授学院、广播电视大学、其他机构等。

中等专业学校

指经县或县以上教育行政部门批准设立，招收初中毕业生实施中等专业课程教育的教学机构。

职业中学(职业高中、职业初中)

指经县或县以上教育行政部门批准设立，招收小学或初中毕业生实施中等职业技术教育的教学机构。按学校性质类别可分为：独立设置的职业中学(包括：职业初中、职业高中、职业初高中合设学校)；附设有普通中学班的职业中学。

普通中学(普通高中、普通初中)

普通中学分为普通高级中学和普通初级中学两个阶段。普通初级中学是指独立设置的招收小学毕业的适龄人口进行初级中等基础教育的机构；普通高级中学是指独立设置的招收初中毕业的适龄人口进行高级中等基础教育的机构；完全中学是指普通初、高中合设的教育机构；一贯制学校是指在一所学校连续实施中小学教育的机构。其中包括实施九年义务教育的九年一贯制学校和实施高中教育的十二年一贯制学校。(说明：一贯制学校的办学条件如能划分为小学、初中、高中，则分开填报；如不能划分清楚，可按就高不就低的方法填入初中、高中报表中，不能重复填写。)

普通小学

指由区或区以上教育行政部门批准，招收学龄儿童实施初等教育的教学机构。

幼儿园

指招收三周岁以上(含三周岁)学龄前幼儿，对其进行保育和教育的单位。

特殊教育学校

指本市独立设置的招收盲聋哑和智残儿童，以及其他特殊需要的儿童、青少年进行普通或职业初、中等教育的教学机构。

小学学龄儿童净入学率

小学学龄人口中正在接受小学教育人数所占比重。

初中学生净入学率

是指初中阶段教育（接受普通初中教育和职业初中教育)在校学生总数占初中阶段教育学龄人口数的比重。

预算内教育经费

指中央、地方各级财政或上级主管部门在年度内安排，并计划拨到教育部门和其他部门主办的各级各类学校、教育事业单位，列入国家预算支出科目的教育经费，包括教育事业拨款、科研经费拨款、基建拨款和其他经费拨款。

SHANGHAI STATISTICAL YEARBOOK

EXPLANATORY NOTES TO MAJOR STATISTICAL INDICATORS

□ School Institutions

School Institutions refer to education establishment set up according to the government evaluation and approval procedures, enrolling population of the right age, providing various phase education activity.

□ Regular Institutions of Higher Education

Regular Institutions of Higher Learning refer to educational establishments set up according to the government evaluation and approval procedures, enrolling graduates from senior secondary schools and providing higher education courses and training for senior professionals. They include full-time universities, colleges, high professional schools, high professional vocational schools and others.

Universities and colleges are mainly providing undergraduate courses; those high professional schools and high professional vocational schools are mainly providing professional trainings; and others refer to educational establishments, which are responsible for enrolling students but not covered in the total number of schools, including: branch schools of universities and colleges, and universities and colleges that have been proved and prepared to construct.

□ Institutions of Higher Education for Adults

Institution of Higher Learning for Adults refer to educational establishments, set up in line with relevant rules approved by the government, enrolling personnel with senior secondary schools or equivalent education, and providing higher education courses in many forms of correspondence, spare time, or full time for adults. Institutions of higher schools for adults include schools of higher educations for staff and workers, schools of higher education for peasants, colleges for management cadres, pedagogical colleges, independent correspondence colleges, Radio and TV universities and other educational establishment, etc.

□ Specialized Secondary Schools

Specialized Secondary schools refer to educational establishment set up according to approval and permission by educational administration department of district and above government, enrolling graduates from junior secondary schools and providing secondary professional education courses.

□ Vocational Secondary Schools (senior secondary schools and junior secondary schools)

Vocational Secondary Schools (senior secondary schools and junior secondary schools) refer to educational establishment set up according to approval and permission by educational administration department of district and above government, enrolling graduates from primary schools and junior secondary schools and providing secondary vocational education courses.

□ Regular Secondary Schools (senior secondary schools and junior secondary schools)

Regular Secondary Schools (senior secondary schools and junior secondary schools) are classified as senior secondary schools and junior secondary schools. Junior Secondary Schools refer to educational establishment enrolling graduates from primary schools and providing junior secondary educational courses. Senior Secondary Schools refer to educational establishment enrolling graduates from junior secondary schools and providing higher secondary educational courses.

□ Regular Primary Schools

Regular Primary Schools refer to educational establishment set up according to approval and permission by educational administration department of district and above government, enrolling graduates from children of school age and providing primary educational courses.

□ Kindergartens

Kindergartens refer to nursery and education establishment, enrolling children in 3 years old and above.

□ Special Education Schools

Special Education Schools refer to educational establishments set up independently, enrolling blind, deaf, dumb, amentia or other special children, and educational establishment, providing regular or vocational junior and senior secondary education for hobbledehoy.

EXPLANATORY NOTES TO MAJOR STATISTICAL INDICATORS

□ Enrollment Rate of School-age Children

Enrollment Rate of School-age Children refers to the proportion of school age children enrolled at schools to the total number of school age children both in and outside schools.

□ Enrollment Rate of Students in Junior Secondary School Phase

It refers to the proportion of total quantity of student in junior secondary school to the population of junior school age.

□ Budgetary Fund for Education

Budgetary Fund for Education refers to education fund that is planned to allocate to various schools and education institutions by central and local financial departments at various levels within the reference year, which is within the state budgetary expenditure, including: appropriate funds for education, science and research, capital construction and others.

第二十一篇

CHAPTER 21

卫生、社会保障和社会福利业

HEALTH, SOCIAL SECURITY AND SOCIAL WELFARE

表21.1 卫生事业基本情况(1978~2010)
BASIC STATISTICS OF PUBLIC HEALTH

年 份 Year	卫生机构数(个) Health Care Institutions (unit)	其中 of which #医 院 Hospital	卫 生 技术人员(万人) Medical Professionals (10 000 persons)	其中 of which #医 生 Doctors	卫生机构床位数(万张) Hospital Beds (10 000 beds)	其中 of which #医 院 Hospital	每万人口医生数(人) Doctors per 10 000 Persons (person)	每万人口医院床位数(张) Hospital Beds per 10 000 Persons (bed)
1978	4 823	388	8.50	3.35	5.47	4.68	30	42
1979	5 627	394	8.88	3.58	5.56	4.78	31	42
1980	6 067	399	9.41	3.92	5.80	4.94	34	43
1981	6 337	403	9.57	4.37	5.84	4.99	37	43
1982	6 445	408	9.88	4.72	5.93	5.11	40	43
1983	6 451	415	10.09	4.87	6.00	5.20	41	43
1984	6 318	420	10.24	4.84	6.16	5.34	40	44
1985	7 245	405	10.42	4.85	6.02	5.32	39	43
1986	7 306	419	10.71	4.91	6.22	5.47	39	44
1987	7 330	431	11.00	5.05	6.38	5.60	40	44
1988	7 471	444	11.46	5.40	6.79	5.89	42	46
1989	7 550	460	11.65	5.73	6.87	6.04	44	46
1990	7 690	462	11.84	5.82	6.96	6.21	44	47
1991	7 554	463	11.92	5.89	7.01	6.31	44	47
1992	7 363	454	11.82	5.88	7.07	6.42	43	47
1993	6 077	486	11.53	5.75	7.12	6.75	42	49
1994	5 606	497	11.20	5.52	7.20	6.81	39	49
1995	5 286	485	11.06	5.37	7.10	6.69	38	47
1996	5 200	477	10.95	5.24	7.00	6.73	36	46
1997	5 028	474	10.89	5.13	7.00	6.78	34	46
1998	4 637	473	10.84	5.03	7.02	6.83	33	45
1999	4 620	465	10.81	5.06	7.24	7.06	32	45
2000	4 400	459	10.71	4.99	7.53	7.31	31	45
2001	3 813	432	10.51	4.85	7.88	7.63	29	46
2002	2 422	436	10.16	4.38	8.15	8.13	26	47
2003	2 319	452	10.22	4.41	8.44	8.11	25	46
2004	2 577	489	10.17	4.38	8.64	8.50	24	46
2005	2 527	487	10.35	4.40	9.08	8.93	23	47
2006	2 519	505	10.90	4.55	9.44	9.28	23	47
2007	2 646	288	12.24	4.88	9.59	7.54	24	37
2008	2 809	301	12.77	5.12	9.78	7.78	24	36
2009	3 013	296	13.09	5.11	9.97	7.95	23	36
2010	3 270	306	13.54	5.13	10.51	8.48	22	37

① 本表数据由市卫生局提供。
② 2002 年开始，卫生指标按照新的《中国卫生统计调查制度》统计。其中，医生为执业医师和执业和助理医师；护师、护士为注册护士。
③ 2007 年开始，医院统计范围按照新的《2007 国家卫生统计调查制度》统计，不再包括社区卫生服务中心、妇幼保健院和专科防治院。

❶ Data in this table are provided by Shanghai Municipal Health Bureau.
❷ Since 2002, statistics of health care has been based on "China Health Care Statistical Investigation System". Of which, Doctors refer to certified physicians and certified assistant physicians, senior and junior nurses refer to registered nurses.
❸ Since 2007, statistics of hospital has been based on "2007 National Health Care Statistical Investigation System", not including the community health care service center, maternity and child care hospital and special disease hospital.

表21.2 各类卫生机构、床位及人员数(2010)
VARIOUS HEALTH CARE INSTITUTIONS,BEDS AND PERSONNEL

机构类别	Type of Institutions	机构数（个）Health Care Institutions (unit)	床位数（张）Beds (bed)	工作人员数（人）Personnel (person)
总　计	**Total**	**3 270**	**105 083**	**169 985**
医疗机构合计	Medical Institutions	3 182	105 083	163 342
医　院	Hospitals	306	84 825	115 316
综合医院	Comprehensive Hospitals	185	52 335	83 986
中医医院	Hospitals of Traditional Chinese	17	4 987	8 128
中西医结合医院	Hospitals of Combination of	5	1 894	2 656
专科医院	Special Diseases Hospitals	85	22 324	19 567
老年护理院	Nursing Home for Aged Persons	14	3 285	979
社区卫生服务中心	Community Health Care Centers	931	18 618	30 082
专科疾病防治院、所	Special Disease Hospitals and Institutions	19	168	1 308
#专科疾病防治院	Special Disease Hospital	5	168	504
妇幼保健院、所	Maternity and Child Care Hospital and Institutions	21	1 195	2 757
#妇幼保健院	Maternity and Child Care Hospital	8	1 195	2 145
疗养院	Sanatoriums	2	265	147
门诊部	Policlinic	429	12	6 165
诊所、卫生所、医务室	Clinic,Health Center and Infirmary	1 463		5 506
急救中心(站)	First-aid Centers	11		2 061
疾病预防控制中心	Disease Prevention and Control Centers	21		3 141
卫生监督所	Health Supervision Centers	20		1 291
医学科学研究机构	Institutions of Medical Science	9		493
采供血机构	Blood Collection and Supply Institutions	8		631
其他卫生机构	Other Health Care Institutions	30		1 087

注：本表数据由市卫生局提供。
Note: Date in this table are provided by Shanghai Municipal Health Bureau.

表 21.2 续表 continued

机构类别	Type of Institutions	其中 of which		
		# 卫生技术人员 Medical Professionals	其中 of which	
			# 医生 Doctors	# 护师、护士 Senior and Junior Nurses
总计	**Total**	**135 411**	**51 278**	**55 871**
医疗机构合计	Medical Institutions	131 155	49 870	55 534
医院	Hospitals	93 566	31 694	43 426
综合医院	Comprehensive Hospitals	69 080	24 024	31 824
中医医院	Hospitals of Traditional Chinese	6 659	2 548	2 679
中西医结合医院	Hospitals of Combination of	2 145	729	925
专科医院	Special Diseases Hospitals	14 978	4 199	7 654
老年护理院	Nursing Home for Aged Persons	704	194	344
社区卫生服务中心	Community Health Care Centers	24 468	11 000	7 967
专科疾病防治院、所	Special Disease Hospitals and Institutions	1 042	525	316
# 专科疾病防治院	Special Disease Hospital	376	172	110
妇幼保健院、所	Maternity and Child Care Hospital and Institutions	2 303	897	1 059
# 妇幼保健院	Maternity and Child Care Hospital	1 805	632	926
疗养院	Sanatoriums	72	26	33
门诊部	Policlinic	4 883	2 503	1 706
诊所、卫生所、医务室	Clinic, Health Center and Infirmary	4 037	2 759	980
急救中心(站)	First-aid Centers	784	466	47
疾病预防控制中心	Disease Prevention and Control Centers	2 218	1 202	61
卫生监督所	Health Supervision Centers	1 019		
医学科学研究机构	Institutions of Medical Science	263	105	6
采供血机构	Blood Collection and Supply Institutions	443	25	184
其他卫生机构	Other Health Care Institutions	313	76	86

表21.3 各区、县卫生机构基本情况(2010)
STATISTICS OF HEALTH CARE INSTITUTIONS BY DISTRICTS AND COUNTIES

地 区	District	机构数(个) Health Care Institutions(unit)	床位数(张) Hospital Beds(bed)	卫生技术人员(人) Medical Professionals(person)	其 中 of which	
					#医 生 Doctors	#护师、护士 Senior and Junior Nurses
总 计	**Total**	**3 270**	**105 083**	**135 411**	**51 278**	**55 871**
浦东新区	Pudong New Area	586	15 164	18 921	7 646	7 448
黄浦区	Huangpu	113	5 766	8 896	3 210	3 495
卢湾区	Luwan	111	4 481	7 061	2 363	3 058
徐汇区	Xuhui	282	13 268	16 669	5 832	7 132
长宁区	Changning	211	4 694	7 537	2 754	3 100
静安区	Jing'an	123	5 173	8 608	3 103	3 752
普陀区	Putuo	157	5 324	6 597	2 545	2 734
闸北区	Zhabei	113	4 928	5 541	2 064	2 402
虹口区	Hongkou	139	6 556	7 989	3 117	3 308
杨浦区	Yangpu	165	6 395	8 509	3 117	3 849
闵行区	Minhang	272	7 514	8 132	3 195	3 430
宝山区	Baoshan	221	4 672	6 379	2 421	2 605
嘉定区	Jiading	206	3 023	4 531	1 955	1 823
金山区	Jinshan	103	3 746	4 476	1 641	1 833
松江区	Songjiang	165	4 087	4 904	2 095	1 842
青浦区	Qingpu	119	2 265	3 329	1 361	1 304
奉贤区	Fengxian	71	4 553	3 855	1 471	1 474
崇明县	Chongming	113	3 474	3 477	1 388	1 282

注：本表数据由市卫生局提供。
Note: Date in this table are provided by Shanghai Municipal Health Bureau.

表21.4 医疗机构病床使用情况(2010)
STATISTICS OF HOSPITAL BED USAGE IN MEDICAL TREATMENT INSTITUTION

机构类别	Types	平均开放床位数(张) Average Beds Opened(bed)	病床周转次数(次) Turnover Times of Beds(time)	病床使用率(%) Usage Rate of Beds(%)	出院者平均住院日(日) Average Days to Inpatient in Hospital(day)
总　计	**Total**	**108 715**	**23.14**	**95.72**	**14.24**
卫生部门	Medical Institutions	90 168	24.15	98.09	14.29
#医　院	Hospital	70 649	27.92	101.08	12.70
#综合医院	Comprehensive Hospitals	44 023	33.87	100.96	10.91
中(西)医医院	Hospitals of Chinese (Western) Wedicine	6 823	26.06	95.16	13.41
护理院	Nursing Hospitals	1 124	4.12	100.85	95.60
社区卫生服务	Community Health Care	18 319	7.18	86.86	43.03
其他部门	Other Departments	18 547	18.25	84.19	13.91

表21.5 医疗机构诊疗人次和入院人数(2010)
PATIENTS TREATED AND INPATIENTS IN MEDICAL TREATMENT INSTITUTION

机构类别	Types	诊疗人次(万人次) Total Patients Treated(10 000 person-times)	其中 of which #门、急诊 Outpatients and Emergency Patients	入院人数(万人) Inpatients (10 000 persons)	每百诊次的入院人数(人) Inpatients per 100 Patient-times (person)
总　计	**Total**	**21 002.46**	**20 676.24**	**285.68**	**1.4**
卫生部门	Public Health Sector	19 138.92	18 858.50	251.72	1.3
医　院	Hospitals	11 009.45	10 950.45	230.85	2.1
综合医院	Comprehensive Hospitals	8 285.11	8 234.30	177.44	2.1
中(西)医医院	Hospitals of Chinese(Western) Medicine	1 438.96	1 437.12	17.75	1.2
传染病医院	Infectious Diseases Hospitals	49.21	49.21	1.42	2.9
精神病医院	Mental Hospitals	101.02	100.92	1.22	1.2
结核病医院	Tuberculosis Hospitals	53.92	53.92	3.58	6.6
肿瘤医院	Tumor Hospitals	70.88	70.82	3.41	4.8
儿童医院	Children's Hospitals	412.25	412.25	6.34	1.5
其他专科医院	Other Specialized Hospitals	568.40	562.61	18.65	3.3
护理院	Nurse Hospitals	29.70	29.30	1.04	3.5
社区卫生服务中心	Community Health-care Service Centers	7 342.23	7 163.38	13.10	0.2
妇幼保健院	Maternity and Child Care Hospital	222.49	211.20	7.39	3.3
其他医疗机构	Other Medical Facilities	564.75	533.47	0.38	0.1
工业及其他部门	Industry and Other Sectors	1 863.54	1 817.74	33.96	1.8

表21.6 前十位疾病死亡原因和构成(2010)
THE TOP 10 DEATH-CAUSING DISEASES AND COMPOSITION

死亡原因	Cause of Death	死亡专率(1/10万) Death Rate(1/100 000)	占死亡总数(%) Percentage of Total Death(%)
循环系病	Circulation Diseases	272.12	35.28
肿　瘤	Tumor	239.91	31.10
呼吸系病	Respiratory System Diseases	83.26	10.79
损伤中毒	Damnification and Poisoning	41.84	5.42
内分泌营养代谢病	Endocrine-Immunity-Metabolic Diseases	32.69	4.24
消化系病	Digestive System Diseases	20.3	2.63
传染病及寄生虫病	Infectious & Parasitic Diseases	9.36	1.21
神经系病	Nervous System Disease	8.69	1.13
精神病	Mental System Diseases	8.13	1.05
泌尿生殖系病	Genitourinary Diseases	6.99	0.91

表21.7 婴儿前五位疾病死亡原因和构成(2010)
THE TOP 5 INFANT DEATH-CAUSING DISEASES AND COMPOSITION

死亡原因	Cause of Death	死亡专率(1/10万) Death Rate(1/100 000)	占死亡总数(%) Percentage of Total Death(%)
先天异常	Congenital Anomaly	209.83	48.65
新生儿病	Neonatal Disease	125.05	28.99
神经系病	Nerwns System Disease	24.37	5.65
损伤中毒	Damnification and Poisoning	15.90	3.69
呼吸系病	Respiratory System Diseases	13.78	3.19

表21.8 婴儿死亡率、新生儿死亡率、孕产妇死亡率(2008~2010)
DEATH RATE OF INFANT,NEW BORN,PREGNANT AND LYING-IN WOMAN IN MAIN YEARS

指　标	Indicators	2008	2009	2010
婴儿死亡率(‰)	Death Rate of Infant(‰)	5.61	6.58	5.97
新生儿死亡率(‰)	Death Rate of New Born(‰)	2.08	1.94	2.03
孕产妇死亡率(1/10万)	Death Rate of Pregnant and Lying-in Woman(1/100 000)	12.23	9.61	9.61

①婴儿死亡率、孕产妇死亡率2008年开始从户籍口径改为全市口径。新生儿死亡率为户籍人口口径。
②本页数据由市卫生局提供。
❶The scale of death rate of infant and death rate of pregnant and lying-in woman have been changed from registered pulation to all population in shanghai since 2008. The scale of Death Rate of New Born is registered population.
❷Date on this page are provided by Shanghai Municipal Health Bureau.

表 21.9 主要年份防病工作情况
BASIC STATISTICS OF DISEASE PREVENTION IN MAIN YEARS

指 标	Indicators	2000	2009	2010
传染病发病总例数(甲、乙)(万例)	**Cases of Contagious Diseases Reported (A,B)(10 000 cases)**	**3.58**	**2.68**	**2.22**
发病率(1/10万)	Disease Rate(1/100 000)	271.66	195.37	161.17
传染病死亡总人数(人)	Quantity of Deaths Caused by Contagious Diseases (person)	179	159	127
死亡率(1/10万)	Death Rate (1/100 000)	1.36	1.16	0.92
结核病登记病人数(千例)	T. B. Patients Registered (1 000 cases)	3.09	2.75	3.26
登记患病率(‰)	Registered Disease Rate(‰)	0.23	0.20	0.23
结核病新发病人数(千例)	Newly Reported T. B. Cases(1 000 cases)	5.18	3.75	3.76
登记新发病率(1/万)	Registered Newly Diseased Rate (1/10 000)	3.94	2.68	2.67
结核病死亡人数(人)	Quantity of Deaths Caused By T. B (person)	293	129	112
死亡率(1/10万)	Death Rate (1/100 000)	2.22	0.92	0.8
牙病受检人数(万人)	Quantity of People Undergoing Tooth Disease Check (10 000 persons)	51.89	84.55	54.85
龋牙患病率(%)	Rate of Caries Patients(%)	28.3	35.3	38.61
小学生视力不良率(%)	Nearsight in Primary School Rate(%)	26.0	35.1	36.14
初中生视力不良率(%)	Nearsight in Junior High School Rate(%)	55.0	68.9	69.98
高中生视力不良率(%)	Nearsight in Senior High School Rate(%)	78.5	85.7	85.73
“五苗”接种率(%)	“Five Vaccines”Recipients Rate(%)	99.7	99.4	99.8
乙肝疫苗全程接种率(%)	Hepatitis-B Inoculation Rate(%)	99.9	99.9	99.8

表 21.10 家庭病床情况(2010)
FAMILY SICKBEDS

机构类别	Types	开展工作机构数(个) Running Institutions (unit)	上门诊疗总次数(次) Total Times of Family Call (time)	年底实有病床数(张) Year-end Sickbeds (bed)	年内开设总病床数(张) Sickbeds Set up in 2009 (bed)
总 计	**Total**	**181**	**1 212 219**	**22 781**	**43 947**
医 院	Hospitals	8	84 162	1 038	1 553
社区卫生服务中心	Community Health-care Centers	173	1 128 057	21 743	42 394

注：本页数据由市卫生局提供。
Note: Date on this page are provided by Shanghai Municipal Health Bureau.

表21.11 主要年份妇幼卫生工作情况
BASIC STATISTICS OF GYNAECOLOGY AND PAEDIATRICS IN MAIN YEARS

指标	Indicators	2000	2009	2010
妇女病普查人数(万人)	**Quantity of People Surveyed for Female Diseases (10 000 persons)**	**40.27**	**76.69**	**86.54**
患病率(%)	Sufferers Rate(%)	35.0	31.8	33.3
治疗率(%)	Patients Treated Rate(%)	91.1	97.0	98.7
胎儿娩出顺产数(万人)	Quantity of Smooth Delivery (10 000 persons)	4.05	8.62	8.81
顺产率(%)	Smooth Delivery Rate(%)	47.5	43.4	45.1
出生低体重儿(人)	Quantity of Low-weight Newborns (person)	2 567	6 420	6 961
占活产总数(%)	Proportion in All Deliveries(%)	3.0	3.5	3.6
出生缺陷人数(人)	Quantity of Newborns with Innate Problems(person)	764	2 189	2 496
出生缺陷率(‰)	Disabled Among All Deliveries Rate (‰)	8.96	1.18	1.28
0~6岁儿童保健管理率(%)	Children, 0~6 Years Old under Health Programm Rate(%)	94.3	84.4	97.0
婚前检查人数(万人)	Quantity of People Undergoing Pre-marriage Checkup(10 000 persons)	17.36	10.52	8.53
婚检率(%)	Pre-marriage Checkup Recipients Rate(%)	98.4	37.5	35.4

表21.12 主要年份公民献血、用血情况
BASIC STATISTICS OF BLOOD DONATION AND USE IN MAIN YEARS

指标	Indicators	2000	2009	2010
无偿(义务)献血(万人份)	Volunteer or Compulsory Blood Offer(10 000 person unit)	35.19	45.50	46.27
临床用血量(万人份)	Clinic Blood Use Volum(10 000 person unit)	34.7	42.5	42.02

注：本页数据由市卫生局提供。
Note: Data on page are provided by Shanghai Municipal Health Bureau.

表21.13 主要年份社会保险参保人数
QUANTITY OF PARTICIPANTS IN SOCIAL INSURANCE IN MAIN YEARS

单位:万人(10 000 persons)

指 标	Indicators	2000	2009	2010
城镇基本养老保险	**Urban Basic Pension Insurance**			
城镇职工	Urban Staff and Workers	431.27	489.06	522.44
个体工商户和自由职业人员	Individual Businessman	9.82	17.80	20.43
领取养老金的离退休人员	Retired Veteran Cadres and Retired Staff and Workers with Pensions	234.23	338.85	352.02
城镇基本医疗保险	Urban Basic Medicare Insurance			
城镇职工	Urban Staff and Workers	364.59	578.66	608.41
享受医保的离退休人员	Retired Veteran Cadres and Retired Staff and Workers with Medicare	202.14	372.54	391.33
城镇职工失业保险	Unemployment Insurance of Urban Staff and Workers	434.86	523.53	556.20
城镇职工生育保险	Generational Insurance of Urban Staff and Workers		625.14	657.30
城镇职工工伤保险	Injured Insurance of Urban Staff and Workers		555.62	556.12
农村社会养老保险	Rural Social Pension Insurance	121.00	72.31	69.06
小城镇社会保险	Town Social Insurance		155.39	114.44
#被征用土地农民参保人数	Land Expropriated Peasant Participated		97.77	96.72
来沪从业人员综合保险	General Insurance of Employment of Migratory Population		378.41	404.84
高龄无保障老人保险	Insurence of Old Ages without Living Securing		5.62	5.22
普通高等院校学生基本医疗保险	Basic Medicare Insurance of Ordinary High Education Institutions Student		65.85	66.08
农村合作医疗	Cooperartion Medicare Insurance in Country		166.55	148.95
少儿住院基金	Medicare Fund of Children	212.47	188.38	197.19

注：本表数据由市人力资源和社会保障局、市医疗保险局、市红十字会提供。
Note: Data in this table are provided by Shanghai Municipal Human Resource and Soccial Security Bureau, Shanghai Municipal Medicare and Insurance Bureau and Red Cross Society of China Shanghai Municipal Branch.

表21.14 主要年份社会保障标准
SOCIAL SECURITY STANDARD IN MAIN YEARS

单位:元/月(yuan/month)

指 标	Indicators	2000	2009	2010
职工工资最低标准	Minimum Standard of Wages of Staff and Workers	445	960	1 120
城镇基本养老金最低标准	Minimum Standard of Urban Basic Pension Insurance	460	460	460
城镇居民生活保障最低标准	Minimum Standard of Urban Living Security	280	425	450

注：本表数据由市人力资源和社会保障局、市民政局提供。
Note: Data in this table are provided by Shanghai Municipal Human Resource and Soccial Security Bureau, and Shanghai Civil Affairs Bureau.

表21.15 社会福利院、儿童福利院、社会福利医院和收养性老年福利机构情况(1980～2010)

INSTITUTIONS OF SOCIAL WELFARE, CHILDREN WELFARE, SOCIAL WELFARE HOSPITALS AND ADOPTIVE SENIORS WELFARE INSTITUTIONS

年 份 Year	社会福利院 Social Welfare Institutions			儿童福利院 Children Welfare Homes		
	单 位 (个) Units (unit)	床位数 (张) Beds (bed)	年末在院人数 (人) Year-end Population Housed(person)	单 位 (个) Units (unit)	床位数 (张) Beds (bed)	年末在院人数 (人) Year-end Population Housed(person)
1980	9	1 555	1 337	2	600	559
1981	9	1 621	1 313	2	650	634
1982	9	1 525	1 495	2	650	672
1983	9	1 644	1 491	2	600	676
1984	10	1 948	1 635	2	600	633
1985	10	1 727	1 630	2	580	625
1986	10	1 697	1 648	2	550	612
1987	10	1 991	1 770	2	378	449
1988	13	2 189	1 790	2	387	458
1989	14	2 418	2 012	2	538	481
1990	15	2 679	2 019	2	589	586
1991	14	2 687	2 138	2	611	592
1992	14	2 776	2 431	2	665	651
1993	14	2 874	2 554	2	708	690
1994	15	2 931	2 648	2	878	862
1995	15	3 006	2 722	2	988	919
1996	17	3 294	2 866	2	988	943
1997	21	4 012	3 441	2	988	946
1998	24	4 596	3 678	2	1 004	984
1999	20	4 215	3 498	2	981	958
2000	23	4 884	4 137	2	1 100	1 092
2001	26	5 570	4 410	2	1 221	1 221
2002	27	5 590	4 760	3	1 491	1 429
2003	26	5 818	4 779	2	1 087	1 512
2004	26	5 876	4 848	6	1 300	1 893
2005	23	5 999	4 809	6	2 016	1 986
2006	25	6 583	5 024	6	1 252	2 142
2007	24	6 499	5 068	6	1 252	2 341
2008	26	6 864	5 215	6	2 490	2 454
2009	26	7 686	5 351	6	2 584	2 552
2010	25	7 944	5 774	6	2 454	2 423

注：本表数据由市民政局提供。
Note: Date in this table are provided by Shanghai Civil Affairs Bureau.

表21.15 续表 continued

年 份 Year	社会福利医院 Social Welfare hospitals			收养性老年福利机构 Adoptive Seniors Welfare Institutions			
	单 位 (个) Units (unit)	床位数 (张) Beds (bed)	年末在院人数 (人) Year-end Population Housed (person)	机 构 (个) Institutions (unit)	床位数 (张) Beds (bed)	年末在院人数 (人) Year-end Population Housed (person)	其 中 of which #老 人 Elder
1980	3	1 475	1 424	42		630	
1981	3	1 460	1 430	53		762	
1982	3	1 490	1 422	58		1 022	
1983	3	1 490	1 432	90		1 402	
1984	3	1 460	1 380	135		2 328	
1985	3	1 480	1 360	199	3 870	3 038	2 786
1986	3	1 510	1 354	249	4 655	3 446	3 100
1987	3	1 497	1 342	277	5 520	4 262	3 893
1988	3	1 497	1 313	322	5 969	4 754	4 429
1989	3	1 433	1 324	349	6 281	5 129	4 835
1990	3	1 497	1 298	332	6 275	5 031	4 452
1991	3	1 391	1 285	341	6 731	5 763	5 642
1992	3	1 510	1 404	351	7 002	6 035	5 655
1993	3	1 510	1 394	331	7 143	6 365	5 934
1994	3	1 510	1 392	333	7 533	6 838	6 541
1995	3	1 510	1 409	330	8 576	7 405	6 633
1996	3	1 510	1 429	333	10 270	8 361	7 867
1997	3	1 500	1 452	323	11 253	9 295	8 647
1998	3	1 500	1 455	339	13 958	11 122	10 826
1999	3	1 710	1 703	331	16 526	12 698	12 013
2000	3	1 840	1 779	398	22 244	16 988	16 541
2001	3	1 894	1 894	378	23 627	17 363	16 923
2002	3	1 917	1 901	417	33 413	20 900	20 309
2003	3	1 680	1 881	422	36 791	23 451	22 682
2004	3	1 780	1 829	414	33 891	26 993	25 902
2005	3	1 811	1 811	450	43 131	31 301	30 181
2006	3	1 860	1 796	479	52 427	35 946	34 447
2007	3	1 852	1 806	536	64 115	42 665	40 731
2008	3	1 851	1 809	556	72 365	46 107	44 226
2009	3	1 842	1 808	589	84 714	51 974	49 789
2010	3	1 835	1 800	635	102 180	66 872	60 634

表21.16 主要年份社会福利事业机构数和职工人数
QUANTITY OF SOCIAL WELFARE INSTITUTIONS AND STAFF AND WORKERS IN MAIN YEARS

指 标	Indicators	2000	2009	2010
机构数(个)	**Total Institutions (unit)**			
收养性福利单位	Adopting Social Welfare Institutions	427	625	635
优抚类	Subsidy	1	1	1
福利类	Welfare	426	624	634
社会福利企业	Social Welfare Enterprises	3 352	1 373	1 375
优抚安置单位	Subsidy and Arrangement Institution	45	41	41
救助类单位	Salvation Institution	16	21	22
婚姻登记服务单位	Marriage Rigister Service Institutions		14	16
殡仪服务单位	Funeral and Interment Service Institution	68	79	79
福利彩票发行单位	Issue Institution of Welfare Lottery	16	18	19
社区服务单位	Community Service Institutions	92	145	177
职工人数(人)	**Staff and Workers (person)**			
收养性福利单位	Adopting Social Welfare Institutions	7 793	17 878	19 966
优抚类	Subsidy	35	45	47
福利类	Welfare	7 758	17 853	19 919
社会福利企业	Social Welfare Enterprises	177 260	100 148	92 351
优抚安置单位	Subsidy and Anargment Institution	745	716	714
救助类单位	Salvation Institution	472	357	403
婚姻登记服务单位	Marriage Rigister Service Institutions		87	110
殡仪服务单位	Funeral and Interment Service Institution	2 577	3 311	3 201
福利彩票发行单位	Issue Institution of Welfare Lottery	86	77	87
社区服务单位	Community Service Institutions	1 014	2 850	4 697

表21.17 主要年份民间组织情况
STATISTICS OF CIVIL ORGANIZATIONS AND CHARITY IN MAIN YEARS

指 标	Indicators	2005	2009	2010
民间组织数(个)	**Quantity of Civil Organization (unit)**	**7 556**	**9 472**	**10 104**
社会团体	Social Organizations	2 952	3 512	3 634
民办非企业	Civil Non-Enterprises	4 537	5 857	6 353
基金会	Fonndations	67	103	117

注：本页数据由市民政局提供。
Note: Date on this page are provided by Shanghai Civil Affairs Bureau.

表 21.18 主要年份养老服务
ENDOWMENT SERVICE IN MAIN YEARS

	指 标 Indicators	2005	2009	2010
机构养老服务	**Endowment Service of Institutions**			
机构数(家)	Quantity of Institutions (unit)	474	615	625
床位数(张)	Quantity of Beds (bed)	49 529	89 859	97 841
#新增养老床位	Newly Added Endowmet Beds	10 094	10 084	10 843
养老床位占60周岁及以上老年人口比例(%)	Ratio of Endowment Bed in Population above 60 (%)	1.9	2.8	3.0
居家养老服务	**Household Endowment Service**			
社区老年人日间服务机构机构数(家)	Community Service Institutions for Aged People Daytime Quantity of Institutions (unit)	83	283	303
日托老年人数数(人)	Population of Daytime Service Aged People (person)	2 108	8 000	9 000
社区助老服务社(个)	Community Service Center for Assisting Aged People (unit)	233	234	233
社区居家养老服务月服务人数(万人)	Monthly Population of Community Household Endowment Service (10 000 persons)	5.48	21.90	25.20
获得政府补贴的老年人(万人)	Population of Aged People Gained Governmental Subsidy (10 000 persons)	3.94	12.90	13.00

注：本表数据由市民政局提供。
Note: Date in this table are provided by Shanghai Civil Affairs Bureau.

表 21.19 主要年份老年医疗服务
MEDICARE SERVICE FOR AGED PEOPLE IN MAIN YEARS

	指 标 Indicators	2005	2009	2010
老年护理院	**Nursing Home for Aged People**			
独立老年护理院	Independent Nursing Home for Aged People			
机构数(所)	Quantity of Institutions (unit)	13	12	14
建筑面积(平方米)	Structure Area (sq. m)	59 742	86 897	101 048
床位数(张)	Beds(bed)	2 353	2 668	3 285
住院人次(人次)	Person-time in Hospital (person-time)	4 346	7 369	10 322
非独立老年护理院(机构数)(所)	Dependent Nursing Home for Aged People(unit)	56	55	50
老年医院	**Hospital for Aged People**			
机构数(所)	Quantity of Institutions(unit)	3	4	4
住院人次(人次)	Person-time in Hospital (person-time)	9 124	14 072	15 520
家庭病床总数(张)	**Total Quantity of bed in home (bed)**	**40 745**	**42 050**	**43 880**

注：本表数据由市卫生局提供。
Note: Date in this table are provided by Shanghai Municipal Health Bureau.

表21.20 主要年份红十字会基本情况
BASIC STATISICS ON RED CROSS SOCIETY OF CHINA SHANGHAI MUNICIPAL BRANCH IN MAIN YEARS

指 标	Indicators	2005	2009	2010
红十字会组织机构	**Institutions(unit)**			
红十字会各级组织机构(个)	Organizing Institutnions(unit)	2 934	3 292	3 134
红十字会医疗机构(个)	Medical Institutions(unit)	67	70	72
志愿工作管理机构(个)	Administrative Institutions on Voluntary Work(unit)	20	20	20
红十字会会员人数(万人)	**Quantity of Member(10 000 persons)**	**61.62**	**85.83**	**86.52**
#青少年会员(万人)	Hobbledehoy Member(10 000 persons)	37.16	51.20	58.64
红十字会团体会员单位(个)	Team Member(unit)	970	1 467	969
社区服务工作	**Community Service**			
社区公益服务站点(个)	Community Commonweal Service Station (unit)	1 589	3 300	3 077
社区志愿者人数(万人)	Quantity of Volunteer(10 000 persons)	1.75	5.71	5.3
组织各种宣传活动	**Times of Publicizing Activity(time)**			
在报刊登载宣传文章(篇)	Articles on Newspaper and Periodical (piece)	831	714	609
电视台播报宣传节目(条/次)	Programs on Television (piece/time)	459	223	200
参加艾滋病预防宣传救助活动人次数(万人次)	Person-time Attended AIDS Prevention Activities (10 000 person-times)	9.86	37.57	18.84
参加普及宣传无偿献血活动人次数(万人次)	Person-time Attended Publicizing Volunteer Blood Donation Activiies (10 000 person-times)		47.45	23.76
卫生救护工作	**Sanitation Rescue**			
救护普及培训(万人次)	Rescue Popularization Training (10 000 person-time)	24.72	59.20	37.35
造血干细胞捐献工作	**Contributing Trunk Cell**			
当年参加造血干细胞捐献库人数(万人)	Quantity of Subscribers (10 000 persons)	5.60	9.70	10.42
配型相合人数(人)	Matching(person)	316	748	301
累计移植人数(人)	Transplanting (person)	68	154	197
遗体捐献工作	**Contributing Reliquiae**			
遗体捐献登记站(个)	Register Center(unit)	27	26	25
遗体捐献接收站(个)	Accepting Center(unit)	8	7	7
全年接受捐献遗体登记(人)	Quantity of Contributing Reliquiae(Person)	1 284	1 396	1 170
全年接受角膜捐献登记(人)	Quantity of Contributing Cornea(Person)	133	50	73
社会救灾和社区救助工作	**Working on Social Relieving**			
救灾投入(万元)	Relieve Devotion (10 000 yuan)		38 772	19 268
受益人次(万人)	Quantity of Beneficiaries (persons-times)		2 514	23 075
社区救助款物投入(万元)	Community Salvation Devotion (10 000 yuan)	1 538.12	3 732.6	4 780.71
受益人次(万人次)	Quantity of Beneficiaries (10 000 persons-times)	2.87	3.29	4.11

注：本表数据由市红十字会提供。
Note: Data in this table are provided by Red Cross Society of China Shanghai Municipal Branch.

上/海/统/计/年/鉴

主要统计指标解释

卫生机构

是指从卫生行政部门取得《医疗机构执业许可证》,或从民政、工商行政、机构编制管理部门取得法人单位登记证书,为社会提供医疗保健、疾病控制、卫生监督服务或从事医学研究和医学在职培训等工作的单位。

医疗机构

指从卫生行政部门取得《医疗机构执业许可证》的机构,包括医院、疗养院、社区卫生服务中心(站)、卫生院、门诊部、诊所(卫生所、医务室)、妇幼保健院(所、站)、专科疾病防治院(所、站)、急救中心(站)和临床检验中心,但不包括村卫生室(单纯统计)。

医　院

包括综合医院、中医医院、中西医结合医院、民族医院、各类专科医院和护理院,不包括专科疾病防治院、妇幼保健院和疗养院

卫生技术人员

包括执业医师、执业助理医师、注册护士、药师(士)、检验技师、影像技师(士)、卫生监督员和见习医(药、护、技)师(士)等卫生专业人员。不包括从事管理工作的卫生技术人员(如院长、副院长、党委书记等)。

执业(助理)医师

一律按领取医师执业证书且实际从事临床工作的人数统计,不包括从事管理工作的医师。

优抚对象

优抚指政府对革命烈士家庭、病故残疾工作人员以及参战负伤致残的民兵、民工的抚恤和人民群众对其的优待。优抚对象包括革命烈士家属、因公牺牲和病故军人家属、革命伤残人员、现役军属、退伍红军老战士、红军失散人员、复员军人、退伍军人、在职退役军人、在乡退役军人、带病回乡退伍军人、复退军人精神病员、孤老优抚对象等。

社会福利事业单位

指集中收养社会孤老、残、幼的机构。包括由民政部门管理的社会福利院、儿童福利院、精神病人福利院和城镇集体办的福利院,以及农村集体办的敬老院。

基本养老保险

1.(参保)职工人数:指报告期末按照国家法律、法规和有关政策规定参加基本养老保险并在社保经办机构已建立缴费记录档案的职工人数,包括中断缴费但未终止养老保险关系的职工人数,不包括只登记未建立缴费记录档案的人数。

2.(参保)离退休人员人数:指报告期末参加基本养老保险的离休、退休和退职人员的人数。

3.基本养老保险基金收入:指根据国家有关规定,由纳入基本养老保险范围的缴费单位和个人按国家规定的缴费基数和缴费比例缴纳的养老保险基金,以及通过其他方式取得的形成基金来源的收入。包括单位和职工个人缴纳的基本养老保险费、基本养老保险基金利息收入、上级补助收入、下级上解收入、转移收入、财政补贴和其他收入。

4.基本养老保险基金支出:指按照国家政策规定的开支范围和开支标准从养老保险基金中支付给参加基本养老保险的离休、退休、退职人员个人的养老金、丧葬抚恤补助,以及由于保险关系转移、上下级之间调剂资金等原因而发生的支出。包括离休金、退休金、退职金、各种补贴、医疗费、死亡丧葬补助费、抚恤救济费、社会保险经办机构管理费、补助下级支出、上解上级支出、转移支出、其他支出等。

5.基本养老保险基金累计结余:指截止报告期末基本养老保险基金收支相抵后的累计余额。

基本医疗保险

1.参保人数:指报告期末按国家有关规定参加基本医疗保险的人数。包括参加保险的职工人数和退休人员人数。

2.基金收入:指根据国家有关规定,由纳入基本医疗保险范围的缴费单位和个人,按国家规定的缴费基数和缴费比例缴纳的基金,以及通过其他方式取得的形成基金来源的款项,包括:单位缴纳的社会统筹基金收入、个人缴纳的个人账户基金收入、财政补贴收入、利息收入、其他收入。

主要统计指标解释

3.基金支出：指按照国家政策规定的开支范围和开支标准从社会统筹基金中支付给参加基本医疗保险的职工和退休人员的医疗保险待遇支出，和从个人帐户基金中支付给参加基本医疗保险的职工和退休人员的医疗费用支出，以及其他支出。包括：住院医疗费用支出、门急诊医疗费用支出、个人账户基金支出、其他支出。

4.基金累计结余：指截止报告期末基本医疗保险的社会统筹和个人帐户基金累计结余金额。包括银行存款、财政专户、债券投资和其他。

失业保险

1.参保人数：指报告期末按照国家法律、法规和有关政策规定参加了失业保险的城镇企业事业单位的职工及地方政府规定参加失业保险的其他人员的人数。

2.失业保险基金收入：指按照规定从企业、事业及其他单位筹集的失业保险费及其他并入失业保险基金收入的总额。包括单位和个人缴纳的失业保险费、失业保险基金利息收入、上级补助收入、下级上解收入、转移收入、财政补贴和其他收入。

3.失业保险基金支出：指报告期内为保障失业人员和下岗职工基本生活、促进其再就业等支出的基金总额。包括失业救济金、医疗费、死亡丧葬补助费、抚恤救济费、转业训练费支出、失业保险经办机构管理费、补助下级支出、上解上级支出、转移支出和其他支出。

4.基金累计结余：指截止报告期末失业保险基金收支相抵后的累计余额。

工伤保险

1. 参加保险人数: 指报告期末依据国家有关规定参加工伤保险的职工人数。

2.享受保险待遇人数: 指劳动者因工负伤致残、死亡或因患职业病致残，根据有关规定享受工伤保险待遇职工或供养直系亲属人数。包括伤残人数、职业病人数、因工死亡人数、供养直系亲属人数。

3.基金收入: 指根据国家有关规定，由参加工伤保险的单位按国家规定的缴费基数和缴费比例缴纳的工伤保险基金，以及通过其他形式取得的形成基金来源的款项。包括：单位缴纳的社会统筹基金收入、财政补贴收入、利息收入、其他收入。

4. 基金支出: 指按照国家政策规定的开支范围和开支标准从工伤保险基金中支付给参加工伤保险的人员及供养直系亲属工伤保险待遇支出及其他支出。包括工伤医疗费、伤残补助金、工亡补助金、护理费、丧葬补助费、工伤预防费用、职业康复费用和其他支出。

5. 基金累计结余: 指截止报告期末工伤保险基金累计结余金额。包括银行存款、财政专户、债券投资和其他。

生育保险

1. 参保人数: 指报告期末依据有关规定参加生育保险的职工人数。

2.基金收入: 指根据国家有关规定，由参加生育保险的单位按照国家规定的缴费基数和缴费比例缴纳的生育保险基金，以及通过其他方式取得的形成基金来源的款项，包括：单位缴纳的基金收入、利息收入和其他收入。

3. 基金支出: 指按照国家政策规定的开支范围和开支标准，从生育保险基金中支付给参加生育保险的职工，因妊娠、分娩和计划生育手术而享受的待遇及其他支出。包括：生育津贴、医疗费用支出及其他支出。

4. 基金累计结余: 指截止报告期末生育保险基金累计结余金额。包括银行存款、财政专户、债券投资和其他。

SHANGHAI STATISTICAL YEARBOOK

EXPLANATORY NOTES TO MAJOR STATISTICAL INDICATORS

□ Health Care Institutions

Health Care Institutions refer to the unit which have been qualified the Certification of Health Care Institution by the administration of public health, or qualified the Certification of Corporate Unit by the civil affairs, administration for industry and commerce, commission office for public sector reform, and engaging in medical care, disease prevention and control, health supervision and inspection, medicine research and health professional education, etc.

□ Medical Organizations

Medical Organizations refer to the institutions which have been qualified the Certification of Health Care Institution by the administration of public health, including: hospitals, health centers, community health service centers (stations), health centers, clinics (health stations and infirmaries), women and children care agencies (centers and stations), special disease prevention and curing agencies (centers and stations), first-aid centers (stations) and clinic inspection centers, but excluding village health care rooms.

□ Hospitals

Hospitals includes comprehensive hospitals, traditional Chinese medicine hospital, traditional Chinese and western medicine hospital, ethnic minority medicine hospital, various special disease hospitals and nursing homes, but excludes special disease prevention and curing agencies, women and children care agencies and health centers.

□ Medical Technical Personnel

Medical Technical Personnel includes licensed doctors, licensed assistant doctors, pharmacist (assistant pharmacist), inspection technician, image technician (assistant image technician), health care inspector and practice doctor (pharmacist, nurse, and technician), excludes medical technical personnel engaging in administrative jobs.

□Licensed Doctors (Assistant Doctors)

It refers to the medical workers who have obtained the licenses of qualified doctors of assistant doctors and are employed by medical institutions, but excludes the doctors engaging in administrative jobs.

□ Special Care

Special Care is offered by the government to the family member of the martyrs, disabled or demobilized servicemen or laborers who were injured on duty. Entitled to the special care are family members of the revolutionary martyrs, family members of servicemen who dies on duty or died of an illness, disabled servicemen, family members of servicemen on active service, retired veteran Red Army soldiers, scattered Red Army soldiers, demobilized servicemen, ex-servicemen, servicemen who were demobilized while on duty, ex-servicemen back to their rural homes, ex-servicemen who were demobilized because of an illness and have gone back to their rural homes, ex-servicemen who suffer from mental illness and elderly persons with no family.

□ Social Welfare Institutions

Social Welfare Institutions refer to institutions taking care of old people without children, handicapped people and orphans. They include social welfare institutions run by civil affairs departments, children's welfare institutions, welfare institutions for mental patients, and collectively-run old people's homes in rural areas.

□ Basic Pension Insurance

1.Number of staff and workers covered refer to staff and workers participating in basic pension insurance programme in line with national laws, regulations and related policies by the end of reference period, who have already had payment records in social security management agencies, including those who interrupt payment without terminating the insurance programme. Those who have registered in the programme with no payment records are not included.

2. Number of retirees participating in basic pension insurance programme refer to number of retirees participating in basic pension insurance programme by the end of reference period.

3. Revenue of basic pension insurance refer to payments made by employers and individuals participating in pension insurance programs in accordance with the basis and proportion

EXPLANATORY NOTES TO MAJOR STATISTICAL INDICATORS

stipulated in state regulations, and income from other sources that become source of pension insurance fund, including the premium paid by employers and staff and works, interest income, subsidies from higher level agencies, income as transfer from subordinate agencies, transferred income, government financial subsidies and other income.

4. Expenses of basic pension insurance refer to payment made to those retired and resigned people covered in pension insurance program in terms of pension or compensation within the scope and standards of expenditure according to related national policies, and expenditure occurred due to shift of the insurance relationship or adjustment of funds among agencies, including pension for resigned people, pension for retired people, pension for people quitting jobs, various subsidies, medical fees, funeral subsidies, compensation pension, management fees for social security agencies, expenses on subsidies to lower subordinates, expenses as transfer to agencies at higher level, transferred expenditure and other expenditure.

5. Balance of basic pension insurance refers to the balance of basic pension insurance at the end of the reference period after deducting expenses from revenue

□ Basic Medical Care Insurance

1. Number of people participating in the insurance programme refers to people participating in the basic medical care insurance programme according to related regulations by the end of reference period, including number of staff and workers and retirees participating in this insurance programme.

2. Revenue of insurance programme refer to payments made by employers and individuals participating in medical care insurance programs in accordance with the basis and proportion stipulated in state regulations, and income from other sources that become source of medical insurance fund, including income of social comprehensive funds paid by employers, income from individual accounts, government financial subsidies, interest income and other income.

3. Expenses of insurance programme refer to payment made from social comprehensive funds to those retired and resigned people covered in basic medical care insurance within the scope and standards of expenditure according to related national policies, and medical care payment made from individual accounts to staff and workers and retirees, and other expenses, including medical expenses of hospital inpatients, medical expenses for outpatients and emergency patients, payment from individual accounts and other expenditure.

4. Balance of basic medical care insurance refer to the balance of medical care insurance of social comprehensive funds and individual accounts at the end of the reference period, including bank savings, special fiscal accounts, investment in bonds and others.

□ Unemployment Insurance

1. Number of people covered refers to staff and workers in urban enterprises or institutions who have participated in unemployment insurance programme in line relevant policies and regulations, and other people who have participated according to local government regulations, by the end of reference period.

2. Revenue of unemployment insurance refer to payments made by employers and individuals participating in unemployment insurance programme in accordance with relevant regulations and other income contributed to this programme, including unemployment insurance premium made by employers and individuals, interest income, subsidies from higher level agencies, income as transfer from subordinate agencies, transferred income, government financial subsidies and other income.

3. Expenses of unemployment insurance refer to total expenses during the reference period to guarantee the basic livelihood of unemployed people and laid-off staff and workers and to encourage their re-employment. Included are unemployment relief, medical fees, funeral subsidies, compensation pension, training expenses, management fees for unemployment insurance agencies, subsidies to lower level agencies, expenses as transfer to higher level agencies, transferred expenditure and other expenditure.

4. Balance of unemployment insurance refer to the balance of unemployment revenue deducting unemployment expenses at the end of the reference period.

□ Work Injury Insurance

1. Number of people covered refers to staff and workers who have participated in work injury insurance programme in line with relevant national regulations.

2. Number of beneficiaries refers to staff and workers and their direct dependents who can, in line with relevant regulations, benefit from work injury insurance, as a result of work injury leading to disability or death of the staff/worker, or occupational disease leading to disability. Included in this category are number of injured and disabled people, number of people with occupa-

EXPLANATORY NOTES TO MAJOR STATISTICAL INDICATORS

tional diseases, number of deaths at work places, and number of direct dependents.

3. Revenue of work injury insurance refer to payments made by employers participating in work injury insurance programs in accordance with the basis and proportion stipulated in state regulations, and income from other sources that become source of work injury insurance fund, including income of social comprehensive funds paid by employers, government financial subsidies, interest income and other income.

4. Expenses of work injury insurance refer to payments made from work injury insurance funds to those who participated in the work injury insurance programme and their direct dependents within the scope and standards of expenditure according to related national policies, and other expenditure, including medical fees for work injury, injury and disability subsidies, death subsidies, nursing fees, funeral subsidies, injury prevention fees, rehabilitation fees for occupational diseases and other expenditure.

5. Balance of work injury insurance refer to the balance of the work injury funds at the end of the reference period, including bank savings, special fiscal account, investment in bonds and others.

□ Maternity Insurance

1. Number of people covered refers to staff and workers who have participated in maternity insurance programme according to relevant regulation at the end of the reporting period.

2. Revenue of maternity insurance refers to payments made by employers participating in maternity insurance programs in accordance with the basis and proportion stipulated in state regulations, and income from other sources that become source of maternity insurance fund, including income of funds paid by employers, interest income and other income.

3. Expenses of maternity insurance refer to payments made from maternity insurance funds to staff and workers who participated in maternity insurance programme within the scope and standards of expenditure according to related national policies, expenses paid for pregnancy, child delivery or surgeries related to family planning, and other expenditure, including allowance for child bearing, medical fees and other expenditure.

4. Balance of the maternity insurance refers to the balance of the maternity insurance funds at the end of reference period, including bank savings, special fiscal account, investment in funds and others.

第二十二篇
CHAPTER 22

文化和体育
CULTURE, SPORTS

表 22.1 主要年份文化机构数
QUANTITY OF CULTURAL INSTITUTIONS IN MAIN YEARS

单位：个（unit）

年份 Year	图书馆 Libraries	群众文化活动机构 Mass Culture	艺术教育事业 Art Education	文艺科研 Art Research	文物机构 Agency of Historic Relics	档案机构 Archives Institutions
1978	23	364	3		7	
1980	21	367	2	2	8	
1985	46	369	3	2	9	
1986	49	403	3	2	11	
1987	50	407	3	2	13	127
1988	54	416	3	2	16	125
1989	52	405	3	2	19	134
1990	51	410	3	2	18	137
1991	31	397	3	2	18	671
1992	31	394	3	2	20	745
1993	31	376	3	2	21	720
1994	31	371	3	2	23	
1995	31	332	3	2	23	768
1996	32	348	4	2	24	674
1997	32	352	4	2	24	681
1998	32	355	4	2	23	643
1999	32	349	4	2	24	994
2000	31	340	4	2	24	792
2001	32	276	3	2	23	614
2002	32	270	1	2	26	652
2003	35	261	1	2	26	656
2004	28	251	1	2	99	513
2005	28	248	1	2	106	545
2006	28	250	1	2	106	439
2007	30	247	1	2	111	524
2008	29	245	1	2	111	524
2009	29	242	1	2	112	533
2010	28	240	1	2	115	707

①本表数据由市文化广播影视管理局、市文物管理委员会、市档案局提供。
②自 2004 年始文物保护机构中包括系统外的机构数。
❶Data in this table are provided by Shanghai Municipal Culture, Radio, Film and TV Administration, Shanghai Municipal Committee of Culture Heritage and Shanghai Municipal Archives.
❷Agency of Historic Relics Preservation refers to total quantity of Agency Bureau since 2004.

表 22.2 影剧院、艺术表演场所、艺术表演团体数(1978~2010)
QUANTITY OF CINEMAS,THEATRES AND ART PERFORMANCE TROUPES

单位:个(unit)

年 份 Year	电影放映单位 Film Projection Units	其 中 of which #影、剧院 Cinemas and Theatres	艺术表演场所 Art Performance Places	其 中 of which #剧 院 Theatres	#书 场 Storytelling Places	艺术表演团体 Art Performance Troupes
1978	803	109	31	26	4	17
1979	799	115	46	32	5	45
1980	770	119	47	43	6	48
1981	804	127	60	56	6	49
1982	815	134	31	48	6	46
1983	822	140	54	49	8	46
1984	815	146	54	48	8	44
1985	847	156	52	47	8	44
1986	859	169	53	49	9	42
1987	890	199	51	48	8	42
1988	734	215	53	50	8	40
1989	579	213	52	49	8	37
1990	577	211	49	46	8	38
1991	548	229	51	47	9	38
1992	530	249	51	47	9	37
1993	462	254	49	40	9	34
1994	462	254	47	39	8	35
1995	452	249	43	35	7	31
1996	488	280	45	38	7	31
1997	466	263	45	38	7	31
1998	445	242	44	39	5	29
1999	445	242	44	41	4	29
2000	445	242	44	39	5	29
2001	370	273	41	35	3	28
2002	370	273	37	31		28
2003	328	238	180	174	4	72
2004	311	225	177	163	7	75
2005	236	193	160	150	5	85
2006	245	186	148	137	2	97
2007	233	175	150	140	6	103
2008	235	172	139	134	5	107
2009	226	169	104	100	0	77
2010	152	136	97	86	2	89

①本表数据由市文化广播影视管理局提供。
②2003 年起文化统计范围扩大到全行业。
❶Data in this table are provided by Shanghai Municipal Culture, Radio, Film and TV Administration.
❷The scope of statistics to culture expands to total sectors in 2003.

表 22.3 主要年份主要文化机构从业人员数
QUANTITY OF EMPLOYEES IN MAJOR CULTURAL INSTITUTIONSS IN MAIN YAERS

单位：人(person)

机构类别	Category of Institution	2000	2009	2010
总　计	**Total**	**217 572**	**264 874**	**274 267**
艺术机构	Art	4 759	8 432	9 779
图书馆	Libraries	2 513	2 376	2 400
档案机构	Archives Institution	2 330	2 501	3 822
群众文化活动机构	Mass Culture	3 874	4 632	4 702
文物机构	History Relic	1 136	2 379	2 558
文化市场经营机构	Cultural Market Operation Institutions	63 297	54 158	60 358
新闻出版机构	Institutions Engaged in News and Publishing	138 492	186 996	185 620
其他文化机构	Other Cultural Institutions	1 171	3 400	5 028

表 22.4 主要文化机构和人员数(2010)
MAJOR CULTURAL INSTITUTIONS AND PERSONNEL

机构类别	Category of Institution	机构数（个）Institutions(unit)	从业人数(人) Employees(person)
艺术机构	**Art**	**194**	**9 482**
艺术表演团体	Art Performance Troupes	89	6 766
艺术表演场所	Art Centers	97	2 425
艺术创作机构	Art Inditing	2	13
艺术展览机构	Art Exhibition	3	191
艺术教育机构	Art Education	1	40
文艺科研机构	Literaturde and Art Research	2	47
图书馆	**Libraries**	**28**	**2 180**
#少儿图书馆	Libraries for Children	5	120
档案机构	**Archives Institution**	**707**	**3 822**
群众文化活动机构	**Mass Culture**	**240**	**4 702**
群众艺术馆	Mass Art Centers	1	53
文化馆	Cultural Centers	26	1 139
文化站	Cultural Stations	213	3 510
文物机构	**Historical Relic**	**115**	**2 558**
博物馆	Museums	114	2 482
文物商店	Cultural Relic Shop	1	76
文化市场经营机构	**Cultural Market Operation Institutions**	**4 647**	**60 358**
新闻出版机构	**Institutions Engaged in News and Publishing**	**13 973**	**185 620**

注：本页数据由市文化广播影视管理局、市文物管理委员会、市档案局、市新闻出版局提供。
Note: Data on this page are provided by Shanghai Municipal Culture, Radio, Film and TV Administration, Shanghai Municipal Committee of Culture Heritage, Shanghai Municipal Archives Bureau and Shanghai Municipal Press and Publication Bureau.

表 22.5 群众艺术馆和文化馆(站)情况（2010）
MASS ART AND CULTURAL CENTERS

指 标	Indicators	合 计 Total	群众艺术馆 Mass Art Centers	文化馆 Cultural Centers	文化站 Cultural Stations
单位数（个）	Quantity of Units（unit）	240	1	26	213
从业人员（人）	Employees（person）	4 702	53	1 139	3 510
组织活动	Organizing Activity				
文艺活动（次）	Literary Activity(time)	35 600	161	4 807	30 632
理论研讨和讲座（次）	Theoretics Conference and Chair(time)	355	110	245	
举办训练班	Conducting Training Courses				
班 次（次）	Quantity of Classes（time）	21 078	118	2 204	18 756
结业人次（万人次）	Persons Completing the Courses（10 000 person-times）	116.36	0.38	4.26	111.72
举办展览个数（个）	Exhibitions Conducted（unit）	2 403	5	241	2 157

表 22.6 艺术表演团体情况（2010）
BASIC STATISTICS OF ART TROUPES

类 别	Types	剧团数（个） Troupes (unit)	从业人员（人） Employees (person)	国内演出场次(场) Times of Domestic Performance (time)	观众人数（万人次） Spectators (10 000 person-times)
总 计	**Total**	**89**	**6 766**	**19 753**	**1 036.7**
按隶属关系分	**By Administrative Relationship**				
市 级	Perfectural level	17	2 859	8 553	493.3
区 级	District level	69	3 861	10 975	517.4
县 级	County level	3	46	225	26.0
按剧种分	**By Type of Drama**				
话剧、儿童剧、滑稽剧团	Drama, Children's Play & Comedy Troupes	12	522	1 515	86.7
歌剧、舞剧、歌舞剧团	Opera and Dance Troupes	5	535	850	102.8
乐团、歌舞团、轻音乐团	Philharmonic, Song & Dance, Light Music Troupes	24	3 483	2 437	175.8
戏曲剧团	Local Opera Troupes	26	1 493	9 876	368.5
曲艺、杂技、木偶、皮影团	Recitation & Ballad, Acrobatics & Cirus, Puppet Show, Shadow Puttet	11	598	3 594	270.3
综合性艺术表演团体	Comprehensive Art Troupe	11	135	1 481	32.6

注：本页数据由市文化广播影视管理局提供。
Note: Data on this page are provided by Shanghai Municipal Culture, Radio, Film and TV Administration.

表22.7 艺术表演场所基本情况(2010)
ART PERFORMANCE PLACES

类别	Types	机构数(个) Institutions (unit)	从业人员(人) Employees (person)	座席数(个) Seats (unit)	演(映)出场次(场) Quantity of Art Projections & Performances (time)	其中 of which #艺术演出场次 Quantity of Art Performances	观众人次(万人次) Spectators (10 000 person-times)	其中 of which #艺术演出场次 Quantity of Art Performances
总计	**Total**	**97**	**2 400**	**82 820**	**22 843**	**10 761**	**784.5**	**615.7**
市级	Municipal Level	17	1 066	30 479	4 952	4 910	427.7	416.0
#上海大剧院	Shanghai Grand Theater	1	36	2 500	663	663	83.0	83.0
上海音乐厅	Shanghai Concert Hall	1	26	1 243	224	224	20.2	20.2
贺绿汀音乐厅	He Luting Concert Hall	1	14	744	203	203	15.0	15.0
上海商城剧院	Shanghai Center Theater	1	18	991	278	264	25.4	23.2
上海话剧艺术中心	Shanghai Dramatic Arts Center	1	319	700	818	818	21.0	21.0
上海美琪大戏院	Shanghai Majestic Theater	1	25	1 328	134	134	14.5	14.5
逸夫舞台	Yifu Theater	1	33	928	356	356	26.4	26.4
兰心大戏院	Lyceum Theater	1	25	681	169	169	10.5	10.5
上海艺海剧院	Shanghai Yihai Theater	1	24	1 377	317	317	28.0	28.0
上海马戏城	Shanghai Circus World	1	55	2 143	533	533	49.1	49.1
上海大舞台	Shanghai Stadium	1	131	12 216	46	38	34.5	28.0
区级	District Level	79	1 322	51 297	17 775	5 780	344.7	192.4
县级	County Level	1	12	1 044	116	71	12.1	7.3

注：本表数据由市文化广播影视管理局提供。
Note: Data in this table are provided by Shanghai Municipal Culture, Radio, Film and TV Administration.

表 22.8 博物馆、纪念馆情况(2010) STATISTICS OF MUSEUMS AND MEMORIALS

指 标 Indicators		机构数(个) Quantity of Institutions(unit)	馆内藏品实际数量(万件) Real Quantity of Collections (10 000 pieces)	其中 of which #一至三级藏品 Collections of Class One to Three	展览活动(个) Exhibit Activity (unit)	参观人次(万人次) Visiting Person-times (10 000 person-times)
总 计	**Total**	**114**	**293.14**	**19.65**	**219**	**1 114**
综合性	Comprehensive	15	2.49	1.42	82	205
历史类	Historical	17	9.56	2.35	28	127
艺术类	Art	6	100.86	13.30	24	142
科学类	Scientific	3	27.07	0.39	4	339
人物类	Character	18	11.91	2.19	45	96
行业类	Industrial	43	135.20		29	195
高校类	University	12	6.04		7	10

表 22.9 主要年份文物保护维修情况 PRESERVATION AND MAINTAIN OF HISTORICAL RELICS IN MAIN YEARS

指 标 Indicators		2005	2009	2010
保护维修项目数(个)	Items of Preservation and Maintaining (item)	44	41	45
#国家级	National	4	7	10
市 级	Municipal	18	16	6
维修面积(万平方米)	Areas of Maintaining (10 000 sq. m.)	2.3	8.5	13.51
项目总预算(万元)	Aggregate Budget of Items (10 000 yuan)	19 650	24 798	20 555
#专项补助	Special Assistance	934	842	8 463
已拨入专项补助(万元)	Special Assiatance Appropriated(10 000 yuan)	1 209	842	8 463
当年保护维修支出(万元)	Expend on Preservation and Maintaining (10 000 yuan)	19 571	13 176	20 554

注：本页数据由上海市文化广播影视管理局提供。
Note: Data on this page are provided by Shanghai Municipal Historical Relic Administrative Committee.

表22.10 主要年份广播电台、电视台情况
TELEVISION STATIONS AND BROADCASTING STATIONS IN MAIN YEARS

类别	Types	2005	2009	2010
广播电台	**Broadcasting Stations**			
中、短波发射台(座)	Relaying Stations of Medium and Short Wave Broadcast (uint)	4	4	4
发射功率(千瓦)	Transmited Power (kw)	390	440	240
公共广播节目套数(套)	Public Radio Program (set)	21	21	21
付费广播节目套数(套)	Pay Radio Program(set)	1	1	1
日均播音时间(小时)	Broadcasting Time a day (hour)	347	360	360
全年制作节目时间(小时)	Length of Programs Produced (hours)	83 665	91 660	85 262
电视台	**Television Stations**			
发射台(座)	Realying Stations (uint)	11	11	11
发射功率(千瓦)	Transmitted Power (kw)	170	172	172
公共电视节目套数(套)	Public TV Programs (set)	25	25	25
付费电视节目套数(套)	Pay TV Programs (set)	15	16	16
周均播放时间(小时)	Broadcast Time a week (hour)	2 879	3 341	3 371
全年制作节目时间(小时)	Length of Programs Produced (hours)	62 819	63 401	49 507
广播电视卫星收转站(座)	**Satellite Transmission Station of Radio and TV Programs (uint)**	**822**	**826**	**855**

表22.11 电视和广播公共节目播出时间(2010)
PLAYING HOURS OF TELEVISION AND BROADCASTING PUBLIC PROGRAMS

单位:小时(hour)

类别	Types	电视台 Television Stations			广播电台 Broadcasting Stations		
		合计 Total	市级 Municipal Level	区县级 District Level	合计 Total	市级 Municipal Level	区县级 District Level
总计	**Total**	**175 304**	**124 882**	**50 422**	**131 433**	**74 808**	**56 625**
新闻资讯类节目	News Program	28 411	21 204	7 207	36 630	19 402	17 228
专题服务类节目	Subject Service Program	37 403	30 198	7 205	26 143	17 967	8 176
综艺类节目	Recreational and Artistic Program	8 809	7 103	1 706	45 359	26 377	18 982
影视剧类节目	Film and TV Program	67 415	42 661	24 754			
广播剧类节目	Broadcasting Drama Program				6 118	1 156	4 962
广告类节目	Advertising Program	19 430	11 648	7 782	15 114	9 711	5 403
其他类节目	Others	13 836	12 068	1 768	2 069	195	1 874

表22.12 主要年份有线电视基本情况
BASIC STATISTICS ON CABLE TELEVISION IN MAIN YEARS

指标	Indicators	2000	2009	2010
有线电视总用户数(万户)	Quantity of Cable TV Users (10 000 households)	303.0	553.3	573.0
#数字电视用户	Digital TV Users		77.6	235.6
有线电视入户率(%)	Popularity of Cable TV (%)	64.50	109.21	112.36
有线广播电视传输网络干线总长(公里)	Lines Total Length (kilometer)	604	35 387	36 211

注:本页数据由市文化广播影视管理局提供。
Note: Data on this page are provided by Shanghai Municipal Administration of Culture, Radio, Film & TV.

表22.13 电影摄制、译制和放映情况(1978～2010)
PRODUCTION, DUBBING AND SHOWING OF FILMS

年 份 Year	摄制和译制电影片 Production and Dubbing				电影放映 Film Showing			
	故事片(部) Feature Films (film)	美术片(本) Cartoons (reel)	科学教育片(本) Popular Science Films (reel)	译制片(本) Dubbed Films (reel)	放映场次 (万场) Showing (10 000 times)	其 中 of which #影、剧院 Cinemas and Theatres	观众人次(万人次) Spectators (10 000 person-times)	其 中 of which #影、剧院 Cinemas and Theatres
1978	10	24	84	275	35	17	27 405	15 291
1979	14	25	95	315	40	20	32 763	29 743
1980	17	30	105	382	39	20	29 304	18 039
1981	17	32	109	289	38	19	26 823	16 203
1982	19	35	112	604	38	20	25 828	15 586
1983	19	34	116	666	37	20	25 204	15 124
1984	19	40	117	633	36	21	24 149	15 539
1985	15	43	140	426	34	21	21 885	14 748
1986	19	38	150	450	36	24	23 220	16 720
1987	17	38	151	378	37	28	21 985	17 067
1988	13	29	156	501	38	30	20 461	16 742
1989	17	29	140	398	37	32	20 776	18 216
1990	16	47	142	340	38	33	19 351	17 021
1991	17	37	146	272	36	31	15 766	13 615
1992	17	42	146	325	29	25	9 145	8 089
1993	16	35	91	251	16	14	3 862	3 332
1994	14	13	69	162	22	20	4 001	3 617
1995	17	37	22	266	23	20	4 419	3 913
1996	10	58	6	283	27	25	4 420	3 783
1997	11	17	8	312	25	23	3 670	3 023
1998	4	16	6	271	23	21	2 924	2 451
1999	17	10	14	372	20	19	2 055	1 678
2000	10	20	12	438	18	17	1 794	1 452
2001	12	2	8	237	18	17	1 553	1 315
2002	10	2	11	204	20	17	1 198	921
2003	9	10	2	216	20	19	971	870
2004	12	1		248	24	23	1 364	1 183
2005	13			183	28	26	1 509	1 323
2006	9			312	27	26	1 254	1 173
2007	9			211	33	32	1 385	1 277
2008	17	8		248	35	34	1 456	1 381
2009	11			284	44	43	1 938	1 844
2010	19	2		151	55	54	2 289	2 174

注：本表数据由市文化广播影视管理局提供。
Note: Data in this table are provided by Shanghai Municipal Administration of Culture, Radio, Film & TV.

表 22.14 主要年份电影发行放映情况
BASIC STATISTICS OF FILM DISTRIBUTION AND PROJECTION IN MAIN YEARS

	指 标 Indicators	2005	2009	2010
放映场次(万场)	**Projection Times (10 000 times)**	**27.60**	**44.46**	**54.63**
#电影院	Cinema	22.20	41.21	51.72
影剧院	Theater	3.90	2.44	2.19
开放礼堂、俱乐部	Open Auditorium and Clubs	1.16	0.76	0.68
观众人次数(万人次)	**Quantity of Audience (10 000 Persontimes)**	**1 509.31**	**1 938.20**	**2 287.84**
#电影院	Cinema	893.92	1 693.19	2 052.62
影剧院	Theater	428.63	150.47	121.33
开放礼堂、俱乐部	Open Auditorium and Clubs	36.24	43.98	55.99
放映收入(万元)	**Projection Revenue (10 000 yuan)**	**27 192.03**	**66 737.07**	**93 875.11**
#电影院	Cinema	23 591.47	62 665.32	89 302.91
影剧院	Theater	2 389.52	2 584.98	2 697.84
开放礼堂、俱乐部	Open Auditorium and Clubs	1 009.58	1 406.04	1 807.88
平均每一放映场次	**Average on per Projection Time**			
观众人数(人)	Quantity of Audience (Person)	54.69	43.59	41.88
放映收入(元)	Returns (yuan)	985.22	1 501.06	1 718.38
日均放映场次(场)	**Projection Time a Day (time)**	**756.16**	**1 218.08**	**1 496.71**
日均观众人次(万人次)	**Average Audience a Day (person)**	**4.14**	**5.31**	**6.27**

表 22.15 电影公益场放映情况(2008～2010)
FILM PROJECTION FOR PUBLIC GOOD

	指 标 Indicators	2008	2009	2010
放映影片(部)	Film Projected (reel)	868	799	821
放映场次(万场次)	Projection Times (10 000 times)	5.58	8.72	9.20
观众人次(万人次)	Quantity of Audience (10 000 persontimes)	1 017	898	960
放映费用(万元)	Cost of Projection (10 000 yuan)	1 072.20	1 212.68	1 849.92
#政府补贴	Government Subsidies	1 125.80	814.99	1 378.60

表22.16 文化娱乐机构基本情况(2010)
BASIC STATISTICS OF CULTURE AND ENTERTAINMENT INSTITUTIONS

类别	Types	从业人员（人）Employees (person)	主营业务收入（万元）Major Business Revenue (10 000 yuan)	主营业务利润（万元）Major Business Profits (10 000 yuan)	房屋建筑面积（万平方米）Floor Space of Buildings (10 000 sq. m)
总 计	**Total**	**56 110**	**1 504 552**	**392 903**	**292.0**
歌舞娱乐场所	Singing & Dancing Rooms	26 636	236 854	31 790	117.6
游戏电子游艺经营场所	Gaming Rooms	4 146	32 567	9 060	39.2
其他娱乐场所	Other Places	5 700	74 770	13 063	63.9
网 吧	Internet Bar	7 708	49 777	16 034	54.0
经营性互联网文化单位	Internet-Culturel Business Unit	11 920	1 110 583	322 956	17.3

表22.17 公共图书馆情况(2010)
PUBLIC LIBRARIES

指标	Indicators	合计 Total	市级 Municipal Level	区级 District Level	县级 County Level
机构数（个）	Institutions (unit)	28	2	25	1
从业人员（人）	Employees (person)	2 180	838	1 305	37
总藏量（万册、件）	Collection (10 000 copies)	6 808.73	5 364.21	1 395.38	49.14
#图 书	Books	2 766.06	1 483.89	1 233.35	48.82
报 刊	Newspaper and Magzines	355.01	315.44	19.56	0.01
本年新购藏量（万册、件）	Publications Newly Bought (10 000 copies)	176.45	56.01	117.14	3.30
#图 书	Books				
建筑面积（万平方米）	Floor Space of Buildings (10 000 sq. m)	37.03	12.38	23.94	0.71
#书 库	Stack Room	9.51	6.09	3.30	0.12
阅览室	Reading Room	9.88	1.38	8.35	0.15
阅览座位（个）	Seats in Reading Room (unit)	19 427	2 332	16 595	500
图书借阅情况	Books Lending				
人 次（万人次）	Readers (10 000 person-times)	579.12	54.65	524.47	…
册 数（万册次）	Books (10 000 copy-times)	1 461.23	256.74	1 204.49	…
信息化装备	Information Equipment				
计算机（台）	Computer(unit)	5 502	2 203	3 209	90
#电子阅览室终端数	E-reeding Romm Terminals	1 774	200	1 516	58
为读者举办各种活动	Activities Held for Readers				
次 数（次）	Times(time)	3 723	654	2 989	80
参加人次（万人次）	Participants (10 000 person-times)	110.89	22.23	80.65	8.00

注：本页数据由市文化广播影视管理局提供。
Note: Data on this page are provided by Shanghai Municipal Administration of Culture, Radio, Film & TV.

表 22.18 图书出版数量(1978～2010) BOOKS PUBLISHED

年 份 Years	种 数 (种) Quantity of Publications (type)	其中 of which #新出版 Newly Published	总印数 (亿册) Total Printed (100 million copies)	总印张数 (亿印张) Total Ptrinted Signatures (100 million signatures)
1978	1 666	1 332	3.92	12.19
1979	2 040	1 563	4.58	15.54
1980	2 338	1 804	5.62	17.73
1981	2 801	1 949	6.01	22.89
1982	3 395	2 057	6.07	21.76
1983	3 653	2 254	4.65	21.31
1984	3 848	2 328	5.37	25.58
1985	4 176	2 634	4.96	23.95
1986	4 531	3 045	3.66	17.81
1987	5 103	3 151	4.26	19.84
1988	5 538	3 658	4.33	19.04
1989	6 765	4 960	3.28	14.52
1990	7 767	4 887	2.98	14.66
1991	8 141	4 756	3.11	17.30
1992	8 095	4 179	2.75	17.19
1993	7 721	4 272	2.26	15.34
1994	7 812	4 382	2.35	17.01
1995	8 338	4 185	2.44	17.92
1996	9 234	4 445	2.79	20.1
1997	9 928	4 844	2.70	18.00
1998	10 718	5 083	2.83	18.69
1999	11 381	5 880	2.68	18.69
2000	12 682	6 936	2.54	19.05
2001	14 000	7 947	2.68	21.24
2002	14 537	8 156	2.59	21.38
2003	15 636	8 726	2.74	23.27
2004	16 449	9 391	2.67	23.54
2005	16 504	9 286	2.59	23.65
2006	17 283	9 338	2.54	24.86
2007	16 958	9 085	2.40	24.05
2008	17 780	9 945	2.64	24.97
2009	18 873	10 615	2.74	25.46
2010	19 519	11 241	2.89	26.34

注：本表数据由市新闻出版局提供。
Note: Data in this table are provided by Shanghai Municipal Press and Publication Bureau.

表22.19 期刊出版数量(1978～2010)
PERIODICALS PUBLISHED

年 份 Years	种 数 (种) Quantity of Publications (type)	每期平均印数 (万册、份) Average Publications Issued (10 000 copies)	总印数 (亿册) Total Printed (100 million copies)	总印张数 (亿印张) Total Printed Signatures (100 million signatures)
1978	42	459	0.47	1.12
1979	90	721	0.73	2.08
1980	126	1 061	1.22	3.37
1981	266	1 873	2.03	5.95
1982	308	2 203	2.31	6.37
1983	349	2 572	2.51	7.07
1984	402	3 502	3.1	8.56
1985	491	3 424	3.45	9.21
1986	541	3 073	3.03	8.17
1987	546	3 058	3.13	8.05
1988	535	2 624	2.66	6.63
1989	527	1 793	1.86	4.58
1990	522	1 735	1.73	4.24
1991	504	1 749	1.79	4.44
1992	527	1 794	1.84	4.59
1993	535	1 668	1.82	4.95
1994	556	1 569	1.72	4.87
1995	565	1 583	1.78	5.3
1996	582	1 530	1.66	5.14
1997	587	1 513	1.66	5.35
1998	591	1 503	1.65	5.81
1999	606	1 493	1.78	6.87
2000	613	1 489	1.85	7.38
2001	616	1 413	1.85	7.58
2002	621	1 332	1.80	7.77
2003	626	1 335	1.83	8.51
2004	612	1 184	1.93	8.94
2005	612	1 130	1.90	8.96
2006	616	1 125	1.83	8.76
2007	624	1 117	1.83	8.75
2008	623	1 105	1.90	9.27
2009	621	1 039	1.79	9.02
2010	632	1 019	1.78	9.04

注：本表数据由市新闻出版局提供。
Note: Data in this table are provided by Shanghai Municipal Press and Publication Bureau.

表 22.20 报纸出版数量(1978～2010)
NEWSPAPER PUBLISHED

年 份 Years	种 数 (种) Quantity of Publications (type)	每期平均印数 (万份) Average Publication Issued (10 000 copies)	总印数 (亿册) Total Printed (100 million copies)	总印张数 (亿印张) Total Printed Signatures (100 million signatures)
1978	5	257	6.41	6.20
1979	8	349	7.32	7.08
1980	12	464	8.55	8.20
1981	15	640	10.28	9.77
1982	31	936	14.93	13.13
1983	34	1 185	18.13	15.49
1984	41	1 429	19.63	16.57
1985	89	1 656	19.54	17.07
1986	93	1 750	19.94	18.37
1987	90	2 003	22.45	20.49
1988	83	1 958	21.38	22.07
1989	81	1 477	15.85	16.25
1990	81	1 510	16.16	16.76
1991	75	1 506	18.48	19.16
1992	77	1 506	24.76	24.76
1993	81	1 506	32.27	32.27
1994	87	1 369	30.43	30.43
1995	86	1 358	19.04	34.00
1996	87	1 357	18.93	36.96
1997	87	1 397	19.34	43.19
1998	80	1 441	19.73	49.84
1999	75	1 311	18.42	46.26
2000	103	1 135	16.77	44.57
2001	101	1 060	16.98	47.67
2002	101	983	16.46	51.42
2003	101	886	17.05	66.13
2004	103	939	19.71	83.66
2005	102	903	19.06	89.94
2006	101	850	17.89	87.33
2007	101	815	17.04	86.75
2008	100	787	17.24	88.29
2009	100	741	16.33	77.94
2010	100	752	15.9	78.65

注：本表数据由市新闻出版局提供。
Note: Data in this table are provided by Shanghai Municipal Press and Publication Bureau.

表 22.21 主要年份新闻出版机构和人员数
NUMBER OF INSTITUTIONS AND EMPLOYEES ENGAGED IN NEWS AND PUBLISHING IN MAIN YEARS

指 标	Indicators	2000	2009	2010
图书出版机构	**Publishing Houses**			
机构数(个)	Institutions(unit)	37	40	40
从业人员(人)	Employee(person)	3 666	4 006	3 949
书刊印刷机构	**Printing Houses**			
机构数(个)	Institutions(unit)	4 543	4 614	4 606
从业人员(万人)	Employee(10 000 persons)	11.54	15.62	16.02
发行机构	**Issuing Houses**			
机构数(个)	Institutions(unit)	6 743	8 862	9 327
从业人员(万人)	Employee(10 000 persons)	1.94	2.68	2.14

注：发行机构数中包括发行网点数。
Note: Issuing Houses include quantity of net places.

表 22.22 图书出版数量(2010)
BOOKS PUBLISHED

类 别	types	种 数(种) Number of Publications (type)	其中 of which #新出版 Newly Published	总印数(万册) Total Printed (10 000 copies)	总印张数(万印张) Total Printed Signatures (10 000 signatures)
总 计	**Total**	**19 519**	**11 241**	**28 864.45**	**263 441.69**
书 籍	**Books**	**14 898**	**9 730**	**14 271.57**	**136 533.68**
#哲学、社会科学	Philosophy and Social Science	3 340	2 582	2 009.79	27 205.98
文化教育	Culture and Education	5 195	2 891	6 438.72	59 006.87
文学艺术	Literature and Art	3 573	2 390	2 449.31	29 983.36
自然科学技术	Natural Science and Technology	1 741	1 228	834.09	11 328.91
少年儿童读物	Children's Reading Materials	1 049	639	2 539.66	9 008.56
课 本	**Textbooks**	**4 567**	**1 458**	**14 563.83**	**126 737.55**
#大专课本	University and College	2 660	1 059	4 001.90	63 912.38
中专技校教材	Specialized Secondary and Technical Worker School	136	67	133.40	1 469.90
中学课本	Secondary School	632	105	5 761.81	40 479.75
小学课本	Primary School	397	34	4 358.10	17 000.61
业余教育课本	Spare-time Education	119	57	120.85	1 891.87
教学用书	Teaching References	623	136	187.77	1 983.04
图 片	**Pictures**	**54**	**53**	**29.05**	**170.46**

注：本页数据由市新闻出版局提供。
Note: Data on this page are provided by Shanghai Municipal Press and Publication Bureau.

表 22.23 期刊出版数量(2010)
PERIODICALS PUBLISHED

类别 Types		种数(种) Quantity of Publications (type)	出版期数(期) Quantity of Issue (issue)	总印数(万册、份) Total Printed (10 000 copies)	总印张数(万印张) Total Printed Signatures (10 000 signatures)
总计	**Total**	**632**	**5 983**	**17 677.23**	**90 406.12**
综合	Comprehensive	14	146	1 065.77	5 524.86
哲学、社会科学	Philosophy and Social Science	123	1 430	4 423.92	26 724.23
自然科学技术	Natural Science and Technology	364	2 965	2 771.26	20 415.64
文化教育	Culture and Education	77	786	1 645.95	10 596.21
文学艺术	Literature and Art	32	336	6 385.32	22 708.47
少年儿童读物	Children's Reading Materials	21	308	1 375.41	4 389.59
画刊	Pictorial	1	12	9.60	47.12

表 22.24 报纸出版数量(2010)
NEWSPAPER PUBLISHED

类别 Types		种数(种) Quantity of Publications (type)	期数(期) Issue (issue)	每期平均印数(万份) Average Publication Per Issue (10 000 copies)	总印数(万份) Total Printed (10 000 copies)	总印张数(万印张) Total Printed Signatures (10 000 signatures)
总计	**Total**	**100**	**11 013**	**752.18**	**159 016.03**	**786 487.28**
综合报	Comprehensive	12	3 468	272.74	94 953.92	577 694.55
专业报	Specialized	88	7 545	479.44	64 062.11	208 792.73

表 22.25 音像电子出版数量 (2010)
AUDIO, VIDEO AND ELECTRON PUBLISHED

类别 Types		种数(种) Quantity of Publications (type)	出版数量(万张、万盒) Quantity of Publications (10 000 piece box)	发行数量(万张、万盒) Quantity of Issued (10 000 piece box)	发行总金额(万元) Total Values (10 000 yuan)
总计	**Total**	**3 104**	**5 599.83**	**4 406.56**	**21 663.04**
电子出版物	Electronic Publication	679	2 679.17	1 680.62	5 086.57
数码激光视盘	DVD	132	67.65	82.53	694.10
高密度激光视盘	EVD	379	480.20	314.77	3 555.17
激光唱盘	CD	1 024	566.22	429.71	3 887.39
录音带	Tape	624	1 314.03	1 449.72	6 621.71
其他	Others	266	492.56	449.21	1 818.10

注：本页数据由市新闻出版局提供。
Note: Data on this page are provided by Shanghai Municipal Press and Publication Bureau.

表 22.26 档案机构基本情况(2010)
BASIC STATISTICS OF ARCHIVE INSTITUTIONS

	指 标 Indicators	合 计 Total	档案行政管理部门	档案馆 Archives Library	档案室(处、科) Archives
机构数(个)	**Quantity of Institutions(unit)**	**707**	**19**	**50**	**647**
从业人员(人)	**Employees(person)**	**3 822**	**375**	**719**	**2 728**
专 职	Full-time	2 172	375	719	1 078
兼 职	Part-time	1 650			1 650
馆藏档案	**Archives Collected**				
全 宗(个)	Overall Rolls(unit)	6 897		5 619	1 278
案 卷(万卷)	Rolls(10 000 rolls)	2 464.89		1 148.87	1 316.02
以件为保管单位档案(万件)	Archives(10 000 pieces)	363.84		113.36	250.48
录音、录像、影片档案(万盘)	Recprd, Video and Film (10 000 disks)	10.35		2.40	7.95
照片档案(万张)	Photo Records(10 000 pieces)	169.91		78.52	91.39
底 图(万张)	Base Maps(10 000 pieces)	1 646.42		18.23	1 628.19
电子档案(万张)	Electronic Records(10 000 disks)				
磁 盘	Disks	2.93		0.06	2.87
光 盘	Compact Discs	12.90		6.09	6.81
微缩胶片	Microfilm				
平 片(万张)	Flat Film(10 000 pieces)	14.31		8.64	5.67
开窗卡(万张)	Open Window Card(10 000 pieces)	56.92		22.82	34.10
档案利用	**Records Utilized**				
已开放档案	Records Opened				
案 卷(万卷)	Rolls(10 000 rolls)	249.44		188.39	61.05
案 件(万件)	Cases (10 000 cases)	343.18		318.99	24.19
开放档案目录(万条)	Catalog of Records Opened(10 000 pieces)				
案卷级	Roll Grade	131.45		131.45	
文件级	Document Grade	318.99		318.99	
本年利用档案	Records Utilized in 2008				
卷 次(万卷次)	Roll-times(10 000 roll-times)	108.51		47.46	61.05
件 次(万件次)	Piece-times(10 000 piece-times)	54.13		29.94	24.19
人 次(万人次)	Person-times(10 000 person-times)	49.50		31.39	18.11

注：本表数据由市档案局提供。
Note: Data in this table are provided by Shanghai Municipal Archives Bureau.

表 22.27 主要年份优秀运动员、教练员情况
BASIC STATISTICS ON EXCELLENT ATHLETES AND COACHES IN MAIN YEARS

指标	Indicators	2000	2009	2010
等级裁判员(人)	Certified Referees(person)	880	669	559
优秀运动员(人)	Excellent Athletes(person)	899	1 641	771
# 女运动员	Women	402	470	371
优秀运动队专职教练员(人)	Full-time Coaches(person)	196	258	73
# 女专职教练员	Women	30	56	22

表 22.28 体育系统职工人数(2010)
STAFF AND WORKERS IN SPORTS SECTORS

单位:人 (person)

指标	Indicators	总计 Total	其中 of which # 优秀运动队 Excellent Sports Teams	# 体育运动学校 Physical Education and Sports Schools	# 普通业余体校 Popular Sparetime Sports School	# 公共体育场(馆) Public Stadiums and Gymnasiums
总计	**Total**	**6 192**	**603**	**449**	**1 094**	**1 784**
# 专职教练员	Full-time Coaches	1 119	75	109	596	78
运动员	Athletes	771	192	17	19	8
管理干部	Administraive Staff	1 589	85	84	215	669
专职教师	Full-time Teachers	431	243	82		
科技人员	Scientific and Technical Personnel	71	2	2	15	
医务人员	Medical Personnel	82	6	12	6	8

表 22.29 主要年份群众体育健身活动场所情况
MASS PHYSICAL ACTIVITIES IN MAIN YEARS

指标	Indicators	2008	2009	2010
社区体育健身设施数(个)	Quantity of Community Fitness Facilities(unit)	4 845	4 845	4 845
# 健身点	Fitness Centers	4 586	4 586	4 586
社区健身场地面积(万平方米)	Area of Communtiy Fitness Space(10 000 sq. m)	301	301	301
社区公共运动场(个)	Quantity of Community Public Playground(unit)	220	261	316
社区公共运动场面积(万平方米)	Area of CommuntiyPublic Playground (10 000 sq. m)	234	239	246.7

上 / 海 / 统 / 计 / 年 / 鉴

主要统计指标解释

文化机构

是指专门从事文化工作具有法人资格，独立核算的事业，企业单位，以及单独核算，附属于事业单位的经营性专业文化活动单位。包括从事艺术、图书馆、档案馆、群众文化、文物保护、艺术教育、艺术研究、文化娱乐、新闻出版等机构，以及其他文化机构。

电影放映单位

指具有放映机器设备、固定或不固定的放映场所与专职或兼职的放映技术人员，经有关部门登记批准，经常为一定的观众对象放映电影的机构。包括电影院、影剧院、开放礼堂、俱乐部、放映队、对内礼堂俱乐部。

艺术表演团体

指从事戏曲、音乐、舞蹈、杂技等专业艺术表演，有独立账户的单位，不包括半工半艺、半农半艺和民间职业剧团。该指标主要反映上海专业艺术表演团体发展规模水平。

艺术表演观众人次

指售票、包场演出或民族地区免费演出的艺术表演观众人次数，不包括彩排审查和内部观摩演出的观看人次数。该指标主要反映上海观看专业艺术表演团体演出的效益规模。

等级运动员人数

指经考核正式批准授予等级运动员称号的人数。运动员等级分为国际级运动健将、运动健将、一级运动员、二级运动员、三级运动员、少年级运动员。该指标主要反映运动员队伍的技术质量水平。

等级裁判员人数

指经考核正式批准授予等级裁判员称号的人数。裁判员等级分为国际裁判、国家级裁判、一级裁判、二级裁判、三级裁判。该指标主要反映裁判员队伍的技术质量水平。

SHANGHAI STATISTICAL YEARBOOK

EXPLANATORY NOTES TO MAJOR STATISTICAL INDICATORS

□ Cultural Institutions

Cultural Institution refers to undertaking and business institutions which specialize in cultural work and have legal personality and independent accounting system, and those professional cultural institutions attached to undertaking institutions and have independent accounting system. It includes institutions specialize in art, library, archives, mass culture, historical relic protection, art education, art research, entertainment, news and publication and other cultural institutions.

□ Film Projection Units

Film Projection Units refer to units with film projection equipments, full or part-time projectionists, permanent or non-permanent places, approved by related administrative departments to show films regularly for certain groups of audience, including cinemas, theaters, public auditoriums, clubs, film projection teams, and interior auditorium clubs.

□ Art Troupe

Art Troupe refers to the troupe which is engaged in drama, opera, music, dance, acrobatics or other art performance, opens independent accounts with banks and has self-supporting accounting system; excluding the troupes which are engaged partly in industrial or agricultural activities, partly in art performance and the professional troupes organized by the people. This indicator reflects the development of Shanghai's professional art troupes.

□ Quantity of Spectators at Art Performance

Number of Spectators at Art Performance refers to the number of attendants at commercial shows, completely booked shows or free shows given in minority national areas, and does not include the number of spectators at rehearsals for examination and internal shows for study. This indicator reflects beneficial results of spectators at Professional Art Performance.

□ Quantity of Athletes in Grades

Number of Athletes in Grades refers to the number of athletes who have been given titles through examination. The titles of athletes include international masters of sports, masters of sports, first-grade, second-grade and third-grade sportsmen and young athletes. This indicator reflects skill of the athletes.

□ Quantity of Referees in Grades

Number of Referees in Grades refers to the number of referees who have been given titles after examination. They are classified as international referees, national referees and referees of the first, second and third grades. This indicator reflects the skill of referees.

第二十三篇

CHAPTER 23

法律、公证和其他

LAWS, NOTARY AND OTHERS

表 23.1 主要年份律师、公证及调解工作基本情况
BASIC STATISTICS OF LAWYERS, NOTARIZATIONS AND MEDIATIONS IN MAIN YEARS

指 标	Indicators	2000	2009	2010
律师工作	Lawyers			
法律律师事务所（个）	Law Offices (unit)	415	970	1 064
专职工作人员（人）	Full-time Staff (person)	5 127	11 405	15 050
#专职律师	Full-time Lawyers	3 522	10 167	11 749
取得法律职业资格（人）	Qualified Law Occupation (person)	4 642	10 701	13 027
#专职律师	Full-time Lawyers	3 522	10 167	11 749
兼职律师	Part-time Lawyers	731	534	549
全年办理	Total Transacted			
民事案件诉讼代理（万件）	Civil Lawsuit(10000 cases)	7.05	7.84	7.69
刑事诉讼辩护及代理（万件）	Criminal Lawsuit and Vindication(10 000 cases)	1.13	1.81	1.49
非诉讼法律事务（万件）	Non-litigation Action(10 000 cases)	2.65	4.01	3.32
解答法律询问(万人次)	Legal Advisory Services (10 000 person times)	10.36	15.67	13.09
代写法律事务文书（万件）	Legal Documents Written on Behalf of Clients(10 000 cases)	1.92	3.60	2.67
公证工作	Notarizations			
公证处（个）	Notarial Offices (unit)	22	22	22
公证人员（人）	Notarial Personnel (person)	366	759	821
#公证员	Notaries	243	343	359
办理公证文书（万件）	Documents Notarized (10 000 cases)	47.72	42.11	40.76
#国内经济合同公证	Domestic Economic Contracts Notarized	18.73	8.23	8.17
在办理公证文书中	Documents Notarizing			
涉外公证（万件）	Foreign (10 000 cases)	19.93	19.80	20.98
国内公证（万件）	Domestic (10 000 cases)	27.79	20.42	18.54
公证费收入（亿元）	Revenue of Notarial Fees (100 million yuan)	1.13	4.51	4.70
人民调解工作	People's Mediation			
专职司法助理员（人）	Full-time Judicial Assistants (person)	416	613	734
人民调解委员会（万个）	People's Mediation Committees(10 000 units)	0.89	0.60	0.63
调解人员（万人）	Mediators (10 000 persons)	3.55	2.91	3.41
调解民间纠纷（万件）	Civil Disputes Mediated (10 000 cases)	6.37	18.10	23.24
#婚姻家庭	Family Disputes	1.97	2.80	3.63
邻 里	Neighbor Disputes	2.51	5.04	5.12
赔 偿	Compensation	0.25	2.43	3.02
房屋宅基地	Housing and Housing Sites	1.04	1.10	1.29

①本表数据由市司法局提供。
② 办理公证文件中包括涉及港、澳、台公证文件。
❶ Data in this table are provided by Shanghai Municipal Justice Bureau .
❷ The number of notarized documents handled included Hong Kong, Macao, and Taiwan's.

表 23.2 主要年份国内和涉外公证文书分类情况
DOMESTIC AND FOREIGN NOTARIAL DOCUMENTS BY TYPE IN MAIN YEARS

单位：件(case)

指 标	Indicators	2000	2009	2010
国内公证	**Domestic Notarized**	**277 949**	**204 155**	**185 425**
经济公证	Business Notarized	187 304	82 267	81 662
#贷款合同	Loans Contracts	80 980	30 704	24 100
招标、投标	Bidding	55	312	82
劳务合同	Labour Contracts	4 982	1	9
财产租赁	Property Leases	22	604	711
法人资格	Legal Person dentification	109	36	116
法人委托书	Legal Person Certificate of Entrustment	227	2 626	3 643
民事公证	Civil Legal Relations Notarized	90 645	121 888	103 763
#继承权	Rights of Inheritance	5 217	16 785	17 482
遗 嘱	Testaments	1 709	4 750	4 468
委托书	Certificate of Entrustment	4 520	61 696	48 788
赠与书	Presentation Documents	5 196	1 134	1 062
声明书	Declarations	10 424	5 454	5 404
其他民事协议	Other Civil Agreements	15 552	1 430	1 563
涉外公证	**Foreign Notarized**	**199 323**	**197 974**	**209 813**
#出 生	Births	28 535	26 632	28 627
学 历	Schoolihg	21 644	4 380	2 107
亲属关系	Kinship	22 488	20 203	19 286
婚姻状况	Marriages	20 274	7 843	7 246
受、未受刑事处分	Criminal Records & Uncriminal Records	20 669	20 999	22 850
文本相符	Confirmation of Copies and Photo-Offset Copies to Originals	23 645	63 061	58 999

注：本表数据由市司法局提供。
Note: Data in this table are provided by Shanghai Municipal Justice Bureau .

表23.3 主要年份公安机关立案的刑事案件情况
CRIMINAL CASES REGISTERED IN PUBLIC SECURITY ORGANS IN MAIN YEARS

单位:起(time)

类别	Types	2000	2009	2010
总计	**Total**	**104 946**	**132 361**	**119 691**
杀人	Homicide	252	175	174
伤害	Injury	1 553	2 621	2 545
抢劫	Robbery	3 033	2 298	1 558
强奸	Rape	396	413	448
诈骗	Fraud	8 425	16 063	16 598
盗窃	Larceny	77 912	90 036	78 322
其他	Others	13 375	20 755	20 046

表23.4 主要年份公安机关查处治安案件情况
OFTENSE CASES AGAINST PUBLIC ORDER HANDLED BY PUBLIC SECURITY ORGANS IN MAIN YEARS

单位:起(time)

类别	Types	2000	2009	2010
总计	**Total**	**194 141**	**428 745**	**566 607**
#扰乱工作、公共秩序	Disturbing Work and Public Order	23 568	25 907	25 787
结伙斗殴、寻衅滋事	Gang Fightingor Picking Quarrels and Making Trouble	3 373	5 973	3 315
阻碍国家工作人员执行职务	Obstructing the Goverment Workers to Perform Their Duty	1 029	670	658
殴打他人	Beating Other Body	16 973	53 855	59 876
骗取、抢夺、敲诈勒索财物	Defrauding,Snatching or Extoring and Racketeering Valuables	2 936	19 798	24 510
伪造倒卖票券、证件	Forging and Fraudulently Selling Bills or Certificates	5 551	444	524
卖淫、嫖娼	Prostitution or Going Whoring	4 631	7 222	7 281
赌博	Gambling	17 464	19 521	21 760

注：本页数据由市公安局提供。
Note: Data in this page are provided by Shanghai Municipal Public Security Bureau.

表23.5 交通事故和火灾情况(1980～2010) BASIC STATISTICS OF TRAFFIC ACCIDENTS AND FIRES

年 份 Year	交通事故 Traffic Accidents				火 灾 Fires			
	次 数 (万次) Times (10 000 times)	死亡人数 (人) Death (person)	受伤人数 (万人) Injuries (10 000 persons)	损失折款 (万元) Losses Converted -into Cash (10 000 yuan)	次 数 (万次) Times (10 000 times)	死亡人数 (人) Death (person)	受伤人数 (人) Injuries (person)	损失折款 (万元) Losses Converted -into Cash (10 000 yuan)
1980	1.10	445	1.01	96	0.08	17	126	457
1981	1.18	507	1.06	119	0.09	33	81	202
1982	0.83	434	0.77	98	0.07	33	76	255
1983	0.73	443	0.70	99	0.06	24	67	533
1984	0.83	503	0.75	123	0.05	21	71	177
1985	0.71	687	0.57	318	0.05	30	74	374
1986	0.84	678	0.62	576	0.06	25	54	790
1987	1.01	811	0.67	959	0.06	51	56	575
1988	0.84	707	0.56	1 117	0.06	58	53	460
1989	0.75	652	0.49	1 137	0.03	30	30	394
1990	0.76	608	0.47	1 345	0.21	45	137	1 868
1991	0.75	594	0.45	1 530	0.17	38	112	937
1992	0.45	591	0.18	2 029	0.17	40	57	2 742
1993	0.81	699	0.29	4 652	0.14	73	128	2 252
1994	1.26	722	0.33	8 337	0.11	51	95	2 378
1995	1.67	788	0.38	12 077	0.11	47	86	2 100
1996	2.01	783	0.44	13 462	0.09	87	96	2 206
1997	2.16	780	0.58	13 682	0.74	51	138	2 639
1998	2.40	781	0.65	15 186	0.72	42	114	2 205
1999	2.61	726	0.78	15 924	0.66	43	90	1 487
2000	4.13	1 492	1.61	20 391	0.52	40	57	1 919
2001	4.21	1 503	1.57	23 883	0.32	31	65	966
2002	4.71	1 400	1.57	30 052	0.60	39	58	1 313
2003	5.42	1 406	1.12	39 721	0.58	47	85	1 724
2004	2.71	1 543	1.13	19 149	0.51	30	47	1 681
2005	0.92	1 393	0.88	7 961	0.43	54	84	1 731
2006	0.66	1 231	0.67	3 292	0.45	45	54	2 292
2007	0.40	1 171	0.38	1 943	0.42	50	45	2 650
2008	0.27	1 100	0.26	1 469	0.35	50	57	14 523
2009	0.28	1 042	0.27	1 226	0.61	63	41	3 990
2010	0.22	1011	0.19	967	0.57	101	125	22 949

注：本页数据由市公安局提供。
Note: Data in this page are provided by Shanghai Municipal Public Security Bureau.

表 23.6 交通事故情况(2010)
BASIC STATISTICS OF TRAFFIC ACCIDENTS

类 别	Types	发生数(起) Number (case)	死亡人数(人) Death (person)	受伤人数(人) Injuries (person)	损失折款(万元) Losses Converted -into Cash (10 000 yuan)
总 计	**Total**	**2 176**	**1 011**	**1 866**	**966.74**
# 死亡事故	Death Accident	948	1 011	321	589.37
伤人事故	Injury Accident	1 225		1 545	369.93
机动车	Motor-driven Vehicles	1 683	837	1 459	857.20
# 汽 车	Automobiles	1 330	672	1 113	764.97
摩托车	Motorcycles	309	134	323	55.81
非机动车	Non-motor-driven Vehicles	382	118	339	80.48
# 自行车	Bicycles	94	29	73	12.81
行人乘车人	Pedestrians and Passengers	103	52	60	26.53
其 他	Other	3	1	3	0.03

表 23.7 火灾事故情况(2010)
BASIC STATISTICS OF FIRES

指 标	Indicators	合 计 Total	按事故发生程度分 By Serious Degree of Fires	
			较 大 Serious	一 般 Ordinary
次 数(起)	Number (case)	5 702	1	5 701
死亡人数(人)	Deaths (person)	43	3	40
受伤人数(人)	Injuries (person)	54	2	52
损失折款(万元)	Losses Converted into Cash (10 000 yuan)	7 100	25	7 075
平均每起事故损失(万元)	Average Loss per Fire (10 000 yuan)	1.25	25.40	1.24

①本页数据由市公安局提供。
②"11·15"火灾事故夜为建筑工地安全生产事故,暂未列入火灾统计范围。
❶Data in this page are provided by Shanghai Municipal Public Security Bureau.
❷"11·15"fire isn't included in the range of fires statistics because it is a corstructon safety acaident

表 23.8　检察院直接立案侦查案件情况(2010)
CASES UNDER DIRECT INVESTIGATION BY PROCURATOR'S OFFICES

类　别	Types	受　案 (件) Cases Accepted (case)	立案件数 (件) Quantity of Cases Registered (case)	立案人数 (人) Person of Cases Registered (person)	侦查终结件数 (件) Quantity of Cases Settled (case)	侦查终结人数(人) Person of Cases Settled (person)
总　计	**Total**	**1 574**	**362**	**422**	**358**	**423**
贪污贿赂案件	**Quamitity of Cases on Corruption and Bribery**	**1 413**	**336**	**393**	**336**	**398**
#贪　污	Corruption	558	72	90	76	91
贿　赂	Bribery	743	234	268	231	274
挪用公款	Misappropriation of Public Funds	59	27	30	20	21
集体私分	Ollective Illegal Possession of Publice Funds	17	3	5	8	11
渎职侵权案件	**Quamitity of Cases on Abuse and Dereliction of Duty**	**161**	**26**	**29**	**22**	**25**
#滥用职权	Abuse of Power	92	17	17	13	13
玩忽职守	Dereliction of Duty	24	6	6	7	7
徇私舞弊	Fraudulent Practice	39	3	4	2	3

表 23.9　检察院民事、行政案件办理情况(2010)
CIVIL CASES AND ADMINISTRATIVE CASES HANDLED BY PROCURATOR'S OFFICES

单位:件(case)

类　别	Types	受　案 Cases Accepted	审查处理 Cases Investigated	其中 of which: 立　案 Cases Registered	结案处理 Cases Settled	其中 of which: 抗　诉 Appeals Rejected
总　计	**Total**	**1 624**	**1 663**	**566**	**566**	**103**
民事案	**Civil Cases**	**1 488**	**1 530**	**551**	**549**	**103**
#合同纠纷案	Contract Disputes	669	698	324	308	56
权益纠纷案	Rights and Interests Disputes	424	421	127	156	30
劳动争议	Labour Disputes	177	183	35	60	10
婚姻家庭、继承纠纷案	Marriages and Inheritance Disputes	105	112	31	25	7
行政案	**Administrative Cases**	**136**	**133**	**15**	**17**	

注：本表数据由市检察院提供。
Note : Data on this page are provided by Shanghai Municipal People's Procurator's Offices.

表 23.10 检察院申诉案件处理情况(2010)
APPEALS HANDLED BY PROCURATOR'S OFFICES

单位:件(case)

类 别	Types	受 案 Cases Accepted	审查处理 Cases Investigated	其 中 of which 分送本院其他部门 Dilivering to Other Department of Such Procurator's Offices
总 计	**Total**	**10 070**	**10 063**	**2 568**
首次申诉	**Appeals First Time**	**5 263**	**5 265**	**2 107**
#不服不立案	Appeals Against Rejection of the Case	257	257	219
不服逮捕	Appeals Against Arrest	9	9	2
不服刑事判决	Appeals Against Judgment of Criminal Case	263	263	21
不服民事行政裁决	Appeals Against Aadminnistration Arbitrament of Civil Case	2 193	2 196	1 603
不服劳教	Appeals Against Judgment of Reeducation Through Labor	6	6	1
重复申诉	Appeals Repeated	4 807	4 807	461

注：本表数据由市检察院提供。
Note：Data on this page are provided by Shanghai Municipal People's Procurator's Offices.

表 23.10 续表 continued

单位:件(case)

类 别	Types	其 中 of which 移送其他检查院 Removing to Other Procurator's Offices	移送公安机 关 Removing to Public Security Organs	移送其他机 关 Removing to Other Organs	直接答复 Direct Reply
总 计	**Total**	**2 590**	**616**	**2 810**	**688**
首次申诉	**Appeals First Time**	**884**	**326**	**1 014**	**576**
#不服不立案	Appeals Against Rejection of the Case	27	3		5
不服刑事判决	Appeals Against Judgment of Criminal Case	36	1	18	33
不服民事行政裁决	Appeals Against Aadminnistration Arbitrament of Civil Case	291		66	208
不服劳教	Appeals Against Judgment of Reeducation Through Labor		1	2	2
重复申诉	**Appeals Repeated**	**1 706**	**290**	**1 796**	**112**

表 23.11 法院各类案件办理情况(2010)
CASES HANDLED BY COURTS

单位:件(case)

类别	Types	收案 Cases Accepted	结案 Cases Settled	其中 of which 判决 Judgement	裁定 Arbitration	调解 Mediation
一审刑事案件	**First Trial Criminal Cases**	**19 803**	**19 762**	**19 637**	**87**	**8**
#侵犯公民人身权利、民主权利罪	Offences Against Citizens' Personal and Democratic Rights	2 481	2 506	2 432	55	8
侵犯财产罪	Offences Against Properties	8 505	8 481	8 460	14	
妨碍社会管理秩序罪	Offences Against Social Management of Order	5 308	5 301	5 292	4	
一审民事案件	**First Trial Civil Cases**	**251 631**	**251 051**	**82 585**	**98 022**	**69 572**
婚姻家庭、继承案件	Marriages and Inheritance Cases	29 711	29 652	9 104	6 661	13 705
婚姻家庭案件	Marriages and Fimily Cases	25 750	25 772	8 284	6 089	11 221
继承案件	Inheritance Cases	3 961	3 880	820	572	2 484
合同纠纷案件	Contract Disputes Cases	162 160	162 353	49 577	77 005	35 148
#买卖合同纠纷	Trade Contracts	17 044	17 018	6 870	5 572	4 397
房地产开发经营合同纠纷	Real Estate Development Contracts	3 272	3 344	1 492	1 067	782
借款合同纠纷	Loan Contracts	19 276	19 255	8 525	6 166	4 450
租赁合同纠纷	Lease Contract	9 943	9 963	3 578	3 921	2 452
劳动争议	Labor Disputes	20 502	21 438	9 049	4 287	8 013
劳务合同	Labor Contracts	765	765	334	174	255
权属、侵犯纠纷及其他民事案件	Disputes of Right Infringement of Right and Other Civil Affaires	59 760	59 046	23 904	14 306	20 719
#所有权及与所有权相关权力纠纷	Ownership and Related Rights	15 935	15 839	5 642	5 531	4 610
人身权纠纷	Personal Rights	36 067	35 546	15 465	4 826	15 242
一审行政案件	**First Trial Administrative Cases**	**1 877**	**1 844**	**829**	**1 014**	

注：本表数据由市高级人民法院提供。
Note: Data in this table are provided by Shanghai Municipal Senior Court.

表 23.12 法院执行案件情况(2010)
CASES EXECUTED BY COURTS

单位:件(case)

类别 Types		收案 Cases Accepted	结案 Cases Settled	其中 of which 自动履行 Automatic Performance	和解 Mediation	强制执行 Compellent Execution
总计	**Total**	**101 607**	**102 221**	**41 065**	**9 240**	**30 939**
刑事	Criminal Cases	2 443	2 455	1 480	18	615
民事	Civil Cases	87 330	87 688	35 909	8 368	25 820
行政	Administrative Cases	120	135	64		47
行政非诉审查与执行	Non-litigious Investigation and Execution of Administration	2 832	2 886	775	158	560
仲裁	Arbitration	8 391	8 550	2 795	626	3 806
公证债权文书	Notary Creditor's Rights	276	291	42	70	91
其他	Others	215	216			

表 23.13 主要年份法院各类案件结案情况
CASE ENDED BY COURTS IN MAIN YEARS

单位:起(time)

类别 Types		2005	2009	2010
总计	**Total**	**283 230**	**384 122**	**406 582**
刑事案件	Criminal Cases	17 353	23 242	22 137
婚姻家庭、继承案件	Marriages and Inheritance Cases	28 563	29 779	31 114
合同纠纷案件	Contract Disputes Cases	128 118	174 862	180 459
权属、侵犯纠纷及其他民事案件	Disputes of Right Infringement of Right and Other Civil Affairs	31 153	46 393	64 395
行政案件	Administrative Cases	3 016	2 235	2 135
申诉、申请再审	Second Trial on Appeals and Requisition	4 023	4 730	4 120
司法赔偿	Justice Compensation	6	3	1
执行案件	Executed Cases	70 998	102 878	102 221

注:本页数据由市高级人民法院提供。
Note: Data in this page are provided by Shanghai Municipal Senior Court.

上 / 海 / 统 / 计 / 年 / 鉴

主要统计指标解释

律　师

指依法取得律师执业证书，担任法律顾问，民事(刑事、行政)案件代理人、刑事案件辩护人、办理非诉讼业务，解答法律询问，代写法律事务文书等，为社会提供法律服务的人员。

公证人员

指在国家机关依法办理公证事务的司法人员。包括公证员、助理公证员和在公证处工作的其他人员。

公证文书

指公证处根据当事人申请，依照事实和法律，按照法定程序制作的，具有法律效力的司法证明文书。根据公证书用途和使用地，公证书分为国内公证书、国内经济公证书、涉外民事公证书、涉外经济公证书四类。

调解民间纠纷

指调解委员会按照法律规定，根据自愿原则，用说服教育的方法调解民间发生的有关民事权利和义务争执的件数，包括调解成功数和调解未成功数。该指标主要反映人民调解委员会的工作量。

立　案

指人民检察院对受理的报案、控告、举报或自首及自行发现的犯罪线索、犯罪嫌疑人进行初步调查后，认为存在职务犯罪事实和应追究刑事责任，并决定作为刑事案件进行侦查的诉讼活动，是追究犯罪的开始。该指标主要反映人民检察院依法将职务犯罪线索作为刑事案件进行侦查的诉讼活动。

申　诉

指经检察机关信访部门审查处理后，移送到检察机关申诉部门的申诉案件，包括不服检察机关处理决定和不服法院刑事判决和裁定的申诉的案件。

SHANGHAI STATISTICAL YEARBOOK

EXPLANATORY NOTES TO MAJOR STATISTICAL INDICATORS

□ Lawyers

Lawyers are certified legal workers according to law, and who are employed by legal counseling firms to act as legal advisers, agents in criminal or civil lawsuits, or defenders in criminal lawsuits, or to handle non-litigious legal affairs, to advise on matters of law or to write legal papers for others, and provide service to the public.

□ Notary Personnel

Notary Personnel are judicial workers of the state notary organs handling notarization work according to law. They include notaries, assistant notaries, and other people working in notary firms.

□ Notary Documents

Notary Documents refer to the judicatory notary documents drawn up by the request of the party and are in accordance with facts and laws and following certain legal proceedings. According to usage and locality, the notary documents are divided into following 4 types: domestic notary documents, domestic economic notary documents, foreign-related civil notary documents and foreign-related economic notary documents.

□ Mediation of Civil Disputes

Mediation of Civil Disputes refers to number of cases made by mediation committees in mediating in civil disputes concerning civil rights and duties through persuasion and education in accordance with the provisions of law on a voluntary basis, so as to solve disputes by helping the parties involved come to an agreement and understanding, including those unsuccessful ones. This indicator reflects the workload of the mediation committees.

□ Acceptance of Case

Acceptance of Case refers to the decision made by the people's procuratorate office on reported cases, prosecution, impeachment, surrender, self-found criminal clues or suspects after initial investigation to confirm the act of crime and to start legal proceedings of the case as criminal case.

□ Appeals

Appeals refer to cases transferred to the appeal departments of procurator's offices after initial review by departments dealing with complaint letters and calls of the public. Included are appeals against decisions made by procurator's offices and appeals against court rules and verdicts.

中国统计出版社最新图书简目

（仅供参考，以最后出书为准）

统计资料

中国统计年鉴-2011
2011中国发展报告
中国劳动统计年鉴-2011
中国建筑业统计年鉴-2011
中国商品交易市场统计年鉴-2011
中国民政统计年鉴-2011
中国科技统计年鉴-2011
中国高技术产业统计年鉴-2011
全国农产品成本收益资料汇编-2011
大中型批发零售和住宿餐饮企业统计年鉴-2011
中国县（市）社会经济统计年鉴-2011
第二次全国R&D资源清查资料汇编-综合卷
2010年中国第六次人口普查公报
中国统计摘要-2011
中国第三产业统计年鉴-2011
中国社会统计年鉴-2011
中国人口和就业统计年鉴-2011
中国房地产统计年鉴-2011
中国贸易外经统计年鉴-2011
中国农村统计年鉴-2011
中国教育经费统计年鉴-2010
中国科学技术协会统计年鉴-2011
中国城市(镇)生活与价格年鉴-2011
中国农村住户调查年鉴-2011（中、英文）
第二次全国R&D资源清查资料汇编-工业企业卷
国际统计年鉴-2011
中国区域经济统计年鉴-2011
中国城市统计年鉴-2009
中国工业经济统计年鉴-2011
中国能源统计年鉴-2011
2011中国地区经济监测报告
中国农产品价格调查年鉴-2011
中国农村贫困监测报告-2011
工业企业科技活动资料-2011
中国农村全面建设小康监测报告-2011
中国零售和餐饮连锁企业统计年鉴-2011

2011年省级综合统计年鉴系列

北京　天津　河北　山西　内蒙古
河南　湖北　湖南　广东　广西
新疆　新疆生产建设兵团
辽宁　吉林　黑龙江　上海　江苏
海南　重庆　四川　贵州　云南
浙江　安徽　福建　江西　山东
西藏　陕西　甘肃　青海　宁夏

2011年市(县)级综合统计年鉴系列

天津滨海新区
运城　忻州　临汾　呼和浩特
上海浦东新区
杭州　宁波　绍兴　台州　温州
厦门经济特区　南昌　上饶
十堰　荆州　咸宁　长沙　广州
贵阳　昆明　庆阳　西安
石家庄　唐山　邯郸　太原　大同
包头　沈阳　大连　长春　吉林市
苏州　无锡　常州　徐州　南通
金华　嘉兴　衢州
济南　青岛　潍坊　郑州
东莞　惠州　深圳　桂林　南宁
兰州　银川　乌鲁木齐
长治　阳泉　晋城　朔州　晋中
四平　哈尔滨　黑龙江垦区
盐城　镇江　江阴　丹阳
福州　福州经济技术开发区
洛阳　三门峡　南阳　武汉　宜昌
柳州　来宾　河池　海口　成都　绵阳

“十一五”规划教材

非参数统计　医学统计学
多元统计分析　经济计量学教程
统计数据处理概论
企业经营管理统计
统计学:从数据到结论
概率论与数理统计　统计学
应用时间序列分析
质量管理统计方法　社会统计学
市场调查与预测
国民经济核算教程(国民经济统计学)
现代金融投资统计分析
统计指数理论及应用
多元统计分析实验
统计学原理（非统计专业使用）
概率论与数理统计(经济、管理类专业使用)

重点图书

挑大学选专业2011—高考志愿填报指南
挑大学选专业2011—考研择校指南

(京)新登字041号

图书在版编目(CIP)数据

上海统计年鉴. 2011 ：汉英对照 / 上海市统计局编
——北京：中国统计出版社，2011.6
ISBN 978-7-5037-6239-0/C·2477

Ⅰ. ①上…
Ⅱ. ①上…
Ⅲ. ①统计资料－上海市－
2011－年鉴－汉、英 Ⅳ. ①C832.51-54

中国版本图书馆CIP数据核字(2011)第114586号

上海统计年鉴—2011

作　　者/上海市统计局
责任编辑/佘竞雄　熊　威
E-mail/yearbook@stats.gov.cn
执行编辑/曹美芳
封面设计/蔡旭洲
出版发行/中国统计出版社
通信地址/北京市西城区三里河月坛南街57号　中国统计出版社
邮　　编/100826
电　　话/(010) 63376907
印　　刷/上海万卷印刷有限公司
经　　销/新华书店
开　　本/889×1240毫米1/16
字　　数/125.32万字
印　　张/30
印　　数/1～4000册
版　　别/2011年6月第1版
版　　次/2011年6月第1次印刷
书　　号/ISBN 978-7-5037-6239-0/C·2477
定　　价/400.00元